A World History of Christianity

A World History
of Christianity

Edited by Adrian Hastings

William B. Eerdmans Publishing Company
Grand Rapids, Michigan

First published 1999 by Cassell, Wellington House, 125 Strand, London WC2R 0BB UK

This edition published by special arrangement with Cassell by Wm. B. Eerdmans Publishing Co. 255 Jefferson Ave. S.E., Grand Rapids, Michigan 49503

Printed in the United Kingdom

Library of Congress Cataloging-in-Publication Data:
Hastings, Adrian.
   A world history of Christianity / by Adrian Hastings.
     p.   cm.
   Includes bibliographical references.
   ISBN 0–8028–2442–0 (cloth : alk. paper)
   1. Church history.   I. Title.
 BR145.2.H37   1999
 270—dc21   98–42984
                                        CIP

The chapter by Philip Walters, 'Eastern Europe since the fifteenth century' (pp. 282–324) includes, by permission, a few paragraphs from the author's chapter 'The Russian Orthodox Church' in Pedro Ramet (ed.), *Eastern Christianity and Politics in the Twentieth Century* (Duke University Press, 1988).

Typeset by Ensystems, Saffron Walden
Printed and bound in Great Britain by The Bath Press

Contents

List of maps

Preface

This book originated in the course of 1994, in correspondence between Judith Longman, at the time a Religious Editor at Cassell, and Peter Hinchliff, Regius Professor of Ecclesiastical History in the University of Oxford. He had recently contributed a chapter to the *Oxford Illustrated History of Christianity*, but, in retrospect, felt that that book, impressive as it surely is, remained rather too Eurocentric, perhaps even too ecclesiocentric, in the way it was shaped. He wanted to attempt something in which the history of Christianity was seen as related more organically to the diversity of the world's cultures and regions and in which full justice was done to Asia, Africa, America, Australasia and the Pacific.

The plan was agreed, a submission date of early 1997 set, and thirteen contributors were signed up for its various chapters. Peter himself was due to write no more than the Introduction. Then, in October 1995, he died very unexpectedly and Cassell invited me to take over the editing. As I was already part of the team, commissioned to write the Latin American chapter, and as I certainly did not want Peter's project to fall apart without him, I agreed to do so. In 1996 one contributor withdrew on grounds of ill health and was replaced. Then in 1997 two more did the same, inevitably disrupting the programme for publication. Benedicta Ward and Gillian Evans gallantly agreed to take over the Western medieval chapter at very short notice. When, however, in October, the writer of Chapter 2 on the Graeco-Roman world withdrew, I decided to write that chapter myself in order to avoid the considerable delay which could be occasioned by seeking an entirely new contributor when most of the rest of the book was already complete. This is the explanation of why two chapters have been written by the editor, together with the Introduction.

I am enormously grateful for the collaboration and patience of all who have taken part in the production of this book with its somewhat troubled history. Perhaps in that it reflects its subject! I can only hope that it remains, more or less, the way Peter hoped it would be. Without him it would never have been begun. The basic chapter plan is entirely his. He wanted the chapters to appear in order, according to when the area in question first entered the story, thus avoiding any impression that the whole of Western European history comes first, to be followed by its 'expansion' elsewhere. Peter's too has been the lack of detailed guidance as to content given to the individual writers. Very rightly he insisted that there could be no one dominant theme or consistent emphasis. Each chapter should be structured differently so as to reflect the varied themes – spiritual, intellectual, political or social – which have been most significant at different times and places within the history of Christianity. The aim throughout has been to provide a history focused upon those dominant themes, rather than a history of everything. Quite deliberately, this is a history of plurality, but because it is a history, not a chronicle, it is focused selectively upon what appears to have most significance for the reader today within each of the different stories it relates.

The differentiation extends as far as the methodology. Thus, while some contributors, writing about areas less generally well known, have included quite a range of footnotes, others decided that there was little point in doing this for subjects already massively covered by readily available literature. This seems to make good sense. Crucial for every chapter, however, are the select bibliographies intended to enable readers to carry the subject further, and it is hoped that they will prove of the greatest use, especially as they are thoroughly up to date. Here again, however, more extended guidance has been provided for some areas where it is less readily available. All this has depended upon each contributor.

In preparing this volume, I owe a very special debt of thanks to Ingrid Lawrie, who has not only typed all my own sections but throughout acted as an additional editor. Without her ever-competent and tireless assistance, the work involved would simply have been too much for me to manage.

Adrian Hastings
Leeds
March 1998

The contributors

Mary B. Cunningham is Honorary Research Fellow in the Institute for Advanced Research in the Humanities and in the Centre for Byzantine, Ottoman and Modern Greek Studies at the University of Birmingham. A specialist in Byzantine homiletics and text editions, she has edited and translated *The Life of Michael the Synkellos* (Belfast, 1991) and has published articles on Andrew of Crete and other Byzantine preachers.

G. R. Evans lectures in history in the University of Cambridge. Her books include works on Anselm, Alan of Lille, Augustine, Gregory the Great, Bernard of Clairvaux and *The Language and Logic of the Bible*, 2 vols (1984–85).

Robert Eric Frykenberg was born and reared in India and is Emeritus Professor of History/South Asian Studies, University of Wisconsin-Madison. His books include *History and Belief: The Foundations of Historical Understanding* (1996), *Delhi Through the Ages* (1993) and *Guntur District, 1788–1848; A History of Local Influence and Central Authority in South India* (1965).

Martin Goodman is Professor of Jewish Studies in the University of Oxford. He is a Fellow of Wolfson College, a Fellow of the Oxford Centre for Hebrew and Jewish Studies and a Fellow of the British Academy. He has published widely on both Jewish and Roman history.

Adrian Hastings is Emeritus Professor of Theology in the University of Leeds. His many books on Christian history in Europe and Africa include *A History of English Christianity 1920–1990* (1991), *The Church in Africa 1450–1950* (1994) and *The Construction of Nationhood: Ethnicity, Religion and Nationalism* (1997). He is General Editor of the *Oxford Companion to Christian Thought* (forthcoming, 2000).

Mary Heimann lectures in Modern History at the University of Strathclyde in Glasgow and is an Associate Editor of the *New Dictionary of National Biography*. Her first book, *Catholic Devotion in Victorian England*, was published by Oxford University Press in 1995.

David Hilliard is Reader in History at the Flinders University of South Australia. He has published widely on Christian missions in the Pacific Islands and on the religious and social history of Australia.

Robert Bruce Mullin is the Society for the Promotion of Religion and Learning Professor of History and World Mission at the General Theological Seminary (New York). He has written extensively on topics in American religious history. His books include *Episcopal Vision/American Reality: High Church Theology and Social Thought in Evangelical America* and *Miracles and the Modern Religious Imagination*.

Andrew Pettegree is Professor of Modern History at the University of St Andrews and Director of the St Andrews Reformation Studies Institute. He is the author of several studies of the English and European Reformation, including *The Early Reformation in Europe* (Cambridge University Press) and *The Reformation World* (Routledge).

Gary Tiedemann teaches Modern Chinese History in the University of London. His particular research interests include the history of Christianity in northern China. He is currently completing a monograph on the social context of anti-Christian conflict in Shandong province, 1860–1900.

Philip Walters has a PhD in Russian religious philosophy. Since 1979 he has worked at Keston Institute (formerly Keston College), the information centre on religion in Communist and post-Communist countries, where he is Head of Research and editor of Keston's scholarly journal, *Religion, State and Society*.

Benedicta Ward SLG is Reader in the History of Christian Spirituality in the University of Oxford. Her works include *Miracles and the Medieval Mind* (1987) and *The Venerable Bede* (1991).

Kevin Ward lectures in African Religious Studies in the University of Leeds, with special research interests in the interaction of religion and politics in East Africa.

Introduction

Adrian Hastings

Christianity occupies a unique position in world history, being today the predominant religion in four and a half of the world's six continents (Europe, North and South America, Australasia and the Pacific, southern Africa) while even in Asia, the world's most populous continent, where it includes in all a very small proportion of the population, it still has hundreds of millions of adherents and is predominant within several countries – the Philippines, South Korea, East Timor. One could reasonably claim that it is, in historic reality, the one and only fully world religion.

This is not a matter of making competitive claims but of insisting upon the unique importance of its study for any understanding of world history. Yet its study is particularly difficult because Christianity has been such a chameleon and so varied in its manifestation that most people fail to begin to understand either its nature or its history. Generally they impose upon the whole of Christianity, past and present, the image of that bit of it they have themselves experienced, whether through membership or through mere observation or opposition. The contrasts it embraces are extraordinary. Let us list a few of them. It has been a rather unritualistic religion, both in its origins and in forms such as that of the Quakers, but it has also at times been reduced to a pattern of almost ceaseless ritual, whether in the monastic liturgy of Cluny or in a Byzantine cathedral. Christianity has been a very apolitical minority religion, yet it has been no less an imperial and persecuting one, just as it has acted as the other side of the coin to the nation-state. In some forms it is exceptionally activist, evangelistic and missionary, in others predominantly monastic and contemplative; it has so lauded virginity and monastic life as to come close to rejecting sex and marriage, and yet it has also in other circumstances appeared as committed above all to the social glorification of monogamy. It has pursued poverty as an ideal, yet become intricately linked with the growth and triumph of capitalism. It has been

1

both pacifist and the instigator of holy wars. It has on one side produced the most lasting, centralized and complex ecclesiastical system of government in Rome and on the other been intensely fissiparous, sectarian and multi-centred. One could go on and on. How does one portray the history of such a many-faced monster?

Of course, Christianity also has its unifying characteristics. It is, above all, the religion of Jesus Christ. The centrality of the figure of Christ, however variously portrayed, holds it together, combined with the acceptance of the scriptures of the New Testament, all of which are centred upon him. Nevertheless here too there is at once ambiguity: the Jesus of History or the Christ of Faith? The Gospels focus upon the one, Paul appears to proclaim the other, almost unrelated to Jesus' actual life. In a way, that was already the question which divided the ancient theological traditions of Alexandria and Antioch. If the Christ of Faith, the divine figure in whose regard the life story of a human being almost ceases to matter, represents not only the choice of Alexandria but the Pantocrator of Byzantium, as well as the theology of Rudolf Bultmann, the Jesus of History keeps coming back, not only in the ancient theologians of Antioch, represented most controversially by Nestorius, but in medieval popular devotion and much modern liberal theology. We may know little about him with absolute scholarly certainty, but that has not made him any less authoritative. The fact that he wrote nothing, and that nothing we now possess was written to record his life until some 40 years after his death, both increases the mystery in the figure of Jesus and permits a pluriformity of interpretation. It can actually enhance his authority.

The authority of scripture too is highly ambiguous, above all because the Christian Church insisted on retaining the Hebrew 'Old Testament' with the result that by far the greater part of the Christian Bible is pre-Christian. The Church has never, however, formulated a way of relating the two parts of the Bible. Are they of equal weight? Is the Old there merely to provide a context for the New, which, effectively, nevertheless replaces it? Is there some far more subtle relationship whereby the one continues, completes, fulfils the other? In practice the unitary authority of the Bible is inevitably in some way undermined by its size, diversity and divergences. Throughout history – and this is true in regard to the New Testament as well as the Old – there has been a constant shift in appeal from one book, author or text to another as providing what one may call a canon within the canon. For most early Christians, especially those living in Jerusalem under the leadership of James, the 'Brother of the Lord', the 'Scriptures' were above all the Hebrew Torah. For many later generations, the 'Scriptures' have been above all the Gospels and Paul's letters. Thus, if the unity of Christianity remains grounded in the unity of Jesus Christ's centrality and biblical authority, the diversity of

Christian history is no less grounded in both the figure of Jesus and the pluralism of the Scriptures.

However the New Testament provided three other figures which have also always remained, each in its own way, determinative for the shaping of Christianity – Paul, Peter and Mary, the Mother of Jesus. Paul's letters are the first Christian literature we possess and Paul's theological brilliance, universalist message and prophetic power have continually dominated the Christian tradition. One cannot get away from Paul. But neither can one get away from Peter. He had no comparable intellectual ability but the exceptional delineation of his role, both in the Gospels and subsequently, is unquestionable. Martyred in Rome, he was seen as providing an authority for the Church there which has remained central to every phase of Christian history and remains so today, when more than half of all the world's Christians accept the jurisdiction of the papacy, while those who do not are still compelled to relate to it, if only to denounce it. Yet Mary may be the most enigmatic of the three. Even the references to her within the New Testament may well be read in very different ways, but there is no doubt about how central she has remained in the main Christian traditions – Greek, Latin, Armenian, Ethiopian. The third ecumenical council was called chiefly to defend her position as the Mother of God. Yet, almost more than Peter, she has been the object of fierce Christian rejection, which has done so much to shape the Protestant quarter of Church history. Did this not, perhaps, represent an eleventh-hour determination of the patriarchalism which has so dominated Christianity to exclude the one major element of femininity which its tradition had hitherto allowed?

Friedrich von Hügel defined the 'three elements of religion' as the mystical, the intellectual and the institutional.[1] In their way our three figures represent these three elements well enough: Peter, the institutional; Paul, the intellectual and prophetic; Mary, especially as linked with the figure of John, the beloved disciple, in the Fourth Gospel, stands for the mystical. Christian history can well be seen as a constant jostling between these three strands, in which one or another is either given a too dominant part or, alternatively, cast intolerantly aside. While one is tempted to characterize Orthodoxy as Marian or Johannine, Roman Catholicism as Petrine and Protestantism as Pauline, that would be a considerable oversimplification, for all three elements of religion are to be found, if unevenly balanced, in each of the three main branches of Christianity.

An extraordinarily large amount of Church history is one of internal conflict, of disagreement about the nature of the tradition. There is no reason to think that this is going to cease and a realistic history has to give its full due to conflict and its underlying causes within the very nature of Christianity. Newman made two remarks which may be of use here. The first comes from a sermon of 1839: 'Controversy, at least in this age . . . is a sort of night battle, where each fights for himself and friend and foe stand together.'[2] The image of the 'night battle', frequently employed since his time, was not in fact original to Newman but is to be found already in the account that Socrates, a fifth-century historian, gave of the Arian controversy of the fourth: 'the situation was exactly like a battle fought by night'.[3] Twenty-five years later, Newman remarked in his *Apologia pro Vita Sua* that 'It is the vast Catholic body itself, and it only, which affords an arena for both combatants [authority and private judgement] in that awful, never-dying duel. It is necessary for the very life of religion, viewed in its large operations and its history, that the warfare should be incessantly carried on.'[4] Whether we see it more in terms of a 'night battle', in which the antagonists hardly understand why they are at war and on whose side they struggle, or rather as an 'awful, never-dying duel' in which contrasting values have each to be championed, whatever the anguish, we have to recognize that Christian history is very much a matter of turmoil and tension — at times creative, at times simply destructive — in which a variety of emphases relating symbolically to the figures of Paul, Peter and Mary, but behind and above them to the Jesus who is also the Christ, can hardly be held together within a single stable synthesis, despite the no less enduring struggles of many to maintain the unity of the disparate strands.

In reality, then, Christian history has many contrasting themes, phases and alternative centres. It is a history of change and translation, of the regular reinvention of itself in new languages and regions. This volume has been structured, more than most of its predecessors, on the basis of this undeniable fact. It is a plural history, looking at the story from the viewpoints of different ages and continents, in which very little attempt has been made to impose any single dominant line. Of course, there are many more centres than we can have chapters in a single, manageable volume. Important countries, whole areas, have been almost left out. I am sorry there is no chapter on the Caribbean, nor on the history of the Christian Churches within the Muslim world. I am sorry too that Ireland does not get more consideration, because the refusal of the Irish (both Gaelic speakers and the long-settled 'Old English' in Ireland) to accept Protestantism, despite huge pressure from the English state to do so, has been one of the most overlooked factors in the modern shaping of Christianity. If Ireland had turned Protestant in the sixteenth century as did Scotland, the whole religious picture of Britain, America and Australia would be very different, and indeed that of all the countries affected by the modern Irish missionary movement. Islands, it seems, do tend to be overlooked in wide-ranging studies such as ours. Not only Ireland and the

Caribbean, but Sri Lanka, Madagascar and Iceland have exceptionally interesting histories not included here.

Again, our commitment to a territorially-based history has meant that less than justice is done to the most specifically international dimensions of modern Christian history – the later papacy, the missionary movement, the Ecumenical Movement and the World Council of Churches, now 50 years old. Twentieth-century Church history needs a strongly international, yet unified, dimension, more than we have been able to offer here. It could be argued that a separate final chapter is needed on the global reshaping of Christianity in the nineteenth and twentieth centuries but that is such a huge subject in itself and one still so much in the making that it has seemed reasonable to retain Professor Hinchliff's original territorially-based plan without modification. At least it emphasizes a primary truth: that the writing of Christian history needs to escape imprisonment within a Europe-centred story in order not only to serve the needs of the many hundreds of millions of Christians who live elsewhere but also to provide an objectively balanced account of a straightforwardly historical kind of something which has for long been seen in too Eurocentric a way.

Notes

1 F. Von Hügel, *The Mystical Element of Religion* (2nd edn; London: Dent, 1923), 1, p. 65.
2 *Fifteen Sermons Preached before the University of Oxford* (London: Longmans, 1871), p. 201.
3 Socrates, *Ecclesiastical History*, 1.23, trans. in Nicene and Post-Nicene Christian Fathers, 2nd series, II (1890).
4 *Apologia pro Vita Sua* (1865), p. 252.

1

The emergence of Christianity

Martin Goodman

In the first century of its existence Christianity evolved from an obscure group of Galilean Jews to become the religion of thousands, most of them non-Jews, in the wider world of the eastern Mediterranean. Both Christian contemporaries and later generations came to see this expansion as evidence of divine intervention in human affairs. For enthusiasts and opponents alike it was an extraordinary achievement without close parallel in the religious history of the ancient world before this time. By *c.* 120 CE, by which time all the books now included in the New Testament had been written, Christianity was a clear-cut religion distinct from Judaism with already an extensive history of its own.

Jesus the Jew and his first followers lived in the Jewish homeland during the period when it was coming under the sway of the Roman Empire. Thus the early Church was a product both of late Second Temple Judaism and of the Roman world and must be understood against both these backgrounds. This is not to suggest that Christianity fitted perfectly into either. On the contrary, the new religion proved in some vital respects unique, and it is by the isolation and appreciation of those unique qualities that its appeal and eventual success can best be comprehended.

Judaism, the Roman Empire and Jesus

By the time of Jesus the myths of the Jews about their ancient history were already enshrined in the Hebrew Bible. Jews believed that their people had come to the land of Israel long ago in the time of Abraham. They preserved traditions both about a time in the distant past when they had enjoyed political independence and national glory under the rule of kings descended from their great leader David, and about the calamity in 587 BCE when their capital Jerusalem and the first temple built there had been destroyed and most of the people had been carried off into exile in

Babylon. Since those days the nation had grown used to political subservience. The small group which returned to Judaea from the Babylonian exile *c.* 537 BCE did so under the aegis of the Persian Empire, and the demise of Persian suzerainty in 332 BCE was followed directly by the control of new masters, the Macedonian Alexander the Great and the generals who succeeded him. The Jews did enjoy real independence when, during the break-up of these successor states, the priestly dynasty of the Hasmonaeans established themselves first as High Priests in Jerusalem and, from 104 BCE, as kings. But their power, which reached its peak in the first quarter of the first century BCE, was not to last. It was broken by the advent into the region from the West of the ruthless superstate of Rome.

The Roman Empire was close to its peak at the beginning of Christianity. It was not by accident that Rome had gained control of the western Mediterranean world by the end of the third century BCE and of the eastern Mediterranean in the second and first centuries BCE. The Romans were a profoundly militaristic people led by a deeply competitive aristocracy and success in war was the main route to political power in Roman society. In the mid-first century BCE such competition had led to civil war by which most of the Mediterranean world was affected, but by 31 BCE, after appalling bloodshed, a single victor emerged: Octavian Caesar, named from 27 BCE by a grateful senate and people as Augustus. Augustus was to rule until his natural death in 14 CE, proclaiming throughout his magnanimity, but as a precaution retaining a standing army of exceptional size and competence. Thus the Roman world of the last years before the birth of Jesus witnessed the consolidation of the power of a military autocrat over an empire which stretched from the English Channel to the borders of Sudan, in which internal peace was achieved by terror and occasional brutal force.

Unification even under tyranny had advantages. Although staple food products were still grown locally, the economy of the Roman world was unified to a surprising degree, both through the extraction of wealth by the state and through the efforts of entrepreneurs who took advantage of secure communications to market between regions manufactured goods of all kinds. The people ruled by Rome had widely differing cultures, from Celts to Egyptians, but in the eastern Mediterranean the Roman state showed a marked preference for the encouragement of urban life on the model first developed in classical Greece. In part this preference had a political origin, in that Rome had no civil service and therefore relied on the co-operation of a wealthy urban elite for such crucial tasks as the collection of taxes, but the effect was a superficial cultural unity, so that town centres in one part of the empire looked much like those in another.

Thus, whatever the popularity of continuing local languages, Latin and Greek became the lingua francas of a cosmopolitan culture.

Within this society the Jews of Judaea were somewhat marginal. Rome had first come into contact with Judaea in the mid-second century BCE but the country only came under Roman sway in 63 BCE, when the great general Pompey captured Jerusalem, ostensibly in support of one native Jewish ruler of the Hasmonaean dynasty in his struggles against his brother. The region did not lie in a position of any notable strategic or economic importance for Rome, and the Romans were content to exercise control first through the native Jewish dynasty and then, when in 40 BCE the last eligible adult male of the Hasmonaean dynasty chose to transfer his allegiance to Rome's enemies, the Parthians, to Herod, a 'half-Jew' adventurer from Idumea, a region south of Jerusalem converted to Judaism by force in the late second century BCE.

Herod's family had risen to prominence in Judaean society precisely because their low status in Jewish eyes made them unthreatening to the Hasmonaeans. Herod himself won his kingdom through the efforts of Roman legionaries in 37 BCE and proceeded to rule Judaea with an iron hand until his death in 4 BCE. The extent to which he relied on repression became clear when after his death rebellions broke out all over his kingdom. Thus his son Archelaus proved unable to emulate Herod's tight grasp and in 6 CE was sent into exile in Gaul, leaving Judaea administered directly by a Roman governor. In Galilee a different son of Herod, Herod Antipas, continued to rule until 39 CE, and other descendants – including Agrippa, King of Judaea from 41 to 44 – remained active in the political life of the Jews, but their power was wholly dependent upon the support of the Roman state, and it gradually became standard Roman practice to control all the provinces, including Judaea, directly through a Roman governor.

The start of direct Roman rule in Judaea was greeted by a revolt against the imposition of a census (intended to ensure efficient collection of the taxes needed primarily to pay for Augustus's standing army), and the relations of the Jews with their Roman governors continued to be occasionally fractious until in 66 CE a general revolt broke out, leading in 70 to the destruction of Jerusalem and the Temple.

Up to its destruction the Temple was a central feature of Jerusalem architecturally, socially and economically. The importance of this city, one of the greatest of the Roman world, was entirely based on its religious function. For almost all Jews the sacrificial cult in Jerusalem was believed to be the main form of worship desired by God. In this emphasis on sacrifice on an altar in a temple, Judaism differed little from the other religions of the Roman Empire. Jews were strange in this respect only in the insistence of most of them that such sacrifices were only permitted in the one sanctuary in Jerusalem, and in the unique custom of mass pilgrimage on special festivals to which this belief led.

For other inhabitants of the Roman world it was obvious not only that the gods would cheerfully accept sacrifices in numerous locations, but also that there were numerous gods. Polytheism was taken for granted; just as people now explain illness in terms of germs because, although they cannot be sensed, their impact can be deduced from their effects, so too the actions of the gods could be gauged from what they did. The gods brought prosperity or misfortune as they saw fit. The notion that they might extend the health of humans into an afterlife was rarely entertained, and views about life after death varied greatly. There were by definition innumerable gods, certainly more than could be worshipped by any one individual, but this was a problem only for the superstitious. Most people expected to have a relationship only with the gods traditionally worshipped by their communities, and innovations usually came about only at the behest of a previously unrecognized divinity, announced perhaps by a dream or a prodigy. Ancient polytheism was thus inherently conservative and varied according to local custom. Literary attempts to create a mythological relationship between divinities were fairly spurious.

This is not to suggest that ancient paganism was static. On the contrary, subtle changes can be observed, not least at the time when Christianity emerged. Thus inscriptions reveal a greater sense that the gods will behave responsibly and fairly, and there was increased recognition, especially in cities, of elective cults such as those of Isis, Mithras and others, into which an individual could opt in addition to his or her participation in traditional worship. The reasons for the spread of such elective cults were doubtless varied. Adherents could become part of a new community within the wider society. In the Mithraic cult, for instance, devotees passed through various grades of initiation proudly recorded on inscriptions. It is probably significant that such cults were envisaged as having originated elsewhere than the Graeco-Roman environment in which they were now found: thus Isis and Serapis came originally from Egypt, and Mithras from Persia, even though their worship within the Roman environment entailed essentially a quite different cult from that in their homeland. In any case the model of the organization of such cults would prove important in the acceptance of Christian communities as religious groups in the cities of the empire in the first generations of the Church.

Pagan writers give a good idea of the ways in which Judaism appeared odd against this background. That Jews had particular ethnic customs, such as food taboos and the circumcision of males, was found amusing and bizarre, as was the observance of the Sabbath as a day of idleness, but more vehement opposition was reserved for two strictly theological issues in which early Christians were to follow Jews: the avoidance of images as the object of worship (leading to the accusation among others that Jews worship a God 'of uncertain name') and, above all, the refusal of Jews to pray to other gods, a refusal that seemed as crazy to polytheists as (to continue the parallel) would a claim by a modern doctor that all medical ills are due to only one germ.

Into this world Jesus was born in 4 BCE or thereabouts. The details of his career and teaching are hard to reconstruct because they were recounted and adapted for ecclesiastical purposes already in the first generations after his death – hence the discrepancies in the different versions preserved in the Gospels. In the non-Christian record his life passed almost wholly unnoticed: the brief reference by the Jewish historian Josephus to his career, which includes the description of Jesus as a 'wise man . . . who did remarkable deeds and was a teacher', has been extensively altered by a Christian scribe in the surviving manuscripts. Nonetheless some 'almost indisputable facts' can be deduced from the record by the cautious procedure of accepting as probably true any tradition about Jesus with which the early Church seems to have been uncomfortable. This procedure does not require disbelief in the many other early traditions about Jesus, only a recognition that they are uncertain.

Thus it is almost certain that Jesus was brought up in Nazareth of humble origin, but taught and gathered followers first in Galilee, and then in Judaea, especially Jerusalem. Those followers were all Jews. Some had been previously attached in some way to John the Baptist, an ascetic holy man who encouraged Jews to repent. Jesus himself seems to have been a follower of John before becoming a similarly charismatic teacher. Although the precise content of Jesus' teaching was already much debated in the first decades of the Church, the power of his personality was accepted by all. His popularity brought him to the attention of the Jewish authorities in Jerusalem and he was put to death by crucifixion by the Roman governor, Pontius Pilate.

Such violent death at the hands of the Roman state was not uncommon in first-century Judaea, for this was a society under great social pressure with which the political system could deal effectively only with a heavy hand. The reasons for this social pressure were quite complex.

In Judaea, the main social, economic and political institution, the Temple, was administered by an hereditary caste of priests, whose prestige simply by virtue of their role gave some of them political clout and access to a disproportionate share of the wealth which flowed into Jerusalem from offerings and tourism. The overall economic state of Judaea was prosperous – this was a period of massive public building, especially by Herod the Great, who turned the Temple site into one of the wonders of

11

the world – but there is much evidence that disparities of wealth were deeply resented, leading to banditry and class warfare. Since the local leaders through whom Rome controlled Judaea were by definition rich, because it was only to such individuals that Rome handed over power, the ruling class lacked the natural authority which might have enabled them to control their society in the constant state of low-level ferment which came to a head at the pilgrim festivals when huge and volatile crowds were mustered in Jerusalem. It is uncertain whether these factors had as much impact on Galilee in the north, where Jesus was raised and began his teaching, for there were few cities in Galilee, and these were very small compared to Jerusalem. Most Galileans were peasants living in villages, and they will only rarely have witnessed the economic and cultural sophistication of the capital. But there is evidence that some Galilean land was owned by Judaean priests, and this may explain tensions between landlords and tenants.

It is probable that, despite claims to the contrary by some scholars, such economic and social tensions were a greater source of unrest in both Galilee and Judaea than any anti-Roman ideology. Banditry was endemic in parts of Galilee but there was no serious opposition in the area to Rome even during the revolt of 66–70 CE: the historian Josephus, who commanded the Jewish rebels in Galilee in 66–67, described the Galileans as particularly prone to rebel, but in the detailed description of his campaign preserved in his autobiography the Galileans are described as strikingly ineffectual. There was a revolt in Judaea in 6 CE in opposition to the imposition of the census, and a great uprising in 40 in protest against the attempt of the Emperor Gaius (Caligula) to have his statue erected in the Jerusalem Temple, but these revolts were exceptional: up to 66 the Roman state stationed only a small number of auxiliary troops in Judaea, and the province was clearly considered by the Romans to be moderately peaceful.

The same economic problems of Judaea were a prime cause of the growth of an extended Jewish diaspora by the first century CE. Jews left their homeland for a variety of reasons, of which overpopulation (itself encouraged by Jewish opposition to abortion, contraception and infanticide) was only one. Some Jews were carried to Rome and other cities as prisoners after wars, either by Hellenistic kings or by Rome. Others left Judaea to find employment as mercenaries. At least some of the Jews in the diaspora were converts or descended from converts. In any case, by the time that Christianity emerged Jewish communities were to be found in many of the coastal cities of the eastern Mediterranean as well as in the countryside of Egypt, in the city of Rome and, in rather larger numbers, in Babylonia.

The religion of these widely scattered Jews was very varied, but all pious Jews held to a common core of belief. They all worshipped the God to whom sacrifices were made in the Jerusalem Temple, and they all believed that this God had established a covenant between himself and Israel which was enshrined in the Torah, a term which might sometimes be applied only to the Pentateuch (the first five books of the Hebrew Bible), sometimes more widely to the whole gamut of divine teaching preserved by Jews through both writings and tradition. There were still debates about the precise limits of the corpus of texts held sacred by Jews, but the central importance of the Pentateuch was universally acknowledged, and Pentateuchal scrolls were held in great reverence. The prime function of synagogues as local meeting places for Jews wherever they lived was to permit the reading and interpretation of the Torah; communal prayer was less important, since most prayer was said in private.

Judaism was by definition the ethnic religion of the Jews, but one of the most significant changes in Jewish life during the Persian period was the acceptance that any non-Jew could become a proselyte to Judaism simply by adoption of Jewish customs. This custom was an oddity in the ancient world, for no other people is recorded into which it was possible to enter simply by self-definition. Converts adopted Jewish history as their own and saw themselves as part of the covenant between God and Israel. Acceptance of them by Jews laid open the possibility that Judaism could, in theory, become a universal religion. There is no sign that any Jews in antiquity wished or expected this to happen, except perhaps in the last days, but Jewish proselytism was to provide an important model for the growth of the early Church.

Variety within Judaism began with the different modes of interpretation of the Torah, for, like all law codes, the Pentateuch left many issues unresolved. Thus some Jews, such as the authors of rabbinic Midrash, tried to make sense of difficult biblical passages by attempting to reconcile them with other passages; other Jews, like the Pharisees, incorporated common customs into their understanding of texts; yet others used the additional teachings of specified revered leaders to amplify the text, as in the sectarian writings found among the Dead Sea scrolls; a very small number, referred to only once by the philosopher Philo and nowhere else in antiquity, even claimed that the practical injunctions of the Torah did not need to be literally obeyed but could be validly observed in their allegorical meaning alone.

A belief is widely attested that true prophecy like that of the ancient prophets of Israel had come to an end, and it is probable that this explains the common use by authors of religious texts of a pseudepigraphic persona in order to give authority to their writings, but this belief coexisted with a claim by many individuals to prophetic-style inspiration which might still lead Jews in new directions.

Jews of different persuasions seem to have been remarkably willing to accept such diversity. Records of open breaches between groups are rare and mostly concern the operation of the Temple. Even here Sadducean priests are said to have carried out the Temple cult in accordance with Pharisaic procedures despite their own misgivings. The only truly sectarian group attested in Second Temple Judaism was the community who produced the Dead Sea scrolls.

Nonetheless the emergence of distinct groups with identifiable religious programmes, and in some cases distinctive organization and leadership, was among the more noticeable of the general trends in Judaean Judaism in the time of Jesus. The issues around which these groups clustered also show distinct features. Foremost among these was the performance of the Temple cult in Jerusalem. For all Jews the correct offering of sacrifices on behalf of Israel was a matter of supreme importance: doubtless only those who lived near Jerusalem could make the Temple the main focus of their everyday religious life, but the Temple as an idea was important for all, and such issues as the observance by the priests of the correct calendar and the right procedures for purification were hotly debated. Also much disputed were more general theological issues, such as the relationship between fate and free will and the possibility of life after death, while for many groups physical purity achieved by washing according to various different ablution systems became an important metaphor for spiritual cleanliness.

Evidence for these trends is largely confined to Judaea, but there are no good grounds for believing that the Judaism of Galilee was markedly different. It is probable that some Galilean Jews were descended from those gentiles converted by the Hasmonaean Aristobulus in 104–103 BCE but there was no reason why their genetic origin from three generations earlier should have affected the Judaism of the Galileans of Jesus' day. Galilean Jews came on pilgrimage to the Temple when they could, but presumably not three times every year as in theory they were required to do. Some customs (for instance, with regard to financial arrangements within marriage) were different in Galilee from Judaea, and it is possible that the admiration accorded to the pious Galilean holy man Hanina ben Dosa, who was strikingly unconcerned about issues of purity which concerned many other Jews, was a distinctive element of the Judaism of the region. But in general the distinctions between Galilean and Judaean Judaism were minimal.

The same is probably true of diaspora Judaism. Diaspora Jews in the Mediterranean world spoke and thought in Greek rather than in Hebrew, and treated the Septuagint, the Greek translation of the Hebrew Bible, as a sacred text in its own right, but there is little evidence that diaspora Jews syncretized their religion with the pagan cults around them; on the contrary, their position as minority communities in diaspora cities may have encouraged them to stress their differences all the more. Gentiles who became proselytes to Judaism will have been attracted precisely because Judaism was different and bizarre, not because of its similarity to the religions they already knew. There is no reason to suppose that the highly sophisticated allegorical interpretation of the Torah to be found in the philosopher Philo, the only Jewish theologian of this period whose writings were extensively preserved by early Christians, was typical of diaspora Jews.

All Jews believed that history progressed under divine guidance and that it was moving towards an eventual culmination. In the time of Jesus speculation on the nature of that end was rife and the views expressed were very varied. The precise dating of the extant eschatological writings by Jews from this period is very difficult, but it is probably significant that some are in the form of apocalyptic, giving the impression that the nature of the future had been divinely revealed and was thus beyond dispute. Many thought that the last age would be ushered in by cataclysmic disasters and great wars in which Israel would triumph over her enemies, followed by a time of bliss in which the land would be the centre of a holy kingdom blessed with supernatural prosperity. Speculation centred on the future of the Jews – on the eventual fate of gentiles views differed widely, some claiming that they would be destroyed, others that they would be attracted to the Jewish God or even converted to Judaism in the new age.

The role in all this of a messianic figure also varied greatly. In some depictions of the eschaton no reference was made to a leader of any kind. Some Jews looked forward to a political leader of the line of David, others to the advent of a supernatural heavenly figure, yet others to more than one messiah. Nor was there agreement as to how imminent the messianic age might be. Some Jews seem to have believed that they were on the threshold of the last days, others that this was something to which they could look forward in the distant future. Thus a messianic faith was integral to almost all types of Judaism in this period, but it is unlikely that it dominated the religious life of more than a few: of all the known Jewish movements of the first century, only one, Christianity, was defined by its messianism.

How were the life and teachings of Jesus viewed by Jews accustomed to such varied forms of their religion? The Gospels themselves give only a partial answer, since they were composed at a time after Jewish rejection of the Christian message was already widespread, but some plausible suggestions are possible. Jews will have seen Jesus as a holy man from the rustic region of Galilee whose prophetic inspiration was confirmed by his power to heal the sick and to predict the future. The performance of miracles gave authority to his teaching despite his minimal learning. His utterances in turn gained force from references to the imminent kingdom of God, probably a reference to the last days, encouraging some of his followers to see in him the long-awaited messiah.

According to the Gospel accounts Jesus taught an idiosyncratic interpretation of the Torah, showing leniency in some areas and strictness in others, but none of his ideas would have been incomprehensible or outlandish to his fellow Jews. Thus, for example, he taught that the laws of the Sabbath were to be interpreted leniently and that contemporary concerns over physical purity were not important, but that laws against taking an oath in vain were to be taken with exceptional seriousness and that marriage agreements were too important to be set aside by divorce. Similar disputes on such matters between other Jews in this period are widely recorded, so it would be wrong to see Jesus as marginal within Jewish society on account of the views he propagated. On the other hand, something in Jesus' behaviour was to lead to his crucifixion by the Roman governor with the approval of the High Priest and his entourage.

If Jesus was as charismatic an individual as he is described in the Gospels, drawing crowds by his oratory and his powers to heal in a fashion dangerously close in the eyes of others to magic, it is not surprising that he drew down upon himself the hostility of the political authorities as John the Baptist had done before him. Thus it is very hard to envisage a theological reason for Jesus' eventual crucifixion since nothing he was alleged to have preached was more shocking than is found elsewhere in Jewish literature of this period, whereas a political explanation is easily forthcoming. The Judaean ruling class, led by the High Priest Caiaphas, knew that their control of the Jerusalem crowds was shaky, above all at the time of the pilgrim festival of Passover when the city was packed. They had few troops, but their political position depended on their success in imposing their authority, for the Roman governor could and did replace High Priests at whim. When a Galilean appeared with a crowd following him it might seem an act of political prudence to have him put out of the way.

The emergence of the Church

At any rate it is with the crucifixion of Jesus in or around 30 CE that Christianity can be said really to have begun. There were many other charismatic teachers and healers in first-century Judaea, but for no other similar individual did a movement in his name spring up after his death. In the explanation of this fact lies the clue to the emergence of the Church.

In the Gospels much emphasis is laid on the impact on his followers of reports about the resurrection of Jesus, and the resurrection already appears in the early creeds in the letters of St Paul. In some ways this is odd, for it is hard to see why Christ's resurrection should have seemed so important as evidence of a divine plan in action or as 'the first fruits of the harvest of the dead' (1 Cor 15:20), since the possibility of various types of life after death for all was widely canvassed among first-century Jews. Whatever the explanation, it is certain that the earliest extant Christian texts, Paul's letters, reveal an emphasis on the mission, crucifixion, resurrection, exaltation and lordship of Jesus rather than on his teachings. It is indeed remarkable that, in contrast to Jesus' mission to Jews alone, Paul rapidly proclaimed himself as the apostle to the gentiles; hardly less remarkable, when Paul taught his gentile converts that conversion to Judaism would demonstrate a lack of faith in Jesus and some of those converts took this to imply an ethical vacuum, Paul seems to have invented a morality for them rather than appealing, except obliquely, to the sayings of Jesus.

After the crucifixion and news of the resurrection of Jesus, his followers in Judaea and Galilee, led by his immediate disciples (the apostles), continued as an identifiable group. All these followers were by definition Jews by birth. About the Jewish Christians of Galilee almost nothing is known, but in the picture provided of the Jerusalem Church in the New Testament, they appear as one Jewish group among many, living for the most part in peace, participating in the Temple ritual, and keeping the Torah in their own fashion while they awaited the second coming of Jesus as Christ and with it the end of the present age. According to the picture painted by the author of the Acts of the Apostles, writing probably some time in the late first century (though both earlier and much later dates for the composition have been canvassed by scholars), these Jewish Christians lived as an ideal community, sharing all in common (cf. Acts 2:46; 4:32, 34). From outside they appeared to Paul as a group firmly administered by the three 'pillars' of the Church, Peter, James and John (Gal 2:9). This model of an ascetic authoritarian community would not have been out of place in first-century Judaea, where both the Essenes and the Dead Sea sectarians (if these are not to be identified one with the other) lived within similar communal structures. The beliefs of these Jewish Christians about Jesus cannot now be discovered with any certainty since nothing known to have been written by them survived. They may have seen Jesus simply as their teacher whose words continued to resonate after his death, just as the sayings of the Teacher of Righteousness were preserved by the Dead Sea sect. But in any case the future of the Church was not to lie with such people, for the number of Jewish Christians in the Jewish homeland seems always to have been quite small. The great expansion of Christianity was to occur outside Judaea.

The Acts of the Apostles provides a detailed account of the missionary journeys of Paul and his circle in the first generation of Christians after the death of Jesus. The narrative may have been partially distorted by the author's hindsight and his desire to demonstrate the essential unity of the Church and the compatibility of Christianity with the culture of the Roman Empire, and there are differences from the account given by Paul of his own career in his own letters written at the time and soon after, but the main outlines of the story may be accepted. Paul and others travelled the cities of the Mediterranean world such as Antioch, Ephesus and Corinth, preaching enthusiastically a new and dramatic message that the future of all mankind had been changed by the life and resurrection of Jesus. Most of the places visited were coastal towns, but in Turkey Paul and Barnabas penetrated into Galatia on the upland plateau, and early on the Christian message reached Rome.

The intensive missionary activity of Paul was, so far as is known, unique in the ancient world. Mission was unknown in ancient polytheism, and although Jews welcomed outsiders who chose to become proselytes, there is little reason to suspect an active proselytizing movement in this period. By contrast Paul marked his success by the number of converts he won. It is of course possible to explain his enthusiasm as a reaction to the specific injunctions of Jesus as recorded for instance in Matthew 28:19-20: 'Go and teach all nations, baptizing them and bringing them instruction', but this can provide only a partial answer, since not all Jesus' alleged sayings have been followed with equal enthusiasm by Christians of all periods, and in any case this injunction, which sits uneasily with Jesus' own career as a teacher of Jews alone, does not seem to have been taken to heart by the Jewish Christians in Jerusalem as they are described in the Acts of the Apostles. One sociological explanation, itself only an inspired guess, may provide a partial clue. It has been observed that groups disappointed in their expectations of some dramatic event often react to disappointment ('cognitive dissonance') by intense activity to demonstrate the truth of the beliefs which seem to be under threat, and that Christians awaiting a dramatic but constantly delayed second coming of Christ may have been such a group. In any case, it is important to note that the missionary urge of the first generation did not continue indefinitely into the later history of the Church.

Who were these new Christians in the first generation of the Church outside the land of Israel? Some were Jews, but many, probably most, were not. Hostile outsiders described them as the dregs of society, in particular women and slaves, but the social backgrounds of converts were in fact quite broad. Some new Christians were well educated and had far-flung contacts, all spoke Greek and belonged to the wider culture of the eastern Mediterranean world. Most will have had little or no contact with the native Jewish Christians of the Holy Land, but the Greek-speaking Jewish Christians in Jerusalem (the 'Hellenists') such as Stephen, whose martyrdom in *c.* 35 is recorded in Acts 7 – 8, had presumably come from the diaspora either before or after their conversion.

So much can be culled from the New Testament texts, but they say less about the *reasons* for converts having desired to become Christians. Jews who joined the Christian community did so presumably in expectation that they would be well placed for the fulfilment of the messianic hope, but for non-Jews the Christian message was not easily understood. A surprising amount of extant Christian exhortatory literature from this period describes the fulfilment of prophecies which will have been previously unknown to their gentile audience, or promises of an afterlife despite the fact that pagans generally lacked concern about the whole topic. Many gentile converts must have been attracted by the sheer novelty and exoticism of Christian communities. Becoming a Christian involved, at least in theory, a dramatic social shift, since if the convert followed the instructions of Paul and other Christian teachers he or she was required to exclude himself or herself from the normal social life of the community and even the family by refusing to participate in the pagan cults which permeated nearly all activities. By contrast the new Christian communities provided social support, mutual aid and comfort from others whose own social identity also derived entirely from their Christian identity. It is likely that converts were encouraged rather than discouraged by stories of martyrdom: a knowledge that some had believed the Christian message to be of sufficient importance to be worth dying for strengthened those who were compelled to suffer lesser problems for their faith. At the same time Christian toleration of mixed marriages (in the hope of the eventual conversion of the non-Christian partner) made the social break more bearable for some.

Suffering, although rarely to the point of martyrdom, was integral to the early Church. Those who underwent such suffering naturally tended to explain it all in theological terms – they suffered for Christ's sake – but the type and severity of suffering and the motivation of the persecutors varied widely. It has already been argued that Jesus was crucified probably on political grounds as a threat to the good order of Jerusalem; the execution was carried out by the Roman governor, with the clear support of the Jewish ruling class. Few of Jesus' followers were perceived as a similar threat: the Jewish historian Josephus recounts the martyrdom of James the brother of Jesus at the hands of a later High Priest, Ananus, in 62, but for the most part the Jerusalem Church was allowed to increase in peace down to the outbreak of the Jewish revolt against Rome in 66 when, at least according to later Christian tradition, the Christians abandoned the city for a refuge in Transjordan.

But the fact that most Christians were not killed by Jews does not imply a wholly happy relationship between them. It is simply not known why Christians were thrown out of Jewish synagogues, but it is possible that it was because of their theological claims about the status of Jesus rather than because of their behaviour. At least according to Acts (6:13–14), it was for his theological assertions about the Temple and the Torah that Stephen was accused, and eventually stoned to death by a mob, in Jerusalem. Theologically-based hostility may also account in part for the refusal of Jews in the diaspora to accept the message preached to them by Paul.

But only a political motive can explain the decision of synagogue authorities to subject Paul to extensive beatings as a formal punishment. Paul as a Roman citizen could have brought his punishers into deep trouble by appealing to the Roman authorities to intervene, and it might have been thought easier simply to ignore Paul's speeches altogether rather than to seek to persecute him. If Paul could not be ignored by diaspora Jews this was probably because he portrayed himself to the gentile authorities as a Jew. As such he was dangerous: if the city authorities believed that the local Jews allowed one of their number to go from city to city openly urging ordinary gentiles to give up their ancestral worship on which, in their view, social stability depended, then the privileged position of the Jewish community as a protected minority could all too easily vanish. It was a sign of Paul's universalism that, despite his mission as apostle to the gentiles, he would not renounce his Jewish status, of which indeed he was most proud.

By the end of the New Testament period opposition to the Church by Jews was already less important than that by gentiles. In theological terms the pagan objection to Christianity was less for what Christians did than for what they did not do. The refusal of gentile Christians to worship the ancestral gods was seen as both wicked and dangerous to society as a whole. Objections were increased by the fact in the early years of the Church that all gentile Christians had opted out of traditional religion: unlike Jews, who were also treated with suspicion for their refusal to worship the other gods, Christians did not have the excuse that they were born into a people for whom this was itself traditional. Hence Nero after the great fire in Rome in 64 could capitalize on popular suspicion to portray Christians as responsible for the disaster. Rumours that Christians indulged in vile practices such as cannibalism and orgies became widespread in the second century in part as a result of Christian secrecy, but the worst calumnies are not attested until the middle of the century, and in his letter to the governor Pliny, who had asked advice about the best way to deal with Christians in the countryside in Pontus and Bithynia (in modern Turkey) in *c.* 110, the Emperor Trajan revealed that at least some representatives of the Roman state paid no heed to such rumours: Trajan advised Pliny that Christians were not to be hunted out, and that when they were discovered they were to be set free unpunished whatever their previous behaviour so long as they were now prepared to make a sacrifice to the gods. Christians reacted to this ambiguous attitude of the state with ambiguity of their own. Some, like the author of Acts, denied any conflict between the aims of the Church and those of Rome, portraying a Roman governor as a sympathizer of Christians. Others, like the author of Revelation, the last book of the New Testament, revelled in the idea that the scarlet whore of Babylon would eventually reach her demise.

By the time of Hadrian, emperor 117–137 CE, early Christian literature revealed that Christians were to be found in cities in Greece, Asia Minor and Syria, and in Rome. Pagan texts record a Christian presence in the countryside of Pontus, and the discovery of Christian texts of the second century in the Egyptian countryside points to the existence of communities there also. A movement that spread so fast without strong central control was bound to take on varied hues in different places. Already the letters of St Paul reveal widely diverse views among Christians about the precise behaviour and ideas required of them. Such variety was treated by Church historians in later antiquity, such as Eusebius, as the product of the implantation of heretical error into the originally pristine Church. More recent scholarship has argued, on the contrary, that an insistence on uniformity of belief and practice emerged only in the second century, and that the first Christians were tolerant of great diversity. The truth probably lies between these two extremes. On the one hand, early Christian documents portray those in the faith as belonging in effect to a 'third race' different from either Jews or gentiles, and the epistles of St Paul to various Christian communities show his attempt to impose some uniformity and discipline on all his 'brothers' in the faith. On the other hand, the same letters reveal the difficulties he encountered in achieving precisely this aim, and his failures, and the survival of evidence from the second century of gnostic gospels and other literature with messages wildly at variance with the Christianity endorsed in the New Testament, encourage the view that the canonization of the New Testament itself was prompted by the need to define orthodoxy and expel heresy.

Thus, despite the coexistence in practice of varied forms of Christianity, the attempted authoritarianism of the early Church was far more severe than was customarily to be found either in ancient paganism or in Judaism, although it was not wholly without precedent. Both pagans and Jews were generally inclined to allow wide latitude in beliefs: precision mattered only in the minutiae of cult practice, so that it mattered less what worshippers thought while they lived their daily lives than how they petitioned the divine on behalf of the community. In contrast, as soon as the apostolic age, characterized by the leadership of charismatic preachers, reached its end in *c.* 75, Christian communities characteristically entrusted their offices to a single overseer (*episcopos* in Greek or 'bishop') with quasi-monarchical powers. Communal rules like the *Didache* were composed to instruct novice Christians in correct behaviour. Furthermore the nascent desire of some Christians for uniformity of belief and practice, already evident in the so-called 'Council of Jerusalem' in *c.* 50 described in Acts, when the leaders of the gentile mission came to a mutually satisfactory agreement with the Jewish Christians of Jerusalem on Christian teaching to gentiles, was strengthened by a system of letter writing which tried, with only partial success, to ensure communal discipline over an extraordinarily wide geographical area, though after the martyrdom of James the Just in *c.* 62 no single figure of authority for the whole Church emerged. On the pagan side the closest parallels to such authoritarian attitudes towards communities were to be found in the philosophical schools, whose leaders went to great length to weed out wrong beliefs. On the Jewish side the most similar organization was the community which produced the sectarian documents found among the Dead Sea scrolls, with their insistence on the teachings of the Teacher of Righteousness and the prescription of penalties for infringements of numerous communal rules. But neither the pagan nor the Jewish parallels to early Christian communities are exact.

By the time of Hadrian, most Christians were born into the faith rather than converts, and most lived within well-established communities with their own rules and systems of mutual support. The ethics by which they lived were in part derived from traditions inherited from the teaching of Jesus and the earliest apostles, but apart from the few Jewish Christians who still followed the Torah, most lived by the ethical norms standard in the rest of Roman society. In the nature of things the exceptional ethical stances were what most people noticed. Thus Christians espoused an unusually rigorous attitude towards sex, praising asceticism, and strongly opposing homosexuality and extramarital fornication, abortion and infanticide, while the fierce Christian disapproval of divorce was unique.

Christian worship differed markedly from standard forms of worship in the surrounding society because of the lack of temples, altars and sacrifices to express devotion to their divinity. The parallel with Jewish synagogues as places for reading and interpreting the Torah is not exact, since all Jews recognized the importance of sacrifices in the Jerusalem Temple in addition to synagogue liturgy, but it is clear that some of the liturgy of the early Church developed out of synagogue practices, with, for instance, a new Christian significance given by Paul to the Passover Feast: 'For

Christ, our paschal lamb, has been sacrificed. Let us, therefore, celebrate the festival, not with the old leaven, the leaven of malice and evil, but with the unleavened bread of sincerity and truth' (1 Cor 5:7–8). Christians early developed the custom of regular meetings, probably on Sundays to mark the distinction from the Jewish Sabbath. These meetings were occasions for teaching. Jewish Christians may have followed in some way the pattern of readings from the Hebrew Bible (or its Greek translation) normal among Jews. Gentile Christians probably did not, but for all in the Church this was the main context in which the Gospel stories about Jesus and his teachings were transmitted.

Already in the first generations Christians also evolved rites for public worship, such as the symbolic transfer onto the individual of the spirit of the divine by the laying on of hands and baptism with water to signify forgiveness of sins as well as entry into the assembly of Christ. The advent of the spirit could be recognized in some by their ecstatic utterances before their fellow-worshippers, taken as important evidence of the workings of the divine (cf. 1 Cor 12:28), even if not all Christians behaved in this way. In the regular weekly gatherings the central act of worship, already assumed in many places in the New Testament, was the Eucharist, a ritual breaking of bread and drinking of a cup of wine in memory of Jesus intended both to express joyful thanks and to bring celebrants into sacramental communion with their Lord. As with the rest of Christian life attempts were made by some Christians to impose uniformity upon this liturgy (cf. *I Clement* 40:2), with partial success. Beyond such communal worship individual dedication to the faith could be shown above all by regular fasts, a technique shared with other Jewish groups, and (more novel) by abstention from sexual relations.

There is still much debate as to how settled these forms of Christian life had become by the time of Hadrian. In almost every aspect it was possible to find some individuals who defined themselves as Christian and yet conducted themselves differently. This was not simply a matter of wide geographical dispersal, although this was an important factor. Widely differing types of Christians lived alongside each other even in longer established communities. Thus in Rome at the end of the first century the attitudes of the conservative Clement, with his desire for harmony and order within the Church and society, contrast markedly with the eschatological speculation of *The Shepherd of Hermas*, a work whose claim (*Vis.* 2.4.3) to have been written by a contemporary of Clement is probably to be accepted despite a tradition in antiquity that it was not produced until the mid-second century. In Asia Minor Cerinthus seems to have held in *c.* 100 CE that the world was not created by the supreme God; it was said that John, 'the disciple of the Lord', ran out of the bathhouse at Ephesus on learning that Cerinthus was there, in fear that the building might collapse on the enemy of truth (Eusebius, *H.E.* 3.28.6), and the sober defence of orthodoxy and social order by Polycarp, Bishop of Smyrna and the most significant Christian leader in Asia Minor in the mid-second century, contrasts markedly with the wild apocalyptic imaginings of the author of the book of Revelation.

This variety is reflected in the lack of any clear consensus on the relationship required between Christian worshippers and Christ himself. Thus in the synoptic Gospels Jesus was portrayed as a prophet and teacher as well as messiah but also as the son of God, while Paul described him at times as Lord, at times as the personification of the wisdom of God (1 Cor 1:24); the author of Hebrews portrayed him as the effulgence of God's splendour (Heb 1:2–3); and the author of the Gospel of John saw him as the word of God (John 1:1–3). From the perspective of the pagan outsider Pliny (*Ep.* 10.96), Christians simply worshipped Christ as a god; and the docetic doctrine that the humanity of Christ had never been real because it would have detracted from his divinity is attested (and opposed) in the New Testament (e.g. 1 John 4:1–3). It is not in doubt that there was a general move among Christians in this period towards the apotheosis of Jesus; what remains uncertain is the speed of this process.

In any case, learned theological debates about such matters lay in the future. In the first century of Christianity, the main focus of the Church rested still in hope: hope for eternal life for the individual, and for salvation for all when, in the fullness of time, Christ would come again in glory and the world would end. In the mean time those in Christ saw themselves as part of a people in exile, presenting themselves as 'a living sacrifice, holy, acceptable unto God' (Rom 12:1).

2
150–550

Adrian Hastings

The second and third centuries

In July of the year 180 a number of very insignificant people, led by a man named Speratus, coming from the small, now unidentifiable townlet of Scillium, were brought before the proconsul Saturninus in Carthage and charged with the practice of an illicit religion. The proconsul was reluctant to order their execution and begged them to 'return to a right mind' or, at least, think it over for 30 days, but they remained adamant in adherence to 'the religious rites of the Christians'. They insisted that they lived in the most moral way, abhorred murder, theft and bearing false witness. They willingly paid tax but absolutely refused to do as the proconsul required and 'swear by the genius of our Lord the Emperor' because they did not recognize 'the empire of this world' but served instead the 'God whom no man has seen nor can see'. Such are the simple words of Speratus. Donata, one of his companions, added 'Give honour to Caesar as unto Caesar, but fear to God', while Secunda remarked that 'I wish to be none other than I am'. Speratus had brought with him a bag containing the letters of St Paul, in case, perhaps, they might need to refer to them, but there was no need. As they persisted in their obduracy, Saturninus read out a sentence of execution and the twelve of them, seven men and five women, were immediately beheaded. They reign, concluded the undoubtedly authentic account of their martyrdom, 'with the Father and Son and Holy Spirit'.

It may seem surprising that already in the year 180 one could find a little group of highly committed Christians in some obscure corner of North Africa. Our text demonstrates how fast this new religion was spreading across the Roman world and, in fact, already beyond it. Seventy years later, there were more than 130 North African bishops, each presiding over a separate Church, sometimes hardly ten miles apart. Their congregations may well have been small enough but the figure still suggests how Christianity had spread out from the large towns to many quite insignificant places. It is right to assert that it was still an urban rather than a rural religion – urban and literate – but its attraction was less to the kind of upper urban class present mostly in the large cities, and more to the lower orders, craftsmen and shopkeepers, who will have been little different in Carthage or in Scillium. While few of these people were slaves, they were certainly of no great worldly importance.

The responses of the Scillian martyrs show too what sort of a religion theirs was: an intensely monotheistic and moral commitment with a very strong belief in the next life and an absolute refusal to compromise with the powers of this world. They had, too, Paul's letters with them, already translated into Latin. In an uncomplicated way it was, then, a bookish religion but not a very ritualistic one. In defending themselves they speak about their morals, not about their rites. Undoubtedly these people had been baptized and met regularly to celebrate the Lord's Supper, their single regular ritual. Beyond that it was a matter of spiritual conviction and moral imperative, grounded in an unambiguous Trinitarian belief: 'The Father and Son and Holy Spirit'.

The picture that Pliny's letter to the Emperor Trajan already presented of Christians brought to trial before him in Bithynia around 112 CE was little different, though it indicated that there were not only Christians willing to die for their beliefs but others willing to deny them or to insist that they had already abandoned them years before. The hundred-per-cent commitment to martyrdom of the Scillians would certainly not prove to be the norm in coming persecutions. We may compare with this evidence a text of a rather different sort, but much the same date, the anonymous 'Epistle to Diognetus'.

> Christians are not distinguished from the rest of mankind by country, or by speech, or by dress. For they do not dwell in cities of their own, or use a different language, or practise a peculiar life . . . but while they dwell in Greek or barbarian cities according as each man's lot has been cast, and follow the customs of the land in clothing and food, and other matters of daily life, yet the condition of citizenship which they exhibit is wonderful, and admittedly strange . . . every foreign land is to them a fatherland, and every fatherland a foreign land. They marry like the rest of the world, they breed children, but they do not cast their offspring adrift . . . They exist in the flesh, but they live not after the flesh. They spend their existence upon earth, but their citizenship is in heaven. They obey the established laws, and in their own lives they surpass the laws . . . In a word, what the soul is in the body Christians are in the world.

Second-century Christians were remarkably sure that theirs was a unique, divinely revealed, doctrine about which no compromise was possible. They expected to be persecuted but this did not make them cut themselves off from society around them. They were preoccupied with their personal lives, without any public ambition or desire to change the structures of society, except in regard to themselves in the fields of marital and sexual custom and business practice. Here their standards were indeed different from those of their neighbours. The abandonment of unwanted babies horrified them as did any kind of marital irregularity. They admired virginity, which seemed already to present a form of perfection of life, but only extremists decried the goodness of marriage.

We should not presume that, because there were Christians in Scillium in 180, there were Christians in every such little town. For the Latin West, North Africa was already far more penetrated by Christianity than anywhere else, even Italy. We know that a couple of years before the Scillian martyrs suffered, a larger group had been executed in Lyons and, doubtless, there were Christian Churches in other parts of Gaul. But the Lyons group, while including Latin-speakers and natives of Gaul, appears to have been predominantly Greek-speaking. In general throughout Gaul, Spain and Britain, the spread of Christianity was far less extensive than in North Africa, Egypt or parts of Asia Minor. Few of the congregations which did exist were of any great size; that of Lyons may well have been among the largest in the Western Empire. There nearly 50 people were martyred, a few reneged under threats or torture, others escaped arrest. The impression given is that there can hardly have been more than a couple of hundred in all before the persecution broke.

There was, at least after the close of the Pauline era, almost no specifically 'missionary' activity, so far as we know. The Christian community had no organizing centre, no missionary task force, no specially trained clergy. It spread through a network of family, friendship, business contacts, through the migrancy of its members, at times through the scattering effect of persecution, through the striking moral example its members offered – especially when persecuted – and through the impact of its rapidly increasing body of literature. Judaism had already proved attractive to many non-Jews on account of its combination of clear monotheistic doctrine, moral integrity and a remarkable body of scriptures, but Judaism was unattractive too through the necessity of circumcision for males and the way in which it imposed incorporation within an ethnic tradition. Christianity took over the attractions of Judaism without these encumbrances. Its stress was on universality, its direct appeal to people of every background and language to be incorporated within a single human community. Neither class nor sex held one back from this community in which there was a strong sense of equality. It was a slave woman named Blandina who proved the real leader of the Lyons martyrs and was hailed as such in the Church's reporting of the events quite uninhibitedly – 'she, the small, the weak, the despised' had 'put on Christ, the great and invincible champion' and was 'crowned with the crown of immortality'.

Most early Christians had undoubtedly been Jews but by 180 this had changed decisively. The separation between the two communities was complete and almost all new converts came directly from a 'pagan' background but also a local one. The leap had been achieved not only from a migratory Jewish environment but also from a necessarily Greek one. It was probably a delay in accomplishing that second leap which lies behind the impression of somewhat slight progress through the middle years of the second century, while it was the achievement of localization in more and more places which made possible the much more rapid growth which seemed to be happening from around the close of the century.

If there was no centralized authority, there was a very clear sense of authority, basically unitary and structured locally in a remarkably unified way. In the early, subapostolic, days each church appears to have had a collegial leadership: a group of 'presbyters' with, most probably, a leader among them who was either called a 'bishop' (*episcopus*) from the start or came so to be called quite soon. The balance between the 'college' and the single 'bishop' will have varied slightly according to place. Almost everywhere the movement was probably from the more collegial to the more episcopal, and it may be that in some places there was at first no one who could have been described as 'episcopus'. In small towns like Scillium with, maybe, no more than a tiny handful of faithful, it would be natural to have no 'episcopus' but a 'presbyter', dependent on a larger community nearby. But we do not know. Certainly, whatever he was called, he will have been a married elderly man of known rectitude of life who supported himself. The reason for the arrival of a single 'bishop' in each church was clear enough – the role of presiding at the Eucharist was likely to have belonged to a specific person and as the Eucharist constituted the heart of Christian life, so its regular presider was naturally recognized as the head of the local church. However important other duties within the community might be, and there could be many in the larger congregations, this held the primacy.

As the Christian movement spread, becoming rooted in an ever wider area, the strain upon its unity and uniformity, given the lack of any single authority, was inevitable. What is remarkable is the degree of uniformity in fact maintained, despite the new situations, challenges and ideas with which it came to be faced. The clear consciousness of belonging to a single fellowship of belief and practice remained decisive. This was achieved in various ways and despite very considerable pressure to incorporate all sorts of additional ideas mostly deriving from what has come to be described as 'Gnosticism' – a dualistic mysticism, claimed as providing a special additional revelation, a movement which probably derived from Egypt, but was spread elsewhere by various travelling teachers of whom Valentinus, who arrived in Rome about 136, was the most influential. It mixed Christian ideas and vocabulary with all sorts of basically incompatible beliefs, mostly related to a rejection of the intellectual inheritance of the Jewish scriptures with their insistence upon the creation of a good world by the one God. Marcion, the son of a bishop in Pontus, developed a theology which systematically rejected everything to do with the Old Testament and he built up quite a network of Marcionite congregations right across the Mediterranean world. Whereas Christian orthodoxy, for such it can already be called, insisted upon the identity of the Jewish God with the Father of Jesus worshipped by Christians, Gnostics proclaimed a vastly more complex theology and cosmology in which there were all sorts of intermediate beings who had created and still controlled the world, on account of whose activities the material universe could be perceived as a prison from which souls needed to escape. The similarities between the two essentially incompatible theologies were nevertheless sufficient for Christian beliefs to be reread, not too implausibly, in Gnostic terms.

Throughout the second century, local Christian communities were only too likely to be infiltrated by Gnostic teachers and ideas, bringing with them a multitude of additional scriptures – further 'gospels' and 'acts' named after various apostles. What seems striking is the firmness with which they were rejected by the Christian community generally, through insistence upon the essential unity of the two covenants and the decisive authority of a limited group of writings known throughout the Churches to derive from apostolic times, centred upon the four Gospels and the letters of Paul. We see the clearest formulation of a 'catholic', anti-Gnostic, position in the writings of Irenaeus, Bishop of Lyons towards the close of the second century. Irenaeus may have come from Smyrna, he had spent some years in Rome and he wrote in Greek. He had experienced the width of the Church's communion of his time as well as anyone. While he still represents Greek, rather than Latin, Christianity, it is symbolic that his major book, *Against the Heresies*, survived in full only in Latin. Irenaeus's insistence on the recognized scriptures, the authority of bishops derived directly from the apostles and a doctrine of God at once monotheist, Trinitarian and incarnationalist, was in no way his invention. It was the defence of what we can call an early Catholicism, something predating the Gnostic challenge, but he was the first great theologian to set it out so systematically. Faced with this sort of response, the Gnostic movement, at least as located in part within the Christian community, seems to have faded fairly fast.

There can be little doubt that the last years of the second century witnessed not only a large expansion but also a certain defining of Christianity. The separate books of the New Testament were by now – apart from one or two rather marginal pieces such as Jude – collected into a unity seen as constituting a single 'New' set of scriptures to be put beside, but not replace, the Hebrew 'Old' scripture within a listed 'canon' of inspired books. Other excellent works, such as *The Shepherd* of Hermas, probably the brother of a Bishop of Rome, were well respected but nevertheless not placed on the same level.

Expansion brought with it the need to surmount the barrier of the Greek language. It was, of course, remarkable that the early Church became so quickly a predominantly Greek-speaking community given that Jesus may well never have spoken Greek at all. Its scriptures were written in Greek, its rituals were in Greek, its early literature was all in Greek. Thus the Church in Rome undoubtedly used Greek in its liturgy for at least a century, but its replacement by Latin was inevitable if Christianity was to maintain its claim to universality. Latin had probably taken over within the African Church well before it did so in Rome and it looks as if it was an African Pope, Victor (189–198), who masterminded the switch in Rome itself. The translation of the Scriptures into Latin was early and unproblematic. As it was a literary language used by Christians unfamiliar with Greek, it was simply the obvious thing to do. No one thought that the Scriptures had less authority in Latin than they did in Greek, though mistranslations once recognized – and the first translations were quite rough – needed to be put right. The same thing happened in Syriac and, just a little later, for Coptic, indeed into more than one form of Coptic. This is particularly significant because Coptic was not hitherto a language much used for literary purposes. By the middle of the fourth century the Scriptures were also being translated into Gothic, then Armenian and, by the fifth century, Ethiopic and then Georgian.

This impressive series of translations can produce no great surprise once the Christian sense of universality is recognized, that sense stressed in the 'Epistle to Diognetus' of being at home in any language and culture. The privileging of Greek, as Christianity's 'sacred' or original language, came later: first, with Byzantine clerics from the late fourth century who increasingly identified the Church with the empire centred in Constantinople; secondly, with post-Renaissance biblical scholars preoccupied with the original text of the New Testament to an extent far beyond the concern of the early or medieval Church; thirdly, with modern theorists of religion anxious to provide every religion with a 'sacred' language. Christianity had none.

If Irenaeus appealed to a canon of scripture and defended the goodness of created matter, especially the 'flesh' which the Son of God had assumed, he also insisted upon the authority of the episcopate as interpreter of correct teaching, an authority derived, person to person, from the apostles: 'Anyone who wishes to discern the truth may see in every Church in the whole world the apostolic succession clear and manifest. We can enumerate those who were appointed as bishops in the Churches by the apostles and their successors to our own day.' This sounds a large claim and many historians have questioned its plausibility but there is really no compelling reason to deny the core of it or to doubt that Irenaeus, who had known Polycarp in his youth, as Polycarp had known John, had adequate ground for what he said. What matters to us is anyway that by the late second century this is how it could be conceived. In the principal cities where the apostles had worked they had appointed bishops, and more bishops had been appointed as the churches multiplied in places where the apostles had never been, but all could be included within a framework of apostolic authority.

There was, however, no clearly formulated way of relating these bishops to one another. Each was thought to preside in his own church with apostolic authority. In practice most of them were simple, poorly informed ministers who could not conceivably have coped with a theological conundrum with the insight of an Irenaeus. What happened in consequence was that they consulted with one another and met in local synods, first informal, then formal. By the middle of the third century this was happening on a large scale. We know of major episcopal gatherings at both Carthage and Rome in 251, at Carthage again in 256 and at Antioch in 268, among others. At such meetings, called undoubtedly by the bishop of the see where the meeting was held, most of the rest said little or nothing. In practice a sharp distinction was developing between the bishops of a small number of major cities, who were backed by a numerous clergy of their own, and other bishops belonging to small towns in their neighbourhood who mostly did as they were told.

The authority of the major sees was based on the size and wealth of their church, the theological and administrative expertise they had at hand and the civil importance of their cities within the imperial order. Nevertheless they sought as well specific ecclesiastical justification and tried to find it in a claim to apostolic foundation. Unfortunately the evidence for this was mostly none too good. Alexandria could only lay claim, somewhat dubiously, to St Mark; Antioch admittedly had been visited by both Peter and Paul but they had moved on elsewhere, so that Antioch lacked the prestige of an apostle's grave to guarantee a sort of continued presence. Carthage had nothing at all. Jerusalem, which had the incontestable authority of James, the Lord's brother, had been so disrupted by the Roman destruction and subsequent rebuilding as a Greek city, that its ecclesiastical authority had been considerably diminished. Ephesus probably had John, though this honour was disputed by other churches. Corinth, Athens and other Greek cities were all proud to have been preached to by Paul. But it is clear that in reality the emerging regional primacy of a few churches by the third century had little to do with the apostles and much with a combination of secular importance and the contemporary strength of their Christian community. Alexandria, Antioch, Carthage, Athens and Rome stood head and shoulders above anywhere else and – apart from Irenaeus – all the Christian writers of significance in this period were connected with one or other of these five churches.

However, in apostolic terms Rome remained in a class of its own because it did possess the burial place of both the principal apostles of the Gentile world – Peter and Paul. It could claim in consequence to be an 'apostolic see' in a way that none of its potential rivals could plausibly imitate. And it did so. It was probably Pope Anicetus (155–166) who erected a noted memorial shrine for St Peter on the Vatican Hill at the place of his burial about 164, maybe precisely the centenary of his death. With the emphatic gospel promises to St Peter of texts like Matthew 16:18, 'You are Peter and upon this rock I will build my Church', it is hardly surprising that the bishops of Rome came to stress that their succession derived especially from him and that this gave them a uniquely extensive authority. The way Irenaeus put it may represent a common second-century perspective: 'It would be very long, in a book of this kind, to enumerate the successions of all the Churches', hence it is sufficient to refer to that 'in the greatest, most ancient and well-known Church, founded and established by the most glorious apostles, Peter and Paul, in Rome . . . For to this Church on account of her more powerful principality it is necessary that every Church should agree [or 'come together'] . . .' Few non-biblical texts have been so argued over as this one, but it should be obvious enough that in apostolic terms the church of Rome had no rival bar Jerusalem, and Jerusalem's church with its strongly Jewish-Christian character had been marginalized and effectively cut off from developing by political and military history. Irenaeus could already point to the way Clement of Rome in the late first century had intervened when there was a conflict within the church of Corinth.

Rome was not only, however, an apostolic church *par excellence*, it was also the church of the imperial capital. That did not make its life any easier, indeed it bore the brunt of more frequent persecution than anywhere else. Moreover there was no necessity for Christians to acknow-ledge some sort of centrality for the church where the Empire was centred. On the contrary, as the Empire was often viewed as 'Babylon', a sink of worldly iniquity, a highly other-worldly religion might be expected to want little to do with it. All the same, in periods of peace it was natural enough that the church of the capital should take the lead in all sorts of things and that Christians from elsewhere, Gnostics and heretics included, should turn up in Rome far more than they did in any other city.

Given the size of the population of Rome it is not surprising that its church should have grown so much in numbers and should have acquired a fair amount of property. The digging of its catacombs for burial was a considerable enterprise in itself. About the year 250 its bishop had beneath him 46 presbyters, seven deacons, seven subdeacons, 42 acolytes, 52 exorcists, readers and doorkeepers and over 1,500 widows and others in distress for whom it provided relief. The seven deacons and subdeacons were responsible for organizing the seven ecclesiastical districts into which Pope Fabian (236–250) divided the city. These figures are not huge, nevertheless the Roman church clearly had staff and resources well beyond those of most other places, especially in the West.

Little by little one can see out of all this the 'papacy' emerging, exercising an undefined but incontestable role, one recognized to some extent throughout the Christian world. There was at this time still no question of any conscious division between East and West, Greek and Latin, in the Church any more than in the empire, to separate Rome from the East. If its own liturgy was now principally in Latin, it certainly continued to be open to numerous Christians from the eastern parts of the empire who gravitated to the capital, and several third-century Popes – Anterus, Sixtus II and Dionysius – were Greeks.

One thing in which Rome certainly did not excel was the writing of theology. Among Latin writers those of Carthage, Tertullian and Cyprian, were more powerful thinkers than anyone connected with Rome, but the most creative centre of Christian theology was undoubtedly Alexandria. Here the intellectual tradition of the large Jewish community had been taken over and, stimulated by the challenge of Gnosticism, two remarkable theologians, Clement (c. 150–215) and Origen (c. 185–254), developed a systematic and subtle approach both to the interpretation of Scripture and to the relation of Christian belief and its formulation to the current philosophy of the secular world, far beyond anything else achieved in this period. It is to be noted too that, though Christians formed a quite small proportion of the total population, their literature in the second and third centuries was already far more impressive, in vigour of thought, imaginativeness and diversity, than that of anyone else.

There were two short but sharp periods of persecution in the middle of the third century, one under the Emperor Decius around the year 250, in which the Bishops of Rome, Jerusalem and Antioch were all martyred, and another, enforced particularly in Africa, under Valerian in 258, of which Cyprian of Carthage was the most prominent victim. For most of the century, however, Christians were allowed to exist in peace and the churches to own property, enter into negotiation with the civil authorities where they needed to, and grow steadily in numbers. It is hard to say quite how numerous Christians were by the close of the third century and it is easy to exaggerate their proportion within the general population. Perhaps in a few areas they could have exceeded 20 per cent, even more in certain towns in Egypt and Asia Minor, but in general the figure must be lower and in most of the West far lower – less than 10 per cent. Nevertheless there was no other remotely comparable religious or civil body. Christians formed a well-organized, self-aware community; they appeared to be represented virtually everywhere; they had even begun openly building churches – including a cathedral in the eastern imperial capital of Nicomedia – instead of, as earlier, simply worshipping within private houses; they included a few members of the wealthy, even senatorial, class, mostly women; they appeared to have built up a coherent intellectual and literary system of their own, and, most serious of all, they appealed confidently and directly to divine authority which they unquestioningly put above that of the emperor. It held them back from military service and much else. It is not surprising that again and again emperors had concluded that this was something which could not be tolerated – an empire within the Empire – and that as Christians became ever more confident and numerous, an imperial decision was taken that, at whatever cost, it was necessary to crush them.

The 'Great Persecution' was the result. It is linked with the Emperor Diocletian (285–305), though it actually began only in 303 and was probably chiefly the responsibility of his deputy and successor, Galerius. Diocletian's original aim was the destruction of an institution, not the killing of people. He was well aware of the counter-productive consequences of martyrdom. But it proved impossible to separate the two. The churches went up in flames, all sacred books were to be handed over and destroyed, church services were forbidden, but there was at first no insistence that Christians should be compelled to sacrifice to the gods. In some places the authorities did not look too closely at what books were actually surrendered – perhaps just heretical ones or even a medical textbook. Most Christians and many of the clergy hoped to avoid the disobedience which would lead to execution but others were wholly uncompromising: anyone handing over anything was for them a 'traitor'. Pope Marcellinus in Rome was one such *traditor*. At Abitina in Africa the bishop too had handed over the Scriptures but his congregation rebelled and continued to worship in the house of a lector named Emeritus. The authorities eventually struck: 47 Christians were arrested and imprisoned in Carthage, including their presbyter, Saturninus, and his four children.

In prison, before execution, the Christians of Abitina emphatically condemned any *traditor*: to hand over the Scriptures to be burnt was to merit eternal damnation. This divide between the compromisers and the uncompromising was soon to tear the Church apart, but also to force systematic reconsideration of the handling of both sin and sinners.

After the death of Diocletian, the persecution quickly died down in the West, but in the East it was renewed by Galerius and his deputy Maximin Daia with ever increasing violence. Everyone was ordered to sacrifice to the gods and the names of those who did so were checked by the military against taxation rolls. Punishments grew worse and worse. In Egypt especially whole villages were massacred. Yet it was clearly not succeeding. There were too many martyrs and too much sympathy for them. In the ceaseless jockeying for power between emperors in East and West, the absence of persecution in the latter and the bitterness it was producing in the former could only strengthen the hands of the tolerant. Egypt was being alienated and on the verge of rebellion, while Christian writers like Eusebius of Caesarea were winning the propaganda war. In 311, about to die, Galerius called it all off. The decree in which he did so is revealing: all that he had done, he claimed, was for the advantage of the state and to bring Christians back to common sense so that they would stop 'making laws for themselves . . . and assembling in different places people of different nationalities'. It was recognition that Christianity had developed into a kind of alternative state, of universalist dimensions, which seemed so threatening. But, Galerius continued, seeing that in their obstinacy they had mostly failed to return to the worship of the gods and were now in consequence worshipping no one, he had decided to exercise indulgence and allow them to re-establish their churches once more.

Constantine and an imperial Church

The very extent and purposefulness of the Great Persecution underlined the significance of its failure. The Christian Church was now a power in the empire, not because it used force, but because it did not and yet — despite the inevitable compromises of many of its members when faced with a threat of execution or deportation to the mines — it held the minds and hearts of a large proportion of the population in a way that nothing else did. But what if military force and Christian faith could only be united, would not that create a new and glorious empire? At some point, and it was impossible to know just when, this became the conviction of the young Caesar in the north-west, Constantine, son of the former emperor Constantius and his first wife, Helena, who had herself become a Christian. He had been proclaimed emperor at York by the legions stationed there on his father's death in 306 but he had the advantage of being brought up in Diocletian's court at Nicomedia, so he knew the Eastern situation well enough even though his power base was in the less Christianized West. When Constantine marched south from Gaul to defeat his Western rival, Maxentius, he claimed to have seen a heavenly vision promising him victory and he certainly had a Spanish bishop, Hosius of Cordoba, among his advisers. From the time that he won the battle of the Milvian Bridge in 312 and occupied Rome, he was already publicly identified with the Christian cause, although he did not, to begin with, wholly distance himself from other cults. The last pagan symbols disappear from the coinage only in 323. The so-called Edict of Milan of 313, agreed with the new Eastern Emperor Licinius, simply decreed that 'every man may have complete toleration in the practice of whatever worship he has chosen' – an admirable principle which Constantine's Christian successors would quickly abandon. His patronage of the Church, together with personal interference in its affairs, grew and grew until his baptism, on the eve of death, in 337.

The rapidity of the change in Christianity's public status must have been extremely hard for both Christians and pagans to relate to. Property and exemptions from tax were rained on the clergy. The gift of the Lateran Palace in 313 remains especially symbolic. It had been the property of Constantine's wife, Fausta, but now became, and remained for centuries, the Pope's principal residence. In it medieval councils were regularly held. From then on the Bishop of Rome would have two homes, the Lateran and the Vatican, one reflecting his imperial inheritance, the other his apostolic one. Few could tell which mattered more. While the famous 'Donation of Constantine', a document purporting to bestow upon the Pope huge ecclesiastical and political authority, is a forgery of the eighth century – though one actually inimical to the papacy's best case for primacy – the Lateran was in point of fact donation enough. It signified a massive accretion in political status. But it is not irrelevant to an understanding of its significance to remember that, if the gift was part of Constantine's power game, the later murder of Fausta – asphyxiated in her bath – was another part, just one of many political murders for which he was responsible. Constantine would later be named 'the thirteenth apostle' and venerated in the Eastern Church as a saint. It was a sanctity of rather a new kind.

Constantine was persuaded that he had been divinely chosen to rule the world and that this responsibility most certainly included ensuring as well the unity and orthodoxy of the Church. Ecclesiastically he was faced with an immediate crisis. North Africa had been the scene of the worst persecution in the West and its termination had been followed by bitter conflict between the new Bishop of Carthage, Caecilian, who took a fairly mild line in regard to those who had compromised under persecution, and opponents led by Donatus, for whom *traditores* were to be shunned and sacraments connected with them judged invalid. Constantine could not, he wrote to a Christian official, ignore such quarrels lest 'the Highest Divinity may be moved to wrath not only against the human race, but against me myself, to whose care he has by his heavenly will committed the government of all earthly things'. Such was the new imperial ideology by which the Church had now to be steered. Constantine told Miltiades of Rome to resolve the matter and, when the Donatists rejected Miltiades's judgement, remitted the question to an interprovincial council held at Arles in August 314, a council which included three British bishops and confirmed what Miltiades had decided. Arles was important, not only as the first regional council in the West but because its very calling demonstrated so clearly the Church's new imperial regime. It all happened so quickly that no one had time to interrogate the change which was taking place. It seemed so providential and exciting that the emperor should show such intense personal interest in ecclesiastical issues that the risks this brought could hardly be envisaged.

In 324 Constantine defeated the mildly anti-Christian Licinius and united the empire firmly beneath his own, by now emphatically Christian, rule. In the East as already in Africa, however, he found a Church divided – between Bishop Alexander of Alexandria on the one side, and a priest named Arius on the other. The conflict here was about the divinity of Christ and, while Alexander enjoyed by far the greater support, it happened that the two Eastern bishops closest to Constantine sympathized with Arius: Eusebius, Bishop of the imperial capital of Nicomedia, and the historian and apologist Eusebius of Caesarea. At once Constantine resolved to settle the matter and a general council of bishops was called to meet at Nicaea in May 325. Nicaea was conveniently close to his capital of Nicomedia and, when some 230 bishops arrived, he himself opened the assembly. What is really remarkable is that the Council of Nicaea came down so emphatically, and almost unanimously, against Arius, despite the views of the two Eusebiuses. If at the time Constantine acquiesced, it was partly because this was the view of his old Western adviser, Bishop Hosius, but perhaps also because, with the eye of a superb political strategist, he knew he needed Egyptian loyalty and the Egyptian bishops were overwhelmingly behind Alexander and his brilliant deacon, Athanasius. Later he would have second thoughts. Eusebius of Nicomedia became his most intimate religious confidant and the person who baptized him on his deathbed. A year later Eusebius was promoted by Constantius to be Bishop of Constantinople – a model for the new courtly ecclesiology. Athanasius, who had succeeded Alexander as Bishop of Alexandria, on the other hand was sent into exile, but the ferociously complicated ins and outs of doctrinal history in the post-Nicaea period matter less than the imperial framework which from now on so largely controlled the surface of ecclesiastical life. Only someone with the intellectual power, obstinacy of will and longevity of Athanasius could stand against it.

It is hardly surprising that Constantine should come to be venerated as the 'friend of God' and thirteenth apostle. Upper-class Christians were proud of Rome and it was not hard to see one supreme providential plan running through the course of history. Luke had taken pains to tie the life of Jesus into the reigns of Augustus and Tiberius (Luke 2:1; 3:1) and in the Acts to carry on the story to the arrival of Paul in Rome. It was not hard to see the Empire as divinely ordered to provide space for God's universal Church or to recognize that part of the plan must be the linking of the two into one, something now achieved. Eusebius of Caesarea was the principal theorist of this new imperial view of Christian history: the Church's leading historical scholar, whose *History of the Church* ends with Constantine's victory over Licinius, his praise as 'pre-eminent in every virtue that true religion can confer' and a picture of the world where everyone now 'danced and sang in city and country alike'. In his *Life of Constantine*, Eusebius describes how on one occasion amid a company of bishops Constantine remarked 'You are bishops whose jurisdiction is within the Church: I also am a bishop, ordained by God to overlook those outside the Church'. He watched over all his subjects, commented Eusebius, with a truly episcopal care. Finally, when in 336 Constantine celebrated his *Tricennalia*, 30 years of rule, in Jerusalem, Eusebius was there once more to delineate the divine order: one God, one Word and Saviour, one emperor whose role it is to interpret to the whole human race the knowledge and love of God. Eusebius in his oration for the *Tricennalia* provided the ideal norm for Church and state which would govern Eastern Christianity for many centuries.

If it was now to be an imperial Church, it was also to be, far more explicitly than hitherto, a Greek Church. In 330 Constantine moved from Nicomedia, east of the Bosporus, to dedicate his new capital of Constantinople on its western side, transforming the old Greek city of Byzantium. It was to be a thoroughly Christian capital as Rome at that time could not possibly be. From the third century the emperors had increasingly realized that they needed for all sorts of strategic reasons to be based well to the east of Rome, but they had never made of their various working capitals a new Rome in the way that Constantine now did. For almost all of them, however, old Rome was an unattractive place, too aristocratically conservative, too dominated by the great senatorial families, to allow a somewhat *parvenu* emperor to feel quite at home. On the Bosporus they could do so. For Constantine the revulsion from Rome was above all religious. It remained too pagan a city. However much property he might bestow on its bishop, that could not alter its real character and Constantine wanted something very different. Rome was left to the Senate and its old gods, but Constantinople would become the true centre of the new political and ecclesiastical order: Nova Roma, the capital of a new 'Roman People', a Christian people. While at first its diocese was subordinate to that of Heraclea, inevitably it quickly came to be recognized as a see equal at least to Alexandria and Antioch.

In 381 the third canon of the Council of Constantinople decreed that 'the Bishop of Constantinople shall have the privileges of honour after the Bishop of Rome, because it is new Rome'. It was in other ways an important and reconciling council, bringing the long Arian dispute to a close, but this canon was declaring something quite new and, inevitably, controversial. It is not surprising that the following year a council held in Rome insisted that 'the holy Roman Church has been set before the rest by no conciliar decrees but has obtained the primacy by the voice of our Lord and Saviour . . . "Thou art Peter" . . . the second see was consecrated at Alexandria . . . the third see . . . at Antioch.' It is significant that when, the year before the Council of Constantinople, the Emperor Theodosius declared Christianity the Empire's official religion, the latter had been defined in terms of the doctrine taught by the Bishops of Rome and Alexandria with no mention of Constantinople. The ecclesiastical conflicts of the fourth and fifth centuries were in point of fact to a large extent due to the attempts of the Church of Alexandria to prevent Constantinople from ousting it in the pecking order of episcopal power. In the 70 years following the Council of Constantinople, the Bishop of Alexandria contrived the deposition of the Bishop of Constantinople no fewer than three times. In the short run the Bishops of Constantinople, whatever 'privileges of honour' were accorded them, were peculiarly vulnerable to the pressures of the court, the Constantinopolitan populace and the rest of the empire. Until a later period they lacked the backing, which Alexandria, Antioch and Rome possessed, of a secure local tradition. But this was not just a matter of rivalry between two sees or two theologies. The continual aggrandizement of the see of Constantinople was an inevitable part of the way the empire was going. It would provide a norm for Christianity of a specifically Greek sort. By the sixth century the Bishop of Constantinople would have assumed the title of 'Ecumenical Patriarch'. With that title, there was no longer a question of claiming an equality of the five patriarchates of Rome, Alexandria, Antioch, Jerusalem and Constantinople – a slightly earlier Eastern view of how the world Church's government should be shaped. Instead the logic of Constantinian Christianity in which one empire was seen as providentially renewed in Christian form and focused upon the 'New Rome' on the Bosporus was bound to lead to the concept that here, and here alone, was a truly universal patriarchate.

This ecclesiological development could only mature, nevertheless, little by little. What happened much more quickly in the wake of Constantine's original revolution was a vast public Christianization of society. The numbers poured in. The majority of senior people in power were soon at least nominal Christians. Bishops everywhere became figures of importance in society and large churches were erected at public expense in all the main cities of the empire. It was no longer thought improper, except by the more austere, for a Christian to take arms and be a soldier. Already in 321 Sunday was declared a public holiday. People began to go on pilgrimage to Jerusalem, following Helena, Constantine's mother, who founded basilicas on the Mount of Olives and in Bethlehem. Even in provinces like Britain where Christianity was a somewhat late arrival and there was only a handful of dioceses, it was penetrating into the countryside and accepted by wealthy landowners, while in North Africa or lower Egypt the rural population was by the late fourth century overwhelmingly Christian.

In 360 Julian became emperor on the death of his cousin Constantius II. A successful general, he had been given the rank of Caesar by Constantius and named as his successor. A brilliant philosopher-king who had been brought up a nominal Christian but had come to hate Christianity and the regime which had murdered his father, a half-brother of Constantine, and so many of his family, he set himself to restore Hellenic civilization and the worship of the gods. Christian privileges were withdrawn, religious freedom granted to every dissident group on the assumption that if left free to do so Christians would quickly tear themselves to pieces 'in their deadly hatred of one another', as Ammianus Marcellinus, a contemporary pagan chronicler, bitingly reported. Temple worship was to be restored and Julian himself spent his time sacrificing to one god or another, while attempting to persuade non-Christians to pull themselves together and even adopt a religious organization and practice of charity modelled on the Christian. 'Why do we not observe', he complained, 'that it is their benevolence to strangers, their care for the graves of the dead and the pretended holiness of their lives that have done most to increase atheism [i.e. Christianity]?' He offered instead a mix of Neoplatonism, classical literary culture, a Mithraistic worship of the sun and a general revival of all local cults, as of the traditional gods of the Greeks.

Such a programme appealed to plenty of upper-class people for whom attachment to Christianity had been little more than a matter of political convenience. But it was intensely artificial. The religious revolution had gone too far to be turned back even by a highly imaginative emperor. He tried moreover to do everything at once, marched into Persia and, despite initial military success, was defeated and killed less than two years after coming to power. It is striking that absolutely no one attempted to maintain Julian's policy after his death. Christian political control was immediately resumed. There was no alternative group of people capable of leading society. If one considers the leading figures of late fourth-century Christianity – Athanasius, Basil, John Chrysostom in the East, Ambrose, Hilary of Poitiers and Martin in the West – one is looking at an exceptional group of people, in both intelligence and moral commitment, who were carrying across a great deal of the culture of Athens and Rome in the revolutionary construction of a new socio-religious order. There was simply no one to rival them upon the other side, except for Julian himself, and he was too idiosyncratic to be convincing. While conversion to Christianity in the post-Constantinian world was undoubtedly for many people a matter largely of political convenience, it was also for a dynamic minority a matter of philosophical and moral conviction. This was a generation still on the frontier between two vast religious views, but that frontier could certainly not be decisively crossed or recrossed simply by the power of the state. When Julian died in Persia, his troops elected a Christian general, Jovian, to replace him and within three months Athanasius was riding into Antioch in triumph with the new emperor.

Ambrose represents the new Christian establishment at its most decisive. The son of the Pretorian Prefect of Gaul, he was Governor of Aemilia and Liguria with his base in Milan, when in 370 the Christians of Milan were contentiously seeking a new bishop. As a conscientious governor, he had intervened in an attempt to keep the meeting calm when suddenly his own name was proposed. The idea proved irresistible though he was at the time unbaptized. Within a week baptism and episcopal consecration had followed. Milan was, at the time, the Western imperial capital and Ambrose's public role was enormous, his political experience reinforcing his episcopal prestige. He forced Theodosius to do penance after his appalling massacre at Thessalonica in 390, but he prevented him from restoring a synagogue burnt down by Christians at Callinicum two years earlier. The new Christianity was already becoming alarmingly intolerant, and this was particularly noticeable in regard to the Jews, whom the pagan empire had treated far more kindly than it had treated Christians. Theodosius produced laws against Manichaeans, Apollinarians and Arians among others. In 380 he formally declared Christianity the official religion of his empire, but the most irreversible step was probably that of 391 forbidding the celebration of pagan sacrifices. Constantine's age of religious tolerance – far from complete but still basically genuine as between Christians and non-Christians – was now replaced by one of ecclesiastical establishment and the official exclusion of alternatives, other than a tolerated Judaism. The closure of the temples or their wholesale transformation into Christian churches began the age of a permanently persecuting Church though, doubtless, in practice in many more remote areas that was still far from the reality, and many temples continued to function well into the fifth century.

In much of this Ambrose was the guiding light, combining the confidence of a Roman ruler with Greek culture and a rather self-righteous sense of inheriting a biblical prophetic mantle. He almost always got his way. The last major intellectual battle between the old and the new religious outlooks came in 384 with the appeal to the emperor by Symmachus, the Prefect of Rome, for the maintenance of the altar of Victory in the Senate House. Why abandon the gods through whom Rome has won so many victories? Why cannot everyone live and believe in his own way? There cannot be only one road to so great a mystery. The arguments of Symmachus were dignified, traditional and pluralist. But Ambrose ensured that the appeal was rejected.

Ambrose's main contemporary in Rome was Damasus (366–384). It was he who had appealed to him to take up the issue of the altar of Victory with the Western emperor. Damasus was hardly an attractive figure. He had come to the position by disposing of his Christian opponents in a couple of very nasty massacres, one in the Julian basilica, the other in the Liberian. He lived in a grand way, socializing rather too frequently with senatorial ladies, and proving very unhelpful in regard to St Basil's patient attempt to sort out the continuing confusion left in Antioch by the Arian conflicts. Basil finally described him as impossibly arrogant. Damasus spent his time harping on the authority of his 'apostolic see' and his position as direct successor of St Peter, while showing very little understanding of what was actually going on in the East. But he built churches, restored catacombs, wrote epigrams about the martyrs and had them elegantly inscribed in marble by a friend. Moreover he commissioned his secretary, St Jerome, the outstanding scholar of his age, to revise the existing Latin translations of the Gospels on the basis of the Greek texts. He behaved, then, very much like many a later Pope, and he represents the way in which the withdrawal of the emperor from Rome left room for its bishops to expand the exercise of their authority even though, for the time being, that of the Bishop of Milan where the imperial government in the West had its base was politically more important.

The monastic movement

If Damasus, Ambrose and Theodosius provide a political face for the post-Constantinian Church which is not altogether appealing, it needs to be balanced by consideration of a very different side of fourth-century Christianity, that of monasticism, the development of whole communities of people committed to a life of prayer and asceticism, including both poverty and celibacy. It was not new in principle. The admiration of virginity goes back to apostolic times and virgins had long held a recognized position in the Church. Even the new monastic movement dates from late third-century Egypt and probably Palestine too, well before the age of Constantine began. In this as in much else the new political context would hasten, rather than originate, the way things would go. A common error in Church historical interpretation is to underestimate the dependence of developments in the fourth century upon what went before.

It was in the 270s that Antony, about twenty years old, heard the words of the Sunday Gospel read in Coptic: 'If thou wilt be perfect, go and sell all that thou hast and give to the poor, and come, follow me.' But his immediate response was no different from that of many people before him: he moved to a shed on the edge of his Egyptian village, continued to share in public worship, supported himself by making mats and baskets and learnt from older ascetics living in the same way. Considerably later he moved out to the edge of the desert, developing a new model of emphatically eremitical life, a model that many others soon came to imitate, until, in Athanasius's later hyperbolic words, 'the desert was made a city by monks coming out from their own and enrolling themselves in the heavenly citizenship'. If Antony's way remained that of a hermit, we have almost at once another dimension – some sort of communion between a network of ascetics, each living alone, but not far apart, while supporting one another spiritually and materially, probably even coming together at least occasionally for common prayer. Both at Nitria in Egypt and in various Palestinian sites a pattern of monastic life was evolving which came to be called a *lavra*, where a group of solitaries shared a church and a bakehouse, so that the element of community obtained institutionalized form, however limited. Total withdrawal of a hermit into the isolation of purely personal prayer was too contrary to the liturgical nature of Christianity and too dangerous psychologically for the individual to become normative for long. But it was Pachomius, a young Egyptian ex-army conscript who was converted to both Christianity and the monastic vocation about 313, who took the decisive step in constructing the first fully cenobitic monastery at Tabennesis, close to the Nile in

Upper Egypt. The Pachomian community was a simple, almost military, institution, in which hundreds of monks could be housed, educated and disciplined. It was broken into a number of residential blocks, each for 20 to 40 monks, with a common assembly hall, refectory, kitchen, bakehouse and guesthouse. Soon numbers required a second foundation and then a third and a fourth, with another for women. Monasteries of this size really needed considerable resources, including the means to transport their products and buy necessities. It is not surprising that the Pachomian communities were all close to the river.

There were similar developments in Palestine. Then, shortly after Antony's death in 356, his life was written by Athanasius, whose anti-Arian struggles Antony and most other monks had vigorously supported. The 'Life of Antony' quickly became something of a spiritual best seller. In Book VIII of his *Confessions*, Augustine vividly describes the effect of reading it on a group of civil servants at Trier. The story was told to him by another civil servant, Ponticianus, in 386 and it had happened some time before. Everywhere monasticism was spreading, first in the Greek world but then also in the Latin, and that is the more interesting, given that Antony, Pachomius and most of the early Egyptian monks, whose experience became in a way paradigmatic for the whole movement, spoke neither Greek nor Latin, only Coptic. But as it spread, so did it change.

The figure of St Basil, 'the Great' (*c.* 330–379), is the best signifier of what happened. A member of one of the most devout Christian families of Caesarea, Basil had St Macrina the Elder for his grandmother, St Macrina the Younger for his elder sister and St Gregory, Bishop of Nyssa, for his younger brother. Everyone in the family was both extraordinarily good and extraordinarily well educated. After schooling at Caesarea, Basil went for further study in Constantinople and Athens before deciding to become a monk at just about the time of Antony's death. After a year or two learning how to do it in Egypt and Syria, he set up as a hermit near his home town, but was soon involved in all sorts of theological and evangelical work until in 370 he was elected Bishop of Caesarea, the same year Ambrose became Bishop of Milan, but, whereas the election of Ambrose was something of a miracle, Basil's represented the natural choice of a maturing Church. He was one of the most balanced of Christian leaders in this formative period, the man who did more than almost anyone else to bring to a close the fearful rifts produced through the decades of Christological controversy subsequent to Nicaea, reconciling the extreme anti-Arians, like Athanasius, with the moderates, strong in Asia Minor, who were alarmed by the tendency of Alexandrian theology to underplay the humanity of Christ. His influence on monastic development was even more decisive. At Caesarea he established a vast monastery which included both the episcopal residence and extensive hospitals and hostels for the poor. He also wrote a series of rules which effectively provided the shape of most subsequent monastic life in the Eastern Church.

With Basil, monasticism has already moved from the isolation of the Coptic countryside to incorporation within an episcopally-led urban Church, where an extensive liturgical life and participation in the wider pastoral care of the community had replaced the extreme asceticism of the earliest ideal. That is not, of course, to say that after Basil remoteness of location or the rigours of ascetic competition would be abandoned by all monks. Far from it. Simeon Stylites, the first of numerous anchorites to spend most of his life sitting on the top of a tall pillar, was born ten years after Basil died. The Stylites flourished especially in Syria, not far from Basil's Caesarea. Monasticism took a great many different forms in its first two hundred exciting years, some of them decidedly odd. What is striking is that while beginning with the most poorly educated, it could so quickly appeal to the most highly cultivated people, while becoming at the same time a mass movement. It was the multitude of monks, perhaps more than anything else, which explains why by 360 a counter-revolutionary movement of the sort Julian hoped to lead really had no chance at all. And yet, while monasticism was in its origins a withdrawal from the rather tight organizational shape of local dioceses, it was quickly harnessed to strengthen rather than divide existing Church organization and came to provide centres for religious specialization and theological learning of a sort that had not hitherto existed.

It was natural for Basil to be called to the episcopate. He had every qualification, of class, education and holiness, but as a monk he represented the beginning of a new type of bishop who would profoundly alter the ethos of ecclesiastical leadership. In 372, just two years after Basil became a bishop, Martin, founder of the very first monastery in Gaul, was made Bishop of Tours and became a pioneer evangelist of the Gallic countryside, although some criticized his appointment because he was grubby and lower-class. He was certainly a different type from Ambrose, but Basil and Martin provided henceforth the norm for the best kind of bishop in both East and West for 800 years – someone who had first been a monk. It brought with it, among other things, a shift from the elderly married man to the younger celibate.

The monastic movement can be seen as many things. On one side it was a reaction of a traditionally ascetic religion to the wealth and worldliness inescapable in the new Church order. No longer was martyrdom a likely way to heaven. Monasticism could replace it as the best exemplific road to spiritual perfection. It was equally a road back to the holy simplicity of apostolic times, the lifestyle described in the early chapters of Acts: 'No one claimed for his own use anything that he had, as everything they owned was held in common' (Acts 4:32). In this sort of restorationism early monasticism was very similar to many later movements in Christian history, an attempt to recreate a primitive New Testament purity. Undoubtedly it provided a freshness of spiritual teaching and example which, however much monks appeared to be withdrawing from the Church and public life, in fact became central to the way Christianity was conceived. The serious pursuit of holiness came to be seen as requiring celibacy. In the West, Ambrose was the principal sponsor of such insistence. It is clear, for instance, that Augustine and his friends took it for granted that if they became committed Christians, they would also want to become monks. Thus his friend Verecundus was reluctant to become a Christian, just because he was already married – to a baptized believer – and therefore could not be the only sort of Christian he found attractive, a monk.

Evagrius Ponticus appears to have been the first monk, apart from Basil, who quickly became a bishop, to write extensively. Originating by the Black Sea, he was a preacher of note in Constantinople before abandoning his public ministry in 382 to join the monastic community in the Nitrian desert of Egypt, led by Macarius the Great. His works on monastic behaviour and the ascent within the practice of prayer to contemplation were foundational for most subsequent spiritual teaching in both East and West. They represent the Hellenization of a Coptic movement even within its homeland. John Cassian, a younger man who also came from around the Black Sea, went to Egypt soon afterwards and learnt to be a monk from Evagrius. Some thirty years later he had moved west to found two monasteries near Marseilles and write for them the *Institutes* and the *Conferences* which provided the Latin world with a full introduction to both the rules and the spiritual teaching of the leading fathers of the Egyptian desert. The monastic ideology was thereby Latinized. All subsequent Western monasticism fed on Cassian, including the Rule of St Benedict written in central Italy rather over a century later. Latin as the Rule was in its balance and sobriety, its spirit was permeated with that of the pioneers of two centuries before and the bridge linking the one to the other was the writings of Cassian.

Dogma and theology in the fourth and fifth centuries

It was a great strength in Athanasius that he combined his doctrinal battle for the faith of the Council of Nicaea with the patronage of the new monastic movement. As a friend and biographer of Antony, he had behind him a spiritual force which could be on occasion a fairly physical one too, if the monks descended with their staffs upon the streets of Alexandria. Fourth- and fifth-century Church history is often written as if there was little else except doctrinal controversy, but the latter can only be understood within the new political and monastic framework we have, hitherto, been exploring. Nevertheless, the theological struggle from Nicaea in 325 to the Council of Chalcedon in 451 remains decisive for the evolution of both doctrine and the geographical shape of Christianity. Nothing mattered more to people like Basil, Ambrose, Athanasius and their successors. In considering it we have, however, always to remember three factors which decisively shaped it and, indeed, collectively ensured that every dispute would be extended to the maximum possible length, in a way that was both pastorally disastrous and quite unnecessary from the viewpoint of the issues themselves.

The first was that of imperial intervention: the political imposition of whatever view the current emperor favoured. While this explains neither the origin of the issues disputed nor the final form any doctrine was given, it does to a large extent explain why controversies, the Arian above all, went on so long and with such devastating consequences. The second was a matter of rivalry between sees. It was inevitable that Christian thought had evolved somewhat locally in the first centuries. Alexandria, Antioch, Carthage and Rome had all generated recognizably distinct theological traditions, though all adhered without question to the shared inheritance of the New Testament and a Eucharist-centred liturgy whose local divergences were not very great. It was less the theological differences in themselves than the determination of leading Churches to insist on getting their own doctrinal way which ensured that the bitterness of *odium theologicum* would go on and on. In this as in many a later age theologians could be unpleasantly vituperative in what they said about each other. Thirdly, there was the ongoing problem of translating biblical ideas into the words and concepts of a Greek and Latin civilization. However much theologians wished to base themselves on the Bible – and almost everyone at work in this period was overwhelmingly anxious to do so – it simply was not possible to write lengthy books about God, Christ and the spiritual life without using words borrowed from philosophy, law or poetry. It is of the nature of Christianity to relate its beliefs to the culture and needs of every age, to be a translating community, rather than a fundamentalist one, confined to repeating the formulas of the past. From the early second century we can see this process at work, philosophizing and argumentative. We see it above all in the writings of Origen, by far the greatest theologian of the early centuries, great as a biblical scholar but great too in the daring with which he made use of contemporary philosophy. It was, of course, a dangerous thing to do and in later centuries Origen would be repeatedly blamed for fathering this error or that, but it was intrinsic to the intellectual enterprise of Christian understanding that this sort of thing was attempted.

About 319 a dispute began between Alexander, Bishop of Alexandria, and one of the leading priests in the city, named Arius. It concerned the nature of Christ. There is no reason to think that either side was doing other than attempting to interpret correctly the, in places apparently contradictory, teaching of the New Testament. Arius (though little indeed of anything he wrote survives) appears to have taught that Christ was neither absolutely God (because 'the Father is greater than I') nor absolutely man (because he was 'the word of God'). He came before all the rest of creation but was himself created. Alexander condemned this doctrine (which Arius had probably learned from his teacher, Lucian of Antioch, who had also taught Eusebius of Nicomedia) and in this he was supported by the great majority of his fellow bishops. Eusebius, sympathizing with Arius, raised the matter with Constantine when he arrived at Nicomedia and Constantine hastily called a council to resolve the matter, just as he had done for Donatism with the Council of Arles. The Council met, proved thoroughly unsympathetic to the Arius–Eusebius alliance, ratified Alexander's position but added one word, *Homoousios* (consubstantial), to describe the relationship of Father and Son. This pleased Alexander and his deacon, Athanasius, but worried a great many other people who feared that it could imply a revival of 'Sabellianism' (Sabellius was an almost unknown third-century theologian accused of denying any real distinction between Father and Son). The problem could be formulated by asking, how can one avoid 'Subordinationism' (making the Son *less than* the Father) without falling into 'Sabellianism' (making the Son *one with* the Father)?

There was another problem with *Homoousios*: it was not scriptural. Christian orthodoxy was here being defined in terms of a Greek philosophical word, *ousia* (essence), which everyone did not understand in the same way. Theologians had already used many such terms in their writings but the idea that biblical revelation actually required for its exact interpretation the use of a non-biblical term in a dogmatic statement was hard for many thoroughly orthodox traditionalists to accept. It certainly constituted a considerable leap towards the 'development' of doctrine, but the final, almost universal, acceptance of the Nicene Creed proved paradigmatic for Christian orthodoxy ever after. Its formulation would go beyond that of the Bible.

Throughout the whole series of controversies from the early fourth to the late fifth century, a contrast remains between a typical Alexandrian approach and a typical Antiochene one. The Alexandrians stressed the divinity of Christ, veering at times towards Sabellian-like phraseology, while the Antiochenes insisted on his humanity in a way that might on occasion suggest undermining anything more than a moral relationship between him and the Father. So, while people in the Antiochene tradition, such as Eusebius of Caesarea, were unhappy with the *Homoousios*, they were no less opposed to the doctrine of Arius because it appeared to undermine Christ's true humanity as much as his divinity. Over the next half-century the Eastern emperors, in particular Constantius (337–360) and Valens (364–378), consistently backed the Arian party, following in this a line Eusebius of Nicomedia had established in Constantinople, while the Western emperors (Constans, 337–351, Valentinian, 364–375, and Gratian, 375–383) were almost equally consistent in support of Nicaean orthodoxy. The reason for that was that the less theologically minded Latin Church had no problem with Nicaea and was already very firmly committed to the divinity of Christ. The worst years for Nicaean orthodoxy were between 351 and 360, when Constantius was sole emperor and endeavoured to impose a sort of simplified Arianism upon the whole Church. On the theological front Athanasius, for much of the time in exile in the West or in hiding with monastic friends in Egypt, was staking out the Nicaean position by his most famous work, *On the Incarnation*, and a series of later treatises. But what in the end mattered most was the viewpoint of the 'Eastern' or Antiochene bishops, whose Trinitarian orthodoxy was in reality unimpeachable but who were deeply unhappy with Nicene and Alexandrian terminology and have come, in consequence, to be termed 'Semiarians'. In due course, after the death of Constantius and with Athanasius growing less pugnacious and more conciliatory in old age, the upholders of Nicaea and the Easterners came together, helped particularly by St Basil to recognize that it had been terminology, not belief, that divided them. But it was only after the death of almost all the main protagonists that peace was fully established with the Council of Constantinople of 381, made possible by the accession as emperor in 379 of Theodosius, whose background was Western and who, unlike his predecessor Valens, had no doubt that the Council of Nicaea was to be adhered to. At that point the whole thing simply came to an end, with one major exception, and it would have done so much earlier if emperors in Constantinople had not consistently thwarted the Church's own mechanisms for finding agreement.

The one exception, however, mattered a great deal. About 341, Eusebius of Nicomedia, by then Bishop of Constantinople, had consecrated a young man named Ulphilas as Bishop of the Goths. He spent the next 50 years evangelizing them both outside and within the empire, and he translated the Bible into Gothic, a remarkable achievement for a proto-missionary. But the doctrine he had learnt from Eusebius was straight Arianism and, in consequence, both the Goths and related peoples like the Vandals adopted Christianity in an Arian form. The result of this for Western Europe in the fifth and sixth centuries when most of Gaul, Italy, Spain and North Africa had been conquered by Visigoths, Ostrogoths, Vandals or Burgundians was enormous. The trail left behind him by Eusebius of Nicomedia proved a very long one.

Nearly 50 years after the Council of Constantinople a new wave of theological controversy suddenly engulfed the Eastern Church, a natural sequel to the earlier one. In 428 the Emperor Theodosius II appointed Nestorius, a monk from Antioch, to be Patriarch of Constantinople. Nestorius was a friend and confidant of Bishop John of Antioch. Zealous to put things to right in his diocese but wholly inexperienced as to how to do so, he found Constantinople – as did many another bishop – a veritable wasps' nest. He was not a great theologian but someone pedantically anxious to put across the Antiochene line in Christology which stressed the full reality of Jesus's humanity. Hence he objected to the title *Theotokos*, 'Mother of God', as applied to Mary, because it seemed to imply that she was Christ's mother according to his godhead, not his manhood. Yet it had been around for a couple of hundred years, though its usage had much increased of late and was greatly favoured by Pulcheria, the extremely devout and influential elder sister of the some-what weak-minded Theodosius II. While some who objected to the title of *Theotokos* would only allow her to be called *Anthropotokos*, 'mother of the man', Nestorius insisted that the right word must be *Christotokos*, 'mother of Christ'. The reaction was immediate on the part of numerous monks within the capital who heckled him in his sermons and sought the protection of Pulcheria.

How could the Bishop of Alexandria not intervene in this heaven-sent opportunity to defend the divinity of Christ, while humiliating the Bishop of Constantinople and the Antiochene theological tradition at the same time? To insist that Mary was not *Theotokos* but only 'the mother of Christ' seemed clearly to impugn Christ's divinity or even to suggest the old heresy of 'two sons' – one divine, one human – linked only morally. Cyril of Alexandria, as productive and brilliant a writer of theology as Athanasius, had been its bishop since 412, when he succeeded his uncle Theophilus. His pugnacity was equal to that of any of his predecessors. Theophilus had successfully engineered the deposition of St John Chryso-stom from the see of Constantinople in 403. Chrysostom had unwisely incurred the hostility of the Empress Eudoxia through the tactlessness of his preaching and it was singularly unwise of Nestorius to lay himself open, so soon after appointment, to a similar attack. But Cyril was not alone in condemnation. While the Bishop of Rome in 403 had unsuccess-fully spoken up for Chrysostom against his enemies, Pope Celestine in 430 had no doubt that Nestorius had fallen into error and formally condemned him in an Italian synod held that summer. Meanwhile the bishops of the provinces of Antioch, Nestorius's home area, were offering him only rather lukewarm support. Cyril now issued a public condemnation which was delivered in December at Constantinople, requiring Nestorius's retraction within ten days. In no time at all an inexperienced archbishop's attempts to suppress what he regarded as a misleading development in Marian devotion had escalated into an empire-wide ecclesiastical crisis. Theodosius, who had for a while sympathized with Nestorius whom he had himself chosen hardly two years earlier, now called a council to resolve the dispute and, perhaps at Pulcheria's suggestion, ordered it to meet at Ephesus where Marian devotion was particularly strong. In June 431 Cyril and the Egyptian bishops arrived there before the Antiochenes, who might have sympathized with Nestorius. Refusing to wait for them or for the papal legate and backed by Memnon of Ephesus, he condemned Nestorius while affirming the doctrine of the *Theotokos*. When John of Antioch and the Syrians arrived they held a rival council and condemned Cyril, but their numbers were only 34, while almost two hundred bishops supported Cyril, as did the papal delegates when they arrived. For a time a confused emperor and his officials actually put Cyril, Memnon and Nestorius alike under arrest, but soon came down on the side of the majority. Nestorius alone was deposed while Antioch and Alexandria were eventually reconciled largely through the good offices of Bishops of Rome, Celestine and then Sixtus III, who, while backing the decisions taken at Ephesus, refused to regard John of Antioch as excommunicated.

Such is the somewhat absurd story of the third ecumenical council. The intensity of the conflict derived from the foolishness of Nestorius, the passions engendered both in monasteries and among the common people by Marian devotion and the aggressiveness of Cyril. But the underlying tension between theological traditions was in no way resolved and the very success of Cyril at Ephesus paved the way for the next, still more disastrous, round of conflict. It all began again at Constantinople in 448 and centred around Eutyches, an aged monk in the city, Archimandrite of a community of 300, and a fervent upholder of Alexandrian teaching. By then the Bishop of Constantinople was named Flavian, while in Alexandria Cyril had died in 444 and been succeeded by his archdeacon, Dioscorus. Eutyches was condemned by a local Constantinopolitan synod for denying that Christ had a human nature, but that was just what the Alexandrian tradition had also come to deny. Its huge stress on the divinity allowed little room for any formulation which safeguarded a distinct humanity. At an extraordinary council held once more in Ephesus in August 449, Dioscorus dominated the proceedings, denounced Flavian, together with his supporter Domnus of Antioch, and had them both deposed. The representatives of Pope Leo who had brought with them his *tomus*, backing Flavian and setting forth a doctrine of one person but two natures, were insulted and ignored. Flavian was so ill-treated that he rapidly died. The Emperor Theodosius accepted what had happened and it looked like just one more victory for the power of Alexandria.

But within a few months Theodosius died from a fall from his horse and Pulcheria became empress, choosing as her consort an elderly general named Marcian. For Pulcheria, Leo's word was decisive. Moreover, she had admired Flavian, and his body was brought back for solemn burial. In 451 a new council was summoned and met in Chalcedon, a suburb of Constantinople, in October. Dioscorus arrived, arrogant as ever, and promptly excommunicated Leo. This was too much. The acts of the 449 Council at Ephesus, now called 'the robber Council' — a phrase of Leo's — were annulled and Dioscorus deposed. Still more important, a new definition of faith affirmed Christ to be one Person in two natures which are united 'unconfusedly, unchangeably, indivisibly, inseparably', a definition based partly on Cyril and partly on Leo's Tome. While the Council insisted that it was moving in no way from the doctrine of Cyril, it was in reality slightly shifting its terminology back towards the Antiochene. The dominance of Alexandria ended at that moment but, effectively, so did communion between the greater part of Egyptian Christianity and the Roman–Constantinopolitan alliance. The tension which had for long been building up between a Constantinople-centred Greek Empire and Coptic society broke out in ecclesiastical schism and when a new Chalcedonian bishop was appointed for Alexandria, he was rapidly lynched. The Coptic Church insisted that the 'in two natures' formula of Chalcedon was a betrayal of its own theological tradition and, indeed, the unity of Christ. From then on it could be described as 'Monophysite'.

When one considers the doctrinal history expressed in the early ecumenical councils as a whole, one may well conclude that it demonstrates the disaster of pursuing something called 'orthodoxy'. In his first years as Bishop of Alexandria Cyril spent much of his time refuting Sabellians, Arians, Novatianists, Adoptionists, Manichaeans and dispossessing them of their churches, while at the same time harrying the Jewish and pagan communities. He was not unusual in so behaving. Indeed, imperial order almost required it, although the Urban Prefect found the bishop's interference in matters of civil order intolerable. The Christian Church by the fifth century appears, especially in the East, as exaggeratedly preoccupied with doctrinal correctness. The cult of the concept of orthodoxy proved inherently self-destructive but it is not surprising that, in the end, this became the very word by which the Greek Church and its offspring are described. It is ironic that a generation after Cyril those most loyal to his teaching were themselves excluded from the communion of the orthodox. His formula, 'one nature of God the Son incarnate', did not quite tally with Chalcedon's 'in two natures' and the Church of the eastern Mediterranean never recovered from the resultant dislocation. In retrospect it is highly questionable how much real difference in Christological belief there was between the varied formulas canvassed at the time, all making use of a range of Greek philosophical terms referring to person, nature and substance – *hypostasis, physis, prosōpon, ousia* – whose exact meaning there was no way of defining. One may well hold that the Chalcedonian formula did something to prevent effective denial of Jesus's real humanity in a way that the Alexandrian formulas did not, and one may also judge that the Antiochene tradition was less intolerant than the Alexandrian. The authority of the see of Antioch itself over neighbouring cities was less great, while there is more sense of a diffused theology whose proponents were to be found in many different places, while in Alexandria theological correctness had come to be closely identified with the person of the bishop, Athanasius and then Cyril. It was also the sheer personal aggressiveness of three Bishops of Alexandria in a row, Theophilus, Cyril and Dioscorus, which finally led to a débâcle as disastrous for the leadership of Alexandria as for the Greek Church as a whole.

Behind the ecclesiastical struggle one may, however, also discern a wider social divergence, a sense of alienation in Egypt and elsewhere with the evolving character of the empire in what we may call a 'Byzantine' direction. Up to the end of the fourth century the emperors, even though Constantinople was now the capital, remained extremely peripatetic. Theodosius I, like Constantine, was still essentially a Roman emperor who might actually be found almost anywhere, but as the fifth century progressed, this notably changed. The emperors remained in Constantinople, while the more remote provinces, particularly a wealthy and powerful province like Egypt with its own historic traditions and written language, felt excluded from the inner circle of power. Alexandrian ecclesiastical aggressiveness was in part at least reaction to that sense of exclusion, but it precipitated an even greater exclusion which undermined the Empire, preparing the ground for its collapse under Arab attack in the seventh century. Despite various attempts at reconciliation, particularly by the Emperors Zeno (474–491) and Anastasius (491–518), assisted by Acacius, the Patriarch of Constantinople, nothing lasting was achievable. Every attempt to placate Alexandria meant a retreat from Chalcedon, unacceptable in Rome, and while Roman authority was seldom evaluated in Constantinople in fully Roman terms it was never happily disregarded for long. Meanwhile Chalcedon itself helped ensure that the primacy of Constantinople as asserted in the Council of 381 but hitherto ineffectual now became a reality. It did so both by effectively undermining its principal practical rival, the Church of Alexandria, and by reasserting and extending what the earlier council had decreed: the Bishop of 'New Rome' was now assigned 'equal honours' to the Bishop of old Rome. The Roman legates inevitably protested but in terms of ecclesiastical history Chalcedon, by its precise definition of Christological orthodoxy, its insistence upon the authority of Constantinople as equal to that of Rome and its undermining of the Church of Alexandria, established the norms and boundaries of Byzantine Christianity with a decisiveness which would endure ever after.

The situation in the West was far less clear. It is striking how small a part anyone from the West played in the ecumenical councils we have discussed, almost no one other than representatives of the Pope. One could even ask whether they were ecumenical at all. By the time of Chalcedon most of the West had been lost to imperial rule, but Rome and central Italy still remained part of the Empire and Rome's representation was important to the emperor for that very reason. The more he lost military control over the Latin world, the more valuable it was to retain a hold on Rome and even to encourage its bishops to extend their working jurisdiction over Gaul, Spain and elsewhere, which had – as he hoped but temporarily – slipped from his control. Rome remained, then, a bridge between Latin and Greek worlds but, for the time, the former was in too great confusion to fuss greatly over the doctrinal leadership of the latter.

Latins were anyway less philosophically-minded than Greeks. Rome itself had produced no Christian theologians of any distinction, while the Church of Carthage, the only one in the West to do so, was quite torn apart by Donatism. Papal preoccupations were always more with jurisdiction than theology, while Latin theological interests, such as they were, seemed to take a more down-to-earth direction, centred on the moral life, the nature of grace, the sacraments and the Church rather than on the mysteries of the Godhead. By far the most serious doctrinal controversy in the West, apart from the Donatist conflict confined to Africa, was that surrounding the teaching of Pelagius and his followers, about grace, original sin and the moral life. What is striking is how low-key the ecclesiastical response to it actually was, apart from Augustine's fierce rejoinders. Only in Carthage, under his influence, was there a council of any size to condemn Pelagianism, while the so-called 'semi-Pelagianism' of Cassian and other spiritual writers in Gaul escaped unjudged until the sixth century. If the West was, nonetheless, to be for generations plagued by schism, it was due to the importation by Germanic tribes from the Balkans of the Arianism of the East. Only with the conversion to Catholicism of Clovis, King of the Franks, *c.* 496 and of Recared, King of the Visigoths in Spain, almost a century later, would this be effectively overcome. The Catholic–Arian schism was, nevertheless, simply an extension of the wider civil crisis – the collapse of imperial rule, the sacking of cities, the general social devastation brought about by Germanic migration.

The course of Western Church history in this period following so soon on the apparent golden age of Christian Latin society as seen in the career of Ambrose may best be approached through the life of the man about whom we know far more than anyone else in the ancient world, Augustine of Hippo. This is the case because while Augustine was an intellectual giant, far transcending anyone else of his period, his career remained in many ways typical of his generation. Through him we can see the transformation of both society and Church.

Augustine was born in 354 in Thagaste, a small Roman inland town in Numidia, part of modern Algeria. His mother was a Christian, his father was not. He was not baptized but imbibed a kind of Christian culture which, until he was over 30, he could neither completely identify with nor definitively reject. They were far from wealthy but fortunate in being somehow connected to a wealthy local landowner, Romanianus, who took care of Augustine's education and ensured that he went to the university in Carthage where he studied and taught until in 383 he moved to teach rhetoric in Rome. Throughout his years in Carthage he was caught up in Manichaeism, dualist, semi-Christian, the fashionable form of the religious approach which two centuries earlier we described as 'Gnostic'. It seemed more intellectually respectable than either orthodox Catholicism or its local schismatic variation, Donatism. What is quite clear is that the academic atmosphere of Carthage and Rome was still essentially traditional. It was hard to meet an orthodox Christian who was also a thoroughly educated man. In due course he decided that Manichaean doctrine, while claiming a sort of scientific foundation, was actually rubbish. He was helped to this conclusion, not through any sort of Christian theology, but by reading some Platonist literature, probably Plotinus, translated into Latin by Marius Victorinus, a distinguished Roman scholar who, in old age, had become a Christian. It was only after Augustine moved to Milan as Professor of Rhetoric in the autumn of 384 that he even learnt that Victorinus had done so. It was clearly something of a revelation that anyone so intelligent could accept orthodox Christianity. But in Milan everything seemed different. On one side Augustine had reached the geographical centre of the Western Empire, its imperial capital, and could even hope to move from his academic chair to a provincial governorship. On another, he was in a city intellectually dominated by Ambrose.

The central crisis in Augustine's life took place in the next couple of years. The lower-class mistress with whom he had lived happily for years was sent away so that he could prepare to marry an upper-class girl, a suitable wife for a successful political figure. But a deeper crisis swept all that aside. Augustine read Paul's letters, listened to Ambrose's sermons, discussed the most basic philosophical and religious issues with a group of friends and decided to be baptized. But baptism at the hands of Ambrose at Easter 387 meant beginning a wholly new life. For Augustine and his friends it meant an end to an academic career, political ambitions or even marriage. Augustine and his closest friend, Alypius, returned to Africa and founded a monastery back home at Thagaste.

It was, however, hard to imagine that a man as distinguished as Augustine would be left to live a monastic life. If one dominant movement within fourth-century Christianity was out of the world and into a monastery, another movement no less decisive for the reshaping of the Church was out of the monastery into an episcopal chair. The first step was ordination to the priesthood. The Bishop of Hippo, a coastal town some 50 miles north of Thagaste, took advantage of Augustine's presence in the congregation to preach on the need for new blood in the ministry, especially in the circumstances of the somewhat demoralized local Catholic community, under pressure from both Donatists and Manichees. Augustine was effectively kidnapped into the priesthood, and then compelled to preach by his far-sighted bishop, despite the rule that only bishops should do so. When Bishop Valerius died, in 395, Augustine was his inevitable successor. He established a monastery beside his cathedral so that he could be at once both bishop and monk, and, of course, writer as well. Books had been pouring forth already and they would continue to do so for the next 35 years of his episcopate. Alypius meanwhile became Bishop of Thagaste.

Outwardly Augustine's life from the moment that he arrived in Hippo was quiet enough. He never left Africa again and seldom travelled further than Carthage. He engaged in the theological controversy apparently inseparable from the work of a bishop, arguing with Manichees, Donatists and Pelagians. He wrote the *Confessions*, the story of his own conversion, one of the few books of antiquity which is absolutely readable today. He became increasingly an establishment figure, relying on imperial authority to suppress Donatism. He had moved from a world where Christianity still appeared marginal to one where it was entirely central. And yet he saw all that fall to pieces too. In 410 the Goths under Alaric sacked Rome. The legions were withdrawn from Britain at the same time. Gaul and Spain were overrun by Germanic tribes. The really great work of Augustine's later years, prompted by the sack of Rome, was the writing of the 22 books of *The City of God*. Here, bypassing the sort of providential idealization of the Roman Empire which Eusebius of Caesarea had developed to explain the triumph of Constantine and which remained ever after the core philosophy of the Byzantine Empire, Augustine worked out a vast and sombre philosophy of history in which empires rise and fall, essentially unlinked to a divine city manifest in, though not identical with, the Catholic Church. It was an interpretation desperately needed at a time when Christians could naturally be accused of having brought about the fall of Rome. Had not they, after all, suppressed the altar of Victory in the Senate House? Nor was this only relevant to some temporary upset in Rome. In 429 the Vandals invaded North Africa. As Augustine lay dying in August 430 their fleet stood outside the harbour of Hippo. Hardly was he dead than it too fell and was devastated though, amazingly, his disciples smuggled his entire library to safety so that we still possess almost everything which Augustine wrote.

Augustine was *sui generis*, a theologian, philosopher, preacher and letter-writer whose work wholly eclipses that of anyone and everyone else writing in Latin in his age. Apart from Augustine the theologians of the Latin West were very pedestrian in comparison with the Greeks, but there is no Greek theologian of the period whose work is really comparable in range, precision and a consistent depth of interrogation of both biblical teaching and human experience. He knew little Greek so that his own work was not greatly affected by that of his Eastern contemporaries. Nor were his writings much known in the East. Theologically this was the point of separation. Ever after, Augustine would be the schoolmaster of the West, through not only the Dark Ages already beginning when he died, but also the high Middle Ages and the Reformation. Everyone would appeal to Augustine and would be profoundly affected by his gloomy view of fallen nature, his absolute insistence on the necessity of grace, but also on an extraordinarily rich spectrum of ideas about God, love, the Church and history. The East would know nothing of this. It would be spared Augustine's pessimism, but it would also lack his disciplined precision and a certain scepticism about any and every political achievement. Its range of theological resources would remain, nevertheless, richer and more diversified than that of the Latin world.

If one considers the 60 years between the year 370, in which Ambrose became a bishop in the West and Basil in the East, and 430, when Augustine died, they include by far the greater part of the most creative and enduring writing which we associate with the high patristic age. In the East these years embrace almost all the work of Basil, Gregory of Nyssa, Gregory of Nazianzus, John Chrysostom, Cyril of Jerusalem and Cyril of Alexandria; in Latin the writings of Ambrose, Jerome, Augustine and Cassian. There were many lesser figures, but the sheer wealth of theological thought and spiritual insight to be found in those ten names in particular would be hard to rival in any other period of Christian history. Doubtless it could not go on, and the ease with which theological creativity turned into a self-destructive heresy hunt is all too obvious. It was, nevertheless, a moment of genius. Many of this group – Basil, the two Gregorys, Chrysostom and Augustine above all – had been deeply educated in the traditional learning of Athens and Rome before turning to theology. That may have had something to do with the freshness of their thought, a sense of diverse stimulation possible only for those inhabiting a philosophical frontier. Several of them, too, had quite chequered careers in other ways as well. Where they became monks it was out of an entirely adult decision. The tension in many of their lives between ecclesiastical service, in the episcopate or otherwise, and the call to contemplative prayer remains evident. The circumstances of this still rather open age would pass as a Christianized political order and established monastic institutions created in the East a more religiously and intellectually predictable world, while in the West the collapse of town life and imperial rule would not encourage the kind of career which was possible for Augustine. With the passing of this generation and the sealing of theological speculation at Chalcedon, the shape of theology would change very little until the emergence in the West of scholasticism in the twelfth and thirteenth centuries.

Missionary expansion and political disintegration: surpassing the empire

There was no intrinsic reason why Christianity should be confined to the Roman Empire and it never was so confined. Its universalist momentum was bound to take it well beyond even the Empire's wide frontiers. If for long it remained largely inside, that was all the same understandable. The ease of communication around the Mediterranean, the presence of a Jewish community in so many towns, the wide expansion of the Greek language all made it natural that the Christian faith, having begun within the Empire, should expand particularly there. If its scriptures were quickly translated into languages other than Greek – Latin, Syriac and Coptic – these were all languages used within the Empire. Advance across the imperial frontiers, especially to the East, came however quite early but the fixation of Church historians with the Graeco-Roman world has led to its being rather little considered. The key point here is Edessa, an independent kingdom until its absorption into the Roman Empire in 241. Edessa and Nisibis, further to the East, became the centre of Syriac Christianity, Syriac being a form of Aramaic. Christianity had certainly penetrated into these parts well before 241 as on into Persia. Edessa may well have been the first place in which Christian churches were built publicly, because there was no persecution before the Roman takeover.

We know that they existed already in the second century. An important theological school also developed at Nisibis, well across the Persian border. It may well have been from Edessa that the faith was taken north into the kingdom of Armenia and on into Georgia, just as it was carried through Persia on into India and, somewhat later, China. All these Churches belonged initially to the Antiochene theological tradition, although Armenia was later persuaded to switch more to the Alexandrian. When the Roman Empire and the kingdom of Armenia became Christian in the fourth century, the hitherto fully tolerated state of Christians within the Persian Empire altered and they became subject to intermittent persecution. It was therefore important to demonstrate that they were not Roman agents and, while they accepted the Council of Nicaea, they did not adhere to that of Ephesus, with its humiliation of the Antiochene tradition, and in consequence came to be branded 'Nestorian', though there is no real connection between them and Nestorius. If the Syriac Church rejected Ephesus, the Armenian Church rejected Chalcedon. Each by so doing asserted its independence from the Byzantine Empire and Greek ecclesiastical hegemony, but the consequent absence of full communion between them may have inhibited the larger movement east. Yet this early wave of evangelization well beyond the Empire's frontiers undoubtedly brought into being strong local traditions of faith in Armenia, Georgia, Malabar and elsewhere which have never ceased to be a significant part of the Christian world.

From Egypt and Syria Christianity also spread south, first to Arabia, and then to the Red Sea kingdom of Aksum, from which Ethiopia developed. The decisive moment here was the early fourth century. A young Syrian from Tyre named Frumentius was among a group of traders captured on their way home from India. Taken into the service of the king, he began to spread Christianity and then, on reporting this to Athanasius in Alexandria, was consecrated by him as Bishop of Aksum. Then or somewhat later the king, Ezana, became a Christian and in the following century the Bible was translated into Ethiopian together with other Christian books, mostly of an Alexandrian provenance. By the early sixth century, Aksum had become a powerful independent Christian state with its own ecclesiastical tradition but still linked hierarchically with Alexandria from where it received its bishops and its 'Monophysite' commitment. To the west of Ethiopia on the Upper Nile, Christianity had also penetrated by this time into various small Nubian kingdoms, though we know little about it before the mid-sixth century. Where it did not advance in Africa was much further to the west, across the Sahara from Carthage and Numidia, and much of the reason for that may well lie in the bitter struggle within the North African Church between Catholics and Donatists which continued for far more than a century and turned the efforts of both sides into either convincing or intimidating the other, so that little energy can have been left for encouraging a movement south across the Roman border.

In the fourth century, Christianity was still somewhat sparsely represented in many of the north-western parts of the Empire, but we know far too little about its spread in, for instance, Britain to make very confident assertions about it. This remained an area in which the Church was still very much of a minority and present in the towns more than the countryside. It had produced one martyr, Alban, in the Roman city of Verulamium during one or another persecution and, a century later, it produced one devout and ascetic, but somewhat heretical, theologian in the person of Pelagius. Pelagius, however, had left Britain well before his ideas became known. It was in Rome that he acquired his reputation as a teacher of moral theology but only in Africa, when Pelagius left Rome on account of the Gothic invasion, that he came to be denounced. However, twenty years later Germanus, the Bishop of Auxerre, made two visits to Britain to preach against Pelagianism. By then the legions had gone, while the Germanic invasion had not yet begun, whereas most of Gaul was already under the control of one or another German tribe, almost all of them nominally Arians. Much of the Gallic countryside had certainly not been deeply Christianized before the invasions and everywhere the Church was in a tottering state, though doubtless still strongest in the south where it had for long been best established – around Arles, Lyons, Marseilles and the island monastery of Lérins, from which so many of its best bishops came.

It was, nevertheless, from the mid-fifth century British Church of which we know so little that Patrick came to become the evangelist of Ireland – the first major advance in the West beyond what had once been the Empire. Whatever urban character may still have survived in the British Christianity of his day, nothing could be carried across to Ireland. Here what mattered could only be tribal leadership and the influence of monastic communities. But much the same would soon be the case in Britain too as its Christians retreated from conquest by Saxons, Angles and Jutes west into Wales. While the Church in Britain had hitherto possessed the usual town bishoprics common throughout the Empire, at London, York and elsewhere, it was left, when these were all lost to the invaders, with no clear structure of leadership, other than that of monasteries and bishops based within them. In fact this proved in the long run a more effective missionary organization. We know almost nothing about the Christian history of Ireland in the first hundred years after Patrick, but clearly the Church survived and grew, as did that of Wales, and by the second half of the sixth century was able to expand outwards. Just as monks from the Welsh Church in the lifetime of Illtyd and Dyfrig, two powerful but shadowy figures of the early sixth century, were carrying their mix of asceticism and evangelism to Cornwall and Brittany, so would the Irish go to Scotland, England and mainland Europe. Columba left Ireland for Iona in 563. Both Welsh and Irish monks clung proudly to the use of Latin, but because their grasp of it was somewhat limited, given their extreme isolation from the rest of the Latin world, it is understandable that they began to write in their own languages as well. Welsh and Irish enjoy in consequence the earliest vernacular literatures of Europe.

The point is that here in the far west of Europe, just as in the far east beyond Edessa, Christianity was still quite capable of maintaining and spreading itself, and proving creative, without the paternal control and protection of an imperial state, without, too, the supervision of the papacy. While in some circumstances both of these umbrellas assisted the mission, in others they could inhibit or twist it. While the picture of the early sixth century Western Church is undoubtedly a somewhat chaotic one, it is not without its brighter sides. In general, the Catholic majority in Italy, Gaul and Spain had settled down with its German Arian rulers pacifically enough. Only in North Africa did it, for a time, suffer persecution. Each had come to need the other and the ecclesiastical gap between the two had the one great advantage that it made the persecution of dissident Christian groups unlikely. The relationship between the papacy and the Ostrogothic monarch based in Ravenna, in particular, for long engendered a certain tolerance upon both sides. The two surviving baptisteries in Ravenna, dating from the fifth century, that of the Arians and that of the 'Orthodox', symbolize the *modus vivendi* established by Theodoric, the Gothic king. The superb basilica of Sant'Apollinare Nuovo, built by him for Arian worship, though after the Byzantine reconquest made into a Catholic church, has an ecclesiastical importance seldom appreciated. It must remain the most splendid church ever built in Italy for other than Catholic use.

This balance, however, would not continue. At a still disputed date in the 490s, Clovis, the brutal but successful ruler of the Franks, was baptized by Remigius, the Bishop of Reims, thereby establishing an alliance between the Catholic Church and the Frankish monarchy which would remain one of the most decisive features in Church history until the French Revolution. From then on the Church and the Gallo-Romans tended to side with the Franks against the Goths and anyone else until, quite rapidly, Gaul began to turn into France. In Italy, the collapse of Arian rule came 50 years later with the Emperor Justinian's vast strategy of recovering the Western Empire. Italy was devastated but Ostrogothic rule destroyed and with it an official Arian presence which had held the institutional hegemony of Catholicism at bay. The Vandal kingdom in

North Africa had already fallen to Justinian's army. From then on the Catholic Church would have no Christian rival, but would instead within a century have to face the far greater peril of Arab Muslim invasion.

If we take a last look at the way things stood around 525 we see a Rome which had managed to weather the storms of the previous century tolerably well. The very confusion of the secular order had helped recognition of the need for a Roman jurisdictional authority throughout the Church in the Latin West, an authority to be regularly exercised. That would not have been the case in the fourth century. Indeed, for a moment, recognition went far further than that. Hormisdas was Pope from 514 to 523. It was a Persian name but he was at least born in Italy. He is the only Pope whose son (Silverius) later became Pope too. Like every Pope of the period he needed to walk a tightrope between the emperor in Constantinople and the Ostrogothic king in Ravenna. For some years Constantinople had veered back towards Monophysitism, producing the 'Acacian schism' with Rome which made the popes more friendly towards the Goths. In 518, however, the Emperor Anastasius died, to be replaced by the pro-Roman Justin. The result was the most striking reconciliation in history between the two traditions, in which the 'Formula of Hormisdas' was solemnly signed at Constantinople in the imperial palace by the Patriarch and some 250 Eastern bishops. This statement not only reaffirmed the doctrinal teaching of Chalcedon and the Tome of Leo, but emphatically asserted the unique authority of the Roman pontiff in a way that was unprecedented.

However if reconciliation (of a sort) between Constantinople and Alexandria under Anastasius brought schism with Rome, reconciliation between Constantinople and Rome under Justin could only further alienate Alexandria. Moreover, Monophysitism had been spreading and much of the old patriarchate of Antioch now supported it. Thus Severus, a monk educated in Alexandria, had been made Patriarch of Antioch by Anastasius. Deposed by Justin, together with 55 other bishops of the patriarchate, he fled back to Alexandria, from where he authorized the establishment throughout the East of a rival, anti-Chalcedonian, Church.

Meanwhile, Hormisdas's reconciliation with Constantinople inevitably upset the Ostrogoths. While Rome and Byzantium were in schism, Ravenna could feel reasonably sure of the loyalty of Italian Catholics, especially the old senatorial families whose influence was still so considerable around Rome. Most distinguished among them was Boethius. He had held the honour of the consulate, was utterly fluent in Greek and, apart from serving King Theodoric as 'Master of the Offices', had translated a whole series of philosophical works into Latin. He now fell under suspicion of conspiracy, was imprisoned and then executed in October 524. While awaiting death he composed one of the great classics of the early Middle Ages, *The Consolation of Philosophy*, the last work written by a Western Christian to breathe the living air of classical culture.

There were very few people in the West who could still read Greek. That is why Pope Gelasius at the beginning of the century had appointed a monk from Scythia named Dionysius Exiguus ('Denys the Short') to work in his archives translating documents. Denys was a friend of Boethius and skilled in the art of calculating the right date for Easter. This led him on to construct an entirely new way of counting the years so as to begin with the birth of Christ. It was around 525 that he invented the concept of the Christian era, 'the years of the Lord', *anni Domini*, AD. There was no necessity to do this, practical as it has proved, and years could be calculated in many other ways. But it is because Denys had his bright idea, working in his Roman scriptorium in 525, that the whole world is now so preoccupied with the passing of the second millennium. At the time, however, no one paid much attention. His manuscript was passed to his friend Cassiodorus and eventually, two hundred years later, the English monk Bede read what he wrote, adopted the system and popularized it through his book *The Ecclesiastical History of the English People*. Cassiodorus was another member of the Roman aristocracy who served the court of Ravenna. When the Byzantine army invaded Italy, he retired into private life and, later, founded the monastery of Vivarium on his estate near Naples. At Vivarium he too did his best to build up a centre of study and arranged for numerous Greek books to be translated into Latin. Boethius, Denys and Cassiodorus were just about the last generation in the West which felt at home in the Greek world as well as the Latin, and it was a very small group which still did so. The Byzantine–Gothic war devastated Italian society more than anything that had gone before. While Justinian's reconquest was a military success, it proved a social disaster.

If the central agenda of Church politics in the century after Chalcedon was how to hold together Rome, Constantinople and Alexandria, and Constantinople in the middle had veered back and forth between the one and the other, in the end it effectively lost both. Communion between Rome and Constantinople continued unquestioned for many hundreds of years, apart from fairly brief schisms, but mutual understanding, confidence, a shared theology continually grew less as the logic of politics, culture and language separated the one from the other. Yet it was too late to restore the Constantinopolitan–Alexandrian axis either. Distrust between Chalcedonians and Monophysites had simply grown too deep. Moreover, once both Jerusalem and Alexandria fell to Arab invasion and were definitely separated from Byzantium, there was little secular reason left even to try.

At much the same time as Boethius was beheaded and Denys the Short invented the Christian calendar, a British monk may have sailed in a tiny boat from Cornwall to Brittany. Samson came from south Wales. Ordained by Dyfrig, he was for years abbot of a monastery on Caldey Island off the coast of Pembrokeshire. Later, it seems, Dyfrig consecrated him a bishop and sent him across the sea to serve the churches dependent on Welsh monks far to the south of Caldey. He went first to Cornwall, then via the Scilly Isles to Brittany, where he founded further monasteries and became Bishop of Dol. He even attended a council in Paris in 557, signing his name 'Samson peccator episcopus' – a bishop but a sinner. Again, on the eastern frontier of Christianity towards the end of the fifth century or early in the sixth, a group of Syrian monks, the 'Nine Saints', travelled south to establish monasteries in the newly converted country of Aksum. Perhaps they were anti-Chalcedonians, fleeing the enforcement of orthodoxy by Justin – we do not know. But they founded a number of monasteries in the hinterland of Eritrea, including Dabra Damo, some of which still survive as monastic communities today, and surely contributed to the translation of Christian texts – the Bible, the writings of Cyril of Alexandria and much else – into Ge'ez.

Boethius and Cassiodorus were highly civilized gentlemen, survivors within an ever more restricted society, cherishing its continuity with the imperial past. They would have seemed different indeed from the strange figures who travelled in their little boats from Cornwall to Brittany or up into the mountains of Ethiopia. Yet all alike were concerned with a work of translation – of Greek into Latin or Ge'ez, of Latin into some Celtic or Germanic tongue. And Cassiodorus at Vivarium as much as Samson at Caldey or Aragawi at Dabra Damo saw the future of the Church especially in terms of founding a monastery, a centre of prayer and books. Rome and Constantinople could still look central enough to our story in the early sixth century, and the breathtakingly beautiful cathedral of Hagia Sophia at Constantinople was about to be built, the quintessence of Greek Christianity. But who could judge what in reality would prove central, what peripheral? From Patrick in the fifth century to Boniface in the eighth, the remote western islands of Britain and Ireland, so apparently peripheral, were in fact the missionary centre of the Western Church, while Bede, quietly inhabiting his Northumbrian monastery, would so litter his work on the history of Christianity and the English people with dates, *Anno Domini*, that he successfully transformed our whole way of conceiving the past, in its unity. If he took the idea from Denys in Rome, he applied it as no one in Rome had quite the vigour to do. So, too, when a century later Alfred, having saved his little West Saxon kingdom from the destruction by pagan Danish invaders which had overtaken every other part of the English Church, set about translating Boethius on *The*

Consolation of Philosophy into English, together with Pope Gregory's *Pastoral Care* and Bede's *Ecclesiastical History*, he was being faithful to the task of carrying on a tradition through the work of translation, just as Boethius himself had done.

The shape of things as we see them in the early sixth century is that of a still extremely confident, bureaucratically sophisticated and city-based Christian Greek empire in the eastern Mediterranean. In political and cultural, even ecclesiastical, terms, Constantinople was the secure centre of the Christian world, near to which every ecumenical council had hitherto been held. The Gospels had been written in Greek, the Creed defined in Greek. The Roman Empire had been converted into a Greek one and a Christian one. Everything else must have seemed provincial, if not peripheral. Contrast that picture with one of the West, of people in hard and uncertain times desperately struggling to rescue what they could of a tradition they cherished, while at the same time shaping a new pattern of Christian presence which would change in its essentials rather little for several centuries. It had to live with insecurity, the regular sack of cities, even of Rome, the rise and fall of many a monastery. It was a pattern more of the country than of the town, yet it still possessed the strength of a network of bishoprics, constructed on an urban hypothesis and held together by the occasional council of bishops and the sense that they were all in communion with the Pope in Rome. It was a pattern whose vitality and attraction depended enormously on being the sole possessor and communicator of literacy, of the power of the book. But, almost more decisive in the struggle to Christianize the West, was the power of the holy man – a multitude of Samsons, unthinkable without the monastic movement, but unthinkable too without a sort of peregrinatory evangelicalism which went well beyond the normal frontiers of earlier monasticism. They sanctified the geography of Western Europe and captured the imagination of illiterate rural populations. It was holy men, not kings or emperors, who made some sort of rough Christianization of Europe a reality over the next few centuries. When Samson became Bishop of Dol, Cassiodorus founded Vivarium and Benedict Monte Cassino, this process was only just beginning. The collapse of Christianity rather than its reconstruction could have seemed most probable, and yet in reality it stood poised on a decisive frontier, just beginning to break through into a new age when its history would be empowered from Paris and London, Ireland and Germany, when Latin would be accepted unquestioningly as the Church's characteristic tongue, and when in consequence a huge, if for long unformulated, problem would arise as to how this new Church could relate to its Greek elder brother.

3

The Orthodox Church in Byzantium

Mary B. Cunningham

> Then we went to Greece, and the Greeks led us to the edifices where they worship their God, and we knew not whether we were in heaven or on earth. For on earth there is no such splendour or such beauty, and we are at a loss how to describe it. We know only that God dwells there among men, and their service is fairer than the ceremonies of other nations. For we cannot forget that beauty.[1]

This famous passage describes the reaction of a group of Russian emissaries to the Great Church in Constantinople in the eleventh century. Sent by their king, Vladimir of Kiev, to the Khazars (Jews), Germans (Catholic Christians), Bulgars (Muslims) and Greeks (Orthodox Christians) in order to choose which of these religions he should adopt, the emissaries decided that there could be no comparison with the Church and liturgy of the Greeks. This Church seemed indeed to represent heaven on earth.

Constantinople and the Great Church of St Sophia stood at the centre of Eastern Orthodoxy in the Byzantine period, but the territory under the jurisdiction of the four Eastern patriarchates included in some periods most of Asia Minor, Greece, the Near East, Egypt, the Balkans and eventually even Russia and the Ukraine. At the beginning of our period, during the reign of the Emperor Justinian in the sixth century and partly due to his military activities, the sovereignty of the Roman Empire still encompassed the Near Eastern territories and North Africa. By the end of the seventh century, however, the Arabs had conquered most of these areas, causing Orthodox Christianity to become a minority religion and its faithful to be subject to the laws and taxes of a Muslim caliphate. Doctrinal differences also split the Eastern Orthodox Church, leading to the creation of the Assyrian Church of the East, often called Nestorian, and the five non-Chalcedonian Churches which are usually known as Monophysite. From the fifth century onwards, rival Patriarchs and Christian dioceses existed side by side in the Near East. Whereas successive

Byzantine emperors and ecumenical (i.e. Constantinopolitan) Patriarchs strove in the early centuries to heal this rift and to unify the Orthodox Church, these efforts seem to have been abandoned after the Arab conquests, perhaps owing to the recognition that these lands had in any case been lost for ever to the Eastern Roman Empire.

The aim of this chapter is to provide a general outline of the history of the Eastern Orthodox Church, beginning in the sixth century during the reign of Justinian and ending with the fall of Constantinople to the Ottoman Turks in 1453. In some ways these dates represent purely arbitrary limits. The history of the Orthodox Church begins as does that of all the other Christian Churches with the descent of the Holy Spirit at Pentecost and it continues in the areas in which it was founded up until the present day. If we define this chapter as a history of the *Byzantine* Orthodox Church, including its offshoots in the Near East and missions to the Slavs, however, then 527 to 1453 CE becomes an appropriate choice of dates. It is only in the sixth century that Orthodox Christianity achieved its definitive character as the dominant religion of the Eastern Roman Empire, as seen in the way the liturgy was celebrated and the increase in popular devotion to such holy objects as icons, relics and above all the Virgin Mary. With the building of the Great Church, Constantinople came to represent the true centre of Chalcedonian, Byzantine Orthodoxy. Eastern Orthodoxy lost its protection in the secular arm of the state when Constantinople fell to the Turks; thus, 1453 does represent the end of the association of the Orthodox Church with the Eastern Roman Empire. The account which follows will not focus purely on the institutional history of the Orthodox Church, however; it is our aim to trace as well its social and cultural background. Ordinary lay people, monks and clergy, aristocrats, emperors and empresses all played a part in the Church and contributed in various ways to its spirituality. The artefacts and texts which survive represent our primary witnesses to this development and all tell a varied, sometimes contradictory tale. It is clear that in the Byzantine Orthodox Church, as in any other Christian tradition, we are dealing with a spiritual and institutional structure which was influenced as much by the laity as it was by those individuals who occupied the highest ranks in the priestly hierarchy.

The Byzantine state was seen by its own rulers and subjects as an earthly image of the heavenly kingdom above. This meant that its social organization was hierarchical, with one absolute ruler, representing Christ, holding sway over all his subjects. The emperor was responsible for maintaining harmony within the Church, for this would both ensure divine favour for the empire and contribute to the effective governance of the secular state. The Patriarch, backed by the synod of bishops, exercised considerable authority as well, however. He could, and occasionally did,

oppose imperial policy as, for example, during the Monothelite controversy in the seventh century, Iconoclasm in the eighth and ninth and
during negotiations for reunion with the papacy in the thirteenth and
fifteenth centuries. The fact that a Patriarch could be deposed if he
disagreed with an emperor reveals the extent of the latter's power in
dictating ecclesiastical policy; on the other hand, if an emperor faced
opposition not only from the Patriarch but from the rest of the clergy,
the monastics and even the laity, his chances of enforcing an unpopular
policy were much reduced.

The theoretical basis for absolute rule under a Christian monarch was
elaborated in the fourth century by Constantine the Great's historian and
apologist Eusebius of Caesarea.[2] Eusebius skilfully combined Christian
ideology and imagery with Hellenistic conceptions of divine kingship in
order to create a new, specifically Byzantine political ideology. While the
Byzantine state cannot be described as 'Caesaro-papist', since the emperor
was not ordained as a member of the clergy, nor could he officially enact
ecclesiastical policies, the religious and the secular spheres were much
more closely integrated than they are in most modern states. Just as
important as his military and political functions was the emperor's role in
the Church's liturgical celebrations. The emperor was responsible for
ensuring that Orthodox belief was enforced throughout the Empire and
that his subjects worshipped God in the correct manner. Not only could
this provoke either divine wrath or favour in this world, but it could
determine salvation in the next.

The sixth century: the revival of the Christian Roman Empire

The Emperor Justinian, succeeding his uncle, Justin I (518–527), came
to the throne of the Eastern Empire in 527. Justinian came from a peasant
background in the Balkan provinces, but he was in fact highly educated
and intensely interested in Church policy and doctrine. Seeking to restore
the original boundaries of the Roman Empire, including the Western
territories which had been lost to Germanic tribes in the course of the
fourth and fifth centuries, Justinian undertook an ambitious plan of
military reconquest, beginning in North Africa and moving on to Italy
and finally even Spain. Linked to his military campaigns was the emperor's
overriding ambition to reunify the Church, by either reconciling or
abandoning the powerful Monophysite movement which had its base in
the Eastern territories and by restoring a friendly understanding with
Rome. The Monophysite policies of some of Justinian's predecessors,
especially the Emperor Anastasios (491–518), had strained the relationship between the papacy and the patriarchate in Constantinople. One of

Justinian's main ambitions seems to have been to restore unity within the Christian Roman Empire as a whole, at the same time enforcing his own military dominance as its supreme ruler.

Even in 527, pagan cult practices and cultural attitudes were still to be found in the Eastern Roman Empire. One of Justinian's religious aims was to eradicate paganism entirely from public life, as is revealed by his closing of the Academy of Athens in 529. On the other hand, the Orthodox liturgy and its accompanying imperial ceremonial was being elaborated as never before in this period. It was in the sixth century, during the reign of Justinian, that the Byzantine rite became fully imperial. The eucharistic service, called 'The Divine Liturgy', acquired new splendour through the addition of hymns such as the *Cheroubikon*. The Church calendar grew in complexity as new feasts were added and special hymns and readings were produced in their honour. One of the most striking features of the imperial rite in Constantinople must have been the stational liturgies, or processions from one church or holy place to another, each of which represented stages in the celebrations for a particular day. Processions such as these, which probably began in the late fourth century and in which not only the patriarch and all his clergy but also frequently the emperor himself participated, provided occasions in which the population at large could play a part, both as spectators and as participants. The Byzantine liturgy, although it later became much more confined to the church interior, still retains elements both of these elaborate processions and of the imperial vestments worn by both emperors and clergy.

Among the greatest achievements of Justinian's reign were the building of churches such as St Sophia in Constantinople and the production of liturgical poetry and other literature. Numerous contemporary writers recorded their reactions to the awesome proportions of the Great Church:

> the church has been made a spectacle of great beauty, stupendous to those who see it and altogether incredible to those who hear of it.[3]

> He [Justinian] . . . built an incomparably great pile such as has never been recorded – I mean the Great Church that is so beautiful and glorious as to exceed the power of speech.[4]

While such accounts are exaggerated, they unanimously convey the sense of innovation which accompanied the building of St Sophia. From this period onward, most Byzantine churches imitated the Great Church in their construction. Symbolically, they represented a heaven on earth, based on a Platonic conception of the cosmos reaching from God's throne in heaven to the earthly realm below. Accompanying the architectural developments in this century was the production of liturgical texts, including, above all, the hymnographic form known as the *kontakion*, a narrative sermon in verse, characterized both by dramatic dialogue and by theological teaching. Romanos the Melodist, probably the most famous of all Byzantine hymnographers, lived and worked during the reign of Justinian. Many of his hymns survive, covering important events in the Old Testament and in the life of Christ.[5] In the eighth century another hymnographic form, the *kanon*, was introduced into the service of *orthros* (matins) in the monastic rite. The two genres continued to be composed for the appropriate rites, the monastic and the cathedral, until as late as 1204.[6]

In order to understand the developments in dogmatic theology which took place in the sixth century, it is necessary to go back to the events and personalities surrounding the Council of Chalcedon in 451. Partly because of the influence of two distinct schools of theology which had developed in Alexandria and Antioch in the preceding centuries, the former emphasizing the allegorical, or spiritual, meaning of the Scriptures, and the latter their literal meaning, disagreement broke out concerning the definition of Christ and the relationship between his human and divine natures. The Council of Chalcedon in 451 succeeded to some extent in formulating a compromise between the Alexandrian and Antiochene views of the Incarnation of Christ, but its final text included insistence on Christ's existence 'in two natures', a wording which many Monophysites found that they could not accept. It is one of the tragedies in the history of Christianity that the formula which was eventually agreed at Chalcedon, which in fact represented a carefully worded compromise between the ideas of Christ's two distinct natures and his personal unity, should have led to a split between the Monophysite ('one nature') and Dyophysite ('two natures') Churches which has lasted until the present day.[7]

The dogmatic formulations of the sixth century represent part of an imperially led movement to reconcile the Monophysites which continued until the end of the seventh century. The Emperor Justinian saw the unification of the Christian Church as closely connected with his political restoration of the Roman Empire. Although his efforts in this direction ultimately failed, they did deeply influence the Byzantine dogmatic tradition. At the beginning of the sixth century, various events served to place Christological controversy firmly back on the agenda. In 519, a movement called Theopaschitism, probably introduced into Constantinople by four Scythian monks, argued that 'One of the Holy Trinity suffered in the flesh'. Believing that this formula would serve to reconcile the Monophysites, Justinian decided to accept the doctrine. Fierce opposition to the Theopaschite formula, however, centred in the Monastery of the *Akoimetoi* ('the Sleepless Ones'), who saw it as undermining the reality of Christ's human Incarnation. Other Dyophysite theologians, perhaps also in an effort to reconcile the Monophysites, embarked on a mission to reclaim Cyril of Alexandria for the Chalcedonian cause. Their argument, expressed in a variety of texts including the *Florilegium Cyrillianum*, sought to prove that Cyril's teachings were in fact consistent with the principal formula of the Fourth Ecumenical Council at Chalcedon.

This movement encountered powerful opposition, however, in the Monophysite theologian Severos, who was Bishop of Antioch between 512 and 518. Severos fiercely opposed the appropriation of Cyril of Alexandria by the movement which has come to be known as 'neo-Chalcedonian'. Severos of Antioch's powerful intellect dominates the Monophysite cause in the sixth century. Whereas Monophysite theologians such as Sergios the Grammarian and Julian of Halicarnassus adopted extreme views such as that the body of Christ remained incorruptible even before the resurrection, Severos, who frequently found it necessary to oppose extreme Monophysites such as these as well as Chalcedonians, adhered to a moderate Monophysitism, teaching that there is one divine nature in Christ, but that he also possessed genuinely human qualities. The difference between this doctrine and that of the Chalcedonians rests primarily on their various understandings of the union of the two natures of Christ in the Incarnation. Whereas moderate Monophysites found the teaching of two distinct natures in Christ illogical, they did not reject his humanity altogether. Instead they argued that while he possessed one *divine* nature, this was formed *out of* human and divine qualities.

The Fifth Ecumenical Council in 553 reflects Justinian's recognition that Chalcedon and moderate Monophysitism were to some extent reconcilable. The conclusions agreed in this Council included (a) the unity of Christ in one divine *hypostasis* (note that the terms *physis* ('nature') and *hypostasis* ('entity') are by now carefully distinguished); (b) the orthodoxy of the Theopaschite formula; (c) the condemnation of the so-called 'Three Chapters', that is, three of the most important proponents of the Antiochene school, Theodore of Edessa, Theodoret of Cyrrhus and Ibas of Edessa. The anathemas of the Fifth Ecumenical Council have been seen by some scholars as a fatal attempt to reconcile the Monophysites at the expense of Antiochene theology; certainly, the definitions of Christological doctrine endorsed in the sixth century determined the development of dogmatic theology in the Orthodox Church thereafter. On the other hand, the acceptance and reintegration of the theology of the fifth-century theologian Cyril of Alexandria can only be seen as enriching Orthodox Christological doctrine.[8] It is unfortunate that in spite of such an achievement, the Fifth Ecumenical Council completely failed in its primary objective: that of reconciling the majority of Monophysites.

Another major obstacle to the reunification of the Monophysite and

Chalcedonian Churches in the sixth century lay in the missionary activities of figures such as Jacob Baradaeos. Jacob, who was patronized in Constantinople by the Monophysite Empress Theodora, was ordained bishop in Edessa at her instigation in order to counterbalance the anti-Monophysite activities of Ephrem, Chalcedonian Bishop of Antioch (527–545). With an independent Monophysite jurisdiction now extending over many parts of the Near East, Jacob Baradaeos was able to appoint bishops in many cities, including some in the Aegean and the west coast of Asia Minor such as Chios and Ephesus. Many of these bishops were drawn from Syrian monasteries so that the Monophysite hierarchy soon displayed a distinctly Syrian character. It was the establishment of this rival episcopal hierarchy which enabled Monophysite Christians eventually to regard themselves as a completely independent and autonomous Church. The persecution which these Churches suffered during the reign of Justinian and his successors may have contributed to their sense of cultural and ethnic identity and to their opposition to the imperial Chalcedonian Church. It is likely, however, in view of the strong religious tendencies of the population at large, that Monophysites and Chalcedonians backed their local Church leaders because they believed that their dogmatic teaching was correct. It is also noteworthy that doctrinal persuasion was not determined completely by geographical location in the late fifth and early sixth centuries. The Near East, including present-day Syria, Lebanon, Jordan and Palestine, included adherents to all the rival Churches, whereas emperors and empresses in this period could choose to back either Monophysite or Chalcedonian Christology. Thus, the Emperors Zeno and Anastasios were Monophysites, while Justinian, who officially backed the Chalcedonian cause, sought some compromises. It is possible that the solution which Byzantine theology ultimately adopted, namely the recognition that a hypostatic union of two natures could be understood in various ways, came just too late. There can be no doubt that political factors played some part in the tragic and apparently irreconcilable division of the Church in this period.

Parallel to developments in dogmatic theology were those in the tradition of monastic teaching, which was based partly on the practical living out of the ascetic and spiritual life by hermits and monks throughout the Byzantine Empire and partly on a highly developed and subtle genre of philosophical literature which accompanied this. This monastic tradition of ascetic teaching was indebted most of all to the fourth-century father Evagrios who in turn was influenced by the teachings of Origen (c. 185–254). While Origen, with his attempt to create a complete Christian cosmology in his book *On First Principles*,[9] represents one of the most innovative early Christian writers, most of his writings were later condemned by the Orthodox Church. Origen's hierarchical view of the Trinity was seen as subordinationism and, above all, his teachings concerning the pre-existence of souls and his separation of 'intellect' from the material body came to be regarded as dangerously dualist in a Christian context. The monastic followers of Origen and Evagrios became sufficiently numerous in the fifth and sixth centuries, however, to cause serious disquiet, especially in the monasteries of Palestine. According to contemporary sources, some monks claimed to be 'equal to Christ' by restoring their original 'intellectual' relationship with God through prayer and contemplation.[10] This extreme and obviously heretical form of Origenism was condemned, first by imperial decree in 543 and then at the Fifth Ecumenical Council in 553. The writings of Evagrios and Origen were largely destroyed and survive only partially in Latin and Syriac translations or under pseudonymous titles. It is important to note, however, that the condemnation of Origen and the writers whom he influenced did not eradicate their ideas from the Byzantine spiritual tradition. Like all other heresies in the early Church, 'Origenism', by forcing a debate concerning certain issues, significantly influenced the development of monastic theology.

In addition to its importance in the formulation of Church doctrine, the sixth century is regarded by most historians as the turning point between the still outwardly secular jurisdiction of the later Roman Empire and the development of a fully Christian medieval state. The development of the imperial liturgical rite has already been discussed; this was accompanied by an increase in popular devotion to various cults, including those of the holy relics of saints, icons and above all the Theotokos ('God-bearer' or 'Mother of God'). Religious devotion of this kind was not confined to the lower and middle classes but was promoted by the government itself as a way to focus the loyalties of the population towards a divinely led and sanctioned emperor. Imperial ceremonies, involving processions with icons, relics and other holy objects, served to emphasize the saving power of the divine in this world. The Virgin Mary became the most powerful of these symbols of divine intercession. The unforgettable image of the siege of 7 August 626, when the Virgin appeared and helped to fight off the Avars and Slavs who were at the very gates of Constantinople, represents a high point in the history of her cult.[11] Poetry in the form of both homilies and hymns had been appearing in honour of the Mother of God from the fifth century onwards. It is after the end of the sixth century, when the last of her feasts, the Dormition, had been instituted, however, that these genres reached their most developed form.

The increase in devotion to the Virgin Mary in this period was accompanied by the growth in the popular use of holy images, or icons, both in church and at home. As this cult gained importance a long-standing opposition to images, which had always existed within the

Church because of Old Testament prohibitions against idolatry, began also to re-surface. Texts both for and against the cult of icons do testify to its existence, however, and there can be no doubt that by the beginning of the eighth century, when Iconoclasm first acquired imperial backing, Orthodox Christians' dependence on holy objects and images operating as channels of divine power had increased significantly since the late sixth century.

Holy men, sometimes under the protection of monasteries and sometimes as free agents, also continued to wield considerable spiritual power in late sixth- and early seventh-century Byzantine society. At the beginning of the seventh century, John Moschos wrote a collection of edifying stories about the ascetics and monks of Palestine and Egypt known as the *Spiritual Meadow*. This includes a number of miracle stories, such as the following vivid account involving an icon:

> The same fathers also told us that in those days, a Christ-loving woman of the district of Apamea dug a well. She spent a great deal of money on the project and dug very deep, but she found no water. Having put so much money and effort into the project, she was very discouraged. Then one day, she had a vision of somebody saying to her: 'Send for and bring the picture of Abba Theodosios at Skopelos and by that means God will give you water.' The woman sent two men at once. They took the icon of the saint and let it down into the well and immediately water began to flow; it filled the well-shaft up to the half-way point. The men who drew the icon up out of the water brought us some of it; we drank of it and all gave thanks to God.[12]

Other sources which reveal much about popular and monastic spirituality in the early seventh century include John Klimakos's *Ladder of Divine Ascent*[13] and Anastasios of Sinai's *Questions and Answers*.[14] The latter text in particular provides valuable insight into the sorts of questions which occupied ordinary people's minds at this time. Such day-to-day problems as how often the laity should partake of the Eucharist, what sort of preparation was required for participation in this great mystery and many others are addressed in a clear and practical way.

The seventh century and Monothelitism

The seventh century was dominated by military confrontations, first with the Persians, who succeeded in taking most of the Byzantine Empire's Near Eastern territories, including the Holy Land in 614. The Persian capture of Jerusalem's most holy relic, the True Cross, and its removal to

Ctesiphon represented for Orthodox Christians a spiritual catastrophe. In addition to other material and territorial losses, the church of the Holy Sepulchre, built by Constantine, was destroyed by fire in the Persian sack of the city. Avar and Slav advances also began from the north so that the empire slowly lost control of most of its Balkan territory. In spite of these reverses, however, the Emperor Heraclius managed to rally the imperial army to the extent that all of these threats were eventually overcome or at least put into abeyance. Concentrating first on overcoming the Persians, Heraclius bribed the Avars to delay their offensive. In the years between 619 and 628, he was able to defeat the Persians and to recapture Jerusalem, along with most of the other territories which they had invaded, while the Avars, having been defeated by the Byzantines at the very walls of Constantinople, retreated into the Balkans, where they were eventually overpowered by the Slavs.

One result of Heraclius's recovery of the Eastern territories was the reopening of the issue of Church unity and reconciliation with the Monophysite Churches. Now that Syria, Palestine and Egypt were once more under Roman rule, it seemed imperative to Heraclius and his ecclesiastical advisers that the long-standing misunderstanding between Chalcedonian and Monophysite Christians should be resolved. Sergios, Patriarch of Constantinople between 610 and 638, was responsible for devising a new attempt at a formula of compromise. The doctrine, called Monoenergism, taught that whereas Christ has two natures, one divine and one human, he possesses a single activity (or 'energy' in Greek). With the backing of Pope Honorius in Rome, Monoenergism appears initially to have met with some success in local Eastern Churches. The Armenian Church agreed to the formula and was welcomed back into the imperial Church in 630 while, even more importantly, in 631 the Metropolitan of Phasis, Kyros, agreed to Monoenergism and was soon after appointed Patriarch of Alexandria. Persuasion was reinforced by persecution, but even so, Monoenergism seems at first to have been fairly successful among the Monophysite population of Egypt.

Opposition to Monoenergism as a theological doctrine, however, soon began to be voiced by the Patriarch of Jerusalem, Sophronios, a venerable and eloquent figure who had travelled with John Moschos through the monasteries of Palestine and Egypt in the course of his long and distinguished career. In 634 Sophronios issued a synodical letter to his fellow patriarchs in which he argued that Monoenergism represented a form of Monophysitism. This letter seems to have had the effect of turning the popes in Rome, beginning with Honorius, against the doctrine of Monoenergism. Partly in response to this opposition, the Patriarch Sergios, backed by Heraclius, issued first his *Psephos* (Decision) and then in 638 the *Ekthesis* (Statement), a document in which the formula of a single energy had been transformed into one of a single will (Monotheletism).

At first even Sophronios seems to have accepted the new formulation, at least as it was set forth in the *Psephos*. By 638, however, he had begun to have doubts and directed his efforts towards convening a Church council to discuss the Monothelite doctrine. When this failed, Sophronios appealed to Rome again, but organizing resistance to Monothelitism, which had just received official endorsement from the Pope, proved to be difficult. Sophronios soon acquired a powerful ally, however, in one of the greatest of all Byzantine theologians, St Maximos the Confessor. Maximos, born in 580, led a wandering monastic life in Asia Minor, North Africa and Rome.[15] During his travels Maximos succeeded in stirring up opposition to Monothelitism, most notably in Rome. After Constans II issued an imperial decree known as the *Typos*, which forbade 'any discussion of one will or one energy, two wills or two energies', Pope Martin II convened a council in October 649 at which 105 bishops agreed to reaffirm the doctrine of Chalcedon, to make explicit the doctrine of two energies and two wills in Christ and to condemn both the *Ekthesis* and the *Typos*. In what represents one of the most shameful episodes in Byzantine Church history, the emperor then ordered the arrest of the Pope. He was taken to Constantinople, tried and convicted of treason and exiled to the northern province of Cherson where he died soon after, on 16 September 655, a tired and broken old man. Maximos, like Pope Martin, was condemned for treason, tortured and mutilated, and finally exiled to Lazica. He died as a martyr to the Orthodox faith, and only later received the recognition and veneration which he deserved.[16]

Maximos the Confessor's theology developed in response to Monotheletism, but it transcended that controversy in its importance to the Byzantine theological synthesis. Deeply influenced by Origen and by the fifth-century mystical writer ps-Dionysios the Areopagite, Maximos understood Christian theology as a message of salvation which redeems the whole of creation as well as humanity. Christ's Incarnation, he argued, could not be seen as anything other than the fulfilment of God's original plan when he created the world out of nothing. Every human being, created in the image of God and representing in himself the whole of the cosmos, has the potential not only to be saved but to regain his original state as an image of God. Such an aim can be achieved through ascetic discipline, through the grace bestowed by the sacraments and by faith in the Incarnate Lord. Maximos's all-encompassing theology influenced the development of Byzantine Christological doctrine especially in the subsequent century, as Orthodox theologians such as John of Damascus developed a theological response to the attack on holy images.

Monotheletism as an imperially backed Church doctrine lasted for another generation, but it ultimately failed in its political aim. The opposition of such figures as Sophronios of Jerusalem and Maximos the Confessor, backed by a succession of Roman popes, led to the abandonment of the doctrine at the Sixth Ecumenical Council in 680–681. With the rise of Islam and the rapid loss of most Near Eastern territories to the Arabs in the mid-seventh century and the deterioration in relations between East and West, it is likely that the Byzantine Emperor Constantine IV (668–685) and his advisers realized that their ecclesiastical policy was divisive rather than unifying. After this period, no further efforts were made by the imperial Chalcedonian Church to reintegrate the Monophysite Churches into its fold; the fact that the Christian Church was irrevocably divided, mainly along political boundaries, seems instead to have finally been accepted. Another serious implication of the Monothelite controversy was its place in the slow but irreversible drift apart of the Western and Eastern halves of Christendom. The arrest of Pope Martin II by Byzantine imperial envoys is shocking in itself, but it also provided a dangerous precedent for future interaction between the sees of Rome and Constantinople. Perhaps it is already in the seventh century that we perceive the seeds of the mutual distrust, misunderstanding and eventually schism which were to characterize East–West relations in future centuries.

The Iconoclast controversy (726–843)

The controversy over icons, known as Iconoclasm, dominates the history of the Byzantine Church in the eighth and early ninth centuries. This event, which has been described by most historians as a watershed in Byzantine history, affected many aspects of political, social and religious life. The adoption of an Iconoclast policy by a series of emperors beginning with Leo III in 726 was to some extent unprecedented in Church history and had serious implications for Church–state relations thereafter. The role which monks and monasteries played in resisting Iconoclast policy, especially during the first period of Iconoclasm between about 760 and 787, was to contribute to the growing importance of monasticism in Byzantine society in subsequent centuries. East–West relations were affected, as Iconophiles appealed to the Pope for support, while the long imperial support for the Iconoclasts soured relations between the two Romes, despite the warm reception of the Roman delegates at the Seventh Ecumenical Council, held at Nicaea in 787. Finally, the debate over the nature and uses of images in religious worship helped Iconophile theologians to develop a dogmatic theology in defence of icons which became central to Orthodox doctrine. The final rejection of Iconoclasm in 843 opened the way for the development of a distinctive iconography and the extensive decoration of Byzantine churches in subsequent centuries.

The causes for the outbreak of Iconoclasm in the early eighth century have been discussed extensively by scholars.[17] Whereas some have seen Leo III's Syrian origins and undoubted contact with iconoclastic groups in that area, including Muslims, Jews and Paulicians, as a possible cause,[18] others have seen Iconoclasm as a reform movement which originated in the Byzantine ecclesiastical hierarchy itself.[19] The chronicler Theophanes states that Leo interpreted an earthquake and tidal wave in the Aegean Sea as signs of God's wrath at Christians' relapse into superstition and idolatry.[20] It is likely that the debate concerning the causes of Iconoclasm will never be resolved. What historians are increasingly studying, however, is the entire political and theological background of the conflict; there can be no doubt that the conquest of the entire Near East and North Africa by the Muslims and their continuing incursions into Byzantine territory in the late seventh and early eighth centuries influenced ideological developments in the Eastern Roman Empire in this period.

The debate concerning the production and veneration of holy icons centred first on the prohibition against idolatry in Exodus 20:4–5: 'Thou shalt not make unto thee any graven image, or any likeness of any thing that is in heaven above, or that is in the earth beneath, or that is in the water under the earth: Thou shalt not bow down thyself to them, nor serve them.' Jews, Christians in the early Church and, later, Muslims all remained faithful to this commandment, although in all three religious traditions exceptions were occasionally made. It was the Christians, however, who introduced images into collective and private worship to the greatest extent in the centuries following the Christianization of the Roman Empire and who began to develop a theological defence of this practice even before the outbreak of Iconoclasm. Early eighth-century Iconophiles defended themselves against the charge of idolatry with various arguments, including the long-standing tradition of religious imagery in the Church, the existence of miraculous icons 'made without hands', some of which were thought to date to the time of Christ himself, and the unanswerable statement that since the Incarnation of Christ, no form of Christian worship could be called idolatry. Germanos, Patriarch of Constantinople until 730 when he was deposed by Leo III for resisting Iconoclasm, developed some of these arguments in his writings,[21] but the defence was raised to a much higher level by his contemporary in Arab-ruled Palestine, the monk and theologian John of Damascus. Using a Neoplatonic frame of reference which had been developed by ps-Dionysios the Areopagite and Maximos the Confessor, John examined what an image actually is and how it is used in Christian worship.[22] In three treatises directed against the teachings of the Iconoclasts, John distinguished between various types of images, separating man-made ones, such as icons, from those which are 'natural', such as the relation of Christ the Son to the Father. Just as the nature of these images differs, so does the veneration (*proskynesis*) or worship (*latreia*) paid to them by Christians. John further argues that in the Incarnation of Christ an eternal and decisive change took place in the relationship between God and his creation. Since God appeared in the flesh and lived among men, it became possible to depict him in his human form. To deny this, as the Iconoclasts were currently doing, would be to deny the reality of the Incarnation and, in effect, to believe with Monophysites that the divine nature of Christ dominated the human one. By using these arguments, John of Damascus succeeded in raising the debate concerning the use of religious images within the Church to a Christological level. Judging by the few surviving Iconoclastic texts, the opponents of images seem to have failed to formulate an adequate response to the theology developed by John of Damascus and his successors. The fundamental difference between their approach to images and that of the Iconophiles was that they regarded images as essentially identical to their prototypes. Thus, to attempt to depict God, even in his human Incarnation, represented to the Iconoclasts a form of idolatry.[23]

Iconophile theology advanced further in the second period of Iconoclasm (815–843) as theologians such as Theodore, Abbot of the monastery of Stoudios, and Nikephoros, Patriarch of Constantinople (806–815), explored the philosophical implications of the controversy. Following in the footsteps of John of Damascus, they examined further the hierarchical relationship between images and their prototypes, as well as the Christological dimensions of the debate. Ultimately, Iconophiles stressed not only the acceptability, but also the *necessity*, of Christian images. They accused the Iconoclasts not only of denying Christ's Incarnation, but also of a dualist denial of the essential goodness of the material world as God's creation. The Orthodox theology of images asserts that God is present in the created world, that he does manifest his power through certain sanctified objects such as icons and that these objects reflect in some way the mystery of the Incarnation. It is important nevertheless to remember that a hierarchy exists in the created world as well as in the heavenly one in Orthodox theology; the sanctity of an icon does not, for example, take precedence over the Holy Gospels or the Eucharist.

Another issue of scholarly debate in this period has been the attitude of Iconoclast emperors, especially Constantine V in the mid-eighth century, towards monks and monasteries.[24] Polemical Iconophile writers such as Theophanes state that monasteries were confiscated and turned into public buildings for secular purposes, while monks were rounded up and imprisoned or exiled if they refused to renounce their monastic calling. Theophanes also describes how Constantine forced the abbots of all the monasteries in Constantinople to parade in the hippodrome, each one holding a woman by the hand.[25] In other passages he mentions the torture and execution of various holy men. The biased nature of Theophanes's narrative, which also dwells on Emperor Constantine V's excesses and moral depravity, however, renders the truth of these stories suspect. On the other hand, there can be no doubt that sporadic persecution of monks did take place in this period. It is likely that Constantine held a particular grudge against monks and monasteries and that this was connected with his distrust of icons, relics and other popular cults. In the second period of Iconoclasm (815–843), the division between Iconophiles and Iconoclasts was by no means so clear-cut. Many monasteries in this period seem to have adopted Iconoclasm, whereas the secular clergy backed either party. The fact that Theodore of Stoudios, who was responsible for organizing Iconophile resistance at this time, also initiated a movement of reform which led to a widespread revival of monasticism in Constantinople, may account for the fact that even in this period the sources associate the defence of holy icons mainly with monks and monasteries.

As in 787, the restoration of icons to the Church came about in 843 under a female ruler, in this case the Empress Theodora, who acted as regent for her young son Michael III until 856. The motivation for maintaining Iconoclasm as an imperial policy had been waning since before the death of Theodora's husband Theophilos in 842. Since the devastating Battle of Amorion in 838, when this central Anatolian stronghold and, more significantly, the home town of Theophilos's father Michael II, fell to the Arabs, Iconoclasm could no longer be linked convincingly with Byzantine military success. Like various other women in influential positions in this period, Theodora was a secret Iconophile throughout her husband's reign and had a personal interest in restoring the holy icons in 843. She also had the backing of members of the Church hierarchy and of key figures in the secular government. Methodios, appointed Patriarch of Constantinople in 843, did his best to eradicate Iconoclast elements from within the Church, replacing Iconoclast bishops with Iconophiles, some of whom had suffered persecution and imprisonment under the Iconoclast emperors. The overturning of the old order and the inauguration of the new was officially celebrated on the first Sunday of Lent, 11 March 843, by a ceremony in the Great Church during which the *Synodikon of Orthodoxy*, a document probably composed by Methodios himself, was read out.[26] This text, which represents a crucial source for the Byzantines' own perception of what constituted Orthodox or right belief in this period, is also a splendid example of theatrical display. The document consists mainly of a list of the figures who defended icons, followed by the acclamation, 'Eternal memory!' Those who opposed the veneration of icons, on the other hand, are anathematized. An abridged version of the document is still read out on the 'Sunday of Orthodoxy' in many Orthodox Churches today.

The revival of monasticism and the patriarchate of Photios

The second half of the ninth century was characterized by increasing tension between two opposing parties within the Church, the secular clergy, headed by Methodios, and the monastic party, which, owing to its association with the defence of Orthodoxy during the Iconoclast period, had become increasingly influential and vociferous. Regarding themselves perhaps as the guardians of Orthodox doctrine and canon law *par excellence*, the monastic group, led by monks associated with the monastery of Stoudios in Constantinople, opposed many of the appointments and decisions enacted by the Patriarch Methodios. In return, he insisted that they repudiate many of the writings of their spiritual leader, Theodore, against the policies of the earlier Patriarchs Tarasios and Nikephoros. When they refused, he anathematized them. This conflict remained unresolved until Methodios was eventually forced to retire and was replaced as Patriarch by Ignatios, a strong supporter of the monastic party.

It is generally accepted that, partly as a result of the overthrow of Iconoclasm and monastic association with this victory, monasticism entered a period of rapid expansion in the mid-ninth century. Many different forms of religious life were available in this period, catering for every sector of the population.[27] Hermits could live in desolate places such as on mountain tops or deserts, following the way of life adopted by early ascetics such as St Antony, whereas groups of monks could follow the cenobitic life advocated by Pachomios, Basil the Great and, most recently, Theodore of Stoudios. Between these two extremes existed many variations; it was common for a cenobitic house in the ninth century, for example, to have an anchorite or two under its protection. Saints' lives of the period suggest that abbots, or *hegoumenoi*, were responsible for guiding monks towards the goal of solitude (*hesychia*) or, alternatively, recommending the communal life. The reforms in cenobitic monasticism introduced by Theodore into the monastery of Stoudios and its daughter houses seem to have included changes in liturgical observances. Some of these reflected the influence of Palestinian monasteries, especially the monastery of St Sabas. The morning and evening offices, *esperinos* (vespers) and *orthros* (matins), were lengthened by the addition of new hymnographic material and all-night vigils were introduced into Constantinopolitan monasteries. Thus, a monastic liturgical office developed, parallel to the existing tradition of the cathedral office; these two traditions coexisted in Constantinople and surrounding regions until the Latin conquest of Constantinople in 1204.

When the Patriarch Ignatios was eventually deposed in 858 for attempting to play too influential a role in the political life of the palace, he was replaced by the cultured layman and civil servant Photios. It was during the patriarchate of Photios that two key events in ninth-century Byzantine Church history occurred: the beginnings of schism with Rome and the first Orthodox missions to the Slavs. The causes of disagreement with the Pope were initially political, when he refused to authorize Ignatios's resignation and to recognize the ordination of Photios as Patriarch of Constantinople. Photios, however, widened the discussion to include a doctrinal issue, namely the acceptance by Rome of an addition into the Creed of the words 'and the Son' in the clause describing the procession of the Holy Spirit. Whereas the papacy had not yet approved the inclusion of the clause (known as the *filioque*) in the churches of Rome in this period, it did overlook its use in Frankish and other Western churches.[28] Photios wrote a letter to the Pope in which he attacked his acceptance of the *filioque* and outlined its heretical implications. In stating that the Holy Spirit proceeds from the Father *and the Son*, the revised Creed appears to admit two principles, or sources, of creation. In 867, after an exchange of hostile letters, Photios held a synod in Constantinople in which he deposed and anathematized Pope Nicholas II.

Ninth-century missions to the Slavs and the emergence of the Slavic Churches

Tension concerning ecclesiastical jurisdiction in Illyricum and rivalry over missions to the Slavs had in fact precipitated the conflicts between Photios and Pope Nicholas II. The papal jurisdiction of Illyricum, which had been removed by the Iconoclast emperors in the eighth century, was one of the powers which Nicholas II had hoped to recover in his diplomatic embassies to Constantinople. Owing to their other disagreements, Photios refused to consider this request, thereby further infuriating the Pope. Rivalry over the form of Christianity adopted by the Bulgarian Khan Boris, who had been baptized by the Greeks in 864 but remained subject to the influence of Latin missionaries in the region, also contributed to the discord between Rome and Constantinople during Photios's first patriarchate (858–867).

Taking place at roughly the same time as the conversion of the

Bulgarian khan to Christianity were the missions to the Slavs in Moravia. Photios appears to have regarded Christian mission, and in particular Byzantine Orthodox mission, as one of his most important patriarchal duties. The fact that the conversion of alien peoples such as the Slavs furthered the expansionist aims of the Byzantine Empire in this period must have contributed to the patriarch's enthusiasm. Photios found able and enthusiastic agents for his missions in two brothers from Thessalonike, Constantine (later Cyril) and Methodios. Constantine, sometimes called 'the Philosopher', was an outstanding philologist and scholar, besides being a skilled theologian. His brother Methodios had been governor of a region near Thessalonike and was an obvious choice for his companion. The first mission on which the brothers embarked was to distant Khazaria in the northern Caucasus. The Khazars had already converted to Judaism during the eighth century, but Photios must have hoped that this might render them receptive to the teachings of Christianity. The mission was a failure, however, and after this Byzantine attention turned to the Slavs in the north. In 862, Ratislav, the ruler of Great Moravia, wrote to the Byzantine Emperor Michael III asking for a teacher to give Christian instruction to his people in his own language. Up until this time, missionaries from the East Franks (Germans) had been working in the area, but their Church services were all celebrated in Latin. It was Constantine and Methodios, both fluent in the language because of their contact with Slavs settled in and around Thessalonike, who conceived the idea of inventing an alphabet and translating the Scriptures and Orthodox liturgical texts into Slavonic. The mission to Moravia was ultimately unsuccessful due to the opposition of the German missionaries already in residence there. Although the two Greek missionaries appealed to the Pope for protection and were granted his blessing, this proved ineffectual. While Constantine died in Rome in 869 after entering a monastery and taking the name of Cyril, Methodios, on returning to Moravia, was imprisoned for a short time and subjected thereafter to continuous harassment. After his death in 885, Methodios's followers were either driven out of Moravia or sold into slavery.

The methods which Constantine and Methodios adopted in their missions to the Slavs were nevertheless to have a lasting impact on all the other Slavic Churches. Whereas the mission to Moravia had been unsuccessful, other Churches in the Balkans and in Rus' took over the translation of Greek liturgical texts into Slavonic. The Glagolitic alphabet invented by Constantine and also employed by his successors Clement and Naum, who worked first at the court of the Bulgarian ruler Symeon (893–927) and later in Macedonia, gave way slowly to the simpler Cyrillic one, which was based mainly on Greek letters.

After the Orthodox baptism of the Bulgarian Khan Boris in 864, he became dissatisfied with the Greeks for refusing to grant autonomy to his national Church. After a brief period in which he allowed Latin missionaries into Bulgaria in the hope of gaining more favourable terms from Rome, Boris eventually turned back to the Byzantines. In March 870 a Church council placed Bulgaria under the patriarchate of Constantinople and Boris expelled the remaining Western missionaries from the nation. In consequence the Bulgarian ruler welcomed the disciples of Constantine and Methodios who had been forced to leave their mission in Moravia. They at once introduced their Slavonic translations of the liturgy and the Scriptures into the churches of Bulgaria and thereby helped to lay the foundations of a Slavic Christian culture. Boris's third son Symeon was educated in Constantinople for an ecclesiastical career – but was recalled in 893 to replace his brother Vladimir as Prince of Bulgaria. While Symeon's education and exposure to Orthodox Christianity in Constantinople meant that he was a strong supporter of the nascent Bulgarian Church, he was also an ambitious political leader who hoped to conquer Constantinople and become emperor of the Greeks and the Bulgarians. In spite of the hostility between the Byzantines and the Bulgarians during Symeon's reign (893–927), this was a period in which Orthodox Christianity flourished and spread in Bulgaria. In 927, the Bulgarian Church was at last granted autonomy by the patriarchate of Constantinople.

Byzantine missionaries also went to Serbia in the second half of the ninth century and many Serbs were converted to Orthodoxy between 867 and 874. It is probably due to influence from Bulgaria that Slavonic service books were introduced early, thereby strengthening local allegiance to the new religion. Although Serbia remained under the jurisdiction of Constantinople until 1219 when St Sava was consecrated archbishop of a semi-autonomous Serbian Church, it early developed its own distinctive culture which was manifested in religious art and literature. After taking over most of the liturgical and patristic texts translated by Constantine and Methodios and their successors, the Serbs made further translations of biblical commentaries, homilies and mystical texts. The greatest flowering of Serbian culture took place during the reign of King Stefan Nemanja (1165–96) and his successors.

There can be no doubt that the use of the vernacular language also played a part in the conversion of the princess Olga in Kiev and her grandson Vladimir, the first Christian ruler of the Rus', in the middle and late decades of the ninth century. Before discussing these conversions, however, it is necessary to provide some background on the emergence of the Rus' and the Varangians, who ruled over them for a period and later were absorbed into Slavic society. According to the earliest document on this subject, the *Primary Chronicle*, the Varangians pushed southwards from Scandinavia and settled in the region around Novgorod in the mid-ninth century. Elements of this group travelled further south around 856 and, seizing the district of Kiev on the way, reached Constantinople in 860 and laid siege to the city. The Patriarch Photios delivered two homilies on the occasion of this siege.[29] It was the successors of the Varangians and the Rus' remaining in the region of Kiev who came to be influenced by the religious beliefs of the Byzantines. In 957, Olga, regent for her son Svyatoslav, paid a ceremonial visit to Constantinople. Here she seems to have been granted a cordial reception and to have been welcomed into the court. It is not clear whether she was baptized on this occasion or whether she had already embraced Christianity in Kiev, but in any case she returned to her native land determined to win more converts to Orthodoxy. Olga failed to persuade her son Svyatoslav to be baptized, but a generation later, in 988, her grandson Vladimir became a Christian. The passage from the *Primary Chronicle* describing the delight of Vladimir's envoys on beholding the liturgical celebrations in Constantinople's Great Church was quoted at the beginning of this chapter; it forms part of the writer's account of the Kievan ruler's conversion to Orthodoxy. More pragmatic reasons for his baptism may include the Byzantine Emperor Basil II's desire for an ally in his efforts to quell a rebellious uprising and Vladimir's own desire for an imperial bride, Basil II's sister Anna. Whatever the actual causes of Vladimir's adoption of Christianity, it is clear that the conversion of his people followed relatively quickly. From this time onwards, Kievan Christianity remained closely linked to its mother Church in Constantinople. Not only did it receive from Byzantium the riches of Orthodox religious art and literature, but it was also influenced by the Greek monastic tradition, in particular that of the eremetical ascetics.

The early period in Russian history, called the Kievan period, lasted from 988 to the early thirteenth century when the Mongols invaded and seized control. This represents in many ways an attractive start to the history of the Russian Church since Vladimir and his successors seem to have taken the ethical teachings of Christianity seriously. Whenever Vladimir feasted with his court, food was also distributed to the poor and sick. It is possible that nowhere else in medieval Europe were there such highly organized social services as in tenth-century Kiev. Vladimir also abolished capital punishment and his sons, Boris, Gleb and Svyatoslav, chose to be killed rather than to take up arms against their relation Svyatopolk when he seized power. All of these figures are still revered in the Russian Church, as saints and 'passion-bearers'.

The tenth, eleventh and twelfth centuries

The so-called 'Tetragamy' crisis dominates Byzantine Church history in the early tenth century. This debate was important because it revealed the willingness of the Constantinopolitan synod of bishops to uphold Byzantine canon law against the wishes of the emperor, and because it represented one more occasion on which he appealed to Rome for support against his own ecclesiastical hierarchs. The background to the controversy was as follows: Leo VI, Byzantine emperor between 886 and 912, became worried that he had not been provided with a legitimate male heir. His first wife, the pious Theophano, died in 893 and he took a second wife, Zoe, who also died without male issue in 899. According to Byzantine canon law, two imperial marriages were acceptable, if not totally approved; a third and a fourth marriage were positively prohibited. Any offspring of such marriages should be considered illegitimate. Undeterred by canonical rulings, Leo married a third wife, Eudocia Baïane, and when she died in childbirth in 901 he took a mistress, Zoe Carbonopsina. Her son, Constantine, was actually born in the palace, or as the Byzantines put it, 'in the purple' (*porphyrogennetos*). Controversy erupted first when the Patriarch, Nicholas I Mystikos, agreed to baptize the baby in the Great Church on the feast of Epiphany (6 January 906). According to Nicholas himself, who wrote a letter justifying his action to Pope Anastasius III, he performed the baptism on condition that Leo would separate himself from his mistress Zoe immediately. Instead, probably around Easter 906, Leo and Zoe were secretly married by a priest called Thomas and Zoe was crowned Augusta by the emperor himself.

Significantly, the Byzantine synod of bishops and the Patriarch were united in their condemnation of the emperor's actions. Leo was forbidden entry to the Great Church and his wife's name was not added to the diptychs. The emperor decided to appeal to the four other members of the pentarchy, the three Eastern patriarchates and the Pope in Rome, for a special dispensation. This was forthcoming and papal legates arrived in Constantinople in 907. The hierarchs who remained opposed to Leo's marriage, including the Patriarch Nicholas, were deposed and exiled to monasteries. Even Nicholas's successor Euthymios, however, refused to acknowledge Leo's marriage and he proceeded to depose the priest who had performed the ceremony. Eventually, after the death of Leo VI in 912, Nicholas Mystikos was returned to office and the whole affair was to some extent resolved. Constantinople's insistence that a fourth marriage should be utterly banned by canon law was acknowledged by Rome, whose support, along with that of the other three patriarchates, was still seen to be necessary.

Another of the achievements of the brilliant and forceful Patriarch Nicholas I Mystikos was his attempt at diplomatic negotiations with the Bulgarian ruler Symeon in the early tenth century. The letters which the Patriarch sent to Symeon after 912 reveal that Nicholas sought to direct the Bulgarian ruler's ambition for the Byzantine throne into peaceful channels, suggesting an alliance by imperial marriage.[30] Nicholas's diplomatic efforts were unsuccessful due to the misguided intervention of the Empress Zoe, but his vision of a peace based on the common faith of the Byzantines and the Bulgarians represents a fine example of the perceived link between diplomacy and Christian mission in the middle Byzantine period.

Monasteries, both privately and imperially owned, continued to increase and to expand in the tenth century. Not only the reigning imperial family, but also the nobility and even ordinary civilians, perceived donations to monasteries as a useful way to invest their money. If a family had no heir apparent, bequeathing land to an existing house or even founding a new monastery ensured that it would remain intact, with the added advantage that the family or individual donor would gain spiritual credit. The donor could compose his own testament and monastic rule, or *typikon*, both of which might enumerate not only his long-standing virtues, but also his formal renunciation of any remaining transgressions. Prayers of intercession for the individual or family could be demanded of the monks in perpetuity.

As monastic houses acquired land and movable property, it became a primary concern for them to safeguard their ownership by law. In the course of the tenth and eleventh centuries, the legal terms on which monasteries held their lands became increasingly complex. At the same time, a succession of emperors felt impelled to enact legislation aimed at restricting the power of monasteries and at preventing their further acquisition of land to the detriment of imperial revenues. The fact that such legislation was frequently overruled or at least modified shows how unpopular such measures were, even in the eyes of the emperors who were forced to promote them. To begin with the various obligations of monastic founders, canon law initiated in the fourth and fifth centuries and updated in the late ninth states that donors and their families must see that building work is completed within three years of the foundation of churches and monasteries. If they fail to achieve this, the leading men (*archontes*) of their neighbourhood should compel them to complete their work. Furthermore, the descendants of donors are responsible for completing or carrying out maintenance on foundations. The need for such laws stems from the long-standing existence in the Byzantine Empire of private monasteries; these foundations continued to be viewed as private property and were not subject to episcopal or imperial authority. In addition to their legal exemptions, monastic foundations deprived the imperial treasury of tax revenues since their land frequently remained uncultivated. The mechanism of *charistike*, or the legal grant of a monastery into the ownership of a layman, who might thereafter receive all its revenues, represented another drain on the resources of the central government. Much of the imperial legislation enacted in the tenth century is aimed at preventing the further acquisition of land by monasteries and the consequent dispossession of peasants. In 934, the Emperor Romanos Lekapenos issued a law which forbade wealthy individuals, including lay magnates and abbots, from acquiring more land at the expense of peasants. Constantine VII Porphyrogennetos reconfirmed these restrictions in 947, and in 964 Nikephoros II Phokas banned all new foundations of monasteries and philanthropic institutions. Throughout this edict, perhaps in order to emphasize its moral underpinning, the emperor stresses the distinction between monastic founders' justifiable concern to ensure the survival of their houses and the avarice which led some to accumulate excessive amounts of property. He also deplores the large number of new monasteries currently being founded and the state of disrepair into which many existing foundations have fallen. In 988, however, the Emperor Basil II repealed Nikephoros's law. This was perhaps a concession to the wishes of the landed magnates whose support he needed to gain. Subsequent laws reverted to the old practice of favouring monasteries and their wealthy founders. By the reign of Alexios I Komnenos (1081–1118), tradition and spiritual considerations seem to have prevailed over the recognition that the privileges of the monasteries were inexorably depleting the resources of the state. The fact that monastic foundations retained so many rights and exemptions in spite of their negative effect on the imperial government in economic terms testifies to the extent of their influence in Byzantine society throughout these centuries.

One of the most famous monastic foundations of the tenth century was that of the Great Lavra monastery on Mt Athos by St Athanasios the Athonite. Mt Athos, an isolated and mountainous projection of the Chalkidike peninsula in northern Greece, had been inhabited by hermits from about the late eighth century. Like other 'holy mountains' in Asia Minor, such as Mts Ida, Latros, Auxentios and Olympos, Mt Athos represented a refuge from the world which was seen as closer to God. St Athanasios, who was seen even by his own contemporaries as an innovator, transformed the monastic life on Mt Athos from one of solitude to cenobitic monasticism. It should be noted, however, that he himself saw no opposition between the two ways of life. His own *Typikon* or 'Rule' for the monastery allows for 'Hesychasts', or those who wish to pursue a solitary existence, to live within the Great Lavra.[31] Of all the Byzantine 'holy mountains', Mt Athos is the most important because it remains to the present day, with a total of about twenty working monasteries, and because monastic documents dating back to the Byzantine period survive in its libraries, providing valuable information concerning the monasteries' property, legal affairs and many other matters.[32]

It is also in this century that one of the great mystical fathers of the Orthodox Church, St Symeon the New Theologian, lived and wrote his spiritual treatises. Born in Paphlagonia in the mid-tenth century, Symeon began his monastic life at the monastery of Stoudios in Constantinople under his spiritual father, Symeon Eulabes. He then moved to the monastery of St Mamas, where he was appointed abbot some time between 979 and 991. Owing to the policies of reform which he imposed on his monastery, Symeon's monks rebelled and he was forced to resign, although he eventually gained permission to found a new monastery, called St Marina, near the capital city. In his writings, Symeon promoted the idea that individuals can follow their own path to salvation, through strict asceticism and prayer under the guidance of a spiritual leader. Symeon himself experienced mystical visions of God at various times in his life, which he describes as appearances of divine light. Symeon's stress on direct experience of God as the heart of theology represents an intensely personal vision, but also grows out of a spiritual tradition based in the early monasticism of the Byzantine Empire.

The Emperors Nikephoros II Phokas (963–969), John I Tzimiskes (969–976) and Basil II (976–1025) were jointly responsible for a period of military reconquest and political stability in the late tenth and early eleventh centuries. In the East, parts of Syria, including Antioch, southeast Anatolia and most of Armenia were recaptured for the Eastern Roman Empire. Nikephoros Phokas regarded war against the Muslims as a holy war; he decreed that all Christians who fell fighting Arabs should be declared martyrs. Byzantine efforts to convert conquered Muslims to Christianity seem on the whole to have been unsuccessful. On the other hand, the recovery of territories in the East led to renewed contact with Monophysites, especially the Jacobite Syrian and Armenian Churches. After the depopulation of enormous tracts of land in Cilicia and Armenia due to Byzantine military advances, Monophysite Christians were encouraged to expand into the newly instituted themes. They moved into many parts of northern Syria and south-east Anatolia and were allowed to establish new, non-Chalcedonian bishoprics. The imperial acceptance of heterodoxy within the Empire was without precedent and was strongly opposed both by ecclesiastics in Constantinople and by local Chalcedonian minorities. Nevertheless, the policy did ensure the repopulation and continued defence of these frontier regions. When it was reversed by a succession of emperors after 1028, the consequences were disastrous.

After the military advances of the tenth century, the eleventh was dominated by political power struggles and a succession of weak rulers. The main contenders for the imperial throne came from two very different backgrounds: landed families based in Asia Minor or Europe and a well-connected class of civil servants in Constantinople. It is possible that territorial expansion led to a false sense of security and that a number of imperial policies, including the replacement of military service by taxation, the failure to establish adequate frontier protection and the neglect of the fleet, were to begin the long process of Byzantium's decline. In addition, the Eastern Roman Empire was now at risk from a number of external enemies whose appearance could not have been predicted. In the East, Turkish tribes were establishing themselves in many of the frontier regions so recently won back by the Byzantines. Their method of military attack was to make frequent raids into Roman territory; contemporary sources suggest that the imperial government failed to adopt adequate measures to repel these invaders. In the north and west, Slavic states under Byzantine rule were becoming increasingly rebellious. Although most of these peoples had by now adopted Orthodoxy as their religion, they continued to play off Greek against Latin ecclesiastical authority. Further north, other Turkic tribes, including the Pechenegs, were becoming troublesome. The traditional Byzantine method of controlling neighbouring peoples by diplomacy or bribery was no longer proving effective.

It is against the background of the growing power of the Normans and the Germans in the West during this period that increasing tension between the ecclesiastical sees of Constantinople and Rome should be placed. At the same time, differences in cultural and religious outlook contributed to their separation. We have seen how political tensions, centring on the issue of papal authority, had begun as early as the seventh century as a result of the Monothelite and Iconoclast controversies. The immediate cause of conflict in the eleventh century, however, was the dispute concerning sovereignty in southern Italy and the threat of a Norman invasion. Both Rome and Constantinople saw the need for political unity in this area, but it soon became apparent that they were unable to agree on a number of doctrinal and practical matters. The main topics of debate were the Western inclusion of the word *filioque* in the Creed, an addition which implied the double procession of the Holy Spirit, the Roman prohibition against married clergy and its use of unleavened bread for the Eucharist. The Byzantines saw all these practices as unnecessary innovations and argued passionately against their acceptance. There can be no doubt that the personalities of the leading contenders in this debate contributed to its bitterness. In Rome, Pope Leo IX, who belonged to a growing party of reformers, was backed by the uncompromising Cardinal Humbert. In Constantinople, the Patriarch Michael Kerularios (1043–58) proved to be an equally redoubtable defender of what he regarded as correct Church doctrine and practice. With the addition of a relatively weak emperor, Constantine IX, dispute between the two Churches became inevitable.[33]

The sequence of events was as follows: in 1054, papal legates brought two letters from the Pope to the Patriarch in Constantinople. This embassy was led by Humbert, the Pope's chief adviser who had been prominent in recent efforts to cleanse the Western Church from the errors of simony and other forms of corruption. When the legates arrived in Constantinople in April 1054, they were well received by the emperor but denied access to the Patriarch Kerularios. Frustrated and angered by the Patriarch's unyielding attitude, Humbert left a bull on the altar of the Great Church on 16 July, excommunicating the Patriarch and all his associates. The Latin delegation then left Constantinople, having parted on friendly terms with the emperor. When Constantine learned of the bull of excommunication, however, he recalled the Roman legates so that they might debate the contentious issues with the Patriarch. Then, fearing for their physical safety at the hands of Kerularios's followers, he hastily dismissed them again. When the synod of Constantinopolitan bishops met, it drew up a document which refuted the charge of heresy brought against Kerularios. The Patriarch further argued that the papal legates were impostors and that their letters had been tampered with en route. In his subsequent correspondence with impartial bystanders such as Peter III, Patriarch of Antioch, it is clear that Kerularios exaggerated the charges brought by the Latin legates and that he suggested that they revealed an unprecedented attempt at papal supremacy. Whereas many of his correspondents, including Peter of Antioch, Theophylact of Ochrid and others, urged Kerularios to forget the matter and to show tolerance and understanding, the patriarch appears to have refused.

The significance of the events of 1054 were certainly not recognized at the time and have perhaps been exaggerated by posterity.[34] Excommunications of particular patriarchs or popes by either see had occurred before and later been healed. The dispute between Pope Leo IX and Patriarch Michael Kerularios represents only one incident in a process of cultural and political separation which had begun much earlier. The lack of mutual trust and understanding between Latins and Greeks became completely evident in the events of the Fourth Crusade and the sack of Constantinople by the Latins in 1204. Historians have rightly pointed to this as the true date of the schism, rather than to the largely personal misunderstandings of 1054.

Another feature of eleventh-century imperial policy was a renewal of persecution of Monophysite Christians. This represented an unfortunate reversal of the more tolerant policies of the previous century and the result was to weaken support for Byzantine imperial rule in outlying territories such as Armenia and eastern Asia Minor. The Patriarch John Xiphilinos (1064–75), a highly educated and otherwise enlightened religious leader, undertook to drive out Monophysite influence within the empire. In 1064 and 1065, Xiphilinos summoned various Monophysite hierarchs to Constantinople for questioning, including both secular and religious leaders of the Armenians. Such measures intensified the Armenians' long-standing religious and ethnic prejudices towards the Greeks and fatally weakened Byzantine support in their territories.

Further repression of heterodox beliefs within the Orthodox Church may be seen in the trials which took place in the late eleventh century under the Emperor Alexios I Komnenos. The first of these trials involved John Italos, a teacher who employed philosophy as a tool for the study of theological doctrine. Italos was the student of the better known scholar and writer Michael Psellos, who had himself been questioned on one occasion, but who had defended himself with a formal profession of faith.[35] For both men, as for earlier patristic thinkers, pagan philosophy, especially the writings of Plato and his Neoplatonist followers, represented a resource which could be used in conjunction with theology – provided of course that it did not conflict with the teachings of Christianity. In the highly charged atmosphere of late eleventh-century Constantinople, however, classical humanism was equated with heresy. John Italos does not appear to have been as adept as Psellos in refuting the charges brought against him; whereas the first trial in 1076–77 did not mention his name and only condemned various teachings, the second, held in 1082, found him guilty and forced him to retire into a monastery.

In evaluating the significance of the second and final trial of John Italos, it is important to emphasize its connection with a deliberate imperial policy on the part of Alexios I Komnenos. Alexios's intention was to reassert the importance of a strong and unified Orthodox Church for the Byzantine polity. His choice of the feast of Orthodoxy, the first Sunday of Lent, which commemorates the final overthrow of Iconoclasm in 843, for the condemnation of Italos was deliberate. The philosopher's dangerous heterodoxy could in this way be associated officially with the earlier heresies, especially Iconoclasm, which had threatened the Church. The anathemas against Italos were added to the official document which was read out annually in church to commemorate the restoration of icons in 843, the *Synodikon of Orthodoxy*. Whereas this document had remained relatively unchanged since that date, it was during and after the reign of Alexios that more heresies began to be added to it. Thus the *Synodikon* became for the Byzantines, in the absence of further ecumenical councils, an authoritative statement of right belief. The trial and condemnation of John Italos also had an effect on Byzantine Church–state relations thereafter. By promoting the established Church at the expense of independent theologians and philosophers such as Italos, the Emperor Alexios reinforced the power and influence of the Constantinopolitan patriarchate.

Alexios I Komnenos also had other heresies with which to contend, including the dualist sect of the Bogomils. Bogomilism probably originated in tenth-century Bulgaria and it seems to have appealed to disaffected subjects of the Byzantine Orthodox commonwealth. Drawing on the Gnostic belief that the material world is the creation of the Devil, the Bogomils denied the basic doctrines of the Orthodox Church, including the Incarnation of Christ. They imposed, at least on a group of selected initiates, an ascetic way of life which included abstinence from sexual intercourse, meat and wine and they taught their adherents to resort to civil disobedience in their resistance to established ecclesiastical authority. The relationship of Bogomilism to the earlier, and largely Armenian, heresy of Paulicianism has been much debated and there can be no doubt that the sects influenced each other.[36] According to the Byzantine sources, including Anna Comnena's *Alexiad*, the Bogomils had spread by the late eleventh century over the entire Balkan peninsula and parts of Asia Minor.[37] There were even adherents in aristocratic circles in Constantinople, led by a figure called Basil the Bogomil, who wore monastic clothing but probably came from the Constantinopolitan professional classes.

Alexios proceeded to arrest Basil and to question him in private, before condemning him to be burned. The emperor also commissioned a book called the *Dogmatike Panoplia*, or a description of heresies, to be compiled by Euthymios Zigabenos. This compendium, along with a work composed at the behest of Manuel I Komnenos, Andronikos Kamateros's *Sacred Arsenal*, reveals much about late eleventh- and twelfth-century attitudes towards heresy. A growing mood of intolerance to doctrinal outsiders, including not only dualists, but also Jews, Muslims and other earlier ideological adversaries, is evident in this period.

Even judging by the hostile Byzantine sources, however, it is clear that Bogomilism and Paulicianism were extremely popular religious sects. It is worth reflecting on what, besides dualism, these groups had to offer to their adherents. Perhaps one of the most attractive aspects of Bogomilism and Paulicianism was their emphasis on ethical and ascetic ideals. In the face of an increasingly rich and powerful established Orthodox Church, represented by clergy who were engaged in an endless round of imperial ceremonial, the heretical sects offered an opportunity for lay involvement, probably with significant spiritual rewards. The Bogomils, like the early Paulicians, emphasized a return to New Testament ethics and inspiration in addition to the esoteric teachings of a dualist philosophy.

Along with heretical movements, Orthodox holy men attracted a share of official disapproval in the twelfth century. This new attitude is somewhat surprising when we think of the importance accorded to holy people engaged in solitary ways of life or even more eccentric behaviour, such as standing on columns or wearing chains, in early Byzantine society. Men with a vested interest in the established ecclesiastical or secular hierarchy began in this period to resent ascetics with few academic or spiritual credentials who attracted notice by their outrageous behaviour. Various texts, written by intellectuals such as John Tzetzes and Eustathios of Thessalonike, castigate the ostentatious and fraudulent practices of people whom they obviously regard as charlatans.[38] During the reigns of the Komneni and the Angeli, and most especially during the reign of Manuel I Komnenos, the Church hierarchy encouraged well-regulated, cenobitic monastic life and frowned on more individualistic forms of religious piety. The lack of extant saints' lives from the twelfth century further testifies to a decline in active, or at least publicly recognized, holy men.

While late eleventh- and twelfth-century emperors may have been repressive towards heretics and unconventional would-be saints, this period is also characterized by an upsurge in literary production and patronage of the arts. The courts of the Komneni attracted intellectuals of all kinds and, in spite of such events as the trials of John Italos, this resulted in an increasing openness to rationalist and humanist theology. This is also the period in which genres of secular literature were revived after a period of decline: historiography, the romances and 'satyrical' poetry represent only a few examples. The combination of enlightenment and repression in the eleventh- and twelfth-century Byzantine Church reflects a society which was on the verge of change – a transformation which was certainly hastened by the appearance of Crusaders from the West.[39]

The first four Crusades (1097–1204)

Before discussing the Crusades, it is necessary to turn once again to the topic of East–West relations in the years leading up to 1097. It is striking that Alexios I Komnenos does not appear to have regarded the schism between Constantinople and Rome as irreparable. Conscious of the threat which the Normans, now firmly entrenched in southern Italy, presented to mainland Greece and potentially to the rest of the Byzantine Empire, Alexios undertook to reopen negotiations with a succession of Roman popes. He was confident that if friendly discussions could take place, doctrinal and practical differences would be overcome and military aid forthcoming. The Byzantine emperor reckoned without a fundamental difference of opinion between East and West, however. Popes of this period, like their predecessors in previous centuries, took their own supremacy throughout Christendom for granted. The Greek and Near Eastern patriarchs, on the other hand, sought to preserve the ideal of a pentarchy: five patriarchates which, if not equal in authority, must all play a part in major doctrinal or disciplinary discussions. This basic misunderstanding dominated East–West negotiations from this period onwards. Secondly, the papacy was by now dominated by a powerful drive in the West to reopen access to sites in the Holy Land and, above all, to recapture Jerusalem from the Muslims. It is against this background that Alexios made his ill-advised request to the Pope for Western aid against the Seljuk Turks, who had been making incursions into Byzantine territory throughout the eleventh century and whom the Byzantines were increasingly unable to repel. In March 1095, Alexios's envoys met Pope Urban II at Piacenza and appealed for military help. The Pope then made a public appeal at Clermont on behalf of the Eastern Christians, also calling for the rescue of the Holy Sepulchre in Jerusalem.

The response of Western Christians was immediate and dramatic. Waves of Crusaders passed through the Balkans and Thessaly to Constantinople, marching on from there to Antioch and the Holy Land. Whereas some contingents were well organized and led by noblemen such as Godfrey of Bouillon and the Norman Bohemund of Apulia, others represented disorganized mobs; it was the latter who fared worst in their encounters with the Turks and many of the survivors blamed Alexios Komnenos for failing to provide them with adequate protection and sustenance. Misunderstandings between the Latins and the Byzantines concerning the actual objectives of the First Crusade added to the confusion. While Alexios prevailed on many Frankish knights to sign oaths, pledging to return territories reconquered from the Turks to the Byzantines, some refused, aiming to acquire new kingdoms for their own use. The first successful battle occurred at Nicaea, which the Turks surrendered to the Byzantines in May–June 1097. When the Crusaders reached Syria and the Holy Land, however, the cities which they seized remained in their possession. Thus, Bohemund took Antioch, and Jerusalem itself was captured for the Latins on 15 July 1099.

While the Byzantine emperor and Orthodox hierarchy in Constantinople no doubt felt cheated by the outcome of the First Crusade, relations between the Near Eastern patriarchates and the Latins were on the whole friendly. The Franks certainly placed their own Latin bishops in command in Antioch and Jerusalem, but they allowed Greek and Syriac Churches under their jurisdiction to carry on much as they had before. Indeed, it is likely that the non-Chalcedonian Churches experienced less oppression than they had several centuries earlier under Byzantine rule. The Greek monasteries in Syria and Palestine remained intact and were visited by both Greek and Latin pilgrims. What is perhaps most important about the reconquest of the Holy Land by the Latins is the great increase in cultural and spiritual contact between East and West which it allowed.

The Second, Third and Fourth Crusades are all distinguished by increasing distrust and hostility between the Greeks and the Latins. The Second (1147–49) consisted of a German army led by Conrad III and a French one led by Louis VII. Conrad's forces clashed with the Byzantine army in Thrace in 1147, after which the Emperor Manuel I Komnenos agreed to transport them across the Bosporus. Both German and French armies fared badly against the Turks in Anatolia and eventually, after reaching Antioch in 1148, the Crusaders decided to withdraw. Later in the twelfth century, the Crusader states came under increasing pressure from Arab generals such as Nur al Din and Saladin. After Saladin conquered most of the kingdom of Jerusalem in 1187, the Byzantine Emperor Isaac II tried to restore good terms with him by leading a large section of the army of the Third Crusade, under the command of Frederick I Barbarossa, into an ambush in Thrace. This action did nothing to improve relations between the Greeks and Latins. After this, the French and English Crusaders failed to recapture Jerusalem, but did regain the fortress of Acre in 1191.

Most disastrous of all was the Fourth Crusade (1202–04), which was diverted into attacking Constantinople. This led to the capture and plundering of the city and the brief establishment in it of a Latin Empire. As the Latin kingdoms established by the Crusaders slowly crumbled in the East in subsequent centuries, the failure of these Christian Holy Wars became evident. To some extent, the Crusades represented the beginning of the end of the Byzantine Empire. They actually weakened the latter while contributing to Greek distrust of the Latins and to the ultimate rise of Turkish power in Syria and Anatolia.

The sack of Constantinople in 1204 made an indelible impression on the Greek Orthodox mentality which persists to some extent to the present day. Whereas before this date the Western Church could be viewed with respect, as *primus inter pares*, even if minor doctrinal and practical differences set it apart from the Greek Church, everything was now changed. Deep resentment was felt at the fact that Latin Christians, whom the Byzantines had summoned initially for aid against non-Christian invaders, could turn upon their fellow Christians. It is correct to place the beginning of true schism in 1204; it is from this date onward that, efforts at reconciliation by various Palaeologan emperors notwithstanding, the healing of the rift between Eastern and Western Christendom became increasingly difficult.

The period of Latin occupation, 1204–61

When Constantinople fell to the Western Crusaders on 13 April 1204, a period of division within the Byzantine Church and state began. The Latins did not succeed in confiscating all the territory of the Eastern Roman Empire from the Greeks; three small principalities ruled by rival Byzantine emperors remained, in western Greece (Epiros and somewhat later, Thessalonike), western Asia Minor (the Nicaean kingdom) and the south-east coast of the Black Sea (the kingdom of Trebizond). Rivalry between these separate kingdoms, each of which was ruled by a self-proclaimed Byzantine emperor, delayed the reconquest of Constantinople from the Latins long after their weakening position might have allowed this to take place. Instead of joining together to seize the former capital, the rival claimants to the throne vied with each other and with the rising Balkan kingdoms, Bulgaria and Serbia, which also had ambitions to rule a revived Byzantine Empire from Constantinople.

The remainder of the former Eastern Roman Empire was divided up by the Latins, however, and the churches were placed in the care of the Roman Pope. The result of this policy, outlined in a partition treaty agreed by the Crusaders before the fall of Constantinople, was that former Greek territories came to be ruled by various Western overlords. In Constantinople, Venice, as the dominant power, arranged for Baldwin of Flanders and of Hainault to be elected emperor. The majority of new clergy appointed to St Sophia, including the Patriarch Thomas Morosini, were Venetians. Much of the rest of the Latin Empire, known as Romania, was parcelled up between Franks and Venetians, the two most powerful groups among the Westerners. Thus, Macedonia and Thessaly, Central Greece, the Peloponnese peninsula, the Aegean islands and Crete, as well as the north-west corner of Asia Minor, all came to be ruled by different leaders, many of whom transferred the Western feudal form of government to their new Greek territories. Whereas Greek Orthodox bishoprics and parishes fared differently according to the religious tolerance or otherwise of their Western overlords, the Latins' ecclesiastical policy was based on one shared assumption, namely that union between Eastern and Western Christians would ultimately prevail. The gradual replacement of the Greek ecclesiastical hierarchy by a Latin one was seen as the best way to advance this goal. Pope Innocent III appears to have believed that the Greek clergy in the new Latin Empire would be happy to remain in their posts, recognizing papal jurisdiction and thus being subsumed into the Roman Church. In fact, many Orthodox bishops and priests preferred to leave their parishes, remaining constant to their own traditions and doctrines. Many flocked to the small Byzantine kingdoms based in Epiros and Nicaea, whereas others, such as the Bishop of Athens, Michael Choniates, departed from their sees.

After the plundering of Constantinople in 1204, the Pope condemned the widespread appropriation of Greek property by the Latins. It is due to Innocent III's protests that an agreement was finally reached whereby Latin clergy were granted one-fifteenth of all property in Romania outside Constantinople. This rule was also to apply to future conquests and, in addition, churches were required to pay the usual Western annual tithe. Monasteries and their property remained sacrosanct and were thus spared any looting by Western rulers or their subjects.

Within the Greek Orthodox Church, reactions to the Latin conquest varied, as some clerics failed to come to terms with the situation and others responded pragmatically. The exiled Greek Patriarch of Constantinople, John X Kamateros, refused to join Theodore Lascaris, son-in-law of the Emperor Alexios III, who had set up court in Nicaea and claimed to be the imperial successor to the dynasty of the Angeli. Fortunately for Theodore, the old patriarch died soon after in 1206 and the learned and pragmatic Michael IV Autorianos was chosen as his successor. This patriarch worked closely with the Lascarids and supported the Nicaean imperial claims. In northern Greece, on the other hand, Theodore Angelos (1215–30) dramatically increased his dominions after a series of impressive victories. He had himself crowned emperor in Thessalonike but the threat of Epiros to the claims of the Lascarids came to end with the defeat of Theodore by the Bulgarians in 1230 and the subsequent decline of the kingdom. Theodore's successors, who ruled over separate parts of the kingdom which he had so quickly conquered, eventually acknowledged the imperial claims of Nicaea.

The Nicaean emperor who followed Theodore Lascaris, John III Dukas Vatatzes (1222–54), laid the foundations with much skill and patience for the recapture of Constantinople from the Latins. Gradually extending his sway northwards into the areas seized by the Bulgarians from the Epirotes, he reclaimed territories in Thrace and Macedonia and in 1246 seized Thessalonike. He even sought union with the Church of Rome, hoping to request the surrender of the Latin Empire in compensation for his own concessions to Latin demands. In fact, Vatatzes must have been aware that sacrificing the independence of the Orthodox Church was no longer necessary; his own military advances rendered the surrender of the increasingly moribund Latin government in Constantinople a foregone conclusion. In the end, however, it was not John Vatatzes, who had so carefully rebuilt the economic and political foundations of the Byzantine Empire, who was destined to recapture Constantinople. He and his son, Theodore II Lascaris (1254–58), both suffered from epilepsy and died prematurely from this illness. It was Michael VIII Palaeologos, regent for

Theodore's young son John IV, who, with the help of the Genoese, stormed Constantinople in 1261 and promptly had himself crowned emperor. The legitimate emperor John IV Lascaris was blinded shortly afterwards and Michael appointed his own son Andronikos as his heir.

The Slavic Churches in the last centuries of Byzantium

The ambition of the Bulgarian 'tsar' John Asen in the early thirteenth century to become the ruler of Constantinople illustrates the danger posed to the Byzantines by the Slavic nations which had accepted Christianity in the late ninth and tenth centuries. There can be no doubt that conversion to Orthodoxy added impetus to various rulers' perceptions of themselves as potential emperors of an enlarged empire which would encompass not only Byzantine but also their own territories. Not only John Asen, but also his predecessor, the early tenth-century monarch Symeon of Bulgaria, cherished this ambition. Conversion to Orthodox Christianity thus not only provided the emerging Slavic nations with a sense of national and religious unity, but also encouraged them to adopt imperialist ambitions.

Symeon of Bulgaria conquered Serbia in the early tenth century, but after his death the Serbian Prince Časlav was able to establish an independent state. In the mid-twelfth century, after a period of subservience to Byzantium following a defeat to the Emperor Manuel I, Serbia gained independence again under another strong leader, Stefan Nemanja. It was one of Nemanja's sons, St Sava, who obtained recognition of an autocephalous Serbian archbishopric from the Byzantine emperor and Patriarch in exile at Nicaea in 1219. Medieval Serbia reached its height in the fourteenth century under Stefan Uroš IV Dušan (1331–55), who created an empire which dominated the Balkans throughout his reign. This empire represented a serious threat to the Byzantines, who were split by a civil war and unable to fight off his advances into regions as far south as Epiros, Thessaly and Albania. Much Byzantine influence is visible in Serbian art and architecture during this period. The many churches and monasteries which survive reveal a rich assimilation and creative adaptation of Byzantine Orthodox iconography. In 1346, owing to the powerful influence of Stefan Dušan, an independent Serbian patriarchate was created; this was only recognized by Constantinople in 1475.

The political history of the Rus' after Prince Vladimir's conversion to Christianity in the late tenth century followed a course of greater fragmentation than that of the Bulgarians and the Serbs. It is clear that by the mid-twelfth century Kiev had lost its domination over many principalities, including Galitza, Suzdal, Novgorod and Smolensk. In

1237, Kiev was overrun by the Mongol Tatars, but when the power of this great nation waned in the late fourteenth and early fifteenth centuries, the Russian princes were able gradually to build up a power base again, this time centred around the principality of Muscovy. In 1448, the Russian Church finally obtained autonomy from the patriarchate of Constantinople. Nevertheless, Russia's roots in the liturgical and monastic traditions of Greek Orthodoxy provided the spiritual background for its development in the centuries to come. The influence of Byzantine art, architecture, literature and many other cultural forms is evident not only in the early Kievan period but also in medieval Russia. During the period of Mongol rule, a number of notable Russian saints deserve special mention. These include Alexander Nevsky (died 1263), a prince of Novgorod who decided to fight German invaders while submitting to the Tatars. His reason for pursuing this course of action was primarily religious: whereas the Tatars exacted a tribute but refrained from interfering in the life of the Church, the avowed aim of the Teutonic Knights was to bring the Russian 'schismatics' back under the jurisdiction of the Pope. Stephen of Perm was another saintly figure to emerge during the period of Mongol domination and was renowned for his missionary work among the pagan invaders. Stephen and his followers, according to the example set by Cyril and Methodios, translated the Orthodox service books into the languages of the peoples to whom they ministered. Finally, Sergei of Radonezh (?1314–92) carried the Byzantine tradition of eremetical asceticism into the forests of Muscovy. After several years of solitude, St Sergei gathered a number of disciples to whom he acted as spiritual guide (*starets*) and eventually founded a regular monastery. St Sergei carried on a tradition which had also featured in the Monastery of the Caves near Kiev in an earlier period; this style of monasticism, based on a recognition of the value of private contemplation and prayer, continued to play an important role in the Russian Orthodox Church in subsequent centuries.

It is also necessary to mention here the origins of the Orthodox Church in Rumania, a nation whose origins are complex and obscure. Parts of the territory covered by medieval Rumania formed the Roman province of Dacia, which was Christianized in the second and third centuries. After the Romans withdrew from the area, however, Christianity appears to have died out. Some of the Rumanians were subsequently converted to Orthodoxy by Bulgarian missionaries in the late ninth and early tenth centuries. They also received the Slavonic liturgy and the Cyrillo-Methodian literary tradition from the Bulgarians. In the fourteenth century, the principalities of Wallachia and Moldavia were converted and it is in this period that the Orthodox Church became dominant throughout Rumania. It is interesting that this people, who spoke a Romance language and who lived relatively near the areas where Latin juridiction prevailed, should have followed the Slavic, Orthodox lead of the Bulgarians. When Wallachia and Moldavia each gained a metropolitanate from the Patriarch of Constantinople in 1359 and 1401 respectively, they gained international status in the eyes of their East European neighbours and also a belated entry into the Byzantine commonwealth.

The Palaeologan period, 1261–1453

The efforts of successive emperors in the Palaeologan period to achieve union with the Church of Rome can only be understood in the light of the political and military background of the late Byzantine Empire. The period of Latin dominion left the empire in a very different state from the position which it had occupied at the end of the twelfth century. Constantinople was vulnerable to attack on many sides and represented the capital of only a small section of what had once been the territories of the Eastern Roman Empire. Much of Greece was still under Frankish rule, while Epiros, together with Thessaly, although ruled by Greeks, refused to be reunited to the rest of the Empire. The Bulgarians and Serbs dominated the northern Balkans and in Asia Minor the Turks represented a constant and menacing threat. Michael VIII saw reunification with Rome as solving the problem of a threat of renewed aggression by the Latins against the Byzantine Empire. At the Council of Lyons on 6 July 1274, the Grand Logothete George Acropolites signed the declaration of union, acknowledging the primacy of the Pope and also Latin doctrines and practices, including the addition of the *filioque* to the Creed and the use of azymes, or unleavened bread, in the Eucharist. It is significant that the Patriarch of Constantinople did not attend the council, nor did any representatives of the three eastern patriarchates.

In spite of Michael VIII's best efforts to convince his clergy and people that the union agreed at the Council of Lyons was in their interest, he encountered severe opposition in Constantinople. The incumbent patriarch, Joseph, was deposed by the synod for his anti-unionist stance and he was replaced by the more accommodating John Bekkos. Many influential figures, both secular and ecclesiastical, opposed the union on the grounds that it betrayed the sacred tradition of the Orthodox Church. As Michael's reign progressed, relations with Rome worsened, while at the same time he was forced to continue persecuting recalcitrant anti-unionists within the empire. When the emperor finally died in 1282, he appeared to have failed either to gain Roman approval or to reconcile his subjects to the union. John Bekkos was dismissed and Joseph declared patriarch for the second time, only days after Michael VIII's death.

That union with the Roman Church represented not only a political, but also a doctrinal issue in the eyes of contemporary Greeks is made clear by the writings inspired by the events just described. After his deposition from the patriarchal throne, the pro-unionist John Bekkos undertook to write treatises in his own defence. The main topic of doctrinal debate with the Latins as he saw it was the *filioque*, or the procession of the Holy Spirit from the Father *and the Son*, according to the Latin creed. John Bekkos argued that the prepositions ἐκ ('out of') and διά ('through') have the same meaning and that early Greek Fathers affirmed the proposition that the Holy Spirit's procession was *through* the Son. Partially in response to this, a later Patriarch, Gregory of Cyprus, drew up a statement, or *Tomos*, on the *filioque* issue. The ideas expressed in this document were taken up in later writings by the same author on the procession of the Holy Spirit.[40] Gregory attempted to show that whereas the Spirit did not proceed, or obtain its existence, from both Father and Son, it was eternally revealed through the Son. The distinction between eternal, unknowable existence and eternal, but revealed, manifestation represents one step towards the fourteenth-century theologian Gregory Palamas's teaching on the uncreated essence and energies of God. Thus, the controversy over the *filioque* prompted by union with the papacy helped to stimulate wider theological debate in the late thirteenth and fourteenth centuries.

The Palaeologan period in Byzantine history represents on the one hand a time of political and economic decline as the empire shrank into a fraction of its former territory due to the relentless expansion of the Turks, but paradoxically also one of cultural and spiritual revival. A renaissance in literature and art occurred during these years, much of which was inspired by religious themes. The writing of saints' lives, to take one example, which had suffered a decline during the twelfth and early thirteenth centuries, was revived and numerous texts were composed or rewritten during this period. Eulogies, spiritual treatises, letters and sermons also flourished at the hands of highly educated humanists and spiritual teachers such as Theodore Metochites, Theoleptos of Philadelphia, Nikephoros Gregoras and many others. In the field of art, the so-called 'Palaeologan renaissance' produced numerous examples of icons, ivories and other objects, while some of the churches built in this period display the most beautiful fresco and mosaic decoration ever produced in Byzantium. It is likely that scholars and artists alike were aware of the impending threat to their diminishing empire, but this consciousness seems to have stimulated their reaffirmation of their Orthodox heritage and shared cultural values.

Monasticism also flourished in the Palaeologan period, although the state managed to curb the growth of monastic estates somewhat more than in earlier periods. Cenobitic houses for both men and women existed as havens to which not only ordinary people, but also members of the nobility and imperial family, could retreat. At the same time, it is important to bear in mind the important role which monasteries played in Byzantine society. Many lay people received spiritual advice from monastic spiritual fathers or mothers, monasteries provided homes for orphans, old people and others in need, and many included hospitals or soup kitchens within their premises. The popularity of bequeathing money to monastic institutions continued in late Byzantine society as it had earlier. Not only were monasteries seen as safe and stable institutions, but they assured the commemoration of a family or individual for ever.

Within many monasteries, especially the foundations on Mt Athos in northern Greece, the practice of *hesychia*, literally 'solitude' or solitary contemplation, was revived. This represented a fundamental part of the Byzantine ascetic and monastic tradition and it was based on the belief that prayer has the power to transform an individual and to bring him closer to God. Indeed, the doctrine of *theosis*, 'deification', is central to Orthodox theology, teaching that through discipline and prayer a holy person may actually be transfigured, i.e., returned to the state of perfection in which Adam was first created. In the fourteenth century, Gregory Palamas, a monk trained on Mt Athos who eventually became Archbishop of Thessalonike, further defined the aim of contemplative prayer. Palamas argued that a distinction exists between the uncreated and unknowable essence of God and his energies which may actually be apprehended by mankind. Strict ascetic discipline and solitary prayer may lead to a vision of the uncreated light of God, exemplified by the light which shone around Christ at his transfiguration on Mt Tabor (Luke 9:28–36). It is by means of this light or energy that deification (*theosis*) is achieved. Gregory Palamas was opposed by certain members of the Orthodox clergy and especially by Barlaam, a Greek monk from Calabria. The basic philosophical differences concerned the two questions, how can the gap between man and God be bridged and how can the unknowable God be understood by man? Both sides used the fifth-century mystical writer ps-Dionysios the Areopagite to support their points of view. Whereas the opponents of Palamas argued that ps-Dionysios's negative or 'apophatic' theology teaches that God is beyond knowledge altogether, including the experiential knowledge claimed by the Hesychasts, Palamas and his supporters suggested that what ps-Dionysios meant by apophatic theology was exactly this experience of God through prayer, an encounter which goes beyond rational understanding. A further issue of contention was the physical techniques of prayer used by the Hesychasts. This involved the repetition of the Jesus prayer ('Lord Jesus Christ, Son of God, have mercy on me, a sinner') and rhythmic breathing carried out in a crouching position. In spite of the philosophical and practical arguments mounted against Hesychasm, Gregory Palamas's teachings were eventually accepted by the Orthodox Church in a series of Constantinopolitan local councils (1341, 1347 and 1351). The acceptance of Palamism into the Orthodox tradition had a lasting impact on the Church for centuries to come. It represented a complete assimilation of ancient monastic traditions as well as the rejection of the philosophical, or scholastic, approach offered by Barlaam and his followers. While the latter movement did have an effect on late Byzantine humanism, it is significant that its preoccupations did not endure in Orthodox theology as did the monastic, or 'interior', wisdom of monks like Symeon the New Theologian and Gregory Palamas.

Opposition to Rome and to reunion with the papacy persisted throughout the reigns of Michael VIII's successor, Andronikos II Palaeologos (1283–1328). The Palaeologan emperors were however forced to maintain diplomatic links with the West as they sought to strengthen their interests in central Greece and the Peloponnese. During the reigns of subsequent emperors it was the threat of the Turks which prompted further efforts at reconciliation with Rome. These culminated in the final attempt at lasting union in the Council of Ferrara–Florence in 1438–39. Negotiations at this council seem to have taken place in a somewhat different atmosphere from that of the Council of Lyons in 1274. The Byzantines, because of increased contact with the West resulting from imperial inter-marriages and from the presence of Western ecclesiastics and monks in Greece and Constantinople, had by now a better understanding of the Latins' doctrine and way of life. It is also possible that the presence of Turks in former Byzantine territories, some already in the immediate environs of Constantinople, injected a greater sense of urgency into the proceedings. The emperor, John VIII Palaeologos (1425–48), was eager for the definition of the council to be agreed so that he could be given military aid against the Turks. As in 1274, however, the announcement of union with Rome was not met with favour in Constantinople. Some of the delegates who had signed the decree in Florence now repudiated it, while one of its most prominent opponents, Bishop Mark of Ephesus, effectively rallied the support of an anti-unionist party. Hopes of defeating the Turks by a crusading army organized by Pope Eugenius IV were quenched once and for all at the battle of Varna in November 1444. Hereafter, the Byzantine emperor was forced to face the fact not only that the Turkish threat was unstoppable, but also that his agreement to union with Rome had been in vain. The definition agreed at Florence was finally allowed to be forgotten after the fall of Constantinople in 1453 when Gennadios II became the first Patriarch under the Turks. Promoted for political more than for theological reasons, the definition of Ferrara–Florence never received enough backing from the Orthodox clergy and laity to ensure its survival. As a result of its demise, the official schism between the Catholic and Orthodox Churches has continued to the present day.

The fall of Constantinople to the Turks in 1453 represented only the final act in a process of disintegration which had begun much earlier within the Byzantine Empire. Nevertheless, it was seen by both contemporaries and posterity as a catastrophic end of the second Rome, the imperial city founded by Constantine in 330 CE. After three days of plundering by the Sultan's army, in which many icons, manuscripts and other ecclesiastical treasures were destroyed, Constantinople became the capital of the Ottoman Empire. The remaining Christian population of the city were, as in any Muslim state, allowed to practise their religion although their freedom to worship openly was much restricted. Although Constantinople fell in 1453, her religious and political tradition lived on to a large extent within the Orthodox Churches. The Slavic Churches of Serbia, Bulgaria, Rumania and Russia assimilated not only the ecclesiastical structure and liturgy of the Byzantine Church, but also its monastic and spiritual traditions.

Conclusion

The Byzantine Orthodox Church, in addition to preserving the liturgy and theology of the early Church in Greek-speaking Christendom, succeeded in making several important contributions to Christianity as a whole. First, the gift of mystical theology, worked out in a long tradition of spiritual practice and writings from the fourth century onwards, is one of deep, inner wisdom. Saints such as Symeon the New Theologian in the eleventh century and Gregory Palamas in the fourteenth, instead of being condemned for their innovative teachings, were granted a place in the heart of Orthodox tradition. The concept of *theosis*, or deification, which was identified as the goal of spiritual endeavour *in this life* by earlier fathers, was further elaborated in the writings of Palamas, who distinguished between the essence of God which remains unknowable to mankind and his energies which may be perceived and participated in by saints who have achieved complete union with God. While obviously only those committed completely to a life of spiritual training and prayer are likely to achieve this goal, the possibility is open to all Orthodox Christians, both lay and monastic. In 1782 a book called the *Philokalia* ('Love of [Spiritual] Beauty') was compiled by St Makarios of Corinth and St Nicodemos of the Holy Mountain (Mt Athos).[41] This represents a unique collection of spiritual texts from the fourth through the fifteenth centuries, dealing with the Hesychastic (solitary) life, asceticism, prayer and mystical union. Widely read by both monastic and lay faithful, the book was quickly translated into Slavonic by a Ukrainian monk, St Paisii Velichkovskii. It became very influential in nineteenth-century Russia, helping to shape the development of monasticism and mystical theology there as well as in other Orthodox nations.

A second legacy of Byzantine Christianity is the fully developed liturgy which is still celebrated in Orthodox Churches today. The words of the Russian envoys quoted at the beginning of this chapter, who did not know whether they were 'in heaven or on earth', could still be uttered by Christians participating in an Orthodox liturgy. The Church symbolizes the whole cosmos, encompassing heaven as well as earth. As the seventh-century theologian Maximos the Confessor put it, 'God's holy church in itself is a symbol of the sensible world as such, since it possesses the divine sanctuary as heaven and the beauty of the nave as earth. Likewise the world is a church since it possesses heaven corresponding to a sanctuary, and for a nave it has the adornment of the earth.'[42] In the Divine Liturgy, the clergy and the laity join together in the unending praise offered by the angelic choirs to God. The Orthodox worshipper literally feels that he has entered heaven and experienced the presence of Christ himself, first in the entrance of the Gospels and second, in the holy gifts. In the Eastern Church, the emphasis was always on salvation, summed up in the mystery of the Incarnation of Christ. This vision was to exert a unifying influence on Orthodox Christians for centuries to come, as they struggled to maintain their faith under the rule of Turks or of Communist governments in the twentieth century.

Notes

1 S. H. Cross, and O. P. Sherbowitz-Wetzor, *The Russian Primary Chronicle: Laurentian Text* (Cambridge, MA: The Medieval Academy of America, 1953), p. 111.
2 Eusebius, *The Life of Constantine the Great* and *Oration in Praise of Constantine*, trans. in Philip Schaff and Henry Wace (Nicene and Post-Nicene Fathers, I; Peabody, MA: Hendrickson Publishers, Inc., 1890; repr. 1995), pp. 411–610.
3 Procopius, *The Buildings*, I, i, 23ff.
4 Evagrius, *Ecclesiastical History*, IV, 31. Both of the above quotations are taken from the translations provided in Cyril Mango, *The Art of the Byzantine Empire 312–1453: Sources and Documents* (Englewood Cliffs, NJ: Prentice-Hall, 1972), pp. 72–4, 79.
5 An English translation of some *kontakia* appears in *St Romanos the Melodist, Kontakia on the Life of Christ*, trans. Archimandrite Ephrem Hall (San Francisco and London: HarperCollins, 1996). The Greek text of many more *kontakia*, with a French translation, may be found in J. Grosdidier de Matons, *Hymnes*, vols I–V (Paris: Sources Chrétiennes, 1964–81).

6 See J. Grosdidier de Matons, 'Liturgie et hymnographie: kontakion et kanon', *Dumbarton Oaks Papers*, 34–35 (1980–81), pp. 31–43; E. Wellesz, 'Kontakion and Kanon', *Atti del Congresso Internazionale di Musica sacra* (Rome/Tournai, 1952), pp. 131–3. The long accepted view that the *kanon* replaced the *kontakion* after the seventh century has been disproved recently by A. Lingas, 'The liturgical place of the Kontakion in Constantinople', *Byzantinorossica*, 1 (1995), Papers of the XVIII International Byzantine Congress (Moscow, 8–15 August 1991), pp. 50–7.

7 Note however that the separation of the various theological viewpoints into three groups, 'Monophysite', Chalcedonian or 'Dyophysite', and 'Nestorian', conceals the fact that many variations, some of them extremely subtle, in fact characterized the views of Christians within these groups. See S. Brock, 'The "Nestorian" Church: a lamentable misnomer', *Bulletin of the John Rylands University Library of Manchester*, 78, no. 3 (1996), pp. 23–35.

8 On the life and teaching of Cyril of Alexandria, see John McGuckin, *St Cyril of Alexandria: The Christological Controversy* (Leiden: E. J. Brill, 1994).

9 An English translation may be found in *Origen, On First Principles*, trans. G. W. Butterworth (Gloucester, MA: Peter Smith, 1973).

10 See, for example, *Cyril of Scythopolis: Lives of the Monks of Palestine*, trans. R. M. Price (Lives of Sts Sabas and Cyriacus) (Kalamazoo, MI: Cistercian Publications, 1991), pp. 206–9, 253.

11 See Averil Cameron, 'The Theotokos in sixth-century Constantinople', *Journal of Theological Studies*, n.s. 29, part 1 (1978), pp. 79–80; F. Barišić, 'Le siège de Constantinople par les Avares et les Slaves en 626', *Byzantion*, 24 (1954), pp. 371–95.

12 The entire collection is published in PG 87.3, cols 2851–3116. This translation is taken from J. Wortley, *The Spiritual Meadow of John Moschos* (Kalamazoo, MI: Cistercian Publications, 1992), p. 66. A critical edition of the *Spiritual Meadow* will soon be published by P. Pattenden in the series Corpus Christianorum.

13 The name *tou klimakos* means simply 'of the Ladder'. The text appears in Migne, PG 88, cols 632–1209 and a translation in C. Luibheid and N. Russell, *The Ladder of Divine Ascent* (London: SPCK, 1982).

14 The Greek text, which is in the process of being re-edited by J. Munitiz, appears in Migne, PG 89, cols 329–824.

15 Note that two different accounts of the birth and early life of Maximos exist. See Andrew Louth, *Maximus the Confessor* (London and New York: Routledge, 1996), pp. 4–7; S. Brock, 'An early Syriac life of Maximus the Confessor', *Analecta Bollandiana*, 91 (1973), pp. 299–346.

16 See J. M. Garrigues, 'Le martyre de Saint Maxime le Confesseur', *Revue Thomiste*, 76 (1976), pp. 410–52.

17 See, for example, Leslie W. Barnard, 'The Emperor cult and the origins of the Iconoclastic controversy', *Byzantion*, 43 (1973), pp. 7–13; P. Brown, 'A Dark-Age crisis', *English Historical Review*, 88 (1973), pp. 1–34; J. F. Haldon, 'Some remarks on the background of the Iconoclast controversy', *Byzantinoslavica*, 38 (1977), pp. 161–84.

18 See Patricia Crone, 'Islam, Judaeo-Christianity and Byzantine Iconoclasm', *Jerusalem Studies in Arabic and Islam*, 2 (1980), pp. 59–95; S. Gero, *Byzantine Iconoclasm During the Reign of Leo III* (Corpus Scriptorum Christianorum Orientalium, vol. 346, Subsidia, vol. 41; Louvain: 1973), pp. 1–31.

19 J. Pelikan, *Imago Dei: The Byzantine Apologia for Icons* (New Haven and London: Yale University Press, 1990).

20 Theophanes, *Chronographia*, ed. C. De Boor (Hildesheim: Georg Olms, 1963), I,

p. 404, ll. 18–19. A partial English translation may be found in H. Turtledove, *The Chronicle of Theophanes (AD 602–813)* (Philadelphia, PA: University of Pennsylvania Press, 1982), p. 96. A new, much improved translation is now available in C. Mango and R. Scott, *The Chronicle of Theophanes Confessor: Near Eastern History AD 284–813* (Oxford: Clarendon Press, 1997). Unfortunately this appeared too late for consultation.

21 Germanos, *Epistolae*, published in Migne, PG 98 (1863), cols 147–222.

22 *St John of Damascus, On the Divine Images. Three Apologies Against Those Who Attack the Divine Images*, trans. David Anderson (Crestwood, NY: St Vladimir's Seminary Press, 1980).

23 It is of course difficult to judge fully the Iconoclastic arguments in the debate, owing to the systematic destruction of all their writings after the Triumph of Orthodoxy in 843. Part of the Horos of the Iconoclast Council of Hiereia in 754 survives in the Acts of the Council of Nicaea in 787: see D. J. Sahas, *Icon and Logos: Sources in Eighth Century Iconoclasm* (Toronto: University of Toronto Press, 1986).

24 See S. Gero, *Byzantine Iconoclasm during the Reign of Constantine V with Particular Attention to the Oriental Sources* (Corpus Scriptorum Christianorum Orientalium; Louvain: 1977).

25 De Boor (trans.), Theophanes, *Chronographia*, I, p. 438; Turtledove, *The Chronicle of Theophanes*, p. 126.

26 The text is published with an extensive introduction and commentary by J. Gouillard, *Le Synodikon de l'Orthodoxie: Édition et Commentaire, Travaux et Mémoires*, 2 (Paris: Éditions de Boccard, 1967), pp. 1–316.

27 See Rosemary Morris, *Monks and Laymen in Byzantium, 843–1118* (Cambridge University Press, 1985), pp. 31–34.

28 *Filioque* had originally appeared in the Creed in Spain and in Carolingian Gaul as a measure against Arianism. See J. Herrin, *The Formation of Christendom* (Oxford: Basil Blackwell, 1987), pp. 230–1.

29 C. Mango, *The Homilies of Photius, Patriarch of Constantinople* (Dumbarton Oaks Studies, 3; Cambridge, MA: Harvard University Press, 1958), pp. 74–110.

30 *Nicholas I Patriarch of Constantinople, Letters*, ed. and trans. L. G. Westerink and R. J. H. Jenkins (Dumbarton Oaks Texts II; Corpus Fontium Historiae Byzantinae, vol. 6; Washington, DC, 1973).

31 See Kallistos Ware, 'St Athanasios the Athonite: traditionalist or innovator?' in A. A. M. Bryer and M. Cunningham (eds), *Mount Athos and Byzantine Monasticism* (Society for the Promotion of Byzantine Studies, vol. 4; Aldershot: Variorum, 1996), p. 12.

32 These archives are published in the continuing series *Archives de l'Athos* by the Centre National de la Recherche Scientifique in Paris.

33 See Michel Kaplan, 'La place du schisme de 1054 dans les relations entre Byzance, Rome et l'Italie', *Byzantinoslavica*, 54 (1993), pp. 29–37; idem, 'Le "schisme" de 1054. Quelques éléments de chronologie', *Byzantinoslavica*, 56 (1995), pp. 147–57.

34 Steven Runciman, for example, sees the real schism between East and West occurring in 1204: S. Runciman, *The Eastern Schism* (Oxford: Oxford University Press, 1955). See also Paul Lemerle, 'L'Orthodoxie byzantine et l'oecuménisme médiévale: les origines du "schisme" des églises', *Bulletin de l'Association Budé* (1965), pp. 228–46.

35 A. Garzya, 'On Michael Psellus's Admission of Faith', *Epeteris Hetaireias Byzantinon Spoudon*, 35 (1966–67), pp. 41–6.

36 N. Garsoïan, *The Paulician Heresy* (The Hague, 1967); idem, 'Byzantine heresy. A reinterpretation', *Dumbarton Oaks Papers*, 25 (1971), pp. 85–113.
37 See *The Alexiad of Anna Comnena*, trans. E. R. A. Sewter (Harmondsworth, Middlesex: Penguin Classics, 1969 and subsequent reprints), pp. 496–505.
38 Paul Magdalino, 'The Byzantine holy man in the twelfth century' in S. Hackel, *The Byzantine Saint* (London, 1981), pp. 54–5.
39 P. Magdalino, 'Enlightenment and repression in twelfth-century Byzantium: the evidence of the Canonists' in N. Oikonomides, *Byzantium in the Twelfth-Century: Canon Law, State and Society* (Athens, 1991), pp. 257–74.
40 See Gregory of Cyprus, *De processione Spiritus Sancti*, Migne, PG 142, cols 269–300.
41 Four volumes of a complete English translation of the *Philokalia* are now available in G. E. H. Palmer, P. Sherrard and K. Ware, *The Philokalia*, vols I–IV (London: Faber and Faber, 1979–95).
42 *Maximus Confessor: Selected Writings*, trans. George Berthold (London: SPCK, 1985), p. 189.

4

The medieval West

Benedicta Ward and G. R. Evans

The medieval idea of the Church

Biblical images of the Church were a powerful influence on the way it was understood in the Middle Ages. To see Christ as the Bridegroom, the Church as the Bride, is to borrow the imagery of the Song of Songs. That idea influenced thinking about the pastoral role of the Church's ministers. Traditions of spirituality adapted the image in miniature, taking the soul to be the Bride.

It was also important to medieval ecclesiology that the Bible sees Christ as the 'Head', the Church as the 'Body'. Images of the body assume that different parts have different functions; that they cannot change places; that one part (the Head) directs the rest. This fitted in well with medieval assumptions about the natural, God-given shape of society. Each person was born to a place in it, and would live his or her life best by remaining in that place. This was not a recipe for social change, and it encouraged a strongly hierarchical pattern in both secular and religious arrangements.

By the early thirteenth century the dominant idea had shifted. The Church was now beginning to see itself more as a parent to children in the faith. The Fourth Lateran Council of 1215 spoke of the Church as 'mother and teacher' (*mater et magistra*). 'Mother Church' taught the faithful what they ought to believe and nurtured their spiritual development so as to fit them for heaven. This assumption went with an enlargement of papal claims to plenitude of power, which by the thirteenth century had made the Pope a figure seen by many as standing in Christ's place as Head.

There was a reaction against this assertion of an authority which seemed to press ever further beyond the boundaries set by the biblical images, and the last medieval centuries saw polarization between dissidents – those who argued that this dominant papal figure was actually Antichrist and the true Church was 'invisible', a purely spiritual reality, a non-hierarchical community of all the faithful – and the powerful in the institutional Church, who were engaged in their own struggles for dominance. That, in outline, is the story of the thousand years of the Middle Ages.

Spreading Christianity through northern Europe

In 404, the river Rhine froze over and a horde of Germanic tribes entered Roman Gaul, pressing always south, leaving a trail of loss and destruction, but settling with no intention of leaving. They were followed by others in the ensuing years: Goths, Huns, Vandals, Ostrogoths, Visigoths and Lombards. They twice entered and sacked Rome before the final cessation of the Western Empire in 476. Some of these people had not heard of Christianity before, and this was also, for some, their first encounter with the civilization of the Mediterranean world. Others were Christians, mostly Arians, followers of the Arius whose teaching had been condemned at the Council of Nicaea (325).

Before the sixth century a natural division in the Roman Empire down the linguistic frontier between Greek-speakers in the East and Latin speakers in the West had begun to harden. Fewer and fewer people in the West understood Greek. The result of that, with huge consequences for the history of the Church, was the evolution of two very different mindsets. The Greek half continued to go its own way, cultivating a taste for mysticism and adapting for Christian use many of the ideas of late Platonism, while the West took more interest in structures of ecclesial governance, sacramental theology and felt a Platonic influence only at second hand and much tempered by a preoccupation with the heritage of Aristotelian logic which Boethius transmitted in Latin.

The invasions, or rather settlements, by successive waves of barbarian peoples flooding the Roman Empire from the north were matched from the early seventh century by a threat to Christendom from Islamic forces invading from the south. The West found decisive leaders in the popes, most notably in Gregory the Great (590–604). Born c. 540 into a senatorial family in Rome, Gregory learned to respect the ancient Roman civic virtues; to these he added Christian ideals through his choice of a monastic life, converting his family home on the Caelian hill into a monastery. Before becoming Pope, he lived for seven years in Constantinople as *apocrisiarius* at the imperial court, an experience which influenced his later policy, but during which – revealingly – he failed to learn Greek. On his return to Rome and election as Pope, he assumed responsibility for the administration of the city of Rome, as well as other Italian cities.

He also negotiated with the Lombards, the latest wave of Germanic invaders, and concluded a peace treaty with them in 592–593.

A prolific writer, indeed later named as one of the four Latin Doctors of the Church, Gregory administered, wrote and prayed with a power that impressed his influence on his own and many subsequent generations, despite a life of constant ill health. His works include the *Dialogues*, the commentary on *Ezekiel*, the *Moralia on Job*, a book on pastoral care and many sermons and letters, all widely copied and read and therefore extremely influential throughout the Middle Ages. In his sermons and writings, Gregory set a pattern for prayer for future generations in the West. He used the vocabulary of the inner senses of the spiritual man, encouraging his listeners and readers to spend their lives seeking heaven. His influence on the public prayer of the Church is more difficult to assess, but is reflected in the use of the term 'Gregorian' to describe the plainsong which was so central to liturgy thereafter.

Before becoming Pope, Gregory had planned to go on a mission to the island of Britain. In 596–597, he implemented this idea by sending in his stead Augustine, the prior of his own Roman monastery, and a group of companions. They landed at Thanet and made contact with the pagan king of Kent, Aethelberht, and his Christian Frankish queen, Bertha.

Britain had had Christians before, and parts of it were far from pagan still. The greater part of the island of Britain had been a province of the Roman Empire for centuries and Christianity had begun to flourish there. The withdrawal of the legions in 410 led to an invitation to the Saxons to assist the British against the northern Picts; the ships came, their men fought and eventually stayed. Angles, Saxons and Jutes took over most of Britain south of Hadrian's Wall. Their many little kingdoms were at first all pagan, and it was this community to which Gregory addressed his mission.

But the British Church had survived in Wales and Augustine's relations with it were not among his happiest endeavours. It was not surprising that the British Christians, driven out of their homes by the English, maintained links with Scotland, Ireland, Cornwall and Brittany, rather than Anglo-Saxon England. Four of the great Welsh monasteries, Llandaff, St Asaph, St David and Bangor, eventually emerged as bishoprics.

The Irish tribes attributed their own conversion to Christianity to the mission of Patrick (*c* .390–*c*. 460). While Patrick came from Britain and his Christianity was no different from the rest of the Western Church in his time, it was acclimatized in Ireland in a form of its own, because Ireland had not been part of the Roman Empire and had for a time very little contact with the wider ecclesiastical world. Irish Christianity produced its own great scholars and missionaries, such as Columba

(c. 521–596) and Columbanus (c. 543–615) and later John Scotus Erigena (c. 810–c. 877). The Irish founded great monasteries and produced beautiful books, such as the Gospel Books of Kells and Durrow. The participation of the Irish in the conversion of northern England was seen by Bede as a continuation of the simplicity of apostolic witness in preaching and holy living among the poor, an image which may in part account for the continued idealization of the Celts by the English.

After the baptism of the king of Kent, Augustine of Canterbury sent one of his companions north when Aethelberht's daughter married the pagan Edwin of Northumberland and there also a kingdom was converted. After a year of pagan reconquest, the new ruler Oswald introduced Irish missionaries from Iona, notably Aidan (died 651) who became Bishop of Lindisfarne. Thereafter a complex web of conquests, alliances, marriages and baptisms enabled the missionaries to work closely with the kings, in a conversion of the whole island by persuasion and political self-interest rather than by force. Relations between the 'Irish' and the 'Roman' Christians could occasionally still be tense. They had different styles of life and celebrated Easter on different dates, which amounted in contemporary minds to dividing the one Body of Christ. The issue proved divisive throughout Europe, and generated a considerable literature of 'pamphlet warfare', but its significance should not be exaggerated. Ireland itself accepted the revised Roman dating for Easter willingly enough.

Anglo-Saxon Christians did not remain idle on the missionary front; while there remained everything to be done to establish the basis of Christian thought and behaviour in their own land, their energy and enthusiasm for their faith caused them to send missionaries to the German tribes on the continent. Within a century of their own conversion they were sending evangelists back to Europe. Willibrord (died 739) was among the first of these, and it is significant that he first spent years in Ireland. The English mission and the Irish mission were not so different. He became the evangelist of Frisia with the protection of Pippin II. Consecrated bishop for the Frisians by Pope Sergius I in 695, he established his see at Utrecht. This link with the papacy, supported by an equally strong link with secular government, was confirmed in the mission of Boniface of Crediton (c. 680–754), the 'Apostle of Germany', whose activities ranged over Hesse, Bavaria, Westphalia, Thuringia and Württemberg. He was made Archbishop of Mainz by Pope Gregory II in 732, founded numerous other bishoprics in Germany and reformed the Church in France in association with Pippin III, King of the Franks. In old age he returned as a missionary to Frisia where he was attacked and martyred by a pagan band at Dokkum. It was a characteristic of this Anglo-Saxon mission to the European mainland that it was carried on with such close and continuous reference to Rome. Gregory's sending of Augustine to England certainly paid dividends in the large extension of papal authority in northern Europe to which it led.

The story of these missions (up to and including Willibrord) and the conversion of the English was recorded in *The Ecclesiastical History of the English People* by Bede the Venerable (*c.* 673–735). Bede was born in Northumbria and when he was seven years old his kinsmen offered him to the new monastery at St Peter's, Monkwearmouth, founded by Benedict Biscop (*c.* 628–689); he lived there and in the twin monastery of St Paul's, Jarrow, under Abbot Ceolfrith (died 716), all his life. Benedict Biscop, one of the most remarkable figures of his age, had visited Rome no fewer than five times and spent two years in the monastery of Lérins, where he assumed the name of Benedict. He had retrieved from Italy many classical and patristic writings which were to prove a huge influence on Western culture through the use Bede made of them. St Wilfred at Ripon together with Biscop ensured that English monasticism would come to be shaped according to St Benedict's Rule with its spiritual restraint, balanced division of the day between the 'work of God' (the eight canonical 'hours' of common prayer), manual work and spiritual reading, and insistence upon the virtues of community and obedience to the abbot. Bede was as stable a monk as Boniface, his close contemporary, was itinerant. Between them, they represent the two most powerfully influential faces of Western monasticism.

Through his numerous writings Bede both preserved the most complete account there is of the conversion of a barbarian people, and himself influenced the intellectual deepening of that faith. His influence on the Church in England was profoundly formative. Almost all that is known about individuals in that age comes from Bede. Important as his *Ecclesiastical History* is, in his own time he was known nevertheless mainly for his commentaries and homilies on the Bible, in which he conveyed the teaching of the Fathers of the Church, along with his own insights. He also wrote on grammar, poetry and natural science, and made significant contributions to the understanding of time, especially by popularizing the system of dating years *anno Domini* (AD).

Bede was conscious of the problems raised by the practical implications, for the governance and pastoral work of the Church, of the conversion of the English, and wrote about them in his last letter to Egbert of York. They were problems that had already, before Bede's time, faced the seventh Archbishop of Canterbury, the Greek Theodore of Tarsus (668–690), who had done so much to organize the structures of the English Church as a whole while his friend, the African monk Hadrian, had built up a notable school at Canterbury. They had come from Rome together in the company of Benedict Biscop, and their formative influence in England demonstrates the continuity which still just survived in the late seventh century, tying the new Churches of northern Europe to the old heartlands of Christianity east and south of the Mediterranean, which in their own lifetime had been engulfed by Muslim conquest.

The Germanic tribes of the Franks and Thuringians had been converted after the baptism of Clovis in 496, a century before the English. The account by Gregory of Tours (c. 540–594) of the history of the Franks provides valuable sources for understanding these early years of the conversion of the invading barbarians. A new stage in the conversion of Europe was reached with the reign of Charlemagne (King of the Franks, 771–814). The son and successor of Pippin III, he inherited not only the kingdom of the Franks but, equally, the rule of the Gaul they had conquered, a land which had a continuous tradition of Christianity from the earliest times. On Christmas Day 800, Charlemagne was crowned in Rome by the Pope with the title of Holy Roman Emperor. The event and its significance was, and remains, much disputed, but the effect was to replace the Emperor in Constantinople with the King of the Franks as the temporal protector of the Church in the West, a fact of continuing significance for both Church and state. The new title was intended to replace that of the Eastern Emperor, signalling an end to his involvement in Western affairs. It was intended by the addition of the word 'holy' to forge a definitive link between the papacy and Charlemagne's empire. The coronation was only a beginning. For the next eight hundred years the affairs of northern Europe revolved at all levels around the question of what it meant: what in fact belonged to God and what to Caesar. If Pope Leo III crowned Charlemagne, he also knelt in homage before him – the only Pope ever to do so to a Western emperor.

The difference made to the Church by Charlemagne lay partly in his concept of it as a department of state, which it was his duty to supervise and regulate along with other departments of life throughout his empire, a concept very similar to that held by emperors in the East. In a series of wars he secured a vast territory from the Pyrenees to the Danube and enforced Christianity on Saxons, Lombards, Croats and even the Moors in Spain, both by force of arms and by legislation. On the interior level of Church life, Charlemagne was influential in several ways. First, he and his son and successor, Louis the Pious, with the help of the principal monastic figure of the time, Benedict of Aniane (c. 750–821), insisted that the monasteries in his vast domains conform to the Rule of St Benedict. Henceforth the latter provided a precise norm for monastic life throughout the Latin world in a way that had not earlier been the case. Secondly, he received as a coronation present from the Englishman Alcuin of York (c. 725–804) a copy of the complete Bible, a revised text of the Vulgate, St Jerome's Latin translation. Alcuin arranged for a number of copies of this revised text to be made, and this standardization of the Vulgate provided an important foundation for medieval biblical scholarship. Thirdly, Charlemagne influenced what has been called the Carolingian Renaissance of learning. His biographer, Einhard, tells a picturesque story of the arrival of two Irishmen at court, with 'learning for sale'; in fact Charlemagne encouraged the advancement of learning at all levels. He himself tried to learn to read and write in Latin, though with no success; he encouraged better handwriting in his own chancery; he made provision for the education of children. The cathedral schools established and sustained a level of learning in Western Europe which was able in due course to provide a foundation for the rise of the first universities. Bishops were required to train their clergy and examine them for their ability to read and write and know Latin for the services and for preaching. By the General Admonition of 789, service books were revised and a copy of the Gregorian Sacramentary was made, which remained the norm for liturgy until this century. And above all there was the palace school at Aachen, where his own family was educated as an example and inspiration to his subjects. Here Alcuin, a great admirer of Bede, was in charge, surrounded by a group of friends: Peter of Pisa, a grammarian, Paul the Deacon, who wrote the history of the Lombards, Theodulf, a Spanish bishop, Einhard, the biographer of Charlemagne, as well as the princes and princesses.

In this setting, a revival of classical learning took place, in a profoundly Christian context. Alcuin spoke of 'a new Athens, only much more excellent because Christian'. The fervour and ability of these scholars touched every sphere, from the church buildings to illuminated manuscripts, such as the Golden Bible. Charlemagne himself, an administrator as well as a soldier, the Emperor of the West, husband of two wives (as well as having several concubines), would always remain one of the most amazing, yet ambiguous, figures of history. Later imperial ideologists would endeavour to elevate him to the rank of a saint, calling him, like Constantine, the 'thirteenth apostle'. But after his death his legacy would prove even more difficult to hold together than that of Constantine.

In England the resistance to the Viking attacks under the leadership of Alfred the Great (849–899) resulted in not only the unification of the kingdom and the survival of Christianity in the south, but also the conversion of the Danes in the northern part of the country. The Viking leader, Guthrum, after his defeat by Alfred at Ethandune in 878, agreed to be baptized and took the noble Saxon name of Athelstan. Like Charlemagne, though with more personal scholarly ability, Alfred took care that his victories with the sword were followed by a conquest of ignorance, particularly facilitating the reading of the Bible and the Fathers by encouraging education and his own translations into English of key texts, such as Gregory the Great's *Pastoral Care*. Alfred went twice on pilgrimage to Rome. In doing so, as in much else, he was a model early medieval Christian king, but in his extensive promotion of writing in English, he was unique in pointing the way towards one of the great achievements of the Middle Ages – the development of a range of national vernacular literatures grounded in the classics of Christianity.

If the Christian world was steadily advancing in the north despite the attacks of the Vikings, it was equally shrinking in the south as the Muslim conquest continued. In the seventh century it swept across North Africa, Carthage finally falling in 698. In the eighth, most of Spain as well as Sicily was conquered. In the ninth, Rome itself was threatened, though Charles Martel's victory at Poitiers in 733 effectively put a stop to a further northward advance. The Christian 'reconquest' of Spain, begun from the north already by Charlemagne, was not completed until 1492, and the marks of that period of Muslim domination are clearly visible in the marvellous medieval architecture of Seville and Granada. For many centuries, the Western Church rested precariously between Muslim south, pagan north and Byzantine east.

The conversion of Scandinavia and the Baltic lands came later than that of most other European countries. Missionaries reached Denmark and northern Germany only in the ninth century when King Harold was baptized on a visit to the court of Louis the Pious, as a result of which a monk of Corbie, Anskar (801–865), established a school in Schleswig and then built the first Christian church in Sweden. In 832 he became Bishop of Hamburg and in 848 first Archbishop of Bremen. In 854 he converted Erik of Jutland, but after his death Scandinavia relapsed into paganism, to be partly re-Christianized only after the baptism of Guthrum by Alfred and, more completely, in the reign of Cnut in the eleventh century. Sweden, too, was first evangelized by Anskar, but the conversion was reversed by pagan conquest, and only effectively achieved in the eleventh and twelfth centuries with missions from England. Lund became an archbishopric in 1104 and Uppsala in 1164.

In the East, Bohemia became Christian in the tenth century and Poland followed soon after when Prince Mieczyslaw was baptized; in 1000 Gniezno became a metropolitan see, while much the same was happening under King Stephen in Hungary, where the archbishopric of Esztergom was established in 1001. It was from Hungary that, a little later, the see of Zagreb was established in Croatia. In all these countries, as earlier in Germany or England, there were many temporary reversals within what looks, continent-wide, like an inexorable process. What is striking is how quickly in each case Christianity and the first Christian kings, such as Wenceslaus and Stephen, became symbols of national identity, while the Church fell largely under royal control. Lithuania and the lands east of the Baltic were the last to be converted in this onward march of Latin

Christianity northwards and eastwards. Here it occurred only in the thirteenth century and largely due to force. Elsewhere conversion had been, for the most part, a freely chosen option, here it was brought about by external crusade, a 'holy war', conversion by conquest, authorized by the papacy – a very different thing from the way it had started in the western islands in the sixth and seventh centuries.

The conversion of the main block of European countries was not the end of medieval missionary endeavour. The beliefs of Islam remained obscure to the West until the contact brought about by the Crusades sharpened interest. In the mid-twelfth century, Peter the Venerable, Abbot of Cluny, sponsored a translation of the Qur'an into Latin by the English scholar Robert of Ketton. For Peter, Islam was not another religion but, rather, a defective form of Christianity. Particularly in Spain there was much intellectual contact between Muslims, Christians and Jews as well. The transmission of Muslim versions of Aristotle and Plato as well as Muslim medicine and science was to be foundational to Western scholarship and this establishment of a dialogue was valuable in helping to give access to the Arabic culture which had preserved and worked upon the classical texts.

During the thirteenth century the Franciscans and Dominicans made preaching expeditions to distant countries, and were to be found far afield in Asia, the Persian Gulf, India and China, striving particularly to convert the Mongols, who at the time ruled China. The Franciscan John of Monte Corvino arrived in Khanbaliq (present-day Beijing) in 1294 and was later appointed its first archbishop, but distance and conquest by the Chinese Ming dynasty meant that this Christian beginning had disappeared before the end of the fourteenth century.

Interfaith dialogue is a modern ideal. 'Mission' throughout the Middle Ages meant the attempt to convert. Islam created some intellectual interest among medieval scholars, but the nearest to a real encounter of faiths was the intercourse between Christians and Jews. For a few this became true dialogue, and in such works as *On Conversion* of Hermannus Judaeus it is possible to see a mind being won from one faith to the other. The roughly contemporary *Dialogue* of Gilbert Crispin, Abbot of Westminster, with a Jew, Anselm of Canterbury's *Cur Deus Homo*, Peter Abelard's *Dialogus*, all reflect Christian interest in this conversation. But, for the most part, contact with Jews living in Christian society meant at the best centuries of mutual coexistence and at the worst persecution.

The Bible and the Church

Throughout the Middle Ages, the Bible was held to have an authority which derived directly from God. It was taken for granted that God 'wrote' the Bible by dictating it directly to the human authors whose names are attached to the various books of the Bible. A common picture at the beginning of copies of the Gospel is of the evangelist sitting and writing his Gospel with the Holy Spirit in the form of a dove, with its beak in his ear, dictating the text. There was discussion in the later Middle Ages of the exact role of the 'human' authors of Scripture, such as the prophets and St Paul. The puzzle of a prophet saying 'I am not a prophet' (*propheta non sum*) threw up sharply the question whether the human authors of Scripture had not perhaps made at least some human, and therefore fallible, contribution. Theologians like Thomas Aquinas, however, took it for granted that divine inspiration did not replace the normal mental functioning of the human writer. The general presumption was that even if a writer was capable of error God would not allow mistakes to creep into the text. So that did not diminish the Bible's high authority. Another kind of mistake did arise and had to be allowed for. This was the error not of authorship but of copying. In thirteenth-century Paris it became necessary to repeat what Alcuin had attempted and prepare a new standard text which was to provide the basis for the first printed Bible, the 'Gutenberg' edition, of 1456.

There were three 'levels' of 'authority' in medieval thinking. Scripture came indisputably first and highest. Then came early Christian authors, and some much respected later ones. In twelfth-century compilations of 'authorities' surviving in some of the English cathedral libraries and elsewhere, the eleventh- and twelfth-century figures of Anselm of Canterbury, Bernard of Clairvaux and Hugh of St Victor appear alongside Augustine and Gregory the Great as of equal standing. Last in authority came classical 'pagan' writers such as Cicero and Aristotle, who were respected for their antiquity. If the authorities disagreed, the Bible was taken to be right, but it was the Bible as interpreted by the Church.

From the patristic period to the Reformation the Bible was the most important book in every monastic and cathedral library. That did not mean that ordinary people, or even most parish priests, had access to a copy, or any way of knowing exactly what it said. For most people the Bible was literally a closed book. Those who did have a copy had it, of course, in the Vulgate, as only a handful of scholars could read it in Greek. When Jerome made this translation in the fourth century, he was turning the Bible into the vernacular, because Latin was the language people spoke in the western half of the Roman Empire. He was also tidying up considerable confusion caused by the availability of a number of different Latin translations. But as Latin dropped out of use and was replaced by the modern European languages, the Church became the Bible's custodian in a new way. Only those who had been educated as clerics or at the new universities could read it, and they had a pastoral responsibility to teach the uneducated masses what it said. The misinterpretation of the Bible, it was held, could easily lead to heresy. Ordinary believers were therefore dependent on their parish priest to explain the Bible as well as he could, and many such priests were poorly educated and idle and did not do the job well. Until the later Middle Ages, when they could hear sermons preached by the friars, the faithful might have no other source of instruction. In worship week by week there was reading of the Bible, but a 'ministry of the Word' in Latin would tell people nothing unless there was some interpretation of the passage for them in their own language. Something could be learned from frescoes, pictures on church walls; and many of the stories from the Bible were memorable. But the theoretical framework of doctrine was less easily transmitted that way, and it is not surprising that for many people during the earlier Middle Ages their Christianity remained close to primitive superstition, and that their ideas about God were often confused with beliefs in magic. Angels and devils and even saints could be hard to distinguish from the deities of paganism for those without education, as Augustine of Hippo and Gregory the Great both recognized.

From the twelfth century the rise of an articulate middle class began to create a pressure for direct access to the Bible, and, with it, texts in the vernacular. In fact the Gospels had already been translated into English by the eleventh century, but their circulation remained very limited. One of the features of the Waldensians which most troubled Church authorities in the late twelfth century was their skill in responding smartly with a biblical quotation when their teachings were challenged. Lollard groups in the fourteenth century conducted Bible studies in one another's homes, sometimes reaching a strikingly high level of critical expertise.

At the other end of the scale of understanding of the faith, scholars analysed the text of the Bible minutely. They gradually built up a running commentary on the whole text. This, known as the *Glossa Ordinaria*, was completed during the twelfth century. The notion that a text might mean more than one thing was recognized very early in Christian history and the analysis of different types of meaning was further developed in the Middle Ages. The first task was to explain how many senses there were. The system in established use in the West throughout the Middle Ages appears to have been worked out by Gregory the Great, who took the surface meaning of the text, its literal or 'historical' sense, as the foundation, and built upon it three 'higher' senses.

The first was the allegorical. 'Allegory' involved some transference from the ordinary meanings of words to give them a spiritual application: for example, the 'lion of Judah' is Christ. The second sense was the tropological or moral. When Gregory composed his *Moralia on Job*, he concentrated especially on bringing out the moral lessons he found in the book. The third was the anagogical or prophetic. To draw that out was to show how the text pointed forward to the future, either in this world or the world to come. A controversial exponent of this method was Joachim of Fiore (died 1202), who tried to work out when the end of the world would come and to point to signs of the 'old age of the world' in contemporary events. Rupert of Deutz and Anselm of Havelberg in the first half of the twelfth century had done something similar, if less controversially.

These spiritual senses were an important help in the task of explaining the Bible to the simple faithful, because they could be colourful, touching people's lives and interests directly. They could make sense of passages in Scripture which appear to be brutal or to show God in a vengeful light. No book of the Bible was explored more thoroughly for this purpose than the Psalms. Monks and nuns sang the Psalms again and again in their worship and many Christians dwelt on them reflectively. Unsurprisingly, it was one of the books most frequently translated into the vernacular. The Song of Songs also became important in this way during the twelfth century, when Bernard of Clairvaux preached his long series of sermons to explain the spiritual meanings of this story of a Bride and Bridegroom in terms of the relationship of the soul and Christ and of the Church and Christ.

One of the most practical ways of unfolding the meaning of the Bible to believers was by preaching on it. Augustine of Hippo had preached for an hour or more, with his audience as involved as though they were at a theatre. He gave several long series (for example on the Psalms, on St John's Gospel) in the course of which he expounded whole books of the Bible. Gregory the Great preached in the same extended exegetical way at the end of the sixth century and Bernard of Clairvaux did the same in the early twelfth century, sometimes breaking off in the middle to admit to his listeners that he knew the sermon was becoming rather long, before continuing for as long again. Bernard's powers as a preacher were not merely verbal, although his skills with words were outstanding. He understood, as the ancient rhetoricians had done, that delivery is important. There is a story of his preaching in Latin to a German-speaking audience and reducing it to tears. When the translator got up to explain to them what Bernard had said the audience was far less moved by the sense than they had been by the delivery.

During the early Middle Ages preaching underwent a series of changes. The number of individuals capable of preaching freshly composed sermons depended upon the number educated to a sufficient level, and those were very few. For a long time preaching, even in monastic communities, was often a mere reading of the surviving 'published' sermons of Augustine, Gregory and other Latin Fathers. In the late eleventh century Guibert of Nogent wrote a pioneering book on how to preach a sermon. At the end of the twelfth century Alan of Lille's 'the art of preaching' set a new fashion. Formally taught in his way, the technique was to take a short passage of Scripture as a 'text', rather than to progress through a whole book of Scripture. The theme was then developed by dividing the meanings of the key terms in the text and analysing each in turn. Numerous manuals on how to do this had appeared by about 1230.

The orders of Friars were founded in the early thirteenth century, first and foremost to carry on the work of preaching. The Franciscans were wandering preachers trying to follow the example of poverty Jesus himself had set, and to spread the Gospel. The Dominicans were founded to preach against heresy in the north of Spain and the south of France. The friar preachers devised a variety of *practical* aids, 'dictionaries' of biblical terms, so that they could look up a word which was to feature prominently in a sermon and see where else, and in what other senses, it occurred in Scripture. They also put together reference books of illustrative stories and parallels and brief patterns of argumentation. One of the results of the friars' work was to make more obvious the lack of teaching about the Bible in the Church's routine worship. They were supplying in sermons in the open air what the Church was not providing in church buildings, although, of course, the friars soon had buildings of their own in every town of importance, if not in the countryside. An absence of truly biblical teaching was, nevertheless, an important complaint in the list the reformers put to the Church in the sixteenth century, and which led to some of them placing a perhaps disproportionate emphasis the other way, suggesting Christians did not need the help of the Church to obtain salvation. *Sola Scriptura* was the cry: 'the Bible alone!' The question of the relationship between Bible and Church thus became contentious in a way it had not been when the Bible was first put together within the Church and by its authority.

Church and state and papal authority

During the Middle Ages 'the theory of what the Church is' ('ecclesiology') was extensively worked out for the first time. Since state recognition of the Church in the fourth century, relations between Church and state had been in a fairly stable balance. The Donation of Constantine, a forged text of the Carolingian period – though it was believed throughout the Middle Ages to be genuine – gave the Church a dominant position in theory, but it was well understood that there were lines it could not cross.

The main problem by the eleventh century was that the Church held lands within states. A bishop was also a baron, and his lands had to be entrusted to him by the king or the emperor when he was made bishop. Kings and emperors therefore had a strong interest in these appointments, and themselves selected bishops, who were frequently drawn from the leading families. Inevitably power games were played. The secular authorities developed a tendency to encroach upon that part of the making of a bishop which was properly the Church's concern alone, the ordination and consecration, by seeking to 'invest' the new bishop with the ring, symbol of his marriage to the Church, and the staff, symbol of his pastoral office. They thus crossed the symbolic boundary between 'temporal' and 'spiritual'.

Gregory VII (born Hildebrand; Pope 1073–85), was one of the most significant architects of change in the history of the papacy. He set out to be a reformer. The *Dictatus Papae*, a curious little document in form, possibly surviving from notes, is a bold statement of papal claims to plenitude of power in the Church and supremacy over the secular authorities. He took a high line on the effect of the succession from Peter, extending it from the ecclesiastical to the political sphere more explicitly than his predecessors. Gregory claimed the right to depose all princes and to have all Christians as his subjects. He claimed supreme legislative and judicial power.

Drives to stop the widespread practice of simoniacal ordination and to enforce clerical celibacy had begun under his predecessors. Both these were connected with the main problem of where the boundary lay between the temporal and the spiritual. Buying office in the Church (simony) was a secular intrusion. If clergy were not celibate they had children, and they naturally wanted their children to be able to 'succeed' to their fathers' positions in the Church, just as a temporal monarch or baron wanted his children to have his lands after him. Gregory re-enacted decrees on these subjects at the Lenten synods of 1074 and 1075. The most far-reaching of his moves was the prohibition of lay investiture. There were three stages in the making of a bishop: the choice or election of the individual to fill the vacant bishopric, the consecration, and the handing over of control of the 'temporalities' or lands and possessions of the see. The consecration was clearly a sacramental act, which only the Church could perform, and the 'temporalities' appeared to be in the gift of the secular authorities. But the election could be interfered with by either, and the actual ceremony of consecration was being muddled by the handing over of ring and pastoral staff, symbols of pastoral office, by a king or emperor, not by the Church authorities. Gregory wanted to see not only a proper separation of roles, but also the diminution of secular intrusion in the process.

The emperor of the day, Henry IV, slowly awoke to the implications of Gregory's claims and from 1075 he asserted himself by making his own nominations to the see of Milan and to sees in Germany, as also Fermo and Spoleto. Gregory reproved him. The emperor called a synod of German bishops at Worms in 1076, at which he deposed the Pope, while the bishops of Lombardy allied themselves with those of Germany. Gregory responded by excommunicating Henry and releasing his subjects from their duty to obey him. It worked. Henry partly capitulated, going to Canossa in northern Italy, where Gregory was residing, to appeal for absolution in the winter of 1077. Gregory kept him waiting in the snow outside the castle gates for several days before granting the emperor's appeal. There followed further years of manoeuvring, while Henry and his rival (and elected anti-king) Rudolf of Swabia struggled for supremacy, with Gregory partly holding the balance of power. Gregory died at Salerno, an exile from Rome and far from apparently successful in his struggles, but the ideal of a Church 'free' from secular control was upheld by his successors and generations of reforming clergy to provide the central model for medieval Christendom. In 1122 the Concordat of Worms was arrived at after lengthy negotiation between Pope and emperor. It settled that the 'temporalities' in the appointment of a bishop were to be the business of the state, the 'spiritualities' that of the Church.

Gregory VII had made papal claims to plenitude of power. Bernard of Clairvaux wrote a book *On Consideration*, for Pope Eugenius III (1145–53), who had been a Cistercian monk, and for whom Bernard continued to have a fatherly concern. He wanted to make Eugenius think hard about his priorities, and the book expanded over the years into five. He taught Eugenius that he was to be supreme over all authorities in the world. This was a line of thought congenial to succeeding Popes. Innocent III (1198–1216) was an outstanding figure in his grasp of the need for the Church to establish clear policies. He systematically sought out the best scholars graduating from Europe's new universities for his civil service, and for strategically important bishoprics. He was, for example, respon-sible for the appointment of Cardinal Stephen Langton as Archbishop of Canterbury, and he placed England under an interdict when King John refused to accept him. Stephen had been a professor of biblical theology in the University of Paris, where Innocent had known him, and he proved indeed to be an outstanding archbishop, although one less amenable to papal directions than Innocent had expected.

Innocent called the Fourth Lateran Council in 1215, bringing together representatives from all over Europe to give it the maximum credibility.

It issued no fewer than 70 decrees, which appear to have been prearranged by Innocent and were largely just rubber-stamped by the council itself. The importance of this council for the pastoral reform of the Church was very considerable and yet Innocent was playing a dangerous game with papal control by reawakening the idea of an authoritative council of bishops. It was the first of a series of truly major medieval councils: Lyons (1274), Constance (1414–18) and Florence (1438–45). One of the most contentious issues of the later Middle Ages was the question whether the Church was ultimately under the authority of a single bishop, the Pope in Rome, or under the control of all the bishops working together in councils. That question had been sharpened by the assertion of papal plenitude of power in the eleventh and twelfth centuries, and the attempted exercise of 'papal monarchy' across Europe above all in the century between Innocent III and Boniface VIII (1294–1303). Boniface's humiliation by King Philip of France and the subsequent transfer of the Pope's residence from Rome to Avignon in France effectively brought the Pope's temporal claims to a halt, but theologically it was the 'Great Schism of the West' (1378–1417), when there were rival Popes in Rome and Avignon, which made the Church as a whole naturally ask, who can decide between them? Must not a council be the ultimate authority?

The Council of Constance put forward robust proposals for the reform of Church governance by council, but, once the various rivals had been compelled to resign and a single papacy was firmly re-established at Rome, they came to very little. Meanwhile, during the last medieval centuries, reforming movements were becoming more and more critical of 'papal monarchism', even arguing that the popes had become 'Antichrist'. There was a call for rule of the Church not by bishops in council, but, much more radically, by the people in their local congregations, expressing the *consensus fidelium*, the agreement of the people, in the ancient way. So, closely parallel to patterns of dispute in the secular sphere were patterns of call for reform within the Church, but the central problem always remained: how to limit the power of the papacy without allowing control of the Church to be taken over by king and barons.

The Church and the individual: sanctity, feasts and sacraments

For most Christians these grand movements and huge shifts, the power games of Church and state, remained remote. The texture of Christian life was experienced in a more modest and domestic way by the majority of the people of Europe. Perhaps the most striking illustration of this is the cult of the saint, the outstanding figure of Christian virtue, the hero or heroine of the faith. Saints were made by popular acclaim, because they were recognized by those who had come into contact with them locally, as persons of exceptional holiness. Sometimes – especially at the end of the eleventh century and the beginning of the twelfth – the process was helped along by hiring a professional writer of saints' lives (hagiographer) to tell the story of the new saint's life in the conventional terms required to show everyone he had the necessary characteristics. After the death of such a person the water the body had been washed in, or a finger nail, or a piece of the saint's clothing, might become associated with miracles; people would travel to the place where the saint had lived or died and especially where he had been buried. Thus the shrine of Archbishop Thomas Becket at Canterbury became an outstanding place of pilgrimage. Martyred in 1170 because of his resistance to royal control of the Church, Thomas had become a symbol of the sort of free Church which progressive clerics were struggling for everywhere. His Roman 'canonization' was a sign of the takeover of this area as well by papal control, but his shrine was popular with everyone as a focal point of holiness. The standing of a saint was reflected in the distance his fame or 'cult' would spread, bringing people to visit him in death and to pray for miracles. So the 'great Christian' was a lively attraction to medieval minds, as someone to whom all could come, and whom they might seek to emulate.

Popular devotion in the Middle Ages took comfort in tangible things, signs of the holy, pictures, relics of saints, holy places. In all these, it was believed, there resided a power derived from the goodness of the saint in question, or directly from God himself. Veneration of the shrines of the saints drew local devotion from those seeking miraculous cures or protections. But such shrines were supplemented by the large wealth of relics brought to Europe from Jerusalem and Constantinople by returning Crusaders or cunning traders. People were credulous and did not ask too many questions about the authenticity of the relics, so something like a modern tourist trade developed, and pilgrimage churches of increasing splendour were built.

The creation of new feasts reflected new interests, popular as well as theological. For instance, the feasts of Corpus Christi, the Sorrows of the Virgin, the Crown of Thorns, and the Precious Blood, show a growing popular concern in the later Middle Ages with the sufferings of Christ and his Mother. In the fourteenth century, the feast of St Anne, Mary's mother (though the name nowhere appears in the Bible), became popular, and then in the fifteenth century a devotion to St Joseph, Mary's spouse, also began to grow.

The Middle Ages was the period during which the theology and practice of seven sacraments became fully developed. A sacrament is 'the outward and visible sign of an inward and spiritual reality'. In practice it was through the sacraments that ordinary people mostly encountered the Gospel and participated in the life of the Church. It began with baptism administered in infancy in the font of the parish church. Many late medieval fonts were decorated with images of the seven sacraments. They represent how Christian life was actually shaped from infant baptism through communion, confession and confirmation to marriage and then, before death, to a last anointing. The 'outward signs' in baptism were the pouring of water and the words invoking the name of the Father, the Son and the Holy Ghost, the inward reality was something which changed them for ever. It took away the guilt of their sinfulness, inherited from Adam, and replaced it by membership of the Church and a state of 'grace', a sharing in the life of God. Except for Jews, everyone in the Christian lands, which gradually included the whole of Europe, was baptized in infancy. Everyone looked towards an eternal life after death which would be spent in heaven or in hell, and most believed that the Church had a large part in deciding their future because only in the Church could they obtain various effective helps towards heaven.

Since at least the time of Augustine of Hippo it had been generally held in the West that all human beings were born in 'original sin', that is, with an inherited guilt which they carry for the sin committed by Adam and Eve, even if they have not committed sin yet for themselves. Being tainted by original sin made it inevitable that people would in due course commit actual sins. It also made it hard for them to act logically, so that it was common human experience to know what was the right thing to do and still do the wrong one. If someone died in a sinful state it followed that he or she would spend eternity in hell, for God was perfectly just and that was what they deserved. That was why baptism to remove the taint was regarded as essential, and why, from at least the fifth century in the West, people were baptized as babies, in case they died in infancy. They were then 'confirmed' when they were old enough to declare for themselves that they believed in God.

But although baptism was believed to take away the stain of sin, it had been obvious to everyone since the earliest days of Christianity that it did not stop people sinning. That raised a considerable problem, because it was agreed that no one could be baptized more than once. In the first centuries of the Church, someone who committed a grave sin – particularly a denial of the faith in persecution – might never be allowed back to full communion. But, mostly, Church authority, and particularly Roman authority, was anxious to moderate this, and find ways whereby the sinner could be publicly forgiven. So a system was gradually devised to deal with repeated sinning, so as to implement Jesus' words 'whose sins you forgive, they are forgiven; whose sins you retain, they are retained' (John 20:23). This was the 'penitential system', which developed a long way in the medieval Church. For many centuries it consisted primarily of lists of heavy penances to be imposed publicly for various sins.

During the twelfth century an increasing emphasis was placed on the importance of personally confessing sins to priests, and manuals were written to help them in their work. The priest was to satisfy himself that the sinner was genuinely sorry and then declare God's forgiveness; he gave the repentant sinner a penance, as a sign of the sincerity of his sorrow. This might be fasting, almsgiving, or prayer, of a certain quantity or duration, but was generally less onerous than the listed penances in the earlier penitentiaries. The understanding was that the Church had authority to impose such penances as a condition of the forgiveness or 'absolution' which restored the sinner to the state he had been in when baptism purified him. At the Fourth Lateran Council of 1215 a ruling was given that all Christian people should confess their sins at least once a year. The switch here was from the public to the personal and even the secret. The Church's authority over the forgiveness of sin had not changed, but the mode of exercising it had done so, in a way that was less onerous for the individual and also more realistic, given the number of sins that most ordinary people were thought to commit.

But of course frequently people died penitent but with penances uncompleted, or even with their sins unconfessed. The twelfth century saw an important development of thinking in that area too. The penitent could hardly go to hell but if they had done no penance they could not go straight to heaven. There had, for centuries, been the germ of an idea that somewhere 'between' heaven and hell there might be a place where the work of refashioning souls could be completed to make them fit for an eternity in heaven. This was now described as 'purgatory'. There the souls of the dead could finish their penances. But that had a further pastoral consequence. The relatives of those who had died wanted to help shorten their time in purgatory, and people looking to the future for themselves also wanted to ensure that they would escape purgatory, or spend as little time in it as possible. The penalties of penance were imposed by the Church, so in principle the Church must be able to lift them again. That led to the development of a system of 'indulgences', which, like the idea of purgatory, had much earlier roots. Indulgences are the remission by the Church of the temporal penalty for forgiven sin.

People wanted to win indulgences, to stockpile them even, and the Church was glad enough to provide them, as a means of encouraging good works of various sorts, including raising revenue, especially for the building of churches. They could be used as a reward in another way too. When he preached the First Crusade Urban II made a new departure in promising a plenary indulgence to all who took the Cross and stayed with the Crusade all the way to Jerusalem, or who died on the way. That would mean that however many penances remained uncompleted in their lives, they would arrive in eternity with a clean slate. Saints were thought to have died with more than enough goodness to get them to heaven. They could therefore help others by lending them goodness from the 'treasury of merit' in the Church. The desire for the intercession and favour of the saints grew accordingly.

There was obviously enough room for abuse in all this. The Church became greedy. Ordinary members of the faithful, with no very clear idea of the theology – which was indeed confused and had to be rationalized by theologians such as Bonaventure (1221–74) after the event – began to think they could buy themselves a place in heaven. Getting there seemed principally a matter of accomplishing certain 'good works' of a pious kind. It was against this pastoral damage that Luther (1483–1546) reacted so strongly when he began to argue against indulgences. Many of his 95 theses, posted on the church door at Wittenberg in 1517, are concerned with this subject. So the abuse of penitential helps originally designed to meet a pastoral need became a major cause of the divisions of the Reformation.

The other sacrament of central importance in the Middle Ages – as in every period of the Church's life – was the Mass (the Eucharist). While the Lateran Council of 1215 decreed that every Christian should receive the sacrament of communion at least once a year, the focus of interest, both theologically and in popular debate, was more on what the priest did than on what the laity did. Here, most of all, religion had been clericalized. A central theological question throughout this period was to define what really happened when a priest repeated Jesus' words 'This is my body' and 'This is my blood'. The early medieval emphasis was that this was a way for believers to participate in the one sacrifice Christ had made when he died on the Cross for the sins of the world, and that it was thus both a way of binding Christians to their Lord in 'communion' and a means by which they could share in the benefits of the sacrifice.

In the Carolingian period there was already a dispute as to whether the bread and the wine were really changed into the body and the blood of Christ or whether the presence of the latter should be conceived more symbolically. This came to a head in the late eleventh century, when Berengar of Tours took a firm symbolist line and the Church reacted by insisting upon a doctrine of 'transubstantiation' (a term used from the twelfth century), which stated that what happened was the exact reverse of the change which takes place when bread goes mouldy. Then its outward appearance changes, but everyone agrees that it is still bread. When the bread of the Eucharist is consecrated, it was taught, its outward appearance stays the same, but inwardly it becomes the actual flesh of Christ. This was not a new belief, depending as it does upon a literalist interpretation of Jesus' own words as given in the Gospels and by St Paul, but it was now given a much more carefully thought-out technical explanation.

The formulation of this doctrine had huge consequences for the history of the Church. It encouraged people to venerate and even to worship the consecrated bread, and that was one reason why in the later Middle Ages the new feast of 'Corpus Christi' or the Body of Christ became so popular. The consecrated bread or 'host' was believed to have miraculous powers. Caesarius of Heisterbach tells stories of popular devotion sliding sideways into the cult of magic. One woman kept the consecrated bread in her mouth after she had been given it at the Mass and placed it in her beehive for safety. The bees had more respect than she, and built a tiny shrine of wax to keep it in.

The doctrine of transubstantiation also placed a new emphasis on the powers of the priest as able to perform this miracle. This led to a diminution of emphasis on people worshipping together and the encouragement of the saying of more and more private Masses, for which people paid, in the belief that they would be of value in wiping out their own sins or those of their loved ones who had died. This in turn encouraged a new development of the idea of the Mass as sacrifice. It was agreed by all that Christ himself made a fully sufficient sacrifice on the Cross, so that, as the Epistle to the Hebrews stressed, no repetition was needed. The Eucharist was a memorial of that sacrifice but it looked like becoming instead a repetition. Reformers would argue against this multiplication of Masses which appeared to diminish the sufficiency of the Cross for all the sins of the world. Popular beliefs in the efficacy of the Mass in the late Middle Ages easily led that way.

If marriage was a sacrament, then it could most suitably be celebrated in church and before a priest, although in the Middle Ages it was never denied that a marriage could quite validly be entered into by two people on their own. But in practice this too had become part of a cycle of life seen as sacramentally supported throughout, controlled by the Church and ending, ideally, with anointing on one's deathbed and a final reception of communion.

The sacrament of ordination was the only one of the seven which ordinary people would never receive, but it became contentious with the rise of popular disquiet about the powers of priests. Was it actually needed? Reforming groups at the end of the Middle Ages began to claim that there was no need for the right to exercise Christian ministry to depend upon the Church's ordination; local congregations could choose, indeed, they could hire and fire, their own ministers. This was potentially hugely disruptive of order in the Church and such groups were fiercely opposed, but the issue would be central to the sixteenth-century Reformation.

Religious life, prayer and mysticism

Throughout Christian history some have felt called to a dedicated form of life in which they give themselves up to prayer and live apart from the rest of the world, either alone as hermits, or in communities. Medieval monks and nuns still took their inspiration from the first examples of Christian monasticism in the fourth century in the deserts of Egypt and Palestine, especially as mediated, for instance, by Cassian's early fifth-century works. The second book of Gregory the Great's *Dialogues* was written in praise of St Benedict of Nursia (*c.* 480–*c.* 550), whose *Holy Rule* became the standard manual for monastic life in the West from about 800 until the twelfth century. The last chapter of the Rule refers to Cassian's *Institutes* and *Conferences* as foundational documents for Western monks. While the Rule of St Benedict gave the ideals of the Egyptian desert a lasting place in Western monastic life, the structure of the life it proposed was rather different, as reflecting a fully developed community of work and prayer, governed by both detailed regulation and the authority of the abbot.

Such a life was not regarded by medieval Christian society as selfish. The prayers were for the world, and influential people were willing to support the monks by making them gifts of lands for their communities to live on. Its centrality in society and the multiplication of monastic houses across Europe made monasticism one of the major influences on the world of Western Christendom in the ensuing centuries; monasteries were centres of intellectual excellence and of instruction, as well as places for the copying of books. The eleventh and twelfth centuries saw the expansion and diversification of the monastic life. Several new types of rule emerged with different variations on the basic theme of monastic commitment for life. There were the hermits, solitaries, such as Godric of Finchale, Christina of Markyate, Wulfric of Haselbury, Stephen of Grandmont; they pursued a life of intense prayer alone, though the accounts of their lives edified others. From the same ideology grew groups who lived together but whose members continued to spend most of their time in solitude, such as the hermit orders: the Camaldoli founded by Romuald (*c.* 950–1027) and the Carthusians founded by Bruno of Cologne (1032–1101). There were also the Premonstratensians, the white canons founded by Norbert (1080–1134), an order of preachers who became especially influential in Hungary. Another new order was founded by

Gilbert of Sempringham (*c*. 1083–1189) a long-lived and influential parish priest from Lincolnshire. The Gilbertines were the only new order to originate in England and the only one to include both men and women, in shared communities or 'double monasteries'. Gilbert never became a member of his own order though he always controlled its complex arrangement (nuns, lay sisters, canons and lay brothers).

The Benedictines themselves underwent reform at the central abbey of Cluny and its related houses, first in the tenth and eleventh centuries and then, again, under the abbacy of Peter the Venerable (*c*. 1092–1156). The first Cluniac reform had introduced into the Benedictine pattern many detailed refinements, including a highly ceremonial and extended liturgy, which allowed time for almost nothing else. In the eyes of some contemporaries this went against the spirit of the Rule and prompted attempts at reform on different principles. A major redefinition of the *Rule of St Benedict* emerged with a small group of hermits in the forests of Colan, who finally settled at Cîteaux, becoming known as the Cistercians. Led later by St Bernard (1090–1153), abbot of the Cistercian foundation at Clairvaux, they became a dominant force in Europe for the next hundred years. The Cistercian movement fostered a spirituality of simplicity and poverty of life, as well as increasing tenderness and emotional appeal in devotion. Men who could not read or write and had traditionally been servants in the monasteries were admitted as lay brothers. The Cistercians undertook sheep farming in remote districts, instead of agriculture in and near villages, so that they could preserve a separation from the rest of society they thought necessary for full concentration on prayer. They also ceased to receive children into the cloister. This recruitment only from adults had the effect of confirming religious life as a vocation freely chosen.

In the thirteenth century, a new kind of religious life appeared with the orders of friars and of the Beguines. Mention has already been made of the friars as preachers. The Order of Friars Minor or Franciscans was founded by a young Italian, Francis of Assisi (1181–1226), one of the greatest spiritual figures in the whole of Christian history. His mystique of poverty and powerlessness contrasts very strikingly with the power and wealth of the Church and yet he did not in any way himself challenge Church authority. No one was more anxious to obey the Pope. Francis's friars made their profession for life not to an individual monastery but to the whole order. They could therefore be moved around the world at any moment, and since their work was preaching and serving the poor in the rapidly rising cities and towns, they were enormously successful. Originally a group of laymen with no pretensions to scholarship, the Franciscans nevertheless produced some of the greatest thinkers of their time, men such as Bonaventure, John Duns Scotus (*c*. 1265–1308) and William of Occam (c. 1285–1347). Difficulties developed rapidly in the Order after Francis's death about the implementation of the ideal of absolute poverty, causing the split between 'Spirituals' and 'Observants'. A debate was set in motion which divided the whole Church, for although it might seem that a life of poverty was what Christ had intended for his disciples, the Church was by now extremely wealthy and there were strong vested interests in the protection of that wealth.

The Order of Friars Preachers (the Dominicans) was founded by a Spaniard, Dominic (1170–1221), at almost the same time. Like the Franciscans they practised poverty and were ready to move as need required, but their chief work was to preach and to combat heresy, especially that of the Albigenses in the Languedoc. Up to the late twelfth century, the Church had resisted the use of physical force against heresy. The Albigensian threat persuaded it to change its mind, but the idea that the true faith could be imposed and heretics punished needed agents to enforce it. Perhaps unfortunately for their own reputation, the Dominicans arrived on the scene and seemed appropriate people to staff the newly established Inquisition. However in many countries, such as England, there never was an Inquisition, and the preaching of the Dominicans was unaffected by an inquisitorial note. Their kind of work, however accomplished, demanded clear knowledge of the faith as well as skill in argument, qualities deriving from their involvement in the new universities of Paris, Oxford, Naples and Cologne. Their most renowned scholar was Thomas Aquinas (c. 1225–74), who brought together the Augustinian theological tradition of the West and the Aristotelian philosophy which dominated universities in the thirteenth century, due to the recent translation of much of Aristotle's work into Latin for the first time. Aquinas established a theological and philosophical synthesis which came under attack at the time for its novelty, but was little by little accepted, especially from the sixteenth century, as the most coherent intellectual expression of Catholic orthodoxy.

Respect for those who were not formally religious had taken a step further with the friars by the formation of the third orders for both men and women. This was developed too with a new style of non-cloistered religious life which emerged in the Low Countries, that of the Beguines and Beghards. The former were secular women mostly of the middle class who lived a religious life without enclosure. Their antecedents were the holy women of ancient Rome, living lives of prayer and chastity at home, to whom Jerome wrote letters of guidance. The Beghards were their male equivalent. They followed their accustomed trades, and gave time to charitable activities in the towns, as well as pursuing a life of prayer and contemplation. They had no common rule or central house or superior; they were at times suspected of heresy and their teaching was condemned by the Council of Vienne in 1321. Like the Franciscans who wanted to remain poor they were perceived by the Church authorities as dangerous, a fringe group, but many Beguine communities survived.

Not everything to be said about monastic life in the Middle Ages is good. The major monasteries grew too rich, while there were far too many small houses with no sound religious or worldly purpose. There was in every order a tendency for the style of life to grow lax or even corrupt over time. It was this at which reformers, like Wyclif, of the late Middle Ages pointed an accusing finger; but at the same time a need was being met, and the continuing popular trust in the value of the religious life cannot be denied.

The eleventh century saw a major redirection of devotion through the influence of the *Prayers and Meditations* of Anselm of Canterbury (1033–1109). This 'Anselmian revolution' drew the long tradition of compunction (that is, the use of the mind and the emotions to enable a person at prayer to break through natural torpor) into a new apprehension of life in God, using his or her own words. This 'interiority' spread widely and rapidly, and in the fourteenth century reached another stage in its evolution among mystical writers and the devout praying laity.

Earlier medieval mysticism involved rational effort to 'climb' towards an encounter with God by prayer. The style changed in the later Middle Ages, in favour of a risky opening of the soul to the darkness and apparent absence of God, which is known as 'negative mysticism', something far closer to Byzantine conceptions. It was an acknowledgement of how little creatures can know about God, and how impossible human language finds it to say anything more than what he is not. Meister Eckhart (*c.* 1260–1327), a quirky German theologian and Dominican friar, was among the most famous preachers and mystics of his time, numbering Tauler and Suso among his disciples. He wrote in both Latin and German, being the first major theologian to write in a European vernacular, and reached new heights in the attempt to express the inexpressible in the language of prayer. In describing the union with God that is the purpose of prayer, he appeared to some to make God and soul into a unity and was accused of heresy before the Archbishop of Cologne in 1326. Appealing to the Pope, he died before his case could be heard. Eckhart's contemporary, the Flemish mystic Jan van Ruysbroek (1293–1381), founded a group of canons regular at Groenendael, which became prominent in the movement known as the *Devotio Moderna*, later connected with such influential spiritual writers as Thomas à Kempis (*c.* 1380–1471) whose book, *The Imitation of Christ*, formed the basis of a 'new devotion' and has remained one of the classics of Christian spirituality as a way of following Christ intensely without entering a monastery.

There were in England also major new spiritual voices, writing mostly in the vernacular. There were, for instance, poets such as Langland (1330–86) and university theologians such as John Wyclif, but there was also a remarkable group of mystical writers, men and women, laypeople and priests: Richard Rolle (1300–49); the author of the *Cloud of Unknowing* (*c.* 1345); Walter Hilton (1330–96); Julian of Norwich (1342–*c.* 1413); and Margery Kempe (*c.* 1373–*c.* 1433), all connected in some way with the increasing numbers of laypeople undertaking a life of devotion in solitude.

Earliest in time was the northern hermit and preacher Richard Rolle. He was born at Thornton in Yorkshire, began his education in Oxford and possibly also studied in France. He became impatient with the formality of the schools, which he soon left in order to become a hermit in Yorkshire. He is an instance of the popular unrest with academic learning and the desire for a more personal following of Jesus. Rolle was a prolific writer and preacher, in both Latin and English, and was best known in his own day through treatises such as *The Fire of Love* and *The Emending of Life*. His English religious lyrics have found a permanent place in vernacular literature. He was an exponent of 'affective' mysticism, which drew on bodily sensations of heat and sweetness. Devotion to the person of Jesus Christ especially in his passion found a new and refined form in Rolle in regard to the 'Name of Jesus', another popular devotion of the times expressed both personally in his lyrics and at the same time liturgically in the new feast of the Name of Jesus (7 August).

A little later in time and less influential than Rolle, Margery Kempe was in some ways the most typical mystic of her age and was noted for an emotional understanding of religion very similar to, and influenced by, that of Rolle. Born at King's Lynn in Norfolk, she married John Kempe in 1393, and had fourteen children. A severe mental illness followed the birth of her first child during which she had a vision of Christ and thereafter regarded herself as bound by a special duty of devotion. It was not until 1418, when she was 45, that she left home and undertook a life of pilgrimage. On her journey she was accompanied by visions and ecstatic experiences. These were dictated by her (she could not read or write) and form the first autobiography in English, *The Book of Margery Kempe*. Margery was emotional and she wept often and publicly; her 'cryings' were the thing for which she was most famous, but the tenderness of her devotion and the strong sense of penitence in her work show her to be representative of a new and lay spirituality.

Julian of Norwich also, like Richard Rolle and Margery Kempe, was a mystic outside the institutional boundaries of monasteries and convents. She lived at the end of her life as a solitary in an anchorage in Norwich which was built onto the wall of a church dedicated to St Julian, from which she drew the name by which she is known. She wrote two works, one a longer version of the other, called *Revelations of Divine Love*. The title itself indicates the direction of her writings, which explore the way in which God loves humanity rather than the way in which prayer and life can be directed to him. She can be regarded as the first writer to discuss major themes of theology in English.

Margery Kempe does not appear to have heard of Julian of Norwich's *Revelations of Divine Love* but on the advice of a friar in Norfolk she consulted her about her inner life and its problems. She recorded Julian as listening with courtesy and recommending obedience, charity and above all patience. There is a great contrast between this emotional, affective, talkative woman and the wisdom of Julian, Hilton and the author of the *Cloud of Unknowing*, but in many ways Margery reflects the eager and vigorous devotion of the times as truly as do her more restrained contemporaries.

Walter Hilton and Julian of Norwich were the serious theologians of the group, but Hilton's *Scale of Perfection* and *Epistle on Mixed Life* were more books of instruction than was the work of Julian. *The Scale* covers a whole range of teaching about a life of prayer. Hilton was a priest in Northamptonshire. He wrote to his 'spiritual sister in Jesus Christ', an anchoress who had requested the book, with advice she had asked for about prayer and spiritual life, drawing on his own experience to do so. A firm and clear picture of the life of prayer emerges, carefully arranged, set out with gentleness and tolerance, though with the austere theme of the cross: in order to reach the vision of peace (which is the literal translation of the word 'Jerusalem'), he says, one must go through the 'night of murk'.

Hilton was reserved about the emotional and affective devotion connected with Margery Kempe and Rolle, as was the most brilliant and original of all these writers, the anonymous author of *The Cloud of Unknowing* and other related pieces, some very short, the most important of which is *The Book of Privy Counsel*. *The Cloud of Unknowing* was also a response to a request for help, in this case from a would-be solitary of 24 who asked the author for advice about prayer. The writer was a clear and decisive person, full of wit and acute observation, with no time or patience for sentimentality and hypocrisy. He wrote in a racy English prose style with a single theme, which he explained with wisdom, patience and confidence, offering specific guidance about the way of prayer which is called 'apophatic' because of its emphasis on the utter transcendence of God and his unknowableness by human faculties. The *Cloud* author insisted that the way of prayer he described was not to be undertaken lightly but only by those called to it by God, not those qualified by learning or self-confident ability, but those seriously seeking God.

All these writers were representative of the fourteenth century, with a freedom within structures, an intense care for the interior life of the individual, and the use of the vernacular. Their positive sense of the love of God towards humanity came not from an ivory tower mentality but from deep involvement in the griefs and dangers of life leading them to a still deeper apprehension of Jesus and his redeeming love. In an age when institutions in Church and state seemed to many distant and incomprehensible, delight in the Lord and his works remained alive among such vigorous but basically ordinary people. The fourteenth century saw the emergence of a distinctively lay spirituality, which was given a sharp turn by Wyclif and the Lollards in the anti-institutional direction which was to lead to the Reformation, but it is necessary to stress that the concern to write for the laity and therefore in the vernacular had as such nothing to do with heresy or an attack on the contemporary Church. No one was more orthodox than Hilton – and few writers were more popular. Richard Rolle translated the Psalms into English and Hilton stressed that the uneducated as much as the educated can and should come to grips with the Scriptures. Finally, these writers were either women or writing, at least in part, for women. The importance of devout women, whether in their requests for guidance about prayer or as visionaries and mystics, or again as royal patrons anxious to read and listen to religious books in the vernacular, was a vital part of medieval Church life. Women mystics like Catherine of Siena (1347–80), Catherine of Genoa (1447–1510) and Bridget of Sweden (1303–73) were immensely influential, both through their writings and through the impact they made personally. Catherine of Siena, in particular, was largely responsible for persuading Pope Gregory XI in 1377 to return from Avignon to Rome.

The Church and war

War was endemic in medieval society. The upper classes were, in feudal societies, under an obligation to give so many days of knight-service a year to their lord, in the expectation that fighting would be a regular occurrence. But Christians are called to be peacemakers. So the Church lived with a paradox. That gave rise to discussion of the situations in which war might be just, or even holy. A just war, as defined by Augustine of Hippo, was one designed to redress a wrong already done by the other side. But medieval warfare was often aggressive. The introduction of the Truce of God and the Peace of God were attempts to curb that tendency.

With the late eleventh century came the opportunity for an entirely new and dangerous development – holy war. Muslim rule in the Holy Land began to be seen as a problem which had to be tackled. The Eastern emperor had encouraged that view when he asked for the help of the

West because Eastern Christendom as a whole was threatened by Turkish invasion. The rise of the Seljuk Turks had posed a new threat to access to Jerusalem; after the battle of Manzikert in 1070 had destroyed the armies of the natural protector of the Holy Land, the Byzantine emperor (Alexius Comnenus) appealed for help to the West. Here was an opportunity to rechannel the destructive propensities of knighthood and make it a form of pilgrimage. It was the sense of undertaking a pious effort to protect the places where Jesus Christ had lived and died that perhaps most deeply motivated the Crusaders; it remained important alongside the desire for travel, for booty or for land which were also strong incentives to go on crusade. It also stirred up a new aggressiveness against non-Christians, manifested at home in violent attacks on Jewish communities.

In his proclamation of the Crusade at the Council of Clermont in 1096–97, Pope Urban II (*c.* 1042–99) urged Christians to go East and liberate the place where Christ had died and risen, offering a full indulgence for all and the status of martyr for any who died in the process. The movement eastward that followed was to prove the beginning of the opening up of the West to many new influences in all spheres of life. The armies of the First Crusade were remarkably successful. They took many of the main strongholds in Palestine, where younger sons from the families of the West established their own principalities, at Tripoli, Edessa and Antioch, as well as in Jerusalem. The coronation of a King of Jerusalem seemed an extraordinary achievement but it was not one that the Crusaders, despite the huge castles they constructed in the Holy Land and along the Mediterranean coast, had the resources to maintain, once the initial mass fervour had passed. This kingdom of *Outre mer* ('over the sea') lasted patchily for about a hundred years, with its own king, and with a Western bishop as Patriarch of Jerusalem.

A Second Crusade in 1147 was called after the loss of Edessa in 1144; it was preached by Bernard of Clairvaux and led by Louis VII of France and the Emperor Conrad III. The Crusaders failed to achieve anything of importance, and Bernard had to preach explanatory sermons, for it was a blow to find that God did not ensure that the Crusaders succeeded. Bernard argued that God had wanted to bring Christians up short with the realization of their unworthiness and the need for them to attain a far higher standard of holiness before they could fight a holy war successfully. This had the effect of heightening the sense that the Crusades were something to be thought of as spiritual exercises, and enhanced their 'theological' dimension.

Jerusalem was captured by Saladin in 1189. This disaster provoked a Third Crusade, led by Richard I of England, Philip Augustus of France and the Emperor Frederick Barbarossa. They regained land in Palestine but failed to take Jerusalem, though they arrived within sight of its walls.

In 1202 Innocent III attempted to remedy this by calling for yet another, a Fourth Crusade. This time the army was deflected from its objective and proceeded instead to sack the most Christian city of Constantinople, a scandal which has never been erased from the memory of the Eastern Church. A Latin Empire was set up there in 1204 and lasted for 60 years. All in all the Crusades were enormously damaging. They weakened the Eastern Empire, turned Greeks against Latins and militarized the whole sense of Christian discipleship for the laity of the West. Nevertheless, murderous, intolerant and deeply destructive as the Crusades in large part were, the ideals of the early Crusaders were linked with better things, including the twelfth-century cult of chivalry. Honour, daring and the protection of the weak against the powerful for no gain to self were high ideals common to both the crusading knights and writers of courtly love poetry. The piece of literature most clearly linking the two is *The Quest of the Holy Grail* which reflects the way in which the high idealism of the knight could be linked with an interior spiritual desire for union with Christ in the Eucharist. The Arthurian legends in their twelfth-century revival embody such ideals through the motif of the 'quest'.

Later Crusades were called to reclaim *Outre mer*, but with little success. The idea of the Crusade degenerated into the use of Crusaders as a papal army, most of all against the Albigensian heretics in the Languedoc, but also against the political enemies of the papacy such as the Hohenstaufen in Italy. The crusading idea, which had always been an aberration in terms of the Christian tradition but had appealed to the romantic ideals of the twelfth century, became confused and died a natural death except as a metaphor of the spiritual life. However, the ideal persisted long after the reality, and still informs Chaucer's *Canterbury Tales*, late in the fourteenth century. The pure-hearted knight, the Soldier of Christ, fighting for his Lord and not for himself, was a long way from the crude realities of medieval warfare, even during the Crusades themselves. But it was a necessary justification of war that it should be presented in that way as something a Christian could rightly engage in, without danger to his immortal soul. The penitential codes are less sanguine; they lay down penances for killing or injuring others in battle.

Education and theology

Monasteries and (especially from the time of Charlemagne, who fostered them) cathedral schools kept learning alive in Europe after the collapse of the Roman Empire. The latter differed from the former in that the monastic schools of the West, all still Benedictine until the twelfth century, were normatively 'enclosed'. Exchange of books for copying and of letters went on between them, and the occasional scholarly traveller might bring new ideas. But in general such schools were only as good as the best teachers in the monastery at any given time. Bec in the time of Anselm (late eleventh century) was exceptional in that, it was said, Anselm could make 'seeming-philosophers' even out of 'rustics'. The cathedral schools were much more open to scholarly exchange and could become centres of controversy, as did Laon at the end of the eleventh century. Peter Abelard went there to listen to the famous but ageing master Anselm of Laon, and declared himself unimpressed; he captured Anselm's pupils for himself by lecturing on the notoriously difficult book of Ezekiel, as a direct challenge to the old man.

The twelfth century saw the rise of schools which were to grow into the first universities, under pressure of student requirements for a syllabus and systematic instruction. Students 'read' a text with a master, who 'lectured' upon it to them. That meant taking a short portion of the text and expounding it. Students were unlikely to have the full text before them as they listened. In early commentaries, from the Carolingian period, the tendency was to concentrate at a fairly elementary level upon the difficult words. The trend thereafter was more and more to address the ideas in the text. Then came the need to tackle larger and larger problems to which portions of the text pointed. An example is a passage on 'why God became man' in Peter Abelard's commentary on Romans, written in the middle of the twelfth century. He rehearsed all the arguments currently fashionable in order to reject them, and then advanced his own.

But it was becoming a problem that the sequence of the lecture could be badly disrupted by such large pieces of 'commentary'. In the course of the next century these 'topics' began to swell to a size which made them disruptive of the sequence of the lecture, and it is clear from surviving lectures that students would interrupt with questions. So 'lectures' led to 'disputations'. The disputed passage or theme would be set aside for special consideration later in the day at a *disputatio*. These, too, grew, until it became an essential part of a scholar's training that he learn to handle disputed questions in a formal way, first posing the problem, then assembling all the arguments on one side and on the other, and finally deciding or 'determining' the matter.

A higher degree in the later medieval universities (Master or Doctor) was a warrant that a scholar had reached a level where he could lead such *disputationes* and thus be a university teacher himself. The most used textbook of theology in the Middle Ages was a product of this development. Peter Lombard wrote his *Sentences* in the second half of the twelfth century to try to put the perplexing proliferation of theological topics into a logical order and thus provide a reference book for students. The basic degree was one in arts, while the higher degree subjects were law, medicine and theology, but theology was universally recognized as the queen of the sciences.

The twelfth-century schools became the first universities. The *universitas* was a guild of scholars, exactly like any other guild of craftsmen. It was independent and self-regulating, and the histories of Paris, Oxford and Cambridge in the later medieval centuries reveal a continuing struggle to maintain the privileges of independence. The Church made use of academic expertise in controversies and at councils, but it was always wary of letting scholars have a free rein to teach what they pleased, though the established universities were largely self-regulating. If Wyclif left Oxford and returned to his parish of Lutterworth, where he died in peace, it was not because the Church's hierarchy had condemned him, but because the university authorities had done so, in 1381. A generation later, however, John Huss, for a time Rector of the University of Prague, was condemned as a heretic by the Pope and condemned to death at the Council of Florence in 1415, but his university proclaimed him a martyr. Important as Wyclif and Huss were in theological history, the universities themselves were far more important, and for religion as much as for the wider development of society. As the university system spread across Europe in the thirteenth and fourteenth centuries, they educated many thousands of people, raising the general scholarly standards of the clergy and providing a large literate class able to staff the growing bureaucracy of the state as well as of the Church. As a network of well-organized centres for the study of theology, philosophy and law, they represent one of the supreme achievements of the later Middle Ages, an achievement grounded on a respect for reason just as important as that for faith.

Reform and revolution

Most medieval Church councils were called in order to reform something. The Fourth Lateran Council of 1215 was particularly effective in doing so, but some of the things councils tended to condemn were actually attempts at reform seen as threats by those in authority. The Church has had to deal with two kinds of threat from within itself. The first has been a division between Churches based primarily on non-theological grounds. In medieval Europe there was only one major schism, that between Latin West and Greek East. After some centuries of growing unease between them, they came into bitter conflict in 1054 and, though that was for a time overcome, the Latin sacking of Constantinople in 1204 created a permanent division never overcome, despite many medieval attempts upon both sides. The deep roots of this division lay in the gradual separation of East from West down the language divide between Greek-speakers and Latin-speakers, which had been going on since the fifth and sixth centuries, and the running dispute of the same period as to whether the Bishop of Rome could exercise authority ('primacy') over the Patriarch of Constantinople and the other Eastern patriarchs. The ostensible reasons for the schism included other matters. In the eighth century the Western Church had begun to add the word *filioque*, 'and the Son', to the Creed at the point where believers affirmed their faith in the Trinity, so that they were saying that the Holy Spirit proceeds from both the Father and the Son, and not just from the Father. The Greeks objected to that, more because it was an addition than because of the theological principle involved. They took a very strong view that nothing could be added, at least unilaterally, to the Creed as defined at an ecumenical council.

Various attempts were made to mend this schism during the Middle Ages. Anselm of Canterbury was asked by Pope Urban II at the Council of Bari in 1098 to stand up and make a speech to convince the Greek representatives present that the West was in the right about the *filioque* too and he published a book on the subject, *On the Procession of the Holy Spirit*, four years later. Anselm of Havelberg in the middle of the twelfth century got together with the few Westerners who could speak Greek well enough and representatives of the Greek Church and tried to find a solution. Both at the Council of Lyons in 1274 and at that of Florence in the mid-fifteenth century there were further attempts. The Turkish threat to what remained of the Byzantine Empire persuaded the Greek emperors to offer almost any concession in the hope of obtaining Western help. Once the city of Constantinople had fallen to the Ottomans in 1453, there was no reason to go on. Divisions once begun tend to be persistent and the schism has never been mended.

Dissident groups within Western Europe began to present another kind of schismatic threat from the twelfth century. They raised the question 'what is the Church?' in a new way, because they were, when they began, often very small in number, and had no distinct history as Churches. It was not like the two giants of East and West facing one another. The foundation of the position of the dissident groups was that the visible Church – by which they meant the Church with the Pope or Bishop of Rome at its head – had taken a wrong turning and ceased to be the true Church, so that they were themselves the remnant of God's people, with a responsibility to speak up for the truth. From about 1200, partly thanks to the prophetical writings of Joachim of Fiore, who tried to foretell the end of the world, writers began to take up the cry that the Pope was Antichrist. They looked at the Book of Revelation with its talk of Satan being bound for a thousand years. By the fourteenth century, they were pointing out that the Roman Empire had become officially Christian in the time of the Emperor Constantine at the beginning of the fourth century, and that the thousand years was now perhaps at an end, with Satan freed and dominant over the Church.

None of these dissident groups became separate Churches in any recognized way during the medieval period. It was one of the most important changes of understanding during the Reformation of the sixteenth century that a multiplicity of bodies calling themselves Churches then came into being, and with them a tendency to look for a visible Church only at a local level.

That takes us to the second threat from within the Church: heresy, persistence in an opinion which goes against the faith of the Church. There were two main types of heresy in the Middle Ages. The first overlapped with schism. It arose among many of the same groups as were calling the Pope Antichrist, and for some of the same reasons. In the late twelfth century in Lyons a group formed round a townsman called Waldes and they came to be known as 'the Poor Men of Lyons' or the 'Waldensians'. They were offended by the conspicuous wealth of many bishops and abbots, and they argued that that could not be right. Christ had set an example of poverty and simplicity of life and he had sent his disciples out to imitate him. It also offended them that such corrupt and unworthy persons should claim to hold in their hands the power of eternal life and death through the sacraments.

In fact this issue of 'unworthy ministers' had been addressed much earlier in the Church's history but it had been argued by Augustine and generally agreed (except by his opponents, the Donatists in Africa, whose schism depended precisely upon this issue) that God could act by grace even through an unworthy minister, so that no one's soul was in danger because a priest was evil. But, faced with the worldliness of many of the clergy, medieval dissidents began to attack the whole system, not merely individuals who fell short of the standards of holiness which ought to have gone with their ministry. They began to argue that laypeople did not need the assistance of the clergy to get to heaven. They wanted to read the Bible for themselves, in their own language, and to organize their own worship, which meant appointing their own ministers.

The Lollards of the fourteenth century were the heirs of the Waldensians, and throughout the Middle Ages and into the sixteenth century, these lines of thought were extremely persistent.

The other main type of heresy in the Middle Ages was dualism. In the early Christian period there was already a problem with dualist Gnostics, and Augustine was a dualist himself for the decade during which he was a Manichee. Dualism arose again in the late twelfth century, right across northern Italy, southern France and northern Spain, among the Cathari, or Albigensians, and other similar groups. Dualism provides an alternative solution to the problem of evil from that proposed by Christianity.

Dualists believed that there are two powers in the universe, Good and Evil. They took spirit to be good and matter evil. They believed that human souls are portions of the Good trapped in evil bodies, so that in every human being there is an enduring war of flesh and spirit. The believers were divided into the followers and the elect, with the followers serving the elect. The elect were thought to have the power to transmute evil matter into good spirit by (for example) eating material food. Elements in this system – such as a stress on fasting and especially the avoidance of eating meat; the cultivation of the ascetic ideal; the repression of sexual feeling; the sense of a duality of body and soul in which the body is believed to be constantly trying to lead the soul astray – have also historically been strong in the Christian tradition, and, as Augustine found, it could be hard as a Christian to shake off the heritage of dualism.

The hard philosophical core of this system was that it provided a solution to the Christian dilemma that if God is all-powerful and all-good it is hard to see why there is such a thing as evil. Christians in the West had answered this since Augustine's day by explaining that evil in itself is nothing other than an absence of good. But it was easier for ordinary believers to be carried away by the idea of a war in the world between opposing forces, and the dualist solution was always attractive.

The Church reacted to both types of heresy at first by preaching and then repressively. Repression seemed necessary if the sheer numbers of adherents were to be discouraged. The dualists were attacked by sending a crusade against them, which behaved extremely brutally, and then by setting up a new institution, the Inquisition, authorized by Pope Gregory IX in 1233. This involved sending investigators into a suspect locality and asking questions about the beliefs of local people. Informers were encouraged, and that meant that petty local jealousies could lead to attacks on persons who were not heretics at all. The heretical sects contained mostly ordinary people of little or no education, who were called before the Inquisition and confronted with a set of articles of false belief which they were accused of holding. Many of them must have had the greatest difficulty in understanding what they were accused of or in stating orthodox beliefs when asked. While punishments were imposed and a few convicted heretics were handed over to the secular authorities and burnt, the virtual disappearance of dualism in southern France by the fourteenth century was probably due chiefly to the pastoral preaching of the mendicant orders.

The capacity of heretics to use the Bible to give strength to their arguments, noticeable from the twelfth century, was linked to the desire to have Scripture in the vernacular, though the translation of, for instance, the Gospels into English had been undertaken already in the tenth century, and quite unlinked to dissidence. The Bible was printed in

German in numerous editions well before the Reformation. Nevertheless in England, in particular, the idea of Scripture in the vernacular became linked with Lollardy. This was a reflection in part of the rise of an urban middle class, in and after the thirteenth century, who were articulate and entrepreneurial and did not take kindly to the notion that they must depend upon a priesthood which might be both poorly educated and unworthy in other ways, for their salvation and for the instruction of their souls.

The Waldensians of the twelfth century became the Lollards of the fourteenth and fifteenth, not necessarily by direct inheritance, but certainly in the close similarity of many of their preoccupations. There is evidence that the Lollards formed Bible study groups in private houses, and that on occasion they reached a remarkably high standard of criticism. They were looking to be pilots of their own souls, and to minister to themselves in matters of the Word. There is an irony in this, in that one of the main objects of Wyclif's own hatred was the friars, whom he described, with members of other religious orders, as sects (*sectae*). Much of his ill-will was generated by internal warfare in the University of Oxford, where there were academic parties representing the various orders. But in fact it was the friars, perhaps above all, who were actively providing a ministry of the Word in a period when this had become partly separated from the ministry of the Sacraments. In ordinary parishes the focus of the Eucharist was the act of consecration, and Masses were commonly said without the inclusion of sermons. The friars, like Wyclif, were committed to reuniting sacrament and Word.

The history of the medieval Church was in one sense a disaster for Christendom. It ended with the first multiple and comprehensive schism in the West, and the entrenching of the division between East and West became unavoidable after the failure of the Council of Florence in the fifteenth century. But the thousand years we have been looking at were centuries of enormous achievement. If they are often called an 'age of faith', they are hardly less an age of reason – indeed the protests of the sixteenth-century reformers were in part against what they regarded as an inappropriate use of reason within the realm of faith. But medieval theology, which produced books still appealed to today, depended upon a highly sophisticated application of logic and metaphysics learned from Aristotle and Plato to the realm of belief. The issue of just how reason and revelation relate was always a contentious issue within medieval thought, but virtually everyone was agreed that neither could be abandoned.

In other ways too the medieval Christian achievement was a surprisingly rational one. The great cathedrals, which remain one of the most astonishing examples of human artistic creativity, may be acclaimed as the products of faith, but they were possible only because of an immense advance in engineering. Without the latter, the high stone vaults of a thirteenth-century nave, or, even more exciting, the spire of Salisbury or the octagon at Ely, both products of the fourteenth century, would have been simply impossible. Again, the growth of universities and of a wider literate culture required a massive increase in books and it was out of this demand that printing was invented – a quintessentially medieval response to a medieval need. And nearly all the first books to be printed were religious ones.

Medieval Christianity's greatest failure may perhaps be seen in what was, for a time, its most striking and indeed successful characteristic: the power of the papacy to unify the Church and direct every aspect of society. It had grown and grown, from roots in the early Church and the age of Gregory the Great, to include a hugely extended political and administrative programme formulated by Gregory VII and almost realized by Innocent III. That crashed with the humiliation of Boniface VIII by King Philip of France in 1301 and the physical removal of papal residence from Rome to Avignon by a French pope, Clement V, in 1309. The 70 years of 'Babylonian Captivity' of the papacy at Avignon followed, with a succession of French popes. When this further led, after 1378, to a 40-year-long schism between a pope in Rome and another in Avignon, the Church was sufficiently scandalized for there to be a widespread movement to limit papal authority through that of councils. The scandal provided, in effect, a supreme opportunity for reform, a way out of a papacy which had turned, theoretically, into an absolute monarchy. It was the failure of the conciliar movement to rein in papal autocracy which may well be seen as making the break-up of the Church's visible unity in the next century virtually inevitable. Oddly enough, it was a sort of biblical fundamentalism appealing to Gospel texts like 'Thou art Peter', typical of the later Middle Ages, which made it so difficult for the conciliarists, who lacked any comparable scriptural text, to argue their case convincingly. The medieval centuries saw in consequence of such struggles the first full formulations of ecclesiology, a theory of the Church itself. They saw immense developments in the theology of the sacraments. On every side, the assumptions of orthodoxy were stretched and tested, with great benefits to the Church's ultimate sense of itself and its purpose. The Church which tumbled into the Reformation was, for good or ill, an enormously more sophisticated and complex body than that which had emerged from the patristic period.

5

India

R. E. Frykenberg

The 'arrival' or 'rising presence' of Christians in India[1] was neither sudden nor simple. The spread of Christian belief and congregations within the continent, or subcontinent, of India, moreover, is still an ongoing, uneven process. This process is believed to have begun nearly two thousand years ago, stretching from *c.* 52 CE to the present. No single arrival marks a clear starting point. Broken bits or shards of the Gospel came in small increments; believers also emerged one by one and sometimes in clusters. Each new presence was different in dimension and texture. Main features of this development can be conveniently, if arbitrarily, divided into three conventional categories. For simplicity, identifying waves of Christian arrival as ancient, medieval and modern corresponds roughly to Thomas (including Babylonian/Chaldean/Syrian Orthodox), Catholic (Roman), and Evangelical (Protestant) phases. These terms themselves suggest kinds of particularity in relation to the universality of Christian history: 'Thomas Christians' are the oldest and most narrowly focused; 'Catholic' and 'Evangelical' Christians each have possessed distinctive attributes which, in normative terms, might be applied to Christians almost anywhere. What began as a small and thin stream of Christian presence in Malabar and Mylapur (Mylapore), peoples claiming descent from converts of the Apostle Thomas, has been joined and mingled in complex ways by innumerable later accretions. Each later arrival, moreover, has generated its own kind of internal 'reformation', 'revival' or 'reawakening'. Each also has brought some further particularity or specificity. Obviously, however, as these waves of arrival have turned into ongoing streams and rivers, attention cannot be focused upon all at the same time. The procedure followed here is to assume ongoing but developmental processes within each tradition, even though all details cannot be specified. More concentrated attention is focused upon each new arrival or development at the time of its occurrence.

R. E. Frykenberg

First waves of arrival: the Thomas Christians

The antiquity of Christian communities in India, along with the origins of Christian institutions, is not easy to identify, trace or understand. Questions of historicity and antiquity are matters of amazing complexity – with answers coming from the south and north, east and west. The 'southern' and/or 'eastern' traditions stress maritime origins while 'northern' and 'western' traditions tend rather to the overland. Yet, before either can be examined more closely, it is useful to appreciate how peoples of India have themselves produced, preserved and perpetuated their own unique forms of historical understanding. This understanding is here woven into the story.

That Christians of India have tended to fashion their own historical understandings in ways comparable to those of other peoples of India is hardly strange. They have preserved their own *itihasa-puranas* and their own *vamshāvalis*. Family members have told and retold their own stories – about how the lineages in their own communities first came into being, settled in their own places and developed their own institutions. Their own traditions have indicated that the Apostle Thomas came by sea from Arabia and landed on the Malabar coast. Alternatively, they have shown that he came overland, down from the north. Details of arrival and subsequent events have been celebrated in song and verse for generations untold. Lyrical sagas, such as the *Margam Kali Pattu*, the *Rabban Pattu* and the *Thomma Parvam*, tell about 'the Coming of the Way of the Son of God'.

Distilled to essentials, these sources indicate that the Apostle, after staying in Malabar, sailed around the Cape of Kanya-Kumari and up the Coromandel Coast; that he stopped at Mylapur (now within the city of Madras, recently renamed Chennai); and that, after going on to China, he returned (*c.* 52–58 CE) to Malabar, settled in Tiruvanchikkulam (near Cranganore) and established congregations at Malankara, Chayal, Kokamangalam, Niranam, Paravur (Kottakkayal), Palayur and Quilon. Finally, they indicate that, having trained leaders (*achāryas* and gurus) from high-caste families for each congregation, the Apostle departed from Malabar for the last time (*c.* 69?), leaving behind a strong, self-propagating and self-sustaining community. One poetic source goes so far as to give a demographic and social breakdown (*varnāshramadharma*) of lineage groups (castes) making up this earliest Christian community: namely, 6,850 Brahmans, 2,800 Kshatriyas, 3,750 Vaishiyas and 4,250 Shudras. Significantly, no mention is made of what 'others' (i.e. aboriginals or untouchables: Adivāsis or Dalīts, in today's argot) might also have become Christians. Such groups, in terms of 'Hindu' traditions, would not have

148

been worth counting. What were worth counting were miraculous healings and deliverances performed by the Apostle – 94 from death, 260 from devils, 230 from leprosy, 220 from paralysis and 250 from blindness.

Oral traditions and palm-leaf, copperplate and stone inscriptions, preserved by leading families who claimed descent from Brahman and Nayar lineages, record details concerning the migrations, habitations and places visited by the Apostle. These, according to Placid Podipara (one of many authorities who have devoted years to studying Thomas Christian texts), make clear that many families of Kerala still trace their conversion to the time of the Apostle or to any number of migrations which occurred for many centuries prior to the arrival of the Portuguese in 1498. *Vamshāvalis* (lineage histories) claim hereditary clerical authority as *kattanars* (pastors) or as local *metrans* (bishops or elders) – on the basis of apostolic succession going back to Thomas – and contain as many as 50, 60 or even 70 unbroken generations of office-holders. Leading families claiming such distinction are Kalli, Kalikay, Kottakali, Kayakkam, Madeipur, Muttal, Nedumpalli, Pakalomattam, Panakkamattam and Sankarapuri. Artefacts, especially stone crosses and monuments preserved by *kattanar* families and villages, further reinforce (or vindicate) claims of hoary antiquity and distinction. Apostolic baptisms near one ancient building at Palayur prompted Brahmans to avoid pollution by bathing or drinking at an older temple tank.

All these traditions take the story further, indicating that Thomas returned to Mylapur, perhaps in 69 CE. They tell how a local raja imprisoned Thomas when money entrusted to him for constructing a palace was distributed to the poor; how the raja's brother who had just died was restored to life in order to tell his sibling of the heavenly palaces which the Apostle had just built; and, finally, how the brother's testimony had convinced the raja and seven hundred members of his court to accept the Gospel and become baptized. Yet another story indicates that the Apostle's days subsequently came to a dramatic end when, while walking near Little Mount, he was confronted by Brahmans leading a procession for the purpose of a blood sacrifice to the goddess Kali: the Apostle, refusing to join the event, so infuriated the crowd that it attacked and slew him, piercing his side with a three-pronged lance (*trishul* or trident). A prayer alleged to have come from the martyr's lips as he died is still regularly sung by Thomas Christians, on 3 July each year, to commemorate the historic arrival and mission of the Apostle to India. Traditions relating to the burial place of the Apostle, whether in Mylapur itself (which seems unlikely) or at the little white shrine which now adorns the top of the hill which for centuries uncounted has been known as St Thomas Mount, continue to give special saliency to this indigenous form of 'Apostolic' Christianity in India. Many centuries before the Portuguese arrival, healing powers were attributed to this shrine and its surroundings, even to the dust on its footpaths. Whatever the historicity of such indigenous traditions, there can be no question as to their great antiquity or to their great appeal in popular imagination. Such imaginings are certainly as strong as those supporting claims concerning the rise of early Christian communities in various parts of Europe.

The oldest literary account of the Apostle's missionary work in India is found in the *Acts of Thomas*. This document is of unknown origin, language or provenance. Its earliest surviving versions, which are in Syriac, have enabled scholars to trace it at least to fourth-century Edessa. These clearly show, from their content and contextual detail, that the document itself could have originated in the second century.[2] This wonderfully colourful narrative, while mingling allegory and romance, also depicts actual people and places. The story itself, repeated in various forms and venues, commences in the Upper Room, with apostolic responses to the Great Commission, 'Go into all the world and preach the Gospel'. The Eleven, after dividing the world into regions and drawing lots over who should go where, assigned India to Thomas-the-Twin (Didymus). When Thomas objected, saying that a Jew would have trouble communicating with Indians, his brother apostles turned to prayer, hoping that God would bring about a change of heart in Thomas. At that moment, even while prayers were rising, a royal commissioner of Gundaphorus arrived in Jerusalem. His name was Abban; and his mission was to recruit a master builder who could build a palace for his royal master. Thomas was a master builder (or carpenter – stone being more plentiful in the area than wood). He had served his apprenticeship as a disciple of Jesus. Such were his credentials that he was immediately offered the task. The offer being too good to refuse, royal agent and apostle set off together on the long journey back to India. Many were the strange and wonderful adventures which befell them along the way. In Andrapolis, for example, a Jewish flute-girl became the apostle's first convert. Then, when the king's daughter proclaimed faith in Christ on her wedding day and then refused to participate in the ceremony, a hasty departure had to be made to avert the royal wrath of her father. On their reaching India, King Gundaphorus advanced funds for the new palace. Thomas, disturbed by the miserable plight of countless poor and by the profligate luxury of the rich, felt compelled to distribute all the funds to alleviate suffering. When the king returned from his journey and asked for a glimpse of his new palace, he was told that it was being built in heaven and that on earth Thomas had given the funds to the poor, all the while 'teaching about a new God, healing the sick, driving out demons and doing wonderful things [in the name] of the new God of whom he was preaching' (*Acts of Thomas* 1:1920 [paraphrased here]). Outraged, the king threw Thomas and Abban into prison. That very night, however, the king's brother (Gad) died and went to heaven where, beholding the glorious palace which Thomas had built for his brother, he begged for a chance to tell his brother what he had seen. This boon being granted, the king heard his brother's words (perhaps in a dream) and immediately became a believer, together with many others. All received three signs of grace from the Apostle: anointing with oil ('the seal'), baptism ('the added seal') and communion ('bread and wine' of the Eucharist) (*Acts of Thomas* 2:22–27). Deacons and elders were trained to lead the new congregation. After this the Apostle again set off and established congregations in other parts of India before meeting his death in the realm of King Mazdai, on the eastern coast. His radical teachings against marriage brought about the conversion of many women, including the queen; when she forsook her marriage bed for the sake of piety, her royal husband became so enraged that he ordered Thomas's immediate execution. The Apostle, facing the spears of his executioners at a mount just outside the city, then prayed: 'My Lord and my God, my Hope and Redeemer . . . I have fulfilled your work and accomplished your command. I have been bound but today I receive freedom' (*Acts of Thomas* 13:167; John 20:28). Whether this romantic tale of questionable historicity contains any residue of historical substance we shall never know; but we do know that Gundaphorus and Gad ruled an empire on both sides of the Indus during the years 19 to 45 CE, years when the Apostle could well have carried the Gospel to that part of the world.

Traders, settlers and refugees came from the West to the shores of India. They came in small groups over many centuries. Commercial relations between the Indian and Roman worlds had increased with the discovery of seasonal (*monsoon*) winds which steadily blew ships to India during certain months and then blew them back to Africa and Arabia. Both Strabo and the *Periplus*, a mariners' manual written about the time of Thomas (*c.* 50–73), describe fleets (with ships of up to seven sails and 300 tons) which moved back and forth across the Arabian Sea. Roman peace brought increasing traffic and prosperity. Romans built colonies on the coasts of India; and Indians moved into Egyptian market places where Greeks and Arabs, Jews and Syrians, Armenians and Persians benefited. Sanskrit and Tamil epics mentioned *Yavana* (Greek) ships, laden with glass, gold and horses, which returned with gems, ivory, pepper, exotic animals and birds, especially peacocks. Greek workmen were used to build a Chola palace. Whatever the historicity of the Thomas story, historical evidence confirms that comparable events did happen, so that items in the story are plausible.

Hints of early Christian presence in India are found in writings which date only a century or two later than the 73 CE date for Thomas's death preserved in local traditions. From Alexandria, citadel of early Christian learning, a remarkably gifted Jewish scholar and Christian convert named Pantaenus (mentor of Clement and Origen) determined 'to preach Christ to the Brahmans and philosophers'. According to Eusebius, he went as far as India and 'found that Matthew's gospel had arrived before him and was in the hands of some there who had come to know Christ'. Whether this was the real India to which Pantaenus went cannot be determined; however, 'Brahmans' mentioned by Jerome could hardly have come from anywhere but India. Moreover, Jewish communities such as the Beni Israel (perhaps dating back to the first Exile) were already settled along the coasts of India; and more Jews also arrived after the destruction of Jerusalem in the year 70 (and again in 136). It seems clear that Christian and Jewish communities were already settled along the shores of the subcontinent from the second century onwards.

Evidence of links between Christians in Parthian Persia and in Edessa (now Urfa in modern Turkey) is strong. Due to the religious pluralism of Parthian rulers, Christians were able to organize a religious community and to become an important minority within the Persian Empire. They were mainly middle-class families who were well off, known for their medicine, science and trusted positions within the government. Edessa, the capital of a tiny principality known as Osrhoene, lay between the empires of Rome and Parthia. Often squeezed by one power or the other, it became a leading centre of Christian culture. Its language, an Aramaic dialect known as Syriac, became the literary and liturgical language for all 'Eastern' (Assyrian, Chaldean and Persian) Christians. Its theological scholars became famous. It was there that Tatian (born c. 150) wrote his polemic against Greek cultural dominance over Christian institutions and his *Diatessaron* or harmony of the Gospels, for long the only Gospel used in the East (but condemned in the West). During the reign of Abgar VIII (c. 190), Christians of Edessa and Persia became caught up in controversies with Christians of the West over the date of Easter. When the Romans conquered Edessa in 216, Christians of Mesopotamia and Persia were again caught in the middle, and became increasingly suspect. Ardeshir, founder of the Sassanian dynasty (in 226) and restorer of Zoroastrian religious dominance, reconquered Edessa and Syria in 258, capturing the Roman Emperor Valerian. Zoroastrian priests (*mobeds*) mounted virulent campaigns against Christians. Calamity struck on Good Friday, 17 April 341: in Seleucia-Ctesiphon, the twin cities bestriding the Tigris, Catholicos Simon Bar Sabbae and over a hundred prominent Christian leaders of the empire were put to death by Shapur II. Years of martyrdom and suffering followed.

After the promulgation of Yezdgerd's Edict of Toleration (c. 401: comparable to the Edict of Constantine 85 years earlier), the Persian Church enjoyed a time of restoration. This reached its zenith under the ecclesiastical rule of Catholicos Isaac, 'Grand Metropolitan and Head of All Bishops'. But theological disputes in the West led to a permanent rift with Eastern Christians. Theologians at Edessa and throughout the Sassanian Empire, beyond the boundaries of Byzantium, rejected the Council of Ephesus and its view of Mary as '*Theotokos*' or 'Mother of God'. After 431, ties with the West became weaker and the patriarchate of Babylon or 'The Church of the East' held sway among Christians in Persia and India.

A century before Eastern Christians fell beneath the shadow of Islam, an Indian traveller from the island of Socotra, with the Greek name Cosmas Indikopleustes, wrote a travelogue entitled *Christian Topography* (*c.* 535). This work shows that he found Syrian Christian bishops and communities along the coasts of India and Sri Lanka. By then wars between Sassanian kings and Eastern Roman rulers of Byzantium had brought more waves of refugees to India; and political pressures in Persia prompted a further severance of bonds with the West. By then also the Patriarch of Babylon had long claimed ecclesiastical authority over Malabar Christians. The term 'Nestorian' as applied to all Christians of India at the end of the sixth century was as much a matter of ecclesiastical and geographical distinction as it was a term applied to doctrine or ritual. Missionary ventures across Asia and into China continued to grow well into the thirteenth century. But Muslim expansion in the seventh century cut the East off from Byzantium and the West, more effectively than any previous event: by diminishing communication, it closed off occasions for theological or ecclesiastical contact or conciliation.[3]

The question of why Christianity disappeared so completely from Persia (as also from certain parts of Arabia) remains unanswered. At least two factors may have played a important part in this disappearance. First, in both Syrian and Persian forms of Christianity – after coming out of Antioch and later stemming out of Edessa – language was allowed to come between clerical leadership and ordinary believers. The language of the Church, Syriac (a form of Aramaic), became the exclusive preserve of the learned and literate, the only vehicle for liturgy, through which the Gospel and biblical literature was transmitted from one generation to the next. In Persia and other lands to the east, Syriac was not the tongue of the common people. Efforts made to translate some Scripture, sermons and religious discourses, especially hymns, into Pahlavi were not effective; and, for the most part, the language of the Church remained foreign and could not be understood by the less learned or less literate. Persians had long held a great affection for the beauty of their language. The failure of Christians to use Persian for purposes of faith, worship and scholarship left an enormous cultural void and residual ignorance, a gulf which could not easily be bridged.

Second, Christianity in the East became increasingly, if not predominantly, monastic in character and celibate in normative social doctrines. As a consequence, very little is known about the daily life of the ordinary Christian believer in Persia, or in other eastern lands. While extraordinary missionary efforts and ventures were undertaken, carrying the Gospel to China and India, if not to islands beyond, both the faith and the faithful became increasingly isolated and relegated. Strict celibacy was equated with spirituality: some even suggested that celibacy might be mandatory for gaining eternal salvation. The Persian sage, Aphrates, had written as early as the fourth century that Christians were divided into two groups: the 'Offspring of the Covenant' (*Bar Qiyama*) and the 'Penitents', emphasizing that only those dedicated to an ascetic and celibate life could be baptized while those who were not so inclined were denied baptism. This virtually Manichaean separation between the tiny elite and the masses, between those dwelling in the Light and those consigned to living in Darkness, coming at a time when the Church faced a strong and hostile state religion that inflicted persecutions over long periods of time, greatly weakened the Christian community and left it vulnerable. And while the bar between marriage and baptism did not last, the strict rules of the Bar Qiyama continued to be upheld – with celibacy, prolonged periods of fasting and prayer, vows of poverty, simplicity of food and garb, ceaseless study and silence. Such world-renouncing was not attractive to Zoroastrians. Such ways were viewed as a blasphemy against life itself. Ironically, with the coming of Islam, both Christians and Zoroastrians were marginalized in Persia. Sunni Islam, at least initially, was averse to asceticism and elitism alike, striving to obliterate all distinctions between the religious and not so religious, between specialists and ordinary people. Only Armenian Christians, coming from the homelands and strongholds to the north and west, managed to maintain a clear identity in Islamic lands. Armenians became a striving Christian community, thriving within the Islamicized societies of the East in the centuries which followed.

From an Indian perspective, processes by which Christians, either as refugees or as settlers and traders, had been coming to the western shores of India, at various times for many centuries, both before and after the rise of Islam, can be documented. Such waves can sometimes be dated by looking at grants of lands and privileges which Christians received. These grants, certified or deeded documents on copper, stone or palm leaf, were often later embellished and reinforced in oral traditions. One such tradition indicates that, as early as 293, a great persecution occurred within the Chola kingdom ('Cholamandalam' along the east coast), that 76 families fled to Malabar and settled among Christians of Quilon, and that some refugees came under the influence of a sectarian Tamil Shaiva (presumably *bhakti*) teacher, insomuch that disputes arose over religious rites, such as smearing ashes on the forehead and venerating the five products of the cow. In the year 345, not long after the great persecutions of Christians within the Persian Empire had begun, a community of Syrian Christians landed on the Malabar coast under the leadership of an Armenian merchant banker named Thomas of Kana. Kana was cordially welcomed by the local king, Cheraman Perumal, and given special privileges: formal grants certified in copper-plate and stone inscriptions, which specified exactly which lands his settlers were to occupy and which prerogatives of high status they were to enjoy. The deeds indicate that Syrian Christians were sought after and highly valued along the Malabar coast. As enterprising traders, their activities generated prosperity wherever they settled. Syriac documents indicate that it was the Catholicos of Babylon who sent 'Thomas of Jerusalem' (alias Thomas of Kana), and that when he arrived at Malankara, he was accompanied by a bishop, deacons and a group of men, women and children.

The processes of separation between East and West which increased after the rise and expansion of Islam brought many more Christian refugees across the Arabian Sea, fleeing from persecution in lands immediately to the west and north. A late eighth-century copper plate in Kottāyam indicates that a grant was given by a king named Veera Raghavan Chakravarthi to a Christian leader named Eravi Korthan. Another set of five plates (known as the *Tarisa Palli* [Persian Christian] plates, two in Thiruvalla and three in Kottāyam) shows that privileges were granted by Aryan Aigal of Venad to Marwan Savriso of Tyre early in the following century (*c.* 825); and, later, that King Ayyan of Vencat [Southern Travancore] (*c.* 880) granted privileges to *Tarisa* (Persian Christians), to *Anjunannam* (Jews) and *Mānigrāmmam* (trade guild members, many being Christians). Lands given were demarcated in the traditional manner, by letting a female elephant roam free; and leaders were granted self-government, protection, corvée labour, and bride-price privileges.

Quite clearly, the different Christian communities which evolved in Malabar became, for the most part, an aristocratic elite. Hindu in culture, Christian in faith and Syrian (or 'Nestorian') in doctrine, ecclesiology and ritual, these Christians constituted a complex of high-caste communities whose occupational position, ritual purity and social ranking, as merchant traders, became ever more firmly fixed and well grounded. Within a Brahmanically framed social order (*vārnāshramadharma*) of a 'four-class' or 'four-colour' (*chaturvārnya*) system, most Christians fell somewhere between Kshatriya and Vaishya. Christian cultures – not all being of the same caste (*jāti*) or lineage (*vamsha*) – were far from uniform. Yet all possessed features which were distinctly native to the land, or 'Hindu' in that sense of the term. A new husband would tie a *thāli* around his bride's neck, and perform a ceremonial of investiture of 'marriage cloth'.

Some of the most exclusive (who claimed a pure lineal descent from Thomas of Kana) wore a tonsure. This elite, known as the Malankara Nazaranis, seems to have paralleled Nayars in the nature of their relations with Brahmans and with each other: their places of dwelling were referred to as *tharavād* and their rituals for removing pollution (from *ghee* and *ghur*, as with food and drink and utensils) were very similar. Even in matters of interdining and intermarriage, as also in disposal of dead bodies, Nayars and Thomas (or 'Syrian') Christians became linked. Indeed, as wealthy merchant bankers and traders whose transactions and travels called for armed protection by skilled warriors, the same kinds of training in martial sciences (*kalāri-pāyat*) were given to boys of both communities. According to the *Villiarvattom Pāna*, Malankara Nazaranis scattered across Kerala even went so far as to form their own 'little kingdom', a domain or realm of authority stretching north and south along the coast, with its capital at Mahadevapatnam (Port of the Great God) on the island of Chennamangalam. This was later moved to Udayamperūr so as to avoid Arab depredations. The Udayamperūr Church's place of worship was built, according to Christian tradition, by the Raja of Villiarvattom (*c.* 510); and the kingdom seems to have survived until after the coming of the Portuguese. Only then, after receiving promises of help to defend themselves from Arabs, were the Malankara Christians betrayed and partially conquered. But they were never completely subdued.

In the centuries which followed (and right down to the present), these earliest expressions of indigenous Christianity to be found anywhere in the subcontinent, in both ideological and institutional forms, survived. At least six communities still claim the apostolic tradition of St Thomas as the historic basis both for their origin and for their doctrinal and ecclesiastical authority. These six groups, as found today, are the Orthodox Syrian Church (in two branches), the Independent Syrian Church of Malabar (Kunnamkulam), the Mar Thoma Church, the Malankara (Syrian Rite) Catholic Church, the (Chaldean) Church of the East and the St Thomas Evangelical Church (or factions thereof), along with (formerly CMS) segments within the Church of South India. Virtually all these groups, or branches and subcommunities` thereof, interacted from the sixteenth century onward with representatives of the Roman Catholic Church. As such, they either answered to or resisted the authority of the Portuguese *Padroado* in Goa or directly communicated with the *Congregatio de Propaganda Fide* in Rome.

Responses to the *Padroado* and Propaganda Fide

The story of Christian peoples in the East and in India, from the time of the Mongol conquests onwards for several centuries thereafter, is really the story of indigenous responses to European (*Farangī/Parangi*) expansion within the Indo-Islamic world – military, mercantile and missionary. While there were still large numbers of 'Nestorian' Christians among the Turkish nomads in the steppes of Central Asia, little is known about them except what can be gleaned from Latin records of special missions sent out from Rome, and from descriptive insights brought back by various European travellers, of whom Marco Polo is perhaps the most famous. Under the regime of the Indo-Islamicate, Armenian Christians moved along trade routes and settled in commercial centres, often enjoying considerable influence as servants of Muslim or Hindu rulers. Only after the fall of Constantinople in 1453 and the arrival of the Portuguese at Calicut in 1498, however, does information about Christians and Christian institutions in the East increase.

The Portuguese *Estado da India Oriental* was unprecedented. Year after year, fleets conveyed thousands of *Farangī* soldiers, draining Portugal of its manpower in order to replace huge losses from disease and war. Portugal's maritime empire of fortified stations – stretching along the shores of the Indian Ocean from Mozambique and Mombasa to Muscat, Mumbai (Bombay), Colombo, Malacca and Macau (along with redoubts in the South Atlantic) – survived for nearly half a millennium. Those common soldiers who survived stayed, settled down and married local women. Their offspring formed a residual nucleus of Indo-Portuguese communities which still exists. Beyond the fortified citadel of viceroys and royal officials in Goa, a network of Portuguese influence extended far and wide. This shadowy presence, consisting of freelance adventurers, mercenaries and merchants, and extending over vast stretches of coastal territory, grew stronger even as the power of Portugal declined. After Portugal's annexation by the Spanish Crown, as military power in the East shrank, much of this 'shadow empire' resided in the vitality of its spiritual and ecclesiastical jurisdiction or *padroado* (royal patronage). The power of the institution of the *Padroado*, originally granted in papal bulls during the fifteenth century, persistently and successfully thwarted and undermined papal authority itself. Among the earliest monastic and missionary orders, many enjoying considerable autonomy both from Rome and Lisbon, were Dominicans and Franciscans. These were later joined by others, such as Augustinians, Carmelites, Capuchins and Theatines. None became more influential or controversial than the Jesuits. Many of these *Farangī* (European) Christians in India manifested remarkable degrees of transcultural adaptability – individually, ideologically, and institutionally. From their monastic and collegial training centres, missionary friars and priests went out into the countryside, winning converts and expanding ecclesiastical domains. This process of conversion and expansion often occurred, however, at the expense of India's most ancient Christian communities, to whom we now return.

Indian Christian leaders of Cochin called upon Vasco da Gama in 1502, during his second trip to India, to ask for protection from Muslim and 'heathen' predators, lest the remnants of Christianity left by the Apostle entirely disappear. They presented him with a staff, ornamented in red and silver. This presentation was interpreted as an act of submission. They gave manifold facts about themselves, which were duly written down in European accounts: letters, books and scholarly treatises. They claimed that one of their own lords had once ruled as 'King of Diamper' and that such rule had vanished when his descendants died out and power was seized by the Raja of Cochin. Thus, at least to begin with, the alliance between Europeans and Indian Christians seemed happy. In that initial time of harmony, this alliance was ratified by the Catholicos (or Patriarch) of Babylon. As war erupted between the Raja of Cochin and the Zamorin of Calicut and as Muslims threatened them, Indians and Europeans in Cochin alike found that the alliance could bring benefit. Christians by themselves were never strong enough to gain lasting security from local rajas and yet were powerful and prosperous enough to bring much of the local spice trade over to the Portuguese. Mar Jacob, *Metran* (Metropolitan, or Archbishop) of Ankamāli from 1504 until his death in 1549, wrote to the Pope in 1523, committing his people to the common cause. The Chaldean Catholicos received reports of parades in which gospel, cross, candles and canticles, consecrations, ordinations and other sacraments were jointly celebrated before high altars.

Recorded accounts coming from encounters between Indian and European Christians are heavily one-sided. Except for one or two Syriac letters between Syrian prelates, virtually all descriptions of the Christians of India and events relating to their interactions with Europeans were made by Europeans and as such were bound to have been alien and biased. Descriptions were produced by explorers, friars, merchants or soldiers – by those who travelled along the shorelines or those few who penetrated the interior of the subcontinent. During their first hundred years in India, from when Pedro Alvares Cabrol landed at Cranganore in 1500 and first met Indian Christians, until the Synod of Diamper in 1599 attempted by fiat to impose European (Portuguese and Roman) control upon the whole community of Thomas Christians, Europeans uncovered and gathered huge amounts of data, collating and documenting their findings. Their mania for information was matched by arguments over its worth. Fortunately also for historians, records and reports were made by several contending European interests, not just in Lisbon and Rome, but also in India. In estimates made by these observers, the numbers of Indian Christians varied, ranging from 70,000 to more than 200,000 persons. These Christians were described, initially, as being located in some fifty to sixty congregations scattered widely throughout towns and villages along the littoral shorelines of Malabar and the adjacent foothill uplands of the Western Ghats. Estimates and figures were to grow in the centuries which followed. Thomas Christians, residing in territories under the rule of some twenty rajas and a multitude of petty warlords in Malabar, were all designated as occupying an ecclesiastical or territorial jurisdiction which they called the *Serra* (suggesting, perhaps, uplands which were away from the coast but running parallel to it).

Harmony did not last. Much as the Europeans and Thomas Christians needed each other, both tiny minorities within a vastly complex and hostile environment, too many complications, competing interests and mixed motives were involved. Once hostile Islamic foes had been cleared away from the high seas and from the shores of the Indian Ocean, Europeans became ever more assertive and coercive. First signs of trouble arose in misunderstandings over business dealings or over ritual practices. Stories of dishonest dealings mingled with rumours of ulterior motives and reports of strange ways of conducting worship. Eventually, as Europeans learned more and more about what doctrines were held and what rituals were observed (or not observed) by Thomas Christians, they expressed dismay and shock. Similarly, as Thomas Christians beheld the beef-eating and uncouth manners of Europeans, they were also shocked and dismayed. Worst of all, *Farangī* Christian clergy, backed by the *Estado da India* and the *Padroado*, incessantly attempted to impose their own rites and ecclesiastical authority. The more this occurred, the more Thomas Christian congregations, in turn, resisted such actions, first covertly and then overtly. Conflicts which arose, however, were fraught with inner contradictions and discontinuities, many overlapping and tangled. For the sake of analysis, these can be broken down into those which were cultural (especially in liturgical or ritual matters), political (especially in ecclesiastical or hierarchical matters) and social (especially in approaches to or relations between communities of different ethnicity, both European and Indian).

Europeans were shocked by the strange beliefs and practices of Indian Christians, many of which they attributed to 'heretical Nestorian' ideas preserved by the Church of the East. Since Indian sacred learning and worship were Syriac, the entire corpus of that sacred writ was held to be suspect and tainted. Thomas Christians, in turn, steadfastly refused to acknowledge the Virgin Mary as 'Mother of God' but only as 'mother of

Christ'. Indian Christians also refused to venerate images. Having for so long been surrounded by Hindu idolatry and in close proximity if not solidarity with Islamic and Jewish communities, they abhorred icons, idols or images of any sort, whether of the Virgin Mary, of the Apostles or other heroic patron saints. Furthermore, they not only waited 40 to 80 days before baptizing their newborn infants (depending upon gender), offering their male offspring to God (emulating Hannah and Mary), but they also performed special baptisms and received special gifts (*chattams* or *srādhas*) for the dead, and used oil as well as water. Their *kattanars* (pastors or priests), while coming from highly respected families, dressed no differently from other believers. Indeed, they engaged themselves in secular as well as sacred affairs, even marrying and begetting children. Among their events of great solemnity, none surpassed occasions in which a newly ordained *kattanar* would lead believers in worship for the first time. Guests would come from far and wide, partake together in a sumptuous 'love feast', and bestow gifts and presents sufficient to provide a living endowment or patrimony, part of which the new *kattanar* would then lay at the feet of his Syriac guru. Great festivals were celebrated annually: at Idapalli, Kuravilangtadu, Mylapur, Palāyur, Quilon and elsewhere. Some of these called for days of fasting, confession and prayer, accompanied by nights of dancing, drums and strange music, with tones, tunes and tempos Europeans could neither understand nor appreciate. Some *kattanars* practised 'Hindu' rites – exorcizing devils, determining auspicious or propitious days (for weddings or journeys), healing and making strange and seemingly weird vows. Trials by ordeal (or 'magic'), such as applying appendages to red-hot iron, walking on fire, plunging arms into boiling oil or swimming among man-eating crocodiles (*muggers*), were offensive to the European observer.

Offensiveness seen in Indians was only half the story. Many things done by *Farangīs* grossly offended the sensibilities of Indian Christians – violations of pollution/purity norms most of all. *Farangī* ways of eating and drinking, not to mention gross sexual activity, rapacity and cruelty, convinced Indians that the kind of life lived by many Portuguese was unspeakably scandalous. Finally, and worst of all, was European intolerance and interference. Thomas Christians found themselves branded as 'heretics' and subjected to the horrors of the Inquisition.

At least until the death of Mar Jacob (Metran 1504–c. 1549/52), a semblance of accord and courtesy and ceremonial protocols was observed. Thereafter, ecclesiastical misunderstandings, controversies and schisms broke into the open. So complex were these conflicts that it is difficult to clarify them entirely. Thomas Christians who were part of the Church of the East (known by several names, stemming from Antioch, Babylon, Edessa, Chaldea and Persia) suffered from their own struggles and schisms.

These, exacerbated by European (*Farangī*) actions, reverberated throughout the Chaldean hierarchy, from the Catholicosate (patriarchate) in Syria down to local metrans (metropolitans, archbishops and/or bishops) and *kattanars* in India. When Patriarch Simon Bar Mama died in 1551, his nephew, Simon Bar Denha, was repudiated by the followers of John, or Simon, Saluka. But Saluka, despite help from Franciscan missionaries and confirmation in Rome, was murdered upon his return to Mosul. His successor, Mar Ebed Jesu ('Abdiso'), was also confirmed by the Pope; and after consolidating his patriarchate over the Chaldean Church which acknowledged his authority, he appointed two metrans for India. These, however legitimate their documents, encountered resistance from the *Padroado*. They were confined in a monastery and subjected to indoctrination into the Latin rite. Upon their release and journey to Cochin in 1558, they encountered a metran from the patriarchate which had not submitted to Rome. Eventually, only one metran, Mar Joseph, remained, the other two returning to Mosul.

Mar Joseph established himself among Indian Christians as their high Metran. Influenced by Indian Christian resentments, he repudiated the Latin rite, reaffirmed his allegiance to the Chaldean Church and renewed his attachment to the old ways, abandoning mandatory confession, condemning image worship and insisting that Mary be known only as Mother of Christ and not as Mother of God. Accused of heresy, he was hunted down and arrested, sent to Cochin, Goa and Lisbon for indoctrination, and then allowed back into India, arriving in 1565. Once again, he no sooner resumed his position than he was found to be preaching doctrines of the East, again suffered arrest and trial for heresy in Goa, and was again deported to Lisbon and Rome. Meanwhile, in despair of ever seeing Mar Joseph again and having sent a deputation to the Patriarch of the other (non-Roman) Chaldean Church, Indian Christians were allowed to take Mar Abraham, a new metran, with them back to India. But no sooner had Mar Abraham begun to assert his new authority than Mar Joseph arrived back from Rome, armed with a papal commission allowing him to preach and teach Eastern doctrines.

With the Indian Church also facing schism, Mar Joseph turned to the Portuguese. The Portuguese, meanwhile, having arrested Mar Abraham and shipped him off to Europe, failed to prevent his escape to Antioch. There, aided by the Patriarch, Mar Ebed Jesu ('Abdiso'), Mar Abraham was himself sent to Rome, where appointment to his see in India was reconfirmed. Both the Patriarch and the Pope, who joined together in sending Mar Abraham to India, gave him authority to divide the sphere of Thomas Christians (the Serra) between the two metrans, Mar Abraham and Mar Joseph. But this new arrangement could never be carried out. Mar Joseph had already again been arrested and, for a third time, sent to

Rome (where he was to die in 1569). Mar Abraham, having reached Goa in 1568, with his letters from both Pope and Patriarch in hand, was now once more repudiated by the *Padroado* (for having tricked the Pope). Escaping arrest, he fled to Malabar and began to reordain all those *kattanars* whom he had ordained during his previous time in India.

Such had Mar Abraham's growing authority in India become that, by 1575, the *Padroado* (i.e., the Archbishop and Council of Goa) determined that the Serra should never again be held by any appointee of any Chaldean Patriarchs and that no Metran of Ankamāli (Bishop of all Thomas Christians) should ever again enter the Serra without prior appointment by the King of Portugal and presentation of documents in Goa. Mar Abraham, in the mean time, sent a special confession of faith to the Pope (Gregory XIII) and, simultaneously, sent warnings to Patriarch Mar Abdiso. He claimed that he was in danger of becoming a suffragan of Goa; that the Patriarch might suffer the loss of all jurisdiction and revenues; and that five new Syrian metrans would be needed to shore up the authority of the Eastern Church in India. Meanwhile, another high Metran (Mar Simon) also arrived, representing the other branch of the Eastern Church and its non-Roman ('Nestorian') Patriarch. Again, after a few years, Mar Simon too was caught and deported to Lisbon (there to die in 1599). However, even so, being apprehensive of such an event and in order to safeguard his flock, he had succeeded in appointing a local *kattanar* (Mar Jacob) as vicar-general to carry on the struggle against the Portuguese *Padroado* and Rome, something he did with some success until his death in 1596.

The final crisis of the still largely undivided and 'uncolonized' ecclesiastical authority over India's Thomas Christians began in 1590 and ended with the confrontation, conquest and capitulation of a segment of those Christians at the Synod of Diamper, 20–26 June 1599. Matters came to a head when Mar Abraham refused to ordain some fifty students trained in the Jesuit seminary at Vaipikkottai. This seminary, founded in 1587 and led by Francis Roz, combined studies in Malayalam and Syriac with Latin and Portuguese, comparing Chaldean with Roman theology and liturgy. It also launched campaigns to 'correct' books and remove all traces of Nestorian heresy. Rivalry between Jesuits and Franciscans aggravated and coloured the controversy, the Franciscans defending Mar Abraham from Jesuit accusations. Thomas Christians saw their whole way of life, nurtured for untold generations, endangered. Told that their faith and forms of worship were flawed and their rejection of images – which had for so long made them distinct from Hindu communities surrounding them – was heresy; that everything handed down to them from their mother Church was unacceptable, and that their family ceremonies, customs and traditions were an abomination, Thomas Christians sought to defend themselves. Mar Abraham refused a summons to attend the Council in Goa. The Pope (Clement VIII) then authorized the Archbishop of Goa, Alexis de Menezes, to inquire into matters and to keep the Metran in custody. Even so no attempt to apprehend the old Metran was dared. Falling ill in 1595, he lingered on at Ankamāli until his death in 1597. Yet, 'the last Metran or Metropolitan of the undivided . . . Christians of St Thomas' did not allow himself to die without making last-ditch deathbed attempts to provide for his people. He made sure to appoint his assistant, a metran known as Archdeacon George of the Cross, as his successor and sent word to the Patriarch asking that a new high Metran should be appointed to take his place.

Archbishop Menezes, aware of these events, sent orders to Ormuz that any cleric coming from Chaldea or Persia was to be intercepted. He then began his campaign to bring the whole of the Serra (i.e. all Thomas Christians) under his authority. Advised that making Francis Roz vicar-general would backfire, he grudgingly agreed to recognize George of the Cross, but only on condition that he make an acceptable profession of faith. The Archdeacon temporized and then retreated into remote and inaccessible locations. Finally, after many months, he summoned all *kattanars* to an assembly in Ankamāli. The entire situation was discussed and all *kattanars* present made a solemn pledge: (1) that they would accept no metran not sent from Babylon; and (2) that they would not accept attempts to enforce the primacy of the Pope and the Church of Rome as sole custodian of all Christians.

Learning of these events, Archbishop Menezes sailed down to Cochin to confront George of the Cross. There he was told that he was only a visiting bishop. A large crowd of Thomas Christians gathered and then carefully approached his tent fully prepared for any eventuality: their metran was accompanied by two *panikkars*, fencing masters, with drawn swords, fifty *kattanars* and three thousand armed retainers. Later, at the Jesuit seminary, Menezes preached on the eternal dangers of disobedience, and led rituals which Indians, Hindu and Christian alike, interpreted as symbols of enslavement. On hearing the Patriarch of Babylon described as the 'Universal Pastor of the Catholic Church', he pulled out a document which anathematized and excommunicated anyone who dared to pronounce such blasphemy. Church buildings were forced open, but people refused to enter them. Libraries were destroyed, to eliminate heretical texts. When extremists vowed to kill the prelate, secret agents were set to watch and report every move. Indignation mounted when the archbishop entered Diamper and announced that he himself would begin ordaining *kattanars* who were properly trained and submissive to papal authority. Even local rajas, worried that the *Padroado* would subvert loyalty among their own Christian subjects, tried to stop him.

On 20 June 1599, amidst colourful processions and choral masses of great solemnity, the Synod of Diamper opened. Sermons admonished obedience to the Vicar of Christ. Anathema was pronounced against the Patriarch of Babylon and against any metran daring to think otherwise. Voices supporting the Church of Rome shouted down all opposition, and doctrines held for twelve hundred years were cast aside. Attempts to show that the legacy of one Apostle (Thomas), while different from that of another (Peter), could still be of equal validity, were condemned; and oaths repudiating submission to Rome were nullified. Speaking against the Pope as Universal Pastor or against the Council of Trent (1545–63) was made a punishable offence. For the sake of administrative efficiency, the Church of the Serra was divided into 75 parishes, each with its own Latinized *kattanar*. The entire structure was firmly placed under the *Padroado* in Goa and its historic see transferred from Ankamāli to Cranganore. There, under the shadow of a Portuguese fortress, George of the Cross was to remain until the Pope could appoint a proper bishop. Two years later, Francis Roz arrived and was installed as archbishop.

Yet, even as Menezes returned to Rome where he was hailed for his victory of the faith, struggles with Thomas Christians continued. These struggles were to go on, year after year and century after century (some even coming down into our own time). Archdeacon George came from the ancient and powerful Pakalomattam family, where nephews had traditionally succeeded uncles for untold generations and where skills of bending and not breaking, dissimulating, evading, manipulating and ceaselessly subverting authority were still carefully cultivated and passed on. For forty years, until his death in 1640, he contended against one European prelate after another, using every kind of stratagem and subterfuge he could devise to defend the ancient institutions. Roz, despite fluency in Malayalam and Syriac, failed to win mastery and died in 1624, a deeply disappointed person. Stephen de Britto, his successor, applied kindness and compromise in attempts to do what excommunication had not done. He died in 1641 having failed also. The severity of his successor, Francis Garcia, eventually drove George's successor (and nephew), Parambil Tumi (or Thomas, known to the Portuguese as Thomas de Campo), into full rebellion.

Thomas Christians simply did not want any *Farangī* to rule over them. In 1653, they made new attempts to bring a prelate from Babylon, Diabekr or Alexandria. When this was thwarted, enraged *kattanars* gathered in solemn assembly at Koonen Cross of Mattanceri, on 3 January 1653. Again, at Vaipikkottai and at Manat thereafter, they gathered to declare, under oath, that they would not accept any *Farangī* prelate or any metran from outside the Eastern Church. The Malankara Church, to this day, marks that event as the moment that their community recovered its independence and rediscovered its own true nature. Thomas Christians then determined to go even further. Since access to all Patriarchs of the East had been denied them by the Portuguese blockade, so that no new metrans could be sent to them, they decided that they themselves would consecrate one of their own. This action, by their calculations, would only require a solemn laying on of hands by twelve *kattanars*. Thus, on 22 May 1653, for the first time in their long history, they installed their own high Metran. Amidst overwhelming support and rejoicing, Parambil Tumi (Archdeacon Thomas) took the title Mar Thoma I and became India's first truly native archbishop. His supporters claimed that, out of 200,000 Indian Christians, only 400 still gave any loyalty to Garcia. Garcia and the authorities in Goa, having lost all ecclesiastical sway in the Serra, strove in vain for ways to counter Mar Thoma.

Meanwhile, keeping itself well informed about the deteriorating situation in India, Propaganda Fide in Rome decided to send four Carmelite missionaries to remedy the situation – an action which, by then, required Dutch assistance. But when they arrived and found they could do little without formal papal authority, they returned to Rome to report their findings. Action was taken to bypass the *Padroado*; but when their Carmelite appointee (Joseph Sebastiani), who had been secretly consecrated and dispatched to the Serra, arrived, he too failed. The Raja of Cochin had already taken the matter into his own hands, to determine which of the two sides should be given ecclesiastical authority. Each side had to appear before him to plead its case. Submission of this kind of dispute to any secular ruler in India was an event of fateful significance. It set a precedent for court cases and appeals which were to continue for centuries (some cases are still pending or being appealed). Nor was this the only such action. Just a decade later, in 1663, the Dutch conquered Cochin and forever ended Portuguese rule in Malabar. Thereafter, neither *Padroado* nor Roman missionaries could ever be strong enough to impose their authority unilaterally upon Indian Christians. Bishop Joseph was given ten days to pack up and leave. Behind him, he left a hastily consecrated Indian bishop, Parampil Chandi Kattanar (Alexander de Campos), as high Metran for the Thomas Christians but he had still to contend with Metran Mar Thoma for their loyalty. The two metrans, however divided by personal and ecclesiastical rivalries, were cousins: both belonged to the same ancient Pakalomattam family and both were well versed in all the old ways of their community – one looking to Rome and the other to Babylon for support.

* * *

Another sphere of *Farangī* Christian influence in India, during the 'high noon' of Indo-Islamic dominance within the subcontinent, was perhaps their most successful. This lay outside Portuguese-ruled areas, both within Hindu realms and within realms in which the high rulers were Muslims, even when most lesser rulers and subjects were non-Muslim. This influence touched different communities in different ways, sometimes being a form of composite ecclesiastic-cum-evangelistic socio-cultural expansion and, in others, more clearly cultural and social in its character. The former was more appropriately applied to low-caste communities, which were often already beleaguered or marginalized segments within essentially hostile socio-political economies; and the latter was aimed at the very highest levels of cultural, social and political privilege. In both kinds of encounter, the ultimate aims were the same: to bring about the conversion of non-Christian communities, and to incorporate them into the larger, worldwide ecclesiastical communion of the Roman Catholic Church.

In either case, and in every instance, efforts were carried forward by monastic orders or societies of disciplined European missionaries working through their native-Indian agents and assistants. These spent their entire working lives in dedicated service to the cause for which they had been ordained, often dying in lonely and obscure places, often suffering from strange maladies and diseases, and sometimes, in words used by Eusebius over a millennium earlier, 'drinking the cup' of martyrdom. Almost invariably, also, many became inextricably involved in conflicts and controversies. These took place as much between fellow missionaries as with peoples around them or among whom they worked. Their stories are among the most fascinating unsung stories of human history, but only a few of the more prominent and well-known can be retold here. They tell what happened among the seafaring Paravas along the Gulf of Mannar; what happened within the courts of those Hindu Nayaks who ruled in Madurai, Ramnad and Shivaganga; what happened within the royal and imperial courts of the Mughals in North India; and, finally, what legacies of scholarship and educational institutions began to expand from the eighteenth century onwards. Interestingly, many of these enterprises, each focusing upon a different and discrete kind of Indian culture, were Jesuit. Each was a manifestation of the revitalized Church of Rome, by then militantly pursuing its post-Tridentine or Counter-Reformation agenda through the agency, after 1622, of its exclusivist and expansionist *Congregatio de Propaganda Fide*.

Paravas are an independent, seafaring people who, for ages uncounted, have inhabited the shorelines on both sides of the Palk Strait. Dwelling in sixty or more hamlets and towns along a hundred-mile coastline of the Gulf of Mannar from Vembar (near Rameswaram) to Kanya Kumari (Cape Comorin), they were fishermen, pearl-divers and seaborne traders (occasionally given to piracy and smuggling). Their hazardous, ritually polluting work required courage, resourcefulness, strength and other survival skills. Yet, hardened adventurers as they were, they were also threatened and oppressed by stronger predators coming from inland fortresses or from deep-water fleets. Arab and Lubbai (Tamil) Muslims constantly threatened, raided, pillaged or enslaved them.

What brought matters to a head was the long and savage maritime war with the Zamorin of Calicut (1527–39). Fearing extermination, Paravas approached a converted Chettiar merchant (John da Cruz) to ask for protection from the Portuguese. Fifteen Paravas accompanied him to Cochin to plead their case, sealing their appeal by becoming baptized. When a formal delegation of seventy followed, led by Vikrama Aditha Pandya, their *jāti thalavan* (caste headman), the Portuguese recognized their strategic importance – and the prospect of also gaining complete control of lucrative pearl revenues. A year later, when Peter Gonsalves (Vicar of Cochin) and three *kattanars* sailed to the Gulf of Mannar on behalf of the *Padroado*, the entire community of some 20,000 pearl-fishers was baptized, the men *en masse* and their womenfolk and children shortly thereafter. By the end of 1537, the entire community of Paravas had declared themselves Christian. At this, maritime Muslims along the Coast took alarm and, with naval support from the Zamorin, launched a major attack. A tiny Portuguese force of three ships fortuitously arrived just in time to join the fight. After a long and furious battle at Vedālai, on 27 June 1538, ending in defeat for the Hindu and Muslim forces, notice was served that the Paravas and the pearl trade would be protected. Henceforth they enjoyed a time of unprecedented prosperity and affluence, especially among their leading families.

At that point, however, the Paravas were Christian only in name. Their forms of worship were still thoroughly Hindu. They knew next to nothing about their new faith or what it entailed. When Francis Xavier landed on the 'Fisher Coast' a decade after their tactical conversion, his orders were to consolidate their attachment and to teach them doctrine. He knew as little about Hindu and Muslim culture as Paravas knew about things Christian. He wrote 'The invocations of the pagans are hateful to God, since all their gods are devils'. As he and three Tamil-speaking assistants walked from village to village, building prayer-houses and baptizing unbaptized children, crowds of quick and bright-eyed boys who clamoured about him day and night were drilled in imperfectly translated essentials of the faith – the Paternoster, the Ave, the Creed and the Commandments. As Xavier had no knowledge of Tamil and no lexicons or grammars, parts of the simply worded catechism were bizarre. The Paravas, like all Indians, literate and illiterate alike, possessed an amazing capacity for learning by rhythmic rote recitation. Words ceaselessly inculcated, details imparted on verandahs at the end of each day, conveyed bare rudiments of worship, pointing out the evils of idolatry, blood sacrifice and various social ills as Xavier witnessed them. Crude copies of the basics were written and left in each village, with the literate asked to write things down. These were to be recited aloud every morning and evening. Attempts were made to train and ordain a *kanakkapillai* (catechist/accountant) for each village, someone to keep track of births, deaths and marriages within each lineage (*vamsha*), thereby preserving community pride and solidarity. When families from other communities – Karaiyars, Shanars, Kaikolars, Pallars and Paraiyars – asked for baptism, they too were drawn into the fold. On the western 'Fishery Coast' (belonging to the Travancore Raja), another fishing community of ten thousand Mukkuvas were baptized (in late 1544).

When Francis Xavier left for Malacca in August 1545, after some months at St Thomas Mount (Mylapur), he made sure that missionaries and clerics would carry on what he had started. One of these, Antony Criminali, was slain when he tried to preach to pilgrims near Rameswaram. But Henry Henriques, despite illness and depression, remained in Tuticorin for fifty years and became the first European missionary to make substantial Christian contributions to Tamil, Sanskrit and Telugu literature. When Xavier returned to the Coast for a last brief visit in 1548, the Paravas paraded him to their main church place in Tuticorin. The Parava Christian identity established by Xavier, and strengthened by his *padroado* successors, has remained firm for more than four and a half centuries.

But the Christian culture which evolved also remained the *jāt* or 'birth' culture for Paravas. In effect, their religion continued to be Hindu or thoroughly 'nativistic' in character. The *jāti thalavan* of all Paravas, for example, became their 'little king' and, as time went on, his position became ever stronger. It was he who led the faithful in processions to the Great Church or Mother Church (*Periya-Koyil* or *Māda-Koyil*) of the Virgin known as Our Lady of the Snows, a cultic patroness whose position became comparable to that of any other tutelary avatar of the Great Goddess (*Mahādevi*: e.g. Minakshi, Kali). It was he who occupied the special throne situated just below her statue and who unveiled her image or adorned it with garlands and jewels on great occasions, such as his installation or marriage. It was he who led the great festival of the Golden Car. This ten-day event, which began to take its modern form in the 1720s, involved thousands of people dragging a huge-wheeled vehicle bearing the statue on its annual *Rath Yātra* through the streets of Tuticorin surrounding the Great Church, doing so to the beat of drums, the chanting of hymns and prayers, and the festooning of garlands from the statue's neck. These rituals of Parava Christianity had the approval of the *Padroado* (but not of all Jesuits).

But what happened in Madurai, not far from Tirumal Nayak's palace, certainly did not win unqualified approval from either *Padroado* or Propaganda Fide. If Francis Xavier had dealt with the lowest, most polluting segments of Tamil society down on the Fisher Coast, Roberto de Nobili dealt exclusively with the highest and most pure. What he achieved called for mastery of the purest forms of classical Sanskrit and Tamil language, literature and lore. Overshadowing Madurai in the ancient Pandya city were the four huge tower-gateways (*gopurams*) of the Minakshi-Sundareswarar Temple. Many thousands of devotees daily entered these gates for its endless rounds of ceremony and festivity. To this centre of Tamil culture flocked throngs of students from the farthest corners of the land, to pursue advanced studies in philosophy and sit at the feet of renowned local master-teachers.

To this place came the young Italian aristocrat, a nephew of Cardinal Bellarmine. Here, in November 1606, Errama Chettiar found him a simple mud and thatch place to lodge. Here, with his two (Thomas) Christian colleagues, Vishvāsam and Malaiyappan, and his newly attracted guru, Shivadharma, de Nobili began his own career as a scholar–missionary. His aim was to win Brahmans for Christ and, as much as humanly possible, to become a Brahman himself. He determined that, aside from matters of faith, he would avoid any action or word which might in any way offend any Indian and that he would do every thing he could to become a master of every possible aspect of Vedic learning. As he gained fluency in the tongues and texts of the Agama and the lore of the Alvar and Nayanar poets, he proclaimed himself also to be a 'twice-born' wearer of the 'sacred thread'. To support such claims, he scrupulously abstained from all possible forms of pollution – eating no flesh, having only one simple meal a day, drinking nothing tainted (except for the Eucharist), touching nothing which defiled, donning only the ochre robe of a *sannyāsi* and strictly observing rules of ritual purity. Public debates, showing his penetration of this intellectual stronghold of Vedanta orthodoxy, brought opposition, especially when he began to baptize high-caste converts, first just a few and then in increasing numbers. By Easter of 1609, after he had withstood a series of accusations and false charges, the number of such baptized converts reached fifty. Twelve, baptized a short time later, included his beloved guru and friend, Shivadharma. In his Tamil manifesto, written on palm leaf and posted in front of his house, he declared: 'I am not a *farangī*. I was not born in the land of the *farangīs*, nor was I ever connected with their [lineages] . . . I come from Rome, where my family holds a rank as respectable as any *rajas* in this country.' By refusing to be linked with *farangīs* (by which he meant Portuguese and perhaps all crude, meat-beef eating, alcohol-drinking barbarians from Europe), he alienated some missionaries and provoked controversy. In determining to be identified only as an Indian, even to taking the name Tattuwa-Bhodacharia Swami, Roberto de Nobili became the 'Roman Brahman'. For fifty years, at least until his death at Mylapur in 1656, he established a remarkable tradition.

The high learned tradition established by Christians of Nayaka Madurai, with its emphasis upon contributions to scholarship and writing in the languages of India, set a standard of excellence for succeeding generations. The great monastery at Shembhaganur became one of the finest repositories for rare manuscripts. The most renowned European–Tamil Catholic sage, known locally as Virumāmani or as Dharya Nāthaswami, was the Italian Jesuit Constanzo Giuseppe Beschi (1680–1747). The long list of his Tamil writings – epic poems in classical (Sangam) style, philosophical treatises, commentaries, dictionaries, grammars, translations and polemical tracts (some intended for Hindu Christians and others for the persuasion of non-Christians) – put him in the very forefront of Tamil scholars during his own day and left a rich legacy for later generations. His epic poem *Tembāvani*, together with his commentary on the *Tiruvalluvar Kural*, had a profound influence in his own day and could well have prepared the way for radical mass movements of conversion which began more than a half century later. Surviving anecdotes about some of the controversial public disputations with Brahman scholars (*archāryas*) and Hindu mendicants (*pandarams*) made him famous and give some indication of the notoriety which he gained.

The royal style in which Beschi lived and moved is indicative of acculturation in south India. As Virumāmani, Beschi's public appearances matched that of the Shankaracharya of Kanchipuram. Travelling in state, wearing a long tunic bordered in scarlet, covered by a robe of light purple, with ornate sandals or slippers, white-and-purple turban, pearl and ruby earrings, rings and bangles of heavy gold and a long carved and decoratively inlaid staff, he was carried in a sumptuous palanquin, with a tiger's skin to sit on, two attendants to fan him, another holding a purple silk parasol surmounted by a golden ball to keep the sun from touching him, and a spread tail of peacock's tail feathers going before him (symbol of Saraswati, the goddess of wisdom). Some years before retiring to a more austere and monastic isolation in Manapad on the Coast, on the occasion of his attending upon Chanda Saheb in Tiruchirapali, the Nawab publicly honoured him in his durbar. He was given the title 'Ismattee Sannyasi', presented with the inlaid ivory palanquin of the Nawab's grandfather, awarded an tax-exempt estate (*inām*) of four villages worth an annual income of 12,000 rupees, and appointed *diwan*, or minister of finance and civil administration. Thereafter, Beschi's 'circuits assumed all pomp and pageantry with which Hindoo gurus usually travel, along with the civil Mahomedan honours, such as chobdars, sawars [horsemen], drums, fifes, caparisoned state horses, hurcarrahs [informers/messengers/

spies], daloyets [shieldmen with spears], nowbuts [kettle drums], and tents . . .'⁴

In the north, meanwhile, Jesuit missionaries enjoyed their greatest access during the reign of the first Grand Mughal, Akbar. Akbar was the grandson of Babur whose skill had enabled a small Timurid army to conquer Delhi, and son of Humayun who had managed to restore Mughal hegemony in 1555. While illiterate, Akbar had an acute and inquiring mind. His durbar was open to notables from every community. His palaces were filled with the daughters of nobles and kings, each from a royal family having a different religion and having a father with whom he forged an astute marriage alliance. With each elite community, of whatever faith, he forged a family bond of mutual loyalty, symbolized by *namak-hallal* ('salt-faith'), so that he became domestically and personally identified with each community's religion. At Fatehpur-Sikri, within his spacious new redstone 'Hall of Discussion' or *Ibādatkhana*, he took delight in his role, as *Imām-i-Adil*, of being the equitable umpire or supreme arbiter of all debates. Seated at the centre of an elevated stone structure which resembled a huge spoked wheel, with disputants from different persuasions sitting around the rim, each occupying a place at one end of a stone spoke, he could turn to face any discussant. Protagonists facing each other around the rim, initially just Sunnis and Shias, soon included Brahmans and Buddhists, Jains and Christians, along with Kayasthas, Kshatriyas, Khattris and representatives of many theological perspectives. It was into this maelstrom of disputations that Jesuits were plunged.

The presence of Christians in the Mughal Durbar was, for the most part, cultural and diplomatic. It left very little lasting legacy in India. While diplomacy brought missionaries into Mughal cities or, when Mughals were on the march, into Mughal encampments, only in the time of Akbar (1556–1605) was there a limited freedom to roam or to spread the Christian message. Three successive missions came during that reign, with adequate communication occurring only during the third. These began when a garrulous secular priest sent by the Bishop of Cochin managed to arouse the emperor's interest, so that he sent an embassy to Goa requesting two learned missionaries and a Persian interpreter. The Jesuits who returned with his ambassador – Rudolf Aquaviva, Antony Monserrate and Francis Henrigues – failed to evoke more than the Padshah's periodic and quixotic enthusiasm and found themselves frustrated and disappointed. Mughals and their nobles were interested in European ideas, and in the latest developments of science and technology. Clocks and firearms, mathematics and medicine, libraries and telescopes interested them much more than disquisitions which qualified the absolute oneness of God. Only the third mission managed to achieve a moderate influence within the Durbar. This was largely due to the accident of its being headed by someone with enough energy, insight and perseverance to master a modicum of Persian. Jerome Xavier (the great-nephew of Francis Xavier) managed to have a long conversation with Akbar and to write what he learned, in a book which he dedicated to the memory of the Padshah. Akbar, ever cautious, refused to be drawn on his own theological views. He merely reminded Xavier that whereas under previous monarchs none would have dared to affirm the divinity of Christ, they could now do so without being concerned about their personal safety. Armenian Christians came and went freely, occupying places in the Durbar and participating in the great discussions. But, beyond diplomatic contacts, Jesuit efforts met with disappointment.

Evangelical and Enlightenment impulses

It is clear that, after the Portuguese arrival in 1498 and the establishment of the *Estado da India*, Catholic orders under the *Padroado* of Goa enjoyed considerable autonomy from either Rome or Lisbon. From monastic and collegial citadels, missionaries went into the countryside, winning converts and expanding clerical domains, often at the expense of ancient Christian communities, gaining whole communities along southern shore-lines, and establishing a high-profile learned tradition, only failing to make significant inroads in Mughal India. Events of the eighteenth, nineteenth and twentieth centuries mark a time of overlapping processes and increasing complexity. While Virumāmani Swami was penetrating and leaving a profound impact upon Tamil learning at its highest levels, German Evangelical missionaries arrived in Tranquebar in 1706. They also began to set in motion a train of events which, while doing the same thing, did so from a radically different direction. Tamil Evangelical Christians soon received land grants from the Rajas of Ramnad, Sivaganga and Thanjāvur, for the support of their model schools.

The modern epoch, initially marked by the decline of Indo-Islamic and the rise of European power, was one in which what was 'Christian' too often became confused with what was European (*Farangī*). Out of the turmoil of the eighteenth century, an all-embracing British Indian Empire emerged. After the coming of William Carey to Bengal in 1793, transcultural interactions and conversions in India increased. Under the impact of the modern missionary movement, Evangelical and Catholic institutions and conversion movements spread until they reached tribal peoples in the remote corners and frontier areas. These events had profound consequences for Hindu and Muslim cultures in the subcontinent. The imperial system was eventually challenged by the Indian National Congress (led by Gandhi and Nehru) and the All-India Muslim

League (led by Jinnah). The politics of protest and the politics of competitive communalism led to the Partition of the Raj in 1947, leaving the successor states of India and Pakistan (from which Bangladesh broke in 1971), Burma, Sri Lanka and Nepal. Thereafter, despite the gradual decline and disappearance of Western missionaries, radical religious movements and remarkable cross-cultural transformations took place within the various 'Hindu–Muslim' environments of the subcontinent. These, in turn, led to the rise of fundamentalisms of many different kinds, some of which have challenged the very existence of Indian Christianity in all its manifold forms. Much of this process, one can perhaps suggest, began in Tranquebar.

* * *

A remarkable blending of Enlightenment Thought and Evangelical Pietism led to the sending of two young Germans as Europe's first Evangelical (non-Catholic or 'Protestant') missionaries to India. Out of the sufferings of the Thirty Years War came the Pietist Movement (sometimes called the Second Reformation) and, subsequently, the Evangelical (or Great) Awakening of Britain and America. Moravian Pietists fleeing from persecution; Count Zinzendorf's shelters for refugees at Herrenhut; Professor August Hermann Francke's theologically based educational innovations at Halle University; and private collaborations between pious royal cousins, Queen Anne of England and King Frederick IV of Denmark: these were but a few components underlying the rise of a new kind of ecumenical voluntarism which led to the forming of a new international missionary consortium. The formation of the SPCK (Society for Promoting Christian Knowledge) in 1698, of the SPG (Society for the Propagation of the Gospel in Foreign Parts: 1702) and of the Royal Danish Mission (supported by the SPCK) can be seen as the precursors of the modern missionary movement which would gradually proliferate and then circle the globe. These agencies carried with them the latest ideas about education and the most advanced forms of scientific thinking and technology. They carried new educational methodologies developed at Halle during the previous generation – ideas which were, at that very time, bringing rapid changes to societies within northern Germany. Francke's dictum – that proper belief was biblical belief, that biblical belief without literacy was impossible and, hence, that universal literacy and education were, in a very fundamental sense, intrinsic to the Great Commission – was unprecedented. Not only should every human being, child or adult, of whatever age or gender, be able to read the Bible in his or her mother tongue; but, Francke also believed, every person should have some useful manual skill (a Rabbinic idea long held among Jewish communities). For Christians, in short, *Kindergarten* and *Kunst Kammer* ('Room of Wonders':

173

combining library and laboratory, with microscopes and telescopes) were essential. The ideal of providing basic literacy and practical aspects of mathematics and modern science to all people, everywhere in the world, had revolutionary implications for any society. To strive for this ideal in Tamil South India was profoundly radical.

Evangelical (or Protestant) Christianity gained its first foothold in India when, in July 1706, Bartholomaeus Ziegenbalg and Heinrich Plütschau landed at Tranquebar (or Tarangambadi). This Danish trading seaport close to rich lands of the Kaveri Delta, which had been leased from Raghunath Nayaka of Thanjāvur in 1620, remained largely sheltered from the wars which were then incessantly devastating the country. Previously, while Dutch Reformed chaplains of Jan Company, such as Abraham Rogerius and Philip Baldaeus, had written about Hindu cultures and while a tiny Brahman-Christian community had grown up in Jaffna, Evangelical efforts had been minimal. Initially, Ziegenbalg and Plütschau encountered hostility: Danish merchants wanted no 'meddling' which might endanger profits. The governor (J. C. Hassius) arrested and harassed the newcomers, even putting Ziegenbalg in Daneborg Fortress for four months. Despite persecution and many afflictions, however, the missionaries were resourceful enough to survive. Help came in 1709, with the arrival of Johannes Ernest Gründler.

University trained as these missionaries were, they began by offering to teach children of resident Europeans. While doing this, they also systematically applied themselves to other tasks: mastering local languages; establishing schools (for as many as possible), including a seminary for training Tamil teachers; translating schoolbooks (including both Scripture and sciences) into Tamil; setting up printing presses (with fonts sent from Halle); and, perhaps most significant of all, collecting and studying as many manuscripts as they could find (so that Halle today possesses one of the finest collections of oriental manuscripts anywhere in the world). As small congregations of Tamil began to be formed, Tamil disciples were trained as catechists, pastors and teachers. Every convert who showed any ability or willingness to help was given responsibility. As the numbers of trained Tamil teachers and pastors proliferated, plans were made to extend the Halle system to the whole of Tamil country, from Madras to Negapatnam (and even to Jaffna).

To accomplish all this, however, something had to be done to end the opposition of the Danish East India Company's Tranquebar governor. When Plütschau's journey to Europe in 1711 for this purpose failed, Ziegenbalg himself decided to go and plead for help. His trip was completely successful: he himself was named Provost of the Tranquebar Mission; the belligerent governor was replaced by an ardent supporter of missionary work; he returned to Tranquebar with Maria Salzmann as his wife; and he completed the building of Jerusalem Church, a large and beautiful edifice, in the place of the ramshackle structure erected in 1707. But, suddenly, a nearly mortal blow fell. The extremely narrow-minded new head of the Home Board, Christopher Wendt, sent a devastating letter to the missionaries. Ziegenbalg – gifted, emotional, sometimes impetuous, but wholly dedicated – was so deeply wounded that he never recovered. Already in precarious health, he penned a careful and judicious reply, 'with his heart's blood', while his condition deteriorated: he died early in 1719, at the age of 36. New missionaries, arriving four months later, delivered another missive heavy with condemnation. Gründler, Ziegenbalg's close and competent friend, was so overcome that he too succumbed within a few months. These fatalities so shocked the home authorities that Wendt, in due course, was dismissed and his theories abandoned. Abandoned also, however, were memories of the Ziegenbalg dreams and plans, with the excitement they had generated.

What made Ziegenbalg's work so distinctive was the level and volume of his scholarly accomplishment. In this, his output can be compared with that of Beschi. Extremely gifted in languages, he became a master of Tamil in both its classical and local forms, using comparisons between palm-leaf manuscripts in his huge collection and some three hundred books to ascertain varieties and idioms. In so doing, he brought learned Tamil closer to ordinary people. He was the first scholar to complete a Tamil translation of the entire New Testament, a work which was printed in Tranquebar in 1715. As early as 1709 his attitude toward Indian peoples and their religions had begun to change, as he became increasingly amazed at the depth and quality of their philosophical insights, learning and wisdom. His most notable work, *Genealogy of the Malabarian Gods* (MSS, completed in 1713), which sought to discover what Hindus themselves believed, was not appreciated at home. Francke, writing that 'Missionaries were sent out to extirpate heathenism, and not to spread heathenish nonsense in Europe', failed to see its significance: namely, that sharing the Gospel required gaining a deeper understanding of Hindu culture. Ziegenbalg's other monument was buried for nearly three centuries under twenty coats of whitewash over the door of an ancient building in Tranquebar. The Tamil inscription *Dharmappallikkūdam* or 'Charity School' symbolized the Francke vision: that every human person should be able to read God's Word in his or her own tongue. In this, he and Francke were united.

On more than one occasion between 1728 and 1731, these new model schools caught the attention of Rajanayakam, a *servaikāran* or captain of the palace guard at Thanjāvur. He and his brother, with fellow soldiers, became instrumental in bringing one of these schools, with a prayer-house, into that kingdom and in obtaining a royal land-grant (*inām*) for its support. Aaron, a high-born Vellālar soon to become the first ordained Tamil Evangelical minister, also began to serve village congregations in the kingdom; Rajanayakam also became a preacher. By then the Evangelical community in India consisted of six Europeans (mainly German Lutheran), dozens of Tamil catechist pastor–teachers (e.g. Savarimuthu) and about fifteen hundred 'confessing' believers (a figure which cannot now be documented).

Among the Europeans who succeeded Ziegenbalg, the most outstanding were Benjamin Schultze (1719; Madras: 1727–43) and Philip Fabricius (Madras: 1740–91). Schultze initiated work with Telugus, compiling a dictionary and producing a grammar, collecting manuscripts and translating the Gospels. Fabricius worked to perfect what Ziegenbalg had begun, completing a Tamil grammar (in English), an English–Tamil dictionary, a translation of the entire Old Testament, and a totally revised version of the New Testament, something Vedanāyakam Sāstri extolled as 'the gold translation of the immortal Fabricius'. Alas, due to fiscal ineptitude, he was to suffer embarrassment and spend his last years in a debtors' prison.

The most renowned of all European Evangelicals in eighteenth-century India was Christian Frederick Schwartz (1750–98). In the annals of Indian Christian expansion, his name stands beside Xavier, Nobili, Beschi and Ziegenbalg. For fifty years, his Indian disciples moved across South India – from Tranquebar to Tiruchirapalli, to Thanjāvur, to Tirunelveli and even to Kanya Kumari (Cape Comorin) and Travancore. Fluent in Tamil, Telugu, Marathi, Persian, Sanskrit, Portuguese and European tongues, both modern and classical; renowned as a preacher, schoolmaster, diplomat, negotiator and statesman, he ended up as protector–regent, *raja-guru*, and 'father' to Serfoji, Maharaja of Thanjāvur. His 'Helpers' extended the reach of Tamil Christianity as never before. This they did during a time of almost ceaseless war and human suffering, and in the face of implacable official opposition to Indian Christians and Missions from the East India Company during the time its forces were inexorably extending British rule over much of the subcontinent. Among these disciples, at least two are particularly noteworthy: Satyanāthan Pillai and Vedanāyakam Sāstri.

Satyanāthan Pillai, a high-born Vellālar of Thanjāvur who became a convert despite strong family opposition, was Schwartz's most active and energetic assistant. His earliest assignment, as pastor to the Company's military garrison at Vallam, seven miles from Thanjāvur, was augmented after the British forces attacked the city in 1772, destroying the local congregation's place of worship. As Stephen Neill aptly observed, 'The progress of the Church in India was at all times linked to the mobility of Christians, and especially of Christian soldiers in the armies of the

Company and of the local rulers'. Meanwhile, by 1765, the Company had established a military garrison town at Palayamkottai in Tirunelveli country far to the south. From there a Vellālar Christian sepoy named Savarimuthu Pillai sent word to Schwartz, in 1769 and again in 1771, that Tamil Christians had settled in Tirunelveli and that he should send them pastoral help. An affluent Brahmin widow at Palayamkottai, living with an English officer, also wrote to Schwartz asking him to visit the congregation and begging for baptism. In 1778, after satisfying himself that she was not 'living in sin', Schwartz came to Palayamkottai, baptized and christened her 'Clorinda'. Thereafter Clorinda and a local catechist, occasionally visited by a Vellālar pastor named Rayappan, cared for the congregation and managed a school (in both English and Tamil). When she subsequently provided funds for the construction of a proper building for her 'prayer-school', Schwartz sent Satyanāthan Pillai to serve as resident pastor and teacher. In 1790, after his ordination in Thanjāvur, Satyanāthan was formally commissioned as the SPCK's first Tamil missionary and sent back to Tirunelveli.

Here, in 1799, Satyanāthan commissioned David Sundaranandam, a convert and disciple who came from the lowly 'Shanar' (now known as Nadar) community. Sundaranandam, in turn, led a mass movement in which whole villages became converted. Thousands of Shanars, a people whose hereditary occupation was toddy tapping, turned to the new faith. In so doing, they incurred the wrath of their landlords. Warlords (*palaiyakarans*) plundered, confined and tortured Christians, destroying their chapel-schools and burning their books. During the years 1799 to 1806, many suffered severe persecution and martyrdom. Thousands lost everything, sometimes being stripped of their clothes and sent into the jungle to die. Their most fiery and radical leader David Sundaranandam disappeared, and was never found. Movements of mass conversion to Christianity, however, continued to break out through the nineteenth century, whole villages often turning Christian. 'Villages of Refuge', such as Mudulur, Megnanapuram, Dohnavur, Suviseshapuram and Ananda-puram, were established to care for those fleeing their homes. The numbers of Christians doubled or even tripled in every decade. Schools proliferated and self-help voluntary societies were formed to care for widows and orphans, social welfare and other projects. As colleges and seminaries and hospitals were built, Tirunelveli Christians transformed the entire area, in its culture and society.

The most renowned of all Schwartz's Helpers, however, was to be Vedanāyakam Sāstri. Born in Palayamkottai, he was noticed by Schwartz among the children of the Vellālar Christian poet Devasahayam Pillai when he was visiting the area in 1785. Seeing the twelve-year-old's remarkable gifts, he asked Devasahayam to let him take the lad to

Thanjāvur for training under his own watchful eye. Vedanāyakam soon became a master teacher, writer and headmaster of one of three modern schools built by Schwartz. These schools, run by the Rajas of Thanjāvur, Shivaganga and Ramnād, became so renowned as models of educational excellence, in which ideals developed by Professor Francke were embodied, that Brahmans strove to get their sons admitted. The Company's directors in London provided an annual subsidy so that Indian recruits for administrative positions within the burgeoning Madras Presidency could be trained in them. The mixed English–Tamil curriculum, while using biblical and Christian texts, also conveyed the very latest in developments, principles and sciences of the Enlightenment, something available nowhere else in India at that time. Maratha Brahman youths who emerged from these three schools soon filled many of the higher-level cadres of the Company's governments in South India, occupying civil service positions immediately below the few 'Covenanted' posts held by Europeans. The culminating symbol of scholarly and scientific achievement in Thanjāvur was the building of the Saraswati Mahal Library within the palace of the Maharaja. Within this work, begun by Schwartz himself, the old classmates fulfilled their dreams. Collections of rare manuscripts and books were preserved; and scientific instruments were placed within the Mahal's own 'Room of Wonders'.

Vedanāyakam Sāstri's main significance, however, lies in his powerful contributions to Tamil literature and, especially, to Tamil Christian thought. His masterly productions in classical Tamil poetry and his equally masterly constructions in modern Tamil prose, of which he was the creator, remain his most enduring legacy, a monument to inventive artistry. The corpus of this writing is astonishing, not only for its sheer volume, but also for its depth, range and subtlety. Hardly a subject can be mentioned on which he did not write and write copiously. His use of the *kuruvanci* genre (drama involving a wandering woman soothsayer or fortune-teller) enabled him to convey profound expositions concerning deep and fundamental elements underlying humanity and society in relation to eternity and the everlasting verities.

Vedanāyakam's *Bethlehem Kurvanchee* is a presentation of the Gospel story in verse. Rendered in dramatic song, sung to various well-known Tamil tunes and tempos within the frame of this particular art form and well-known local idioms, its characters symbolize essential events or truths. Ultimate union between the Lord (*Nathan*) as Bridegroom and the Church (Virgin Daughter of Zion) and Bride (*Devamohini*: Bride of God) requires the actions of Faith Foretold (*Visuvasa kuruvanci*), the wife who is a wandering prophetess, and Reason Conveyed (*Gnanachinkan*), the husband. As a bird-catcher or fisherman (preacher/teacher/catechist), the believer is under obligation (*dharma*) to cast his net (*Veda*: the Word of

God) and bring birds or fish (Mankind) he has caught as gifts to his Lord (King Jesus, the Son of God); but he must also confront and defeat Evil, personifed by the devilish wandering Thief (*Kallakuravan*). Works such as this, composed in 1800 and revised in 1820 for presentation before Christian congregations, received increasingly wide recognition. Vedanāyakam's career culminated with his serving as poet laureate to Serfoji, the Maharaja of Thanjāvur, with the title *Sāstri* being suffixed to his name when he came into the Durbar.

The pathway blazed by Vedanāyakam was followed immediately by H. A. Krishna Pillai. Another Thanjāvur Vellālar who became a convert, he spent most of his life teaching in one of the modern schools. Krishna Pillai's greatest work, his epic *Irakshaniya Vāttirikam*, is a poetic rendering of Bunyan's *Pilgrim's Progress*, set within the context of Tamil culture. It shows how conversion to Christianity could occur without doing violence to the hallowed modes of classical Tamil literature.

Challenges under the Raj

Christians of nineteenth- and twentieth-century India continued to be overshadowed by increasing European missionary activity and by the military, administrative and technological presence of the enormous imperial system. Yet, while profoundly affected by the Raj, contributions made by Indian Christians themselves to the development of their own institutions continued to be as crucial as ever. As before, each new wave of Christian expansion brought changes. These changes were often profoundly radical, especially as the Gospel was interpreted in new ways and extended to new peoples, in ever lower strata of society, in ever more remote jungle areas, or in ever deeper ways in the lives of women and children. Governments came under increasing pressure to open doors, to carry out reforms and to bring help to peoples in want – hitherto neglected peoples such as the outcasts, the impaired and the diseased. Radical notions of humanity and society suggested that all people – men, women and children – should be seen as intrinsically equal to each other, at least in the sight of God, and that they should be given equal access to protection and to basic needs – such as medicine, education and opportunity. Many who graduated from missionary colleges, whether Christian or not, joined movements for reform, national self-determination, or more radical revolutionary changes.

The wheel has turned and come full circle. Hostility toward Christians in India, and toward foreign missionaries, has again become a predominant attitude, if not the reigning policy of the Government of India. This position, based upon clear-eyed and rational assessment of the logic of power, was certainly that of the East India Company's Raj. The entire structure undergirding the imperial system depended upon support from Hindu elites. Armed forces of some three hundred thousand men came from military castes who ruled over agrarian villages across the country; and administrative cadres of roughly another three hundred thousand provided bureaucratic skills which controlled the flow of information and revenue. It was these Hindus, especially Brahmans in the secretariats, who quietly helped to construct and shape what became modern Hinduism. Company Raj under the British became, at least unofficially, a 'Hindu Raj'. Hostility toward India's Christians and towards foreign missionaries was palpable, despite local, occasional and specific contradictions and exceptions. This was true despite times when, out of immediate pragmatic need, Christians who were on the ground were readily exploited – Catholic and Evangelical (Protestant) missionaries alike being used as local military chaplains, schoolteachers or diplomatic emissaries (e.g. sending Schwartz to Tipu Sultan). Except for occasional instances of persecution and martyrdom (e.g. John de Britto SJ, in Ramnād), Indian Christians and alien missionaries often fared better, received kinder treatment and were more successful in domains which remained outside European control (e.g. under Vellama Nayakas of Madurai, Marava Tevars and Setupatis of Ramnād and Sivaganga, Kallar Tondaimans of Pudukottai, Maratha Rajas of Thanjāvur, Nayar Raja Vermas of Travancore and many others). In British-controlled districts, the cries of persecuted Christian villagers, who sent appeals all the way to London during the last years of the eighteenth century, fell on deaf ears. Such indifference, both in London and in India, while it began to diminish after 1813, did not disappear for another fifty or more years.

The 'Father of the Modern Missionary Movement', at least in the eyes of Anglo-Saxon Evangelicals, was William Carey. He and his fellow Baptists in England were the first to initiate the rise of voluntarism among grass-roots believers whose Christian faith was revived during the Evangelical Awakening (or Great Awakening in America). Societies were formed, contributions were solicited and overseas agendas were drawn up for the sending forth of missionaries to the far corners of the world. His *An Enquiry into the Obligations of Christians to Use Means for the Conversion of Heathens* (1792), evoked in part from reading about deeds of German Pietists in India, immediately led to the formation of the BMS and his departure for India. The formation of the LMS, CMS and other societies, on both sides of the Atlantic, quickly followed. Since the Company remained hostile and resisted free entry into British territories, Carey's group had difficulties until he was allowed to settle in the Danish station at Srirampur (Serampore). He could not cross the Hugli to work in Calcutta until he was hired to teach oriental languages at Fort William

College. Only by a sustained campaign in Britain, aided by a converted Company Director, Charles Grant, powerful friends in Parliament (Wilberforce, Thornton, *et al.*) and an alliance with the Free Trade lobby, was it possible to procure an insertion, known as the 'Pious Clause', into the Company's Charter Renewal Act of 1813. Thereafter, anyone denied entry into British India could appeal directly to the Board of Control, which was headed by a government minister. Free merchants and missionaries then began to arrive in ever greater numbers.

Even so, Company directors and officers continued to be both pragmatic and cautious, using missionaries when they were politically useful. Thus, subventions were provided for Roman Catholic Vicars Apostolic in Bombay; Catholic missionaries were used as chaplains for Irish contingents in Company armies; and, due to parliamentary pressures mounted by the Evangelical lobby prior to 1813, some missionary chaplains went to India in the Company's service. During the 1820s, the Company also heeded the cries of Hindu reformers and Christian missionaries for the abolition of female infanticide and widow-burning. Later in the century, moreover, the Company's governments in India welcomed the arrival of increasing numbers of missionary teachers, physicians and nurses. As missionary schools, colleges and hospitals proliferated and spread out across the country in the late nineteenth century, multiplying into many hundreds – staffed by dedicated professionals and volunteers of societies from all over the world (including America, Canada, Australia and New Zealand, and countries of Scandinavia and Southern Europe) – responses in India remained ambivalent. Some Hindus had grounds for feeling that, as Marx put it, foreign missionary activity in India was the 'handmaiden of imperialism'.

At the same time, officials in London had reason for caution. They and officers in India were ever wary of tactlessness which might lead to disorder, and ready to expel summarily any missionary who might provoke social unrest. Westerners who denounced Hindu and Muslim practices, by calling them 'devilish', were admonished and sometimes punished. A Governor of Madras was censured in the 1840s for using the term 'heathen' in official communications. When devout servants of the Company, both civil and military, organized a campaign against the official state involvement in 'idolatrous practices' – e.g. the managing of temple property and functions (for tens of thousands of institutions); protecting pilgrimage sites; requiring Christian soldiers to attend Hindu festivals; forcing hundreds of thousands, including Christians, to pull great temple cars in processions (*Rath Yatras*) which invariably saw some people crushed to death; and allowing temple 'dancing girls' (*devadasis*) to function even though hundreds of thousands were forced to perpetual prostitution – the government summarily reprimanded them, including Bishop Spencer, and sacked their leaders, including General Peregrine Maitland. Some in the Company blamed the 1806 Vellore Mutiny on excessive 'proselytizing zeal' among Christians of India – a charge which resurfaced in connection with the Great Rebellion (Mutiny) of 1857. The Government of India eventually had even less reason for enthusiasm when missionaries sympathized with, or rendered aid to, the nationalist cause. As late as the 1930s and 1940s, missionaries were being either interned or expelled as 'risks' to security – even as other missionaries were exploited as intelligence officers on the Burma border.

Relations between Christians in India continued to be fraught with conflicts and tensions. These occurred among and between Catholic, Evangelical (or Protestant) and Thomas Christians, as well as among missionaries working with them. As numbers and varieties increased, not to mention complexities of relationship, as much attention was sometimes given to 'sheep stealing' between Christian folds as to striving for conversions among non-Christians. This was vigorously done on all sides, with each side looking askance at the others. Each new wave coming from the West represented different or newer perspectives, philosophies and theologies; and each new wave caused intergenerational strife (ardour tending to chill in older missionaries, as in older institutions). Since newer waves of missionaries from abroad could avoid 'sheep stealing' by looking for as yet 'unclaimed' or 'wild' sheep, the latest to come would tend to move into the remotest tribal areas or down into the lowest rungs of social structure (where ritually polluted or subhuman beings had been abandoned, at least by some standards). Among such peoples, people not yet Sanskritized or Islamicized and eager to escape conditions in which they had lived for ages untold, spectacular successes were recorded – insomuch that, for example, virtually all Khasis, Mizos, Nagas and similar peoples became Christians and sometimes did so without ever becoming 'Hindu' or 'Indian' – a circumstance which has hindered their being ever fully nationalized and has caused continuing troubles with the National Government.

But the biggest and most ceaseless and continuous of all ongoing arguments and conflicts, bringing about divisions and mutations among almost all Christian groups in India, regardless of whether they were Indians or Westerners, Catholics or Evangelicals, Anglicans or Dissenters, Mar Thoma or Syrian, conservative or liberal, continued to swirl around issues of caste, culture and acculturation. Indeed, since it is difficult to find any time in the history of Christians in India when this has not been a burning issue, this both remained and still is *the* enduring problem for all Christians in India. It is one which has never gone away and one which is still bringing dissension and strife. Its dimensions are both historical and theological, with intermingling and intricate permutations which remain because every single Christian group which has ever existed in the subcontinent continues to exist, sometimes in a fossilized form but more often in some revitalized and altogether new form. In theological terms, issues of unity and pluralism provide a polarity of seemingly endless and paradoxical contradictions. In historical terms, what has been involved is the challenge of finding acceptance, within the fullest sense of humanity, without, at the same time, causing damage or rejection in the contexts of various specific communities.

But, in addressing these complexities, it is important to recognize that, behind the issue of caste and culture conflicts, in all their manifold forms, lies a shadow (or ghost) issue which, in the harsh light of analysis, never went away. For Indian Christians, what was at issue — as disturbing in recent centuries as in earlier times — had always been the very presence of missionaries themselves. By definition, missionaries were agents of change and disturbers of the *status quo*. This sense of alien intrusion was experienced by Indians, Christians and non-Christians alike. Clashes between alien influences and indigenous institutions were more than simply religious or theological. They were cultural, ecclesiastical and political. If and when alien missionaries were opposed by political regimes within which they worked, then alien Christians and indigenous Christians tended to find common ground and could look to each other for mutual solace and support. But, if and when any alien Christians (or just some out of many missionaries) and alien rulers of the same culture (even if indifferent to religion) found common ground or became inextricably linked politically, then Indian Christians found themselves marginalized and/or obliged both to collaborate and change (or submit to domination). This they resented.

At no time were the majority of missionaries — from some sixty Catholic and some fifty non-Catholic missionary societies, whether British or not — predisposed in favour of colonialism. Indeed, pre-colonial, non-colonial and anti-colonial missionaries, taken together, outnumbered those British missionaries of the Anglican establishment who might have wanted to make India into another fiefdom for their own Christendom. The very fact that so many Catholic missionaries were not British (being French, Italian, Irish and so on), and that so many non-Catholic (Evangelical or Protestant) missionaries were from North America or Northern Europe, was bound to make this so. Opposition to the Raj, moreover, tended to increase as voluntarism drew more and more recruits from lower and lower classes (or cultural levels) of the Western world and as these recruits came from 'faith' societies beyond the control of mainline denominations, with their established systems of ecclesiastical control. Indeed, at every stage during their struggle, anti-imperial nationalism in India received substantial and sympathetic support from missionaries (from

Allen Hume and Verrier Elwin to Charles F. Andrews, Edward Thompson and Amy Carmichael, many of whom became friends of Gandhi).

In both theological and historical terms, therefore, caste was not just a matter of birth, but also of culture. Two Vellālar Christians of Thanjāvur, Muttusami Pillai and Vedanāyakam Sāstri, a Catholic and an Evangelical, crystallized the central question: how could one God give one salvation for one humanity and yet there still exist so many cultures? For them there was no such thing as a Christian in the abstract or in general, but only a Christian or a community of Christians, known in concrete and specific terms – with traits of language, birth, culture, education and style particular to an environment. In holistic terms, primordial mankind was such an abstraction, as were stories of origin, and explanations of birth and caste. Thus, at the 'Lord's Table' or the Eucharist, different peoples 'sat together separately' – enjoying 'spiritual unity' within a context of social diversity that allowed different people to live separately and to organize themselves hierarchically according to distinctions of caste (in India) or class (Europe). In his 'Dialogue on the Difference of Caste' (*Jāti-ārasan-bhāvanai*: 1824), Vedanāyakam told of European Christians sitting on benches, Vellālar Christians sitting on grass mats and Paraiyar or Shanar Christians sitting on the bare (dirt or stone) floor – according to their circumstances. None of these concrete circumstances was to be seen as immutable.

But in waves of the radically changing cultural climate of post-revolutionary America and Europe, there were those who felt they had a divine mandate to make sure that the intrinsic unity of mankind was more than a unit of abstract worth and that such unity not only had to be made concrete but had also to be individualized and made available to every human being. Implicit was the notion of a homogenizing and obliterating of all distinctions, so that cream and skim could no longer separate but remain together. Implicit was a democratizing and levelling ethos which justified, in theological terms, the total abolition of caste. That this was not the first time, nor the last time, that such injunctions were made would become obvious to each generation. Such concrete problems as worshipping together, sitting together, partaking of the same bread and cup together, singing the same songs together, having access to the same education together and being admitted to the same ministry together – at each step along the way, the same conflicts arose. In 1830 Anglican Bishop Wilson reversed positions taken by Bishop Heber just three years earlier. While both Wilson and Charles Rhenius were agreed on being opposed to the persistence of caste among converts, Wilson sacked Rhenius for daring to question apostolic succession. Anglo-Saxon denominations went one way and German Lutherans went another. In Thanjāvur, during the 1850s, an SPG missionary (George Pope) insisted on having 'Tanjore Christians' publicly flogged for refusing to abandon caste rules and strictures. Yet, at that very same time, a CMS missionary was being attacked by fellow missionaries for focusing attention exclusively on Brahmans, to the exclusion of other peoples. Both were Anglicans. Roman Catholic missionaries also were no more of one mind about caste observances and practices among Indian Christians than in previous centuries. French missionaries along the Coromandel were more ready to respect existing caste and cultural norms; Irish missionaries opposed, Italian missionaries were more evenly divided on such issues.

When the great mass movements of conversion occurred among untouchable communities in Telugu country at the end of the nineteenth century, once again caste consciousness kept Malas and Madigas from mixing (and they have remained unmixed to this day). Each birth group had its own distinct sacred story, each its own *vamshāvali*, telling how its particular lineage had come out of the mists of antiquity, and survived. Missionaries, as change agents, may have understood the procedures and values necessary for progress under the Raj or helped to protect Christians and their interests when trouble arose over the law or in relations with Hindu or Muslim neighbours. But, as the evidence shows, they never resolved the caste–culture question. Indeed, evidence also seems to indicate that no mass movement of conversions in India was ever led by a European. Put in the quaint language of Vedanāyakam, as expressed earlier in the century, it took 'an elephant to catch an elephant' and 'a quail to catch a quail'.

As the nineteenth century came to an end, some theologically liberal missionaries, in the post-Darwinian climate, repeatedly confused conversion with civilization as worthy goals, and then went on to exalt and extol Brahmanical civilization. Among upper-class intellectually eclectic missionaries, such as William Miller of Madras Christian College, a 'downward filtration' theory was replaced by 'upward fulfilment' as an excuse for explaining why Europeans had not been effective in bringing about conversions among the high-caste elites of India. The Christian task was not so much to convert people as to permeate Indian society with Christian values. To do this Christians needed to influence the elites who were taking to Western education in droves. Conversion was no longer seen as such a worthy goal. Since much in the life and conduct of Hindus and Muslims was praiseworthy, a new strategy was articulated by J. N. Farquhar. Since all religions were, in some measure, divinely inspired, and since Hinduism was leading Indians towards Christianity, missionaries had only to devote more effort to dialogue and mutual understanding. This kind of thinking in the West, sometimes called 'fulfilment theory', gained some acceptance among some missionaries. It was put forward both in the Parliament of World Religions at Chicago in 1892 and in the World Missionary Conference at Edinburgh in 1910.

Among some Indian Christians also, theological liberalism gained headway. In Bengal and North India, where there were relatively fewer Indian Christians and where there were Brahman Christians, Anglican Krishna Mohan Banerjea argued in 1875 that Hindus could become Christians without abandoning their cultural or social traditions; Kali Charan Banerjea, in his Calcutta Christo Samaj (begun in 1887), required neither liturgy nor clergy; and Upadhyaya, a Brahman Catholic, donned the ochre robes of a swami and held that one could be both a Hindu and a Christian. In Maharashtra, Narayan Vaman Tilak, a prominent Brahman Christian poet, founded a Christian ashram in 1917; and an Anglican Christa Seva Sangh (Christian Service Society) was established. In Madras, the National Church, founded in 1886, only survived into the 1920s. But when they said that Christianity in India should be Indian in culture, many later thinkers were saying something very different, something much less orthodox than what Vedanāyakam Sāstri or Roberto de Nobili would have had in mind, even when they used the same words.

Theologically more conservative and pragmatic missionaries from lower levels of American, British and European societies tended to work within an entirely different cultural ethos and to be ignored by upper-class missionaries. Thus, radical Nonconformists, already critically conscious that Methodism in Britain was no longer working-class but becoming middle-class, saw a dangerous loss of spiritual fire. For them and for many others, theological liberalism was a more serious problem than caste or culture. Such missionaries, from whatever country, criticized those who now failed to bring the Gospel and who only prepared high-caste Hindus for lucrative careers while, at the same time, neglecting the plight of low-caste Christians and failing to help them to overcome cultural, economic and social disabilities. Officers of the Salvation Army arriving in the 1880s, while theologically conservative, abandoned European clothes, furnishings, food and even music, took Indian Christian names and adopted as many elements of Indian culture as possible in order to identify themselves with the downtrodden. Pandita Ramabai, the Brahman widow who had won such renown in Varanasi for her high learning, had become a Christian while in Britain. Fêted among high society women's missionary circles in the eastern states of America, she had turned away from those elites and their rationalizing theologies and ended up among Pentecostals in California before returning to found her Mukti Mission for female orphans and widows. Among Catholic and Thomas Christians also, the same kinds of processes developed.

Theological liberalism was also increasingly challenged by more conservative Christian missionary thinkers. Among these the most influential was Hendrik Kraemer, a Dutch theologian working in Indonesia. Looking at resurgent forms of anti-Christian Islamic militancy, he took a Barthian theological position. His *Christian Message in a Non-Christian World*, written for the International Missionary Conference at Tambaram, just south of Madras, in 1938, reminded Christians that their faith was fundamentally and intrinsically different from any religion. Christian faith, he argued, was not man-made but God-given. All religions, even certain elements found in Christianity, were of merely human origin. It was important to know where the differences lay.

Meanwhile, among Roman Catholics also, old controversies continued, some going back centuries, over such matters as rites of different kinds – Latin and Malabar (as well as Chinese). Pope Benedict XIV (in 1744) held that Catholics of high and low birth alike should hear the same mass, take the same communion and meet in the same building at the same time. Even such regulations could be modified in implementation. Jesuits in South India erected little walls and opened different doors for the high and the low castes. Thanjāvur Christians arranged for different castes to sit in separate quadrants of nave and transept. After all, slave Christians in America worshipped in their own chapels; and servants in Europe sat in back galleries. In problems over training clergy, rival Catholic jurisdictions – *Padroado* and Propaganda Fide – often favoured separate castes. The Mukkavan fisherfolk petitioned Rome, asking how, if a fisherman could be the first Pope, they could be considered not worthy enough for clerical training and ordination. One Apostolic Delegate, in 1902, pointed out that, while no descendants of de Nobili's Brahman converts remained in the Church, many descendants of Paravas converted by St Francis Xavier remained faithful. If anything, problems of caste and culture seemed to become more and more formidable.

Mass movements, with whole villages becoming Christian, a phenomenon which had occurred at the end of the eighteenth century and again in the late nineteenth century, among both Evangelicals and Catholics, became a focal point of nationalist opposition in the twentieth century. Such movements were severely criticized by higher-caste Hindus, including Mahatma Gandhi. Gandhi went so far as openly to chastise India's first native Anglican Bishop, Vedanayakam Azariah, accusing him of betraying the nation for his leadership of mass conversions in Dornakal. But untouchable communities, denied access to temples, common wells or other facilities enjoyed by clean-caste peoples, had hitherto never counted as Hindu. The charge that such converts were only motivated by material considerations was refuted by Indian Christians. Advocates of mass conversion argued that all human motives are mixed and that imperfect motives need not nullify the genuineness of conversions. For despised peoples to desire a fuller life for themselves and their children could hardly be considered something unworthy, ignoble or unpatriotic. Vedanayakam Azariah was himself a Nadar from Tirunelveli, the son of a village pastor. His consecration as Bishop of Dornakal in 1912 and subsequent shepherding of a mass movement of Telugu-speakers into Christianity symbolized both the work of Schwartz, Satyanāthan Pillai and Vedanāyakam Sāstri a century earlier and the beginning of the Indianization of Church leadership in the twentieth century.

The continent since 1947

Since Partition in 1947 and the emergence of India, Pakistan and Bangladesh (not to mention the autonomous neighbouring states of Burma, Nepal and Sri Lanka), missionaries from abroad have almost disappeared (with just a few exceptions). Radical religious and social movements, accompanied by far-reaching cross-cultural transformations generated within 'Hindu–Muslim' (or 'Indian') environments, have, however, continued to accelerate, together with a welter of competitive fundamentalist and revivalist enthusiasms (Buddhist, Christian, Hindu, Muslim and Sikh).

Indian independence in 1947 brought more cries for Christians in India and the Churches to which they belonged to become more Indian. Especially noxious were some of the denominational divisions and boundaries which alien missionaries had drawn. Many mainline groups, such as Anglicans, Congregationalists and Methodists, banded together to form the Church of South India. Bishop V. Azariah was the principal Indian leader in the movement to create the CSI, but he died in 1945, too early to see it inaugurated in the same year that India became independent. In 1970, a much weaker Church of North India and a Protestant Church of Pakistan came into being. Baptists and Lutherans, together with many Anabaptist and Free Church people, retained their separate identities and communities. The same, of course, is true for the six to ten Syrian and Thomas Christian communions of Kerala.

The Roman Catholic Church continued to struggle with the anomaly of the *Padroado*, fully resolved only after the Indian occupation of Goa in 1961. That the Portuguese should continue to have any ecclesiastical authority within an independent India was unthinkable; and in due course elements of this anachronism were gradually ended. Not until the last Portuguese Bishop of Cochin retired in 1952 were animosities there between high-caste and low-caste Christians resolved: two dioceses were formed, with a bishop of appropriate birth for each. Since then the 'Indianāion' of the Catholic Church has developed around three principal themes. The first is how to implement the decrees of the Second Vatican Council (1962–65), encouraging adaptation and pluralism, especially in relation to the liturgy. The high point here was the All-

India Seminar at Bangalore, Pentecost 1969, but the implementation of its resolutions became bogged down in fears that Indianization looked to some too much like Hinduization. The second has been the, often fraught, relationship between Latin Catholics on the one hand and Catholics within the Syro-Malabar and Syro-Malankara Churches on the other. The latter represent some of the most dynamic groups within Indian Catholicism; but only in 1987 did Pope John Paul allow them to expand their diocesan organization away from Kerala. The third theme is the development of Christian ashrams following the example of Jules Monchanin, Abhishiktananda and Bede Griffiths. Particularly significant here is the founding at Kurisumula, Kerala, by Francis Acharya, of an ashram combining a Cistercian pattern of life with the Syro-Malankara Rite.

The Indian Catholic Church appears unique in the southern hemisphere for the number of its clergy, both diocesan and religious. In this it contrasts strikingly with the Church in the Philippines and in most of Latin America and Africa. If in general the number of Jesuits is declining in the world, in India they have grown remarkably, providing distinguished intellectual leadership. In consequence Indian Catholicism has not been as subject to new waves of Pentecostalist Protestantism in the way that the Catholic Church, suffering acute shortages of priests, has been in many countries. On the contrary, India now exports Catholic missionaries just as South Korea, for instance, exports Evangelical (Protestant) missionaries.

Resentments and suspicions remain. Hindu nationalists continue to view Indian Christians as belonging to a foreign power. The Government of Madhya Pradesh, homeland of the RSS, appointed a commission of enquiry which, in its report, labelled Indian Christians anti-national – a 'foreign hand' subject to American influence. The controversy aroused national attention. Evidence was presented to the effect that Christianity in India had a long history and that it had long been truly and authentically Indian. As had been usual since early in the century, Hindu attacks focused upon Christian 'proselytizing' activities. Hindu hostility toward Christianity has grown stronger with each passing decade. This has been led by various political parties and religious agencies, such as the RSS, BJP, VHP, Shiv Sena and Bajrang Dal. These now make up what is sometimes known as the Sangh Parivar (Society of Families) or as the 'Saffron Brotherhood'. Christian church buildings are now regularly destroyed in various parts of the continent, usually on the pretext that they were built under colonial rule and that they stand upon the foundations of some former temple. Indian Christians may in some areas be attacked and killed, usually in rather small, isolated incidents, but that is not entirely exceptional in societies where there is much communal violence.

The response of Indian Christians to such incidents has been mixed. Some, such as the Catholic Shoreline Movement, are militantly self-assertive and ready to take up arms in defence of their own 'territories'. Others, such as the Mennonites, are quietistic, choosing rather to prove themselves to be twice Christian, if not also twice as Indian as anyone else. On the other hand, some Christians still enjoy situations of social privilege. Since most Christians, but especially Catholics, are concentrated in urban areas and since Christians possess some of the finest educational institutions in the country – with elites of the Indian aristocracy often preferring to send their own children to Christian schools – some Christian communities of India enjoy a disproportionate share of positions within the privileged sectors and strata of society. Many Thomas Christians of Kerala, a state with the highest literacy in all of India, enjoy positions in government, business and the professions. In Nagaland, where over 95 per cent of the population are Christians, they inevitably occupy virtually all senior positions.

At the opposite end of the spectrum are Indian Christians from the poorest classes, many of them still located in rural areas and 'untouchable' communities. Legally they should be called 'Scheduled Castes', 'Backward Castes' and 'Other Backward Castes' – within which some Adivāsi or tribal Christian communities are also fitted. But, politically, Christians are not counted among these disadvantaged groups, because of the technicality of their being defined as 'Christian' and not 'Hindu', with the resultant loss of many government welfare benefits which are not extended to them. Yet, two or three powerful movements have begun to stir Christians at this level. First, there is the Dalīt Movement, with a separate Dalīt Christian movement. *Dalīt* means 'broken' or 'crushed' or 'oppressed' – as when a boot grinds a glass bangle into the dirt. For the last two decades, this movement has been growing with ever more intensity. Similarly, there are also resistance movements among Adivāsis, the aboriginal or tribal peoples of the north-east, many of whom are Christian. Nagaland is indeed the one state in India to have a Christian majority. Secondly, perhaps the largest single movement of Christian awakening and conversion is the Pentecostal movement, with all of its manifold branches throughout India. This is particularly active and notable within the large urban areas. Finally, and somewhat related, are continuing conversion movements among various communities.

Growth in numbers of Indian Christians, in all communities, seems clear. But there are claims among Indian Christians that their numbers are undercounted or not recorded, for political reasons partly related to the political manipulation of census gathering and reporting. Whatever the case, the aggregated total is estimated to be not less than fifty millions. Among these, Catholics remain the largest single Christian community; but there are substantial non-Catholic communities, both Thomas and Evangelical, with perhaps the largest aggregations being among formerly Adivāsi and Dalīt populations.

Notes

1 'India' or 'Indian', as used here, denotes anything lying within the continent (commonly also called a subcontinent) that today includes countries now known as India, Pakistan, Bangladesh, Nepal, Sri Lanka and Afghanistan: everything south of the Himalayas, south and east of the Hindu Kush, and west of mountains separating Assam from Burma. 'India' is about as precise a concept as 'Europe'. 'Indic' denotes what is confined to Indo-European languages. 'Asia' is so imprecise as to be useless.

2 This, the oldest surviving narrative account of any congregation beyond the frontiers of the Roman Empire in the East, is noteworthy for its linking of Thomas with India. The 'Babylonian' or 'Chaldean' congregations of Edessa, the capital of the small principality of Osrhoene, were caught in the war between Parthia and Rome. Claiming apostolic legitimacy comparable to that of Antioch and Rome, they published a number of works, such as the Abgar legend of Judas Thomas, their version of the *Acts of Thomas*, and other works (e.g. Ephrem of Nisibis, who died in 373, and wrote hymns stressing links between believers of Edessa and India).

3 A footnote to these events was recorded in far-off England where, for the year 883, the Anglo-Saxon Chronicle reported the conveying of 'alms that the king vowed to send thither, and to India to St Thomas and St Bartholomew'. Some quibble over what was meant by 'India' but we know that other long journeys of that nature occurred, in both directions.

4 'Brief sketch of the life and writings of Father C. J. Beschi, or Virumāmani', trans. from the Tamil by T. Muthusami Pillai, *Madras Journal of Literature and Science* (April 1840), pp. 250–300.

6

Africa

Kevin Ward

Three major religious traditions flourish in Africa: Islam, Christianity and African Traditional Religion. In contrast to the indigenous character of the traditional religion (or religions, since this is a diverse phenomenon) and the inculturated nature of Islam, African Christianity has often been presented as alien to the continent, the religion of the West, of European missionaries. And yet Christianity has strong claims to be reckoned the oldest of the three traditions, with a continuous history on the continent of nearly 2,000 years. Moreover, Lamin Sanneh, the West African historian and theologian, sees Christianity in modern Africa as above all a movement of affirmation and preservation of local culture. This may seem a surprising assertion given the widely held view of missionary Christianity as the despiser and destroyer of the African cultural heritage. Yet, says Sanneh, the paramount emphasis on translating the Bible into the 'mother tongue' has in fact served to enhance African culture in its particularity and diversity, whatever the motives and intentions of the missionaries.

> In doing so missionaries gave local people a standard by which to question claims of Western cultural superiority, and it does not matter whether that was the result of a conscious decision by the missionaries or the perception of Africans as receivers and adapters. Whatever linguistic distortions, compromises, egregious inventions and other forms of invasive interference missionaries may have introduced, the shift into the vernacular paradigm in the long run, if not immediately, would excite local ambition and fuel national feeling. In this respect the Scriptures are unlike Plato or Milton, for they are preserved in a community of memory and observance, so that in their translated form they continue to speak authoritatively to transmitter and recipient alike.[1]

The emphasis on the vernacular in evangelism and worship as well as in transmitting the faith is complemented, especially in the growing urban areas, by the importance of lingua francas – Swahili or Lingala, Amharinya or Hausa, not to mention Afrikaans – languages which have wide currency in regional communication. At an even wider level, Africans have made their own the languages of world communication, notably French and English, Arabic and Portuguese. In the twenty-first century, as the numerical preponderance and dynamic of Christianity continues to shift from Europe and North America, it has been estimated that Africa will contain more Christians than any other continent, and this ability to express Christianity both locally, and on an international, global level will be crucial.[2]

Egypt, North Africa, Nubia and Islam

The interplay between local and metropolitan has not only been a feature of the modern history of Christianity and Africa; it is also an important feature in understanding the early period of African Christianity in the first 600 years of the Christian era. Christianity spread along the Mediterranean coast of North Africa, taking advantage of the *Pax Romana*. Finding Greek and Latin already established as the languages of trade and the army, of administration and learning, the Christian message expressed itself on African soil through these languages: the Greek of Origen, Athanasius and Cyril in Egypt; the Latin of Tertullian, Cyprian and Augustine in North Africa; as well as the dissident traditions of Arius (Greek) and Donatus (Latin). But Christianity was never simply the religion of empire – the witness of the martyrs in the first centuries shows that African Christians could stubbornly and courageously resist the civil power. And from early in its history, Christianity in Africa began to be articulated in vernaculars. In Egypt, the flourishing of the monastic movement was important in enabling Christian piety and theology to be expressed in terms of Coptic culture. St Antony himself knew no Greek; one of the fruits of Athanasius's *Life of Antony* was to emphasize the common concerns of both Greek and Coptic in the upholding of Christian orthodoxy.

As far as Christianity was concerned, the next centuries were disastrous. With the capture of Alexandria by the Islamic armies in 641 CE, Islam spread over North Africa even more rapidly and deeply than had Christianity some 500 years earlier. Islam took over the inheritance of the collapsed Roman Empire, imposing a new metropolitan language – Arabic – for the Greek and Latin of the Romans, and replacing what had become the imperial religion, Christianity, by a new religion of empire, Islam. The unity and moral fervour of a pristine Islam, in stark contrast to what appeared to be a fractious and worldly Christianity, may have some explanatory value for the success of Islam. Certainly, the fact that Christianity in Africa so decisively collapsed in the face of Islam poses difficult historical and theological problems for Christianity in general and African Christianity in particular.

It is tempting, but probably mistaken, to look for explanations in the area of African Christianity's supposed lack of indigenous roots. And yet, as far the language question is concerned, Islam's relationship to Arabic has been even more intimate than the Christian reliance on Greek or Latin. It was not that Christianity had failed to incorporate itself into local culture, and Islam succeeded in this; but rather that world religions (as opposed to local 'traditional' cults) were seen as being inextricably bound up with a universal civilization. When, in North Africa, the Graeco-Roman civilization was replaced by that of the Arabs, this was signified by a change to a new but equally universal monotheistic religion.

Christianity in Africa did survive the advance of Islam, but only narrowly. It survived in Egypt but not further west. Could this really be because of the higher 'quality' of the Church over which Bishop Cyril had presided in Alexandria as compared to Bishop Augustine's Church in Numidia and Carthage? Perhaps a more useful explanation lies in the contrasting nature of the conquest in Egypt and in North Africa: in Egypt the Arab conquest came extremely rapidly, and was accepted pacifically by the population, which had, in any case, been largely alienated from the Eastern Roman Empire. This was bound up with the drive for religious conformity and the persecution of the Copts for their adherence to the 'one nature' (Monophysite) theology which had been condemned at Chalcedon in 451. The Arabs were, by contrast, tolerant of Coptic religious sensibilities. The Eastern Empire had always been more diverse and heterogeneous – not least in the variety of its Christian expressions based on Antioch, Alexandria or Constantinople; and divided, in terms of Christology, into Melchite ('the king's faction', i.e. the emperor's Chalcedonian party), Nestorian or Jacobite. Long before 641 CE these differences had in many parts of the East come to have an ethnic dimension. The Islamic practice of recognizing ethnic minorities in the East, in so far as they followed a 'religion of the Book' – the *Dhimma* or 'protected people' – worked to the advantage of the Egyptian Church. Indeed the Orthodox Copts, proud of their monastic heritage and anchored in the *mia physis* (one nature) theology of Cyril, regarded the coming of the Muslim rulers as a relief from Melchite oppression from Byzantium. The invasion of North Africa was much more prolonged and bitter, and the proximity of co-religionists in south Italy and Spain meant that flight, rather than the 'internal emigration' of Coptic intellectuals, was often easier and more sensible, when resistance became futile.

One aspect of the survival of the Church in Egypt is the fact that, partly as a result of the monastic movement beginning in the early fourth century, Christianity had ceased to be overwhelmingly urban and Hellenic, and had become incorporated into the native Egyptian culture of the Nile valley. The Bible and liturgy had been translated into Coptic languages. They, along with monasticism, became the principal vehicle for the survival of Christianity in an increasingly Arabic and Islamic culture. The Muslim rulers of Egypt continued to rely on the Christian Coptic community for their professional, literary and commercial skills as administrators, traders, fullers, cabinetmakers. By the tenth century, Copts had become a minority in the population, and increasingly they were required to live in special settlements (ghettos), and to wear a distinctive uniform. Christian men were not allowed to marry out of the community. Muslim men could marry Christian women – the children would be Muslim. Active evangelism by Christians was prohibited, and there were incentives, notably relief from the burden of a discriminatory tax system, for Christians who converted to Islam. As a result of immigration from Arabia and the entropy of individual conversion to Islam, Coptic Christianity over the centuries became the minority faith. But the very distinctiveness, introversion and silence imposed on the Copts helped the Christian community to survive even the change to Arabic as the language of the Christian community (Coptic continued as the liturgical and biblical language). The leader of the Copts, their Patriarch or Pope, was chosen by lot (a practice which perhaps minimized state interference in the choice) from a list of monks, preferably young. This encouraged long patriarchates, and reduced the disruption to the community which the death of a patriarch always caused. The Coptic community was always conscious of the fragility of its relationship to a predominantly Muslim power. The Crusades, that incursion of Western Christendom ('the Franks') into the East, put the local Christian community in Egypt under intolerable suspicion without giving any tangible benefits, and forced the Copts to be very wary of contacts with Latin Christendom. These could be so easily misinterpreted as disloyalty to the Egyptian rulers. In any case the Latins showed little sensitivity to the theological and spiritual traditions of Coptic Christianity, now reinvigorated through a wealth of scholarly and devotional literature in Arabic.[3]

Coptic Christianity continued to be the focal point for a wider African Christianity, no longer spread out along the Mediterranean littoral, but flourishing in the Nile valley. The land of Nubia, to the south of the first cataract at Aswan, had never been part of the Roman Empire, but had always been receptive to religious movements coming from Egypt. Christianity spread in an informal way into Nubia through trade and probably also through the establishment of Coptic monastic communities along the banks and islands of the Nile. In the sixth century, just a century before Rome lost its control of Africa, Nubia became the target of rival evangelistic missions from the Byzantine court. The initial impetus for this state-directed evangelism had a lot to do with strategic considerations – providing, in the upper Nile valley, stable regimes allied to the empire. Rivalries between the Chalcedonian Christology of Emperor Justinian and the Monophysite leanings of his wife, the Empress Theodora, resulted in the official mission being held up. The party of Theodora, led by Julian and Longinus, were the first to preach to King Silko of Nobatia (the northernmost kingdom of Nubia). The aim of keeping the southern border quiet remained a strategic consideration for the Muslim rulers who took over Egypt in 641. Peace and security were promoted for many centuries by the *Baqt* treaty with the rulers of Nubia, giving them the space and freedom to develop a distinctively Nubian Christian culture. Nubia continued to look to Byzantine court models for its inspiration; but the Christological divisions, unlikely to have been of great significance either way for rulers or people, were resolved in favour of the Monophysitism of the Copts, who now provided the chief supply of monks, priests and bishops for the Church in Nubia.

Archaeological excavations, conducted by Polish archaeologists (and other national teams) under the auspices of UNESCO in the 1950s and 1960s, have done much to further understanding of Nubian Christianity, emphasizing, for example, the vigour of the mural pictorial representation of the churches excavated on the islands and along the banks of the Nile, and the possibility that there were black (i.e. Nubian) priests and religious as well as Copts. During times when the Nubian kingdoms were strong they were even able to offer some kind of protection for the minority Coptic community – for example, in 745 marching to Cairo to secure the release of an imprisoned Pope. Relations with the Fatimid regime which ruled Egypt from 969 tended to be cordial, but the coming of the Abbuyids in 1171 inaugurated a more aggressive policy towards Nubia on the part of Egypt. The next centuries saw increasing pressures on the Christian kingdoms, Arab invasion and settlement, conversion to Islam and Egyptian backing for Muslim contenders for the throne. The last Christian King of Nobatia was defeated in 1323, though a smaller splinter-kingdom of Dotawo did have a Christian ruler as late as 1494. The large number of churches destroyed during this period testifies to an intense conflict; the rebuilding of churches as fortresses shows equally that there was a strong national resistance to the inexorable Islamification. Although a Christian kingdom in Alwa to the south does seem to have lingered on, by 1500 Christianity had all but disappeared from Nubia.[4]

Ethiopia

Christianity came to Ethiopia earlier. It faced similar pressures to Nubia in the face of Islam. But in Ethiopia, Christianity survived. Ethiopia, too, relied on Coptic support and sustenance, but it should be stressed that the Ethiopian Orthodox Church is not a mission Church of Egypt. It is not 'Coptic', and has its own distinctive life and traditions. The origins of Christianity in the mountain kingdom of Aksum go back to the fourth century, to the visit of two Christian merchants from Syria, Frumentius and Aedesius, to the court of the Negus (king). These young men became important figures during the minority of King Ezana, using their position to spread the Christian message at court; to such an extent that the king ascribed his successful expansionist policy to 'the Lord of Heaven' (echoing the association of conquest and religion which Constantine had made not long before). In 346 Frumentius went to Egypt to discuss the needs of the new Christian community with Bishop Athanasius. He found himself consecrated as the first Bishop (Abuna) of the Ethiopian Church – and became known as Abba Salama. In the succeeding centuries monks from both Syria and Egypt played a large part in spreading the Gospel into the surrounding countryside of Aksum and, as in Egypt and Nubia, making the monastery basic to the health of the Ethiopian Church. Even more crucial was the support of the rulers and the close identification between Church and monarchy and the Amharic culture.

One of the unique features of Ethiopian Christianity is its sense of identity with the Jewish heritage of Christianity. Ethiopia is part of a Semitic world (Amharinya is a Semitic language). There may well have been a Jewish presence (as there was in Arabia just across the Red Sea) long before the coming of Christianity. For centuries a small group of Amharic people, the Falasha, have described themselves as Jewish: they obey the law (Torah) and respect the Sabbath. But the Ethiopian Church also sees itself as the heir of Judah. The greatest of the Zagwe kings, Lalibela, returned from pilgrimage to Jerusalem determined to re-create a 'Zion' in Ethiopia. The great rock churches of Lasta (often with names from biblical topology) are the result. When the Zagwe dynasty, regarded as usurpers, was overthrown in 1270, the new dynasty was anxious to stress its legitimacy. In the *Kebra Negast* (The Glory of the Kings), the descent of the kings from King Solomon was emphasized, with the legend of Sheba returning to her Ethiopian realm pregnant with Solomon's son, Menelik I. According to this foundation myth, Menelik was to return to his father's court to bring back the Ark of the Covenant (the *tabod*) to Ethiopia. Replicas of the ark are placed at the centre of all new churches in Ethiopia, and the churches themselves are designed on an idealized plan of Solomon's temple in Jerusalem.

Kebra Negast was translated into Ge'ez from Arabic in the reign of Amda Siyon (1314–44), whose 'glorious reign' is remembered as the time when the boundaries of the Christian kingdom expanded as never before, through military conquest followed by a process of Christianization and acculturation. Yet the king himself was subject to criticism by the monks for his failure personally to exemplify Christian values. Strong rulers like Amda Siyon and, in the next century, Zara Ya'iqob (1434–68) were successful in forging a strong sense of nationhood. But the variety of peoples incorporated into the empire (for example the disparate Oromo peoples to the south), as well as the mountainous terrain, meant that this unity was always very fragile, and centrifugal forces correspondingly powerful. This was true of the Church too. The Abuna continued to be called from Egypt, in a process which required delicate negotiations with the Muslim authorities in Cairo. He arrived as a complete stranger to Ethiopia, the upholder of orthodoxy, but inevitably circumscribed in his practical power and influence. This tended to be exercised by the monasteries around the capital in Shoa (the centre of power in Ethiopia had gradually moved southwards), one of whose abbots, Takla Haymonot of the monastery of Dabra Libanos, was regarded as having played an important part in the restoration of the dynasty. The abbot became an important official at court. Known as the *Echage*, he was appointed by the Crown, and responsible for the practical management of the affairs of the Church. But, to many of the more ancient monasteries in the northern heartlands of the kingdom, this alliance between monarchy, Abuna and Echage often represented a falling away from the ancient traditions of the Church. One conflict crystallized these different perceptions – the question of the observance of the Sabbath. The northern monasteries, grouped round the figure of Abbot Ewostatewos, conservatively defended the Jewish traditions of the Church and emphasized Sabbath observance as opposed to Sunday observance, which the Ewostatewians claimed was an innovation of the Abuna and the Copts. Eventually a *modus vivendi* was reached at the Council of Mitmaq (1450) in which both Sabbaths were honoured. By this time the Church, and monasteries in particular, had become great landowners, responsible for tax collection and assuming a considerable burden of administration on behalf of the state.[5]

The Christian kingdom of the highlands was by now surrounded by Islamic peoples. There is another important 'foundation myth' in Ethiopia which is used to explain the comparatively good relations between the Christian kingdom and Islam. It relates to the refuge afforded the companions of the Prophet Muhammad when they fled from persecution in Mecca before the Hegira. This act of hospitality established a cordiality which subsisted for many centuries. Islam penetrated the highlands and Muslims became an important minority, including a large merchant community of Amharic speakers. It was in the sixteenth century that this mutual acceptance was disrupted by the violent incursions of the Muslim general nicknamed Gran ('the left-handed'). Between 1529 and 1543 Gran ravaged and devastated the whole of the Christian highlands, destroying churches and monasteries. Ethiopia sought assistance from Portugal, an intervention which may well have been decisive for the survival of the Christian kingdom, and which certainly opened up the way for greater contact with European Christianity. The Spanish Jesuit, Father Paez, after being captured by pirates and forced to work for a number of years as a galley slave, eventually arrived in Ethiopia in 1603. His generous and sympathetic approach resulted in an interest in Catholicism on the part of the emperor, which may well have been prompted by an appreciation of the greater potential assistance which Rome could offer Ethiopia in comparison with a weakened and beleaguered Coptic Christianity, and the crisis provoked by this unprecedented challenge from Islam. The alliance led to the appointment of another Jesuit, this time a Portuguese, Alphonsus Mendez, as the first non-Egyptian Abuna since Frumentius. But the resentment already invoked by these breaks with tradition was exacerbated by the complete insensitivity with which Mendez tried to reform the Ethiopian Church to bring it into line with Roman Catholic theology and practice. He insisted on rebaptism of lay people, the reordination of clergy, the reconsecration of churches – a programme extraordinary in its arrogance and one which almost immediately proved self-defeating. The civil war which ensued resulted in the abdication of Susenyos in favour of his son Fasiladas, who in 1632 formally dissolved the union with Rome and expelled the Jesuits. It left a legacy of bitterness against outside intrusion in the life of the Ethiopian Church, and a fragmented Church often bitterly quarrelling about Christological dogma – quarrels which may have their roots in Catholic attempts to introduce Duophysite notions into the Church. The disputes also reflected the wider fragmentation of Ethiopian society between the seventeenth and nineteenth centuries, as the emperor was reduced to political impotence in the face of regional barons.

The fascination of Ethiopian Christianity lies in its development of a coherent and distinctive form of the faith, built on its own traditions and (for the first time in Africa) to a large extent independent from Hellenic or Roman models (though the eucharistic liturgy was shaped by Alexandrian traditions). It was a Christian culture strongly integrated into African life and ideas of kingship, combined with a vigorous local presence based on a peasant priesthood, hereditary in families which had rights to church land (*gult*) and tithes. Monasticism was crucial in supplying the learning and scholarship which the largely uneducated deacons and priests could not provide. Vital for the life of the local parish were the *dabtara*, the lay cantors responsible for intoning the divine service based on a musical system of chants of great antiquity. *Dabtara* had a rigorous musical training, and could be much better educated people than the village priest. They often combined these skills with a reputation as healers. Christianity became part of the very fabric of peasant life in Ethiopia, incorporating traditional views of the spirit world without the sense of conflict which was to be such a feature of nineteenth- and twentieth-century mission Christianity. But the Christianization of marriage practice was to be as problematic for the Ethiopian Church as it was for later missionary Christianity. Even the most revered, successful and Christianizing emperors found it hard to combine 'Christian' views of marriage with the expediency of using polygamy as a political tool in fostering and sustaining alliances within the state. As a result there was a running battle with the monks, the guardians of Christian monogamy. Christian practice was equally difficult to achieve at a village level. As a result few married in the church, and it became the conventional understanding that participation in the sacrament of the Eucharist was only for the very young (before they reached puberty) and the very old. These patterns have been replicated time and again in many diverse forms in the modern history of Christianity in the rest of the continent.

In Egypt, Nubia, Ethiopia, the Church often seemed woefully ill-equipped to withstand the pressures from an expanding self-confident Islam. Its inability, especially in Nubia, truly to develop a self-sustaining indigenous clergy was a fatal weakness. The development of viable local forms of episcopacy are crucial to this process, and even Ethiopia failed adequately to deal with this issue – to its detriment in both the sabbatarian conflicts and the encounter with Catholicism. That Christianity did survive at all anywhere in Africa in the face of Islam is perhaps as remarkable as its catastrophic decline. As Adrian Hastings has vividly put it: 'Thus at times violently, but more often quietly enough, did Islam advance while Christianity, like an ill-adapted dinosaur, declined and expired in place after place, crushed essentially by its own limitations, its fossilized traditions, and the lack of a truly viable, self-renewing structure.'[6]

The kingdom of Kongo and the Portuguese missionary enterprise

If, at the end of the fifteenth century, the expansion of Islam seemed to threaten the very existence of African Christianity, there was a very different mood in Portugal, a country exhilarated by the *Reconquista*, the expulsion of the Moors from Iberia, and by the pioneering naval exploits of Henry the Navigator and Vasco da Gama in undermining what Europeans conceived as the Muslim stranglehold on the route to the wealth of the Indies. For the Portuguese, Africa was both near at hand and a necessary stage on the way to the distant goal of Eastern wealth. Diplomatic alliances with African rulers would help further to consolidate the anti-Islamic crusade. A mark of such alliance became the acceptance of the Catholic faith, signified by the baptism of the rulers and their wives and the bestowal of new Portuguese, preferably suitably regal-sounding, names. For many West African rulers this was primarily a strategic and diplomatic gesture rather than something with intrinsically religious import – not least since the King of Portugal, following Catholic teaching, condemned the sale of gunpowder and weapons to non-Christians. Baptism thus opened the way to the legitimate sale of arms, with all the advantages which that gave in local struggles for power. The great exception to this shallow cultural and religious contact was the kingdom of Kongo. The *mindele* (the ships, literally the whales) of the Portuguese were first sighted in 1482, and negotiations inaugurated which resulted in the baptism of the Manikongo (the ruler), Nzinga Nkuwa. Christianity became an established cult at the court. Succession disputes were a routine feature of the transition of power from one generation to the next. Now this took the form of a battle between traditionalist and Christian factions.

The baptized son, Afonso, defeated his pagan brother and began a reign of nearly 40 years (1506–1543). What distinguished these events from similar encounters on the west coast of Africa over the previous 50 years, was that Afonso worked actively and assiduously to build a Christian kingdom in Kongo, through the establishment of a strong Christian cult at court. The *Regimento* agreement of 1512 envisaged an ongoing alliance with Portugal, involving trade and a programme of Portuguese acculturation promoted by the clergy, missionary, mixed race and African. Afonso's son, Don Henrique, was sent to Portugal for education, and returned to Kongo having been ordained as 'Bishop of Utica and Vicar Apostolic of the Kongo'. But much of the optimism of this project was undermined by the increasingly exploitative nature of the commercial relationship between Portugal and Kongo, the depredations of the slave trade on the life of the country, the arrogance and insensitivity of Europeans in the face of the genuine attempts of Africans to incorporate Lusitanian culture. The Portuguese clung tenaciously to the *padroado* – the concession from the Pope that the Portuguese Crown would have rights of patronage and appointment to high office in the Church overseas (from China to Brazil) – long after they had declined as a European power and were unable effectively to utilize the privilege for the well-being of the Catholic Church. Kongo was the victim of *padroado* and the mentality it engendered. On Henrique's premature death, there was no attempt to repeat the experiment of an African bishop. In the first flush of enthusiasm for the benefits of Portuguese and Christian civilization, Mbanza Kongo (the capital city) had been named São Salvador. Briefly at the end of the sixteenth century it became an episcopal centre (with a missionary bishop), but this was subsequently moved to the Portuguese colony of Luanda. Portugal proved unable to provide a reliable, regular supply of secular clergy or members of missionary orders; but it was zealous in keeping out missionaries of other nations.

It was only in 1645, taking advantage of the temporary eclipse of Portuguese power in the region to the Dutch, that Italian Capuchin friars, sent by Propaganda, were able to begin work. They were enthusiastically welcomed by the Manikongo, Garcia II. Under Capuchin inspiration Christianity further expanded into the countryside. The friars organized campaigns to destroy *nkisi* (fetishes) and undermine the work of traditional *nganga* (healers). Yet the Capuchins called themselves *nganga*, presenting themselves as the new arbiters of the sacred, to replace the old religious experts. Christianity, which at court had been closely identified with Portuguese culture, was becoming extensively acculturated to the rhythms and exigencies of Kongo life. Baptism became popular and with it the prestige of a Portuguese name and the honorific title 'Dom' or 'Donna'. The other sacraments did not become widespread – the paucity of missionaries and the failure to sustain a programme for training and ordaining local priests made this impossible. Interpreter–catechists accompanied many of the Capuchins on their itinerations and this office developed a status and prestige of its own, enabling local initiative and leadership to assert itself, despite the lack of opportunities and encouragement for ordained ministry. There was a wide level of accommodation to local concepts of the spirit world and its power. But, as Hastings has noted, the mentality of people in the Kongo was anyway not so far removed from that of pre-Enlightenment Catholic southern Europe.[7]

The impact of Christianity on the African environment of the Kongo can be seen dramatically in the emergence of the Antonian movement of Donna Beatrice (her African name was Kimpa Vita) in the early years of the eighteenth century, at a time when Kongo was fast disintegrating as a coherent polity. Beatrice has something of the Jeanne d'Arc about her, though she was a member of the aristocracy rather than a peasant girl. St Antony of Padua, a thirteenth-century Franciscan saint who had been born in Lisbon, was one of the most popular saints of Portuguese sailors, and his devotion was widespread in both Brazil and Kongo. Beatrice claimed to be possessed by Antony, who was telling her to rescue and renew the Christian nation. Under Antony's guidance, she urged the

Manikongo to gather the courage to reoccupy the capital of São Salvador, Christ's holy city, which in Beatrice's spiritual topography was the place of his birth, but was now in ruins, in the hands of usurpers. But as her campaign gathered momentum and became a popular movement, the Capuchins began to be anxious about the heterodox implications of much of what she was doing, not least her attack on fetishes (*nkisi*), since she began to include even crucifixes in this category. The fact that she appointed a male assistant called 'St John' her 'guardian angel', by whom she became pregnant, seemed further to discredit her message in Capuchin eyes. They persuaded the authorities to arrest her and she and her partner were burnt as heretics in 1706. The momentum of national rejuvenation was sustained for a time – in 1709 Pedro IV 'the Pacific' did succeed in reoccupying São Salvador, but there was no real revival of an extensive Kongo kingdom, which continued to disintegrate, along with the organized life of the Catholic Church. By the nineteenth century there was little left in terms of an institutional Church, ordained ministry and doctrinal coherence of what had once been a hopeful establishment of the Christian Church in tropical Africa.

Portuguese Christian influence continued – in the enclave of Luanda, a centre for the Atlantic slave trade; and on the great latifundia of the Zambesi valley – the *prazos* – where Portuguese and mixed-race plantation owners increasingly adopted the African mentalities and world-view of the area, with the rites and doctrines of Catholicism performing an altogether peripheral role: a reverse acculturation. Portugal, for its part, was no longer able to provide the resources of personnel or the conviction of spirit to fulfil much of a role in the evangelization of Africa.[8] In the Zambesi the most active missionary work was undertaken on *prazos* run by Dominicans and Jesuits, whose origins were often Spanish or Italian rather than Portuguese.

The revival of mission in the nineteenth century

West Africa

For three and a half centuries the major contact between Europe and Africa was the slave trade. 'The South Atlantic system consumed people, just as other industries consume raw materials', as Curtin has put it.[9] Such a dehumanizing commerce was hardly conducive to cultural, let alone, religious exchange, as the Abolitionists well recognized. Estimates of the number thus 'exported' to the New World between 1500 and 1870 vary from Walter Rodney's 15 million to Philip Curtin's 9 million. (These figures relate to those who arrived alive in the Americas and do not try to calculate the overall cost in human lives.) The Portuguese were the major carriers in the sixteenth century, to be replaced by the Dutch in the seventeenth, and the British and French in the eighteenth. The British and the French were subsequently to become the most enthusiastic missionaries to West Africa in the nineteenth century. Meanwhile, until the 1860s, the trade itself continued at a high level, with the Americans and Brazilians as major traders. The Society of Friends was the first group of Christians to express the incompatibility of the trade with a Christian view of humanity. At the end of the eighteenth century the evangelical awakening in Britain created a climate of opinion increasingly hostile to the slave trade, at a time when the restrictive mercantilism which the Atlantic trade represented was seen as inhibiting the development of the free trade and economic liberalism so cogently advocated by Adam Smith.

An optimism about the benign world-wide consequences of the diffusion of capitalism was paralleled by a strong sense that *now* was the God-given opportunity to spread the beneficent message of the Gospel. The moral activism of the evangelical movement expressed itself in the creation of voluntary missionary societies, felt to be a much more effective and appropriate instrument of evangelism than the state-sponsored missions embodied in the Portuguese *padroado* system or the British and Dutch trading company chaplains. The fact that abolitionism and the associated missionary movement were from the first British meant that it was Protestant evangelicalism which pioneered the renewed missionary thrust into sub-Saharan Africa. Mission work in the Roman Catholic Church had certainly striven hard to free itself from an exclusive reliance on state patronage, especially after the creation of the Roman Congregation of Propaganda Fide in 1622. But Catholicism was at a low ebb in 1800: the Society of Jesus, hitherto the most efficient missionary order, had been dissolved; the Church as an institution was severely undermined throughout Europe by the French Revolution. It was only after the defeat of Napoleon that Catholicism was able to re-create the morale and the structures which would enable it to grasp the new opportunities presented throughout the world. The state, even where Catholic regimes survived or were restored, could not be relied on to organize mission. Catholic revival sprang from the life of the Church itself, both at the centre and in the parishes, from the Vatican and from the faithful. In Rome, the Congregation of Propaganda was revived in 1817, and Pope Gregory XVI (1831–46) made it an important task of his papacy to promote missions. In France there was also a new enthusiasm for voluntary effort. The mid-nineteenth century saw the creation (or renewal) of orders with a specific African focus: the Holy Ghost Fathers, the Society for African Missions, the White Fathers, the Verona Fathers. This was combined with a new popular interest at parochial level, fostered and directed by agencies such as the Lyons-based Association for the Propagation of the Faith. But the

Catholics were a generation behind the Protestants as far as the renewed missionary interest in Africa was concerned.

One of the unintended consequences of the slave trade was the creation of the 'black Atlantic' – a phrase used by Paul Gilroy to describe the importance of a new cultural diaspora formed by people of African descent, stretching from Africa to the Americas and Europe. One of the first representatives of this tradition to receive fame and recognition was Olaudah Equiano, captured as a ten-year-old from his Igbo homeland in West Africa and enslaved in the West Indies. He spent a number of years as a sailor, before settling in England as a free man. He became active in the abolitionist cause. His book, *The Interesting Narrative of the Life of Olaudah Equiano* (1789), was a powerful abolitionist tract as well as a testimony to Christian evangelical experience.

The first obvious impact of this British interest in Africa was a rather ambiguous one: the creation of a 'colony of freedom', Sierra Leone. In so far as it was a way of 'solving' the London 'black problem' by dumping urbanized black people in an inhospitable tropical rural slum, it was regarded with suspicion by Africans in Britain. Its faltering existence was only given any real viability by the abolition of the British slave trade in 1807, and the establishment of a British Squadron off the coast of West Africa to enforce compliance on reluctant European powers (who, as part of Napoleon's Continental system, were at war with Britain at the time). Freetown became the place where recently enslaved Africans, who had never crossed the Atlantic, were landed back in Africa. They were called 're-captives'. The majority were Yoruba in origin, nicknamed 'Aku' in Sierra Leone. The Anglican Church Missionary Society (CMS) and the Methodist Wesleyan Missionary Society were chiefly involved in building up a new Christian society in Freetown. Parishes (which had both civil and pastoral status) had names like Wilberforce and Waterloo, and social life was based on the solid institutions of church and chapel and school (by the end of the nineteenth century often mirroring the social and religious sectarianism which this entailed in England). There was an aspiration, shared by missionaries and Creoles (as the freed slaves and their descendants came to be called), that there could be a thoroughgoing educative process whose aim was to create African Englishmen. Someone like the Creole lawyer Sir Samuel Lewis (1843–1903) is the epitome of this:

His career provides an outstanding example of an African's successful response to the culture of Western Europe ... The really formative influences of his life had little to do with the culture of tribal Africa, even as handed on through the Aku community of Freetown; though he was known to express his pride in his Yoruba ancestry, this was not a living force. His career was made among, and his character was moulded by, essentially 'Western' institutions – the English bar, the Wesleyan Church, the business world of Freetown, the Legislative Council.[10]

This vignette, though it certainly captures an important facet of Lewis's experience, needs to be read with some caution – 'Western' and 'tribal', European and African, are not the ready-made forms of life implied by the quotation. Sierra Leone middle-class culture was neither simply a reflection of English values a generation out of date, nor an attenuated form of Yoruba tradition. It had a dynamism and creativity of its own.

For many successful Aku, the Yoruba heritage was certainly more than a nostalgic dream, though it was impossible simply to return to the world of one's childhood. From the 1830s many did return to their native land, for business, and also as Christian missionaries. Abeokuta, a Yoruba city state, itself in the process of re-creation after the years of disruption throughout Yorubaland (particularly intense in the early years of the nineteenth century and responsible for the enslavement of so many of the re-captives), became an important community for returning Aku, as did Lagos on the coast. Other Yoruba city states began to invite missionaries (both European and African) to settle within their walls. It seemed highly advantageous to have in one's midst someone who in one way or another could be regarded as a representative of British power. But, with the British takeover of Lagos in 1861, British power came to be regarded with much greater suspicion, and missionaries were required to leave the cities of the interior.

The Yoruba Christian returnees were concerned both to uphold and preserve their native society and to reform it. The translation of the Scriptures into the vernacular was embarked upon, by missionaries and Creole agents. From this literary work grew a desire to establish the validity and legitimacy of local culture, and to contribute to its delineation and preservation, through writing down its history and traditions and customs. The motive was certainly not a nostalgic antiquarianism but a concern for cultural integrity in societies undergoing profound transformations. One can cite the work of a Creole clergyman, the Revd Samuel Johnson's *History of the Yoruba*. This kind of project was not simply the work of those who looked at their culture from one remove, which, of necessity, was the experience of those Creoles who had experienced radical displacement and reorientation. It can also be seen in the work of the Basel mission on the Gold Coast (Ghana) – in the great cultural enterprise among the Akan people undertaken by the German missionary Johannes Christaller and his local collaborator and colleague, David Asante from Akropong.[11]

Edward Wilmot Blyden (1832–1912) was an important figure both in the development of Creole self-consciousness, and in the critique of Creole Christianity. A native of the West Indies, he spent much of his life in West Africa (in Liberia and Sierra Leone). He was a brilliant linguist, more independent in both intellectual outlook and lifestyle than those brought up in missionary institutions and relying on the mission for their livelihood could be. His book *Christianity, Islam and the Negro Race* (1887) brings together articles written over a number of years. One of his recurring themes is the potential of Christianity to speak from within the African condition. But he was critical of the somewhat artificial way in which this had developed within Creole Christianity, as compared with the organic process which he discerned in the slow development over many centuries of West African Islam. He urged the creation of a native African Church – an attractive proposition to many of those involved in the Native Pastorate controversy within the CMS and Anglican circles in Sierra Leone in the 1870s, and its aftermath. This controversy arose from a feeling that the Church was dragging its feet in implementing the 'three selves' policy of Henry Venn, the Secretary of CMS. Venn argued that the missionary task was essentially pioneering. Its aim was to create a self-governing, self-financing and self-propagating local Church which would free the mission to pioneer new fields: the 'euthanasia of the mission'. In Sierra Leone this met with local missionary opposition – a combination of a hard-headed realism from the Europeans on the spot in the face of armchair theorizing, doubts about the actual level of financial self-sufficiency obtainable in the local Church and a tendency to despise or minimize the Creole achievement.

An articulate young priest called James Johnson (1840–1917) was the spokesman of the Creole Christian community in Sierra Leone, especially during the Native Pastorate controversy of 1871–74. He antagonized Bishop Cheetham by the force of his protests against the racial discrimination practised within the structures of Sierra Leonian Anglicanism and was transferred to Lagos to be pastor of the Breadfruit Church. Johnson later became the great defender of Bishop Samuel Ajayi Crowther (1806–91) against his detractors, in the controversy over the last years of Crowther's episcopacy on the Niger. Crowther is probably the most famous West African Christian of the nineteenth century. A Yoruba freed slave, he was one of the first graduates from the Fourah Bay College. Ordained as an Anglican priest, he did missionary work back in his home area, as well as being involved in the ill-fated Niger expedition of 1841. In 1862, when he was looking forward to retirement, Henry Venn appealed to him to accept the call to become Bishop on the Niger. Ostensibly a fulfilment of Venn's theories, in reality it broke all Venn's own rules: rather than a native bishop being the 'crown' of a self-sustaining local Church (Sierra Leone would have been the obvious choice), Crowther found himself in charge of an enormous area with inadequate resources and personnel, and almost completely devoid of local commitment, in finance or personnel. It was, in fact, a missionary diocese. For the next twenty years Crowther tried to build up the Church, with some success, but through the use of Creole pastors and evangelists rather than local people, and without being able to provide the training or the supervision which would have been necessary. Crowther lived hundreds of miles from the diocese in Lagos and did not have transport; and CMS, wedded to the fiction that this was a self-supporting native Church, was slow in giving adequate financial assistance. A number of moral scandals, and one widely reported murder case, implicated Church workers. The CMS missionaries who were introduced to the Niger from 1878 tended to blame Crowther's benevolent but indulgent leadership for these problems.

Then in 1889 a new group of young missionaries arrived under the leadership of Graham Wilmot Brooke, a man of independent means and no profession, who had been prepared for a military life. He was also a man of intense but unbalanced dynamism, impatient with all ecclesiastical and mission structures. The new group was influenced by the Keswick holiness teaching which was such an important stream of English Protestant spirituality at this time. They were rigorous in their criticisms of the spiritual and moral laxity which they saw in the congregations and among the workers. In other circumstances missionaries influenced by the Keswick movement were to do important and good work (for example Pilkington in Uganda), but in this environment their zeal overstepped the boundaries of prudence and good sense. Their moral absolutism combined with the increasing racial stereotyping of the Creoles as being in some sense innately inferior to proper natives – 'the dregs of society' as one missionary outrageously put it. The young missionaries' damning report on Crowther's 'nominal episcopate' reinforced the mood in CMS circles that this 'experiment' had been a failure and should not be repeated. To the great distress of the Christian community in Freetown and Lagos, when Crowther died he was not replaced by an African. The furore which these events created gave new impetus to the growth of 'Ethiopian' Churches – that is, Churches led by Africans independent of missionary control, usually retaining the liturgical and doctrinal standards of their Church of origin, but determined to fulfil in authentically African terms the biblical prophecy that 'Ethiopia [i.e. black Africa] shall stretch forth his hand to God' (Psalm 68:31). Already Mojola Agbebi had in 1888 established the Native Baptist Church. Others were to follow, though James Johnson resisted leaving the Anglican Church. In Hastings's words: 'More painfully than anyone else, Holy Johnson represents an Ethiopianism unable to repudiate its debt to European Christianity.'[12] Having refused to become what he scornfully called 'half-bishop', Johnson did at last become assistant bishop in the Niger delta, part of Crowther's old diocese. But, as West Africa fell under formal colonial rule in the 1890s, there was, in both mission-founded and 'Ethiopian' Churches, a strong undercurrent of African nationalist sentiment, to inform the debate about colonialism.[13]

South Africa

The development of Christian mission in South Africa presents a number of comparisons and contrasts to the West African nineteenth-century experience. One common theme in the development of an African Church is the crucial role played in both areas by Western-educated Africans, people who were conscious of being children of two worlds, bilingual both culturally and religiously. The main difference was the power of white settler Christianity in southern Africa, and the much more substantial European missionary presence. Missionary families, especially in the second and third generations, often merged into white settler society and absorbed its values. The Boer farmers, from Dutch, Huguenot and German stock, had by 1800 begun to identify themselves as 'African': 'ik bin ein Afrikander' was the famous boast of one *trekboer*. But this identification bore little resemblance to the Portuguese Zambesi experience of absorbing and internalizing the mentalities of the local cultures. The Afrikaner sense of being preserved as a People (*Volk*) against the odds (which stems at least partly from the Dutch experience of forging their nationhood in opposition to the sea and the Spanish) was reinforced by that exodus from British rule in the 1830s known as the Great Trek. It was not, at least in this period, as is often suggested, an outworking of orthodox Calvinism; rather one might call it a folk self-consciousness. In the nineteenth century Scottish evangelicalism was deeply to inform the life of the Dutch Reformed Church through the introduction of Scottish *dominies* (ministers), which also brought a more orthodox Reformed character to Afrikaner religion, as did the influence from Holland of Abraham Kuiper's neo-Calvinist theology at the end of the century. The Coloured community has also claims to be regarded as part of an Afrikaans culture, and many Coloured people belong to the Reformed Church – by the latter part of the nineteenth century organized in their own Churches rather than as 'inferior' members of the white congregation. Even the DRC by the end of the nineteenth century was beginning to become active in missionary work to black African peoples – enthusiastic about mission at a safe distance north of the Limpopo, and even as far afield as Nigeria, but increasingly seeing mission also in terms of evangelizing the local South African peoples among whom they lived. White Afrikaner religion is important for a more general discussion of African Christianity, both because it reflected and helped shape the way the Afrikaners conceived themselves, and because this in turn had such fundamental import for the whole of South African life. The Christianity of the English-speaking portion of the white community diverged less from the British norm, though it is interesting that the famous quarrel between Bishop Robert Gray of Cape Town and his fellow Bishop of Natal, John Colenso, whom Gray accused of heresy, had important implications for the development of the Anglican communion, being a major factor in the convening of the first Lambeth Conference in 1867.

The first English-speaking missionaries in the Cape (from 1799), especially the London Missionary Society (representing primarily a Congregational tradition), were extremely critical of the social effects on both indigenous inhabitants and imported slaves of Cape Dutch society. Johannes van der Kemp (a Dutchman employed by LMS) and his successor Dr John Philip (a Scot) campaigned for the human dignity of the Khoikhoi (the original inhabitants of the western Cape), and the growing mixed-race or Coloured community. Often the best means of securing that dignity seemed to be to establish separate and economically independent communities, both at the Cape and in the hinterland (for example, Griqualand) where Coloured people trekked to escape Boer dominance. Afrikaners bitterly resented such missionary interference in the ordering of social and economic relations with native peoples. Taking their cue from the perceived missionary protection of Coloured communities, some African rulers, most notably Moshoeshoe of the Basotho people (regrouping in the aftermath of Shaka's disruptions), invited missionaries as a means of strengthening and preserving their own societies from threatened disintegration in the face of European expansion. Such rulers often became disillusioned as they realized that the missionaries themselves could become conduits of the very forces they were trying to avoid. Increasingly this was not simply Afrikaner pastoralism, but British imperialism, and, with the discovery of diamonds and gold, the intrusion of international capitalism and industrialization. Moreover, missionaries often seemed to have a negative attitude to a whole range of important elements in African social life: polygamy, *lobola* (bride price), levirate marriage (of widows to brothers-in-law),[14] initiation ceremonies. The LMS missionary John Mackenzie talked enthusiastically of 'weakening the communistic relations of members of a tribe among one another and letting in the fresh, stimulating breath of healthy individualistic competition'.[15] The reality was that, though African chiefs were often the patrons of mission, they rarely succeeded in directing and taking charge of the processes of change and transformation which missionary Christianity brought.

Among the Xhosa, Christianity intruded at a time of severe disruption to society through a succession of wars with the settlers (British as well as Afrikaners, for the English had settled in the Port Elizabeth area from 1820). Mission stations often provided a refuge for those made landless by these wars; or those who for one reason or another wanted to escape their obligations to their chief: such people were dubbed *amaqoboka* – 'those having a hole where to hide'. Particularly receptive to the Christian message was a group which came to be known as Mfengu, whose core had originally fled as refugees from Shaka's wars (the *Mfeqane*), and were settled by the British as 'friendlies' in Xhosa areas. Two Xhosa figures from the early nineteenth century have come to symbolize two contrasting ways of responding to Christianity and British power: Nxele and Ntsikana. Nxele was a diviner who had had contact with Boer farmers and knew something of Christianity. In some ways he was a man who could be regarded as an outsider in both his own Xhosa society and in the white settler community, a type of person often regarded as particularly susceptible to religious change. But his initially favourable impression of Christianity turned to contempt and opposition. He saw mission stations as 'instruments of colonial espionage' and came to the conclusion that missionary religion was alien to African spirituality: the correct way to worship God is not, he said, 'to sing M'Dee, M'Dee, M'Dee all day and pray with their faces on the ground and their backs to the almighty – but to dance and enjoy life and to make love, so that the black people would multiply and fill the earth'.[16] All this led him, in 1819, to lead an attack by Xhosa warriors on the colonial frontier town of Grahamstown, advising his followers that the bullets would turn to water (a recurring theme in the African religious resistance to colonialism and informing such diverse movements as the Maji Maji resistance in German East Africa in 1905 and Alice Lakwena's Holy Spirit movement in Uganda in 1986). Captured and imprisoned on Robben Island (one of the first of an illustrious line of political prisoners), he was drowned trying to swim to freedom in 1820.

Contrasted to Nxele is Ntsikana, a respected establishment figure in Xhosa society, councillor to the Ngqika chief. He advocated conciliation with white rule rather than futile opposition. Steeped in Xhosa spiritual values, including the spiritual value of cattle (one of his most famous dreams concerns his favourite ox), his thinking became increasingly influenced by Christian values. He composed praise songs and hymns to the Almighty, which were passed down and altered within the Christian community and became the core of Xhosa hymnody. He was never baptized but wanted to be buried 'in the Christian manner'. He was a profound influence on a whole generation of educated Christian Xhosa, who came into their own in the aftermath of the traumatic failure of the Cattle-killing movement of 1857. This event was associated with the young girl Nongqawuse who prophesied that, if Xhosa killed all their cows and stopped growing maize, there would be a general resurrection of the ancestors, a renewal of the earth and a restoration of prosperity. Cattle were already threatened by an epidemic of lung-sickness, but the overall result was quite the opposite of the prophecy: famine, the collapse of organized resistance to British expansion, an exodus of Xhosa onto white farms, the crumbling of self-confidence by a whole culture:

> Your cattle are gone, my countrymen!
> Go rescue them!
> Leave the breechloader alone
> And turn to the pen.
> Take paper and ink,
> For that is your shield.
> Your rights are going,
> So pick up your pen.
> Load it, load it with ink.
> Sit on a chair
> Repair not to Hoho
> But fire with your pen.[17]

In the aftermath of this terrifying experience, Xhosa turned more than ever before to mission Christianity and to the school, though this was by no means universal — there remains a profound cleavage in society between the 'reds' (traditionalists) and the 'school people'. Missions, Methodist, Presbyterian, Anglican in particular, offered high schools, which, like their equivalents in Lagos and Freetown, provided a high standard of Western education. The most famous was the Scottish mission at Lovedale (established in 1841), in whose vicinity was erected Fort Hare College in 1916. For many years Fort Hare was to offer degrees to Africans from all over the continent, until it was demoted to the status of a Xhosa 'tribal' college under the terms of the apartheid legislation of the 1950s. In the late nineteenth century, an impressive array of educated and articulate Christian Xhosa emerged. Tiyo Soga (married to Janet Burnside, a Scot) was a Presbyterian minister, hymn writer, the translator into Xhosa of *Pilgrim's Progress*. His son John Henderson Soga was the author of an important book: *The Ama-Xosa: Life and Customs*. John Knox Bokwe was a musician and hymn writer. John Tengo Jabavu, an Mfengu, a Wesleyan layman, was a journalist and politician; his son D. D. T. Jabavu was the first African lecturer at Fort Hare. Enoch Sentonga was the composer of *Nkosi Sikelel i'Afrika* (God Bless Africa), eventually to become South Africa's national anthem. It was from this group, combining with others from the Zulu, Sotho and Tswana people, that the first leaders of the African Nationalist Congress of 1912 were recruited. As a group they can be compared with the educated elite of Lagos, Freetown and Monrovia — they have the same moral earnestness, 'pride of race', national consciousness. Perhaps more truly than the Creoles they were bicultural, walking with ease in a Western and a local milieu — but there is a similar sense of alienation as well. One of the greatest representatives is Solomon Plaatje, a Tswana journalist, novelist and Christian layman, who was sent by the ANC to London to make representations to the British government against the 1913 Land Act (a measure which consolidated the racial division of the land, giving whites 92 per cent and Africans 8 per cent). He proceeded to write the great polemical work *Native Life in South Africa*, with its haunting opening statement: 'Awaking on Friday morning, June 20, 1913, the South African native found himself, not actually a slave, but a pariah in the land of his birth.'[18] In many ways, in people like Plaatje, the great campaigning humanitarian tradition of South African Christianity, begun a century earlier by van der Kemp and Philip, was continued.

Eastern Africa

In considering West and South Africa in the nineteenth century, it has been important from the beginning to appreciate the creative ways in which Africans responded to the Christian faith and made it their own. In Eastern Africa, by contrast, the figure of the missionary takes on a greater importance: the missionary as explorer, as visionary of radical social transformation, as strategist concerned with a potential rather than an actual African Christian Church. David Livingstone (1813–73) travelled extensively throughout East Africa, publicizing the harrowing disruptive effects of the growing slave trade in this area (blamed on the Arabs, though its roots at the end of the nineteenth century were connected with the growth of European plantation economies of the Indian Ocean). Livingstone can usefully be contrasted with his contemporary, Ludwig Krapf, a Württemberger Lutheran who worked for the CMS in Ethiopia and, from 1844, at Rabai near Mombasa. Livingstone burnt with indignation at the suffering and oppression borne by Africans; Krapf's pietism led him to see Africans in terms of the fallenness which they share with all humanity.[19] Both missionaries were failures if winning converts is the measure of success. But both inspired many missionaries in their wake. Livingstone was sure that an end to suffering would only come through the radical reordering of society: 'I go back to Africa to make an open path for commerce and Christianity.' That might mean planting white settlers to pioneer a new agriculture; it certainly required a reordering of world trading patterns. Krapf was sceptical of relying on any form of colonialism: 'Banish the thought that Europe must spread her protecting wing over Eastern Africa if missionary work is to prosper in that land of outer darkness. Europe would, no doubt, remove much that is mischievous and obstructive . . . but she would probably set in its place as many but perhaps still greater checks.'[20]

In West and South Africa Roman Catholic missions throughout much of the nineteenth century were at a disadvantage compared with the Protestants who tended to set the agenda. In East Africa Catholics were able to take much more of a leading role. In 1838 the Lazarist priest Justin de Jacobis re-established a Catholic presence in Ethiopia, to be followed by the opening up, by Italian Capuchins under Guglielmo Massaja, of work among the Oromo of southern Ethiopia. Daniel Comboni inspired new efforts to re-establish a Christian Church in the Sudan. All three were to become bishops. Comboni was to create a new missionary order, the Verona Fathers. Another great administrator and mission strategist was Charles Lavigerie, Archbishop of Algiers. He established the White Fathers, who were to have a profound impact on East Africa. Their name referred to the long flowing white cassock (the Muslim-style *gandoura*) rather than to the racial composition of the order – in fact Africans became members of the order, and the first modern Catholic bishop, Archbishop Kiwanuka, from Uganda, was a White Father. Lavigerie created a strong, disciplined society, trained by Jesuits, and inspired by Jesuit spirituality and pastoral theology. The White Fathers insisted on a thorough catechumenate for converts, inculcating the essentials of the faith. They stressed the importance of the mission as a self-supporting community adapted to the environment and, above all, the necessity of their members becoming conversant in the local language.

The Holy Ghost Fathers, another French order, were the first to work on the East African coast. In 1863 they established a freed slave settlement at Bagamoyo. The Anglican CMS made a similar move at Freretown near Mombasa in 1873. Potentially these settlements could have done for East Africa what Freetown did for the West African coast. But they came into being half a century later, in very different circumstances. The European missionaries were more firmly in charge and were much more likely to see themselves as the initiator of missionary work, according much less autonomy for African Christians, whether the 'Bombay Africans', freed slaves who had received an education in mission schools in India, or local people. The settlements were too restrictive socially and too narrowly based economically to sustain the kind of communities which had developed in West Africa, and which gave so much energy and drive to African-initiated missionary work. With the coming of colonial rule in the 1890s the settlements rapidly disintegrated. The establishment of missions upcountry was to be under the direction of the European missionaries rather than something which sprang primarily from the initiatives of East African Christians (though there were individual Africans of note who took part in the missionary expansion of the 1880s and 1890s, such as the Revd William Jones, who accompanied Bishop Hannington on his fateful journey to Buganda, and James Mbotela, employed by the Africa Inland Mission as they began work in Ukambani).

But, even before these events of the early colonial period, there had been a remarkable development in the Great Lakes Region. Buganda was a strongly centralized sophisticated society, expansive and receptive to new ideas. Islam had gained a strong influence among the young pages (*bagalagala*) who resided at court and were in training as the future leaders of the country. In 1875 Henry Morton Stanley visited Buganda. The Kabaka (king), fearful of the political consequences of an overreliance on Muslim outsiders, discussed the possibility of Christian missionaries coming to his country, and Stanley dispatched his famous letter to *The Daily Telegraph* pleading for 'pious, practical missionaries' to come to Buganda. The Anglican CMS arrived in 1877 and the Catholic White Fathers in 1879, and were soon locked in bitter conflict with each other and with the Muslim faction. The vigour and enthusiasm of intellectual controversy stimulated rather than alienated the young Buganda elite, and very quickly each religion developed a substantial following. The Kabaka soon found that Christianity was likely to prove just as subversive as Islam. In attempting to clip its wings, first the Anglican Bishop James Hannington was killed *en route* to Buganda (along with a substantial number of Africans, including Christians and Muslims, from the coast), and then some 100 Christian converts, mainly from the ranks of the young pages, were burnt to death, many at the Namugongo execution site which was later to become a shrine. The main result of this holocaust was to convince the surviving adherents of the new religions that it was necessary to exercise power themselves – this gave rise to a coalition of Muslims, Catholics and Protestants, who overthrew the Kabaka and seized power in 1888. But the different factions were themselves soon involved in an internecine struggle which was only finally resolved by the intrusion of an outside colonial force and the emergence of the Protestant faction as the political victors – but now under British overrule. There are many examples in the modern history of Christianity in Africa of rulers acting as patrons of Christian missions. But Buganda is remarkable in that a whole ruling class became Christianized and, within a remarkably short period of time, initiated a thoroughgoing Christianization of society. Islam survived as an important minority; but the Christian Church, in both its Protestant and Catholic versions, became integral to Ganda society, with a profound effect on the moral, intellectual and cultural life, both nationally and locally. The Churches in Buganda became strong 'folk-Churches', with deep roots in the villages and among the peasantry throughout the land.

At around this time, in 1896, the Christian Emperor Menelik of Ethiopia defeated the Italians at the battle of Adwa – one of the few decisive defeats of a European power by an African nation in the era of the Scramble. It was an event of great significance for African Christians throughout the continent, reaffirming the sense of Christianity as an African faith with roots in the biblical narrative itself (Ethiopia in the Bible signifies black Africa as a whole), and reinforcing the sense that Africa figured in God's plan of salvation, even at this time of colonial intrusion, political, cultural and religious. This strong, unified Ethiopian state enabled the Ethiopian Orthodox Church to overcome its institutional and theological divisions, to reclaim areas lost in the sixteenth century and to engage in a missionary work which involved both an extension of the Christian message and Amharic cultural imperialism. It was an expansion which has been compared to the work of Baganda Catholic and Anglican evangelists and 'sub-imperialists' in extending the Gospel, British rule and Ganda cultural norms in many parts of Uganda in the early years of the twentieth century.

Colonial and missionary scrambles

Throughout much of the nineteenth century missionaries were quite content to live as guests of African rulers. In certain circumstances they did urge what was called a 'forward policy' in terms of their home government's involvement in Africa. Governments tended to be suspicious of such entanglements. Lord Palmerston acidly remarked about the Zambezi expedition of 1858: 'I am very unwilling to embark on new schemes of British possessions. Dr Livingstone's information is valuable but he must not be allowed to tempt us to form colonies only to be reached by forcing steamers up cataracts.'[21] Britain was reluctant to exchange its free trade policy for colonial entanglements; but as such adventures became more attractive for France, Germany and King Leopold of the Belgians (each for their own nationalistic or geopolitical reasons) so Britain felt compelled to stake its prior claim to much of Africa. Between the Congress of Berlin of 1885 and the early years of the twentieth century, most of Africa was partitioned against its will by European aggressors. The missions with long-standing interests in Africa were not at first at the forefront in the demand for colonies, though their presence was often useful to colonial powers in claiming 'spheres of interests'. By the 1880s the planting of new national missions might well be encouraged by European countries anxious for their 'place in the sun'. In the feverish atmosphere which increasingly took hold, missions might become militantly nationalistic – urging their sometimes reluctant home government to protect 'national' interests in the area against foreign predators, or what they saw as increasing anarchy within Africa itself. For example, the Scots missions campaigned for Britain to assert its interest in what became Nyasaland before the Portuguese (with a much longer interest) roused themselves. The CMS campaigned vigorously for the British government to take over Uganda, in the face of internal civil disorder, and German expansionist desires. By and large, African Christian communities might be predisposed, if not to welcome, at least to accept European control and to collaborate with the occupying power. But, equally, in areas of Islamic influence, European powers relied on Muslims to provide a corps of literate clerks and functionaries for the new administrative apparatus. Societies which traditionally had been resistant to Christian mission, like Ijebu in the hinterland of Lagos, might well fiercely resist colonial intrusion. Ijebu provides an interesting case, in that the Ijebu, reacting to their violent defeat at the hands of an imperialist force, became one of the most receptive peoples in Nigeria to the new religions (both Christian and Muslim). Even where missionaries had welcomed and promoted the colonial takeover, this did not necessarily mean that they were uncritical of the results: indeed long-standing missions, conscious of their greater knowledge of the situation, were predisposed to outspoken criticism of the perceived shortcomings or injustices of colonial rule. Missionaries were at the forefront of disclosing the atrocities of the rubber plantation economy of the Congo Free State; they were critical of forced labour in various East African British colonies; they advanced themselves as spokespersons and defenders of 'native interests' in settler-dominated colonies like Kenya or Rhodesia, with all the implications of paternalism which such a claim conveys.

As profound as the colonial takeover was to be, for most Africans it was just one of a whole host of crises to convulse Africa at the end of the nineteenth century: crises in the ecology, in medical pathology, in society and the increasing incorporation of Africa into a global capitalist economy. Robin Horton, in a famous discussion, examined the attraction of both Islam and Christianity in this period in terms of the enlargement of scale, the increasing importance of finding intellectual and conceptual resources to cope with a 'macrocosm' rather than simply a 'microcosm'. Even where the colonial impact at first seemed remote and safe to ignore except in superficial ways (the stance of certain predominantly pastoral peoples), the colonial takeover was, sooner or later, to impinge profoundly on all aspects of life and to be the driving force in a conceptual revolution. Islam and Christianity seemed to offer resources to cope with these radical changes; in sub-Saharan Africa, Christianity, as the religion of the colonial powers, had a definite advantage. It above all was equated with the modern, and modernization was seen as essential for Africa, in material as well as intellectual and even spiritual terms.[22]

Christianity in colonial times: education and 'adaptation'

For missionary Christianity, being a Christian and going to school were two aspects of the same process. Catechumens were called 'readers' precisely because they needed to learn basic literacy skills in order to cope with texts, whether biblical or catechetical.[23] In the nineteenth century, missions had created boarding high schools (in British missions often attempting to replicate a public school ethos), with a 'grammar school' curriculum of classical languages, and with a European language as the medium of teaching. By the end of the century there had developed a more 'modern' curriculum, and there was the beginnings of an emphasis on vocational and technical skills.

There was also the basic elementary catechetical teaching in the vernacular, and this sector everywhere expanded enormously under colonialism. What was the relationship between these elementary schools and the high school, which inevitably could only teach a privileged minority? Could the 'school in the bush' serve as the basis for a colonial education system?

These issues became particularly pertinent in the years after the end of the First World War, when colonial governments developed their own ideas of responsibility for the welfare of their subjects. Missions were anxious that governments would not try to create parallel secular systems in which the Christian ethos would be lost. Equally governments were anxious to be seen to fulfil their new role, preferably as cheaply as possible. There was plenty of opportunity for partnership. In the early 1920s an American charity funded the Phelps–Stokes Commission, which travelled extensively through tropical Africa, directed by the American educationalist, Jesse Jones. The Commission was heavily influenced by the kind of education developed in the Southern states for African Americans, inspired by Booker T. Washington and the Tuskegee Institute, offering an education which was 'adapted' to the particular economic and social conditions of the community, that is, one which did not fundamentally call into question those conditions, even if they colluded with racial inequality and injustice. In the African context the positive part of their message was that education should deal with the realities of African village life rather than with an exotic curriculum which served only to alienate people further from their own culture. But this could easily be interpreted negatively, as an attempt to introduce a separate and inferior type of education, designed to keep Africans from taking advantage of modern conditions. This was especially true in settler-dominated societies where there was often a prejudice against educated mission products and a desire for what were seen as more practically orientated technical courses which fitted in to the requirements of the white economy. But, whatever criticisms the educational philosophy of Phelps–Stokes would subsequently be subjected to, at the time the Commission fulfilled two very important purposes. First, it created a strong climate of opinion that the 'school in the bush' should indeed be affirmed and its Christian character strengthened, but that it needed drastically to be improved educationally. This was best done by a contract between mission and government – the mission to supply suitably qualified teachers and the government to refrain from creating a rival parallel village structure for education, but to support the missions with grants-in-aid, and to develop curricula and an inspectorate. Second, the Commission was important for African Christians, one of its members being Dr James Aggrey, an educationalist of West African origin, who made a great stir wherever he went. He was regarded as a magnificent role model, an example of how education might engender respect and equal status for the black person in a societies where black people were denied that dignity. Aggrey affirmed the importance of co-operation between black and white, using the metaphor of the black and white piano keys popularized by Booker T. Washington in the USA (and rather controversially, as it seemed to condone segregation). In Africa in the 1920s Aggrey's words were invested with much more positive connotations: the possibilities of improvement and progress and the affirmation of human dignity.

Joe Oldham, of the International Missionary Council (one of the forerunners of the World Council of Churches), was supremely active in the inter-war years in setting up a system of mission-government co-operation. Some of the evangelical faith missions (for example the Africa Inland Mission) were rather suspicious of going along this road because they feared that the imposition of government curricula and general interference might well detract from the supreme evangelistic task of mission and encourage secularizing tendencies among their pupils. Increasingly, however, this was seen by African members of those missions as putting their communities at a severe disadvantage – they paid the taxes which government disbursed as educational grants to missions, but these grants were not coming back to their areas.[24]

These tensions were also reflected in Roman Catholic views of co-operation with government. This can be seen clearly in the differing views of Catholic missions on the Niger in West Africa. Carlo Zappa of the Society of African Missions at Lokoja, in rejecting the old discredited style of mission concentrating on freed slaves living in isolated 'Christian' villages, did not want to produce 'detribalized' mission Christians and was equally suspicious of 'Western' education: 'I believe ... that in encouraging them to be instructed we are pushing our young people towards the European business house and towards Government employment.'[25] He refused to have secular schools at all in his mission area, and concentrated on building up an efficient catechetical and seminary system. It paid dividends in that the first Igbo priest, Fr Paul Emecete, ordained in 1920, came from the SMA area. In sharp contrast was Bishop Joseph Shanahan of the Holy Ghost Fathers, some way down the river. He was enthusiastic about co-operating with government: 'Those who hold the school hold the country, hold its religion, hold its future.'[26] This meant whole-hearted co-operation with the colonial department of education, and acceptance of its secular curriculum and inspections. It too paid off: it has been estimated that 40 per cent of schools in Igboland became Catholic, and Catholicism became the major denomination among the Igbo, despite the 30-year head start of the Protestants.[27] Shanahan's enthusiasm was endorsed by Monsignor Arthur Hinsley, the special Visitor-Apostolic to Catholic Missions in British East Africa: 'Collaborate with all your power and where it is impossible for you to carry on both the immediate task of evangelisation and your educational work, neglect your churches in order to perfect your schools.'[28]

If Fr Zappa in Nigeria and the AIM in Kenya were seen as eccentric in holding out against secular education, Zappa's concern about not producing 'detribalized' natives was echoed again and again in the inter-war years. It has been powerfully argued that the idea of 'tribalism' is less to do with the realities of Africa than with the European perception of Africans as living entrapped in small-scale mutually exclusive units, locked in timeless tradition and with a single unchangeable identity. Colonial theories of 'indirect rule' were often premised on this kind of reasoning. It was a powerful stimulus to inter-war missionary thinking – the fostering of what were considered wholesome aspects of tribal life rather than its wholesale destruction, the recognition of the organic nature of society. Working among the Chagga people of the Mount Kilimanjaro region of Tanganyika, the German Lutheran Bruno Gutmann argued that mission should aim at the Christianization of society as a whole, the creation of a *Volkskirche* in which the 'primal ties' of family, clan and community were recognized and honoured: an antidote to the 'individualism' of the West. It has produced a strong cohesive self-confident Chagga Lutheranism. Too often, however, 'adaptation' was a mere tinkering with what were regarded as traditional customs, a romantic conservatism which was resented by Africans who were more aware of the changing realities of life and the need for participation in the modern.

On the other hand, ill-considered interference in custom by missionaries could have explosive repercussions, as happened in the female circumcision crisis which erupted in Kenya in 1929. The attempt to compel Kikuyu Christians to pledge at their baptism or institution as Church elders not to circumcise their daughters became the focal point of what was seen as a frontal attack on the integrity of Kikuyu culture. 'I am a Kikuyu and no water can wash away my Kikuyu nationality', wrote one protester. Had not Moses himself 'refused to be called the son of Pharaoh's daughter, but returned to his own people and threw in his lot with them?' 'Missionaries have tried on many occasions to interfere with the tribal customs and the question is asked whether, circumcision being the custom of the Kikuyu Christians, he is to be a heathen simply because he is a Kikuyu.'[29] One result of this hotly debated controversy was the formation of a number of independent Churches, and the breaking of the missionary monopoly control on how Kikuyu were to receive the Gospel. In the final analysis, the issue was not about the preservation of tradition (the Kikuyu are often characterized as exceptionally progressive and adaptable), but about who is the arbiter of what is or is not acceptable for the Christian ordering of society: missionaries or African Christians.

The rise of independent Churches

Colonialism had an ambiguous role in its impact on Christianity. On the one hand it tended to make the Church more dependent than before on foreign missionaries – they were the ones expected to make decisions, liaise with governments, provide the technical expertise.

In pre-colonial times, missionaries had been on intimate terms with the local community, living alongside people, often sharing a similar standard of material culture, with a fluent and often idiomatic command of the language. Now there was a 'withdrawal upwards' into institutional fortresses – hospitals and colleges and mission compounds. Moreover the colonial mentality tended to force a certain social distance between expatriate and native: what has been called 'verandah Christianity'. On the other hand, colonialism did vastly expand the scope of missionary activity into every part of the land. Much of this work, in fact an increasing amount, was done by African catechists, evangelists and teachers; for many the sight of a missionary was a rare and special occasion. For the vast majority of communities, it is the African catechist, either from a neighbouring ethnic group, or a child of the soil who had received the new faith while working outside the home area, who is remembered as the one who established the Church in that area. The vernacular and local character of Christianity really became established in the colonial era, often for the first time.

To what extent was Christianity concerned with the 'modern'? It encouraged a reliance on the hospital and Western medicine, and that had implications for the whole understanding of the nature of sickness and health and its relation to the spirit world. It insisted on literacy and a long catechumenate. But was there another way of being a Christian? It is interesting that the first breakaway from mission Christianity in Uganda in 1914, the Bamalaki, concentrated on these two issues. It was as wrong, said the founder Yoswa Kate Mugema, to rely on mission medicine as it was to consult traditional diviners and mediums. It was equally wrong to insist on literacy. The Bamalaki offered instant baptism and the prestige of a new (biblical or European) name: as a consequence it was nicknamed 'dini la rahisi' (religion on the cheap). The period just before and after the First World War was a significant time for the birth of African Christian independency in many parts of the continent. In 1913 William Wade Harris, from the Grebo people of Liberia, having had a vision of the archangel Gabriel in prison, began a dynamic evangelistic campaign along the coast of West Africa, preaching, largely in pidgin English, the message of the power of Christ over the spirits. He wore a white gown and black bands, and carried a gourd, a cross, a Bible and a bowl for baptizing. He baptized thousands, without the normal restrictions demanded by missionary Christianity, and 'permanently rewrote the religious geography of the Ivory Coast'.[30] Some years before this, in South Africa, a Zulu prophet by the name of Isaiah Shembe established his 'Nazareth' at Ekuphakameni in the Drakensberg mountains, just one of a plethora of groups which collectively have become known as 'Zionism', stressing prayer and divine healing, gathering at a sacred place (their Nazareth, or Jordan or Zion) and expressing an exuberant combination of biblical and African symbols and motifs.

Another outstanding prophet of this period is Simon Kimbangu, from the lower Congo, home of Kongo Catholicism and the first 'independent' Christian prophet, Donna Beatrice. Kimbangu was brought up in the Baptist Church and was baptized. In 1921 he began a remarkable healing ministry in his home village of Nkamba, attracting crowds of expectant people. The Belgian authorities took fright at the potential disorder and subversive nature of this popular movement, and Kimbangu was sentenced to death, commuted to life imprisonment. And Kimbangu did spend the next 30 years of his life, indeed the rest of his life, in prison. It was only in the last days of colonial rule in the 1950s and early 1960s that a cohesive denomination, L'Église sur la Terre par Simon Kimbangu, was able to emerge, along with other groups, more or less orthodox in Christian terms, which claimed Kimbangu's inspiration. The Kimbangu-ists were to become the largest single independent Church in Africa.

Harris, Shembe, Kimbangu were early, and particularly dynamic and interesting, examples of a movement of 'independency' which became widespread in many parts of Africa. In Nigeria this phenomenon is known as Aladura: the praying Churches. The Cherubim and Seraphim, co-founded by a woman, Christiana 'Captain' Abiodun, is a particularly famous example, partly because of its strength in the post-war period among the Nigerian diaspora in Europe. There are many other examples of women founders and leaders of independent Churches, reflecting the important role women have traditionally played in the spiritual realm: Gaudencia Aoko, of the Maria Legio Church of western Kenya, the largest independent Church to come directly out of the Roman Catholic Church; or Alice Lenshina's Lumpa Church in Zambia. Independent Churches are often contrasted to the mission-founded Churches by their wearing of flowing white garments and headgear, their use of drums and responsive chanting, and their emphasis on spiritual healing. They are interested in locating the cause of sickness in the realm of evil spirits, charms and witchcraft, and in confronting and defeating those powers in the name of Christ. They may be tolerant of polygamy and customs relating to birth, marriage and death which had been condemned as 'pagan' by mission Churches. Often condemned or despised by Christians of mission-founded Churches for 'syncretism' or a superficial understanding of the Gospel, the members of these Churches may well reply with a good deal of cogency that they are much more successful at integrating the Gospel into the African mode of being, and overcoming the painful dichotomy lived by many mission adherents, who worship the Christian God on a Sunday, and consult the traditional medium or diviner from Monday to Saturday.

But it would be wrong to think too much of rigid contrasts between two conflicting traditions. Both are in fact very diverse, and African Instituted Churches demonstrate a whole spectrum of judgements about the relation to African tradition or the place of 'orthodox' doctrine. Nor should one forget the links which the independent movement has often had (especially in Southern Africa) with American Adventist or Apostolic (Pentecostal) groups; not to mention the role of the Jehovah's Witnesses in the movement known as Watch Tower founded by the Malawian Elliot Kamwana, also in 1914, which has had a wide influence in Zambia and Malawi. Independency is a complex and diverse phenomenon.

Other movements of spiritual renewal

One of the reasons for not being too quick to characterize the mission Churches as 'foreign' and independent Churches as 'African', the mission Churches as 'orthodox' and the African Churches as 'syncretistic', is that such a division seriously underestimates the common search of all African

Christians for ways of living both an authentically Christian and an authentically African life. This has often been best expressed in what Hastings has called 'associational religion', characterized by its lay rather than clerical involvement, its African rather than missionary leadership and the larger degree of women's participation than was often accepted in the official aspects of the Church life. In fact one important example of the associational pattern – the Manyano (South Africa) or Ruwadzano (Rhodesia) – was specifically for women: a prayer union or fellowship, a society of mutual help and spiritual uplifting for women.

The most famous movement of renewal is probably the Balokole Revival movement within the Protestant Churches of East Africa (*Balokole* is Luganda for the 'Saved People'). This movement sprang from a remarkable partnership between a CMS medical missionary, Dr Joe Church, and Simeoni Nsibambi, from a distinguished family in Buganda. Members called themselves *Ab'oluganda*. In English the term 'Brethren' is often used (though it should be noted that *Ab'oluganda* in Luganda refers to both men and women). The Revival came to have a decisive influence on the character of many mission-founded Churches. At one level it is a typically Evangelical movement, with a strong emphasis on the need for repentance of sin and on sole reliance on the atoning work of Christ's blood on the cross. The Revival did not fear to be confrontational – fearlessly speaking out ('walking in the light') against a complacent compromise with sin and robustly intolerant of all attempts to incorporate traditional religious 'pagan' practices into the Church. Brethren were also fearless in regarding white people as equals, equally in need of repentance and salvation: a quite radical egalitarianism in a racially stratified colonial society. At another level the movement was profoundly African, seeing itself as a new 'clan', stressing the intense solidarity of the group, arranging marriages, looking after widows. Beginning within the Anglican Church of Uganda and Rwanda, the movement spread to the Mennonite and Lutheran Churches of Tanzania, and the Presbyterian and Methodist Churches of Kenya, where the Balokole became famous for their refusal, at great personal risk, to participate in the oathing ceremonies of Mau Mau – the blood of Jesus, not of goats, being the only acceptable oathing permitted of a Christian.[31]

In Catholicism, the lay apostolate has been encouraged, for example, through participation in the Legion of Mary or devotion to the Uganda martyrs, but clerical direction can often be an inhibiting factor. The Jamaa (family) movement in the Shaba and Kasai Catholicism of Zaire is a notable example of a predominantly lay spirituality which went a long way to overcome a top-down, clerically directed approach. Yet Jamaa has clerical origins. It springs out of the attempt of a priest, the Flemish Franciscan missionary Placide Tempels, to express an affective, Franciscan type of spirituality based on God's love. This could be experienced through people being drawn into the love of Christ and of his mother Mary, which in turn elicits a love for each other, for the Father and for the family of the Church. Jamaa involved initiation of man and wife (Baba and Mama) into a spiritual encounter with each other and with God, mediated by the priest. Like the Balokole, Jamaa saw itself as a movement within the Church, but one can see the scope for overtly sensual interpretations which the Catholic Church found difficult to contain (even the formidably puritanical Balokole had to deal with these problems in its early days).[32]

Women have often played a leading role in the life of the Church; they certainly have for many years been the majority in most congregations. Often their contribution has been overlooked or taken for granted by a largely male leadership. In turn, their historical contribution does not get recorded: they tend to 'fall through the cracks of academic analysis' (Elizabeth Isichei).[33] The case of Moder Lena (Magdalene) Vehegtte Tikkuie provides a vivid early example of this. When Georg Schmidt left the Moravian mission at Genadendal in South Africa in 1742 he left three baptized members of the Christian community: two men and Lena. He commissioned the men to continue the work, but they soon dropped off. Only Lena persevered in the faith, steadfastly teaching others the Bible and Christian prayer for 50 years, until in 1792 a new group of Moravians arrived. Surprisingly, the new missionaries were not sure of the validity of her faith – perhaps her articulation of it did not quite conform to their understanding of heartfelt evangelical religion. She died in 1800, only five days before the new church was consecrated.[34]

In the nineteenth century, missionary service increasingly offered single European women a chance for active ministry denied them in the Churches at home. The faith missions pioneered the use of single women, but by the last decades of the century all Protestant mission societies were following the practice. One of the great heroines of the missionary endeavour was Mary Slessor of Calabar, second only to David Livingstone in esteem in her native Scotland. Slessor was a woman of great energy and initiative, who found a personal fulfilment she might have found difficult to achieve in Dundee. For African women, the benefits of Christianity might be more ambiguous. Certainly the missions had a strong rhetoric about 'raising womanhood', but at times it served to place boundaries on what women could do. As Church institutions became more structured, the ordained ministry and even the work of catechists and evangelists seemed to be confined increasingly to men. Catholic religious orders certainly did provide a clearly defined religious role for women. In Uganda, as in other places where Catholicism has been widely successful, local orders have been successfully established: for example the

Bannabikira (Daughters of the Virgin) and the Little Sisters of St Francis. Both Protestant and Catholic missions have offered secondary education, and domestic science 'finishing schools' for women; often at first they were particularly directed towards providing suitable Christian wives. By the mid-twentieth century they were beginning to stress the independent role of women as professional people in many fields. But it was only in the 1980s that there was much movement in opening up the ordained ministry to women.

However, long before that, the *Manyano* and Mothers' Unions were providing women with a powerful forum for influencing the life of the Church. In stressing the importance of Christian marriage, these types of organizations have sometimes created something of a gulf between women married in church ('the ring wife') and those who, for one reason or another (for society generally militates against straightforwardly Christian forms of marriage), find themselves in relationships which are not blessed by the Church. Throughout Africa, women tend to be the backbone of the rural Churches. Government policy in South Africa often forced women to stay in the homelands while their menfolk increasingly were drawn to the towns. But, even in South African towns, women tend to be the mainstay of Church life. Iris Berger has suggested that, in the particular conditions of apartheid, women in towns were unable to sustain the patriarchal kinship relations in the rural areas which remained of crucial importance to males. The Church provided an alternative community, a supportive network and an important way of making sense of urban reality: 'We pray and cry and think that all our problems will be solved. In church you find two hundred women and ten men' (Lucy Muubelo). 'I think that was the only loving time I had with my children. Just holding their hands and walking with them to church. Even today I love to go to church, only now my company is my grandchildren instead of my children' (Emma Mashinini). Berger also notes that the Churches, both mission-founded and Zionist, provide women with 'religious sanction for their efforts to redirect male resources and responsibility' from anti-social activities, such as drinking in shebeens, to more constructive occupations conducive to family life and well-being.[35]

Decolonialization

Even in the period of high colonialism, there were individual missionaries who were prepared to be extremely critical of colonial policy, especially in areas where the interests of African populations seemed to be subordinated to those of a white settler community demanding economic privilege and political rights for itself. In the inter-war period Archdeacon Owen in

Kenya and Arthur Shearly Cripps in Southern Rhodesia were vigorous campaigners against injustices and spokesmen for African grievances. Moreover there was increasingly a body of educated articulate African Christians (especially from Protestant Churches) who could directly voice such concerns. In his evocatively titled book *Are We Not Also Men?* Terence Ranger has provided a vivid portrait of the Samkange family of Southern Rhodesia. Thompson Samkange was a Methodist minister and a key figure in the development of a nascent modern nationalist consciousness. His wife, Grace, was an important role model, economically and socially, for African Christian women. Their two sons, Stanlake and Sketchley, were key figures in the nationalist politics of the 1950s and 1960s.[36] Often participation in Church councils and synods provided opportunities for African initiative and responsibility in ways which were denied in racially exclusive colonial structures. This was true for both clergy and laity. For in most Protestant Churches the standards of clerical training at theological colleges fell sadly behind those of the mission high schools, which produced the clerks and teachers, the lawyers and politicians of late colonial society. The disparity between a rather poorly educated clergy, geared towards village life, and an educated laity, in varying degrees orientated towards an urban culture, became one of the critical points for the mainline Protestant Churches as Africa entered the era of independence, especially as the Africanization of ecclesiastical hierarchies began to take place rapidly in the 1950s, usually just slightly in advance of the political changes which began to sweep across the continent. Max Warren, the immensely creative and perceptive General Secretary of the Church Missionary Society from 1942 to 1963, was particularly important in interpreting to British government and society the anti-colonial movement of the post-war world, particularly in Africa. John V. Taylor, a CMS missionary in Uganda in the 1940s and 1950s, was equally important within Africa in helping the missionary movement and the African Church to adjust to the great sea change in society in these years.

The Catholic Church had meantime been quietly rectifying its disadvantages vis-à-vis Protestant missions. In addition to catching up educationally, Catholic missionaries were much more visible than their Protestant counterparts at the village level – there was not the same desperate shortage of personnel and the consequent withdrawal upwards into largely institutional life. Catholic catechists had the basic, vernacular religious education which characterized Protestant lay catechists and clergy. In contrast to the large number of African Protestant ministers, there were few African Catholic priests, but they did have the advantage of a long and rigorous seminary education. Especially in areas such as Buganda and Igboland, where Catholicism had become deeply rooted and where priestly vocations could be fostered, this opened up the possibility of an Africanization of diocesan clergy and the episcopate, even ahead of Protestant Churches. In 1939 Masaka, Uganda, became the first Catholic diocese in Africa entirely to be staffed by African clergy, with an African bishop, Joseph Kiwanuka. It was to take the Anglican Church in Uganda another eight years before it consecrated its first bishop, Aberi Balya, and he was only an assistant. It was to be nearly 100 years after the consecration of Crowther before the Anglicans got round to appointing a second African diocesan bishop.

These strengths of African Catholicism were enormously reinforced and reinvigorated by the Second Vatican Council:

> Probably in no other continent did the Vatican Council coincide quite so neatly and sympathetically with a major process of secular change as in Africa . . . The conciliar themes of localization and pluralism, of the recognition of the positive values of different cultures and even other religious traditions, the new use of the vernacular in the liturgy, ecumenical rapprochement, all this conformed with the general early 1960s stress on African political and cultural values, on decolonializa-tion, on the social necessity of co-operation and unity across the divisions of tribe, race and religion. On both sides there was the sense of a fresh, rather optimistic, new start, and the two were easily allied.[37]

Along with this went the rapid Africanization of national hierarchies, an often radical and thoroughgoing inculturation of the liturgy, a vigorous evangelization programme into areas previously hardly affected by Catholicism or any form of Christian expression, a blossoming of Catholic participation in national life that would have seemed difficult to imagine outside the Portuguese and Belgian territories in colonial times, and which has provided the basis for the high profile of Catholicism in independent Africa.

Christianity and the politics of independent Africa

The rapid decolonization process which took place quite suddenly in the late 1950s and 1960s effectually handed over government in many parts of Africa to the mission-educated elite. In mobilizing popular support for independence and 'nation building' in the early years of independence, it was often useful to speak critically of mission Christianity, of the ideological support which mission education gave to colonialism. Nkru-mah expressed a widespread irritation with what appeared to be an overspiritualizing interpretation of mission religion in his much quoted dictum, 'Seek ye first the political kingdom'. Pan-Africanism in the 1960s might seem to be an appropriate alternative both to colonialism and to certain aspects of mission Christianity. But there were also powerful currents which served to reinforce Christianity in the new nation states. Most politicians continued to have links with their Churches. If the mission-founded Churches had often underpinned the colonial state, their establishment mentality also meant that they were potentially just as useful to rulers in independent states. Independent Churches (AICs) seemed less amenable to this kind of co-option. In so far as they had a political profile they were often regarded with considerable suspicion by governments. If they were not political they could be easily ignored or regarded with benign condescension.

There was a strong element of religious idealism in the programmes of many first-generation leaders: Nyerere's Catholicism was an important element in his African Socialism programme for Tanzania; Kaunda's Presbyterian upbringing shaped his African humanism (which did not have the anti-religious streak of the European variety) in Zambia. Independence put no brake on people seeking baptism. Indeed, in their strong urge to extend and broaden the school system (even if they wanted to take the school out of denominational control) governments gave an added incentive for people to seek Church affiliation, especially in the mission-founded Churches, traditionally strong in the educational field.

In the decades after independence, as African states passed through various social, political and economic crises, resulting in army rule or an increasing breakdown of law and order, the Church often proved remarkably resilient both in an institutional sense and as a moral and spiritual focus of hope, in situations where it did not, in fact, make sense to 'seek first' the political kingdom. In the late 1980s Churches (for example in Malawi or Benin) might be at the centre of movements towards democratization, as old authoritarian regimes began to crumble. Nowhere was this more the case than in South Africa. Individuals such as Michael Scott or Trevor Huddleston or Cosmos Desmond had achieved a worldwide fame in the 1950s and 1960s for their personal opposition (taking advantage of the leverage they had as white non-nationals). By the 1980s this had become a more general and broadly based opposition, in which the Churches were seen to represent society as a whole. The role of Archbishop Desmond Tutu and Alan Boesak was significant for the work of the UDF (United Democratic Front), which, in the absence of normal politics and the continued banning of the African National Congress and other political movements, served as a force to mobilize and fatally to undermine the apartheid regime.

In these situations of apparent social disintegration, the Churches were often able to recruit into their ministry people of high educational attainment, who in previous generations might well have looked for jobs in the civil service or the law or journalism or, indeed, in politics. The Churches themselves became for the first time providers of university-level education, often in seminaries designed for ministerial training. At the local level where the Churches had such strength, the bishop or Church leader might be looked to in order to provide political and material goods which the state was no longer able to supply, either because good government no longer existed in corrupt and authoritarian regimes, or because the structural readjustment programmes imposed from outside from the 1980s had a strong bias against 'government' as the chief provider of welfare and services. On the other hand, as the democratization movement did begin to have some success and to make its impact on the governmental processes of many countries, so the fact that the Churches had themselves become deeply entangled in webs of corruption become obvious. The claims of the Churches to offer a moral lead for society had become problematic and needed to be treated with caution.

Nevertheless there has been brave witness from Church people in the face of tyranny or barbarism. In 1977 (the centenary year of Christianity in Uganda) Anglican Archbishop Janani Luwum died a brutal death at the hands of Idi Amin, reminding the Church during that critical time that it was founded on the witness of the martyrs. Luwum represented the best of the Revival (Balokole) tradition. In the ethnic conflicts in Rwanda between 1959 and 1961, which heralded independence, there were also martyrs from the Revival movement (as there had been in Kenya in the Mau Mau period). In a biographical survey of 200 African priests who have died violent deaths over the last 40 years, nine are listed for Uganda, including Fr Clement Kiggundu, the editor of the Catholic newspaper *Munno*, Ananias Oriang from Lango, Gabriel Banduga from Arua and Charles Oberu from Tororo. But this number, depressing though it is, pales into insignificance beside the 31 listed for Burundi, and the appalling 103 for Rwanda – half the total for the whole of Africa, and chiefly relating to the genocide of 1994. What about the countless lay men and women who have been victims? And under what circumstances is one classed as a witness for truth? Clergy have also been accused of condoning and even participating in genocide and indeed, in as Christian a country as Rwanda, the vast majority of the perpetrators of crimes of genocide must have been baptized and have had some kind of Christian upbringing. The Church's witness in Africa, in common with all places and times, is rarely unambiguous.[38]

If ethnicity (with all the problems of definition which this concept has) is often seen as an important element in much conflict at the end of the twentieth century, religion is also a factor, often expressed in Islamic–Christian conflict. In sub-Saharan Africa Islam and Christianity have usually existed side by side, with the minority faith having a secure niche and a valued place in the society. Conflict in the last part of the twentieth century has often been focused on the Sahalian belt of countries like Sudan and Nigeria, with a strong traditional Muslim majority in the north, and a more recent, and increasing, Christian presence in the south. In the case of many West African countries, there was an active policy of Christian evangelization among people who have been influenced by Islam for many centuries without becoming fully part of the house of Islam. Political conflict often hardens ethnic and religious definition, where fluidity and tolerance existed before.

African theology

Even before the process of decolonization properly got under way in terms of practical politics, there were intellectual movements intent on reclaiming the African heritage. A renewed interest in the springs of an African philosophy, a re-evaluation of the spiritual value of African religious consciousness, was particularly notable among African francophone intellectuals from the 1930s: Senghor, in collaboration with others from the African diaspora living in Paris, were exploring concepts like *Négritude*; and after the Second World War, Alioune Diop's review *Présence Africaine* provided a stimulating forum for a French-speaking African intelligentsia. In a specifically Catholic environment, the work of Placide Tempels on *Bantu Philosophy* (published in French in 1945) inspired a generation of francophone Catholic scholars such as the Rwandan Tutsi Alexis Kagame and the Congolese Vincent Mulago. A group of students studying in Rome in the 1950s (including Kagame and Mulago) produced the famous collection of essays *Des prêtres noirs s'interrogent*: 'Are we, African priests, going to defend our hidden complex of being "poor relatives" in the Church of God for ever? Or will we be sowers of Christian enthusiasm, which will force each one of us to rethink this problem of African fundamental theology?'[39] These intellectual stirrings were under way before the Second Vatican Council. For the African Catholic Church, the reforms of the 1960s fell on ground well-prepared. There was to be a great flowering of Catholic theology concerned with 'inculturating' the Gospel in Africa, and giving theological depth and resonance to the transformation of worship through the introduction of vernacular liturgies and music. These transformations were often enthusiastically pushed through by expatriate missionaries, in a Church which still depended heavily on clerical support from outside the continent. But, especially, in the area of pastoral theology, it was increasingly the large number of

African priests coming out of the major seminaries who were setting the agenda.

A milestone of Protestant thinking was the work of the Ghanaian Presbyterian layman (a lawyer and politician) J. B. Danquah. In *The Akan Doctrine of God* (1944), Danquah attempted in a detailed and rigorous way to present African traditional religion as basically monotheistic, and therefore basically compatible with the Christian view of God. This was the first of a long line of West African theologians, both lay and clerical: Bolaji Idowu, Harry Sawyerr, C. G. Baeta, Kwesi Dickson, to name just a few of the first generation, who laid the foundations of an African theology for the Protestant Churches. In East Africa, John Mbiti has had a seminal influence on ordinands since the 1960s, not to mention the religious education syllabuses of secondary schools. If there is a Protestant equivalent to Tempels as progenitor of an African theology, that accolade must surely go to Edwin Smith, the Primitive Methodist missionary, who articulated a synthesis of African views of God and shaped it as a coherent, unified (rather too unified perhaps) theology. Mbiti's *African Religions and Philosophy* continued that work. The tendency to see traditional African society as saturated with religion, and to perceive African religion as basically consonant with Christianity, has been criticized by people like Okot p'Bitek, the Ugandan poet and thinker. For Okot the African world-view has a much more radically secular orientation.

Christian theology in South Africa stood rather apart from these developments. The struggle against apartheid needed a protesting theology of crisis rather than an affirming theology of inculturation. The emphasis on tradition could also be interpreted in the South African context as repressive, reinforcing 'separate development', tribal homelands and the narrowness of 'Bantu education'. South African theologians increasingly adopted a political protest theology, with a certain kinship to North American black theology. This was expressed among black students through the Black Consciousness movement promoted in the early 1970s by the medical student Steve Biko:

> Even at this late stage, one notes the appalling irrelevance of the interpretation given to all Scriptures. In a country teeming with injustice and fanatically committed to the practice of oppression, intolerance and blatant cruelty because of racial bigotry ... the Church further adds to their insecurity by its inward-directed definition of the concept of sin and its encouragement of the 'mea culpa' attitude ... Black Theology, therefore, is a situational interpretation of Christianity. It seeks to relate the present-day black man to God within the given context of the black man's suffering and his attempt to get out of it.[40]

Biko, murdered by the police in 1977, remained a powerful symbol to many young people, both those who wanted to explore the liberating role of Christianity, and those who felt that one should abandon a Church which seemed irrelevant to the struggle. In 1985 a group of black and white South African theologians produced an important document concerning the political situation. They called it the Kairos Document. *Kairos* refers to the Greek word used in the New Testament to indicate a time of decision, of momentous significance for the individual or community involved. The document combined something of the burning indignation of a man like Biko with the white involvement in protest (which had often looked for inspiration to the model of the Confessing Church in Germany in its struggle against Hitler). The document urged the Churches to get beyond a 'state' theology which justified Afrikaner nationalism, or a 'Church' theology preoccupied with its own affairs in a supposed apartheid-free zone, to a 'prophetic' theology which was willing to challenge the foundations of an unjust state.[41]

Conclusion

Christianity in contemporary Africa is an immensely varied and complex phenomenon. It also remains an immensely powerful force, deeply rooted in rural society. Catholicism, which in the early part of the twentieth century was particularly assiduous in cultivating a village Christianity and as a result managed numerically to catch up and overtake the Protestant Churches in area after area, has in the last 30 years or so also put great efforts into maintaining and expanding its educational structures. At the time of independence there was an understandable emphasis on developing national educational systems, and loosening the bonds of mission or Church control. The Catholic Church has been more alert and attentive to the need to keep a foothold in the educational sphere, exploiting whatever residual powers it retained, and continuing to support its former schools in terms of finances and personnel. Governments have become more anxious to involve Churches again in the running of educational systems, which by the 1990s had become a seemingly intolerable burden on national resources due to expanding youthful populations and insatiable demand for educational provision. The Catholic Church has often been able to respond more effectively than most other institutions. By the 1990s, private universities were springing up in many countries, and here it was often Evangelical bodies, with American money and resources, who have grasped the opportunities presented.

The old distinction between mission-founded 'mainline' Churches and the African Instituted Churches may appear to have lost much of its rationale, as all Churches are now African-led and there are few which would reject some form of inculturation. On the other hand there are still suspicions between the two traditions. There is an unwillingness among many Christians from the mission-founded Churches fully to accept independent Churches as properly Christian, accusing them of being unorthodox doctrinally, of incorporating unacceptable practices into their worship and lifestyle. African Instituted Churches naturally resent the often supercilious attitude of the mission-founded Churches, whom they accuse of failing to address the spiritual realities of African life, or to meet the range of needs of ordinary people. This in turn creates a false dichotomy between areas which Christian practice can deal with and those where one should consult traditional diviners and religious practitioners.

The last decades of the twentieth century saw an explosion of new Pentecostal Churches. At one level this is an example of the Americaniza-tion of culture on a worldwide basis, a re-alienation of the African Church under the influence of the strident and uncompromising tenets of the American religious Right. American Evangelical money and personnel, para-Church evangelistic 'ministries', cheap and available literature, an emphasis on personal salvation, healing, deliverance from demons, the 'gospel of prosperity', offering material blessings to believers, charismatic worship in a technologically sophisticated modern idiom – these are some of the constituents of this new wave of Christianity.[42] It can result in a narrowing of perspective and a failure to engage fruitfully with either political or social realities; nevertheless, it does address African needs in ways which some of the traditional forms of Christianity are manifestly failing to do. The appeal is to urban youth – both the successful, for whom it justifies the accumulation of wealth; and the less successful, semi- and unemployed, for whom it opens up new horizons of hope and offers tantalizing possibilities. The Pentecostal movement tends to be even more condemnatory of compromise with 'paganism' than the old established Churches, and consequently more hostile to those African Instituted Churches which are arrogantly dismissed as pagan. On the other hand the Pentecostal movement does focus on, rather than shy away from, the realm of spiritual powers, and so (like the older independent Churches) can be seen as dealing with this important area of life in more honest and direct ways, helping people to cope with the struggle which defines and circumscribes day-to-day life for so many. The Pentecostal style of worship is more in tune with youth culture. The village Christianities which dominated African Christianity for much of the twentieth century are now giving way to a more urban-orientated style of life and worship. Many people in fact retain a double identity – worship-ping in the Pentecostal Church in town, but using their inherited Church tradition for some of the important rites of passage. Also the older

Churches, especially in towns, are introducing charismatic styles of worship and attitudes to modern living which sometimes upset the older members. Christianity, as has been the case for much of its modern history in Africa, is youth-driven in a way which is almost unimaginable in Europe. American evangelists may come and go; increasingly these types of Churches are African-led and are expressing African solutions to African problems.

If the burgeoning urban centres are setting trends, this is not the only important development in Africa. There continue to be areas of primary evangelism. One example is in the Dinka and Nuer areas of southern Sudan, which have seen war, the disruption of the cattle culture central to existence, a renewal of slave trading and what are resented as attempts to introduce an alien (in this case Arab and Muslim) culture from the North. The area has a long history of fairly superficial encounter with Catholic and Protestant mission. In a society which is being torn apart, Christianity is seen as a new force, a new spiritual power.[43]

These contemporary examples give some indication of the enormous variety of forms which African Christianity takes at the end of the twentieth century. It also illustrates the often critical situation in which Africa exists. Whatever the solutions to those problems, if there are solutions, Christianity is bound to have a deep concern. Christianity and Islam are the dominating religions, each claiming the allegiance of about half the population, and now deeply enmeshed in the structures of African society, politics and culture. The traditional African spiritual heritage remains very much alive, expressed as much within Christianity and Islam as outside these religions. It seems likely that, at some point in the twenty-first century, Christians in Africa will become more numerous than Christians in any other single continent and more important than ever before in articulating a global Christian identity in a pluralist world.

Notes

1 Lamin Sanneh, *Encountering the West: Christianity and the Global Cultural Process: The African Dimension* (London: Marshall Pickering, 1993), p. 17.
2 Cf. David Barrett, 'Status of global mission, 1996, in the context of 20th and 21st centuries', *International Bulletin of Missionary Research*, 20, no. 1 (January 1996), p. 25.
3 Still the most accessible general account of Coptic Christianity is A. S. Atiya, *A History of Eastern Christianity* (London, 1967).
4 Giovanni Vantini, *Christianity in the Sudan* (Bologna, 1981).
5 The best single study on this medieval period is Taddesse Tamrat, *Church and State in Ethiopia 1270–1527* (Oxford, 1972).
6 Adrian Hastings, *The Church in Africa 1450–1950* (Oxford, 1994), p. 70.

Kevin Ward

7 Hastings, *The Church in Africa*, pp. 74–5.
8 John Thornton, *The Kingdom of Kongo, Civil War and Transition, 1641–1718* (Madison: University of Wisconsin Press, 1983); idem, 'The development of an African Catholic Church in the Kingdom of Kongo, 1491–1750', *Journal of African History* (1984), pp. 147–67; Anne Hilton, *The Kingdom of Kongo* (London, 1985); Richard Gray, *Black Christians and White Missionaries* (New Haven: Yale University Press, 1990); ch. 3, 'Come vero Prencipe Catolico', pp. 35–56.
9 Philip Curtin, *The Atlantic Slave Trade: A Census* (London, 1969).
10 J. D. Hargreaves, *A Life of Sir Samuel Lewis* (Oxford, 1958), p. 102.
11 Kwame Bediako, *Christianity in Africa: The Renewal of a Non-Western Religion* (Edinburgh, 1995).
12 Adrian Hastings, *The Church in Africa*, p. 356.
13 See E. A. Ayandele, *The Missionary Impact on Modern Nigeria, 1842–1914: A Political and Social Analysis* (London, 1966).
14 See the careful analysis in Michael Kirwen, *African Widows* (Maryknoll, 1979).
15 See A. J. Dachs, 'Missionary imperialism: the case of Botswana', *Journal of African History* (1972), pp. 647ff.
16 See J. B. Peires, 'The origins of Xhosa religious reaction', *Journal of African History* (1979), pp. 51–61.
17 Isaac Wauchope, writing in a Xhosa-language newspaper in 1882. Hoho refers to a mountain where Xhosa had resisted in vain the British guns. This poem is quoted in Les Switzer, *Power, Resistance in an African Society: The Ciskei Xhosa and the Making of South Africa* (Madison: Wisconsin University Press, 1993), p. 161.
18 The opening words of Sol Plaatje, *Native Life in South Africa* (London, 1916; new edn, Johannesburg, 1982, with an introduction by Brian Willan).
19 A point made long ago by a pioneer of East African Christian history, Roland Oliver, *The Missionary Factor in East Africa* (Oxford, 1952).
20 Ludwig Krapf, *Travels and Missionary Labours in East Africa* (1860; 2nd edn, London: Cass, 1965), p. 498.
21 Quoted in A. D. Roberts, *History of Zambia* (London, 1976), p. 153.
22 Robin Horton, 'African conversion', *Africa*, 41 (1971); idem, 'On the rationality of conversion', *Africa*, 45 (1975). For a brilliant discussion of the implications of the impact of the crises of the late nineteenth century on a particular area of Africa, see John Iliffe, *A History of Modern Tanganyika* (Cambridge, 1979).
23 For example in Luganda 'Ngenda okusoma' (literally I'm going to read) could mean, according to context, 'I'm going to school' or 'I'm going to church'. Among the Agikuyu of Kenya the term 'athomi' was used as a generic title both by Christians and non-Christians for members of Christian denominations.
24 Cf. Kevin Ward, 'Education or evangelism?', *Kenya Historical Review* (1974).
25 Quoted in John M. Todd, *African Missions* (London, 1962), p. 121.
26 P. B. Clarke, 'The methods and ideology of the Holy Ghost Fathers in Eastern Nigeria 1895–1906', *Journal of Religion in Africa*, 6 (1974), p. 101.
27 Elizabeth Isichei, *Varieties of Christian Experience in Nigeria* (London, 1982).
28 Roland Oliver, *The Missionary Factor in East Africa* (1952; 2nd edn, London: Longmans, 1965), p. 275.
29 These quotations are taken from *Muigwithania*, a Kikuyu-language newspaper; except for the last quotation, which is a statement by the Kikuyu Central Association (at the forefront of the dispute) to *The East African Standard* (1929) (English-language newspaper published in Nairobi).
30 E. Isichei, *A History of Christianity in Africa* (London: SPCK, 1995), p. 285.

31 Kevin Ward, 'Tukutendereza Yesu: the Balokole Revival in Uganda' in Z. Nthamburi, *From Mission to Church: A Handbook of Christianity in East Africa* (Nairobi: Uzima Press, 1991).

32 See W. de Craemer, *Jamaa and the Church: A Bantu Catholic Movement in Zaire* (Oxford: Clarendon Press, 1977).

33 E. Isichei, *A History of Christianity in Africa* (London: SPCK, 1995), p. 190.

34 Cf. *The Genadental Diaries: Diaries of the Herrnhut Missionaires, 1792–1794* (Belville, South Africa, 1992); B. Kruger, *The Pear Tree Blossoms: History of the Moravian Church in South Africa 1737–1869* (Genadendal, 1966). This story is recounted by Angela Swart, 'Dignity and worth in the Commonwealth of God' in Musimbi Kanyoro and Nyambura Njoroge, *Groaning in Faith: African Women and the Household of God* (Nairobi: Circle of Concerned African Women Theologians, Acton Publishers, 1996).

35 Iris Berger, *Threads of Solidarity: Women in South African Industry 1900–1980* (Bloomington, 1992), p. 243.

36 Terence Ranger, *Are We Not Also Men? The Samkange Family and African Politics in Zimbabwe 1920–64* (London and Baobab, Harare: James Currey, 1995).

37 Adrian Hastings, 'The Council came to Africa' in Alberic Stacpoole (ed.), *Vatican II by Those Who Were There* (London: Geoffrey Chapman, 1986), p. 316.

38 Neno Contram, *They Are a Target: 200 African Priests Killed* (Nairobi: Paulines Publications, 1996).

39 From *Des prêtres noirs s'interrogent*, p. 190. Quoted in John Baur, *2000 Years of Christianity in Africa* (Nairobi: Paulines Publications, 1994), p. 291.

40 Steve Biko, *I Write What I Like*, republished by Penguin (London, 1988). Cf. 'The Church as seen by a young layman', p. 47.

41 Institute of Contextual Theology, *The Kairos Document: Challenge to the Church* (Johannesburg, 1986).

42 Paul Gifford, 'A new and foreign element in African religion', *Religion*, 20 (1990), pp. 373–88.

43 Marc Nikkel, 'Aspects of contemporary religious change among the Dinka', *Journal of Religion in Africa* (1992), pp. 78–94.

7

Reformation and
Counter-Reformation

Andrew Pettegree

The pre-Reformation Church

The influence of the Church in European society in the late fifteenth century was all-pervasive. Leading figures in the Church hierarchy could have reflected on an institution with an unchallenged position at the heart of the community: robust, intellectually vigorous and assured of a role in almost every aspect of human existence. In some parts of Europe up to 10 per cent of the population were members of the institutional Church; collectively the Church was Europe's biggest landowner. The clergy played a vital role in the lives of all late medieval communities, as dispensers of sacraments, managers of hospitals and schools and providers of vital services such as writing and literacy. No European rulers could ignore the Church in their political calculations; the Pope was a major political force in his own right and a constant fixture in the strategic alliances of the day. No one could have anticipated that the Church was about to be faced by a challenge which would shake it to its foundations, and leave it, two centuries later, permanently divided.

The Reformation, in this respect, was a movement of many paradoxes. In its first intention a movement of renewal and reform, the division of Western Christendom was a wholly accidental and unforeseen consequence. And although it would result in the withdrawal of up to one-third of Europe's population from obedience to Catholicism, the Reformation was in no respect a consequence of religious indifference. On the contrary, the Church on the eve of the Reformation gave every sign of being an institution in rude good health. Indeed, it is now argued that the century before the Reformation was characterized by a degree of engagement in matters of worship and theology, especially on the part of the laity, unprecedented in medieval Christianity.

This was an age of church-building and religious enthusiasm. In Suffolk, England, during the fifteenth century, something approaching 50 per cent of parish churches were substantially remodelled, as citizens poured the new wealth generated by a successful wool trade into their religious lives. This was an age of great religious art, stimulated by the growth of the cult of saints. Increasingly during this period, popular medieval saints were adopted and invoked as guardians and protectors, and honoured for their benevolent interventions in the lives of those who invoked them in sculpture, painting and shrines. The collection of relics, small mementoes of saints' lives or preserved parts of their bodies, became almost a cult in its own right; some aristocratic collectors amassed huge collections, each carefully and often magnificently housed in custom-made reliquaries, and each carrying a documented remission from the torments of purgatory for those who gazed upon them. Albrecht of Brandenburg, Renaissance prince and patron of artists, amassed a collection of such magnificence that the assiduous visitor could accumulate a remission of some six million days. One of his greatest rivals as a collector in central Europe was, ironically enough, the Elector of Saxony, Frederick the Wise, later Martin Luther's patron and protector.

This was an age of pilgrimages and ostentatious public devotions; nor was the crusading urge entirely dead. More than one Renaissance prince aspired to lead a new Christian expedition against the Turk when more immediate European conflicts were settled. And this was an age in which the individual's ceaseless search for a sense of the divine was manifested in ever more elaborate devotional practice, and the pious expenditure of much hard-earned wealth. The commitment of the laity received tangible expression in a financial investment of unprecedented proportions: in the provision of funeral Masses, voluntary offices and sermons, and the purchase of indulgences.

What then was required to move people out of this deep, and for the most part unquestioning, commitment and in many cases to turn them furiously against institutions to which they had given so much, in both emotional and financial terms? To such a question there can be no simple answer, and it is worth remembering that the sixteenth-century call for reform would elicit a very different response in different parts of Europe. But for historians with the benefit of hindsight there were sufficient indications even in the robust good health of the late medieval Church of why, when a climate of criticism emerged in the 1520s, it achieved such a popular resonance.

In the first place, the evidence of the Christian layman's ever increasing support for the Church was itself slightly double-edged. With the increasing investment of their wealth and time went rising expectations. The fifteenth century witnessed a great expansion of lay literacy and education. University education was no longer a clerical monopoly; in urban communities and princely courts it was no longer necessary to rely on clerics to act as clerks, scribes and schoolmasters, as had been the almost exclusive tradition of the early Middle Ages. And many of the religious institutions newly popular in the fifteenth century, such as confraternities, represented not only lay commitment to the Church, but a desire on the part of the laity to take greater control over their religious lives. Confraternities were associations of pious laymen, often based around a trade craft and guild, who paid subscriptions for the purpose of having a priest say Masses on behalf of their deceased members. It followed that the priest so engaged was in effect their employee, and in the fifteenth century an increasing proportion of the clerical estate relied on such positions for their livelihood. The German city of Hamburg had no fewer than 99 confraternities in 1517; most urban communities of any size had a variety of such institutions.[1] In some parts of the Church, such as England, even the parochial clergy were increasingly dependent for their salaries on voluntary financial donations, raised by the churchwardens on behalf of the parish. Not surprisingly, lay people in return felt able to insist on a high standard of service in those they employed.

The capacity of the clergy to respond to these increased expectations varied greatly in the different parts of Europe, and even in different parts of the clerical estate. In England, for instance, the parish clergy seem to have enjoyed a high level of confidence among the population at large. Reasonably adequately trained and well disciplined, English priests seem to have given little cause for scandal. In this they were given an exemplary lead by their bishops, few of whom could be seriously criticized for their moral conduct (Cardinal Wolsey, who acknowledged a bastard son, was a great exception among the English bishops). Most English bishops also played an active role in the administration of their diocese.

Pious, conscientious bishops were to be found in most parts of Europe, but in some countries they were clearly very much the exception. In France, most bishops were either non-resident royal officials, or the younger sons of the local nobility. In the Netherlands, the structure of the Church was so archaic that a growing population of over two million was served by only four bishops. But it was in the German Empire that the condition of the Church gave most cause for concern. Germany teemed with clergy, many of them ill-educated and penniless indigents with no hope of a position. At the other end of the scale, Germany's bishops were often great princes of the Church, ruling over an independent princely state, their appointment jealously guarded by the Pope and often the subject of an intensely political negotiation (not to mention the payment of a substantial fee). The prelates, for their part, often exploited the resources of their office with a ruthlessness which differed little from that of secular landlords, except insofar as through their spiritual office they enjoyed access to opportunities to raise funds denied to temporal lords.

Clerical privileges often included the right to sell produce gathered on their lands in neighbouring urban markets without paying the usual duties, an exemption inevitably fiercely resented in these communities. Meanwhile a regular and substantial sum might be generated by the tax bishops collected from the more humble clerics of their diocese who wished to keep a wife. This tax was paid by up to 60 per cent of the clergy in some dioceses, such as Basel. Clerical and monastic landlords also played their full part in the reimposition of serfdom with which landlords secured their workforce in the wake of the Black Death. Less immediately resented was the exploitation of spiritual benefits such as the trade in indulgences, a relatively accessible and highly popular means of seeking some assurance of favour in the afterlife among Germany's Christian population at this date.

The great disparities of wealth, status and education were a source of considerable tension within the clerical estate. Prominent reformers within the clergy, such as Dean Colet in his famous Convocation sermon of 1509, made frequent and passionate calls for a renovation of the quality of religious life, to begin with the clergy themselves. But it was increasingly doubtful whether the traditional institutions of the Church were themselves sufficient to create the momentum for a wide-ranging movement of reform. The history of medieval reform movements was in this respect salutary. The agenda of reform ostensibly lay at the heart of the Conciliar movement of the fourteenth and fifteenth centuries, but increasingly became subsumed in a political struggle for control of the papacy. Prominent individuals who allowed their call for reform to stray into overt criticism of a politicized and often corrupt papacy, such as the Bohemian Jan Hus or the Florentine prophet Savonarola, were condemned as heretics and destroyed.

The conflict of authority that lay at the heart of Conciliarism was eventually resolved in favour of the papacy, but the legacy in terms of practical reform was modest. Prominent laypeople interested in reform could legitimately doubt whether the institutional Church could provide the leadership for the wholesale renovation of the Christian life which many saw as necessary. Some of this scepticism was seen in the movements of popular devotion which posed an increasing challenge to the more traditional piety of the monastic orders, in any case under threat from the increased vitality of parish religion. In England, pious donations to religious houses had declined steeply even while parish-based religious institutions were generously supported. Many religious houses were in difficulties long before the Reformation, with criticisms of the sincerity of vocations and a serious shortage of manpower. The need for reform was widely recognized in parts of the religious orders themselves.

The agenda of change was of obvious relevance to the new intellectual movement known as humanism. Humanism was not in its wider sense primarily concerned with Church reform. The rediscovery and celebration of classical civilizations which lay at the heart of the Renaissance was a development of far wider application, in the world of education, scholarship and the visual arts. But an intellectual movement of such force could not leave the Church untouched. To the extent that the humanism of the Renaissance celebrated the capacities of man to govern his own destiny, it proposed a world-view fundamentally at variance with that of the Church. At the same time, humanists celebrated and acknowledged the growing self-confidence of a newly articulate Christian laity. Such sentiments explain the huge popularity of the *Enchiridion militis Christiani* ('Handbook of the Christian Soldier') of Desiderius Erasmus, a Dutch scholar of humble origins, who became a figure of European renown with the publication of this vision of the active Christian vocation. Erasmus was one of a growing number of writers who employed wit and satire to decry the failings of the institutional Church, criticism which would provide a corrosive background to the more frontal attack of Protestantism in the sixteenth century.

All of this was important, but the greatest contribution of humanist scholarship was in its championing of new standards of critical scholarship in the fields of theology and the classics. Humanism promoted a remarkable renaissance in the study of Greek and the ancient civilizations of the Middle East, including – significantly – the original languages of the biblical canon. The rigorous scholarship which restored the uncorrupted text of many Greek and Latin authors could also be applied to testing the received text of Scripture (principally the fourth-century Latin translation of St Jerome known as the Vulgate) against original texts. This was a process which set the new scholarship on a potential collision with a Church hierarchy which gave great weight to the accrued authority of Church tradition, and which regarded the Vulgate as hallowed and sacred. The potential dangers of the new scholarship in this regard were demonstrated when Erasmus's celebrated new translation of the New Testament seemed to challenge the scriptural basis for the doctrine of penance.

The techniques of the new scholarship were eagerly embraced by many in the expanding university world, including those, like the young Martin Luther, not instinctively drawn to the implicit secularity of the humanist project. But left to itself, humanism posed no particular danger to the established Church. The danger would arise if the theological scepticism of the intellectual critics of the Church could be articulated in such a way as to tap into the broader seams of dissatisfaction which existed among the laity. It was precisely this combination which, emerging from an obscure quarrel among religious professionals in the 1520s, would shake the Western Church to its foundations.

Luther and Germany

Luther's role as a catalyst of change was in many ways ironic. For until his criticisms of indulgence-selling brought him into conflict with the Church hierarchy, with such fateful results, Luther's career had been conventional, indeed notably successful. Luther was a Catholic success story; an example of just what was possible within the pre-Reformation Church. Born the son of a successful mine-owner in Saxony, Luther reaped the benefit of the educational revolution of the late Middle Ages, attending successively the cathedral school at Magdeburg and the University of Erfurt. The decision to enter the Augustinian monastery at Erfurt, taken against his father's will, was a turning point, after which Luther rose steadily through the ranks of his order. A lecturer at the University of Wittenberg in 1507, Luther represented his order on business in Rome in 1510. By 1512 he was Doctor of Theology, and a rising force in the local university, recognized in Wittenberg as a powerful and effective preacher.

It was also during these years that Luther began to formulate the new theological understandings that would later underpin his theology. Luther was prone to depression throughout his life, and this may have been the background to a fundamental reordering of his thought with relation to judgement and salvation. Like many of his contemporaries, Luther found the concept of God as judge almost unbearably oppressive. The breakthrough came from a reading of Romans 1:17: 'For therein is the righteousness of God revealed from faith to faith: as it is written, The just shall live by faith.' Luther came to see that this could offer the prospect of mercy, not the damnation he saw as the inevitable consequence of his fallen state. Far from being judged, the suffering Christian was in fact rescued by God's free gift and Christ's sacrifice on the cross.

There was no sudden revelation, and Luther's concept of 'Justification by Faith' built on a solid body of doctrine within the Catholic Church. But it did mean that when Luther later became embroiled with his own superiors, he had to hand the conceptual framework for a radical disavowal of the traditional framework of authority: a reordering of the theological order which would prove powerfully incendiary in the particular circumstances of the German Empire.

For all that, the issue which made Luther into a public figure was prosaic enough. Indulgence-selling was already a much criticized aspect of late medieval devotional practice. The offering of pious donations against the hope of mercy in the afterlife was obviously prone to abuse, pandering as it did to the most basic fears of ordinary Christians; and the manner in which the St Peter's Indulgence was preached would have offended many less tender consciences than Luther's. The organization of fund-raising through this indulgence in northern Germany was in fact a highly sophisticated piece of Renaissance finance. In 1514 Albrecht of Brandenburg had been raised to the archdiocese of Mainz, but since he intended not to surrender his previous diocese of Magdeburg, and was in addition under the canonical age to be a bishop, the Pope was able to insist on a considerable fee. He agreed in return that 50 per cent of the monies raised from the preaching of the indulgence in Albrecht's two dioceses could be set against this sum. The whole transaction was underwritten by the Fuggers of Augsburg, Germany's principal banking-house.

It was a shoddy enough deal, made more offensive by the vigour and lack of sophistication with which the indulgence was preached around Magdeburg by Albrecht's agent, the Dominican friar Tetzel. Reports of Tetzel's activities spurred Luther to action. In October 1517 he published his 95 theses against indulgences, a call for academic debate wholly justified by Luther's position as university professor. What Luther could not have anticipated was the widespread public interest which followed. Electoral Saxony was some way from the commercial heart of the empire, and despite the growing prestige of its new university, Wittenberg was at this stage not one of Germany's established intellectual centres. Yet within months Luther's theses had circulated widely, reprinted in Leipzig and Nuremberg, and in the great international printing metropolis of Basel. Soon news of Luther's controversial writing was spreading among the intellectual community around Europe: by early 1518 Erasmus in the Netherlands had heard, and approved, of Luther's protest against abuse within the Church. Luther and the debate over indulgences soon became a fashionable cause among humanists and churchmen who had themselves been critical of abuse within the Church in the preceding years.

Public reaction was critical to Luther's fate; so too was the fact that the Church hierarchy was slow to perceive the wider implications of his call for reform. In part this was a result of political circumstances which relegated Luther to the margins of a complicated agenda. The Emperor Maximilian died in November 1518, and it would be a full six months before his grandson Charles had secured the succession. In the meantime those concerned with the future direction of imperial policy were fully engaged, and critically Luther's patron, the Elector of Saxony, Frederick the Wise, had to be courted as a vital influence in the forthcoming imperial election. In consequence Frederick, a devout Catholic but fiercely proud of his new university and its suddenly famous local professor, had to be indulged in his perverse sponsorship of his turbulent friar. It was not until May 1520 that Luther's theses were formally condemned, in the papal bull *Exsurge Domine*. Luther made full use of the interval afforded by the slow processes of papal justice. His first big test was the meeting of the Augustinian chapter at Heidelberg in March 1518. Luther spoke well and effectively; hereafter members of his own order would be his most resolute early supporters. The following year, 1519, Luther confronted in debate one of the most effective of his growing army of Catholic critics, the Ingolstadt theologian Johannes Eck. Eck forced from Luther some damaging concessions. Rather than accept the orthodox judgement first pronounced by the legate Cajetan at Augsburg the previous autumn, Luther now claimed that the Pope himself did not have the final authority to interpret Scripture. The ultimate authority was Scripture itself; this was the *sola scriptura* principle which became, together with Justification by Faith, an intellectual cornerstone of the Reformation.

Through all of this Luther was writing feverishly, a torrent of writings in Latin and German, which simultaneously widened the scope of his criticisms of the Church and brought them to a wider public. As it became clear that his own Church would ultimately disavow his criticisms without the debate he sought, Luther moved to an ever more pessimistic and apocalyptic understanding of the role of the Church hierarchy. Even before Leo X had agreed to condemn Luther, Luther had written off the Pope as an agent of Antichrist. This was radical indeed, and it may be asked why so many Germans were prepared to honour Luther as a prophet and leader despite the increasing violence of his language. It was essentially Luther's gift as a writer which saved him from isolation and destruction. Culminating in his three great tracts of 1520, *The Babylonian Captivity of the Church, On the Freedom of a Christian Man* and *To the Christian Nobility of the German Nation*, Luther developed in numerous tracts and pamphlets a complete manifesto of reform, a call for the radical renovation of the German Church and the life of the Christian. It touched a sensitive nerve both with Christians struggling, like Luther, with their own relationship with an apparently vengeful God, and with secular powers resentful of the power of the Church in the lives of the German cities and princely states. It was a powerful cocktail of resentments, and one largely unique to Germany.

Thus, by the time the new emperor, Charles V, came to meet the Diet of the German princes at Worms in April 1521, Luther was already a major public figure, his image familiar from an increasing flood of pamphlets and illustrated broadsheets. The emperor, a devout Catholic, had no wish to meet Luther, and intended at first merely to proclaim the Pope's recent condemnation of his views. The German princes, however, insisted that Luther be heard; an ominous indication of the shifting balance of power within Germany. Luther therefore appeared personally to answer the charge of heresy. In a famous scene he refused to recant his views; more crucially, his safe-conduct was honoured, and Luther was permitted to leave Augsburg unharmed. Although Charles now proclaimed the imperial ban against Luther, he had lost his last best chance to snuff out the movement.

Luther was now dependent again on his loyal and supportive protector, Frederick the Wise. For a year after the Diet at Augsburg he remained incarcerated in the Wartburg Castle, held there for his own protection by the anxious Frederick. He occupied himself with writing and study, most constructively by beginning the new German translation of the Bible which would be his greatest and most enduring literary achievement. But even in his absence the movement continued to grow. In Wittenberg, his university colleague Andreas Karlstadt ensured that the momentum of reform was not dissipated, introducing into the local liturgy a new German Mass. A similar pattern was established in many towns across Germany, as sympathetic laymen and clergy took up the call for the renovation of Church life.

In many respects this was the crucial moment, as the call for reform finally outgrew the scandal and turbulence raised by the drama of the 'Luther affair'. It now became clear that in pursuing his own increasingly violent quarrel with the Church hierarchy, Luther had tapped into a broad seam of resentment about the German Church, which spoke to the concerns of many of his fellow citizens. In the pamphlet war of 1519–22 Luther certainly pursued his own theological agenda, but he was also careful to embrace a wide agenda of long-held grievances about the Church: the provision of clerical services (and the widely resented fees clerics charged for sacramental offices), tithes, clerical immunities. Thus although Luther's central theological message, Justification by Faith, was a real inspiration to many, what really struck a chord was his call for a return to pure scriptural teaching, with its implicit criticism of scholastic theology and a clerical ethos which left laymen excluded and disadvantaged. The preaching of the pure gospel, *Rein Evangelium*, became the slogan of those who followed Luther in his call for a total renovation of Church life.[2]

This was most clearly expressed in the German towns. Germany in the sixteenth century was a land of towns; the landscape of the empire was densely packed with cities, many of them, like Nuremberg and Augsburg, centres of both a highly developed trade and cultural life. Some 65 were Free Imperial Cities, self-governing territories which enjoyed a wide measure of political independence and separate representation in the imperial Diet. In the years after 1521 most of the cities experienced evangelical agitation from priests and laymen sympathetic to Luther. By 1525 several, led by Strasbourg and Nuremberg, were prepared to follow the example of Wittenberg and proclaim the introduction of a new German service and the abolition of the Mass.

By now the movement had clearly outgrown the theological concerns of its founder. Luther returned to Wittenberg in 1522 and continued to write and preach, a torrent of new writings which scarcely abated, and largely drowned out his Catholic critics. Reprinted freely across Germany, Luther's own writings make up an astonishing 25 per cent of the vastly increased number of printed books published in these years. None was more influential than Luther's German Bible, the practical embodiment of his call for a return to biblical simplicity.

But for all Luther's towering presence, a movement of this complexity could hardly remain under the direction of one man. Inevitably, the call for reform unleashed a vast and unruly surge of emotions, only imperfectly channelled by Luther's own reforming agenda. Not all those inspired by Luther would share his ultimate goals, or his innate social conservatism. Luther had a first inkling of this on his return from the Wartburg in 1522. In his absence Wittenberg had been convulsed by a group of self-appointed lay apostles, the so-called Zwickau prophets, who, supported by Karlstadt, had preached a much more radical reform than was acceptable to either Luther or the Electoral Court. Luther's return nipped this in the bud, but his influence could hardly be felt with the same force elsewhere in Germany.

The most damaging manifestation of this untamed energy was the Peasants' War of 1525. Although Luther's teaching found its most immediate resonance in the German cities, it also found many admirers among Germany's rural population. Here Luther's teaching of the social gospel, the equality of Christians before God, had a particular appeal, especially when applied to long-held grievances about the harsh conditions of rural life. In many parts of rural Germany the Church was deeply unpopular. The clergy were resented as harsh and oppressive landlords, not least for the reimposition of serfdom and the harsh terms of labour services, extracted as a traditional due in addition to rent. In 1525, many parts of Germany rose in revolt. Such peasant unrest was far from unprecedented: a similar series of risings, known as the *Bundschuh*, had smouldered along the Rhine basin for the previous twenty years. But now, ominously, the peasant leaders clothed their traditional grievances in the new language of evangelical justice: 'Third. It has until now been the custom of the Lords to own us as their property. This is deplorable, because Christ redeemed and bought us with his precious blood, the lowliest shepherd as well as the greatest lord.'[3]

To those who had denounced Luther as a social revolutionary, the Peasants' War appeared the final vindication. Luther himself, terrified that his movement would now be abandoned by the socially respectable, denounced the peasants and called for their suppression. By 1526, after a series of bloody engagements culminating in the wholesale slaughter of the battle of Frankenhausen, the revolt had been put down, but at considerable cost. Luther's own reputation was permanently damaged by the frantic violence of his polemic against the peasants; more fundamentally, the war and its aftermath made clear the boundaries beyond which reform could not be extended. In Germany's Free Cities, and in those states where the prince acted as sponsor, reform would proceed, a process which in the long term inevitably led to the increase in the power of the secular authorities at the expense of the Church. But those who had interpreted Luther's call for reform as an opportunity for social levelling were driven out of the movement. Increasingly they were confined to the wilder fringes of evangelism, sustained by self-styled prophets and preachers of little theological training. The defeated and disappointed victims of the Peasants' War were the first adherents of the unofficial Reformation which found its most powerful manifestation in Anabaptism.

The shock of 1525 proved only a temporary setback. In the years immediately following, more of the imperial cities adopted the evangelical agenda, joined now by the first of the princes who officially adopted the movement in their lands. By 1529 they were sufficiently strong to band together to defy the Emperor Charles V, who continued to insist that his condemnation of Luther, proclaimed at Worms in 1521, be enforced. The evangelical 'Protestation' against this decision in 1529 (the origin of the word 'Protestant') was followed in 1530 by the adoption of a common declaration of Faith, the Confession of Augsburg, now in effect the credal statement of a new Church. In the following decades the new movement consolidated its hold in the German lands. Luther himself, now securely established as patriarch of the new movement, accommodated himself to these developments. Mellowed by experience, the apocalyptic energy of his early preaching was replaced by the more practical work of Church building, to which Luther contributed a new genre of instructional literature, his German catechism. In this aspect of his work he was ably assisted by other talented men: Johannes Bugenhagen, who wrote Church orders for many of the first Lutheran lands, and Philip Melanchthon, the quiet intellectual who contributed the first systematic exposition of the Lutheran faith, the *Loci Communes*. By the time of his death in 1546 Luther's Church had transformed the landscape of religious life in Germany for ever.

The Reformation outside Germany

Outside Germany Luther's movement never achieved the same impact. The circumstances which permitted the rapid dissemination of Luther's message were too particular to his homeland. This was partly because of the empire's unique political and social make-up, a highly urbanized society where the central political institutions were exceptionally weak. Although the Emperor Charles V was determined to combat the Lutheran movement, he was ultimately powerless to impose his will on cities more concerned at the reaction of their own populations, and princes eager to exploit the controversies for their own ends. Also, Luther himself was a quintessentially German figure. Alongside an intensely serious and personal theological message, Luther also contrived to speak directly to the immediate concerns of his fellow countrymen, their frustrations with their religious life, their resentment of foreign interference in the German Church. Little of this would have the same force outside the empire; outside Germany, too, those who took up Luther's call for reform often met with far more determined opposition than was the case in the empire. Here, papal condemnation of Luther's teachings tended to carry more weight, and those who espoused Luther's doctrines did so at the hazard of their lives. The first Lutherans to die for their faith were two Augustinian monks from the Netherlands, Hendrik Vos and Jan van der Eschen, executed in Brussels in 1523 as Charles V clamped down savagely on local manifestations of the German heresy. Here in his patrimonial lands, Charles V could sustain the ban on heresy that he was powerless to enforce in Germany.

Yet in the years immediately following the outbreak of the German controversies, the impact of German events was certainly felt across wide parts of Europe. Luther's writings were known and read in most parts of Europe: individual admirers of his works can be identified as far away as Sweden and Scotland in the north, and in Spain and Italy in the south. But the call for reform seldom provoked the same turbulence, or inspired the degree of popular support, as had been the case in Germany. Where Protestant Churches were ultimately established it was generally through the agency of a sympathetic state power, as was the case in Scandinavia or England.

Outside Germany it was not surprising that the Reformation should have its most immediate impact in Switzerland. The Swiss Confederation was in its social and political structure not dissimilar to the empire, well provided with proud, independent cities, grouped around an inner core of rugged mountain cantons. The Confederation had won independence from its Habsburg overlords in 1499, at the end of the Swabian Wars, at which point it was effectively separated from the Holy Roman Empire. The close relationship between Swiss German and High German meant that there was no significant language barrier for evangelical writings to overcome. Most of all, the Swiss Reformation had its own inspirational leader in Ulrich Zwingli. Appointed to the prestigious post of *Leutpriester* (people's priest) in Zurich in 1518, Zwingli pursued a clear-minded agenda of reform which had much in common with that of the German cities. Zwingli had read and admired Luther, but there is no reason to doubt that reform in Zurich proceeded to an independent agenda, and Zwingli was able to call on considerable support from within Zurich's ruling elite. Spurred on by Zwingli, in 1525 the Zurich town council formally abolished the Mass, giving Zwingli and his colleagues a free hand to complete the work of reform.

The Zurich Reformation, so swiftly concluded, became a magnet and inspiration both within and beyond the Swiss Confederation. Many both in the German cities and elsewhere in Europe would in due course prefer the more radical Zurich model of reform to Luther's more conservative version. But within the Confederation, the response was more ambiguous. Zurich was one of the biggest and most powerful of the Swiss cantons, and its zeal to spread the evangelical message could easily be interpreted by its less powerful neighbours as a pretext for asserting Zurich influence over the Confederation as a whole. Thus whereas the urban cantons most equal in size and self-confidence, Bern and Basel, swiftly followed Zurich into the evangelical camp, the smaller inner mountain cantons resisted, a resistance prompted in equal measure by their antipathy to Zurich and their loyalty to Catholicism. Towards the end of the decade, goaded by interference from Zurich, the Catholic cantons went to war twice to defend their independence, in the second war inflicting on Zurich a crushing defeat which also cost the life of Zurich's inspirational leader (battle of Kappel, 11 October 1531).

Zwingli's death at Kappel put a decisive break on the development of the Zurich Reformation. Within Germany the eclipse of Zurich tilted the balance decisively back towards Wittenberg, much to the relief of Luther, whose antipathy towards Zwingli's theological writings had already provoked unseemly and damaging polemicizing between the two men. Within the Confederation, the Catholic cantons had effectively sustained their right to independent religious choice. On the Protestant side too the fronts were drawn; from this point on the most significant development would be the extension of Bern's influence into the French-speaking territories at the western end of the Confederation, which in 1532 encouraged the small city of Geneva to throw off the rule of its prince-bishop and declare for the Reformation. Four years later John Calvin, a young French exile, arrived to assist the process of consolidating the new evangelical order. It was hardly to be anticipated that this was in fact the beginning of the emergence of a new order which would in due course eclipse Zurich as the leading force within the Swiss Reformation.

In other parts of Europe the influence of Luther's movement often travelled in the footsteps of German immigrants and merchants. In both Scandinavia and Eastern Europe it was the small German communities who first read and disseminated his doctrines, enthusiastically seconded by students who had studied in Wittenberg before returning to their homeland to spread the word. The lands of Eastern Europe proved, in fact, surprisingly fertile ground for the Reformation, a circumstance now disguised for posterity by the later success of the Counter-Reformation in reclaiming Bohemia, Hungary and Poland.[4] But in the decades following the German Reformation Luther's movement made a profound impact. Bohemia (now the Czech Republic), and Hungary, in particular, were well integrated into the central European economic system, with strong trading and communication links with Germany; the precious metals of the Czech lands were mined by an international community which included many German settlers from across the border in Saxony. The Bohemians, too, had their own reasons for welcoming Luther's reform, not least its apparent endorsement of their own religious revolt against Rome as followers of the fifteenth-century heretic and martyr Jan Hus. After initial suspicion the Hussites eagerly embraced Luther (and vice versa). Their strong tradition of political independence, established in a brutal war in the 30 years following Hus's execution (1415), meant that they could easily resist Habsburg attempts to call them to order. Secure in their knowledge that the new Habsburg monarchy (rulers in Hungary and Bohemia since the death of King Louis Jagiello in the defeat at Mohács in 1526) could hardly rule these lands without the co-operation of their powerful estates, the Bohemian and Hungarian nobles extracted a high price for their support, and that included the toleration of Protestantism. The ironic result was that the Habsburg emperors, elsewhere the most resolute opponents of the evangelical movement, were forced to accept in these lands well-organized and strong Protestant Churches which became the dominant religious culture in these lands. The restoration of Catholic hegemony was forced to await the Habsburg victory in the early phase of the Thirty Years War.

The kingdoms of Scandinavia, too, became bastions of the new religion, though here the introduction of a robust and orthodox Lutheranism had less to do with local enthusiasm than with the determination of two strong-minded and opportunist kings. Whereas in the case of Christian IV of Denmark conviction possibly outweighed political considerations, with Gustavus Vasa of Sweden the opposite was certainly the case. Whatever the motive, the result was to build royal power at the expense of both the nobility and the clergy. In the case of Denmark, it is possible to talk of an alliance between the king, who had already introduced reform in his German lands of Schleswig-Holstein before succeeding to the throne, and the towns, for both Malmø and Copenhagen showed a considerable propensity to reform. It required a brief but decisive civil war in 1536 to overcome the entrenched opposition of the Catholic landed nobility to Christian's succession on the death of his uncle, the more cautious Frederik I. But after this the conversion of Denmark into a Protestant state proceeded apace; in 1537 the new king signed a Church Order, drawn up by Luther's closest lieutenant Johannes Bugenhagen, who also on this visit ordained the first seven Lutheran superintendents. A Lutheran state Church had been established only a decade after the Reformation had first begun to make an impact.

Sweden pursued a somewhat different course, partly because, in the case of Gustavus Vasa, there is little evidence of any disposition to favour Protestantism for its own sake. Rather, perhaps profiting from the example of the German princes who had adopted the Reformation, Gustavus clearly discerned the potential of the new evangelical teaching to assist his attack on the wealth and influence of the Church in Sweden. The Reformation would experience several setbacks before a parliament in 1539 granted the king full control over the Swedish Church; even so, the country would wait a further 30 years before the promulgation of a Protestant Church Order (1571). The very different character of the Scandinavian Reformation is underlined by the relative scarcity of vernacular religious literature to promote the new doctrines. This was hardly surprising; neither country had the population to sustain a printing industry of any size, nor the critical mass of town dwellers to provide a market. In Sweden and Denmark the task of inculcating the new beliefs would necessarily follow the acts of state which won both lands to Protestantism.

Circumstances were very different in the three prosperous lands of Western Europe where the fate of the Reformation was initially most uncertain, France, England and the Netherlands. England in this period was a land of contrasts: much less urbanized than either Germany or the Netherlands, it nevertheless possessed a thriving international trade centre in London, and in Oxford and Cambridge two universities of outstanding reputation. Both, in fact, would play a significant role in the early campaigns against Luther as Henry VIII turned to their finest theologians for the arguments which allowed him to enter the lists against the growing threat of Lutheran heresy, an initiative which would earn him from a grateful Pope the coveted title Defender of the Faith. The progress of the Reformation in England was closely bound up with Henry's personal affairs, as his increasing desperation to secure release from his marriage to Katharine of Aragon forced him to contemplate radical steps which went very much against the grain of his own instinctive theological conservatism. In this respect the Reformation in England would follow a model much closer to that of Scandinavia than Germany or Switzerland. Although England, like Bohemia, had its own indigenous medieval heresy in Lollardy, Luther's attack on the Church produced little resonance in

England outside the colony of the German merchants resident in London; indeed, although Luther's works were clearly imported into England at an early stage, this may very often have been for the convenience of conservative theologians who bought them to refute them, such as Bishop John Fisher and Sir Thomas More.

All of this changed when Henry made the fateful decision that only drastic action could extricate him from a marriage which, in the absence of a male heir, now threatened the future of his dynasty. In rapid succession from 1532, legislation was passed through Parliament curbing the influence of the papacy in England, and appointing the king Supreme Head of the Church. This and the divorce once achieved, the king moved to take control of much of the Church's property through the dissolution of the monasteries. The political nation was, for the most part, obediently compliant rather than enthusiastic. There is no evidence of any great hostility towards the Church and its institutions before the Reformation; on the contrary, both the English episcopate and parish clergy seem to have been by the standards of other European lands both well trained and living without scandal. On the other hand, few were prepared to defy the king to defend the threatened institutions of the Old Church, and the king was to discover that, largely inadvertently, his own actions had stimulated support for the heresy he had so virulently condemned in his youthful writings. This was predictable enough. In the campaign against the Church Henry and his faithful agent, Thomas Cromwell, necessarily made use of those who had the necessary polemical armoury, and this was most conveniently supplied by continental Protestantism. Several open advocates of the new beliefs, such as the new Archbishop of Canterbury Thomas Cranmer, and the preacher Hugh Latimer, attained positions of influence as a result.

As Henry's health failed in the last years of his life it became clear that his own actions had encouraged the growth of a powerful evangelical party at court. On his death in 1547 they moved quickly to establish their supremacy in the regency government necessitated by the youth of the new king, Edward VI. Thus the short reign of Edward VI saw a determined attempt to introduce a full Protestant Church polity into England, modelled on that of the Swiss and German Reformed Churches, and driven on by a powerful alliance of Archbishop Cranmer and the Lord Protector, the Duke of Somerset. In the five years of the king's life, much was achieved: two evangelical Prayer Books, a new English order of service, the stripping of the remaining Catholic paraphernalia from the churches. But time was too short to put down roots; on Edward's death in 1553, the changes were easily reversed by his Catholic half-sister, Mary. Only Mary's devotion to the papacy (which threatened the continued possession of former monastic property in the hands of those who had purchased it from the Crown), and her determination to marry her cousin, Philip of Spain, provoked a half-hearted reaction. English Protestantism was reduced once again to a persecuted remnant, many of its most able figures taking refuge abroad, to avoid the martyrdom which was the fate of those who remained behind.

English Protestantism at least had its first brief moment of success (and Edward's reign would prove an important benchmark later when Elizabeth's accession allowed a renewed return to Protestantism). The same could not be said of either France or the Netherlands. In both these countries those sympathetic to reform had to suffer cruel disappointment after the evangelical doctrines had made early inroads.

Perhaps nowhere was this disappointment more acute than in France, where political circumstances had seemed for a time to be uniquely favourable to reform. France had its own strongly rooted humanist movement, led by the towering figure of the renowned New Testament scholar Jacques Lefèvre d'Etaples. Equally important was France's strongly developed tradition of independence from Rome, which dated from the time when the medieval French monarchy was the leading force in Conciliarism and the sponsor of the schismatic Avignon papacy. This breach had been healed, but the price extracted by the French Crown was a substantial degree of control over high ecclesiastical appointments in France, a privilege confirmed by the Concordat of Bologna in 1517. The architect of this agreement was the new King Francis I, a monarch with strong humanistic leanings who seemed strongly inclined to endorse much of the reform agenda: his sponsorship of fashionable humanist scholarship sent out signals which could not but alarm conservative forces in France, led by the *Parlement* of Paris and the theology faculty of the University of Paris, the Sorbonne. So from an early stage the battle lines were drawn. The reform-minded, led by Lefèvre and Briçonnet, the evangelical Bishop of Meaux, sought to pursue an agenda of evangelical renewal whilst remaining loyal to the highly independent French Church. Conservatives, meanwhile, tried at every turn to tarnish these initiatives by association with the German heresy.

For a decade the reformers seemed to have the upper hand, secure in the protection of the king, and his sister, Margaret d'Angoulême. The turning point came in 1534, when a small group of radical émigré evangelicals contrived to exhibit in Paris posters denouncing the Mass in language of a ferocity previously unknown in polite evangelical circles. The king was outraged, and now more easily convinced of the dangers which lay behind the speculative preaching of the Parisian humanists. In the persecution which followed this 'Affair of the *placards*', Paris evangelism suffered a setback from which it never recovered, as many of its leading figures, Calvin among them, were forced to take flight abroad. In the years which followed, persecution abated, but French evangelism never recovered, reduced to a string of diffuse and essentially leaderless cells until the emergence of Calvinism in the second half of the century breathed new life into the shattered movement.

In the case of the Netherlands, the hostility of the state power was never in doubt. The provinces of the Low Countries formed part of the Burgundian patrimony of the new emperor, Charles V, whose hostility to Luther was intense and personal. Freed of the constraints which bound him in Germany, in the Netherlands he took rapid and decisive action to inhibit the spread of the new doctrines. This was all the more necessary since there was no doubt that the Netherlands would otherwise have proved fertile ground for the German heresies. The rich provinces of Flanders, Brabant and Holland formed one of the most urbanized regions of Europe. The prosperous cities of Bruges, Ghent and Antwerp enjoyed both a buoyant international trade and a proud educational tradition: this region was the cradle of northern humanism, famed both for its high degree of literacy among the general population and the distinction of its Latin schools. It might have been expected in these circumstances that Luther's teachings would find an eager audience in the Low Countries, and leaders of the German movement were not disappointed. In the first two decades of the Reformation there were more translations of Luther's works into Dutch than any other European vernacular. The poorly structured and ill-led Netherlandish Church was badly equipped to resist the appeal of the new doctrines, and Luther's teachings quickly found a deep resonance among the urban population. 'If there be three men that speak', wrote Cardinal Wolsey's envoy, Sir John Hackett, in 1527, 'the twain keep Luther's opinions',[5] a pardonable exaggeration which nevertheless conveys something of the extent of popular interest in the new teachings.

But even so robust a movement could make little headway in the face of so determined an opponent as Charles V. Luther's teachings were proscribed in the Netherlands even before his appearance at Worms in 1521, and this official condemnation was soon backed by an apparatus of persecution to match any in Europe. A series of proclamations made first the preaching or printing, later even the possession, of Lutheran books a capital crime. The first victims of the edicts were prominent local preachers who had dared to support Luther's call for reform; soon most had either been executed, forced to recant or driven into exile in Germany.

The elimination of this first generation of Lutheran leadership had a profound effect on the Reformation in the Netherlands. Deprived of their theological guidance, Dutch evangelicals turned increasingly to visionaries and prophets whose rejection by the leaders of the evangelical mainstream found expression in a doctrine of violence and apocalyptic despair. This movement, the first, decisive phase of Anabaptism, reached its apogee in 1534 with the seizure of the German imperial city of Münster, just across the border from the eastern Netherlands. The proclamation of the Münsterite kingdom had a profound resonance in the Netherlands, particularly in the northern provinces and Holland, then suffering a sharp economic recession. Although an attempted insurrection which would have made Amsterdam a second Münster failed, thousands from the Dutch provinces flocked to the German New Jerusalem; when Münster was finally suppressed in 1535, many in the Netherlands were caught up in the bloody repression that followed. But Dutch Anabaptism proved a resilient plant; reformed in the 1540s by the Friesland priest Menno Simons, and shorn of its more violent rhetoric, Dutch Anabaptism would survive to mount a plausible challenge to Calvinism in the second half of the sixteenth century.

In his other dominions Luther's movement would not cause Charles V the same problems. Spain was always likely to prove unfertile territory for Protestantism, since this was a land where memories of the struggle to reclaim the Spanish mainland from the Moors were still fresh. The conquest of Granada, completed in 1492, was heralded in the peninsula as the Catholic monarchs' greatest victory, and undoubtedly helped create a strong sense of identification between the Catholic Church and the developing self-identity of the new Spanish kingdom. Another important remnant of that period was the Spanish Inquisition, created as a means of testing the sincerity of those of other religions, Moors or Jews, who had converted to Christianity in order to stay in Spain, but equally easily turned against the rare individuals who showed signs of sympathy for the new heresies.

A more interesting case was that of the Italian peninsula. Here a robust response to Luther's call for reform might well have been expected. The proud city states of northern Italy were not much different from the German imperial cities in their traditions of political independence, and over much of the peninsula relations with the papacy were extremely tense. Many Italian churchmen were prepared to speak out at the slow pace of papally-sponsored reform, and the cynical exploitation of papal power for political ends that had characterized much of the fifteenth century. It was probably also in Italy that theologians engaged most directly with Luther's doctrine of Justification by Faith, since his reformulation of the doctrine of salvation commended itself to several leading figures on the reform wing of Italian Catholicism. Right up until the first session of the Council of Trent men such as Reginald Pole and Gasparo Contarini hoped to persuade their colleagues that agreement on this central Protestant doctrine offered the basis of possible reconciliation between the two Churches.

But Italian evangelism failed to live up to these promising beginnings. Nowhere, apparently, did Luther's call for reform produce the same popular resonance as in parts of northern Europe. Italian evangelism remained an elite movement, and those Church leaders who favoured doctrinal engagement with Lutheranism were too bound up with the institutional Church to follow the Germans into a repudiation of papal authority. Perhaps also cultural snobbery played its part: living in the cradle of humanism and the Renaissance, Italians were reluctant to concede that the reform of the Church could proceed according to an intellectual agenda emanating from the barbarous north. However this was, the polite evangelism of Italy made little progress against the entrenched forces of the Church hierarchy. The decisive moment came in 1542, when two prominent leaders of Italian reform, Bernardino Ochino and Pietro Martyr Vermigli, abandoned their charges and fled abroad. Henceforth Italians would, like Ochino and Martyr, make their most substantial contribution to evangelical reform from outside the peninsula, many of them attaining notoriety as freethinkers and dissidents on the very margins of the mainstream Protestant Churches.

In many lands of Europe, like Italy, the 1540s was a decade of retreat for Protestantism. After the optimistic evangelism of the 1520s, followed by a decade of consolidation, the movement suffered substantial reverses in the middle years of the century. In France, Italy and the Netherlands, promising beginnings had now given way to repression, which forced all of those who wished openly to espouse the evangelical doctrines to seek safer climes elsewhere. Many chose the safer course of conformity. Even in Germany the situation was far from rosy. Luther's death in 1546 was followed by a determined effort to subdue German Protestantism by force, as the emperor finally took to arms in the Schmalkaldic War. The result was a smashing defeat for the Protestant princes, which seemed at one point likely to reverse two decades of systematic Church-building in the German princely states. Even before this, many even of the reformers had begun to question how far these German Churches had progressed with the fundamental renovation of the Christian life which had been at the heart of Luther's call for reform. The Reformation, it seemed, was badly in need of a second wind.

Calvinism and religious warfare in the second half of the sixteenth century

The salvation of Protestantism came from what might at first sight have seemed an unlikely source. Geneva was at this point a small French-speaking enclave surrounded by three powerful neighbours: to the north and west, France and Savoy, to the east, the Swiss Confederation. A latecomer to the Reformation, the city's population converted to Protestantism in consequence of a citizen rebellion intended to free itself from the control of its local bishop. For a decade or more the small city remained very much in the shadow of the larger Swiss Protestant powers, Bern, its heavy-handed protector and sponsor of the revolution of 1532, and Zurich, beacon of evangelical reform both within and beyond the Confederation. Its transformation from this lowly and essentially provincial status owed everything to the clear-minded vision of John Calvin, a French refugee who first came to Geneva intending nothing more than a rapid passage onto a more substantial centre of evangelical scholarship, but who remained to transform the city and its international influence.

John Calvin was by any reckoning a remarkable man. Born in Noyon, Picardy, in 1509, he was very much a figure of the second generation, graduating through a conventional education to the humanist circle which flirted with evangelism in Paris in the early 1530s. Forced to leave France by the persecution which erupted in the wake of the Affair of the *placards* (1534), Calvin now turned his considerable intellectual skills to a justification of French evangelism, which Francis I was attempting to demonize to justify his recent harsh repression; the result was the first version of his *Institutes of the Christian Religion*, an exposition of the new evangelical faith remarkable for its clarity and lucidity of expression. It was the spreading reputation of this book which persuaded Guillaume Farel, the first reformer of Geneva, to detain Calvin to assist him with the work of reformation, when Calvin passed through the city in 1536.

This first ministry was not a success. A stranger to the Swiss Confederation and to Geneva's byzantine factional politics, Calvin was in 1538 outmanoeuvred and expelled, though he quickly found new employment as minister to the small French congregation in Martin Bucer's Strasbourg. Calvin profited greatly from this interlude, taking the opportunity to clarify his ideas of Church organization in one of the greatest of the German Protestant cities; when he returned to Geneva in 1541 he did so very much on his own terms, as the undisputed master of the Genevan reform.

Calvin's recall gave him the opportunity to create in the city his own vision of the reformed Church community. Not without opposition but with the steely determination which would characterize all his enterprises, Calvin introduced the best of what he had observed in Germany and his own small French church in Strasbourg: regular preaching and catechismal instruction for children and adults alike, combined with close regulation of the business and moral life of the community. The cornerstone of the enterprise was the co-operation of a close band of like-minded ministerial colleagues, all of them like himself exiles from France, and the consistory, a new institution made up of equal numbers of magistrates (sitting as elders) and ministers which met on a regular basis to supervise the morals and religious life of the community.

The values of Calvin's Geneva were not intrinsically different from those of other early modern European urban societies; its peculiarity lay in the care and determination with which they were enforced. For many around Europe, Geneva's growing reputation as a community living out the principles of reform, combined with Calvin's own reputation as a preacher and theologian, made it a beacon of hope in an unruly world: in John Knox's famous formulation, 'the most perfect school of Christ that ever was on the earth since the days of the Apostles'.

Geneva's emergence as a powerhouse of reform came at an opportune moment. All over Europe, Catholicism was beginning to recover its confidence, and a brake had been put on the evangelical advance. The Council of Trent finally began its deliberations in 1545, and in its first sessions committed the Old Church to a decisive repudiation of evangelical doctrine. Canon by canon, its doctrinal determinations offered a stark antithesis to the fundamental tenets of Protestantism: 'Canon 12. If anyone should say that justifying faith is nothing other than trust in the divine mercy which remits sins for Christ's sake, or that we are justified by such trust alone, let him be anathema.'[6] Although it would be many decades before the effects of Trent's decrees were felt throughout the Catholic Church, the returning confidence of the Old Church was evident in a much more determined pursuit of heresy in several parts of Europe. Those who had committed themselves to the new doctrines had little choice but to seek safety abroad; Geneva became one of a number of cities strategically placed along the borders of the German Empire to receive a major influx of refugees from the suffering evangelical minorities of western and southern Europe.

This 'Reformation of the Refugees' had a profound impact on the development of the Protestant movement. Liberated from the compromises and equivocations necessary in the constrained circumstances of their homelands, these groups of French, Italian, English and Netherlandish exiles were now drawn into Churches with a much clearer sense of identity and developed organizational structure. Many of these exile groups now committed themselves to the re-evangelization of their homeland; and most drew their inspiration from the structures and ethos of Calvin's Church in Geneva.

The first to feel the effect of this new militant climate within the evangelical movement was, not surprisingly, Calvin's French homeland. Even during the difficult years when Calvin's own position in Geneva was far from clear, he never forgot the scattered evangelical sympathizers left behind in Paris and elsewhere; much of his writing during these years was devoted to encouraging them to hold true to their beliefs. Calvin's fame today rests mostly on his talent as a theologian and Church organizer, but his contemporary influence probably owed as much to his undoubted gifts as a popular writer. In small tracts of remarkable clarity and force, such as his *Traité des reliques* (1543), and the *Excuse à messieurs les Nicodemites* (1544), Calvin spoke directly to the concerns of these French sympathizers; his correspondence also maintained a steady pressure on those tempted to conform to follow their vocation with courage.

For more than a decade Calvin's energy could make no great impact against the policy of persecution maintained by Francis I and his son, Henry II. But from about 1555, the situation began to change. It was significant that in this year Calvin finally imposed his will on his local Genevan opponents; he was now able to direct his whole efforts to the evangelization of France. Over the next years a steady stream of ministers trained in Geneva were dispatched to assist the small secret French Calvinist Churches emerging in the larger French cities (the first was founded in Paris in 1555). These ministers were able to form the congregations in the image of Geneva, and enforce a measure of central control. The first 'national' synod of the French Churches met in Paris in 1559, and although only eleven Churches were represented, nine of their ministers were Genevan-trained.

By 1559 the political climate began to turn decisively in the Calvinists' favour. In June the persecuting King Henry II died, the victim of a freak jousting accident which Calvinists were not slow to interpret as an example of the providential favour which seemed increasingly to shine on their movement. Henry's death left a political vacuum, quickly filled by the ultra-orthodox Duke of Guise, ruling France in the name of the new king, his nephew Francis II. Guise's domination of government provoked a number of nobles excluded by his arrogant assertion of power to join the Calvinist Churches as a vehicle for their political opposition. When in December 1560 the sudden death of Francis destroyed the Guise power base, the Calvinist communities were in a position to demand religious toleration as a condition for their future co-operation.

These were, indeed, years of hope and exultation for Protestants all over northern Europe. In England, the accession of Elizabeth in November 1558 brought an end to the Catholic regime of her Catholic half-sister Mary, and promised a significant shift in the religious balance of power in north-western Europe. This in itself was sufficient to encourage sections of the Scottish nobility who had been keen to challenge the power of the French-dominated regency government of Mary of Guise. In 1559, stimulated by the impending return of the widowed Queen Mary from France, they rose in revolt. Military aid from England tipped the balance in favour of the rebels; a short campaign, encouraged by religious demonstrations orchestrated by John Knox, led in 1560 to the establishment of a Calvinist regime.

It is easy to see why Protestants across Europe took new hope from these events. After a decade of retreat, new life seemed to have been breathed into the Protestant movement. The effect was inspirational, even intoxicating. All Christians in the sixteenth century shared a perception of God as an active force in everyday events, but this sense of providential activism seems to have been particularly developed in Calvinism. 'God's Providence governs all', wrote Calvin in his *Institutes*. 'For he is deemed omnipotent, not because he can indeed act, yet sometimes ceases and sits in idleness . . . but because, governing heaven and earth by his providence, he so regulates all things that nothing takes place without his deliberation.' [7] And this sense of God's active direction of events could easily be applied to the unfolding drama in France. 'Did you ever read or hear anything more opportune than the death of the King?' was Calvin's reaction to the death of Francis II in December 1560. 'He who pierced the eye of the father has now struck the ear of the son.'[8]

It is important to appreciate the atmosphere of the day if one is to comprehend how the triumphalism and defiance of French Calvinists drove France on towards religious confrontation. By this point the beleaguered French Crown was strongly inclined to compromise. Catherine of Medici, widow of Henry II and mother of the new young King Charles IX, was by now securely in control of government, and could see the pointlessness of continuing the policy of persecution. By now religious violence had convulsed most of France's major cities; continuing attempts to control religious dissidence by repression seemed only to exacerbate the problem. So in 1561 Catherine sponsored an attempt to promote religious reconciliation, a conference between the Calvinists and orthodox Catholics. The Colloquy of Poissy was attended by a powerful Genevan delegation led by Theodore Beza, Calvin's principal lieutenant and ultimate successor; when it failed, not least because of a forthright restatement of Calvinist Eucharistic theology from Beza, Catherine in January 1562 issued a unilateral declaration of toleration. But by this time events had moved beyond the possibility of a negotiated settlement. Outraged Catholics were provoked beyond endurance by the arrogance of those of the new religion (or as they called it, the religion which *pretended* to be reformed: *Religion prétendue réformée* or RPR). Bands of Calvinists roamed the streets, chanting their metrical psalms, assaulting priests and desecrating religious buildings. In March the Duke of Guise, the champion of Catholicism, came upon a congregation worshipping at Vassy near his lands in Burgundy, and a massacre followed. Within a month both sides had taken to arms.

The outbreak of the religious wars in France ushered in a new stage in the Reformation conflict. In many respects the resort to arms was an inevitable consequence of the collision of two new and irreconcilable faiths: a more militant Protestantism, and a reviving and newly self-confident Roman Catholicism. Although the religious conflicts which now came to dominate the religious landscape in northern Europe were generally preceded by polite requests for religious toleration on the part of the emerging Calvinist congregations, there is little sign that those of the new faith would ever have been truly satisfied with such an outcome: in France, as in the Netherlands, Scotland and other places where they achieved ascendancy, Calvinists inevitably pressed for the complete abolition of the Mass.

In France this would never be achieved. Indeed in retrospect it appears as if the beginning of the Wars of Religion in 1562 put a decisive brake on the development of French Protestantism. When the two sides took to arms, the Catholic majority still enjoyed a decisive advantage. While the Protestant forces, raised through contributions levied on the congregations, were well led, they lacked the professionalism of the royal army, now decisively committed on the Catholic side. Having lost the only major engagement of the campaign (the battle of Dreux, December 1562), the Huguenots were gradually prised out of many of the northern towns they had occupied at the beginning of the war. The Peace of Amboise, published in March 1563, set a definite limit to their ambitions. Henceforth they would be permitted to worship only on the lands of sympathetic nobles, and in addition in two places in each local administrative unit; a highly unsatisfactory concession for the city churches, since these sites might be situated many miles from the principal centres of population. In areas where the magistrates were hostile to the new religion they invariably were. Such conditions cut off the lifeblood of what had previously been largely an urban movement; the growth of French Calvinism had been decisively checked.

This was not immediately clear to contemporaries; the Wars of Religion continued in France, fitfully and without decisive military engagements, for a further 35 years before Henry IV brought the conflict to an end with the peace settlement known as the Edict of Nantes. But long before this French Protestants accommodated themselves to the status of a privileged minority. The desire to convert France, the providential evangelism of the early 1560s, was much diminished even before the massacre of St Bartholomew's Day in 1572 brought a steep decline. The massacre, which grew almost spontaneously out of a bungled attempt to assassinate the Huguenot leader Admiral Coligny, was a measure of the genuine hatred which now divided the religious communities in France. Its effect was to leave French Protestantism bewildered and leaderless in much of the country. Only in the south of France, secure in strongholds far away from royal armies, did the Huguenots remain a force. In the wake of the massacre the Protestant towns and nobles of this region banded together in a new military and political organization (the United Provinces of the South) which came close to a total declaration of independence from the discredited French Crown. Only the death of the last Valois heir in 1584, an event which made the Huguenot champion Henry of Navarre next in line to the throne, saved royal authority in the south. On his accession in 1589 Henry could rely on the support of his former allies even if pragmatism dictated that he would only make good his claim to the throne by adopting the religion of the majority of his subjects. Henry's conversion to Catholicism in 1593 effectively ended the religious wars, though the negotiation of a settlement required a further five years. The final settlement accorded the Huguenots significant privileges including the right of worship. It was a realistic recognition that Calvinism had, through 40 years of warfare, established a permanent, if limited, presence in the most Catholic kingdom of France.

That French Protestantism survived owed much to the extraordinary resilience of Calvinism, but the French Huguenot movement also drew strength from the increasingly international aspect of the conflict. One of the principal characteristics of the Calvinist movement was a sense of solidarity which crossed national boundaries, and induced members of Churches in one nation to provide help and hospitality to fellow Church-members elsewhere. The role of the Genevan Church was in this respect exemplary, if not unique. Religious refugees from France and the Netherlands could also rely on finding a safe haven in other similar places in Germany and England.

Events in the Netherlands, in fact, closely paralleled the conflict in France. As in France, a previously disparate evangelical movement was revived and reorganized by exile communities drawing their inspiration from Calvinism. As in France, too, the crucial decade from 1555 saw the establishment of small secret congregations back in the homeland sustained by the encouragement and missionary activity of those who remained abroad. In the Netherlands, however, the members of the secret Churches could not rely on any weakening of resolve on the part of the ruling power. On the contrary, the Low Countries' implacable ruler, Philip II of Spain, was determined to do all in his power to stamp out the new heresies, and persecution continued unabated through the period of gathering crisis to 1565. It was a political crisis which had set Philip against the local Netherlandish nobility which gave the Calvinists their opportunity. Exploiting a temporary suspension of the heresy laws in 1566, the result of a collapse of will on the part of the regent, Margaret of Parma, in the face of noble protests against her regime, thousands of religious refugees flocked back to their homeland. Mass open-air preaching became the occasion for a call for full religious freedom; very shortly, the Calvinists took matters into their own hands by descending on the churches to cleanse them of the Catholic images. The iconoclasm, a carefully organized pre-emptive strike against the institutions of the Old Church, radicalized the revolt. Although in the short term disastrous, since the nobility swiftly made up their differences with the Crown and co-operated in the re-establishment of order, the events of 1566 gave Dutch Calvinists an unchallenged position at the centre of the Dutch revolt.

Forced back temporarily to the exile towns, the Calvinist communities did not have long to wait for the opportunity to renew the conflict. In 1572 rebel forces invested two small ports at Vlissingen and Den Briel and Holland rose in support. As the rebels consolidated their hold, the Holland towns became the new Calvinist stronghold of the free north. This was hardly the intention of William of Orange, who after initial hesitations had become the greatest of the opposition nobles to commit himself unambiguously to the revolt. In the period after 1572 he would emerge as an inspirational military and political leader, providing the revolt with a vital social respectability in the search for allies in other parts of Protestant Europe. William's vision was that the revolt should remain patriotic and inclusive, essentially a struggle for religious tolera- tion and freedom from Spanish rule. But the Calvinists exacted a heavy price for their assistance. As the towns of Holland fell under their control, a ruthless religious uniformity was asserted, the Mass prohibited and the chief town churches commandeered for their use. And when after 1576 it briefly appeared that the provinces could unite to expel Spanish troops, the same proselytizing zeal was exported to the other provinces. The result was predictably disastrous for the exponents of an inclusive free state. By 1579 the southern Catholic nobility had made up their differences with a new and more tolerant Spanish commander, the Duke of Parma. The promulgation of two rival unions in this year indicated what would become a permanent division between a free Calvinist north and a client Habsburg state in the south, increasingly firmly restored to the Catholic fold.

For William of Orange, struck down by a Catholic assassin in 1584, the failure of unity was a personal tragedy, but for the Calvinist leadership it was a reasonable price to pay for the opportunity to create a new Calvinist order in the provinces of the Union. As in France, Scotland or other parts of the Calvinist international, the towns under Calvinist control, modelled on Calvin's Geneva, soon felt the effects of the distinct- ive Calvinist concept of religious life. Reformed leaders in all of these lands bent their efforts to a comprehensive remodelling of society. As always in Protestant societies, exhortation from the pulpit played a critical role, but in the Calvinist system the moral force of preaching was backed by a close supervision of life and morals provided by the consistory, the characteristic Calvinist institution. Calvinists wasted no time erecting consistories wherever they achieved political control: for them, the public exercise of discipline was as crucial a mark of the true Church as preaching or the sacraments. In an ideal state of affairs, Calvinists would also enjoy a monopoly of public worship, and the support of the state power for the administration of civil penalties to reinforce the moral persuasion of the discipline. Perhaps, though, only in Scotland and a few of the German principalities was this state of Genevan perfection truly achieved.

Elsewhere the ministers found the local magistrates curiously ambivalent in the face of their righteous zeal. In the Netherlands, for instance, the magistrates of the Dutch towns proved extremely reluctant to concede so much power to the pastors. They had, after all, only recently thrown off one form of religious intolerance, and had little taste for a new theocracy. In the new Dutch state, therefore, the Calvinist Church operated within a system of subtle checks and balances. The Church was recognized as the sole public Church; but the town authorities turned a deaf ear when the ministers urged them to pursue more energetically the other religious congregations which continued to enjoy a flourishing if unauthorized existence. Most significantly of all, neither membership of the Church, nor participation in its sacraments, was made compulsory: only those who chose joined themselves to the Church, and submitted themselves to its discipline. Not surprisingly, this was a small proportion of the population: although perhaps half of the population of the new Dutch state attended services in the Calvinist churches, full membership was as low as 10 per cent.[9]

But even without the wholehearted support of the state, the sheer moral force of the Calvinist project did achieve a significant reordering in the societies where it held sway. Members of the Church would be increasingly recognizable; through the sobriety of their dress, and through their resolute abstention from forms of entertainment which they deplored (such as dancing and the theatre), but to which the mass of the population remained obstinately addicted. And Calvinists in their turn accommodated themselves increasingly to this half victory. In this they were helped by their own theology, for Calvin's doctrine of Predestination made clear that only a small number would be saved. The public adherence of a limited section of society to a severe congregational discipline was in this sense theology made flesh – it was not without cause that non-Calvinist neighbours objected above all to the insufferable self-righteousness of the brethren, even if the social values to which Calvinists adhered were not essentially different from those of society at large. In was in this sense that 'puritanism' was used, as a term of abuse from neighbours less inclined to ostentatious sanctity; but puritanism, or something like it, was a phenomenon which emerged naturally in all Calvinist societies, for the urge to perfection was a quest in which Church members were ceaselessly involved. And for all their faults, Calvinists could congratulate themselves that they had pursued effectively the renovation of Christian society which had been at the heart of Luther's German movement, and had there ultimately been frustrated. Increasingly it was Calvinism which provided the moral energy behind the Reformation movement, as German Lutheranism descended into arid and divisive theological debate.

Later Lutheranism and the second Reformation

Luther's death in 1546 left Protestantism in his homeland perilously placed. True, half of Germany's princely states and a larger proportion of the Free Cities had now officially adopted Lutheranism. But against this even Luther's supporters would concede that the Christian education of the mass of the population had scarcely begun. More worrying still, there were signs that the forces of the Old Church were beginning to revive. In 1544, Catholic armies forcibly prevented the Archbishop of Cologne, Herman von Wied, from turning his lands into a secular Protestant state, a clear indication that the balance of military force was turning against the Protestant Schmalkaldic League. And in 1546 the emperor, Charles V, finally tired of negotiation and embarked on the forced subjugation of the Lutheran princes. A short military campaign succeeded beyond his wildest dreams, when the crushing victory at Mühlberg left the leading Protestant princes as prisoners in his hands. Able now to dictate terms, Charles insisted on a harsh religious settlement (the Augsburg Interim) which presaged the reintroduction of a Catholic order of service throughout the Empire.

Happily for German Lutheranism this crisis was short-lived. The emperor's military advantage proved to be only temporary, and within a few years a sharp turn in the strategic balance forced him to contemplate a more realistic settlement of Germany's religious stalemate. Exhausted and discouraged, in 1555 Charles V retired from active political life, leaving his brother Ferdinand to make the concessions to German Protestantism that were now inevitable. The Peace of Augsburg, signed in 1555, was a landmark settlement, justly recognized as such by both contemporaries and historians. For the first time, the Lutheran Churches of Germany received official recognition. In lands where the prince or city council had formally adopted the Reformation, Lutheran Churches were now formally acknowledged (the principle known as *cuius regio, eius religio*). In this respect the peace signalled the formal end of attempts, by force or by consensus, to bring an end to the confessional divide in Germany. But Germany's Protestants paid a price for their hard-won security. For the peace also laid down that those lands which remained in Catholic hands should equally be respected. In terms of territorial gains, German Lutheranism made little further progress in the half century after 1555.

Even more importantly, the Peace of Augsburg made no provision for other Protestant confessions to enjoy its protections. This was highly significant, because in Germany as in Western Europe Calvin's Church system exercised a strong dynamic pull. Cities and territories which flirted with the Swiss movement in these decades did so without the protection of the provisions of the peace. This omission became almost immediately a matter of some importance when in 1559 the new Elector Palatine, Frederick III, began moving his lands (Protestant since 1546) towards a Reformed confession. With the Palatinate and especially the University of Heidelberg as a focal point, Calvinism proved to be a strong influence for change within the empire, particularly in the years after 1580. In the two decades at the end of the century a whole series of cities and small territories professed the Reformed religion, most concentrated in the same strategic theatre of north-western Germany and Westphalia. Together with the Palatinate, these lands provided the ideal jumping-off point for intervention in the religious conflicts raging in the lands to the west, a phenomenon epitomized in the career of Count John Casimir, younger brother of the Elector Frederick, who actively pursued the role of international Protestant champion by leading a sequence of military expeditions into France and the Low Countries.

The strong dynamic growth in German Calvinism after 1580 was partly a result of developments within German Lutheranism. For some time after the Peace of Augsburg German Lutheranism had remained relatively fluid. But conflicting strains were already beginning to emerge, their origin dating back to the difficult years after Charles V's victory at Mühlberg. Faced with the emperor's overwhelming victory, a significant proportion of the Lutheran leadership had urged compromise, among them Luther's lieutenant and heir, Philip Melanchthon. Such lack of resolution had outraged those who favoured resistance at whatever cost; Charles's eventual retreat from Germany seemed to have vindicated this position. Not surprisingly those who had opposed any compromise regarded themselves as the true heirs of Luther. Strongly entrenched in the Universities of Tübingen and Jena, they took refuge in an ever more rigid defence of Lutheran orthodoxy, and ever more virulent denunciations of those who deviated from this demanding standard.

The difficulties posed by such a hardening of the confessional fronts were amply demonstrated by the later career of Philip Melanchthon, since Luther's death undoubtedly the most illustrious voice of German Lutheranism. Melanchthon's accommodating spirit was little suited to the world of uncompromising factional polemics that had erupted in the empire since 1550. Those who followed Melanchthon in these controversies, the 'Philippists', were mostly men of the same stamp: jurists, physicians and theologians, often strongly influenced by Erasmian humanism, and well represented in the University of Wittenberg.

The decisive showdown within German Lutheranism occurred as the result of developments within electoral Saxony. For much of his long reign, the Elector Augustus tolerated both tendencies in his lands: a coterie of Philippists at his court was balanced by a strongly orthodox clergy and nobility. In 1574, provoked by the publication of a pamphlet openly espousing Calvinist Eucharistic theology, the orthodox persuaded Augustus to purge his court: a number of the leading Philippists were arrested and imprisoned, and some even tortured. A major exodus followed. In the wake of these dramatic events Elector Augustus encouraged orthodox theologians to articulate a clear statement of Lutheran doctrine. The Formula of Concord, proclaimed in 1580 and widely accepted as the new credal statement in Lutheran Churches across Germany, established hardline Gnesio-Lutheranism as the undisputedly dominant tendency within the German Churches.

The expulsion of the Philippists did not arrest the development of German Calvinism. But these events did ensure that the major German princely states would remain true to their Lutheran heritage. When in 1613 the Elector of Brandenburg, Johann Sigismund, announced a personal conversion to Calvinism, there was no question that his subjects would obediently follow. Calvinism in Brandenburg remained almost entirely confined to the ducal court. Events such as these demonstrated that in the long decades since Luther's preaching, his movement had put down deep roots. In the second half of the sixteenth century most of the German princes continued the work of consolidating their authority within their dominions, a process to which the defiance of the emperor's will in the early Reformation had given a decisive impulse. In this process the Lutheran pastors were to emerge as vital allies as local agents and upholders of the princely authority; in return the German princes were careful to defend and enhance the prestige of the ministerial office. Thus the Lutheran pastorate became an increasingly attractive and professionalized occupation as the century wore on. Trained in state-supported colleges and universities, ministers became a new force in the local community. Dominating the village through their social prestige and superior education, the new ministerial family became the natural focus of village life to an even greater extent than had their priestly predecessors in the pre-Reformation period.

This process, often referred to as confessionalization, was not unique to the Lutheran Church. The same process of professional development and close co-operation with the state power was evident in Calvinism and Catholic lands in this period also. And Lutheran Germany, notwithstanding these real advances, would pay a heavy price for the divisions which had preceded the resolution of the theological disputes in the 1580s. The strong passions raised inevitably turned the movement inwards. Preoccupied by their own affairs, the German Churches had little appetite for a leadership role in the wider Protestant community. In the second half of the century this leadership role therefore devolved increasingly on the other major emerging Protestant power, England.

Elizabethan England was in many respects an unlikely, and certainly reluctant, champion of the international Protestant cause. In 1558 Elizabeth had acceded to a troubled throne, after five years during which Catholicism had been re-established in England with little apparent difficulty. Although the changes of Mary's reign were now reversed once more, Elizabeth and her councillors were under no illusions that many of her subjects remained obstinately attached to the old ways. It would be well into the last two decades of Elizabeth's long reign before it could confidently be said that Protestantism was the religion of the majority in England.

For the first decades those who opposed the religious policies of the Elizabethan government could take comfort from the evident insecurity of a regime embodied by a mature childless queen who obstinately refused to marry, and whose nearest heir was the Catholic Mary Queen of Scots. Had Elizabeth died early (as she nearly did in 1563, from smallpox), England too might have plunged into the same religious civil war convulsing neighbouring lands on the Continent.

Given this evident insecurity, the confidence with which Elizabeth and her advisers addressed the complicated problems of domestic and foreign policy, arising from a new restoration of Protestantism, was remarkable. A parliament gathered to settle religion in 1559 compliantly reinstated the Protestant Prayer Book of Edward VI, but Elizabeth balked at the introduction of the full Calvinist Church Order urged upon her by foreign theologians and some of the English exiles who, having withdrawn to the Continent during Mary's reign, now returned to inaugurate the new era. Bishops were retained, and so too ecclesiastical vestments, which many of the hotter Protestants regarded as an unacceptable popish survival. When in 1566 Elizabeth insisted upon uniformity in clerical attire, a substantial proportion of the English clergy (up to 10 per cent in London) refused to submit, and were deprived. Further attempts to move the queen to a more perfect Reformation, whether by parliamentary statute or subtle pressure through the bench of bishops, proved equally unavailing; the Church of England would remain, in the words of its Protestant critics, 'but halfly reformed'.

Despairing at the queen's obstinacy, and at the apparent indifference of broad sections of the population to the call to a more godly lifestyle, evangelicals took refuge in brotherhoods and congregations which became increasingly detached from the mainstream Church. The frustration of reform measures in the parliaments of 1571 and 1572 led some into formal separation. In the latter years of Elizabeth's reign Puritanism gave way to sectarian nonconformity, and eventually into outright confrontation with the established Church. But the numbers involved in such open dissidence were small, the vast majority of the godly preferring to remain in communion, and seek consolation in voluntary associations which provided an appropriate context for the Puritan lifestyle. And in the main, their choice was justified, for whatever their disappointment at Elizabeth's lack of godly zeal, England's general allegiance to the Protestant cause was not in doubt. Even from the beginning of the reign there were evident proofs of this in an ambitious foreign policy which led swiftly to confrontation with the leading Catholic powers. By the last quarter of the century England was destined to play a pivotal role in the survival of Calvinist powers on the Continent, as they faced the most profound threat to their survival from a resurgent Catholicism.

Catholic reform

Catholic reform was not a product of Protestantism. Long before Luther's protest divided the German Church a coherent agenda of reform was already in place; the renewal of worship and Church institutions had been pursued with vision and energy by Church leaders in several parts of Europe since the middle of the fifteenth century. In the Spain of Ferdinand and Isabella, Cardinal Ximenez de Cisneros had introduced a series of reforms which anticipated by the best part of a century the reforming agenda of the Council of Trent, and notable Italians, such as Bishop Giberti of Verona, appointed in 1524, followed suit. With such examples in mind Catholic historians have rejected with indignation the use of the term 'Counter-Reformation' to describe a movement whose roots lay deep in the medieval era. Luther, they remind us, was by no means the first or most influential Catholic reformer of his day.

Nevertheless, there is no denying that the emergence of Protestantism provided an enormous stimulus to the process of reform. The reform of Church structures and established patterns of belief had proved an arduous undertaking, and for every Cisneros in early sixteenth-century Europe there were a dozen bishops who owed their position to family influence or royal patronage, rather than any intrinsic fitness for office. The eruption of criticism of the Church spreading from Germany in the 1520s pressed reform to the top of the agenda, if only because it demonstrated that if the hierarchy proved unequal to the task, others within the Christian community were now wholly determined on a renovation of Church life and institutions.

The problem for the Church was that reform could only really come from the top. The medieval conflict over Conciliarism had eventually been resolved by reaffirming papal authority, but the papacy had also saddled itself with the responsibility for initiating reform. In the early sixteenth century the institution faced a double challenge: to confront and throw back the threat posed by Luther's movement, while at the same time meeting the concerns of those who acknowledged the need for fundamental reform within the established Church. It was hardly surprising that at times during the first years of Protestantism such a task seemed almost beyond a papacy assailed by both friend and foe alike. In the first years after Luther's protest there was considerable disagreement as to how much could be conceded to the Church's critics. Luther was a heretic, but were his theological propositions equally heretical? Many even within the higher reaches of the Roman hierarchy were deeply attracted to Luther's teaching on Justification, which drew on a strong tradition of thought within Catholicism. Gasparo Contarini, the leading representative of this tendency and a cardinal from 1535, is believed to have reached his understanding of Justification prior to and independent of Luther. It inevitably took some time for the Renaissance papacy to adapt to the new scale of the challenge posed by evangelism. Only when the traditional weapons of ban and excommunication had been tried and failed, was it finally recognized that a fundamental review of Catholic doctrine was necessary if the Old Church were to survive.

The chosen instrument of reform was a General Council of the Church, summoned, after years of negotiation and hesitation, to meet at Trent in northern Italy in 1545. The hesitation reflected deep misgivings regarding the merits of such an open assembly, and prolonged dispute between Pope and emperor over the council's location. But in some respects the delays were critical to the council's undoubted success, because by the time the council met the critical doctrinal questions in relation to Protestantism had effectively been resolved. The half decade before Trent had seen a series of meetings designed to promote reconciliation between the divided confessions; the most serious of these, a conference of German and Italian theologians at Regensburg in 1540, revealed that the theological gulf between Lutherans and Catholics was now unbridgeable. The council which gathered at Trent was not therefore intended to promote reconciliation with Protestantism; rather its purpose was to declare Catholic orthodoxy on matters where Protestants clearly deviated from traditional teaching. This purpose is clearly indicated by the resulting theological canons of the council, which declared the validity of the Catholic tradition entirely in relation to institutions and customs challenged by evangelicals. The validity of pilgrimages, images and prayers to saints were affirmed, the doctrine of Transubstantiation confirmed, the value of Church authority proclaimed against an exclusive reliance on Scripture.

The doctrinal pronouncements of the Council of Trent, substantially complete by the end of its first two sessions, were essential to the Catholic revival in Europe. After decades of debate and doubt as to what constituted the essentials of faith, Trent established clarity in the areas of doctrine and Church practice most disputed between reformers and conservatives. These matters once settled, it allowed the fathers of the Church to draw a clear distinction between the heretical assault on Church doctrine, and the call for renovation of the Church's institutions and improvement in standards of clerical performance, which all shades of Christian denomination recognized had some validity.

The reform of the Church's institutions dominated the council's later deliberations, which eventually, after several recesses, stretched over twenty years. Here, too, the council's provisions reflected the impact of the evangelical agenda. Some of the most important of the council's decisions in this area recognized the necessity that the clergy should be properly qualified and worthy of respect; scandalous and ignorant clergy had been one of the most provocative issues in the eyes of many of the laity who had joined the evangelical movement. In response, Trent laid down clear provisions for the training, residence and moral direction of the clergy. To ensure a future supply of adequately educated men, each diocese was to establish a seminary. But the fathers at Trent were careful to do nothing to disturb the traditional hierarchical structures of the Church. The authority of a bishop in his diocese was confirmed, and the council was at pains to do nothing to undermine the authority of the Papal See. The reform of the Curia, widely recognized as essential, was left to the initiative of a series of reforming Popes, notably Paul III (1534–49) and Paul IV (1555–59), inspired but in no way directed by Trent.

The reforms of parish life anticipated by the council took decades, even centuries, to be carried into effect. The establishment of diocesan seminaries proceeded only at a slow pace, and by the end of the sixteenth century many priests were still woefully badly educated. And whilst notable bishops such as Archbishop Charles Borromeo of Milan (1560–84) took up the reforming agenda with exemplary zeal, in the broader mass of the episcopate old habits died hard. Many continued to treat episcopal office as a family property: four successive members of the Gondi family held the Archdiocese of Paris between 1559 and 1662, and it was by such a process that Richelieu first attained high office, when he was promoted to the 'family' diocese. For others, Church positions continued to be held in plurality, or as the adjunct to royal service. Small wonder that the effects of the council's decrees were often scarcely felt at parish level. Historians of Protestantism now recognize that the evangelical programme needed many generations to achieve a substantial reordering of fundamental religious beliefs, and this seems equally to have been the case for Catholicism. Studies of local Catholic culture published in recent years demonstrate that in many parts of Europe, parishioners remained addicted to religious customs that were essentially pre-Reformation in character, or even semi-pagan.[10] The wiser, more experienced members of the local Church hierarchy frequently accommodated themselves to such local customs in their application of the canons of reform.

But all of this is not to say that the impact of Trent was not immediate, or profound. Probably the council's first effect was psychological. The promulgation of its decrees, backed by clear evidence of a will to reform in the papacy, restored self-confidence to a battered movement and, just as important, a sense of mission. This was reflected in a new willingness on the part of a committed Catholic laity to oppose and confront further Protestant encroachment.

Among the religious professionals the most striking manifestation of this phenomenon was the foundation and spectacular growth of the new religious orders. The best known of the orders was the Society of Jesus or Jesuits, founded in 1540 by the former soldier Ignatius Loyola. The saintly piety and organizational flair of their founder, combined with an ostentatious devotion to the papal office, assured the Jesuits of crucial political patronage. Thanks to their rigorous educational programme and a stream of high quality recruits, the Jesuits were able to turn themselves into a veritable missionary elite. But the Jesuits were by no means the first, nor the largest, of the new orders – the Theatines (1524), Ursuline Nuns (1535) and Oratorians all played their part in the new religious life of mission activity, as did the Capuchins and reformed Cistercians. Together they accomplished what amounted to a wholesale renovation of the jaded monasticism of the Middle Ages.

The new religious orders achieved their most spectacular successes overseas, in the mission fields of the New World and Asia. Here their strenuous and often heroic efforts were relatively uncontroversial: these were virgin territories for Christianity, with souls to claim in their millions. The fathers gave themselves to this work with a zeal which was for a time proof against doubts regarding the real chances of bringing native peoples to a profound understanding of Christianity. The Augustinians were in Mexico by 1533 and Peru by 1550. For the Jesuits, Francis Xavier, Loyola's most charismatic lieutenant, wore out his life in repeated voyages around the eastern oceans, among his many achievements opening up China and Japan to Christian influence. This was dangerous work, and many of the missionaries gave their lives to the cause. But this was hardly a useless sacrifice, since the example of these noble martyr-saints gave Catholics exemplars to set against the many evangelicals who had given their lives bravely and without complaint in the defence of their beliefs. The Counter-Reformation, indeed, was an age of new saint-making. Twenty-seven men and five women who lived during these centuries were canonized by the Church before 1770, a clear sign of the Church's desire to promote new models of emulation to set alongside the more various (and sometimes largely mythical) saints of the medieval Christian tradition.[11]

For succeeding generations the mission Churches would pose more difficult questions. European superiors with no experience of native societies were increasingly troubled by the extent to which missionaries were prepared to temper their presentation of Christian teaching to make it more comprehensible to local civilizations. Few, it must be said, shared modern scruples at the havoc wreaked on advanced and sophisticated native societies by the introduction of Western mores and social custom. For European Catholicism, however, the impact of the overseas missions was an almost unqualified success. For their effect in restoring the self-confidence of a bruised and battered Church, the missions were quite irreplaceable. At a basic level the millions of new souls won overseas offered a partial compensation for those lost to Protestantism at home. The overseas missions also offered the opportunity for immediate action at a time when the problems of Christian Europe seemed more intractable.

The impact of the new religious orders on the collective religious psyche of Catholicism is revealed when it is recognized that a full half of the new saints of the Catholic Reformation were members of the new religious orders. These included five Capuchins, three Theatines and no fewer than six Jesuits. Many of these saints had been active in the missions. Alongside Francis Xavier, Jesuit apostle to the East, were the Spanish Observant Francisco Solano and the Dominican Louis Bertran, sixteenth-century missionary to the Indians of Colombia. But the mission field of the new religious orders was not confined to native peoples in faraway places. Among those canonized by a grateful papacy were the Jesuit Jean-François Regius, who laboured to recover souls lost to Protestantism in Languedoc, and Felix of Sigmaringen, who did similar work in the Swiss Grisons.

For while Catholics celebrated and honoured the work of their overseas missionaries, few would doubt that the most critical task was to combat the apparently inexorable spread of Protestantism in Europe. And here, too, the most immediate consequence of the Council of Trent lay less in specific reforming decrees, than in its contribution to restoring Catholic self-confidence. In the 1560s French Catholicism found individuals and groups prepared to engage the apparently rampant Huguenot bands with equal fervour and determination. France in fact witnessed at this time an extraordinary growth of voluntary religious associations, on both sides of the religious divide. The greatest of the Catholic associations was the Catholic League, formed in 1584 to oppose the succession of the Huguenot Henry of Navarre after the death of the last Valois heir. At the end of the decade the League would defy two monarchs to seize the capital, Paris, and establish it as a stronghold of unyielding opposition to the Huguenot succession.

There is little doubt that this resurgent lay Catholicism proceeded in advance of any officially inspired renovation of religious life. Even by the end of the century there were fewer than 300 Jesuits in France, and generally the French bishops had not as yet shown themselves active in the promotion of the Counter-Reformation agenda. French Catholicism survived through a successful alliance between committed elements of the Catholic laity and the leadership provided by the Catholic nobility, notably the family of Guise. At a time when the French Crown was contemplating permitting Protestant freedom of worship as a means of putting an end to religious conflict, this carefully crafted compromise was effectively destroyed by popular opposition.

Events in France were a salutary reminder that for all the careful work of Trent, Catholic revival was first and foremost dependent on arresting the seemingly inexorable spread of Protestantism. As much as it revered and sanctified its missionaries and aesthetics, Tridentine Catholicism owed an even greater debt to its men of war. The first phase of Catholic recovery is epitomized by the careers of successive Dukes of Guise, both of whom would have their careers as leaders of the French Catholic armies cut short by assassination, or the Duke of Parma, whose military campaigns in the Netherlands between 1579 and 1585 recovered for Catholic Spain most of the southern Netherlands. Lying behind much of this martial activity was the sombre figure of the Spanish king, Philip II, a man who more than any other embodied this phase of the militant Catholic struggle. Fiercely committed to both the crusade against the Ottoman Turk in the Eastern Mediterranean, and the battle against heresy in Western Europe, Philip made a clear identification between his global political mission and the struggle against Protestantism. 'You may assure His Holiness', Philip told his ambassador in Rome in 1566, 'that rather than suffer the least damage to religion and the service of God, I would lose all my states and an hundred lives, if I had them; for I do not propose nor desire to be the ruler of heretics.'

Philip's Catholic allies were sometimes less convinced of the purity of the king's motives. 'The King of Spain as a temporal sovereign, is anxious above all to increase his dominions . . . The preservation of the Catholic religion, which is the principal aim of the Pope, is only a pretext for his majesty' was the somewhat more cynical response of Sixtus V (1585–93), Philip's sometimes reluctant partner in the Enterprise of England.[12]

But for all these misgivings it must be said that Philip's ventures did more than any other to turn the tide in favour of Catholicism. Between 1559 and 1571, Philip almost single-handedly gathered a coalition of forces capable of confronting the Turk in the Mediterranean, an initiative rewarded with the crushing naval victory at Lepanto in 1571, the greatest Christian victory of the sixteenth century. Thus encouraged, in the second half of his reign Philip turned his attention to the problems of heresy in northern Europe. The wealth of the New World was poured out in successive campaigns to turn back the rebels in the Netherlands, to shore up the Catholic League in France and finally, in the Armada campaign of 1588, to strike down Elizabeth of England, now in Philip's mind identified as the principal support of continental heresy.

The failure of the Armada campaign was a setback from which Philip's grand strategic plan never recovered; but there is little doubt that for all his eventual disappointment his application of military force had put a crucial brake on the growth of Protestantism. The leadership of the Catholic princes, not just Philip but his Habsburg cousins in Germany, and lesser lights such as Maximilian of Bavaria, had provided Catholicism with a vital breathing-space.

In the next generation reforming churchmen and their allies in the religious orders could begin the serious work of rebuilding the faith in areas of Europe where the prospects of survival had at one point seemed extremely bleak. Even by the turn of the century the fruits of these efforts could be discerned. In Poland, where the monarchy had since the accession of King Stefan Batory (1576) become a staunch supporter of the Counter-Reformation, the Catholic recovery was remarkable after a generation in which Protestantism of all hues had made deep inroads. Most significant of all was the Catholic recovery in France. So secure was the Catholic ascendancy by the last decade of the century that the Huguenot Henry of Navarre saw no way to secure his inheritance other than to announce his conversion to Catholicism. For the religious conflict in Europe it was a signal and telling moment.

The seventeenth century and the resolution of the Reformation conflict

There is little doubt that Henry IV of France did more than any one else both to bring an end to religious conflict and to promote the revival of Catholicism within his realm. Despite the scepticism of his former enemies, Henry clearly took his obligations to his new Catholic faith seriously, and he swiftly emerged as a highly effective exponent of Catholic revival. Following his reconciliation to Rome in 1594 and the end of the religious wars four years later, Henry took a number of measures to rebuild the faith, even going so far as to readmit to France his old adversaries the Jesuits, in 1603. But in 1610 he was struck down by a Catholic assassin; a salutary warning that the wounds caused by two generations of religious conflict could not easily be healed.

The attack that cost Henry IV his life was the twenty-fifth assassination attempt of his twenty-year reign. Nothing illustrates more effectively the extent to which normal political loyalties had been confused by the poisonous confessional politics of the later sixteenth century. It would be many decades before such tensions were wholly dissipated, and genuine toleration between rival confessions was still centuries away: in this era those who advocated religious toleration as a point of principle, such as the Dutch humanist Dirck Coorheert, were very much the exception. But as the century wore on Catholics and Protestants in Europe were at least able to advance to a sort of grudging coexistence. The pace of change varied according to internal political circumstances, but by the century's end a genuine change had been accomplished. Relations between states were now dominated almost wholly by strategic considerations, and hardly at all by the religious solidarity that underpinned the great confessional alliances of the age of Religious Wars. And while bigotry and religious hatred remained widespread, by the end of the seventeenth century the execution of an individual for dissident religious beliefs had become sufficiently rare to be a notorious and somewhat shocking event. The fires of official justice and popular prejudice burned to consume witches, rather than heretics.

In this, as in so much else in the seventeenth century, the new Dutch Republic led the way. By the end of the sixteenth century the division of the Netherlands into a free Protestant north and a group of southern provinces which remained under Spanish rule was effectively acknowledged on both sides. It would not be until 1648 that Spain formally conceded the Dutch their freedom, but long before this the conflict had lost its ideological edge, pursued on both sides more for commercial than for religious reasons. Most of all, the continuing commercial embargo between the two parts of the Netherlands allowed the Catholic south to recover some of the economic ground lost to the north and establish its own identity as a separate Catholic state. In this it was greatly assisted by a great flowering of Catholic devotional art, defiantly different from the austere traditions of the Calvinist Dutch Republic. The brilliant altarpieces commissioned from Rubens, Van Dyck and Jacob Jordaens epitomized a new religious culture which celebrated the restored self-confidence of Catholic society. This new-found confidence was a notable feature of Catholic art in several parts of Europe. Both religious painting and the decorative arts enjoyed an enormous popularity during this period, under the energetic patronage of both Catholic princes and the leaders of the Church, as each sought to outdo the other in an ostentatious piety designed for the glorification of God. It also permitted the Church to erase the memory of the damage done to the fabric of religious life by the Protestant assault on the outward appearance of Catholic worship.

In the Dutch Republic itself the large and mainly quiescent Catholic minority achieved a high level of *de facto* toleration. Dutch Calvinists seemed to reserve their most bitter hatreds for each other, to judge by the prolonged and brutal conflict between orthodox Calvinists and the followers of the Amsterdam professor, Jacobus Arminius, whose unorthodox teaching on Predestination brought the young nation to the brink of civil war in the second decade of the seventeenth century. The reverberations of this conflict were also felt in England where the new century had brought a new dynasty impatient with Puritanism and keen to assert its own royal prerogatives over both Church and state. The tensions remained under control during the reign of James I (1603–25); but the evident admiration of his son Charles I for continental and largely Catholic theories of kingship could not but worsen relations with those parts of the political nation determined to defend both the prerogatives of Parliament and the Protestant settlement. The part that religious tensions may have played in bringing about the eventual conflict between king and Parliament is complex; but it is without doubt that the sense that Charles and his Catholic wife Henrietta Maria posed a dire threat to England's Protestant heritage was the crucial factor which drove many into the parliamentary camp. The man who emerged as Charles's most formidable opponent, Oliver Cromwell, was a dour and committed Calvinist, dangerously convinced of his own vocation to abolish tyranny. The convictions which led Cromwell to establish a government every bit as autocratic as the monarchy he had destroyed brought its own backlash, and the repudiation of Cromwell's joyless Republic. But if Cromwell's regime did not long survive his death, the tumultuous events of this period had confirmed that Protestantism was at least as valued a part of English life as its parliamentary heritage. Kings would meddle with either at their peril, as James II would discover when his short-lived attempt to promote toleration of his own Catholic beliefs brought only his deposition (1688).

Events in England epitomized one of the leading characteristics of the seventeenth century, that although religious persecution was largely a thing of the past, religious convictions were still sufficiently deeply felt to play a vital part in political decision-making. Kings and rulers would meddle with the established confessional identity of their lands at their peril. Nowhere was this more evident than in the German Empire, still the fulcrum of religious conflict a century after Luther first ignited the Reformation conflict. For all the comparative calm of relations between the confessions in the decades after the Peace of Augsburg, tension simmered below the surface. Reviving Catholic fortunes, together with a complicated succession crisis within the ruling Habsburg dynasty, finally brought an end to the uneasy peace, sparking the great pan-European struggle known as the Thirty Years War. Incubated in a steady worsening of relations between the religious confessions in the empire in the first decades of the new century, the conflict sprang into life in 1618 as the thoroughly Protestantized Bohemian Estates sought to avoid the succession of the new Habsburg emperor, Ferdinand, for whom Bohemia formed a part of his hereditary lands. In his place they elected Frederick, Elector Palatine, leading representative of German Calvinism. This confusion of the religious politics of the eastern and western empire inevitably led to decisive action on the part of the Habsburgs to enforce their rights. A swift military campaign put an end to the revolt; Frederick was deposed and stripped for good measure of his electoral title. The punishment of the rebel Bohemian nobility was the deprivation of their lands and their replacement with more amenable Catholic clients.

The intervention of new protagonists, notably Lutheran Sweden, prevented the Habsburgs from forcing home their advantage as the war spread into new areas of the empire. As the years went by the conflict inevitably lost some of its original clarity of purpose, particularly after the intervention of Catholic France on the Protestant side in a traditional anti-Habsburg role. But the eventual peace settlement, the Peace of Westphalia, in 1648, did provide a significant resolution of outstanding religious differences. Uniquely, in these negotiations Catholic and Protestant delegates met in different locations (Münster and Osnabrück); the Thirty Years War would also be the last occasion on which a general European war would be fought with religion as one of the primary motivating forces. Hereafter the rival confessions, now both settled in their own separate identities, would continue to evolve, often in parallel, but manifestly apart.

For all that, the Thirty Years War undoubtedly offered confirmation that Catholicism was once again the more vibrant force in Western Christianity. The Habsburg victory in the first phase of the conflict had permitted the reclamation for the faith of both Bohemia and Hungary – lands where Protestantism had previously enjoyed an unchallenged dominance. In the seventeenth century Poland also witnessed a steady erosion of the previously healthy Protestant Churches; it was in this century that the Polish people first established the identification between Catholicism and their sense of Polish nationhood which was to prove so remarkably enduring. Only the intervention on the anti-Habsburg side of another major power, France, had prevented a total Habsburg triumph; a sure sign that international relations were finally becoming decoupled from confessional considerations.

The decision to revert to France's traditional anti-Habsburg foreign policy was sufficiently momentous to cause much controversy within French governing circles. It was the triumph of the new Bourbon dynasty, and of their ministers, Cardinals Richelieu and Mazarin, that they could combine such alliances with Protestants and the Turk abroad with steadfast support for the Catholic Church within France. Not all French Catholics could comprehend such a policy any more than could the Pope, but for Louis XIV, the great 'Sun King', these were the twin pillars of France's new dominance of European politics. For 50 years Louis pursued a policy of unremitting hostility to the Habsburg monarchies, combined with a steadily mounting pressure on his own Protestant subjects. This reached its climax in 1685 with the ceremonial Revocation of the Edict of Nantes, the settlement which by guaranteeing Protestant freedom of worship had ended the French Wars of Religion. Those who would not convert were given three months to leave the kingdom, and over a hundred thousand of Louis's subjects chose to do so.

Louis XIV intended the Revocation of the Edict of Nantes as a triumphant reassertion of France's Catholic identity. But the expulsion of a community universally recognized as hardworking and peaceable was by this point something of an anachronism, a throwback to a more turbulent age. Other towns and nations in Europe were only too happy to welcome the Huguenots, and the loss to the French economy confirmed Louis's decision as a rash and in many respects counter-productive gesture. By the eighteenth century those Protestants who remained in France had achieved the same grudging toleration that was the lot of religious minorities everywhere. As the years went by, even those on the margins of Christian society, traditionally persecuted by all of the main Churches, were largely free from active persecution. To the extent that Christians had finally abandoned the attempt to convert their neighbours by coercion the era of the Reformation conflicts was finally at an end.

Notes

1 Bernd Moeller, 'Religious life in Germany on the eve of the Reformation' in Gerald Strauss (ed.), *Pre-Reformation Germany* (London, 1972), p. 16.

2 H. R. Schmidt, *Reichstädte, Reich und Reformation* (Stuttgart, 1986).

3 'The Twelve Articles of the German Peasantry', art. 3. Text in Peter Blickle, *The Revolution of 1525* (Baltimore, 1981), pp. 195–201.

4 On Eastern Europe see now the essays collected in Karin Maag (ed.), *The Reformation in Eastern and Central Europe* (St Andrews Studies in Reformation History, 1997); Winfried Eberhard, 'Reformation and Counterreformation in East Central Europe' in Thomas Brady, Heiko Oberman and James Tracy (eds), *Handbook of European History, 1400–1600: Late Middle Ages, Renaissance and Reformation* (2 vols; Leiden, 1995), vol. II, pp. 551–84.

5 *The Letters of Sir John Hackett, 1526–1534*, ed. E. F. Rogers (Morgantown, VA, 1977), p. 81.

6 S. J. Schroeder (ed.), *The Canons and Decrees of the Council of Trent* (Rockford, IL, 1978), p. 43.

7 John Calvin, *Institutes of the Christian Religion*, Book 1, ch. 16, pt 3.

8 Letter to Sturm, December 1560; cited in Alastair Duke, Gillian Lewis and Andrew Pettegree (eds), *Calvinism in Europe, 1540–1610: A Collection of Documents* (Manchester, 1992), p. 80.

9 A. Th. van Deursen, *Bavianen & Slijkgeuzen* (Assen, 1974); idem, *Plain Lives in a Golden Age* (Cambridge, 1991), pp. 260–79.

10 David Gentilcore, *From Bishop to Witch: The System of the Sacred in Early Modern Terra d'Otranto* (Manchester, 1992); William A. Christian, *Local Religion in Sixteenth-Century Spain* (Princeton, 1981).

11 Peter Burke, 'How to be a Counter-Reformation saint' in Kaspar von Greyerz (ed.), *Religion and Society in Early Modern Europe, 1500–1800* (London, 1984), pp. 45–55; and R. Po-Chia Hsia, *The World of Catholic Renewal, 1540–1770* (Cambridge, 1997), ch. 8.

12 John Lynch, *Spain Under the Habsburgs*, vol. I: *Empire and Absolutism, 1516–1598* (2nd edn; Oxford, 1981), p. 273.

8

Eastern Europe since the
fifteenth century

Philip Walters

Europe East and West

There is a religious 'fault-line' in Europe separating East from West.[1] Starting in the north as the eastern border of Finland and then of the Baltic states, it proceeds south through Belarus' and Ukraine, separates Transylvania from the rest of Romania, and Croatia from Serbia, and ends up meandering through Bosnia and Albania to finish on the Adriatic coast. In this chapter we shall be looking at the religious history of the countries to the east of this fault-line, that is to say the countries in which the predominant faith is Eastern Orthodox.

Whereas Catholicism and Protestantism focus on doctrine and teaching, the Orthodox tradition lays emphasis primarily on worship as the most important area of religious experience. Eastern and Western Christianity are different species, and at the best of times this has led to fruitful cross-fertilization; but more often it has meant that the Eastern and Western Christian alternatives have become symbols in a Europe divided along political, economic and social lines. The history of this division, as reflected in the history of Christianity, is one of the themes of this chapter.

The emphasis on worship in the Orthodox Churches has been reinforced by historical circumstances. Even under conditions of the harshest oppression or privation, whether at the hands of Ottomans or Communists, Orthodox priests have continued to serve the liturgy, bringing something of Heaven to earth for the humblest believer and binding together the body of the faithful even when no other religious activities have been permitted (education, social service) and all other signs of a common political or social identity have been obliterated.

Orthodoxy at its best allows considerable freedom to mystics, philosophers and writers to develop spiritual understandings of political and social reality and to translate these into transforming activity: one such period of Christian creativity was the second half of the nineteenth century and the first two decades of the twentieth century in Russia. At the same time, however, the Orthodox Churches as institutions have traditionally co-operated with the secular power, which in most of the countries and periods covered by this chapter has been authoritarian or totalitarian. Most of the Orthodox Churches are autocephalous, running their own affairs within, and identified with, one particular nation-state. The dual loyalty involved here – towards the nation, on the one hand, and towards the secular power, on the other – leads all too often to ambiguities, particularly over how far the Church can identify itself with aspirations towards political freedom on the part of a particular national group. These ambiguous relationships are a second theme of this chapter.

One important fact to establish is that the Orthodox world is not coextensive with the Slav world. One of the richest Orthodox traditions is that of the non-Slav Romanians. Important Slav states have been central participants in the Christian history of Western Europe. Poland has for centuries defined itself by reference to the Catholic faith, and Catholicism kept Polish national identity alive during the long periods when the country as a political entity disappeared from the map. Catholicism provided the moral and intellectual framework for popular resistance to the Communist system in Poland, and in 1978 the Polish Cardinal Karol Wojtyła became the first non-Italian Pope since 1523. The western parts of Ukraine and Belarus' were for centuries in the Polish sphere of influence. Further south, the Habsburg Empire was host to substantial Slav populations. In the Czech lands Catholicism was challenged by Hussitism, one of the earliest European Protestant movements, and the experience of harsh Catholic reaction at the time of the Counter-Reformation was one factor in the gradual secularization of the Czech lands. By contrast Slovakia, under Hungarian rather than Austrian control, remained as staunchly Catholic as Poland. Until the formation of Yugoslavia after the First World War Catholic Croatia and Slovenia were part of the Habsburg Empire. The only substantial difference between Croats and Serbs is their traditional religion.

The territories lying along the fault-line, where East meets West, exhibit distinctive religious characteristics. At the southern end of the fault-line, in Bosnia and Albania, centuries of religious mixing have meant that no one faith has become identified with the nation. Further north, particularly in areas where the reinvigorated Catholicism of the Counter-Reformation was active from the mid-sixteenth century, the phenomenon of Eastern-rite Catholicism is common.[2]

Eastern-rite Catholics (often called 'Greek Catholics' or 'Uniates') are Eastern Orthodox in their liturgy, spirituality, discipline and theology but are in communion with the Roman Catholic Church. The Union of Brest of 1596 brought into union with Rome the majority of the

Orthodox in the Belorussian and western Ukrainian territories inside the powerful Polish–Lithuanian Commonwealth. Between 1697 and 1700 the Romanian Orthodox hierarchy in Transylvania joined Rome and created a Romanian Uniate Church. The initial impulse in all these places was political pressure from the local dominant non-Orthodox power; but over the centuries these Eastern-rite Catholic Churches have acquired a distinctive character and a genuine identity. Unfortunately they have also remained the unwitting (usually involuntary) cause of periodic inter-denominational strife, most recently and most acutely in the Soviet Union from the later 1980s, and now in post-Communist Ukraine and Romania.

1453–1700

Christianity under Ottoman rule

The city of Constantinople fell to Turkish conquest on 29 May 1453, an event which effectively ended a Byzantine Greek Christian Empire which had lasted for eleven hundred years. The Ottoman Empire was founded at the beginning of the fourteenth century. By about 1475 it had expanded to include the remains of the Byzantine Empire and most of the Balkans except for Dalmatia and a tiny enclave in Montenegro. In the next 50 years Ottoman armies crossed the Danube into Hungary and Romania and laid siege to Vienna in 1529. The peace treaty of 1533 marked the beginning of a long period of mainly static confrontation between the Ottoman and Habsburg empires; during the rest of the century each side built up a military frontier zone, guarded by a chain of fortresses and an armed peasant population. From the mid-seventeenth century the Ottomans were on the offensive again, and besieged Vienna for the second time in 1683. Over the next two decades, however, they were driven back out of the Hungarian territories (though retaining control over the Romanian lands of Moldavia and Wallachia) and confined to the area south of the Danube–Sava–Una line, where the frontier remained for almost two centuries.

This long history of confrontation had some important repercussions in the religious history of Western Europe. It enabled the Protestant princes of Germany to consolidate their political power after the Reformation at a time when their potential Roman Catholic opponents were preoccupied with developments in the East. It also helps to explain the tenacity of Reformed Protestantism in Hungary and Transylvania, in contrast with its eclipse further north after the Counter-Reformation. Catholic reaction was delayed in the south almost until the eighteenth century because, while the possibility existed that the Ottomans would make political use of Protestantism as an anti-papal and anti-imperial force, the Habsburg rulers were wary of persecuting their Protestant subjects in these regions and so destroying their loyalty.[3]

Within the Ottoman Empire itself the lives of the Christian communities were radically affected, mainly by two features of the Ottoman system of government, *devşirme* and the *millet* system.

Devşirme was the compulsory regular enrolment of Christian boys into the military and administrative service of the empire. They were required to become Muslims and learn Turkish, and were not allowed to marry. Some became elite troops known as janissaries. While widely resented, the practice was a unique way for children of poor families to reach some of the highest offices of state. They provided the sultan with several grand viziers (chief ministers), including Mehmed Sokolović, the Bosnian who held the post in the sixteenth century. He is held in esteem in his native Bosnia and in Serbia for persuading the sultan to allow the revival of the Serbian Orthodox see of Peć.

The *millet* system affected all Christians and Jews in the Ottoman Empire, who were recognized by the Muslim authorities as fellow 'people of the Book', and were therefore not to be forcibly converted or persecuted for their faith. Each religious community or *millet* was placed under the supervision of its own leaders, who were responsible for civil justice, education, collecting taxes and maintaining order amongst their people. The administrative power of the Orthodox ecclesiastical authorities under Ottoman rule was in fact greater than in the Byzantine Empire. Christians were divided not according to nationality but according to confession. Thus all the Orthodox, whether Greeks, Bulgars, Serbs, Arabs or Albanians, were grouped together as the *millet-i-Rum*. At local level they were under the authority of their own bishops; but at the top level they were all under that of the Ecumenical Patriarch in Constantinople.

The Ottomans depended on their non-Muslim subjects to conduct the trade of the empire and to provide most of its professional specialists. In return, though officially second-class citizens, they were free to practise their religion. Until the Ottoman Empire began to decline in the late eighteenth century, Christians in the Balkans were probably treated no worse than were the peasants of central Europe by their Christian feudal overlords. The impression of conditions in the empire as one continuous 'long Turkish night' arises from the intolerant policies of the last few sultans during the late nineteenth century;[4] but the Ottoman Empire in its heyday has been described as a 'classic example of the plural society'[5] which allowed diverse groups of people to live together with a reasonable amount of social peace and order. It would even be argued that the Ottomans inherited from Byzantium its role as protector of Orthodoxy.

One phenomenon increasingly resented by all the Slav peoples in the Ottoman Empire was indeed a consequence not of Ottoman oppression but of the fact that it was the Greeks who had ultimate authority over the Orthodox *millet*. This was the increasing Hellenization of the Slav Churches and cultures. The struggle between Greek and native Slav influences within the Byzantine Church goes back to the time of Cyril and Methodius, and it continued into the nineteenth century in both the Serbian and Bulgarian Churches. The Phanariots, so called after the Greek Phanar quarter in Constantinople where they originated, engaged in trade and were relatively rich. They were therefore able to buy all the lucrative ecclesiastical and civil appointments open to Christians in the Ottoman Empire, using 'their ostensible ecumenism as a cover for promoting ecclesiastical Hellenism'.[6]

The Christians were allowed to exist in peace, then; but limitations were placed on their activities. Church building and monasticism were restricted. Theology lost originality and vigour, charitable and educational work was reduced to a minimum, many parish clergy were illiterate and missionary activities ceased altogether. The practice of selling ecclesiastical offices spread down from the highest to the lowest levels as each officeholder recovered his expenses from those he appointed below him, and it was the ordinary peasant who bore the final financial burden.

By the time Constantinople fell to the Ottomans in 1453 the city's inhabitants had become resigned to their fate. There was widespread resentment of the Latins who had failed to come to the aid of the Byzantine Empire despite persistent embassies by successive emperors; but the Western price – papal supremacy – was in any case unacceptable to the majority of the Greek clergy and nobility. One grand duke allegedly said that it would be preferable to see the turban of the Turk in the city rather than the mitre of the Latin.

The Greeks in Constantinople and the inner Ottoman Empire were able to keep in contact with developments in the rest of Europe. During the Reformation and Counter-Reformation there was some contact between Protestants and Orthodox which had as its context their perceived common interest in defining a non-Catholic identity.[7] Moldavia and Wallachia under Phanariot rule were an important channel for influences from the West and a valuable school of politics for the Greeks, and Greek academies were set up there. More important was the emergence in the seventeenth and eighteenth centuries of a large class of Greek merchants both inside and outside the empire. They used their wealth to fund schools, libraries and scholarships in their home communities, to which they remained patriotically attached. Under Ottoman rule the ecumenical patriarchate in Constantinople and its school became the natural focus for Greek cultural life.

At the same time, however, the patriarchate became part of the institutionalized corruption of the Ottoman system. The office of Patriarch was soon obtainable only by means of a massive bribe to the grand vizier, and although Patriarchs theoretically enjoyed tenure for life the sultan replaced them at whim. In the seventeenth century the office changed hands some 60 times.

The *millet* system meant that no local Church in the Ottoman Empire kept its autonomy. Nevertheless, the Christian subjects of the empire were allowed to maintain their churches and monasteries, and their religious leaders had a defined role to play; and it was the Churches that did most to preserve the cultural heritage and separate identities of the various Balkan peoples.

Geographically closest to Constantinople, Bulgaria experienced more systematic intervention than other Balkan regions from Turkish officials, Phanariots and cosmopolitan administrators from all over the empire; and the Bulgarians were to be the last of the Balkan Orthodox nations to gain independence. Many churches, especially in towns, and all monasteries were closed, at least in the earlier Ottoman period. Monks, novices, scribes and scholars left the country, depriving Bulgaria of its educated classes. It was in the villages, where Greek influence over the Church was less strong than in the towns, that Bulgarian traditions were best preserved.

From the earliest days of the statehood of Serbia, no clear distinction had been made between the interests of the Church and those of the nation. A characteristic feature of Serbian Orthodoxy is *Svetosavlje*, veneration of St Sava, who is said to have founded the autonomous Serbian Church in the thirteenth century. *Svetosavlje* reflected the tribulations of the Serbs in later centuries in terms of suffering and martyrdom, at the same time apparently endowing them with a mystical purpose.[8] The Serbian Orthodox Church is of overwhelming importance as a rallying point for Serbs, both within and outside the Ottoman Empire – an importance reinforced by the fact that even under Ottoman rule the Serbian Church experienced two centuries of autonomy. In 1557 it was removed from Greek control thanks to the work of the Bosnian-born Grand Vizier Mehmed Sokolović. The area of the restored patriarchate of Peć was much greater than that of its medieval predecessor, and virtually all the Serbian nation came under its authority. It remained in existence until 1766 when it was once again placed under the Patriarch of Constantinople. Thereafter the task of preserving Serbian culture in Ottoman-controlled territories fell to the ordinary parish priests, many of whom were illiterate, and the Church was unable to overcome its institutional weakness until the beginning of the twentieth century. However, as the Ottomans extended their control over the Balkans many Serbs fled north into the military frontier zone between the Habsburg lands and the Ottoman Empire. Serbian churches and monasteries were established here, and these were later to fuel the Serbian national rebirth.

Serbian identity was also preserved in Montenegro (earlier known as Zeta), which thanks to its mountainous remoteness retained its independence throughout the Ottoman period. Here again the Church played a key role. After the expiry of the ruling dynasty in 1516 the bishops took over the secular leadership, electing one of their number as prince-bishop. These rulers maintained close contact with Russia and its Church during the Ottoman period.

Territory which in the 1990s was once again the subject of fierce dispute between Orthodox Serbs and Catholic Croats, Bosnia-Hercegovina reveals its identity as one of the 'fault-line' states of Europe. By the time the first native ruler established himself in Bosnia in the twelfth century the Christian population was already split into Orthodox and Catholic. In the period leading up to the Ottoman conquest, the ecclesiastical structure in Bosnia was weak and fractured, and no one national Church had predominance, as it did in Serbia and Bulgaria. Many parts of Bosnia, moreover, were only mildly touched by Christianity. (In both these respects, Bosnia resembled Albania.)

On the northern border of Ottoman territory, the lands of the Romanians saw yet another variation on the theme of evolution towards self-determination. The Romanian principalities of Moldavia and Wallachia had long been a target of political and cultural expansion on the part of surrounding empires. Romanian political leaders came to see themselves as defending the Christian faith against Islam and protecting the autonomy of their Church. A close interrelationship between national and religious values gradually developed. Although Romania has substantial Protestant, Roman Catholic and Eastern-rite Catholic minorities, Romanian nationality has become firmly identified with Romanian Orthodoxy. The course of Romanian history nevertheless clearly reflects the country's membership of two worlds: the Balkan world, with its Byzantine heritage and subsequent centuries of Ottoman control, and (through Transylvania) the world of Habsburg Central Europe.[9]

After they were conquered by the Ottomans the Romanian lands became a focus for Orthodox culture, conveying financial support to the Orthodox further inside the Ottoman Empire and supplying theological books in Greek, Arabic, Georgian and Slavic. It was natural that the Romanian Orthodox Church in Moldavia and Wallachia would also concern itself with the cultural and religious survival of the Romanians in Transylvania, who, although in the majority,[10] were not recognized as a nation by the Hungarian rulers. Predominantly peasants, they formed the lowest stratum of society. From the mid-sixteenth century the rulers of Transylvania tried to curb the activities of Orthodox clergy in favour of Calvinist superintendents and preachers. Towards the end of the century the Habsburgs began to reassert their authority over the indigenous

Hungarian princes in Transylvania, and their policy was to induce the Orthodox there to accept the Union with Rome. The Union was formalized in Transylvania in 1700, and thus the Uniate Church was created in territory which would eventually become part of Romania. Through their links with Rome the Uniates were to play a distinctive role in maintaining the (non-Slav) identity of Romanian culture.

The three Romanian provinces were in fact united, very briefly, in 1600. One impetus towards unification at the time had been the emergence of printed religious literature in Romanian, as opposed to Old Church Slavonic, in the sixteenth century. During the seventeenth century Slavs were gradually replaced by Greeks in key positions in the churches and monasteries of Moldavia and Wallachia, and Slavonic was eventually supplanted by the vernacular. The first complete Romanian Bible was published in 1688. By the middle of the seventeenth century the Romanian Church was strong enough to respond creatively to the challenges of the Renaissance and Reformation.

At the other end of their empire, in the Caucasus, the Ottomans took over the oldest Christian nation in the world, Armenia, which had officially adopted Christianity in 301. After the Council of Chalcedon in 451 the Armenian Church named itself 'Apostolic' and independent from the Universal Church, but for political rather than theological reasons: the Church was not so much championing Monophysitism as struggling against Byzantine hegemony. Since then, throughout its history, the Church has been the symbol and preserver of Armenian national identity, a particularly important function for a nation which has suffered centuries of war over its original homeland, culminating in genocide, and which today has a diaspora at least as large as the population of its home republic.

The seat of the Catholicos, the head of the Church, moved in response to successive invasions and foreign occupations of Armenia over the centuries, and two rival catholicosates eventually emerged, one at Echmiadzin in the Armenian homeland and one in Cilicia (the region of today's Lebanon). The Armenian homeland in the Caucasus was fought over continually. Leadership of the people fell to the clergy. Armenian culture was preserved in the diaspora in Western Europe. The first Armenian book was printed in Venice in 1512, the first Armenian Bible in Amsterdam in 1666. Under Ottoman rule, the Armenians were treated like all other Christian subjects of the empire, in accordance with the *millet* system. In 1461 an Armenian Patriarch in Constantinople was given authority over all the 'non-Orthodox' Christian peoples of the empire. The post had no connection with Armenian Church tradition and the incumbent was a political appointment.

Russia and its Church

In 1240 Mongol invaders from the East destroyed Kiev. Before the Mongol conquest Kievan Rus' had formed the north-eastern edge of Christendom; politically and socially part of Europe, it had been intimately involved in shaping Europe's early medieval Christian history. For the next hundred and fifty years, however, virtually all the Russian lands, divided into petty princedoms or 'appanages', were to be under Mongol control, and increasingly nominal Mongol rule persisted until the late fifteenth century. While Western Europe experienced the Renaissance and the Reformation, the Russian lands were isolated from the rest of Europe. They received a compulsory new identity as the western edge of an Asiatic empire and the Russian princes had to travel to central Asia to pay tribute to their rulers. At the end of this period, Russia re-emerged as an independent state under the leadership of Moscow, 650 kilometres north-north-east of Kiev.

At the crossing of major trade routes, Moscow began its rise to prominence in the second half of the thirteenth century. Ivan Kalita settled permanently in the city as Grand Prince of Moscow (1328–41). In 1326 the head of the Orthodox Church in Russia, Metropolitan Petr, happened to be staying in Moscow when he died. He was worshipped as a saint and canonized. Kalita persuaded Petr's successor, Feognost, to settle in Moscow. Moscow thus became the new ecclesiastical centre of Russia, and this fact played an important part in Moscow's eventual achievement of political supremacy over all the Russian principalities.

After the fall of Kiev the Orthodox Church survived as the best-organized institution in the Russian lands. The Mongols were not interested in converting their subject peoples, and the Church therefore enjoyed considerable freedom. Monasticism flourished.[11] Russian monasteries differed from their Western European counterparts, which were organized into different orders with different disciplines. All Russian monasteries followed a ritualized communal life, but had a looseness of structure which reflected their centrality to the life of the leading princely cities in which they were situated. Those who took vows there were typically members of local noble families who continued their previous political, economic and military activities. In the 1330s Metropolitan Aleksi began to build churches in the Moscow kremlin.

In a reaction to this rather worldly style of monasticism, a second type was championed particularly by St Sergi of Radonezh (1314–92), who set off into the forest to seek holiness through prayer and self-denial. Communities on his model sought to live by humility, kindness and brotherhood and to follow the Hesychast tradition, which taught that through physical discipline one could achieve inner peace without the sacraments and gain illumination through the uncreated Light of the Transfiguration. One of the greatest exponents of Hesychasm was Gregory Palamas (1296–1359); Hesychasm was confirmed by the Eastern Church in 1351.

Individual monks and monastic communities provided important momentum to the spread of Russian settlement from the steppes of the south-west to the forests of the north-east. St Sergi of Radonezh founded the Holy Trinity Monastery in what became Sergiyev Posad (Sergi's Settlement) near Moscow in 1337. In the following century Sergi's successors founded some 150 new monasteries in one of the most remarkable missionary movements in Christian history. By 1397, with the founding of the Monastery of St Cyril on the White Lake, monastic communities were 300 miles north of Moscow, and by 1436, they were another 300 miles north, with the founding of the Solovetsky Monastery on the White Sea, still the most northerly monastery in the world.

At about the time that the Solovetsky Monastery was being consecrated, the Byzantine Emperor John VIII was travelling to the Council of Florence (1437–39). His empire stood in serious need of help from Western Christendom in order to defend itself against the encroaching Ottoman Turks. The standing price for possible help from the West was acceptance by the Greek Orthodox Church of papal supremacy and union with Rome. At Florence the emperor agreed to these terms. Isidor, Metropolitan of Moscow, who attended the council and who spoke for reunion with Rome, was a Greek, as were many of the leading clergy in Russia at that time. He returned to Moscow but was subsequently compelled to flee. In 1443 a Council of Bishops in Moscow condemned the Union. Despite the Byzantine emperor's ecclesiastical capitulation no substantial Western help was forthcoming. In 1453 Constantinople fell to the Turks.

In 1472 the Muscovite Grand Prince Ivan III (1462–1505) married Zoe Palaiologina, the niece of the last Byzantine emperor; he proceeded to use the title tsar (emperor) and adopted the Byzantine two-headed eagle. In his reign Moscow achieved the 'gathering of the Russian lands' under its control and brought the appanage period to an end. The capture of Constantinople in 1453, it was argued in Moscow, showed God's displeasure with the Greeks, particularly for their submission to Rome. Some held that the fall of the imperial city was a sign of the imminent end of the world, widely expected for 1492, 7,000 years after the Creation. When 1492 came and went (incidentally seeing instead the arrival of Columbus in America), the belief was promoted in Moscow that God would now need to choose another nation to further his purposes and that Moscow and its ruler were the natural heirs to the Byzantine legacy.

The doctrine of 'Moscow the Third Rome' was expounded in a letter written in 1510 by the abbot Filofei to Vassili III (1505–33). The Church in Rome, argued Filofei, fell to heresy, and the Church in Constantinople to the infidel. The Church in Muscovy, however, would like the sun illumine the entire world, and moreover would last for ever: two Romes had fallen, and the third was now in existence; a fourth Rome there would never be. The theory of the Third Rome clearly derived from the Byzantine claim to universalism; but its messianist and even nationalist overtones had less to do with Byzantinism than with a general early sixteenth-century tendency for secular European rulers to strive to create strong centralized monarchies, with the help of, rather than in the service of, the Church.[12]

At this stage in Muscovy, however, it was not only the secular rulers who were working for the integration of Church and state: many leading churchmen were strong advocates of it too. One such was Iosif of Volokolamsk (1440–1515). His convictions placed him in opposition to holy men of the Hesychast tradition such as Nil Sorsky (1433–1508). Leaving the Monastery of St Cyril on the White Lake, Nil Sorsky became a holy wanderer (*skitalets*) and set up an isolated hermit community (*skit*) beyond the River Sora (hence his name). Others emulated him; the number of brothers in any one *skit* was limited, and they lived a life of apostolic poverty and Franciscan closeness to nature. He and his followers became known as the Trans-Volga Elders.

By the end of the appanage period the Church in Russia owned over a quarter of the cultivated land in the country. These large holdings were to create major problems for religious consciousness and the state. Iosif of Volokolamsk defended the wealth of the monasteries, not as the personal possession of the monks but as a sacred trust and a means whereby sanctity would radiate out into society. Those who supported this view became known as the Possessors. Those who disagreed, including the Trans-Volga Elders, became known as the Non-Possessors. The Possessors were supporters of a strong centralized monarchy. They believed that society should be constructed on monastic lines, with rules of behaviour to be observed by all citizens. They laid stress on the accurate celebration of church services. They combined a highly developed ritualism with elements of puritanism and were strongly influenced by the Old Testament. The Non-Possessors, by contrast, held that what was important was not ritual but the holiness and devotion of the human heart. They believed that Old Testament law had been superseded by the New Testament commandment of love in freedom. A Church council in 1503 decided in favour of the Possessors. They then became the dominant party in the Church, and by the mid-sixteenth century it was under their full control. The Non-Possessors retreated into their communities in the forests of the north and east, but by the middle of the sixteenth century they had been pursued and destroyed.

The reign of Ivan IV, the Terrible (1533–84), coincided with the period of the Henrician breach with Rome, the birth of the Church of England, the Marian Counter-Reformation and the development of Anglicanism in the first half of the reign of Elizabeth. There was no Reformation in Russia: on the contrary, Ivan identified himself totally with the programme of the Possessors and the Muscovy of the second half of the sixteenth century was compared by foreign visitors to one vast religious house in which Church canons were as binding on all citizens as the laws of the state. The 1556 book *Domostroi* (Household Management) by the monk Silvestr gave detailed instructions on how a Muscovite should run his life and household: the themes were ritualism, formalism, piety and patriarchalism. The so-called 'Council of the Hundred Chapters' in 1551 regularized Church–state relations. Neither Church nor state was to dominate the other, but each was supreme in its own sphere. The head of the Russian Orthodox Church received the title of Patriarch in 1589. Tsar and Patriarch were equal, the two heads of one Christian Kingdom.

The Council of 1551 was one of a series of councils (1549–51) which were concerned to establish that Russian traditions alone embodied the true tradition of the whole Church. At this period Russian suspicion of the Greeks, dating from the very birth of the Muscovite state, was expressed with particular vigour. Greek visitors were suspected of being tainted with Uniatism or Islam. Greek merchants were denied permission to enter Russian churches. Greek clerics coming to Russia would be put in quarantine for several weeks in a Russian monastery to test their Orthodoxy.

Orthodoxy as established in Muscovy in the Josephan tradition (so called after Iosif of Volokolamsk) thus declared itself to be in sole possession of the truth; at the same time it rid itself of the fertile spirituality of the Non-Possessor tradition and also cut itself off from the rest of Christendom – including the Orthodox who were not Russian. Symptomatic is perhaps the fate of one of the most interesting personalities of that period, St Maksim the Greek (1470?–1556). A native of Greece, he had gone to Italy in 1492 where he took part in the intellectual and artistic controversies of the Renaissance. His arrival in Moscow in 1516 might have offered Russian Orthodox circles an opportunity to engage with contemporary Western European spiritual issues. Instead Maksim was to spend 30 years in prison and confinement.

Church–state symbiosis of the Muscovite kind was to turn out to be a very mixed blessing for the Russian Orthodox Church. The Church's alliance with the state was conceived of in terms of a harmony of equal powers; in time, however, it was to be clear that the secular tsarist programme envisaged rather the subordination – or even, eventually, subjugation – of Church to state. As one scholar notes, 'the Byzantine Middle Ages were well over by the sixteenth century and the further development of the Russian Empire along the lines of a secularized modern state, which in the eighteenth century was destined completely to subject the Church to its will and confiscate its property, justified the misgivings of Nil [Sorsky] and his party a posteriori'.[13]

In the course of the seventeenth century 'High Muscovy' was destroyed and Russians were brought back into contact with the rest of Europe. This process, which was repeatedly traumatic, was catalysed by three periods of particular crisis: the Time of Troubles (1598–1613), the Great Schism (1653–67) and the reign of Peter the Great (1682–1725).

The Time of Troubles was a long period of political turmoil during which Muscovy was invaded by foreign armies in support of various pretenders to the throne. These foreigners were predominantly Poles, and Catholics. Having missed participation in the more creative periods of the Renaissance and Reformation, Muscovy was now suddenly embroiled in the destructive European religious conflicts which from the mid-sixteenth to the mid-seventeenth centuries accompanied the Counter-Reformation. Old suspicions of the Roman Catholics as secular and predatory were violently confirmed.

By the middle of the seventeenth century Russia was reasserting some political influence in Europe. In 1648 the Cossacks in Ukraine under Bogdan Khmel'nitsky rose against the Poles and in 1654 recognized the Russian tsar as their sovereign. In the fourteenth century Ukraine – the area from which Kievan Christianity originally spread to Russia – had come under the control of Lithuania. In 1386 Lithuania was dynastically united with Poland; one of the conditions was that the Lithuanian Grand Duke Jogaila should convert to Roman Catholicism and that this should become the official religion of the new state. Russian Orthodox living in Lithuania and Ukraine were not at first put under pressure to change their religion, but this changed after 1569 when Poland and Lithuania concluded a much closer union at Lublin. In the climate of the Counter-Reformation Catholicism was promoted with new energy. The first to be targeted were the Calvinists; then the Orthodox, particularly in Belorussia and Ukraine, who were induced to accept Union with Rome. The 'Union of Brest-Litovsk' of 1596 created the 'Uniate' Church in the Polish–Lithuanian Commonwealth. Those Orthodox who refused to accept the Union were outlawed and deprived of their bishops, priests and churches. During the Time of Troubles, as Polish armies penetrated as far as Moscow, their plight seemed hopeless. However, the Cossacks in eastern Ukraine took up their cause, and soon the Theological Academy in Kiev became the centre of resistance to Roman Catholicism. In 1620 the Cossacks succeeded in having new Orthodox bishops consecrated, and the Church of the Ukrainians in communion with Rome (or the Ukrainian Greek Catholic Church, as it came to be known) found itself between two hostile Churches, the Roman Catholic Church in Poland and the Orthodox Church in Kiev, neither of which regarded the Greek Catholics as a proper and established Church. That state of affairs has persisted to the present day.

The Kiev Theological Academy understood that it was no longer sufficient simply to train men for the priesthood; they had to be intellectually equipped to enter into debate with the Uniates. This task was addressed under the leadership of Peter Mogila (1596–1647), elected Metropolitan of Kiev in 1633. Educated at the Sorbonne, he realized that those who knew only Old Church Slavonic and Greek had no access to contemporary literature. He therefore made Latin the language of instruction at the academy and put Western texts on the curriculum. This exposure to Western Catholic culture produced more sophisticated clergy but it also inevitably led to some modification of traditional Orthodox practices and doctrines.

War between Russia and Poland lasted until 1667, and in the eventual compromise peace Ukraine was divided. The eastern part, including Kiev and its theological academy, came under Russian control. A body of scholars trained in sophisticated Western debate and familiar with Western textbooks was thus incorporated into the Russian Church, and Russian intellectual and spiritual isolation was further eroded.[14]

Re-exposure to the West in the first part of the seventeenth century was accompanied by a realization that Russia had responsibilities that went beyond its borders. Appeals were reaching the Moscow patriarchate from Orthodox Christians in Poland and Turkey describing persecution at the hands of Catholics and Muslims. Some in the Russian Church, with Patriarch Nikon (1652–58) at their head, believed that Russia would be unable to champion Orthodoxy in Europe at large if it continued to despise those who did not follow Muscovite traditions. He therefore proposed that Russian Orthodox doctrines and practices be critically compared with the Greek models from which they were derived, and adjusted if necessary. Nikon's activities were stoutly resisted by another group within the Church whose most prominent spokesman was the Archpriest Avvakum. In total contrast to Nikon, Avvakum wished to assert ever more strongly, in the face of increasingly intrusive Western heresy and cunning (*khitrost'*), the intrinsic correctness of the Russian way of worship. An ironical feature of the situation was that both men were interested in protecting and promoting Russian Orthodoxy by reforming it; and both were from within the Josephan tradition.

Nikon's proposed reform path was a theocratic one, including the novel proposal that the Patriarch rather than the tsar should exercise the leading authority in the state, an aim which did not accord with the balance of dual power implicit in the Byzantine–Muscovite tradition. Nikon had taken the title *'Veliki Gosudar"* ('Great Lord'), hitherto reserved for the tsar alone. This 'Russian Hildebrand' based his claim to temporal as well as spiritual power on the forged *Donation of Constantine*, the document used by the medieval papacy to pursue its own similar aspiration. Avvakum's solution, with its stress on adherence to correct rituals, was a fundamentalist one. Avvakum was in fact a kind of Protestant; unlike Western Protestants, however, he and his followers did not believe that truth was to be found in the words of Scripture – they exhibited suspicion of the Bible as the product of cunning Western Slavonic scribes – but in the correct forms of worship.

To us today the issues over which the followers of Nikon and Avvakum contended seem superficial: whether you should use two fingers or three when crossing yourself, or whether you should spell the name of Jesus 'Isus' or 'Iisus'. It may appear that the Old Believers, as the followers of Avvakum came to be known, went to their deaths resisting the altering of one iota, literally, of their faith. In fact, however, the Schism was fuelled by fundamental questions about Russia's relationship with the rest of Europe. Both Nikon and Avvakum were condemned at the Church Council of 1666–67. Nikon was condemned for his aspiration to establish the supremacy of the Patriarch over the tsar. The council refuted his proposals by referring to the sixth *Novella* of Justinian, which asserted the Byzantine ideology 'that the king or emperor has pre-eminence in political matters, and the patriarch in ecclesiastical'.[15] However, Avvakum was also condemned, and the bulk of Nikon's reforms accepted.

Like the Non-Possessors before them, the Old Believers were driven out to the north and east and into Siberia. In 1682 Avvakum was burnt alive, and thousands of Old Believers eventually chose to emulate him and die by self-immolation rather than compromise their principles. The Great Schism produced a still unhealed rift in the body of the Church.[16] It weakened it both spiritually and institutionally and left it helpless in the face of the aggressive policies of Peter the Great which involved the secular Westernization of society and the placing of the Church firmly under state control.

1700–1920

Peter the Great and the New Russia

Peter had presumably learned a salutary lesson from the experience of his father, Tsar Aleksei Romanov, at the hands of Nikon. As autocrat, he thoroughly subordinated Church to state so that this kind of interlude would not occur again. When Patriarch Adrian died in 1700 Peter allowed the post to remain vacant for 21 years, until with his *Dukhovny reglament* (Church Regulations) he abolished it altogether.

As part of his policy of Westernization, Peter put the leadership of the Russian Orthodox Church in the hands of clergy from Ukraine who were versed in Western traditions and influenced by developments in the Catholic and Protestant Churches. He brought in Feofan Prokopovich, a churchman from Kiev who had had some training in Lutheran traditions, to draw up the new *Dukhovny reglament*. The Patriarch was replaced as head of the Church by a new collegiate body, the Holy Synod, modelled on Protestant synodal bodies, under a chief procurator, who was a layman appointed by the tsar. Originally the function of the procurator was to communicate the tsar's wishes to the synod and to make sure the synod's decisions did not violate the laws of the land. By the end of the nineteenth century, however, he had become the *de facto* ruler of the Church.

Why did the Church remain passive while Peter introduced his reforms? The triumph of the Possessors had seen to it that Muscovite Orthodoxy would pivot on a close relationship with the tsar. The assumption was of course that the tsar would be a true believer; there was no strategy for coping with a secularist emperor. At the same time the Church, already weakened by the Great Schism, was suffering from continuing inner dissension. From the Ukrainian lands now newly brought within the empire came Orthodox bishops and clergy who had grown sophisticated in their exposure to Western ideas and in their dealings with Catholics and Protestants. The clergy of the Russian heartlands met them with suspicion and hostility.

The eighteenth century saw the Russian Orthodox Church compromised both institutionally and spiritually. The synod was subject to all the vicissitudes of court politics. Bishops, who were always monks, were controlled by the synod; they were regularly nominated without consideration for the interests of the Church and were moved from one diocese to another, promoted and demoted on political rather than spiritual grounds. Meanwhile the parish clergy, who were married men and in whose family the job of priest tended to become hereditary, remained completely dependent on the decisions of remote bishops, often unknown to them, who nevertheless appointed and dismissed them. Under the new legislation parishioners no longer had any say in appointing their own pastors. However, the upkeep of a parish priest and his assistants remained as in the old days a parish responsibility. This often led to friction and discontent and sowed the seeds of later widespread anticlericalism.

Catherine the Great (1762–96), a German who became empress through marriage, was baptized a Lutheran but later espoused the rationalism of Voltaire. She saw her role in Russia as that of enlightened and benevolent autocrat; for her the Orthodox Church was steeped in superstition, a vehicle for keeping a backward people in ignorance. The procurators she appointed reflected her views.

During this period of institutional eclipse, the Church nevertheless continued to nurture men of great spiritual stature, followers of the old monastic Hesychast tradition. St Tikhon Zadonsky (1724–83) lived as a simple monk at the service of all in need of help and advice and wrote books of devotion. He was venerated as a holy man and canonized in 1861. One of the most beloved saints of the Russians is St Serafim of Sarov (1759–1832), an ascetic who devoted himself to the service of others as a healer and seer. Paisi Velichkovsky (1722–94), from his monastery in Moldavia, translated into Russian the Greek classics on asceticism and contemplation and helped revive Orthodox monastic traditions which by the eighteenth century had fallen into decay in many parts of the Eastern world. His disciples brought his revived ascetic tradition to Russia and established monastic communities. The monastery of Optina Pustyn' near Tula was to become famous in the nineteenth century as a place where Westernized intellectuals in search of genuine Christian teaching and practice could meet monks maintaining the authentic patristic traditions of Eastern Orthodoxy.[17]

In the eighteenth century Russia intensified its contacts with the representative bodies of Orthodox populations in other parts of Europe, and eventually assumed the role of self-styled protector of Orthodoxy wherever it was threatened. The Russian Church was of course not only much larger numerically than all other Orthodox Churches put together, but also the recognized spiritual arm of a secular power at a time when all other Orthodox either lived under non-Orthodox administrations or were divided amongst small states. The Slav Orthodox clergy in the Ottoman Empire increasingly saw the Russian Church as a natural ally against the Phanariot Greek clergy imposed on them by the Ottoman authorities. Peter the Great first made contact with the Montenegrins. In 1727 the Russian Church sent a mission which spent ten years forging strong links with the Serbian Orthodox clergy and their flocks. As Russia began to play an increasingly important role in European affairs, the Balkan Slavs became accustomed to turning to Russia for diplomatic and military support, which was usually forthcoming.[18] By the time of the war between Russia and Turkey in the eighteenth century it was not only the Slavs who were looking for help to Russia, but the Greeks themselves. The Russians made direct attempts to incite the Greeks to rise against the Ottomans during the Russo-Turkish war of 1768–74. It was in the treaty concluding this war, the Russians were later to claim, that the Ottomans had conceded them a general right of protection over all the Orthodox Christians of the empire.

The reign of Catherine the Great saw further extension of the western boundary of the Russian Empire. The three partitions of Poland (1772, 1793 and 1795) brought with them large populations of Orthodox Ukrainians and Belorussians as well as territories inhabited by Roman Catholic Poles and Jews. The political, social and religious structure of the empire grew more complex.

For four decades after the partitions the Russian government suppressed the Greek Catholic dioceses in the newly acquired territories and in 1839 all Greek Catholics in the Russian Empire were aggregated to the Russian Orthodox Church. Ukrainian Greek Catholicism was kept alive outside the Russian Empire, in Galicia, which the partitions had given to Austria. For the next century and a half, under the imperial Russian and then Soviet governments, Greek Catholicism was both illegal and officially non-existent.

Russia experienced a period of national revival during the campaign against Napoleon (1812–14). Tsar Alexander I (1801–25) was attracted to German Pietism and mysticism and in the early part of his reign had liberalizing inclinations. He was open to non-Orthodox initiatives: in 1814 the Russian Bible Society was founded on a Protestant model. There were great hopes of political reform. However, before long Alexander drew back, disconcerted by the Europe-wide unleashing of forces apparently seeking to overthrow legitimate authority. When the Greeks revolted against Turkish rule in 1821 and the Ottoman authorities responded by executing the Ecumenical Patriarch, the Russians confined themselves to withdrawing their ambassador from Constantinople.

Under Alexander's successor Nicholas I (1825–55) the pendulum swung decisively back from enlightenment and reform to discipline and reaction. Nicholas I wanted to close Russia's windows on the West. The stream of Western ideas could not now be stopped, however; the flow was simply diverted into side channels. From now on philosophy, history and literature became the vehicles for Russian cultural development, replacing politics and religion, both of which were increasingly identified with the establishment status quo.

One of the few nineteenth-century Church leaders to adopt a critical stance was Filaret, Metropolitan of Moscow from 1821 to 1867. He was politically liberal, tolerant and opposed to confessional chauvinism. The main part of his ecclesiastical career coincided with the reactionary reign of Nicholas I, and this prevented him from making his full contribution to the Church. As Metropolitan of Moscow he had a permanent seat on the synod, though during the tenure of the procurator's office by General Protasov (1836–55) he was not invited to attend the synod sessions. Nevertheless, even during that period no major decision affecting the Church was taken without his views being sought. He was not afraid to dispute the validity of dubious doctrinal pronouncements made in the name of the Church by uncanonical bodies. He lived long enough to see the liberal reforms of Alexander II (1855–81) and himself drafted the 1861 manifesto liberating the serfs.

The mid-nineteenth century saw a remarkable expansion of missionary activity on the part of the Russian Orthodox Church. Missionaries went to Siberia, to Alaska (part of the Russian Empire until 1864), to the Muslim tribes in the Volga and Ural regions and even to Japan. Archbishop Innokenti Veniaminov, who for 44 years devoted himself to missionary work, succeeded Filaret as Metropolitan of Moscow. He founded the Orthodox Missionary Society, which continued its activities up to the Revolution of 1917. In 1899 the Russian Church had twenty missions inside the Empire and five foreign missions, in Alaska, Korea, China, Japan and Persia.[19]

During the nineteenth century the Russian Orthodox Church at once enjoyed extensive privileges and suffered from serious restrictions, both consequent on its legal status as the established religion of the empire. It was supported financially by the government and was defended by law against its religious rivals; it alone had the right to proselytize. The secular authorities welcomed the help of the Church in combating the influence of non-Orthodox denominations. The Church ran an effective system of parish primary schools throughout the empire. At the same time it was not allowed to acquire property freely and was encumbered with an inefficient bureaucracy. Parish priests – the 'white' or married clergy as opposed to the 'black' or monastic clergy from whose ranks the bishops were appointed – still suffered from lack of contact with their bishops, who were moved around too frequently to become effective leaders in their dioceses. Priests were also burdened with financial poverty and a large number of secular administrative duties. There was widespread anticlericalism in society, and particularly amongst the intelligentsia, where atheism or positivism had been characteristic for decades before being further encouraged by the Marxism which took hold in the later 1890s.

Under these circumstances, it is hardly surprising that by the end of the nineteenth century the Russian Orthodox Church had failed to develop any programme for Christian social or political engagement, or even the theoretical basis for such a programme: we may contrast the situation in the Roman Catholic Church, the papal encyclical *Rerum novarum* of 1891 providing the basis for further statements during the following century. Throughout the nineteenth century, however, a certain proportion of the Russian intelligentsia had remained committed to the development of social and political ideas derived from what they believed to be the true doctrines of Russian Orthodoxy. Central was the concept of *sobornost'*, which they understood to define 'community' as 'individual diversity in free unity' and to represent a Russian Orthodox alternative to inappropriate social models derived from Western Enlightenment individualism. These 'Slavophiles' (as opposed to the 'Westernizers') included the Kireyevsky brothers Ivan (1806–56) and Petr (1808–56), the Aksakov brothers Konstantin (1816–60) and Ivan (1823–86), and Aleksei Khomyakov (1804–60).[20]

When hopes for the introduction of liberal Western-inspired reforms in Russia began to fade after 1825, the imperial government adopted a programme which bore some external resemblance to the Slavophile programme but was designed to consolidate the autocracy. It was summarized in 1832 by Count Uvarov as 'Orthodoxy, autocracy and nationality' and guided the policies of the last two Russian tsars and of Konstantin Pobedonostsev, Procurator of the Holy Synod from 1880 to 1905 and a dedicated conservative.

The Caucasus between Russians and Ottomans

In the eleventh and twelfth centuries Georgia produced a distinct Christian culture and civilization, noted for its literature and architecture (churches and monasteries). The official date for the Christianization of Georgia is 330, and the Georgian Orthodox Church gained autocephaly in 1057, over 500 years before the Russian Orthodox Church. From the early twelfth century Armenians fleeing north from their occupied territories settled in Georgian towns, and for centuries Armenian merchants and Georgian nobles lived symbiotically. The medieval Georgian kingdom reached its apogee under Queen Tamar (1184–1212). After the Mongol invasion in 1236, however, Georgia fragmented once again into independent principalities.

It was not until the eighteenth century that growing commercial, political and intellectual ties with Russia led to a period of national revival, accompanied by intensified publication and educational activity which was predominantly religious in nature.[21] From 1780 Catherine the Great decided to risk antagonizing the Turks and began taking control of the various warring Georgian kingdoms. The Georgian social structure remained intact: the king; the nobles with their landholdings and peasantry; the merchants with their prerogatives in the towns; the Church with its monopoly on education. The Church retained its autocephaly, and its head gained a seat on the Holy Synod of the Russian Orthodox Church.

In both Georgia and Armenia general education was in the hands of the clergy. In Georgia the village priest would often be the only local educated person and frequently the teacher of the young nobles. Church services were a central part of village life and the church was where people gathered socially. Russian response to revolts in Georgia in the early nineteenth century included removing the autocephaly of the Georgian Church in 1811, appointing a Russian archbishop as exarch and putting plans in place to replace Georgian with Slavonic rites. These moves stoked further resentment.

In the half-century before the Crimean war, Georgian society underwent fundamental changes. The rebellious semi-independent dynasts were transformed into a service gentry loyal to their new monarch, the Russian tsar. In the process they were introduced to Western education, and this eventually brought with it revolutionary ideas. In the later nineteenth century, after the death of Tsar Alexander II, growing Russian chauvinism clashed with the developing Georgian national consciousness. In 1886 a student at Tiflis seminary fatally stabbed the Russian rector. The seminary had long been a centre of student political activity. Russian reprisals for the murder led to protests of a political nature: thus the Church and its educational institutions were the crucible for nationalist revolutionary protest.

South of Georgia, the historical Armenian homeland had long been under Ottoman control. The Armenians within the Russian Empire, however, became the dominant commercial class in the region in the decades after the Crimean war, and following old traditions gave money to the Church for educational purposes. In 1836 the Russians had given the Armenian Church a large measure of internal autonomy as well as responsibility for education, and this was to work to the benefit of the whole Armenian people. In Constantinople, Patriarch Khrimian Hairik (1869–76), although a political appointment by the Ottoman authorities, did a great deal to awaken the consciousness of Armenians living in various communities throughout the Ottoman Empire, criticizing the Ottoman government and calling openly for a war of liberation in western Armenia. From the later nineteenth century Armenian businessmen in Russia also showed an increasing concern for their brethren in the Armenian homeland and elsewhere in the Ottoman Empire.

This kind of concern soon translated itself into calls for Armenian emancipation within the Russian Empire too, catalysed by developments in education. When the Russian authorities entrusted Armenian education to the Church they believed they were putting it into the ineffectual hands of ignorant clerics. However, the Armenian Church again demonstrated its role as a point of focus for the entire nation. Teachers in the parish schools included men of a modern outlook who, while paying great attention to Armenian history and culture, had been educated in Russia or Europe and taught their disciplines in a critical and scientific manner.

The church schools thus became centres of opposition to Great-Russian assimilation.

After the death of Tsar Alexander II reaction set in and heavy-handed attempts to Russify and then close down Armenian schools led to widespread resentment. Crisis came in 1903 when the Russian government attempted to take over the property of the Armenian Church, provoking a campaign by the Armenian Revolutionary Federation (*Dashnaktsutyun*), whose cause now began to receive support from the clergy and the bourgeoisie. The Russian government thus gradually destroyed the goodwill of the Armenians by clumsily interfering with their religious and national identity.

Within the Ottoman Empire persecution of the Armenians grew steadily more serious from the mid-1890s, killings and massacres culminating in 1915. By the end of the First World War the Armenians on Turkish territory, except for those in Constantinople, had been completely exterminated.

Balkan Christians in a declining Ottoman Empire

The first Balkan people to gain their independence from the Ottomans were the Greeks. The intellectual preparation for the revolt of 1821 came through a small predominantly Western-educated intelligentsia, many if not most of whom lived outside the Ottoman Empire. Throughout the Ottoman period books in Greek had been printed in substantial and steadily increasing quantities, mainly in Venice. At the beginning of the eighteenth century these books were overwhelmingly religious in character. During the 50 years or so before 1821, however, they became increasingly secular, reflecting a revived and intense interest in Greece's classical past supplemented with revolutionary ideas in the wake of the French Revolution.

Inside the empire there had been occasional uprisings amongst the Greek population from the earliest years of Ottoman rule, but it was never clear how the nationalists' aims were going to be realized, given the vested interests of those with a stake in the status quo – the clergy, the Phanariots, the merchants – and the ignorance and passivity of the great mass of the Greeks in the homelands, who were mostly illiterate and under the supervision of a Church which ever more actively opposed modern secularized thinking. The patriarchate in Constantinople published books (under strict censorship by the Ottoman authorities) designed to counter the flood of atheistic and seditious literature from abroad. At the time of Napoleon's invasion of Egypt – part of the Ottoman Empire – in 1798 a book by the Patriarch of Jerusalem published in Constantinople argued that the Ottoman Empire was created by divine will specifically to protect Orthodoxy from contamination by Latin heresy, and that Orthodox citizens should remain loyal to their Ottoman masters. This kind of view was anathema to the new generation of Greek nationalists.

In 1821, as soon as news of the Greek uprising reached Constantinople, Ecumenical Patriarch Grigorios V was killed by the Turkish authorities along with some 30,000 Greeks. Nevertheless international circumstances soon forced the sultan to grant Greek independence. The first king of the new country, chosen by the great powers, was Otto of Bavaria (1833–62). His largely German ministers set about giving Greece the structures of a new state in a conservative European mould. In order to achieve secular control of the Church they set up a synod on the Russian pattern as a department of state. In 1833, with state encouragement, the Greek bishops proclaimed their Church autocephalous (with the Catholic Otto as its head). Deadlock with the ecumenical patriarchate ensued. Meanwhile the Greek government was growing suspicious of a Church that voiced popular anti-foreign sentiments. The number of bishops was reduced from 33 to ten, corresponding to the new political divisions of the country, and the majority of the monasteries were suppressed and their properties forfeited to the Crown.

At first many of the state's policies were unwelcome to the Church, but it developed a robust attitude, prepared to discuss perceived encroachments on its domain and to protest when necessary; mutually acceptable compromise was usually reached. Conditions for the Church improved in the second half of the nineteenth century. The Ecumenical Patriarch recognized the Greek Church's autocephaly in 1850. The number of dioceses was increased to 24, and efforts were made to raise the standard of Christian knowledge and education. As time went on, the Church hierarchy identified more and more with the state's domestic and foreign policies. Meanwhile, although the 'Bavarian Monarchy' was by and large indifferent to the cultural sensibility of its Greek subjects, it operated astutely and set in place a system of Church–state relations which basically survives to this day.

There was one particular area where Church and state were in sympathy from the outset: the 'Great Idea' (*Megali Idea*) of bringing all the 'unredeemed' Greeks of the Ottoman Empire within a single Greek state. From the 1870s Greek irredentist ambitions in Macedonia were to bring Greece into conflict not only with the Ottoman authorities but with the rival nationalist programmes of the Bulgarians and Serbs. In the course of the nineteenth century the Greek government also made strenuous efforts to re-Hellenize the Turkish-speaking Greeks of Anatolia. During the Ottoman period there had been widespread conversion to Islam, particularly in Albania, Bosnia and Bulgaria;[22] and also in Crete, where there was a large population of Greek-speaking Muslims until this century. Amongst the substantial Greek populations on the western and northern seacoasts of Asia Minor and in central Asia Minor itself a marked decline in Christian observance must in part be put down to conversion. Whereas in 1204 there had been 48 metropolitanates and 421 bishoprics, by the fifteenth century the numbers were 18 (including one archbishopric) and 3 respectively.[23] Others in these areas remained Christians but became Turkish-speakers. It was these so-called Karamanli Christians in particular, mainly concentrated in the interior of Asia Minor, whom the Greek government now wanted to bring back into the fold.

The Hellenization of the Balkan Orthodox Churches within the Ottoman Empire did not cease with Greek independence: the Greek Patriarch was after all still located in Constantinople, and he was still responsible for all Orthodox in the eyes of the Ottoman authorities. The tradition in Bulgaria was to appoint not only Greek-speaking bishops but even Greek-speaking priests to purely Bulgarian parishes; 'to have to say confession through an interpreter could excite forceful emotions'.[24] If in the 1820s protests in Bulgarian communities focused on the venality of the episcopacy, some complaining that they paid more in Church dues than in taxes to the state, by the 1840s a growing demand was that they be given bishops who could at least understand their language. Such priorities reflected the steady development of Bulgarian culture throughout the nineteenth century. Most of the early enlighteners in Bulgaria were faithful to the Greek patriarchate and tended to regard, for example, education in Bulgarian as an addition to rather than an alternative to Greek schooling. By the middle of the century, however, schools had been founded which taught the Bulgarian language and propagated the idea of liberation. As the Bulgarians grew more conscious of their cultural identity they clashed first not with the Ottoman state but with the Greek Church.

The patriarchate in Constantinople had grown accustomed to ignoring complaints from the Bulgarian communities. The latter now started demanding the right to appoint their own clergy and to run their churches themselves. In 1848 the Ottoman authorities agreed to allow the Bulgarians to open a church in the Phanar district of Constantinople. This was a success which other religious communities in the Ottoman Empire were keen to regard as a precedent for themselves.

In 1860 a leading bishop declared the Bulgarian Church independent, and during the following decade many dioceses in Bulgaria, Macedonia and Thrace declared for it. The patriarchate put up fierce resistance, and the Ottoman authorities were content to sit back and watch the quarrel, until growing violence and unrest in Bulgaria and international pressure prompted them to respond. In 1870 the sultan recognized the Bulgarian

Church as a separate religious community headed by an exarch. The Patriarch's response was to excommunicate the new Church in 1872 for the heresy of phyletism, or maintaining that ecclesiastical jurisdiction is determined ethnically rather than territorially. One element in the Ottoman recognition of the Bulgarian Church was certainly furtherance of the policy of divide and rule. Russia, whose attitude to Greek ecclesiastical hegemony in the Balkans had cooled since Greek political independence, acquiesced in the move; in its turn Greece, which had always believed that the Russians were champions of Orthodoxy, now began to suspect that the Russians' primary ambitions in the Balkans were pan-Slavist and political.

The other Orthodox Churches in the Ottoman Balkans expressed support for the newly independent Church. They had all had to wait for their states to gain political freedom from the Turks before they had been able to put an end to Phanariot control in ecclesiastical administration. Bulgaria was the only country in which the order of events was reversed. The exarchate became the focus for the continuing Bulgarian national revival; some argue that it was the ecclesiastical victory which encouraged the Bulgarians to claim political freedom. Such was the extent to which the Church was identified with the nation that it was the territories which the Bulgarian exarchate comprised which became the ideal of Bulgarian nationalists for a Greater Bulgaria.

Bulgaria achieved independence in 1878 and its constitution of the following year was one of the most democratic in Europe. The Church was granted state subsidies, on which it has in fact remained dependent throughout modern Bulgarian history, and Orthodoxy was declared the official religion of the state. This led to continuing differences of interpretation, secular leaders taking it to mean state sovereignty over the Church, Church leaders the reverse — frequently to the point of overt political involvement by members of the hierarchy. In fact the whole period between independence and the Communist takeover was marked by embittered confrontations, with Church leaders defending Church autonomy as well as involving themselves in national politics. The politicization of the Church hierarchy was seen by some as a factor causing a decline in religious faith and observance among the population.[25]

Amongst the Serbs, the first revolt against Turkish rule took place in 1804. When this was crushed in 1813 many more Serbs fled to Vojvodina. The second revolt in 1815 under Miloš Obrenović led by 1830 to international recognition of Serbia as a virtually independent state. Turkish garrisons remained in strategic positions, and the Serbs still paid tribute to the sultan; but they had won the right to organize their own administration and were able to build churches and open schools. Serbia won total independence from Turkey in 1882, and the Serbian Church gained its autocephaly. As in other Balkan countries, there was friction between the Church and the new political leadership, who had mostly been educated in France and Germany and who had a secularizing and modernizing programme. By 1881 the Serbian Church had effectively been turned into a department of state. The Serbian constitution of 1903 recognized Orthodoxy as the state religion: as in other Orthodox countries emerging into independence the Church found itself at once honoured and restrained.

Under the Ottomans the Romanian principalities had at first enjoyed a quasi-autonomous status under the rule of native princes, but in the early eighteenth century the Ottoman authorities replaced them with Phanariot Greeks. These posts were the most prestigious and lucrative held by the Phanariots in the Ottoman Empire. At this time of Greek political control the principalities were a significant channel for influences from the West to the Greeks in Constantinople and the inner empire, and a valuable school of politics. The Greek uprising of 1821 was to be inaugurated by Alexander Ypsilantes in the principalities; ironically, this event led to the abrupt termination of Phanariot rule by the Ottoman authorities.

Continuing conflict between Russia and Turkey in the nineteenth century brought Turkish recognition of the autonomy of Moldavia and Wallachia. The two principalities elected the same ruler in 1859; Romania achieved full independence from the Turks in 1877 and recognition as a national state, including Transylvania, by the European powers in 1918. Developments in the Church mirrored these changes. In 1864 the Romanian Orthodox Church declared its independence from Constantinople, and partly in order to diminish Greek influence over the Church the Romanian authorities confiscated the lands of Greek monasteries endowed by the Phanariots. The Ecumenical Patriarch granted the Church autocephaly in 1885. Self-government for the Church meant the disappearance of several forms of restraint and increasing orientation towards the West. Greek control and accompanying Hellenization came to an end. Russian messianism became a less real threat. The Church continued to express concern for the Romanian Orthodox in Hungarian-governed Transylvania, where Metropolitan Andreiu Şaguna (1846–73) was soon exercising statesmanlike leadership.[26] The Church and the Romanian political leadership worked together towards the reunited Romania of 1918.

In independent Romania Church–state relations developed in a similar way to those in other Balkan states. The 1866 Romanian constitution recognized the Orthodox Church as 'the dominant religion of the Romanian state'. Secular governments tended to interpret this as implying loyal subservience and to treat the Church as a department of state. Bishops were appointed to suit political requirements and the parish clergy, recruited from the peasantry, were looked down on by the Westernized upper classes. During the half-century after 1877 the Church was concerned with establishing in concrete form its leading role within the nation, consolidating its own ecclesiastical structure, and working on improved educational standards for clergy, spiritual renewal in the monasteries, social action and intensified publishing activity. In 1890 a theological faculty opened at the University of Bucharest. For its part, the government was concerned both to promote Orthodoxy's dominant position in society but also to bring the Church under regular supervision. Despite its officially favoured position, the Church was nevertheless suspicious at various periods that the government was favouring the rights of Roman Catholics and Uniates; and a continuing and at times heated debate about the value of the Catholic contribution to Romanian history[27] is illustrative of the complex heritage of a region situated on the fault-line between the Eastern and the Western spiritual traditions.[28]

The Russian religious renaissance of the late nineteenth century

In the Russian Empire, and later in the Soviet Union, political and social debate always tended to be initiated in literature. Writers were regarded as prophets and as such taken much more seriously than in Western countries. From the middle of the nineteenth century the great Russian novelists began to transcend the 'realism' which had become the prevailing literary style and to deal with deeper spiritual issues. The creative intelligentsia in general was increasingly beset with seeking spiritual solutions to secular problems. The monastery of Optina Pustyn' became a popular place of pilgrimage, which the writers Gogol', Dostoyevsky and Tolstoy visited, as did the philosophers Solov'yev and Rozanov. Ivan Kireyevsky and Konstantin Leont'yev made it their permanent home. What they found there were holy men, *startsy* or elders, saintly figures who embodied and continued the Hesychast tradition and who stood outside the all-too-compromised hierarchy of the Church. A powerful portrayal of a *starets* is that of Fr Zosima in Dostoyevsky's novel *The Brothers Karamazov*.

Lev Tolstoy moved through the profound psychological analysis of *War and Peace* (1869) and *Anna Karenina* (1877) to a moral and religious crisis; after this his aim was to write simply about spiritual truths in a style which would be accessible to ordinary people. In his desire to adopt a peasant lifestyle and his increasing concern to convey the simple moral teachings of the Gospels he is in the tradition of Russian sectarianism. At the heart of his later teachings lies the doctrine of non-violence, which for him involved repudiation of the state and all its structures. His world-view is best summed up in his *Confession*, finished in 1882. He was excommunicated by the Russian Orthodox Church in 1901. In the last decades of his life he enjoyed immense popularity within Russia and a growing reputation abroad.

Fedor Dostoyevsky spent four years in prison (1850–54) for his involvement with revolutionary socialist circles. Here his own religious crisis led him to conversion to the Orthodoxy of the Russian people. As a journalist he went on to tackle political and social issues from a perspective of mystical populism, and his programme is conservative and frequently chauvinist. However, it is his novels which are of enduring importance, primarily *Crime and Punishment* (1866), *The Idiot* (1868), *The Devils* (1871–72) and *The Brothers Karamazov* (1880). Here he deals more profoundly than perhaps any other writer with the fundamental issues of sin and redemption, and the range of his concern encompasses everything from an individual's responsibility for his own actions to prophecy of the 'universal harmony' which will transcend the tragedy of mankind.

By the last decade of the nineteenth century Russian society had begun to polarize politically as increasingly extremist programmes were adopted by the revolutionaries, and particularly as the growing influence of Marxism meant that materialism and atheism became an ever more integral part of these programmes. At the turn of the century the quest to bring Orthodox values to bear on pressing cultural, social and even political questions took on a new urgency. Some members of the hitherto positivist intelligentsia began to voice deep concern about the implications of such programmes for human freedom. Their increasingly Christian analysis was catalysed through the philosophy of Vladimir Solov'yev (1853–1900) who brought together Hegelian rationalism and mysticism, Westernism and Slavophilism, into a new synthesis for the modern age and a potential source of social and political doctrines for the Church.

It was in this climate that a movement took shape to reform the Church, to free it from the suffocating embrace of the state and to equip it as an institution able to tackle contemporary challenges. The movement was supported not only by members of the intelligentsia but by bishops, ordinary clergy and lay believers. In order to restore canonical self-government to the Church the reformers planned to convoke a Local Council (*Pomestny sobor*), traditionally the supreme ecclesiastical organ. A brief interlude of political liberalization (1905–06) saw religious concessions, including the edict on religious toleration of 17 April 1905 which granted religious freedom to non-Orthodox denominations. The issuing of the edict meant that reform of the Orthodox Church was now urgent: it needed institutional independence in order to join the other newly legalized denominations on equal terms. However, renewed reaction (1906–17) spelt an end to the reformers' hopes and it was only after the February revolution in 1917 that the Church was able to convene a council in Moscow and elect a Patriarch, Tikhon – the first since 1721. The council continued its reform deliberations until September, but by then the Bolsheviks were in Moscow. The only one of its decisions the Council was able to put into effect was the decision to restore the patriarchate.

The most important contribution of the Christianized intelligentsia to the intensifying political debate was the collection of essays *Vekhi* (Signposts) of 1909. The central message was an urgent call to the Russian intelligentsia to repent; a spiritual reorientation was needed if Russia were not to head for self-destruction wrought by maximalist egoism. The unfamiliar message obviously touched a nerve: *Vekhi* aroused intense controversy. The proposed solutions were ineffective, however. Some of the same authors came together in the collection *Iz Glubiny* (From the Depths), published in 1918, where the lament is that it is now too late. Most of the leading figures in the 'Russian religious renaissance of the twentieth century' were sent into exile when the Bolsheviks came to power. Men like Sergei Bulgakov (1871–1944), Semen Frank (1877–1950), Nikolai Lossky (1903–58) and Nikolai Berdyayev (1874–1948) were centrally involved in the development of Russian Orthodox philosophy and theology in the West during the Soviet period; and Berdyayev in particular was to have significant influence on existentialist philosophers as well as Christian theologians in non-Orthodox traditions.

Both Tolstoy and Dostoyevsky have of course had a profound influence on world literature. Despite his pacifism, Tolstoy was held up for adulation in the Soviet Union as a champion of the common man and a critic of the Orthodox Church; Dostoyevsky, by contrast, was never assimilated into the Soviet canon, and many of his works, dismissed as reactionary, were not generally available – especially *The Devils*, which is a spiritual investigation of the revolutionary mentality.[29] But neither Tolstoy nor Dostoyevsky has ever been recognized by the Russian Orthodox Church as any kind of exponent of Orthodox belief.

In the 1960s and 1970s in the Soviet Union there was to be a revival of spiritual searching. Unofficial groups came together in an urgent need to find personal integrity in the Christian faith and to work out how to apply Christian truths to pressing social and political problems. Two of the most important 'spiritual fathers' to these groups were Dostoyevsky and Berdyayev; and behind them stood the figure of Solov'yev, his all-embracing world-view a potential comprehensive challenge to the prevailing Marxist-Leninist ideology.

1920–1990

The collapse of the empires

The First World War brought about the collapse of four empires, the Russian, German, Austrian and Ottoman. The political changes led to changes in the circumstances of Churches throughout the Orthodox world. Some Christian communities disappeared altogether. Five new autonomous Orthodox Churches came into existence in countries which had now achieved political independence: Poland, Finland, Lithuania, Latvia and Estonia. Some of these accepted Constantinople as their head, others remained nominally linked to Moscow. Most of the larger Orthodox Churches increased substantially in size, and a central issue became that of determining the relationship between Church and state, particularly the question of how far a national Church could and should retain freedom for prophetic witness.

Most immediately and drastically affected were perhaps the Churches of Asia Minor and the Near East. In 1908 the Young Turk revolution had brought to power in Constantinople a new generation of politicians who were concerned to reinvigorate the Ottoman administration and were more nationalistically minded than the old guard. They launched a campaign to Ottomanize non-Muslim subjects. Especially vulnerable to this increasingly aggressive nationalism were the Greek Christians in Asia Minor, at that time numbering well over a million. The incorporation of Smyrna and its hinterland into Greece had long been part of the Great Idea. It was accomplished immediately after the First World War as the Ottoman Empire collapsed. However, the new Turkish government of Atatürk would not countenance Greek occupation of what it regarded as the Turkish homeland. In 1922 the Turks seized Smyrna and massacred the Christians there, perhaps as many as 30,000. A 2,500-year Greek presence on the western coast of Asia Minor was thus traumatically terminated.

These events reduced the patriarchate of Constantinople, which included 8 million Christians before 1914, to some 80,000 Greeks living in Constantinople. It was only under foreign pressure that the leaders of the Turkish Republic consented to allow the Ecumenical Patriarch to retain his residence in the Phanar, and they imposed many restrictions on his movements. The Greeks of Rhodes and some other islands and the Greeks in the diaspora (totalling some 500,000) continued to recognize him as their spiritual head. The territory of the patriarchate of Antioch was divided between the two republics of Syria and Lebanon; some 280,000 Orthodox Arabs were left under its supervision, of whom 100,000 were in the diaspora, mostly in North and South America.

This débâcle marked the end of the Great Idea; it also resulted in the arrival in Greece of well over a million Greeks, many of them destitute, and many knowing no language other than Turkish. In 1923 Greece and Turkey reached an agreement on exchange of populations on the basis of their religion. The Karamanlis came from central Asia Minor to Greece; the Greek-speaking Muslims of Crete went to Turkey. Between 1907 and 1926 the population of Greece rose from 2,600,000 to 6,200,000. A large part of the increase was the consequence of substantial territorial gains; but it also included the influx of 1,100,000 Christians in the wake of the 1923 agreement and perhaps another 200,000 refugees from Russia, Bulgaria and elsewhere.

The Churches in the inter-war Balkans

During the first half of the twentieth century the Archbishop of Athens and other hierarchs became progressively more influential and visible in Greek national life. Some of the new generation of archbishops were from families of immigrants from Asia Minor. Archbishop Damaskinos, whose tenure (1941–49) coincided with the Nazi occupation and civil war, played a crucial role in politics as well as Church life, especially in 1944–46 when he served as regent for the absent king and in subsequent political negotiations. He set up relief organizations for the families of those executed by the Germans and worked to protect Jews. Lay renewal and social witness initiatives such as the Zoe brotherhood gained the approval of the Church leadership, which also set up similar initiatives of its own.[30]

The first half of the century also saw continual struggle between Church and state over how much autonomy the Church was to have in running its own affairs, at times focusing on the question of the relative power of the bishops and the government procurator in the synod, but at other times addressing basic questions about how far a state Church identified with the nation can offer effective prophetic witness. These debates continue to the present day. One long-standing problem in the Church, for example, which was still not resolved by the 1980s, was how to improve the low educational standard of the ordinary clergy. The Church has argued that the scale of the needful undertaking would require funding beyond its own resources, and this has been used as a powerful argument against those who would like to see a cut in the state's subsidies to the Church.

In Bulgaria, despite a substantial increase in size from 1.5 million in 1910 to 5 million in 1924, the Church was prevented by the government from organizing itself into a patriarchate. One reason was very probably the monarch's fear that it might present a challenge for national leadership. Church–state relations recalled the Russian synodal system under Peter the Great. The Church was not allowed to elect a successor to Exarch Iosif, who died in 1915; at the same time, it provided the only ideological bulwark protecting the state against increasingly prevalent revolutionary programmes. By 1944 the Church had all too obviously become part of the state machinery, alienated from its flock. Some maintain that the Bulgarians had become the least religious people in Europe.[31]

At the start of the century the Serbian Church saw advantage in the proposed unification of the South Slavs in terms of the unification of its own scattered flock. The Kingdom of Serbs, Croats and Slovenes was established in 1918. In 1920 the Serbian patriarchate was re-established; it absorbed the Church of Montenegro and the Serbian dioceses in Austria and Hungary. Church membership grew from 2.3 million in 1910 to 7 million in 1925. Under Yugoslavia's King Alexander (1921–34) all significant political and military posts were occupied by Serbs. The government was interested in establishing firm state control over the Church. During the 1920s, however, non-Orthodox denominations complained that the Serbian Church was manipulating the state in its own confessional interests. The Church came out in successful opposition to the 1935 concordat between the Vatican and the Yugoslav government on the grounds that it would give the Catholic Church privileges not shared by other denominations. Like many other Orthodox Churches with a leadership co-opted into the service of the state, the Serbian Church nevertheless experienced grass-roots renewal initiatives. A movement resembling the Zoe movement in the Greek Church acquired a nationwide significance, organizing annual pilgrimages and generally exercising a beneficial influence on the Church's spiritual life.

In 1910 the Romanian Church had some 4.5 million members; after the First World War, with the incorporation of the Orthodox of Bessarabia, Bukovina and Transylvania, the number rose to 15 million. In 1925, following the addition of Transylvania to the Romanian state, a Romanian patriarchate was founded.

By the first two decades of the twentieth century two parallel tendencies were evident within the Romanian Church; they were to remain typical of it to the present day. It was clearly a Church of the people, with priests working and fighting alongside the peasants; at the same time appointments at higher levels in the Church were heavily politicized. The first Patriarch of the Church, Miron Cristea, was made prime minister in 1938; he nevertheless proved unable to bring the Church's influence effectively to bear in combating the rise of the Iron Guard, which under Corneliu Codreanu was claiming roots in Orthodoxy and, with justification, extensive support amongst Orthodox clergy and laity. Guardism was rooted in a 'fundamentalist Orthodox populism'.[32] Its main supporters were young men and women, including university students, who were reacting against prevalent Western secularism and who regarded Church membership as a sign of love for Romania. One of the aims of Guardism was to strengthen and purify the life of the Romanian Church. It was also dedicated, however, to 'saving' Romania from foreign ideologies and in particular from the Jews. Anti-Semitism was revivified.[33]

At the same time, the inter-war years also saw positive developments in Church administration and more evidence of the traditional creativity of Romanian Orthodoxy. Charitable organizations were set up. Theological educational establishments were strengthened. New publications encompassed a range of styles from pietist to philosophical. The challenge of new Protestant movements coming in from Transylvania and Ukraine led to the appearance of 'born again' movements within Orthodoxy. One group was expelled from the Church and became a neo-Protestant denomination called the Evangelical Christians (*Creştini după Evanghelie*). The Lord's Army movement started by Fr Iosif Trifa in Transylvania in 1923 remained as a revival movement within the Orthodox Church. It should be noted that the Romanian Baptist Church is the largest in Eastern Europe (excluding the former Soviet Union):[34] evidence once again of the complex spiritual heritage in Romania which has the potential for remarkable cross-fertilization.

Russian Christianity under Communism

Marxism taught that 'religion is the opium of the people'; Lenin was a typical member of the nineteenth-century Russian intelligentsia in his profound hatred of institutionalized religion. For 70 years the Communist Party of the Soviet Union sustained an offensive against religion on a scale unprecedented in history.[35] The Decree on Separation of Church from State of January 1918 opened the way to the confiscation of the Orthodox Church's schools and welfare establishments, the seizure of Church property and valuables and violence against clergy and believers. At this early stage the new regime directed its hostility against the Orthodox Church rather than against religion in general. Patriarch Tikhon condemned Bolshevik atrocities; he was arrested.

From the early 1920s a movement called the 'Living Church' attempted to constitute an Orthodox Church which would be acceptable to the new regime. Its leading members included not only idealists imbued with the aspirations of the Church reform movement of the earlier part of the century but also opportunists and careerists with a political agenda. The authorities at first encouraged the Living Church, on the basis of the principle of 'divide and rule'. To the average believer, however, the preoccupations of the Living Church seemed both obscure and of minor importance, and it was clear that their loyalties still lay with the Patriarchal Church.

The trial of Patriarch Tikhon was put off again and again, and he was released in June 1923. The Living Church quickly faded from the scene. Tikhon signed a confession admitting the anti-Soviet nature of his activity hitherto; when he died in April 1925 he left a Testament confirming his unwavering loyalty to the Soviet state. Nevertheless, the Church was not allowed to elect a new Patriarch. Tikhon's eventual successor, patriarchal *locum tenens* Metropolitan Sergi, issued a Declaration of Loyalty in 1927. This proved a highly controversial document for many in the Church and led to claims by alternative organizations – including the 'underground Church' and the Russian Orthodox Church in Exile – that they alone preserved the integrity of the Church; for it was clear that the Soviet authorities would be content with nothing less than complete endorsement by the Church of all aspects of Soviet reality.

From 1928 the anti-religious campaign under Stalin became comprehensive and all denominations in the Soviet Union suffered. The 1929 Law on Religious Associations meant that from now on the only legally permissible religious activity was meeting for an act of worship in a registered building: and soon it would become practically impossible for most believers to exercise even this right. There was savage and prolonged persecution throughout the 1930s. By 1939 the Orthodox Church had virtually ceased to exist as an institution: in the territory under Soviet control from 1919 to 1939 no more than a few hundred churches remained open out of a pre-revolutionary total of some 46,000; clergy and lay people were in labour camps; only four bishops remained at liberty. Nevertheless, the existence of an underground Church must have warned the authorities that the people were not abandoning the faith; indeed, in the mid-1930s the head of the League of Militant Godless estimated that some 57 per cent of the Soviet population remained believers.[36]

The situation for the Church changed dramatically on the outbreak of the Second World War. The partition of Poland between Hitler and Stalin in 1939 increased the number of open churches by 40 per cent. For the first time Stalin made use of the Church, allowing it to organize Church life in the annexed territories. In 1941, in a further dramatic development, Hitler violated the Nazi–Soviet pact and invaded the Soviet Union. Metropolitan Sergi responded before Stalin did, in the spirit of his 1927 Declaration calling on the faithful to defend the Motherland. Meanwhile a remarkable revival of Church life was taking place in those areas of the Soviet Union now under Nazi control.[37]

In September 1943 Stalin summoned Sergi to the Kremlin; four days later he was elected Patriarch. The government then set up a council to deal directly with the Church hierarchy, a move which amounted to *de facto* recognition of the Church as an institution. The new policy continued after the war. Churches were reopened, the number of clergy and bishops grew, theological schools and monasteries began to function again and the Church was allowed to publish a journal. There was, however, no change in the law of 1929, and the new liberties had no legal status. During the war Stalin realized that the Church could be of positive help to the state in mobilizing public support for the defence of the Motherland. It was soon clear, moreover, that it would continue to be of help in furthering the Soviet state's post-war political agenda. Between 1945 and 1948 the Soviet authorities encouraged the Church to extend its authority over the Orthodox Churches in the countries of Eastern Europe now coming under Soviet political control. When western Ukraine was again incorporated into the Soviet Union, the Greek Catholic Church there was suppressed in 1946 and declared aggregated to the Russian Orthodox Church.

Those deemed reliable enough by state and Church to represent the Church officially were soon providing valuable service in building up the Soviet state's diplomatic relations with the world at large, and spreading a favourable Soviet image abroad. After 1948 Church representatives were regularly to be found promoting the Soviet concept of 'peace' in international gatherings. In 1961 the Russian Orthodox Church became a member of the World Council of Churches; it could not have done so without the consent of the Soviet authorities.

For the Armenian Church too the Second World War saw the general improvement associated with Stalin.[38] The Soviet authorities were always anxious to ensure there was no vacancy for Catholicos at the head of the Church for fear that leadership of the worldwide Armenian diaspora might devolve to the Catholicos in Cilicia and out of Soviet control. Nevertheless they were equally anxious to ensure that any Armenian Church leaders were politically pliable, and this led to bad feeling between Echmiadzin and Cilicia. In 1956 the Catholicos of Echmiadzin was allowed to travel to Beirut in order to ensure that the Soviet-preferred candidate there was elected. The ensuing scandal induced the Soviet authorities to allow the Church in Armenia to announce the reopening of a number of churches and monasteries. From the 1960s the Catholicos was encouraged to travel widely abroad to win over the Armenian diaspora to a positive view of conditions in Soviet Armenia, including religious freedom. Throughout the Soviet period, then, the fact that most Armenians lived abroad helped to restrain the Soviet authorities from curtailing the activity of the Church at home. In the late 1970s some 90 per cent of Armenian babies were being baptized, pilgrimages to holy sites continued to attract huge crowds and Armenia was the only republic where Bibles could sometimes be found on open sale.

With the alleviation of persecution during the Second World War came reconciliation between the Georgian Church and the Russian Orthodox Church, and the latter recognized the former's autocephaly in 1943. Ironically, however, the institutional dependence of the Georgian Church on Soviet power was thereby strengthened: the price of Russian Orthodox recognition of its autocephaly was staunch Georgian loyalty to the Soviet system. In the post-war period the revival of religion in Georgia was less strong than in Russia or Armenia. In the 1970s the Church fell into moral decay and corruption;[39] the most active campaigner against it was Georgian Orthodox dissident Zviad Gamsakhurdia, who identified the Church with the general struggle for national self-expression and who was to enjoy a brief spell as president of a newly independent Georgia after the collapse of the Soviet Union. During the 1980s the Church became increasingly popular and influential as an important focus for growing nationalist sentiment in Georgia.

One of the tasks of Russian Orthodox representatives in the WCC from the early 1960s was to deny that there were any restrictions on religious freedom in the Soviet Union. This was ironical because at that time a massive and unexpected new anti-religious campaign had begun under Khrushchev. It suddenly became obvious to believers that, however useful the Church might be to the Soviet authorities for propaganda purposes abroad, they were never going to be reconciled to the existence within the country of an institution representing an alternative world-view to that of the Communist Party. The Khrushchev anti-religious campaign lasted from 1959 to 1964 and led to the closure of two-thirds of the 20,000 legally operating churches. The total of some 7,000 churches still open in the mid-1960s was to remain more or less unchanged until the later 1980s.

The traumatic shock the Khrushchev anti-religious campaign delivered to religious believers inside the Soviet Union was one of the factors giving rise to the religious dissent movement of the 1970s and 1980s. In 1971 Aleksandr Solzhenitsyn, for the first time publicly identifying himself as a Christian, wrote to the Patriarch exhorting him to stand up to the state's anti-religious policies. The aspirations of religious activists were given a considerable boost by the onset of détente in the early 1970s and by the ratification of the Helsinki Final Act in 1975. In November of that year the Orthodox priest Fr Gleb Yakunin and the layman Lev Regel'son sent a letter to the World Council of Churches assembly in Nairobi, and this initiative sparked off the first ever discussion of religious liberty in the Soviet Union to be held at the WCC. As we have seen, the official WCC representatives from Churches in Communist countries were themselves constantly playing the subject down. Encouraged by the Nairobi response and by increasing world attention, a number of religious rights movements sprang up alongside movements for human rights and national identity in the second half of the 1970s; and in some religious discussion circles an echo of the Christian renaissance of the early twentieth century was to be heard as new converts and those older in the faith came together to try to work out solutions to pressing social and political problems from a Christian perspective. By 1979, however, a new crackdown on dissent had begun, and the first half of the 1980s saw the number of prisoners of conscience in the Soviet Union rapidly increasing.

The trauma of the Khrushchev years of persecution gave way to the 'years of stagnation' under Brezhnev and his successors. For ordinary churchgoers this meant that if they confined themselves to attending services of worship in registered buildings and did not attempt to comment on or involve themselves in political or social matters from a Christian perspective they would be barred from many kinds of educational and career opportunities but otherwise left in peace. The Church was allowed a limited institutional existence, able to train some clergy in a small number of theological educational establishments, to publish limited numbers of official journals and calendars and to produce very small print runs of the Bible. The average believer received no spiritual nourishment beyond attendance at the liturgy: Sunday schools, discussion groups, charitable activity, parish newsletters were all prohibited in a society in which the official ideology continued its systematic occupation of the public space.

Mikhail Gorbachev came to power in 1985, and soon the new policies of 'glasnost' and 'perestroika' had become household words. Gorbachev himself believed the Soviet system could be reformed, but with the active co-operation of 'all citizens of goodwill' – and this soon came to include religious believers. The Millennium celebrations in 1988 for the thousandth anniversary of the acceptance of Christianity in Kiev[40] were already marked by cautious triumphalism on the part of the Church; and in the next two years religious freedom became once again a reality.

While welcoming the new freedoms, the Church was nevertheless seriously shaken as an institution by the events of the late 1980s. The certainties of the status of second-class servant of the state it had enjoyed since the Second World War were abruptly destroyed. In 1989, for example, the Soviet government suddenly relegalized the Ukrainian Catholic Church, and immediately millions of nominal Orthodox in western Ukraine revealed their true allegiance. Since the collapse of the Soviet Union the Ukrainian Catholic Church has become one of the major denominations in independent Ukraine.

The Russian Federation passed a new law on Freedom of Conscience in 1990, replacing Stalin's law of 1929; it granted complete freedom to all religions to engage in worship, teaching and social activity; at the same time, churches and monastic buildings began to be handed back in large numbers.

Balkan Christianity under Communism

Generally speaking the Communist governments which came to power in Eastern Europe after the Second World War attempted first of all severely to restrict religious practice, closing places of worship and arresting and even murdering clergy and believers, and then later attempted to co-opt the Churches for political ends, at the same time neutralizing their capacity for independent witness, harassing individuals with an active faith and keeping religious believers out of higher education and many professions. These policies had least success in countries with a Roman Catholic majority, the obvious example being Poland, where the Catholic Church retained far more authority and legitimacy than the government throughout the Communist period. They also had limited success when applied to certain Protestant Churches: the Church in East Germany succeeded in making its authentic voice heard on important social and political issues, while in the Soviet Union a significant section of the Baptist Church went underground and assumed the freedom of the outlaw. Those Churches which proved to be able to offer least resistance to Communist policies were the national Orthodox Churches.

In Bulgaria the Communists brought Church–state relationships to a logical conclusion. During the 1940s the Church was reduced by persecution and threats of withdrawal of state subsidy to a position of submission; but it was named as the 'traditional Church of the Bulgarian people' in the 1949 law on confessions, and the patriarchate was restored in 1953. Communist leaders regularly paid tribute to the key role of the Church in preserving Bulgarian identity through centuries of tribulation. The Church was thus transformed into an obedient and useful tool in the hands of the government, which consolidated its hold with judicious use of divide and rule tactics, for example promoting a 'priests' union' seeking Church reform along the lines of the Living Church movement in the Soviet Union in the 1920s.

The Communist authorities in Yugoslavia viewed nationalism as potentially the most dangerous dividing force in the country. In this context their tactics towards the Churches, principally the Serbian Orthodox Church and the Catholic Church in Croatia, were aimed at reducing their influence in society. The Catholic Church presented special problems because its administrative centre was in the Vatican; but as far as the Serbian Church was concerned the Party envisaged a tame and co-operative institution which would support its policies, and to this end revived the 'priests' associations', which dated back to 1889, and which the Party now used to criticize the hierarchy. At the same time the Party began obstructing the activity of the Church in education and practical witness. As in other Communist countries, then, the Church was allowed to retain or even rebuild its institutional structure while suffering restraint on its outreach into society.

The Serbian Church remained in a weak position throughout the Communist period. It was nevertheless prepared to oppose the government if its vital interests were at stake, and particularly when it perceived threats within the multinational Communist state to the Serbian nation and culture. The government regime was for example eager for political reasons to see an independent Church in Macedonia, which has always been a meeting place of contrasting cultures and a cockpit of rival political ambitions. Macedonia was in Turkish hands until the First Balkan War of 1912. The memory of its brief period of glory under Alexander the Great remained a source of inspiration to Macedonian nationalists, although their interpretation of its significance was always challenged by Bulgarian, Greek and Serbian historians. With the encouragement of the Yugoslav government the Macedonian clergy unilaterally claimed autocephaly in 1967. Their claim has however never been recognized by the Serbian Church. The Serbian Orthodox Church, then, was an opposition force in the Communist period primarily in so far as it was an institution representing the national interests of the Serbs.

In Romania the new Communist government accused thousands of Orthodox of collaboration with the Fascists, and clergy and lay people were imprisoned. The Lord's Army had been banned in 1947; the Uniate Church was declared reintegrated with the Orthodox Church in 1948. Both continued to operate illegally throughout the Communist period. Latin-rite Catholics also suffered discrimination, as did the Baptists.

Under Nicolae Ceauşescu, who came to power in 1965, overt persecution of the Orthodox Church as an institution came to an end. The Church was presented as a historical expression of Romanian national identity. In the 1980s 17 million of Romania's 21 million population were baptized Orthodox. The Church had a high profile and visibility in the media. The Church funerals of Ceauşescu's father and mother were major media events, with Ceauşescu present while Orthodox ceremonies were performed. At the same time Church leaders, especially when travelling abroad, were required by the state to promote a positive image of Romanian reality and to assert the existence of complete religious freedom within the country.

In Moldavia the monasteries remained centres of spiritual vitality, despite government efforts in the 1950s to cut down drastically on the number of religious. They continued to build on the Hesychast tradition of Paisi Velichkovsky, venerated in both the Russian and the Romanian Churches. Teaching, publishing and ecumenical contacts continued.[41]

Nevertheless, the Communist authorities continued to infringe religious liberty by the promotion of exclusively atheist education; and the general human rights record of the Ceauşescu regime was arguably the worst in the entire Communist bloc. Religious believers of all denominations who attempted to apply their faith to social and political problems were certain to be persecuted. Eastern European movements for human rights reached a peak in the late 1970s and there were sporadic efforts in Romania too. These prominently involved religious believers: first Baptists and then members of other denominations including the Orthodox. Church leaders were prompt to co-operate with the secular authorities by repressing dissent within their own denominations. The most famous case in the late 1970s was that of Fr Gheorghe Calciu, whose preaching and political involvement led to his arrest in 1978 and release to emigrate in 1984: it was clear that even in a Church as apparently tolerated as the Romanian Orthodox there were no possibilities for criticism of the status quo. As the Party's oppression of the people grew, questions were increasingly raised about the close identification between Church and state. Even after the fall of Ceauşescu and end of the Communist system, they continue to be so.

Post-Communist Christianity

In October 1990 the Soviet Union passed a new law on freedom of conscience, at last replacing the harsh Stalinist law of 1929, and later in the same month the Russian Federation followed suit with an even more liberal law. After decades of persecution all denominations found themselves legally among the most free in the world: free to reopen churches, monasteries and theological academies, to publish, to engage in mission, social work and political activity. Similar freedoms of course came to believers in all the formerly Communist countries of Central and Eastern Europe after the events of 1989. State persecution was however soon replaced by a whole range of different problems.

The main task facing the Churches was that of re-establishing themselves as properly functioning organisms within society. In most Communist countries they had been severely restricted in their witness and their infrastructure dismantled; parish life had ceased to exist. They were generally speaking critically short of money, equipment, literature and material resources of all kinds which were taken for granted by denominations in the West, and also lacked trained clergy. Most denominations began receiving back from the post-Communist authorities large numbers of church, monastic and educational buildings illegally seized from them; but for many the costs of restoring them all were quite beyond their means. Meanwhile some denominations, particularly the Eastern-rite Catholics, found it difficult to obtain their former property because of continuing state prejudice or resistance from rival denominations. At the same time, the Churches in post-Communist countries faced a fundamental problem in trying to find a language in which to communicate with their nominal flock and even more so with those who had never had contact with a Church. It was not only the ordinary people who were ignorant; very often the clergy had had no chance to receive theological education or pastoral training.

An internal problem for the Churches was reconciliation of two groups divided by bitterness and distrust: those who had 'compromised' with the Communist authorities and those who had 'resisted' and who had been persecuted or discriminated against as a result. After the end of the Communist system the Bulgarian Orthodox Church, for example, suffered serious schism, partly because of the legacy of political involvement on the part of hierarchs and clergy. The schism did nothing to improve the Church's standing in the eyes of ordinary people.

Another split which developed within the Churches was between 'conservatives' and 'progressives'. Loud voices among clergy and laity began to champion chauvinist programmes and stress the need to return to the traditional teachings and disciplines of the Church, while others struggled to maintain openness to the West and ecumenical dialogue now this was genuinely possible for the first time for decades, and to promote spiritual renewal and a commitment to social and even political involvement. The area in which the Russian Orthodox Church was most successful in rebuilding its activity in the post-Communist period was arguably in the sphere of theological education; yet the dozens of new seminaries and academies tended to be divided into 'conservative' and 'progressive', as did the hierarchy of the Church itself: the Church was thus unable to speak with one voice on important issues of the day.

The Churches in Communist countries had been in enforced and unnatural isolation, generally speaking unable to develop their own responses to social or political problems and cut off from developments of world significance such as the Second Vatican Council. After the end of Communism many Christians in Eastern and Central Europe, coming back into contact with the wider world, were genuinely shocked by the excesses, as they saw them, to which liberalizing tendencies had led in some Western Churches. Some in Orthodox circles decisively turned their backs on Western Europe and its culture, which seemed to them to be suffused with materialism and heresy.

One of the main causes of dismay in the Churches throughout Central and Eastern Europe was the sudden influx of all kinds of foreign missions and sects. Many of these had huge financial and technical resources which could not be matched by the indigenous Churches, and frequently offered jobs, training or material goods to attract converts. Suspicion about the motives of foreign religious organizations was exacerbated in a climate of increasing disillusionment with Western-style capitalism, which in most parts of the post-Communist world arrived suddenly and in a particularly virulent form.

With the end of Communism ecumenical relations between major denominations began deteriorating. The Russian Orthodox Church quickly grew seriously alarmed by what it construed as a policy of aggressive 'sheep-stealing' on the part of the Vatican. Traditional Protestant denominations were also increasingly under attack. Baptists and Pentecostals have been strong in Russia since the last century; yet in the 1990s the Russian Orthodox Church published booklets attacking these 'sects'. There was the danger, particularly in the context of resurgent nationalism in many parts of Eastern Europe, that not only genuinely harmful sects would be targeted, but also well-established but minority denominations with connections abroad.

There was a growing desire amongst the Churches (usually the Orthodox Churches) which regarded themselves as 'traditional' in post-Communist countries to protect their own interests by means of legislation. The new governments came under increasing pressure to revise liberal laws so as to place new restrictions on 'foreign' or 'harmful' sects and evangelical denominations. In the Russian Federation regional governments began introducing their own local laws restricting religious activity, in violation of the provisions of the 1993 Russian constitution, and in 1997 the Russian government itself introduced a new restrictive law to replace that of 1990.

The Orthodox Churches in the post-Communist world began showing interest in the legal status of religion in Greece and the pattern of Greek Church–state relations as it had developed during the twentieth century. The Greek Orthodox Church enjoys a special status. Generally it has avoided sacrificing its principles for the sake of political accommodation, but during the military dictatorship (1967–73), for example, many people found the Church's collaboration with the colonels very offensive. A perennial question is whether the Greek Orthodox Church has a monopoly on the 'truth'. The Church has a history of resistance to liturgical or scriptural change. The new constitution of 1975 now allows proselytizing by 'recognized' non-Orthodox denominations, thus moving towards recognition of religious pluralism, but Orthodoxy is still recognized as the 'dominant' religion. Until the end of Communism the Orthodox Church in Greece was in a unique category in the Orthodox world; but it is now likely that other Orthodox Churches in post-Communist countries will be interested in achieving a similar status.

For it is clear that one temptation for the Orthodox Churches in formerly Communist countries is triumphalism, on the basis of the fact that they have all survived the time of trial with their nominal flocks intact. What is more, they now find themselves championed by a wide variety of nationalist, chauvinist and protectionist groupings, many of which want to restore the old social and economic certainties of the days of totalitarian control − only this time under an Orthodox rather than a Communist banner. With the collapse of Yugoslavia, for example, and the opportunist adoption by the Milošević government of nationalist in place of Communist rhetoric, the Serbian Orthodox Church suddenly found itself centre stage again after decades of weakness and marginalization. 'Lately', comments one expert, 'Serbians have taken their *Serbian* identity far more seriously than their *Orthodox* identity. Leaders of the Serbian Orthodox Church generally promote a close identity of the two terms, seeing that they feed upon each other.'[42] The Church thus proved unable to make a principled stand against the atrocities in the civil war which accompanied the collapse of the Yugoslav state.

Everywhere in the post-Communist Orthodox world there are new signs of growth at grass-roots level: initiatives in spiritual education, social involvement and interfaith understanding. In Russia, for example, many small groups have been activated by spiritual disciples of Fr Aleksandr Men', the well-loved Russian Orthodox priest who was murdered in 1990 and whose legacy is having a growing influence both in Russia and in the West. Generally speaking, however, the Orthodox Churches of the 1990s have been hampered by their split personalities. Triumphalism is undercut by self-defensiveness[43] and a desire to reach out into society by an awareness of internal weakness. They find themselves having to perform new kinds of balancing act in a new age of uncertainty.

Notes

1 For an interesting discussion of this 'fault-line' see Jaroslav Pelikan, *Confessor Between East and West: A Portrait of Ukrainian Cardinal Josyf Slipyj* (Grand Rapids, MI, 1990), pp. 54−5.

2 For a good recent summary of the subject see Serge Keleher, 'Church in the middle: Greek-Catholics in central and eastern Europe', *Religion, State and Society: The Keston Journal*, 20, nos 3−4 (1992), pp. 289−302.

3 See Jean Bérenger, *A History of the Habsburg Empire 1273−1700* (Essex, 1994), pp. 180−4; Leslie C. Tihany, 'Islam and the eastern frontiers of Reformed Protestantism', *Reformed Review* (Holland, MI), vol. 29 (Fall 1975), pp. 52−71;

idem, *A History of Middle Europe: From the Earliest Times to the Age of the World Wars* (New Brunswick, NJ, 1976), pp. 94–103.

4 See Fred Singleton, *A Short History of the Yugoslav Peoples* (Cambridge, 1985), p. 37. For the view criticized by Singleton, see Nicolas Zernov, *Eastern Christendom* (London, 1961), p. 135.

5 Benjamin Brande and Bernard Lewis, *Christians and Jews in the Ottoman Empire: The Functioning of a Plural Society* (New York and London, 1982), vol. 1, p. 1.

6 Spas T. Raikin, 'The Bulgarian Orthodox Church' in Pedro Ramet (ed.), *Eastern Christianity and Politics in the Twentieth Century* (Durham and London, 1988), p. 161.

7 Attempts by Protestants to make contact with the Orthodox Church in a bid to have their views ecumenically validated, reciprocal interest by the Orthodox (particularly the Ecumenical Patriarch Kyrillos Loukaris (1572–1638)) and robust attempts by the Catholics to thwart the rapprochement are described by Nicolas Zernov in his *Eastern Christendom*, pp. 136–9. See also Metropolitan Germanos, *Kyrillos Loukaris 1572–1638* (London, 1951) (a short pamphlet); George A. Hadjiantoniou, *Protestant Patriarch: The Life of Cyril Lucaris (1572–1638), Patriarch of Constantinople* (London, 1961).

8 Geert van Dartel, 'The nations and the churches in Yugoslavia', *Religion, State and Society: The Keston Journal*, 20, nos 3–4 (1992), pp. 274–88. See also Sabrina Petra Ramet, 'The Serbian Church and the Serbian nation' in Sabrina Petra Ramet and Donald W. Treadgold (eds), *Render Unto Caesar: The Religious Sphere in World Politics* (Washington, DC, 1995), pp. 301–23.

9 See François Thual, *Géopolitique de l'Orthodoxie* (Paris, 1993), pp. 61–8.

10 55 per cent of the population by 1910.

11 For a recent short summary see Vladimir Kotelnikov, 'The primacy of monastic spirituality' in Giuseppe Alberigo and Oscar Beozzo (eds), *The Holy Russian Church and Western Christianity (Concilium*, 1996, no. 6; London and Maryknoll), pp. 21–32.

12 For a recent short summary of the context in which this doctrine arose see Emmanuel Lanne, 'The three Romes' in Alberigo and Beozzo (eds), *The Holy Russian Church and Western Christianity*, pp. 10–18.

13 John Meyendorff, *The Orthodox Church* (London, 1962), p. 108.

14 William K. Medlin and Christos G. Patrinelis, *Renaissance Influences and Religious Reforms in Russia: Western and Post-Byzantine Impacts on Culture and Education (16th–17th Centuries)* (Geneva, 1971).

15 Aristeides Papadakis, 'The historical tradition of church–state relations under Orthodoxy' in Ramet (ed.), *Eastern Christianity and Politics in the Twentieth Century*, pp. 37–58, here p. 54.

16 For the history of the Russian Church to the Schism and the origin of Russian sects see Albert F. Heard, *The Russian Church and Russian Dissent* (London, 1887).

17 Nadejda Gorodetsky, *Saint Tikhon Zadonsky: Inspirer of Dostoevsky* (London, 1951); Fr Seraphim (Rose), *Blessed Paisius Velichkovsky* (Platina, 1976); Valentine Zander, *St Seraphim of Sarov* (Crestwood, 1975).

18 Fred Singleton, *A Short History of the Yugoslav Peoples* (Cambridge, 1985), pp. 73–4.

19 Paul D. Garrett, *St Innocent: Apostle to America* (Crestwood, 1979).

20 For a recent short summary of the views of the Slavophiles see Aleksi I. Osipov, 'The theological conceptions of the Slavophiles' in Alberigo and Beozzi (eds), *The Holy Russian Church*, pp. 33–48.

21 See Ronald Grigor Suny, *The Making of the Georgian Nation* (London, 1989), p. 123.

22 For an interesting discussion of some factors predisposing the Bulgarians to conversion to Islam see Jan L. Perkowski, 'New light on the origins of Bulgaria's Catholics and Muslims', *Religion, State and Society: The Keston Journal*, 22, no. 1 (1994), pp. 103–8.

23 Richard Clogg, *A Short History of Modern Greece* (Cambridge, 1986). p. 22.

24 R. J. Crampton, *A Short History of Modern Bulgaria* (Cambridge, 1987), p. 14.

25 Spas T. Raikin, 'The Bulgarian Orthodox Church' in Ramet (ed.), *Eastern Christianity and Politics in the Twentieth Century*, p. 165.

26 R. W. Seton-Watson, *A History of the Roumanians: From Roman Times to the Completion of Unity* (Cambridge, 1934), pp. 390–4.

27 Romanian Orthodox have shown a mixture of hostility and insecurity when dealing with Catholicism. Alan Scarfe, 'The Romanian Orthodox Church' in Ramet (ed.), *Eastern Christianity and Politics in the Twentieth Century*, pp. 208–31, here pp. 209–15, looks at the historical roots of this phenomenon.

28 Ion Bria, *Romania: Orthodox Identity at a Crossroads of Europe* (Geneva, 1995).

29 Vladimir Seduro, *Dostoevski's Image in Russia Today* (Belmont, MA, 1975).

30 In 1938 Zoe had some 80 members, the majority lay theologians, devoting all their time to teaching and preaching. Most had theological degrees; all were celibate and held their property in common. The brotherhood organized Sunday schools, published popular religious literature and a magazine *Zoe*, and was responsible for catechetical instruction. For a brief biography and account of the work of the founder of Zoe, who died in 1929, see Seraphim Papakosta, *Eusebius Matthopoulos* (London, 1939).

31 See Joachim von Koenigslow, *Ferdinand von Bulgarien* (Munich, 1970), p. 104.

32 Stephen Fischer-Galati, 'Autocracy, Orthodoxy, nationality in the twentieth century: the Romanian case', *East European Quarterly*, 18, no. 1 (March 1984), pp. 25–34.

33 Alexander F. C. Webster, *The Romanian Legionary Movement: An Orthodox Christian Assessment of Anti-Semitism* (Pittsburgh, 1986).

34 See Earl A. Pope, 'Protestantism in Romania' in Sabrina Petra Ramet (ed.), *Protestantism and Politics in Eastern Europe and Russia: The Communist and Post-Communist Eras* (Durham and London, 1992), pp. 157–208.

35 For a survey of attempts at a chronology of periods of Soviet religious persecution see Philip Walters, 'A survey of Soviet religious policy' in Sabrina Petra Ramet (ed.), *Religious Policy in the Soviet Union* (Cambridge, 1993), pp. 3–30.

36 The results of the Soviet census of 1937 were never published, apparently because such a high percentage of the population identified themselves as religious believers. See Felix Corley, 'Believers' responses to the 1937 and 1939 Soviet censuses', *Religion, State and Society: The Keston Journal*, 22, no. 4 (1994), pp. 403–17.

37 See Wassilij Alexeev and Theofanis G. Stavrou, *The Great Revival: The Russian Church under German Occupation* (Minneapolis, MN, 1976).

38 For the history of the Armenian Church since the Second World War see Felix Corley, 'The Armenian church under the Soviet regime, part 1: the leadership of Kevork', *Religion, State and Society: The Keston Journal*, 24, no. 1 (March 1996), pp. 9–53; and 'The Armenian church under the Soviet regime, part 2: the leadership of Vazgen', *Religion, State and Society: The Keston Journal*, 24, no. 4 (December 1996), pp. 289–343.

39 Peter Reddaway, 'The Georgian Orthodox Church: corruption and renewal', *Religion in Communist Lands*, 3, nos 4–5 (1975), pp. 14–23; 'The Georgian Church: a controversy', *Religion in Communist Lands*, 3, no. 6 (1975), pp. 45–54.

40 1988 occasioned wide-ranging disputes on the theme 'whose millennium?' Ukrainians in particular were anxious to correct the impression that the celebrations were primarily those of the Russian Orthodox Church based in Moscow. See Andrew Sorokowski, 'The Millennium: a Ukrainian perspective', *Religion in Communist Lands*, 15, no. 3 (1987), pp. 257–63.

41 Alf Johansen, *Theological Study in the Rumanian Orthodox Church Under Communist Rule* (London, 1961). The Romanian Orthodox Church has a long history of dialogue with the Anglican Church. See Hugh Wybrew, 'Anglican–Romanian Orthodox relations', *Religion in Communist Lands*, 16, no. 4 (1988), pp. 329–44.

42 Paul Mojzes, *Yugoslavian Inferno: Ethnoreligious Warfare in the Balkans* (New York, 1995), p. 18. This book contains important material on the creation of mytho-history and the destructive use of memory by the various nations in the former Yugoslavia. See also Geert van Dartel, 'The nations and the churches in Yugoslavia', *Religion, State and Society: The Keston Journal*, 20, nos 3–4 (1992), pp. 274–88.

43 Hence the title of Jane Ellis's 1996 book *The Russian Orthodox Church: Triumphalism and Defensiveness* (Basingstoke).

9

Latin America[1]

Adrian Hastings

Sixteenth-century Spain

The Christianity of South America was, primarily, a precise transportation of the Catholicism of the Iberian Peninsula in the age of the 'Catholic Kings' – Isabella and Ferdinand, Charles V, Philip II. The American conquests became an adjunct of the Crown of Castile, and it is in Castile that an intelligible history of the Latin American Church must begin.

When Columbus 'discovered' America in 1492, believing it, however, to be just the eastern side of Asia, Spain was entering upon the age of its greatest power and the decisive construction of its image as the standard-bearer of Catholicism. The relatively tolerant 'convivencia' of Christianity, Judaism and Islam which had been a striking characteristic of early medieval Spain was brought to an end. That very year the Jews were expelled from Spain, and Granada, the last Iberian Muslim kingdom, was conquered and annexed to Castile. The enforced conversion of the 'Mudejans' began. The identity of Castile, as also of Portugal, had to a quite considerable extent been forged by the long 'crusading' wars which had little by little re-established Christian rule throughout the peninsula. The spirit of crusade, intolerant, aggressive, insistent upon a uniform political–religious orthodoxy triumphed above all under Isabella. It was her establishment of the Inquisition in Castile in the 1480s (soon extended by Ferdinand to Aragon) which ensured for more than two centuries the stability of her particular form of highly state-controlled Catholicism. Its initial purpose was to pursue secret Jews or Judaizers among the numerous 'conversos', Christians of Jewish blood, but its efficiency and ruthless probing of evidence for unorthodoxy of any kind ensured that Protestantism never made any advance south of the Pyrenees and that religious writers of any tendency could quickly come under suspicion.

The Spain of the sixteenth century remained in consequence, it could be said, a very 'medieval' society, rather little affected by the great movements of thought from the Renaissance on, even though parts of Italy and the Low Countries were included within the realms of Charles V and Philip II. But 'medieval' is in some ways a misnomer: medieval Spain quite lacked the systematic intolerance of sixteenth-century Spain. Moreover the Church of the latter, and its Inquisition, was entirely controlled by the monarchy. The exclusion of papal power was almost absolute. It was, however, in many ways a far more religiously intense society than the Spain of earlier centuries. Under the leadership of the highly intelligent and ascetic Franciscan, Cardinal Ximenez de Cisneros, Archbishop of the primatial see of Toledo, who had earlier been Isabella's confessor, the religious orders were reformed and scholarship encouraged, not least in the University of Alcala, which he himself founded. Perhaps more surprising, the first polyglot Bible of modern times, with parallel texts in Hebrew, Greek and Latin, was produced on his commissioning.

Spain was by far the most powerful state in sixteenth-century Europe. If its power was used both for the extension of the greatest empire the world had seen since the fall of Rome and for the advancement of Catholic Christianity, it was linked with a remarkable revival of theology and philosophy, essentially Thomist, in the University of Salamanca and elsewhere. The development by the Dominican theologian Francisco de Vitoria of a theory of international law, based on the Thomist concept of natural law, has remained lastingly important, while the great spiritual writers of the century, notably John of the Cross, Teresa of Avila and Ignatius Loyola, demonstrate the intense quality of its religious life. Sixteenth-century Spain had an army of missionaries – Dominican, Franciscan and, later, Jesuit – at its disposal unrivalled in any other part of Europe. It had then the religious as well as the military resources to respond with enormous vigour to the chance discovery of a new hemisphere by an Italian adventurer moved, it seems, largely by a millennial belief that the history of the world was soon to end and that his transatlantic voyage was part of a providential scheme for beginning its final age. The extraordinary extent, near universality, of the realms of Charles V and Philip II encouraged a powerful sense that they and their empire were favoured by providence in a unique way and part of that favour was that on them had been bestowed dominion over America, its wealth and its millions of people. On them their conversion to Christianity depended, as Pope Alexander VI, a Spaniard and a rogue if ever there was one on the papal throne, had made clear when in 1493 he granted to the kings of Spain and Portugal both sovereignty and the *patronato* – total responsibility for evangelization of all the new lands their subjects were uncovering.

The first hundred and fifty years of Latin American Catholicism

In 1493 neither the Catholic kings nor the Pope had any clear idea of the vastness or character of the societies west of the Atlantic their expeditions had only just begun to explore and to conquer. At that point it was the 'Antilles', the islands of the Caribbean, they had in their sight. Hispaniola with its capital of Santo Domingo constituted the core of this new empire for the first decade, and a diocese of Santo Domingo was established in 1504; then in 1515 came the conquest of Cuba and the establishment of a new centre of imperialist advance at Havana. Only in 1519 was the mainland attacked with Cortés's conquest of Mexico, which became henceforth 'New Spain'. From there bands of Conquistadores fanned out in every direction until Pizarro invaded Peru in 1532. Within another few years the Spanish Empire of the New World was virtually complete. One 'America' was in ruins, a new one imposed.

That now devastated first 'America' had developed over many centuries, a world until 1492 totally apart from the Afro-Asian-European complex of humanity, since many thousands of years earlier the ancestors of American 'Indians' had, it is presumed, crossed the straits from Asia to Alaska. By 1492 the American Indian world consisted socially of three very different groups. There were the two highly centralized states, organized by the Mexicas (Aztecs) in Mexico around their capital, Tenochtitlán, and by the Incas in Tawantinsuyu (Peru) around their capital, Cuzco. These two extraordinarily interesting kingdoms had existed for only a few centuries or less and were still rapidly developing at the time of the Spanish invasion, but they drew upon earlier civilizations both Mesoamerican and Andean, of which the Mayan, extending in central America through Guatemala, Yucatan and central Mexico, was the most important. This too had been in part an urban society. It and many others continued, politically fragmented, within and around the Aztec and Inca kingdoms. Beyond these were a much more geographically extensive range of peoples, far less politically or technically advanced. They included the population of the Caribbean and most of the peoples of South America, broken up into hundreds of language groups and seemingly devoid of any type of statehood. They were hunters, gatherers and fishers. Their European observers commented upon their innocence, gentleness and docility and later upon their uselessness as labourers in mine or plantation.

Undoubtedly it was the Aztecs and the Incas who fascinated and horrified the incoming Spaniards. They possessed wealth in gold and silver, towns of amazing splendour filled with palaces and temples and a highly organized social system, at once religious, agricultural and military.

Their languages – the Nahuatl of the Aztecs and the Quechua of the Incas – were administrative media, lingua francas, imposed for public use on many other tongues, and Nahuatl, as well as Maya, had developed a written form. Religion included many gods, some of them the tutelary deities of peoples now absorbed into a single empire. At Tenochtitlán these were kept in a special temple, the 'common house of the gods'. Among the most important Mexican deities was Tonantzin, a great mother goddess, but the dominant worship both of the Aztecs and the Incas was that of the Sun. They were the 'People of the Sun' and among each the Sun had to be placated by continuous human sacrifice. A primary purpose of war, especially in Mexico, was to obtain new victims for the sacrificial rites to the Sun, Huitzilopochtli, which were central to the life of society. Linked with Sun-worship went an intense preoccupation with the calendar, characteristic already of earlier Maya civilizations. The precision of their calendars, based on the work of priests in the royal observatories, and the span of years they incorporate remain one of the most striking aspects of this whole group of societies. Both Aztec and Inca empires were highly ordered worlds, with moral laws strictly enforced, no alcoholism, common property and systems of collective organization and ritual behaviour which both amazed and horrified their highly individualistic invaders.

The Spanish impact proved incredibly disastrous, as was already clear in the first twenty years before the mainland was assaulted. The papal bull of 1493 established the character of the invasion as one of evangelization. It was that which justified it. In royal eyes this was never merely a specious excuse. On the contrary, it was taken extremely seriously, at times agonizingly so. The motivation and behaviour of the Conquistadores themselves was something very different. Here was a gang of adventurers, mostly men quite insignificant at home, risking their lives in pursuit of gold. Yet there was precious little gold to be found in the Antilles. The growing population of settlers needed native labour if they were going to achieve anything at all and, though Isabella had forbidden the enslavement of her pagan subjects, the Indians were conscripted into one or another *encomienda*, granted to a Conquistador, whereby they were compelled to work for him in the mines or the fields, while the women were seized as concubines. Far from becoming an efficient labour force, however, they simply faded away under the impact of brutal treatment, extreme social disorientation and a wave of European-imported illnesses. When Columbus first arrived, Hispaniola was claimed to be a well-populated island. There was soon next to no native left there or anywhere else in the Caribbean. Seldom has genocide, actually in no way intended, been so rapid or so complete. On the Sunday before Christmas 1511, Antonio de Montesinos, one of the first Dominican party who had arrived in Hispaniola the year before, denounced the settlers from the pulpit of the cathedral of Santo Domingo for their ill-treatment of the Indians: 'Are they not men? . . . You are all in a state of mortal sin . . . because of the cruelty and the tyranny you are inflicting on these innocent victims.'[2] It was the beginning of a long campaign which infuriated the Conquistadores, the governor included, but which the Spanish government, with its devout commitment to evangelization, could not ignore. Yet effectively there was little it could do. The whole enterprise had developed an irreversible momentum which required native labour as much as it destroyed it. The very collapse of the aboriginal population in every place that was occupied forced the Conquistadores to advance into new territories in pursuit of labour as much as gold, while beginning the importation of black slaves from Africa to replace the natives they were wiping out.

In 1519 the focus of the process was transferred from the islands to the mainland where a great deal more gold could be found. Pedrarias Davila, one of the most brutal of all the Conquistadores, founded the city of Panama, while Hernán Cortés invaded Mexico from Cuba. A few hundred men overthrew a magnificent civilization after marvelling at the splendour of Tenochtitlán. How could it happen? It was not so much a matter of a handful of muskets and sixteen horses. The Aztecs were psychologically far more unprepared than the Spaniards for this strange encounter. Montezuma, their king, actually welcomed Cortés as the legendary figure of Quetzalcoatl returned from the east to reclaim the land. Montezuma was seized, the Aztec nobility massacred and, though for a few months the Spaniards were forced to abandon Tenochtitlán, they recaptured it in ruins in August 1521. By then the Aztecs had been ravaged not only by fighting but, still more, by smallpox. Moreover in Mexico as, later, in Peru, the war was not really one between a huge Indian army and a tiny Spanish one, because the Spaniards had persuaded many peoples unwillingly subject to the Aztecs to rise in revolt against them. The very centralization of both Aztec and Inca realms contributed to their quick collapse. The decentralized Maya or the Araucanian Indians in southern Chile proved more effectively resistant, but where there was less evidence of gold or silver the conquering impulse was less sustained.

As the military advance continued, followed by the forcing of Indians into the shackles of the *encomienda* system, two decisive developments resulted. On the one hand was the collapse of the indigenous population, on the other the growth of a network of Spanish towns inhabited, by the middle of the sixteenth century, by a largely creole population (that is to say, people of Spanish blood but born in America) supplemented by a mestizo population of mixed blood. Almost everywhere the Indian population rapidly and steadily declined. Disagreement over probable figures remains considerable, nevertheless it seems most likely that the Indian population of Spanish-ruled America by the late sixteenth century was less than a quarter of what it had been a hundred years earlier, and it continued to be reduced by the enforced labour which became all the worse as total numbers declined. There were major plagues, as in 1575–77, and a general disintegration of society and its moral norms reflected most obviously in the spread of alcoholism.

Meanwhile, a new institutional and ecclesiastical world had come into existence, entirely dependent upon the authority of the crown of Castile, and the Council of the Indies in Madrid, but controlled locally by the two viceroys – of New Spain and Peru. Beneath them were various provincial governors and the nine *audiencias* based in Santo Domingo, Mexico City, Panama, Quito, Lima and elsewhere. But beneath them too by the early seventeenth century were five archbishops, 27 bishops, two universities, over four hundred priories and colleges of religious orders, not to speak of countless parishes. By 1620 there were 36 bishoprics in Spanish America and no further one was created until near the end of the eighteenth century. What did continue to grow was the number of 'universities' or (in many cases) effectively seminaries, opened by the religious orders or the episcopate to cope with the training of the growing number of creole priests. But what needs here to be made clear is that the Church's organization, quite as much as that of the colonial state, depended wholly and solely upon Madrid. At no point did Rome enter into any appointment. Even more than the Church of Spain itself this was a Catholic Church from which, organizationally though not doctrinally, the papacy was wholly excluded. The paradoxical character of the *patronato* was that it both excluded papal intervention and established royal authority over the Church in strictly papalist terms. Moreover the system by no means excluded acceptance of new developments elsewhere in the Catholic Church, especially in regard to the Council of Trent, to which the Spanish contribution had in fact been very considerable. The Latin American Church became, ideologically, emphatically Tridentine. Yet in administrative terms there was but one exception to the totality of royal control. That exception was the Society of Jesus. The Jesuits, as we shall see, became immensely powerful in Latin America but here as everywhere they remained faithful to the central principle of their society, which was one of absolute obedience to the General resident in Rome, who was himself obedient to the Pope. In New Spain as in Old Spain the Jesuits maintained their basic freedom at once from royal control, from episcopal supervision and from the jurisdiction of the Inquisition, this despite a good deal of pressure from Philip II upon the papacy.

Vast indeed must the growth of the Church have appeared in the century and a half following Columbus's first expedition. How providential it all could appear. Even the fact that Cortés invaded Mexico in 1519 just when Martin Luther was disrupting the Church in Europe could be and was interpreted as a supreme expression of providence. God had called the New World into existence to put right the mishaps of the Old. Certainly Philip II could never have carried on his European wars without the support of the American treasure fleet. If God had held back any knowledge of this vast world from Christians until now and then bestowed it entire upon the Catholic kings, this demonstrated almost incontrovertibly the entirely special role that Spain was called upon to play in sacred and human history. The development of the history of Christianity in Latin America was shaped, in consequence, not just by Catholicism, of a mixed medieval and Counter-Reformation sort, not just by its being part of a large colonial empire, but by a very special sort of sacred imperialism, a conviction of the hand of providence, of manifest destiny, which is foundational to the thinking of almost everyone upon the Spanish side and which would not begin to be shattered until, eventually, the Spanish Empire itself was shattered not only politically but intellectually by the emergence instead at the heart of the Western world of power systems inherently opposed to it.

When the various orders of friars, most notably Franciscans and Dominicans, began work in the Americas, it was to convert to Christianity the Indian societies which inhabited them. It is striking that the Catholic kings saw no point in dispatching across the Atlantic any of the more contemplative orders. No primarily monastic tradition took root in Spanish America. The friars came above all as missionaries if with a somewhat simplistic conception of what missionary work must entail. In Mexico at least, where the first twelve Franciscans arrived in 1524, they believed they had found very willing converts. Brutal as Cortés had been in conquest, he more than any other of the Conquistadores was anxious that society should continue to function in a stable way, even if the people were to be compulsorily resettled in villages, each laid out around a church and a prison. It was the religious orders who could supervise his new society and that was what the Franciscans of the strict observance, bristling with the devout enthusiasms that Cardinal Cisneros had inculcated, were anxious to do. Here already a model of separation between Indian and Spaniard informed the missionary plan.

What is more remarkable is the enthusiasm Mexicans at first showed for their new faith. The unity of belief and government in Aztec Mexico had been so absolute that the one collapsed with the other, and if the King of Spain had replaced Montezuma then Catholicism must replace the religion of the Sun. Baptisms took place by the thousand. Mexicans participated in the liturgy with vast enthusiasm, begged to be allowed to build churches and flogged one another remorselessly in the penitential processions of Good Friday. They were quick to learn Spanish and many of the crafts and arts the missionaries taught them, while the latter studied Nahuatl and other Indian languages. Cortés rounded up over a thousand children of the Indian nobility and handed them over to the Franciscans for special education which would, he hoped, lead many of them to the priesthood. The first Archbishop of Mexico, Juan de Zumárraga, himself a Franciscan, composed the first catechism, as well as overseeing the destruction of hundreds of pagan temples and tens of thousands of 'idols', but the man who best expressed the excitement of these early years of Mexican Christianity was Toribio de Benavente, one of the first twelve Franciscans to arrive, who is better known by his Nahuatl name of *Motolinia* – 'the poor one'. He and his brethren stressed the diabolical character of Aztec rule as shown by the unceasing round of human sacrifice and cannibalism, but this provided the backdrop for their interpretation of what had happened as the passing of a new Israel from the idolatry of Egypt into the promised land of the Church. At the same time they studied Indian history, were fascinated particularly by the Mexican calendar and became fluent in Nahuatl.

While Motolinia recognized how cruelly the Indians were treated by the Spaniards and that they had greatly declined in numbers, the central theme of his *Historia de los indios de la Nueva España* (1541) was one of deliverance from darkness into a near millennial light. If the Conquistadores had made it possible for all these people to become Christians and subjects of the King of Spain, they should not be too harshly judged. The Franciscans were optimists. Bishop Zumárraga's College of Santa Cruz at Tlatelolco was intended to produce an Indian clergy who were taught Latin, theology and philosophy, but none was ever ordained as it became clear how unsuitable celibacy was for Indians. The college continued nevertheless for many years educating men who became assistants of the friars in the creation of a Nahuatl Christian literature. The greatest Franciscan scholar of Nahuatl, Bernardino de Sahagún, taught there and his disciples helped him in his researches into Indian culture. A graduate of Salamanca, Sahagún little by little constructed an amazingly valuable account of Indian history and culture, almost an encyclopaedia. The *Historia general de las cosas de Nueva España* was actually written first in Nahuatl, the Spanish version being a translation. It was completed in the 1570s but, tragically, never printed until the nineteenth century. Coming a generation later than Motolinia, and entering into Indian realities with exceptional sympathy, Sahagún was deeply pessimistic about the whole missionary and colonial enterprise. The Indian population had vastly declined and, as the creole population grew, they became ever more marginal in their own land. Even the nobility whose position was recognized in part by Cortés lost its role of leadership as Indian land was alienated and the population relocated by force away from their own villages. It was clearer than ever that only the friars, in their paternalistic way, remained to protect Indian society from becoming no more than an underclass of serfs.

In Peru the picture had always been more sombre. There no early wave of Indian Christian enthusiasm had ever been reported and, on the contrary, it was claimed that Indians were so far from having become genuinely Christians at all that the Council of Lima in 1552 forbade their admission to communion. The reason for this may well have lain in the survival for some decades of an independent Inca state. Pizarro murdered the Inca Atahualpa and captured Cuzco in 1533, but at first made use of Atahualpa's half-brothers Manco Inca and Paullu as intermediaries between the Indian and Spanish power. In this he seemed to be imitating Cortés in Mexico, but the fact that he located the Spanish capital of Peru on the coast at Lima allowed the Inca symbolic tradition to survive at Cuzco in a way that was not possible in Mexico where Tenochtitlán at once disappeared beneath Mexico City. Moreover, Manco soon rose in rebellion and, while failing to recapture Cuzco, established a 'neo-Inca' state in the mountains of Vilcabamba which included the sacred sanctuary of Machu Picchu. The Spaniards, Manco declared, had proved themselves by their deeds to be not sons of God but of the devil. While one of Manco's sons, Sayri Tupac, later surrendered to the Spaniards and was rewarded with a rich estate, another, Titu Cusi, continued the resistance. In consequence, there was no political reason for the people of Peru to abandon their gods wholesale as had happened in Mexico. It was only in 1572 that a ruthlessly determined new viceroy, Francisco de Toledo, overthrew the state of Vilcabamba and ordered the beheading of its captured Inca, Tupac Amaru, in the public square of Cuzco in the presence of an appalled multitude, and despite the protests of the ecclesiastical authorities.

There is a fine early seventeenth-century painting by an unknown Cuzqueno artist depicting the marriage of Martin Garcia de Loyola, the nephew of St Ignatius Loyola, with Beatriz Ñusta, the daughter of Sayri Tupac. Yet Loyola was the commander of the expedition which had defeated and seized Tupac Amaru, his wife's uncle. Twenty years later, in 1598, Loyola himself was captured by the Araucanian Indians and his head paraded on an Indian spear. Few Spanish–Indian unions had been celebrated with the solemnity of Loyola's. For the most part they were cohabitations rather than marriages and their offspring were in consequence canonically excluded from ordination to the priesthood. In the hope of developing an Indian priesthood and one at home in Indian languages, Gregory XIV explicitly permitted the ordination of mestizos and illegitimate sons in 1576, but this hardly began to happen on any considerable scale for another two hundred years.

To Don Martin de Loyola and the Princess Beatriz we might add five other figures to represent the Catholicism of Peru as it was developing towards and beyond the close of the sixteenth century. The first was a Dominican, Domingo de Santo Tomás, who had arrived there in 1540. A theologian and linguist, he published the first grammar of the Quechua language (1560) and became an ardent campaigner for the civic rights of the Indians, returning to Spain for six years as their delegate to argue their case. The second, Toribio de Mogrovejo, was appointed Archbishop of Lima by Philip II in 1580. He had previously worked in the Inquisition in Granada. A man of enormous energy, between 1580 and his death in 1606 he carried out a systematic reorganization of the Peruvian Church, including holding the first ten Lima diocesan synods and three Peruvian provincial councils. His *Catecismo Mayor* was published at Lima in 1584 in Spanish, Quechua and Aymara. Here was the very model of a Tridentine bishop, firm both in his pastoral strategy and even in standing up to the political authorities when he judged it necessary. It was a strategy which increasingly insisted on the extirpation of idols.

Our third figure is St Rose of Lima (1586–1617), the first canonized saint of the New World. She was a creole, her parents Spanish settlers who had speculated in the mines, but unsuccessfully. She joined the Third Order of St Dominic, lived in a hut in the garden and practised the most severe physical penance. There is nothing about her that seems specifically American. She represents the export of a certain type of Iberian spirituality. The fact that she existed and was canonized testifies to the way a creole Church was stabilizing itself, beside and above the Indian Church.

Our fourth choice is another saint, Martin de Porres (1579–1639). He too lived in Lima, the exact contemporary of St Rose. While she was canonized in 1671, being white, he had to wait until 1962, being black. His father admittedly was a Spaniard but his mother was a negro and he was illegitimate. The rules of the Peruvian Dominican Province did not permit them to accept blacks or mulattos even as lay brothers, but Martin was allowed to be a voluntary servant, wear a religious habit and look after the infirmary attached to the priory of Our Lady of the Rosary. He became the very model of a medieval saint. His boundless charity brought crowds of Indians and blacks to seek help. He spent his nights in prayer and penance. Even animals did as he told them. Even Dominicans did, coming for spiritual direction to one who humbly described himself as 'mulatto dog'. The Viceroy of Peru attended the funerals of both Rose and Martin, and the popular cult of both was enduring, but it remains striking that the institutional Church canonized the one so fast and held back on the other so long.

Our final figure is by far the least predictable. Some time around 1614 an extraordinary document consisting of 1,190 folio pages and 496 illustrations was sent from Lima to Spain, where it disappeared, to be discovered in the royal library in Copenhagen in 1895. Its author, Guaman Poma de Ayala, was a very elderly Indian, a scion of the provincial nobility, who knew Spanish of a sort, but interlarded it with Quechua and even the odd phrase of Aymara. His enormous testament was written as a protest to the viceroy at the vast injustices in Spanish rule, but included a whole history of Peru and its customs, inserted within a biblical chronology. Guaman Poma's account of traditional Peru was of a thoroughly moral society: 'How the Indians of old were Christian: although they were pagans, they observed God's commandments and the good works of compassion.' Today, in contrast, 'the poor of Jesus Christ' are persecuted by priests and rulers of every sort, 'at times it is a matter for tears, and at times for laughter and at times for pity'. In Peru, he concluded, 'there is no God or king: they are in Rome and Castile'.[3] This extraordinary book, the disordered yet highly detailed outpourings of an old man, otherwise totally unknown, the work itself saved for us today by sheer chance, must all the same represent the sort of Christian vision which numerous other Indians had acquired by the early seventeenth century. It included an absolute refusal to blacken the Indian past in the way almost all Spaniards endeavoured to do, but it fused that past with the major elements of biblical history and Christian belief, as mediated through the pastoral ministry of a Church led by men like Archbishop de Mogrovejo. Yet the voice of Guaman Poma is not only that of people of his own generation but, one may judge, countless voiceless Indian Christians across the next three centuries too.

Guaman Poma praised Jesuits and Franciscans but spoke harshly of Dominicans, Augustinians and Mercedarians for their pride and ill-treatment of Indians. In other circumstances the praise and blame would be differently divided. What is clear is that there was no one clerical attitude to all the issues troubling the Spanish Empire. Many, probably most, priests were highly supportive of the imperial endeavour in almost all its ramifications. The critics, however, few as they may have been, have proved the more memorable, but no one comparably to Bartolomé de Las Casas. It is more than time that we turn to consider him and his work, controversial as they were both in his own time and almost ever since. Las Casas remains the supreme figure of the religious history of Spanish America. Let us start with a succinct curriculum vitae. He was born in Seville in 1484; his father and uncle were in Columbus's second expedition and he himself crossed the Atlantic at the age of eighteen in 1502. In the following years he lived as a settler but was ordained as a secular priest – the first priest to say his first Mass in America. He joined in the expedition that conquered Cuba and obtained an *encomienda* there – the grant of a number of Indians compelled henceforth to give him labour service. He set them to work in the mines. In 1514, under Dominican influence, he broke with the system, freed his Indians and returned to Spain the next year. He was then 31 and he would henceforth campaign unceasingly in defence of Indian rights until his death 51 years later. In 1524 he joined the Dominican order and in 1543 rather unwillingly agreed to be the Bishop of Chiapas, a poor diocese in the south of Mexico.

It is important that one remembers how deep his own experience had been in his twelve years as a settler in Hispaniola and Cuba. He knew very well what he was talking about when he thundered against the crimes perpetrated in the name of Spain and Christianity. From his 1516 *Memorial de remedios* through his missionary treatise *Del único modo de atraer a todos los pueblos a la verdadera religión* written in Mexico about 1540, and his particularly vehement *Brevísima relación de la destrucción de las Indias* of 1542, to his massive *Historia de las Indias* and *Apologética Historia Sumaria* composed in the 1550s during his final years of struggle in Spain, Las Casas built up a coherent, yet steadily developing, indictment of the entire colonial enterprise. Almost monotonously violent as his denunciations can seem, that reflects only too well the monotonous violence of the Conquistadores as they devastated one society after another.

Las Casas was not an effective missionary or Church administrator and his brief periods in those roles were not a success: they could not be. The situation on the ground was far too unfavourable and he was someone unable to hold his tongue. Yet even in narrowly missionary terms, his critique of contemporary methods of conversion, particularly the mass baptisms by Franciscans in Mexico, is impressive. His role, however, was not that of a practitioner but of a prophet, and it was exercised most forcefully in Spain where he spent most of his later years. That was the right place to be because only the Crown could do something to control the colonizers. However, even the Crown could do relatively little, in a situation where news travelled slowly and royal decrees were hard to enforce against recalcitrant Conquistadores on the ground – particularly when the Crown remained dependent in the last resort on those same Conquistadores to ensure its annual supply of gold and silver. While the 'New Laws' of 1542, intended to end the worst abuses by ordering the immediate emancipation of all Indian slaves and a vigorous reform of the *encomienda* system, were seen as due to the influence of Las Casas, they produced a hugely hostile reaction throughout the Americas and open revolt in Peru. If then and later Las Casas did actually succeed in modifying both royal policy and, to an extent, the actual situation on the ground, it was due not only to his own fierce insistence and power of arguing but also to the support he received from many other churchmen in America as well as from Dominican theologians at the University of Salamanca. Francisco de Vitoria's famous lecture at Salamanca in 1539,

Relectio de Indis, was an application of his Thomist philosophy to the problems of the Indies. He provided the academic grounding in terms both of an evaluation of Indian culture and of the principles of a just war, for the more impassioned writings of Las Casas.

Las Casas, whether he was conscious of it or not, was always faced with a dilemma. The more he challenged almost everything the Spanish had done in the New World, other than the preaching of Christianity, and the more he lauded the political and cultural institutions of pre-Spanish America, the harder it was to justify the conquest or the authority of the Crown of Castile in any terms whatsoever. And yet, if he questioned the latter, his whole case must in practical terms fall to the ground. The only hope of reform was to strengthen not only the moral purpose but also the power of the Crown in regard to America. While Vitoria, more concerned with what was becoming a coherent philosophy of international law, simply denied the papal power to donate the 'undiscovered' world to Spain or Portugal, Las Casas based his justification of Spanish royal authority precisely on the papal donation but limited it, in consequence, to a sort of religious overlordship. There was absolutely no authority for armed invasion or for overthrowing Indian rulers, who had every natural right to resist. The claim put forward by so many churchmen that the cruelty of Aztec religion with its multiple human sacrifice was so diabolical as to justify outside intervention cut no ice with Las Casas. On the contrary, he audaciously justified human sacrifice as a very natural expression of the duty of humankind to offer to God the highest gift available. It is clear that Las Casas knew a very great deal about the Americas – even parts he had never visited. His fellow Dominican, Domingo de Santo Tomás, was probably responsible for providing him with much of his detailed Peruvian information. His *Historia de las Indias* was written precisely to describe and defend Indian culture, Indian history, Indian worth, above all Indian rationality. Throughout these years we see development within both his position and his arguments. This is hardly surprising given the fact that he began not at all as an academic but as a young lay colonial, drawn into the enterprise by his father with little thought as to what it involved. Thus it is noteworthy that in the early stages of his campaign Las Casas argued pragmatically in favour of the importation of black slaves to do the work and relieve the burden on the Indians, and he has often been condemned for saying so. What is less often pointed out is that the mature Las Casas profoundly rejected this proposal, denouncing the African slave trade with considerable vigour.

He was, of course, in consequence both of his uninhibited denunciation of colonial brutality and of his actual influence on royal policy, a very unpopular man, accused of maligning the Conquistadores and blackening the good name of Spain. This continued after his death due to the translation into other languages of his *Brevísima relación* which was published in Dutch in 1578 and then in French, English, German and Latin, illustrated by numerous engravings of Spanish atrocities. It may well be said that the entire subsequent literary tradition of Latin America in regard to its sixteenth-century construction has been formed around Las Casas – the appropriation of his central judgements upon the one hand, an attempted belittlement upon the other. He remains one of the supreme religious figures of the sixteenth century and perhaps the most important missionary intellectual of the post-medieval period.

Las Casas died in 1566. Tupac Amaru was executed in the central square of Cuzco six years later. The Church which was being shaped in the next 50 years by men like Archbishop de Mogrovejo in lands now firmly and irrevocably controlled by Spain no longer thought of itself as just, or even primarily, a mission to Indian societies. It was a Spanish Church glorying in the very Spanish holiness of a Rose of Lima, but it was still a Church trying hard, especially through the work of the Franciscans, Dominicans and Jesuits, to maintain within it a Quechua, Aymara or Nahuatl Christianity. In some ways it succeeded in doing so, as one can surmise through a study of Guaman Poma's amazing pages. Despite the execution of Tupac Amaru, Cuzco and the mountains of Peru did retain a specifically Inca historical identity, an identity which coalesced with a newer Christian one. In the celebrations for the beatification of Ignatius Loyola in 1610, the figures of eleven Inca monarchs were carried in procession and the walls of the Jesuit College in Cuzco came to be adorned with their portraits.

It was, however, not Cuzco, with its surviving assertion of Inca self-awareness, but Lima which was determinative of the character of the Church. When Archbishop de Mogrovejo called together the third Peruvian Provincial Church Council in 1581, he appointed as its chief theologian a distinguished Jesuit named José de Acosta, who had been in Lima for the last ten years, where he had lectured in the university and served as Jesuit Provincial Superior. Acosta is an important figure, in many ways the antithesis of Las Casas, and his intellectual influence was almost as great due to the publication of his highly impressive *Historia natural y moral de las Indias* in 1590, a work quickly translated into all the main languages of Europe. Acosta, despite huge knowledge of the New World, especially its natural history and material conditions, took a far more pessimistic view of Indian society than did Las Casas. The devil was once more in the middle of the picture. Moreover, unlike Las Casas, he had no time for the claim that the Pope could grant jurisdiction over infidel kingdoms to anyone at all. For him the establishment of Spanish rule was essentially a matter of brute force – on an Augustinian perspective every kingdom was achieved by violence, the Spanish no more and no

less than the Inca or the Aztec. The point for him was that by the 1580s
it was all a *fait accompli*. The Spaniards ruled the New World, and it was
simply within that context that one had now to think, building up the
Church kindly but firmly. He had little criticism to offer of current
government policy, believed it would be a mistake to ordain Indians to
the priesthood, but would support their admission to the Eucharist. For
Acosta the Spanish Conquest was unquestionably a providential development, assisted even supernaturally. The 1581 Provincial Council had
pronounced that all who dwelt in Peru prior to the Spanish Conquest
were children of Satan and sentenced to eternal damnation. Acosta had
himself been active in securing the condemnation of a Dominican,
Francisco de la Cruz, who had taught just the opposite. If Las Casas may
be judged the winner in the long-term intellectual debate, Acosta almost
certainly won the immediate battle in terms of ecclesiastical life. Indian
Christianity would survive, despite regular hammering for its retention of
'idols', but the Church as institution would remain for centuries faithful
to the spirit of the 1581 Provincial Council.

'Idols' might, however, survive, if transmogrified into a sufficiently
Christian form. Nowhere was this more striking than in what became the
most famous shrine of the New World, that of Our Lady of Guadalupe
outside Mexico City. There had been a temple of Tonantzin, 'Mother of
the Gods', at Tepeyac, where according to the Guadalupe tradition a poor
Indian named Juan Diego saw a vision of the Virgin Mary on 9 December
1531 asking him to have a chapel built in Tepeyac in her honour. 9
December is, of course, the day after the feast of the Immaculate
Conception. 1531 was barely ten years after the Spanish Conquest. Bishop
de Zumárraga at first rebuffed Diego but at the fourth apparition the
Virgin instructed him to pick the flowers growing unseasonably on the
hill at Tepeyac, fill his cactus fibre mantle with them and go thus to the
bishop. When he opened his cape and the flowers fell out, a miraculous
likeness of the Virgin was found imprinted upon it. The bishop was
convinced and the chapel was built.

The Guadalupe story is extremely intriguing, not least because so little
was made of it for over a hundred years. Did it ever happen, or was it a
seventeenth-century invention? Only in 1648 did a remarkable book
about it, written by a priest named Miguel Sanchez, suddenly make the
Tepeyac image of Mary something which everyone knew about. Everywhere chapels were dedicated to Our Lady of Guadalupe, at Tepeyac a
pilgrim highway to the sanctuary was constructed and then a large new
basilica. Archbishops, nuns and canons vied with one another to do
honour to the Virgin of Guadalupe until, in 1746, delegates of all the
dioceses of Mexico united to proclaim her their universal patron.

The image of Our Lady of Guadalupe is that of a young girl, without a child, standing on the moon and in many ways reminiscent of the woman described in chapter 12 of the Apocalypse. She seems to typify the concept of the Immaculate Conception, a devotion which developed more in seventeenth- than sixteenth-century Spain. Yet it seems that a shrine was already in existence at Tepeyac in 1554 and that the Nahuatl text of the story may have been composed by Antonio Valeriano, leading representative of the early College of Santa Cruz, Tlatelolco. It is decidedly odd that the name of Guadalupe (that of an old Marian shrine in Spain) should have been given to one in Mexico where the image (unlike almost every other such icon) was never claimed to have come from Spain, from the brush of St Luke, or wherever. Its claim from the start was to be Indian, imprinted on the cloak of the poorest of the poor. Its very Indianness and the obvious link with the local cult of Tonantzin could have made the Franciscans for long quite opposed to its acceptance. Here, it could well be argued, was only too clear a case of an old idol reappearing in Christian form, something which did not accord at all with Franciscan theology, though it might fit with a Las Casas view that grace perfected rather than replaced the works of nature. In the sixteenth century Our Lady at Tepeyac would have been too Indian for Spanish creoles to identify with. A hundred years later they had no such problem. It had become their very own, Spanish-named, Guadalupe. It was the canon professors at the cathedral and university who became its most enthusiastic supporters. Guadalupe/Tepeyac represented God's predilection for New Spain over Old Spain or anywhere else because, it could be claimed, unlike every other image, this one came directly from the Virgin. Yet it was pointed out as well that Mexican Indians had pictures rather than script, so it was culturally correct that the Virgin should bring no message but a picture of herself, should give it to someone as poor as Juan Diego and should place it on the absolutely Indian material of a piece of cactus cloth. Thus could Indian and creole Christians be united in veneration of Our Lady of Guadalupe, if often in very little else.

1650–1780

Latin American Catholicism had, by the mid-seventeenth century, acquired its enduring form, a form dominated by creoles, although they still had to accept that most bishops came to them from Spain, as did governors and viceroys, and that the orders still saw it as their special role to protect and supervise the Indians. What had vastly diminished was the effective power of the monarchy together with the intellectual and spiritual strength of the Spanish Church. Spain at home was exhausted, worn down by wars, policy mistakes and inadequate kings. The vitality of

Catholicism, to be found in sixteenth-century Europe pre-eminently in Spain, was now located in France and elsewhere, countries cut off from influencing Latin America. The creoles on their side had multiplied, beautified their towns and churches, distanced themselves psychologically from the *peninsulares* (new arrivals from Spain) and poured especially into the secular clergy – an attractive occupation when there was not so much else to do. No fewer than 1,325 secular priests and 1,080 religious processed through Mexico City at the exequies held for Philip IV in 1665. The overwhelming majority of the former were creoles. It was to educate them that the religious orders kept opening new 'universities' and colleges. The splendour of the baroque churches of seventeenth-century Mexico and Peru testifies to a religious culture anxious to outdo that of its mother country, yet still essentially dependent upon it.

The Council of Trent had stressed that parishes should have parish priests, preferably from the secular clergy, fully subordinate to the diocesan bishop. Religious orders disliked being subject to local bishops. In early America while the secular clergy had staffed the inner town parishes intended for creoles, most of each diocese was divided into *doctrinas*, far larger areas which were devoted to the Indian apostolate. Each was entrusted to a priory or Jesuit house where no individual was specifically named as parish priest. The religious, most of whom came from Europe, regularly preached and taught in one or another Indian language. As the number of creole secular clergy increased, the bishops took over the less remote *doctrinas* and broke them up into parishes, thus apparently implementing Tridentine regulations and strengthening their own diocesan control. One result could be the replacement of the Indian language by Spanish, for few creoles bothered to learn the former. The ecclesiastical marginalization of Indians was further enhanced. When the Indians of the pueblo of Zapotlán in western Mexico complained in 1799 that their priest would only bury non-Indian newcomers in the churchyard of their own village, and that, moreover, the church bells were 'not rung for any Indian',[4] they were protesting about a basic lack of shared identity between priest and people. Nevertheless, as lower-class creole and mestizo diocesan priests multiplied, they too could become part of Indian society and almost more completely than any religious, because many were poorer and more on their own. The two outstanding leaders of the Mexican peasant rising of 1810–15, Miguel Hidalgo and José Maria Morelos, were both priests, Hidalgo a creole, Morelos a mestizo and former mule driver.

The orders of friars were caught in the middle of what was ostensibly more a struggle between creoles and *peninsulares* than between creoles and Indians. There were many hundreds of Franciscan, Dominican and Augustinian creoles who felt that the control of their orders remained in the hands of newly arrived Spaniards. Eventually the *alternativa* had to be adopted, a rule whereby every position of importance alternated between creoles and *peninsulares*. While this arrangement betokened a loss of missionary fervour as the orders settled down into the inward-looking preoccupations of a colonial world only moderately prosperous, tied to medieval structures and deprived of any final political control of its own affairs, which remained in the hands of Madrid and of viceroys coming from Madrid, that loss should not be overstated nor located too early. The Franciscans enjoyed a remarkable revival of missionary fervour in the early eighteenth century, noticeable particularly in Texas but present in many parts of the Spanish Empire. That was mostly, but not wholly, a movement of *peninsulares*.

The religious control of *doctrinas* in areas more remote from creole settlement remained unchallenged. And that was where the Jesuits had concentrated their missionary endeavour. Their work was divided between running colleges in the towns and remote missions on the frontiers where a Christian Indian society could be built up without Spanish, creole, or even episcopal interference. Separation had always been the missionary ideal ever since the time of Motolinia and Las Casas: Indian life could only be preserved and Indians Christianized effectively if shielded from the destructive impact of colonialism. There was in principle little difference between the strategy of the Jesuits and that of the orders of friars. The Jesuits were simply more ruthlessly consistent in carrying it out. While the friars were part and parcel of normal society, subject to pressures from the Crown, the tensions between creoles and *peninsulares* and much else, the Jesuits never faltered in the absoluteness of their centralized control and never hesitated to expel members who in any way failed to perform satisfactorily. Their international character probably increased as time went on, including Germans, Italians and Flemings as well as Spaniards from Europe. This did not at all mean that their ranks did not include creoles, for they had a great many, including the cream of well-educated colonial society. It did mean that as an institution they remained apart, frequently in tension with the bishops as well as with the state, not least because of their considerable wealth – their agricultural estates far exceeded those of any other order. It was wealth, they claimed, needed for the maintenance of their many colleges.

The Jesuits are remembered, nevertheless, mostly for their frontier missions, above all in Paraguay. The latter was only one of many important areas in which they were at work – Lower California, Mainas (east of Quito), much of northern Amazonia (in Portuguese territory) as well as the most extensive area of all, Paraguay. While their methods were everywhere much the same – and not so different from those of the Franciscans – the degree of success greatly varied, depending on their ability both to get the Indian population to adopt a sedentary village life and to hold at bay the intrusion of slave traders and royal administrators. East of Quito they largely failed. In Paraguay among the Guaranis they succeeded in what became one of the most remarkable of missionary enterprises.

It began in 1603. Little by little bands of Jesuits advanced unarmed and alone into the forest areas, often entering a village in procession carrying aloft cross and painted boards.[5] Here the sort of entirely pacific conversion championed by Las Casas was shown to be possible and, with time, extremely successful. The Crown forbade any other Spaniards to enter the area but Portuguese slave raiders from São Paulo began to do so, devastating the mission villages. The Jesuits then obtained permission from Madrid to arm their converts and built up a well-disciplined militia able to provide adequate protection. By the eighteenth century the missions of Paraguay included over a hundred thousand people, living contentedly in villages whose ordered life was a combination of agricultural work, crafts of many sorts and a complex liturgical cycle including a great deal of music. In comparison with the fate of Indians elsewhere, the *Reductions* of Paraguay represented something not far off paradise. But it remained a captive Christianity in which the leadership was provided by the most dedicated of outsiders. Here, as everywhere else, the failure of the mission lay in the lack of any local clergy, a lack rendered almost inevitable by the law of celibacy and the insistence upon a knowledge of Latin. In Paraguay as in Mexico or Peru, the Indian Church would have become far less vulnerable if it had had as local ministers its own Indian priests, but very few even mestizos were ordained before the eighteenth century. While Indians could be catechists in most of the missions and play an active role in the semi-independent religious life of confraternities in the cities – no fewer than 82 separate Indian confraternities took part in the Mexico City procession at Philip IV's death in 1665 – these could not substitute for the absence of priests of their own. It is hardly surprising that in 1768, one year after the expulsion of the Jesuits from Spanish America, a royal ordinance stipulated that at least a quarter of the students entering the seminaries must be Indians or mestizos. Creole priests, many unable to speak an Indian language, could hardly replace the Jesuits in the full range of their achievement. Some, however, did their best and Indian Christian life, as fostered by the Jesuits, had itself a far greater resilience than many commentators have recognized.

If in Paraguay political pressures quickly decreased the population of the Reductions after their expulsion, in their Chiquitos mission, in what became Bolivia, the endurance of the Jesuit legacy even now is what needs stressing. It had been a very holistic mission, ever since it began in 1691 with the founding of San Javier, to be followed by nine further settlements: a mix of agricultural improvement, basic education and religious celebration. Musical instruments (whose relics still survive) were imported from Europe. Some amazing churches were built. The human and religious were integrated making the fullest use of Indian language and culture to create here, as elsewhere, a functioning Indio-Christian synthesis. What is remarkable is that this involved the successful unification of a number of ethnic and language groups and that it survived the expulsion of 1767. The Chiquitenos continued to identify themselves through loyalty to the 'santos padres' so that a stranger could note as late as the 1840s how respectfully silent everyone fell when their memory was recalled. And the creole secular priests who replaced them carried on the tradition as best they could. Thus the District Council of San Rafael wrote to the king in March 1791, 'Our P. Gregorio means a lot to us. He knows our poverty and so we want that he stays with us and dies among us.'[6]

Two remarkable Jesuits of the seventeenth century who were engaged in quite another sort of mission can lead us into a different area. In 1627 Alonso de Sandoval published a book entitled *De instauranda Aethiopum salute* about the apostolate to African slaves. He and his assistant, Pedro Claver, worked indefatigably in the docks at Cartagena where thousands of blacks were unloaded every year, often more dead than alive after their fearful Atlantic crossing. With a group of black interpreters picked to cope with the range of African languages needed, Sandoval and Claver ministered to the slaves materially and spiritually without stopping for more than 50 years. In his book Sandoval denounced the abominable treatment of the slaves, listed the African peoples and languages they represented, while appealing to other Jesuits to join him in this work. He and Claver were undoubtedly two of the most heroically dedicated and saintly men religious history, even Jesuit history, can record. But in the wider context of the Latin American Church they were indeed, even more than Las Casas, voices crying in the wilderness. While there was a vast apostolate to the Indians, there was little indeed to the ever-growing population of, often even worse treated, black slaves. One of the reasons was that the missionary orders already had their hands full with the one, before the other had begun to develop. A second was that they had, as we have seen, largely decided that they could only work effectively by separating their flock from white interference, but it was of the essence of the slave condition that they were wholly subject to white power. A consequence was that while superficially the black population, too, came to accept *en masse* a coping of Christianity, its characteristic synthesis of old and new was far more coherently located, even organizationally, in a reworking of the 'traditional' – in this case West African – side of the mix. Voodoo in Haiti and numerous Afro-Brazilian cults are the result.

In Spanish America, however, it was only in Cuba, Hispaniola and Venezuela that a world consisting principally of black slaves and large slave-worked plantations really developed. Elsewhere they tended to become integrated into the wider society. Already in the early seventeenth century we saw the mulatto, Martin de Porres, at work in Lima. It was in Portuguese America that the multiplication of black slaves absolutely dominated the whole character of society. Brazil is basically a latecomer in our history. The sixteenth-century Portuguese colonial interest lay in Asia. Brazil seemed at first to have little to offer and Portugal's own resources of manpower were far more circumscribed than Spain's. In Brazil they found none of the instant wealth of Mexico or Peru, nor, indeed, any at all advanced Indian society. Its attraction lay in the production of sugar. Sugar plantations required slaves. The Indians wilted, so it seemed easy enough for the Portuguese, who had forts along the West African coast and had already begun exporting slaves to Europe, to develop a massive transatlantic trade to build up the Brazilian economy. While the Jesuits arrived early in Brazil – in 1549 – and were followed by Franciscans, Carmelites and Benedictines, they represented a European Church which had little of the theological and spiritual brilliance of sixteenth-century Spain. Here as in Spanish America, if less pardonably, the orders concentrated on the Indians, unable to see how to tackle the problem of the black population which, in consequence, was never systematically evangelized at all. Until 1676 there was but a single diocese, at Salvador de Bahia. There was an isolation in Portuguese Catholicism far deeper than that to be found in Spain. The Portuguese Empire, and particularly its Brazilian wing, came to be permeated with a slave culture to an extent that the Spanish never was. Moreover Brazil developed in population, economy and extent far more in the eighteenth century, the heyday of the slave trade, by which time both the Spanish and Portuguese empires had entered economically into a somewhat stagnant period, with the sole exception of Brazil. The eighteenth century was, moreover, one in which the Portuguese Church too had lost whatever missionary fervour it had earlier possessed. Almost everything dynamic that happened within the Brazilian Church was done by the Jesuits, though they too were deeply involved in slavery, and their most distinguished intellectual, Antonio Vieira, attempted to justify it, despite his impassioned appeals against the oppression of the Indians. However, when the Jesuits were expelled from Brazil by Pombal in 1759 – eight years before their expulsion from Spanish America – there was no one to replace them. In Pombal's modernizing view there was no room for the preservation of Indians as such; 'the only way to dominate a barbarous people', he declared, 'is to civilize it and establish a bond between conquered and conquerors, who will live in society under the same laws, as one people without any distinctions'[7] – that is to say, as Portuguese. It was the policy which had already wiped out the Indians of the coastal areas. Not only were the Jesuits expelled, but the *aldeias* of the Franciscans too were taken from them and broken up into parishes to be run by secular clergy where Tupi was replaced by Portuguese.

The Jesuits had made plenty of enemies: the bishops resented their independence, slave traders and owners of large plantations resented their protection of Indians from being dragged into the labour force, lots of people resented their wealth, while the Spanish Crown could be persuaded that in Paraguay they were creating an independent state. Yet the underlying reasons for their expulsion had more to do with Europe than America: Gallican hostility in France, Josephite hostility in Austria, a mounting wave of anticlerical Enlightenment opinion linked with a new absolutism which allowed no place for any surviving power in the papacy. The Jesuits seemed to stand, and still too potently, for a system of religious absolutism which accorded neither with rationalism nor with the state's supremacy as late eighteenth-century modernizers understood them. In this Pombal led the way in his expulsion of 1759 but in 1773 Pope Clement XIV would be compelled by the principal powers of Europe to suppress the Society entirely. None of this was very popular in America; indeed their expulsion in 1767 from the Spanish territories produced violent protests across Mexico involving both creoles and Indians. The departure of 2,500 Jesuits, more than half of them creoles, not only involved the effective collapse of a mission to the Indians in many frontier areas, it also removed the best education available for creoles. If Europe's *raison d'état* was responsible for this sudden destruction of the most high-minded and disciplined element within the colonial Church, the revolutions of Europe 30 years later would produce even greater consequences for the upturning of the Catholicism of America.

1780–1900: revolutions and reactions

The American Revolution of the 1780s had not gone unnoticed in the lands to its south. If the Thirteen Colonies could throw off the rule of Britain, the most powerful and progressive of countries, why should Latin Americans not do the same? What had Spain, a land almost as under-developed as its colonies, to offer creoles, except frustration with the imposition of *peninsulares* into most senior positions and the ceaseless milking of its economy, the bullion trade above all, to pay for government in Madrid? The answer is clear enough: creoles remained fearful of dropping the hand of nurse, for fear of finding themselves overwhelmed by something a great deal worse – the vast, unwhite majority in their own lands. Perhaps 15 per cent of the population of Spanish America could now claim to be white, but even in New Spain (Mexico), where immigration had been particularly high, of a population of six million only one million were white. As the bishop-elect of Michoacan, Manuel Abad y Queipo, declared in 1799 commenting on the division between Indians and Spaniards, 'there is the conflict of interests and the hostility which invariably prevails between those who have nothing and those who have everything, between vassals and lords'.[8] The extensive rebellion of Tupac Amaru II in Peru, beginning near Cuzco in 1780, and then the even more bloody black revolution in Saint-Domingue (Haiti to be), the French-ruled half of Hispaniola, in 1791 made it clear enough why creoles did not feel too anxious to be free of the protective control of the mother country.

The Napoleonic Wars, however, created a decisively different situation. While Spain was on the French side, the British fleet blockaded its ports and broke the commercial ties linking Spanish America to Cadiz. When, moreover, Napoleon invaded Spain and, in 1808, imposed his brother, Joseph Bonaparte, as King of Spain, provoking immediate civil war, the political ties were disrupted as well. The intellectual, economic and political bankruptcy of a once great country was only too obvious and it was inevitable that more and more Latin Americans should feel the urge to declare independence. There were still royalists in plenty, especially *peninsulares* in positions of power, to put up a fight over the next fifteen years but by 1824 the whole Spanish American mainland had achieved its independence. It would probably, in fact, have happened a good deal quicker if the Indians and mestizos of Mexico had not risen in revolt in 1810 under Hidalgo, seized control of much of the country, and massacred a good many whites, both *peninsulares* and creoles, especially in the storming of Guanajuato. That forced the mass of creoles back for a while into the support of royalist legitimacy. When independence was achieved it was essentially the victory of the creole upper class unwilling to tolerate any further the irritating oversight of Madrid but no more willing to allow power to slip into Indian, black or mestizo hands. They had never constituted a single American colony and had little sense of being a single community. Loyalties were far more local than that, so a string of new republics from Argentina in the south to Mexico in the north made their appearance. Brazil moved less dramatically. By the start of the nineteenth century it was already clear that Brazil was a far larger and more prosperous country than Portugal. When Napoleon invaded Portugal late in 1807, the royal family and entire government fled to Rio de Janeiro. When, finally, in 1821, João VI returned to Lisbon under huge Portuguese pressure, the Brazilians were quite unwilling to lose the status they had had for fourteen years and declared their independence, with João's young son, Dom Pedro, as Emperor of Brazil.

What influence had the Church on the revolution and what effect did the revolution at once have upon the Church? One might, oversimplifying a little, classify the clergy into three classes, each parallel to the three forces at loggerheads in the revolutionary years. Most of the bishops and many of the religious were *peninsulares* and royalists. They had been appointed by the king and few could easily envisage any safe order of things other than one of 'throne and altar', even though the Bourbon kings of eighteenth-century Spain had proved increasingly unhelpful to religion – expelling the Jesuits and endeavouring to seize the Church's principal funds. Yet the old order was still basically in existence, archbishops could still easily be appointed as viceroys in an emergency, the Inquisition still functioned to ensure the public orthodoxy of society. For most Spanish ecclesiastics, only too aware of what the consequences had been all across Europe for the Church and religion of revolution in France, it was madness to encourage revolution west of the Atlantic as well.

Upper-class creole priests tended to see things rather differently. Many shared and had even sometimes inspired the more progressive aspirations of the revolutionaries. They could see no reason why they provided the cathedral canons of their dioceses but were so seldom chosen to fill the episcopal thrones. Essentially they wanted a creole Church for a creole state – a state which by ideologically adopting an American identity could claim that it was freeing non-white Americans as well as white. Yet the bottom line of their *politique* had been shown clearly enough at the most critical moment in the rising of Tupac Amaru II when the creole Bishop Moscoso of Cuzco had defended the city from his attack. While Tupac Amaru himself had been educated by the Jesuits and wanted an Inca state with Catholicism as its official religion, for many of his followers the Church and its clergy were simply part of a regime of Spanish landowning oppression. Once the siege was over, Moscoso wrote to the tyrannical Visitor General, whose determination to increase the tax yield had led to the revolt. Moscoso denounced his flock in unmeasured terms for their obstinate adherence to pagan beliefs, Inca clothes and even their own language. It had been disastrous, he remarked, to allow a collection of Inca imperial portraits to adorn the walls of the Jesuit college in Cuzco. Everything should now be done to extirpate such uncivilized relics of the past, including even the use of native languages.

There were, however, many other priests, both creole and mestizo, who had lived with, and worked for, the non-white population, had seen how desperately ill-treated it was and deeply sympathized with a far more radical reshaping of society than the creole leadership could tolerate for a moment. More than a hundred priests were executed in Mexico for supporting the rebellion of Hidalgo and Morelos.

The 1810–15 war represents a prism for the exposure of all sorts of ambiguities which it would take the rest of the century and more to sort out. It is part of the built-in tragic irony of Mexico's history that it has been able to identify the start of its War of Independence with Hidalgo's *Grito de Dolores*, the call to arms he uttered from the steps of his parish church on Sunday 16 September 1810. It was an appeal to Indians and mestizos to follow him in the defence of religion, the rejection of Spanish rule and the righting of Indian grievances. The Virgin of Guadalupe was proclaimed guardian of the revolution but the relationship to it of creoles remained decidedly vague. Meanwhile in Guadalajara, before it was captured by Hidalgo, the loyalist Bishop Cabañas was organizing a somewhat laughable *cruzado* regiment which he personally led out of the cathedral day by day, followed by mounted priests, sword in hand, while the lads who followed behind cried 'Long live the Holy Catholic Faith'. Thus were the Church, its symbols and clergy split down the middle. If many devoted creole priests followed Hidalgo, few other creoles did so. He was captured, hanged and his head displayed above the city granary at Guanajuato where his bloodiest massacre had taken place, yet he still became 'the father of independence' and 16 September, the date of his *grito*, Mexico's national independence day, while the Republic which substantially represented those who had defeated him went on to overturn every ecclesiastical privilege in which Bishop Cabañas believed.

The arrival of independence all across Latin America, a regime combining a basic social conservatism with some commitment to modernization, affected the Church in a number of ways. Very few of the new political leaders were consciously anti-Catholic, but most took for granted the elimination of the more archaic elements within the ecclesiastical system. The Inquisition was abolished at once, but it took 50 years or more in some places before the juridical privileges of the clergy disappeared together with state collection of tithe. As Britain soon became the principal trading partner of most of these countries, it was important to allow freedom of worship for Protestants, but that too was slow in coming, as was an ending to the clergy's monopoly control of education. Most of nineteenth-century Church history can be written, depressingly enough, around a struggle over such issues, country by country. Despite a certain to-and-fro movement, including periods when conservative politicians upheld the Church's more antiquated claims, and even guaranteed them in concordats with the Vatican (Guatemala, 1852; Ecuador, 1863; Colombia, 1887), the Church inevitably lost out in this sort of contestation. What is depressing is that the retention of these 'rights' was for long so central to ecclesiastical preoccupation while any concern for the rights of the Indian and non-white majority is harder to detect. A sense of siege was actually enhanced by increased links between the Latin American Church and the European Church centred around the papacy in the long pontificate of Pius IX (1846–78). Ultramontanism was something quite new for a Church hitherto wholly controlled by the Spanish Crown, but, with the loss of both that control and the privileges that went with it, it was inevitable that the Latin American hierarchy should seek a new source of protection in the papacy, though it was a papacy at its most illiberal and itself most buffeted by the pressures of an unsympathetic new political order.

The most immediate question, however, was how the Latin American hierarchy was to continue to exist at all. The kings of Spain and Portugal had been granted the right to make all episcopal appointments and were not at all disposed to forgo that right. Equally the new governments took it for granted that the royal *patronato* must pass to them. In consequence no bishops were appointed for many years. The diocese of Mexico was vacant from 1824 to 1839, that of Buenos Aires from 1813 to 1833, that of Nicaragua from 1825 to 1849. When the Archbishop of Guatemala and the Bishop of Puebla both died in 1829, Central America and Mexico were left without a single bishop. The papacy was caught in a quandary. It was under pressure from both the government of Spain and other European governments not to recognize revolution by appointing bishops except as nominated by the King of Spain. Moreover, the conservative political sympathies of the papacy pressed it in the same direction. Yet, fortunately for the Latin American Church, Leo XII (1823–29) appointed as prefect of Propaganda Fide Cardinal Cappellari who, while intensely conservative in most other ways, had a quite exceptional commitment to reinvigorating and extending the non-European Church throughout the world. On his advice, Leo declared that he would henceforth personally appoint bishops to vacant sees in Latin America and proceeded to do so at once for Colombia. The sharpness of the Spanish reaction caused him and his successor (Pius VIII) to pull back, but when Cappellari himself became Pope, as Gregory XVI, in 1831, the policy was resumed, though its implementation depended on the acquiescence of the governments of each Latin American country, whose right of nomination was soon implicitly, if not explicitly, admitted.

The significance of this change in the control of the American hierarchy cannot be overestimated. It produced a new sort of episcopate, if one actually at times more politically intransigent than its predecessor. An immediate effect of the hiatus between old and new was a sharp decline in the number of priests. In many places there were no ordinations for twenty years. A good many royalist priests had already retreated to Spain. Moreover in the new republics there were far more career opportunities for the educated creole than formerly – in politics, the army and commerce – hence the attraction of clerical life markedly declined. Furthermore, in several countries the government imposed restrictions on entry into religious orders, so that their number decreased even more than that of the secular clergy. In consequence of all this, one of the characteristics of the modern Latin American Church – an acute shortage of clergy – can be dated from this period.

Much of the trouble in Church–state relations was that the state was in most countries at least as disorganized as the Church. Peru, for instance, had six constitutions and eight presidents in a space of ten years. The new governments were effectively moneyless. They also needed an ideology to sustain their regimes. One immediate source of money could be found by disappropriating the Church – rich in some parts, such as Mexico, though poor enough in others. The ideology favoured by the *pensadores* was, almost inevitably, the anticlerical liberalism struggling in southern Europe with absolutist monarchies and a reactionary Church. Damaging as it could actually be for young states, an attack on the Church could appear the gateway to liberty and modernization. The degree of confrontation, however, was by no means everywhere the same. In Peru, the dominant figure for a quarter-century, from the 1840s to the 1860s, was President Ramón Castilla, a mestizo, who showed remarkable pragmatism in pursuing a 'liberal' agenda while managing to avoid a collision with the Church. He was assisted in this by the accommodating attitude of successive Archbishops of Lima. In Mexico the reverse was the case. Its original constitution declared that 'The religion of the Mexican nation is and shall be perpetually the Catholic, Apostolic, Roman religion. The nation protects it with wise and just laws and prohibits the exercise of any other.'[9] In reality the Mexican state was far from protective. Government policy moved, if erratically and across various *coups*, towards the abolition of ecclesiastical legal privilege, the *fuero*, and the confiscation of ecclesiastical property, while Church authority dug itself into an ever more intransigent position. The Archbishop of Mexico responded to the new 1857 constitution, which abolished the *fuero* and arranged for the expropriation of Church lands, by denouncing not only these measures but also freedom of assembly, press and expression. The Three Years War began in consequence late in 1857. The conservatives were roundly defeated and President Juarez proceeded to a still more aggressive programme: the confiscation of all Church wealth, the suppression of all monasteries, the complete separation of Church and state, freedom of religion. Nowhere else in Latin America was the institutional and emotional gulf between the Church and the Republican regime so sharp or so lasting, but almost everywhere the Church's political influence and pastoral presence declined steadily throughout the nineteenth century. It stood aloof, rigid in its newly acquired Ultramontanism, bemoaning both the secularism of the state and the superstition of its peasant followers. While its clergy was now being reinforced by recruits from several parts of Europe, this simply strengthened the commitment to Latinization and the clericalization of Church life, a commitment in which there was no place to sympathize with the popular, highly syncretistic, Catholicism of the rural masses.

The rural population, however, did not lose its addiction to Christianity. On the contrary. Antagonistic as it mostly felt towards the middle-class creoles now fully in control of government and ejecting it from lands it had held hitherto under the umbrella of royal protection, it could identify itself precisely as Catholic in contrast to its oppressors, even though in many countries the Church's hierarchy had effectively made its peace with the decreasingly liberal and increasingly dictatorial regimes which had become established almost everywhere by the latter years of the nineteenth century. They were at one in disgust for the preoccupations of the very poor.

We can best detect something of those preoccupations – what was becoming in reality the characteristic Catholicism of Latin America – at moments of uprising and unrest, of which there were very many. Let us consider three: the Atusparia rising in Peru in 1885, the movement led by Antonio 'Conselheiro' crushed by the Brazilian army at Canudos in October 1897 and the *Cristiada* in Mexico in the 1920s.

The Atusparia rising, named after its leader, an illiterate but dignified local Indian official who had been ill-treated by the departmental prefect, provides a useful example of *mentalité* just because it was in any terms so insignificant as a rising. It came at a moment when Peru, having lost its war with Chile, had particularly weak government. Its 'aims' were little more than to protest against overtaxation and bad treatment. Peasant Christianity shaped its course, even somewhat holding it back, but it was not as such a religious movement. If the rebels wrecked a couple of small towns, they were restrained elsewhere precisely by religious ritual, such as the carrying of the monstrance with the Blessed Sacrament in procession just as Atusparia and his force were entering Caraz. He knelt at once as did his followers. Again, when the government forces arrived at the rebel centre of Huaraz there was little resistance because everyone was celebrating the important local festival of the Lord of Solitude. It is clear that local priests, who were genuinely close to the Indians but no less anxious to avoid strife or revolution, could mediate effectively by ritual and sermon because they did in a way belong to both sides: 'Do you want to rule the land and be condemned to hell forever, or will you suffer on earth and enjoy heaven eternally?'[10] Other-worldly as their teaching was, the Indians did not dispute its objectivity. But it is clear too that the festivals and rituals of the year were central to Indian life, quite apart from the role of the clergy. Even an insurrection had to wait while the feast of the Lord of Solitude was celebrated.

Canudos grew out of a more explicitly religious motivation. Antonio

Vicente Mendes Maciel had been a shopkeeper and lawyer's clerk in the Brazilian north-east. Abandoned by his wife, he became a *beato*, a holy man, a penitent pilgrim, walking for twenty years through the backlands, offering advice and spiritual support, so that he became known as 'nosso conselheiro', our counsellor, though he always referred to himself as 'O peregrino', the pilgrim. Some rural priests, impressed by his devoutness and influence, asked permission for the *Conselheiro* to preach in their churches. The archbishop's reaction was exactly the opposite and prohibited anyone from listening to his words. By that time a considerable crowd followed Antonio around, consisting of landless peasants and ex-slaves. The majority of the population in many parts of the north-east had been slaves, and their emancipation had only come in 1888. When the government announced that taxes would be raised, the *Conselheiro* denounced it and even ordered the crowds to tear down copies of the edict and burn them. Following this incident, he decided to lead 'his people' to a remote and inaccessible wasteland, Canudos, where they settled in 1893. Soon more and more people were joining them and Canudos flourished extraordinarily, growing in numbers in four years from 4,000 to 25,000. The land was free, food was plentiful. Agriculture and animal farming at Canudos had proved a great success. To the landowners, whose labourers were abandoning them to join the new community, and to the government, which saw it as a millennialist and revolutionary threat to order, all this was too dangerous to be allowed to continue. The army was ordered to crush it, but it took four expeditions before, finally, Canudos was destroyed on 5 October 1897, a date the Brazilian army still commemorates. The *Conselheiro*'s body lay dead in the ruins of his church.

Victor Lanternari has claimed that Antonio thought himself to be 'a messiah, a saviour of men, and the reincarnation of Christ'.[11] It seems a great misunderstanding of what was in fact a pretty orthodox expression of popular Catholicism. The *Conselheiro* carried round with him a copy of the *Missão Abreviada*, also a little book in which he wrote down his own sermons – meditations, for the most part, on the sufferings of Jesus and Mary. He saw his mission as the following of Jesus, the proclamation of the law of God and the denunciation of Republicans, Freemasons, Protestants and other evil people who would burn in hell.[12] This reflected, exactly enough, the preaching of many a Franciscan, the religion Catholic peasants had been taught in Brazil for centuries, if just a little archaic for the clergy of the 1890s. What was really insufferable was that it was being said by a layman, and a poorly educated one, and that it was linked with satisfaction of the peasants' yearning to recover a land of their own. It was the combination of other-worldly pieties with a this-worldly liberation – if only the chance to cultivate together a rather arid stretch of land – which made it so dangerous in the eyes of both Church and state.

The twentieth century

The *Cristiada* in Mexico was altogether a larger, more politically danger-ous, affair. Another wave of Church–state confrontation had been building up since the Mexican Revolution of 1910 whose spirit was more consis-tently and aggressively anti-religious than that of any previous govern-ment in post-Independence Latin America. When in the mid-1920s President Calles began the systematic implementation of the anti-religious articles of the 1917 Constitution, the bishops declared an interdict: no religious service would be performed. Calles saw before him a feeble, discredited Church only waiting for its *coup de grâce* from the forces of modernity theoretically anxious to liberate the peasant. What he dis-covered instead was the entire rural population of the highly concentrated central highlands in armed revolt. The first riots took place within days of the suspension of services on 31 July 1926. By the following January the movement was general, and the nastiness of the army's attempts at suppression merely increased it. Three years later the government had effectively lost, unable to defeat a guerrilla army involving some 50,000 men fighting in detached units, 25 to 500 strong. Church authority was almost equally embarrassed. The clergy had little part in encouraging the rising, only one bishop had openly defended it and the Vatican wanted a diplomatic compromise. By June 1929, Church and state were forced to come to an interim agreement, religious services were resumed and within weeks the war ended, as spontaneously as it had started.

Viva Cristo Rey, the battle-cry of the Indian peasantry, gave the war its name, the *Cristiada*. This, the largest of all Latin American rural uprisings, had no specific point other than a religious one, and it differentiated peasant Christianity from the clerical Church almost as much as from the anti-religious state. The bishops had found their surest defenders among those whose Catholicism they trusted the least, mixed as they saw it with every kind of syncretism. In an important pastoral letter of 1916, the Archbishop and future Cardinal of Rio de Janeiro D. Sebastião Leme had described the poor as 'ignorant, superstitious, impertinent and fanatic', but they were the people, effectively the only people, who could ensure by the sacrifice of their lives that Catholicism could not be cut out, as a colonial survival, from a modern Latin America.

By then the ecclesiastical revival had, however, begun. Perhaps it could be dated from 1872 when the Bishop of Recife in Brazil, Dom Vital Maria de Oliveira, was sent to prison for challenging the state's control of the Church in regard to the administration of religious fraternities. It is significant that this should happen in Brazil, whose population was growing fast with immigration from Europe and which would soon become the leading state of Latin America. In the twentieth century the nub of Church history tends to shift from a Mexico–Peru axis to a Brazil–Mexico one, but almost everywhere religious history is profoundly affected by mass immigration which, for the first time, placed the native Indian inhabitants in a minority in most countries. As towns were magnified their slums and shanty lands came to replace the remote rural areas as the focal point of missionary zeal. Only Peru and Colombia would retain an Indian majority. They would retain too a strong, but particularly conservative, Catholicism.

In 1899 Leo XIII convoked a Plenary Council of Latin American bishops in Rome. Ecclesiastically this was the beginning of a new age in which Rome had come to realize the huge importance of this continent. Throughout the nineteenth century the influence of the Church had declined; through much of the twentieth century it would increase. In this, of course, it reflected the fortunes of the Church in Europe and of the papacy in particular. It was after 1920 in the pontificate of Pius XI and then, after the Second World War, of Pius XII, that the renewal was most clear. Dioceses multiplied; priests from Europe, first chiefly from Spain then from many other countries, moved to Latin America to cope with its shortage of clergy; new religious institutions, from Catholic universities to forms of Catholic Action, proliferated. By 1960 the continent included 35 per cent of the world's nominal Catholics, rather more than Europe. Where hardly a middle-class intellectual could be found in the late nineteenth century claiming to be a Catholic, by the 1950s there was a very considerable Catholic intelligentsia, especially in Brazil. A young Brazilian philosopher, Jackson de Figueiredo (1891–1928), began the movement with his submission to the Church in 1917 and subsequent founding of the Dom Vital Centre as a focus for the Catholic intellectual life of the new urban laity, thus recalling the example of the bishop who had gone to prison 40 years earlier.

In many ways this revival fitted naturally with what was happening in society at large. Here the fashionable agnostic liberalism of the nineteenth century with its contempt for the colonial past but lack of success in coping with that past's legacy – particularly the divide between white 'haves' and non-white 'have-nots' – was giving way to new forms of nationalism fed on a romantic *Hispanismo*, which went naturally enough with right-wing Catholicism and could be linked with dictatorial regimes in Portugal and Spain. But it was also giving way in places to a more pragmatic pursuit of democracy, fuelled not only by the example of the Anglo-Saxon countries but also by the rise of Christian Democratic parties in Western Europe. By the end of Pius XII's pontificate in 1958, the sheer importance of the Latin American Church within world Catholicism was obvious. Brazil alone had no fewer than three cardinals. In 1955 the first General Conference of the Latin American bishops was held in Rio de Janeiro during which a permanent council was founded to link them together – CELAM. This provided both a model which other continents were later to follow and a working instrument for mutual assistance, immensely strengthening the capacity of the Latin American Church to respond to problems in a self-fashioned way, a capacity which would prove its value once the Vatican Council was over.

Undoubtedly, looked at from the perspective of the 1950s, the reshaping of the Church throughout the continent must have appeared a great success. Yet the measure of that success masked major weaknesses. The shortage of local priests had led to an invasion of foreigners, possible at a time when priestly vocations in Europe and North America were rather numerous. Yet this transfer of literally thousands of priests from one continent to another not only failed to resolve the Latin American shortage, in numerical terms, but also produced the rather undesirable position that by 1960, 37 per cent of the entire clergy consisted of foreigners. In Venezuela they were over 60 per cent, in Guatemala almost 85 per cent. The importation of foreigners seemed simply to be helping the Church put off the real issue of reshaping its own ministry in viable local terms. In general this period appears in retrospect somewhat uncreative, little more than an application of standard Roman attitudes with almost no attempt at adaptation or inculturation, other than that of going along with local nationalisms. Above all, the basic social issue of the huge discrepancy in wealth between landowners and upper middle-class townspeople upon the one hand, the peasantry and urban proletariat on the other, coupled with the extent to which the Church as institution was tied to the former, remained hidden beneath the pursuit of fairly conventional pastoral objectives. These objectives were not seen as incompatible with exceedingly close links between many senior ecclesiastics and some of the most oppressive and dictatorial regimes in the world.

All that would be challenged in the last stormy period of Church history beginning with the Second Vatican Council (1962–65). Almost every one of the more novel stresses in the Council's teaching resonated in Latin America, perhaps more than in any other continent: social justice, the vocation of the lay Christian, the enhanced value of the vernacular languages into which the liturgy was to be translated, the positive encouragement of pluralism, the duty to attend especially to the poor, following John XXIII's own phrase, 'the Church of the poor', *Iglesia de los pobres*. The immediate response to the Vatican Council of the Latin American Church can be best seen in three ways: first, the Second General

Conference of Latin American bishops held at Medellín, Colombia, in 1968; second, in the development of Liberation Theology; third, in the growth of Christian Base Communities, above all in Brazil.

At Medellín, the Church declared its 'preferential option for the poor', committed itself to the liturgical use of the vernacular, encouraged the laity to be more actively involved in Church life and set about a rethink of the idea of sin in terms less of personal guilt and more of the collective responsibility of society in creating unjust and oppressive structures. Never before had the Church in America defined its role in a way so critical of the socio-political order as it had existed, essentially unchanged, since the sixteenth century. By so doing it opened the doors to a burgeoning theology of liberation and to the exploration of ways in which, given the huge shortage of priests, the laity – particularly among the poorest classes – could actually shoulder an active ecclesiastical role. *The Theology of Liberation*, the seminal text for the new thinking, was published in Spanish by Gustavo Gutiérrez, a Peruvian priest, in 1971 and in English two years later.

Liberation Theology was a combination of the excitement seething through the Catholic Church worldwide in the aftermath of the Second Vatican Council, a widespread willingness among radically minded religious intellectuals to go along with much in Marxism, and the particular circumstances of both society and Church in Latin America. The balance between rich and poor had never been worse, the progressive, developmental policies, characteristic of the Christian Democratic parties in Chile and elsewhere in the post-Second World War years, had proved inadequate to provide a remedy – particularly because they, like all previous governments, had failed to challenge the dominance of the *hacendados*, the great landowners. Latin America appeared ripe for revolution and within the Church there was considerable willingness to back change of a fairly revolutionary sort. The tradition of Las Casas was at last being reappropriated, both by the thousands of European and North American priests who had responded in the 1950s and 1960s to the frequent appeals for help and by a generation of young Latin American priests, of whom the intellectual cream had been sent for advanced studies to Europe, and especially to Louvain, at the time the Catholic university felt to be most deeply imbued with the spirit of Vatican II.

While Liberation Theology came in various forms, some of which made for greater use of Marxist terminology and analysis than did others, its central thrust derived from the insistence of the need to pursue social justice to be found both in the conciliar documents (especially *Gaudium et Spes*, the massive constitution on 'the Church in the modern world') and in recent papal encyclicals, both Pope John's *Mater et Magistra* and Pope Paul's *Populorum Progressio*. In the last analysis the Marxist element was marginal, while the doctrinal position was in general more conservatively orthodox than that of many leading European theologians of the period.

Linked with Liberation Theology was the pastoral strategy which came to be known as the Base Community. The shortage of priests almost everywhere had long made a parish community of the sort hitherto taken for granted in the European Church an impossibility except in certain middle-class urban areas. Clericalism and an absence of contact between priests and people blocked the creation of the kind of local liturgical community with an informed and active laity which Vatican II had proposed as the model. The underlying ecclesiastical barrier to the development of such a Church was, as ever, refusal to accept a married priesthood. The Base Community was, at heart, conceived simply as a way of developing parish-type communities without resident priests – in general smaller in size and consisting entirely of active members. This could only come about through encouraging a new kind of lay leadership, and in shifting the religious centre of inspiration away from the Mass and towards a reading of the Bible as productive both of group prayer and of social action. All this was closely akin to an approach long approved in Europe within movements such as the 'Young Christian Workers' (and Students) founded by Canon (and finally Cardinal) Cardijn, and influential in Latin America especially in the 1950s.

The Base Community, not the university, was the true context for Liberation Theology, and provided the home for its greatest classic, Ernesto Cardenal's *The Gospel in Solentiname*. But it was easier both to develop, and then to attack, Liberation Theology at the academic level. Liberation Theology might be found on the academic agenda of every Latin American country. The presence of Base Communities was a good deal more limited and depended, far more than did Liberation Theology, on the sustained encouragement of the local episcopate. It was above all in the north-east of Brazil that such encouragement was to be found, particularly through the leadership of Archbishop Helder Câmara of Recife. It was from Recife too that came the most outstanding theorist of the practice of a new kind of popular education. Paulo Freire and his philosophy of 'conscientization', as expressed most powerfully in his *Pedagogy of the Oppressed* of 1970, were at the heart of the whole movement of Base Communities.

As Liberation Theology and Base Community developed in the course of the 1970s and early 1980s as a major challenge both to the socio-political system of Latin America and to the way the Church had long been run, they inevitably came up against steadily increasing resistance from the more conservative elements in both Church and state as well as from Rome.

Archbishop Lopez Trujillo of Medellín came to represent this reaction.

Colombia is one of the strongest but also most conservative Catholic Churches in the continent, so it was somewhat ironic that the 1968 General Conference of CELAM should have been held there. Trujillo became CELAM's executive secretary and a long struggle began to be waged in which Rome intervened with increasing weight on the conservative side by condemning aspects of Liberation Theology and appointing new bishops unsympathetic to it. If Peru is the home of Liberation Theology, it is also the country with the world's largest proportion of Opus Dei bishops and Opus Dei represents worldwide the integralism characteristic of traditional Iberian Catholicism at its most conservative. If Liberation Theology's supposed Marxist character was the generally asserted ground of objection, it is probable that what worried Rome considerably more was the undermining of clerical control of the Church through the development of lay-led Base Communities.

At the same time political polarization worsened between left and right, with far more aggressive US intervention in Latin American politics in the final period of the Cold War and the general shift to the right in American policies in the Reagan era. On the one side liberal or socialist governments were replaced by military dictatorships in Chile, Brazil, Argentina and elsewhere; on the other hand in Nicaragua the Sandinista revolution of 1979 brought about a socialist revolution in which radical priests were closely involved. Father Miguel d'Escoto was Minister of Foreign Relations and Ernesto Cardenal Minister of Culture. Rome demanded that both withdraw. In the confrontation which escalated across the continent throughout the 1980s a large number of priests were murdered, from Archbishop Oscar Romero of San Salvador, shot while celebrating Mass in March 1980, to Father Ignacio Ellacuría and his five Jesuit academic colleagues with their housekeeper and her daughter, in the same country, nine years later. If the Vatican had appeared close to total condemnation of Liberation Theology in an 'Instruction' of 1984, it pulled back quite considerably in a further 'Instruction' of 1986 together with a letter of John Paul II to the Brazilian episcopate (9 April 1986) in which he recognized that 'Liberation Theology is not only timely but useful and necessary'.

Meanwhile the collapse of Communism in Russia and the ending of the Cold War removed much of the American rationale for backing oppressive governments in Latin America, and there developed a political movement in many countries towards more centralist positions. Yet the 1990s saw sustained oppression of the peasant majority particularly in the dominantly Indian lands – southern Mexico, Guatemala, Colombia, Peru. Especially noteworthy is the rising of the Zapatistas in Chiapas, Las Casas's old diocese in southern Mexico, where the Indian rural population remains as ill-used as ever, but magnificently supported by Bishop Samuel

Ruiz of San Cristobal de las Casas. It is strangely symbolic of the continuity in Latin American Church history that it can end the twentieth century with a Bishop of Chiapas struggling for social justice much as his predecessor did four and a half centuries earlier. While the apparent unison and excitement of the years around Medellín could not be recovered within the wider Church, and those committed to an effective renewal of the Las Casas tradition were back in a situation far closer to his own, they had not been extinguished and they had, for the first time in the history of Catholicism, made Latin America into a place of leadership and theological construction. Nevertheless, the pastoral potential of the Base Communities had certainly not been generally realized. The majority of the bishops were by the 1990s opposed to any radical renewal of Church structures, while the shortage of priests was growing worse than ever and it was no longer possible to seek any large number of recruits in Europe or North America, because they too were now experiencing an increasing shortage.

Throughout the Christian history of Latin America the gap between popular Catholicism and the ecclesiastical–clerical system has been a decisive factor. The two were in part held together in the first centuries by the activities of the religious orders, Franciscans and Jesuits especially. From the time when the Jesuits were expelled and then, after Independence, the other orders were increasingly discriminated against or even in some countries expelled as well, the gap grew greater. It was made still worse by the Ultramontanism of the late nineteenth-century Church. The basic meaning of the whole movement of ecclesiastical renewal, spreading from the 1950s through to the murder of Archbishop Romero in 1980, was an attempt to close the gap, to reincorporate popular Catholicism within the full recognized life of the Church, by a triple programme of cultural and linguistic adaptation, the empowering of lay leadership, and the pursuit of social justice, which has always been impossible without agrarian reform.

The reaction of the Church's leadership as expressed in the figure of Archbishop Trujillo inevitably threatened to prevent the closing of the gap in Catholic terms and may well have contributed to the encouragement of a very different development – the sudden mass advance of Protestantism in a continent where hitherto it was so marginal that a brief history of this sort could not reasonably refer to it at all.

There had been some sort of Protestantism in the Caribbean since the mid-seventeenth century when the English conquered Barbados and the Dutch conquered Curaçao. However, as both the English and the Dutch were great slave owners but not great missionaries, it made little impact. Moravians, Methodists and Baptists eventually became active in Jamaica and elsewhere, but the Dutch, in particular, appeared happy enough to let their black slaves remain Catholics of a sort, restricting the delights of Protestantism to the purely white. The nineteenth century began with no Protestant presence whatsoever on the mainland, although Protestantism was widely admired by the liberal political elite which came to power after Independence because it was the religion of Latin America's new mentors – Britain and the United States. Yet the consequences were slight. British missionary societies were long unwilling to regard these countries as suitable targets for mission because they were seen as already Christian, while American societies which mostly had no such qualms only became widely active in the twentieth century. Nineteenth-century Protestantism was almost entirely a matter of immigration, mostly into the south of the continent, Argentina, Brazil and Chile. The immigrants kept largely to themselves. The Welsh in Patagonia even continued to speak Welsh. In all, their numbers were not great.

Even in the first half of the twentieth century this position was not substantially altered. Protestant numbers certainly grew. There was a great multiplication of denominations and more direct missionary activity derived from America, particularly from the southern Bible Belt. National Councils of Churches began to be formed: Mexico and Puerto Rico in the 1920s, Brazil and Argentina in the 1930s, Peru, Chile, Ecuador in the 1940s, Colombia and Guatemala in the 1950s. In 1949 the first Latin American Evangelical Conference was held, perhaps significantly, in Buenos Aires. Protestantism at that date still had its firmest base at the southern end of the continent. But the 1950s were to see the beginning of a great change. The long social and political crisis into which the continent was entering provided an opening for new forms of Protestantism as much as for new forms of Catholicism. Moreover, Asia, traditionally the principal field of American missionaries, was now becoming a largely closed area. Evangelicals turned their eyes south just as the American government turned its eyes in the same direction, anxious to ensure in the Cold War that Communism did not get a foothold west of the Atlantic or, if it did, as in Cuba, that it was severely isolated. American Protestant missionaries undoubtedly entered into this large political strategy, at times unconsciously, at least occasionally in full collusion. As Latin America became polarized between conservative 'National Security' regimes, utterly opposed to social justice policies but backed by the United States, and radical, often Marxist-inspired, movements seeking a fundamental reform of the social and economic structure but backed by the new wave of socially active Catholic clergy, it was natural that Evangelicalism should frequently appear as aligned with the former side. Its gospel was one of individual salvation, personal achievement, a limitation of Christian teaching to the traditionally 'religious' aspects of life. Its apoliticism was here, as elsewhere, attractive to the political right because it theoretically removed religion from any applicability to politics. This was particularly true of the latest wave of Pentecostalism, favoured in consequence by dictators like Pinochet in Chile and Somoza in Nicaragua.

Nevertheless, Latin American Protestantism by the 1960s was as fragmented, theologically and politically, as Catholicism. If on the one side newly arrived movements could appear ostentatiously anti-Catholic, anti-ecumenical and anti-Communist, many older Churches were as aware of the necessity of relating the Gospel to the social and cultural realities of the continent as Catholics and some of the leading liberation theologians were, in fact, Protestants, such as the Argentinian José Miguez Bonino and the Uruguayan Emilio Castro. For them the renewed Catholicism of Vatican II was seen no longer as an enemy but, rather, as an ally. The huge growth of the Protestant community in these years, above all in Brazil, cannot possibly be put down to the mere importation of an American-style fundamentalist Evangelicalism. When Castro became General Secretary of the World Council of Churches in 1985, that point was demonstrated clearly enough. The constituency he represented was an utterly different one.

Nevertheless there were areas of rapid growth where American influence was preponderant. Take Guatemala. Its Protestants formed about 2 per cent of the population in 1960 but 35 per cent by 1990. While they included many of the urban middle class, they also included a considerable proportion of the poor. The 12,000 population of the township of Almolonga, 99 per cent Maya, was divided by 1988 into 52 per cent Catholic, 48 per cent Protestant.[13] What produced this sea change? It is hardly a happy story. A progressive Christian Democrat government committed to agrarian reform was overthrown by a military coup in 1954 backed by the small Guatemalan landowning elite and the American government. From then, for 50 years, Guatemala was torn to pieces by revolutionary governments, military terrorism and movements of popular insurrection. Tens of thousands of people were killed, hundreds of Indian towns and villages wiped out. At the height of the government offensive under President Rios Montt (1982–83), little less than genocide of the Indian population was taking place. General Montt was a born-again, neo-Pentecostal evangelical, a member of the California-based Church of the Word (El Verbo). At the same time as the country was torn to pieces and hundreds of thousands of Guatemalans took refuge in Mexico, a huge missionary offensive was launched from America funded by Jimmy Swaggart, Pat Robertson and other TV evangelists, proclaiming a highly anti-Communist and anti-Catholic Gospel of biblical fundamentalism and 'prosperity'. Meanwhile, numerous Catholic priests, organizers of Base Communities and preachers of a message of social justice, were hounded out of the country, and association with them seemed only to lead to the threat of military attack. Protestant broadcasting in Guatemala City amounted to some 5,900 minutes a week, Catholic broadcasting just 300.

Essentially what happened in these years was a huge and concerted campaign to eradicate both traditional Maya culture and Catholic influence, especially modernizing Catholic influence, and replace both by the religious culture of the American Bible Belt. Faced with a calamitous political and economic situation, conversion to what appeared to be American values proved overwhelmingly attractive. Thousands of distinct Churches resulted, most of them at least initially under strong American Pentecostalist media influence, but increasingly self-generating and offering a religious message remarkably like that of Catholic missionaries three hundred years earlier. As Juan Cedillo, pastor of the quickly growing Prince of Peace Church in Nebaj, explained: 'Many left the Catholic Church because of the trauma of war that taught them that man couldn't create heaven on earth. We found that the earthly battle doesn't change anything. We must accept the suffering of this world in order to be saved by Jesus Christ in the world to come.'[14] It may well be that religious life for a peasant inside a Pentecostal Church was not so different from that inside a Base Community, except that the stress in preaching was more on the world to come (which he or she was used to from traditional Catholicism) rather than on the world here and now. But another, important, difference, not only in Guatemala but in Brazil and everywhere, was that an ordinary person could well become a pastor in the one but never a pastor in the other. The Pentecostal ministry multiplied while the Catholic clergy, in most places, was in decline.

'Generally speaking, Brazilians will be Catholics or vague spiritualists. They will never make good Protestants.'[15] So wrote a leading Brazilian intellectual in the 1950s. By the 1990s such a judgement was no longer plausible. Over twenty million Brazilians were Protestants, some 15 per cent of the nation. They constituted over half the entire Protestant population of Latin America but in a number of other countries Protestants were between 8 and 20 per cent – Chile, Nicaragua, Puerto Rico, El Salvador, Panama and Venezuela. Most of the growth was Pentecostalist. Almost everywhere it owed a great deal to North American influence, to situations of grave political unsettlement and to the use of the mass media, combining the flair of TV evangelism with a message of economic advancement for the individual.

It is too soon to decide how far this movement will go in the major countries of South America in altering their basic Christian character. The ecclesiastical history of the continent has up to this point demonstrated an extraordinary stability and public uniformity. The model of Iberian Catholicism, somewhat refashioned by nineteenth-century Ultramontanism, has never hitherto been challenged, interiorly or exteriorly, except for occasional buffetings from an anticlerical state. Since 1960 it has been under attack from both directions. Catholic reformism, with its strength in the religious orders, in university departments and in the Base Community movement, has challenged it from within. Protestantism, and especially Pentecostal Protestantism, has challenged it from without. Yet, paradoxically, the older established Protestantism is often deeply in sympathy with radical Catholicism, while the new Protestantism is often both politically and doctrinally oddly similar to traditional Catholicism. It could well be that the conservative Catholic hierarchy, reinforced so strongly in the pontificate of John Paul II, by undermining the Base Community movement, because of its seeming threat to the traditional pattern of clerical control, has in fact been throwing away the only instrument with which in most countries it could hold the Protestant advance at bay, and do it precisely by both sanctioning and reinvigorating the popular Catholicism of the poor. If the religiosity of the masses cannot find a helpful opening there, it switches easily enough to a neo-Pentecostal form. The complexity of modern Latin American Protestantism is already vast, and it would be highly mistaken to think that its future as a whole could, for instance, be foretold in the light of the Guatemalan experience, significant as the latter must be, given that it has made of Guatemala a country almost as Protestant as it is Catholic.

While Brazil continues to hold the prime role both in regard to Catholic reform and in regard to Protestantization, the story of each country, religious as much as political, is its own. The Latin American may need no reminding, but the outsider does have to beware of homogenizing Brazil and Peru, Argentina and Colombia, Chile and Mexico. Each has had its own religious history, clear enough in the nineteenth century and still more clear in the twentieth. What is certain is that, hitherto, nowhere else in the world did the Catholic Church have so huge a field almost to itself, that this is no longer the case, and that the religious development of the next 30 years from Mexico City to Buenos Aires may quite strikingly determine the entire balance of the Christian world.

Notes

1 I am most grateful to Austen Ivereigh for reading through this chapter, spotting errors and making a number of helpful suggestions.
2 *The Cambridge History of Latin America*, ed. Leslie Bethell (Cambridge, 1984–95), vol. I, p. 513.
3 David Brading, *The First America* (Cambridge, 1991), pp. 152 and 165.

4 Eric Van Young, 'The Messiah and the Masked Man: popular identity in Mexico, 1810–1821' in S. Kaplan (ed.), *Indigenous Responses to Western Christianity* (New York University Press, 1995).

5 This looks remarkably like the way Augustine and his Roman monks entered Canterbury in 597. Las Casas had pointed to Augustine as model for American missionaries. The stability of a working model of mission across a thousand years is remarkable.

6 Johannes Meier, 'Religious developments in the Chiquitos Territories (Bolivia) since the expulsion of the Jesuits', unpublished paper, 1997.

7 Bethell (ed.), *Cambridge History of Latin America*, vol. I, p. 477.

8 Bethell, *Cambridge History*, vol. III, p. 32.

9 Bethell, *Cambridge History*, vol. III, p. 431.

10 William W. Stein, 'Religion and clergy in the Atusparia uprising, Peru, 1885' in János M. Bak and Gerhard Benecke (eds), *Religion and Rural Revolt* (Manchester University Press, 1984), p. 432.

11 Victor Lanternari, *The Religions of the Oppressed* (London and New York, 1963), p. 191.

12 Daniella Klein, 'Canudos and the language of liberation', BA Honours dissertation, University of Leeds, 1994, unpublished. Klein bases herself particularly on Alexandre Otten, *So Deus e Grande: A Mensagem Religiosa de Antonio Conselheiro* (São Paulo, 1990). An understanding of what happened at Canudos, portrayed at the time as a major threat to the Brazilian Republic, was made exceedingly difficult by the account given by a journalist who accompanied the troops: Euclides de Cunha, *Os Sertoes*, translated into English as *Rebellion in the Backlands* by Samuel Putnam (University of Chicago Press, 1957). See also R. Della Cava, 'Brazilian messianism and national institutions: a reappraisal of Canudos and Joaseiro', *Hispanic American Historical Review*, 48 (1968), pp. 402–20.

13 *Crosscurrents in Indigenous Spirituality: Interface of Maya, Catholic and Protestant Worldviews*, ed. Guillermo Cook (Leiden, 1997), pp. 64–5.

14 Steve Brouwer, Paul Gifford and Susan D. Rose, *Exporting the American Gospel: Global Christian Fundamentalism* (New York and London, 1996), ch. 4, 'Guatemala: Protestant modernization or Evangelical apocalypse?', p. 57.

15 Alceu Amoroso Lima, 'Brazil' in Adrian Hastings (ed.), *The Church and the Nations* (London, 1959), p. 205.

10

China and its neighbours

R. G. Tiedemann

The introduction of Christianity into eastern Asia proved exceptionally difficult, for here it encountered highly sophisticated and culturally stable societies based on different ideological and organizational principles. South-east Asia had long been exposed to cultural and religious influences from India, which further added to the significant ethnic and cultural diversity of the region. Theravada Buddhism, in both its elite and folk variants, was strongly entrenched among the dominant ethnic groups of Burma and Siam (modern Thailand) and played a central part in the politico-religious traditions of these kingdoms. In the South-east Asian island world, animist traditions remained strong in spite of the introduction of elements of Hinduism in ancient times and the expansion of Islam into the region since the twelfth century. The East Asian world consisted of the large 'Confucianized high cultures' of China, Japan, Korea and Vietnam. These powerful polities, with their organized religions, hierarchies of priests and monks, sophisticated scriptures and well-endowed temples, proved particularly resistant to the introduction of alien religious systems from western Eurasia.

China before 1500: Nestorians and Franciscans

Much of pre-modern East and South-east Asia was subject to or influenced by China, the dominant cultural and political power in the region. In time this populous but distant empire was to become the principal object of Western evangelization. However, it was an Eastern variant of the Christian faith that first gained entrance into China.

As Nestorian Christianity spread eastward from Persia among the Turkic nomads of Central Asia and along well-established trade routes, it eventually came into contact with Chinese civilization, probably some time in the sixth century. The first reliable evidence of Christian missionary activity in China is found on the famous Nestorian monument – erected in 781 and rediscovered in 1625 – with its lengthy and informative inscriptions in Chinese and Syriac. It states that a certain Alopen arrived in the Tang dynasty's capital of Chang'an (now Xi'an) in 635 during the reign of Emperor Taizong (627–649). This was a period of remarkable cultural openness and religious tolerance, allowing native Daoism as well as foreign creeds such as Buddhism, and to a lesser extent Manichaeism, Zoroastrianism, Judaism and Islam, to exist alongside Confucianism, the orthodox tradition of Chinese culture. As the following passage inscribed on the stele indicates, Christianity, too, had received imperial patronage:

> Bishop A-lo-pên of the Kingdom of Ta-ch'in [Syria], bringing with him the Sutras and Images, has come from afar and presented them at our Capital. Having carefully examined the scope of his teaching, we find it to be mysteriously spiritual, and of silent operation. Having observed its principal and most essential points, we reached the conclusion that they cover all that is most important in life.[1]

With imperial financial support, the first Christian church and monastery were built at Chang'an in 638. In the same year Alopen, with the permission of the emperor and help of Chinese collaborators, completed the translation of *The Sutra of Jesus the Messiah*, which thus became the first Christian book in Chinese. By this time 21 Nestorian monks, probably all from Persia, were active in China.

However, after these auspicious beginnings, two developments were to affect the Nestorian mission in China: the persecutions under the pro-Buddhist Empress Wu (625–705) and the Arab conquests in western Asia which cut off the Nestorian missionary outpost from its Persian heartland. Still, during the reign of Xuanzong (712–756) the Church recovered and made considerable progress. According to the monument, church buildings were restored and new missionaries arrived from Persia by sea in 744. Moreover, the faith spread among the Uighurs, the dominant Turko-Mongolian power on China's north-western frontier.

Yet in the Chinese Empire itself, Nestorianism was in decline soon after the erection of the monument. The great persecution under Emperor Wenzong in 845 proved particularly disastrous. In the final analysis, its fortunes had always been too closely tied to those of the Tang, and when the dynasty was overthrown in 907, China's first Christian Church vanished in the chaos which followed. As Samuel Moffett concludes, the decisive factor which caused the collapse of the Chinese Church 'was neither religious persecution, nor theological compromise, nor even its foreignness, but rather the fall of the imperial house on which the Church had too long relied for its patronage and protection'.[2] However, the Nestorian faith survived among some of China's Inner Asian neighbours.

The Mongol expansion in Asia created relative stability along the principal trade routes which significantly promoted the movement of peoples, goods and ideas between East and West Asia, creating the conditions for the reappearance of Christianity in China. Nestorianism returned to the Middle Kingdom in the wake of the Mongol conquest of North China in 1260. The Mongol world empire also facilitated direct contacts between Chinese and Europeans. The latter responded to stories circulating in Europe by the middle of the twelfth century of a benevolent Christian ruler named 'Prester John', who was said to live among the nomads of Central Asia.[3] Pope Innocent IV and other European rulers conceived the idea of an alliance with the Mongols against Islam. Thus the Council of Lyons in 1245 decided to send fact-finding missions to the Mongols, to establish friendly relations with them and possibly convert them. One of the missions, led by the Franciscan friar John of Plano Carpini (Giovanni del Pian di Carpini), arrived in the Mongol capital at Qaraqorum in time to witness the enthronement on 24 August 1246 of Güyük, the third Great Khān (1246–1248). Although John was received by the new supreme Mongol ruler, the papal letters urging the Mongols to convert to Christianity and abandon their military campaigns in Europe angered Güyük. Consequently, Plano Carpini returned empty-handed, arriving in Lyons in November 1247. Other missions to the East were equally ill-fated, including the one which set out in 1253 under William of Rubruck, a Franciscan in the entourage of crusading King Louis IX of France. An interview with the new Great Khān Möngke (1251–59) merely aggravated long-standing differences.[4] However, Rubruck left a more detailed account of life in the Mongol capital and the various people assembled there from many parts of Eurasia. While it alludes to the presence of Christians, it also reveals more clearly the persisting antagonism between Nestorians and Catholics. Thus, in connection with the Easter celebrations in 1254, 'a great crowd of Christians appeared – Hungarians, Alans, Russians, Georgians and Armenians – none of whom had set eyes on the sacrament since their capture, as the Nestorians would not admit them into their Church, from what they told us, unless they were rebaptized by them'.[5]

During the period of Mongol rule, East Asian Christians also came to Europe. In 1287 Arghun, the Īl-khān of Persia, sent the Nestorian monk Rabban Saumā on an embassy to foster an alliance with the Europeans. He visited Rome, Paris and Bordeaux and met the Pope and the kings of France and England. Originally Saumā had set out on a pilgrimage from China to Jerusalem with a monk named Rabban Markos, but they were unable to reach their destination and remained in the Nestorian heartland in Iraq.[6] Both were Önggüt Turks from Inner Mongolia. Some of the Önggüts, along with elements of other Turko-Mongolian tribes such as the Uighurs, Keraits and Naimans, had converted to Nestorian Christianity several generations earlier.[7]

In this connection, it is interesting to note that the Nestorian Kerait princess Sorqoqtani (died 1252) was the mother of Qubilai Khān, who in 1271 founded the Yuan dynasty in North China and by 1279 had conquered all of China. It was his pragmatic policy of religious toleration which enabled Nestorianism to make a comeback in China proper. Qubilai's vulnerable situation as a foreign ruler of a subjugated but thickly populated and highly civilized China led him to adopt a strategy of administering the country through foreign intermediaries. This in turn gave these advisers, including Eastern Christians, far more power than their small numbers warranted.

The favourable conditions prevailing during the Yuan dynasty also allowed Roman Catholicism to enter the Middle Kingdom itself. A solitary Franciscan friar, John of Montecorvino, after an arduous journey by sea via India, reached Khanbaliq (or Dadu, present-day Beijing) in 1294 and was received by Emperor Temür Öljeitü (1294–1307), grandson of the recently deceased Qubilai. With the help of the influential Prince George of the Önggüts, whom he had converted from Nestorianism (thereby aggravating the smouldering enmity between Nestorians and Catholics), John was permitted to build a church in Beijing in 1299 on land bought by an Italian merchant, Peter of Lucalongo. In a letter written in 1305, he reported some 6,000 converts. He added that 'I have already grown old, and my hair is white from the labours and tribulations rather than years, for I am fifty-eight years old'.[8] By then he had built a second church and assembled and baptized some 150 boys, instructing them in Greek and Latin, and teaching some of them to sing the Divine Office.

In recognition of these achievements, Pope Clement V appointed him Archbishop of Cambaluc (Khanbaliq) and Patriarch of the East. However, it would be several years before reinforcements arrived from Europe. Of seven Franciscan bishops sent out by the Pope, only three reached Khanbaliq in 1308. They spent five years in the capital, supported by generous grants from the Emperor of China. In 1313 the Franciscan China mission was able to expand, when a wealthy Armenian woman provided the funds to build a church in the important port of Quanzhou (Zaitun) in Fujian province. Subsequently a Catholic presence was also established in Yangzhou, Hangzhou (Quinsai) and other places.

Around 1322 a Franciscan visitor, Odoric of Pordenone (c. 1265–1331), arrived in South China, carrying with him the bones of four Franciscans who had been killed in India during an earlier attempt to reach China.

On his way to Beijing he visited members of his order at Quanzhou and Hangzhou. One other, rather large, group of clerics is known to have reached China, led by John of Marignolli. They set out from Avignon in 1338, reaching Beijing in 1342. Five years later John left China via Quanzhou to return to Europe. By this time the Yuan dynasty was already in decline, to be overthrown in 1368. The fifth Bishop of Zaitun, James of Florence, was killed by Chinese patriots in 1362, and in 1369 all Christians were expelled from Beijing. Once again Christianity disappeared with the fall of the dynasty. The new isolationist Chinese Ming dynasty would not tolerate foreigners and their religions, whether Catholic or Nestorian.

The planting of Christianity, 1500–1800

The expansion of Portuguese colonial and mercantile power in Asia during the first half of the sixteenth century was accompanied by a surge of militant Catholic missionary zeal to preach Christianity to the peoples of the newly discovered countries. In accordance with a bull of Pope Alexander VI (1493) and the treaties of Tordesillas (1494) and Saragossa (1529), the world had been divided into two exclusive spiritual jurisdictions under the royal patronage of the monarchs of Spain and Portugal who assumed direct responsibility for the conversion of the 'heathen' and the building of churches and monasteries. Consequently, as the Portuguese proceeded to establish a string of trading stations in Asia, extending from Goa (1510) in India to Melaka (1511) on the Malay peninsula, Ternate (1522), Tidore and Ambon in the Maluku or 'spice islands', Faifo (now called Hoi An) near Da Nang in Vietnam, Macao in China (granted as a trading post in 1557) and Japan, priests came along as chaplains and evangelists under the royal patronage (*padroado*) arrangement.

Except for the major establishments at Melaka, the Portuguese were not particularly successful in planting Christianity in South-east Asia. In the Indonesian islands the high point came in 1546 with the arrival of the Spanish Jesuit Francis Xavier (1506–52). He spent two years in the Maluku region and was said to have made thousands of 'converts' among the non-Muslim tribes. His missionary efforts stimulated a wider interest in Christianity, and by 1555 some 30 villages on the island of Ambon had become Christian. Even so, the lack of priests meant that such congregations were left to their own devices. Moreover, because the Portuguese Crown failed to provide effective support, the missionaries were unable to assist local rulers who had accepted Christianity against their (more often than not Muslim) enemies. The Catholic mission was further weakened after 1605 when the Dutch East India Company drove the Portuguese from Ambon and Tidore. Only some remnants of Dominican mission work survived into the nineteenth century on the islands of Solor and Flores, in the vicinity of Portuguese East Timor. The capture of Portuguese Melaka by the Dutch in 1641 and the destruction of its numerous monasteries and churches severely reduced the Catholic presence in South-east Asia.

The Philippines

Whereas the Christianity promoted by the Portuguese made relatively little impression in much of South-east Asia, the situation was quite different under royal Spanish patronage in the Philippines. After initial contact had been made by Magellan's ill-fated fleet in Cebu in 1521, evangelization began in earnest with the decision of King Philip II in 1570 to commit Spain to the colonization and Christianization of the islands. Following the capture of Manila, the local chief agreed to a treaty accepting Spanish protection and the propagation of Christianity. By 1595 there were 134 missionaries working in the Philippines, and it was estimated that 288,000 baptisms had taken place.

The Christianizing process in the Philippines followed precedents already established in Spanish America, where missionaries had learnt that it was vital to obtain the conversion of chiefs in order to win over their followers and that the most effective way of converting local leaders was to teach Christian ideas to their children. An important factor in the success of Christianity was the fact that many aspects of worship could be accommodated by Filipino culture. It is important to note that – except for Mindanao in the south where Islam had made some inroads – the Spanish did not have to confront the 'high cultures' of mainland Asia. Instead, in a setting where animism was the dominant belief amongst the various local social groupings, Christian practices were vaguely akin to indigenous rituals. It has been suggested that the sprinkling of holy water, the recitation of prayers in Latin and the sign of the cross provided an alternative to animistic healing rites. At the same time traditional popular Filipino practices were included in or adapted to Christian worship, in spite of missionary concern. In a society where spirit worship was widely practised, the vast array of Catholic holy figures was accepted as an effectual and attractive source of power. As had hitherto been the case with the ancestors, the names of saints could be invoked to obtain assistance and protection. Blessed by the priest, rosaries, crosses and holy medals became potent talismans. On the other hand, Filipinos gradually came to accept the Christian idea of monogamy and the indissolubility of marriage. In this way a kind of folk Catholicism was enabled to take firm root in the northern part of the Philippines.

The rise and fall of Christianity in late medieval Japan

The Catholic missionary effort in Japan followed closely on the heels of Portuguese traders who had first reached the country in 1543. On 15 August 1549 Francis Xavier and his confrères Torres and Fernandez landed at Kagoshima, the capital of Satsuma, one of the most powerful *han* (feudal domains) in western Japan. They were accompanied by the Japanese Paul Yajirō (or Anjirō) who, having fled Japan in 1544 in a Portuguese ship to avoid arrest for manslaughter, was baptized and received a rudimentary education at St Paul's College, Goa. He now served the priests as interpreter. The missionaries soon were able to establish cordial relations with some of the important men. In the unstable political environment of sixteenth-century Japan – a time of civil war – all the western *han* feared for their independence and sought to attract Portuguese aid. The Jesuits were particularly successful on the southern island of Kyūshū, where they were able to 'convert' important local *daimyō* (feudal lords), who in turn ordered their subject people to adopt the foreign religion.

Not long after Xavier's departure in 1551, the remaining missionaries began to look to the central area, Japan's cultural heartland, where the old capital was located, as well as what passed for central government. They continued the practice of cultivating friendly relations with and gaining the support of influential persons. Thus Gaspar Vilela SJ (1525–72) was granted an audience with the shōgun (military ruler) in 1559. In time the Jesuits succeeded in gaining the friendship even of the hegemonic ruler Oda Nobunaga (1534–82), who by 1568 was the most powerful man in Japan. The fact that the Buddhist sects had generally sided with his enemies may explain why he treated the Jesuits well during these uncertain years in Japanese history. Toyotomi Hideyoshi (1537–98), Nobunaga's successor as military ruler of Japan, seemed similarly well disposed toward the foreign religion. In 1583, for example, he provided the land for the construction of a church in Ōsaka.

In the mean time, the missionaries were beginning to make greater efforts to adapt to the local culture. The Italian Jesuit Alessandro Valignano (1539–1606), who had arrived in 1579 to conduct the first of three inspection tours, immediately set out to reverse the rigid policy of Mission Superior Francisco Cabral, who had maintained that Japanese Christians would have to adopt the manners and practices of the Portuguese Jesuits. In contrast, Valignano insisted that the foreign priests must as far as possible accommodate themselves to indigenous sensibilities and ways of doing things, as long as they did not run counter to the Christian creed. They were to adopt the Japanese lifestyle in dress, cleanliness, food and housing. Furthermore, the missionaries were to pay careful attention to the niceties of etiquette to ensure success for their strategy of working from the top down. It was, after all, the Jesuits' hope to transform the Asian countries into Christian lands by first converting the rulers and then allowing the faith to trickle down to the populace at large.[9]

As a result of the expanding missionary endeavour in the second half of the sixteenth century, other Western religious and commercial influences entered the country. Initially the Portuguese played a dominant role. By the early 1600s, Dutch and English traders, that is to say, Protestant heretics, began to challenge the Portuguese position. Moreover, the Jesuit missionary monopoly was broken in 1593 with arrival in Japan of the first Spanish Franciscans from Manila. The Jesuits' approach brought them into conflict with other missionaries, with disastrous consequences. Whereas the Jesuits had worked with Japan's leaders, the Franciscan friars began to proselytize among the poor and criticize the Jesuit policy of accommodation.

This proliferation and the ensuing competition and intrigue amongst the foreigners alarmed Japanese leaders. As early as 1587 anti-Christian edicts were published but not rigorously enforced. The shōgun Ieyasu (1542–1616), who in 1603 established the centralized feudal Tokugawa state, and at first had been friendly to the Christians, soon turned against them. In 1606 Christianity was declared illegal, and on 27 January 1614 the famous edict against Christianity was published, which included the following passage:

> The Kirishitan [Christian] band have come to Japan, not only sending their merchant vessels to exchange commodities, but also longing to disseminate an evil law, to overthrow true doctrine, so that they may change the government of the country and obtain possession of the land. This is the germ of great disaster, and must be crushed.[10]

In that year Ieyasu embarked on a long and painful destruction of Christianity which intensified under his successor, commencing with a serious campaign to expel the missionaries. The greatest tragedy occurred, however, in 1637–38 when a peasant uprising in the Shimabara-Amakusa area of western Kyūshū, in which Christians took a leading part, was brutally suppressed by the government. Some 37,000 peasants are said to have lost their lives. As a result of the savage attacks, the number of Christians (300,000 out of a population of some 25 million inhabitants before the persecutions) was much reduced, yet some survived as underground communities into the nineteenth century. Some Christians managed to flee abroad, establishing Japanese congregations in Faifo in Vietnam, and in Ayutthaya in Siam. Japan itself was now closed to virtually all European influences (except for the precarious Dutch establishment at Deshima Island near Nagasaki).

In the end Catholicism failed because it was not compatible with Japanese tradition, in particular with Buddhism. At the same time, the initial missionary successes coincided with attacks of important Japanese military leaders on powerful Buddhist interests. Moreover, Christianity had gained a toehold precisely at a time of internal difficulty, during the brutal age of the Country at War (*Sengaku*), particularly during the period 1560–87. But once the political stability and intellectual orthodoxy had been restored by the Tokugawa shōguns, an alien faith could no longer be tolerated, especially one that had engaged in political intrigue. Christianity came to be seen as potentially subversive, not only of the political order, but of the basic social structure, for it challenged accepted values and beliefs. The work of the Franciscans and Dominicans among the masses rather than the elites was regarded as undermining the established hierarchical order from below. As the Shimabara rebellion seemed to indicate, Christianity was seen to inspire disloyalty and had to be eradicated like a disease. Missionary association with European expansion was perceived as a threat from abroad, most notably from the Spanish in the Philippines. Given the new political realities of early Tokugawa Japan, few of the so-called 'Christian *daimyō*' – or their successors – kept the faith. One notable exception was Takayama Ukon, who remained a committed Christian. Having been dispossessed by Hideyoshi in 1587, he was expelled from Japan during the general persecution of 1614, and died the following year in exile in Manila.[11]

The entire Tokugawa period is marked by persistent and rigorous enforcement of anti-Christian laws long after the early 1600s. In 1640 the Office of Inquisition for Christian Affairs was established in Edo (modern Tokyo) to oversee the surveillance of Christians. Throughout the country Buddhist temples were entrusted with the investigation of Christianity and other 'evil religions'. This control was supplemented with another severe anti-Christian practice, namely the ceremony of *efumi*, or 'picture stepping'. Sacred pictures of Christ or the Virgin Mary were placed on the ground, and all the inhabitants of cities and villages were ordered to trample on them to demonstrate their rejection of the Christian faith. The practice was eventually abandoned in 1857, under pressure from Western powers.

Late imperial China

There is no concrete evidence that some of the Christian congregations of the Mongol period survived into the late Ming and early Qing, although later Christian communities claimed such a link.[12] It would not be until the long-lived native Ming dynasty experienced domestic decay in the late sixteenth century that the opportunity for renewed missionary activity emerged. The early modern mission in China is closely linked to that in Japan. Francis Xavier, having started to work in Japan, hoped to begin work amongst the populous Chinese as well. But he died in 1552 on Shangchuan Island (St John's Island) off the coast of southern China before he could reach his goal. Three further Jesuit attempts to enter China also failed before Alessandro Valignano established a special training centre at the Portuguese settlement of Macao, enabling missionaries to study the Chinese language and culture in preparation for work in China.

The basic rules of accommodation which Valignano had established for Japan were applied by the first two Jesuit missionaries who successfully entered the Chinese Empire in 1583, namely the Italians Matteo Ricci (1552–1610) and Michele Ruggieri (1543–1607). They began to study both the vernacular and classical Chinese languages. After a number of false starts, they were invited by the prefect of Zhaoqing near Guangzhou (Canton) to reside in his city. They arrived there in September 1583 and Ricci remained until 1589. These were important years of preparation and adaptation for the Jesuit mission in China. Between 1589 and 1601 Ricci travelled and established a number of missions in some cities of central China. Finally, in 1601, he was permitted to travel to Beijing, the imperial capital, and the years from 1601 until his death in 1610 mark the peak of his achievement, setting the pattern of activity for the Jesuit mission in late imperial China.

Ricci was determined to win the respect of Chinese scholars and officials in intellectual terms in two ways. He set out to acquire a familiarity with the Confucian classics, so that he could bring references to traditional Chinese literature to bear in his arguments. At the same time he strove to impress the Chinese elite with the achievements of Occidental intellect to convince them that the Europeans were no mere barbarians. He demonstrated the results of Western astronomy and mathematics and the value of mechanical skills such as instruments and clocks. Perhaps the most noteworthy achievement during these years was Ricci's production of a world map with Chinese characters. This approach brought Ricci and his colleagues to the attention of well-known scholars and high-ranking officials. They were even permitted to engage in personal discussion with some of the emperors. In view of their scientific knowledge, some Jesuits were retained by the imperial court as quasi-officials.

Once they had gained the intellectual respect of the Chinese elite, the early Jesuit missionaries would start to preach their doctrines, avoiding unnecessary conflict with Chinese tradition and questions of dogma that might spark off controversy. Ricci, in particular, would interpret the terms used in Chinese classic texts as elements of Christian doctrine where this would be appropriate. By this means he was hoping to show an identity of basic Christian ideas with those of what he called 'ancient Confucianism', before it had become perverted into 'Neo-Confucianism' through the absorption of Buddhist and Daoist notions. In other words, Ricci was willing to accommodate, and by this means managed to achieve limited success in converting some important scholar-officials, most notably Xu Guangqi (1562–1633), Li Zhizao (1543–1630) and Yang Tingyun (1557–1627).[13]

After the Manchu conquest of China in 1644, Jesuit missionaries continued to be employed in official capacities in Beijing. Johann Adam Schall von Bell (1592–1666), Ricci's successor at court, was retained by the new Qing dynasty as their astronomer. Later Jesuits, especially Ferdinand Verbiest (1623–88), gained the favour of the great Emperor Kangxi (1662–1722), the middle years of his reign being the high point of early Catholicism in China, culminating with the promulgation of an imperial edict of toleration for the Christian religion in 1692. Yet not long afterwards developments would come to a head that would severely test the Christian enterprise in China.

In this connection, it should be noted that the Jesuits at court were no longer the only missionaries in China. Other Jesuits, as well as members of different mendicant orders and the Missions Étrangères de Paris, had established themselves in increasing numbers in the provinces. Here the missionaries concentrated not primarily on the conversion of the ruling class, but worked among the common people. In the towns and villages they came face to face with Chinese popular religion, with its beliefs in miracles and exorcism, the worship of images, practices of divination and acts of healing performed by holy men. The indigenous inhabitants were accustomed to worshipping a vast pantheon of popular deities. The practice of ancestor worship was ubiquitous, as was that of geomancy (*feng shui*).

Having been exposed to the realities of popular beliefs and practices, the provincial missionaries were less willing to make the same efforts at accommodation as the court-based Jesuits in Beijing. Thus in time serious differences emerged within the missionary community. For a hundred years or so the notorious 'Rites Controversy' caused a great deal of bad blood. This protracted controversy involved more than simply adaptation to Chinese culture. It was complicated by European national rivalries and the competing ambitions of different religious orders, essentially but not exclusively between the Jesuits and the mendicants. Furthermore, Rome was anxious to assert its own power of jurisdiction and control over missionary activity, with a view to weakening the Portuguese *padroado*. Nevertheless, it was the outcome of the debate concerning Confucian rites and ancestor worship that was to have such dire consequences for the Christian missions in East Asia. Should Christians be forbidden to participate in them? Or did these practices have no religious significance? Should Christians be permitted to contribute to community festivals in honour of non-Christian divinities? These were difficult questions and hotly debated in China and Europe for a century.

As we have seen, from the beginning some of the Jesuits had begun consciously to accommodate their methods to Chinese culture. The honouring of Confucius was a duty of scholars who had obtained literary civil service degrees. The ceremony was, therefore, an act of respect, and Matteo Ricci believed that it did not contain any superstitions. He claimed that 'the ultimate purpose and the general intention' of Confucianism was for 'public peace and order in the kingdom', and for the benefit of the family. He argued that the scholar-officials did not recite prayers to ask for favours from Confucius, and the kowtow (touching the ground with the forehead) was performed solely out of respect for the great sage.

Although Ricci supported a policy of accommodation with 'Confucianism', he did not accept all aspects of it. For example, he rejected the orthodox Neo-Confucianism as superstitious, perverse and leading the Chinese away from the one true God. His policy of selective accommodation is most clear in his attitudes towards ancestral and Confucian rites. He could tolerate those rites in which the superstitious practices seemed minimal. In other respects, however, Ricci forbade converts to say prayers and make petitions to the dead. He also condemned the belief that the dead received benefit and nourishment from offerings of food and the burning of paper money. Similarly, Ricci and other early Jesuit missionaries did impose certain restrictions on converts accustomed to participate in Confucian ceremonies. They forbade the converts of the gentry class from taking part in any ceremony honouring Confucius in which animals were killed and sacrificed. This they considered too superstitious. However, their missionary adversaries found this compromise unacceptable.

Another major issue that gave rise to intellectual controversies and contradictions within the missionary community concerned the nature and rendering of the word 'God'. As part of his strategy of accommodation, Ricci had adopted the policy of taking over or even exploiting the ideas and expressions of Chinese classical tradition, so as to demonstrate that Chinese culture had originally included a belief in ideas that were Christian. It was in this way that he adopted the two expressions *Shangdi*, or 'Sovereign on High', and *Tian*, 'Heaven', as evidence of early Chinese belief in a single deity. At the outset of his mission, in 1583, Ricci chose the term *Tianzhu*, 'Master of Heaven', to render 'God'. But at the suggestion of some Chinese scholars he later tended to use the term *Shangdi*, believing the two terms to be synonymous for his purposes. However, in 1628 the term *Shangdi* was rejected at a missionary conference in favour of *Tianzhu*, and Catholic Christianity henceforth became known as *Tianzhujiao*, the religion of the Lord of Heaven.

In the socio-political context of imperial China, the 'term question' and Rites Controversy were to have grave implications for the future of Christianity in the Middle Kingdom. The Jesuits had appealed to the Emperor Kangxi for an opinion on the key issues of the controversy, and he expressed himself as agreeing with them that honours were paid to Confucius only as legislator, that those to the ancestors were not for the purpose of asking protection but merely a demonstration of love and a commemoration of the good the dead had done during their lives. Moreover, the emperor asserted that the sacrifices to *Tian* were not to the visible heavens, but to the Supreme Lord, the creator and preserver of heaven and earth and all contained therein. The emperor's statements were sent to Rome for consideration. Pope Clement X rejected them and in 1704 sent a papal legate, Charles Maillard de Tournon (1668–1710), to China to convince the emperor that Rome's findings were not in contravention of Chinese imperial prerogatives. But de Tournon managed to antagonize the emperor, who was annoyed that his supreme position as 'Son of Heaven' was being challenged. Furthermore, he was angered by the implicit assumption that some missionaries had a better knowledge of the Chinese classics than the emperor himself. Thus in 1706 he issued an edict to the effect that all missionaries, if they wished to remain in China, had to obtain an imperial licence (*piao*). This was to be granted only to those who agreed to abide by the practices of Matteo Ricci.

While some Chinese scholars were impressed by the Jesuits' scientific knowledge, they found the foreign religious message rather incomprehensible. As a certain Zhang Chao put it in 1699:

> They are extraordinarily intelligent, those people [the missionaries]. Their studies concern astronomy, the calendar, medicine, and mathematics; their customs are loyalty, good faith, constancy, and rectitude; their skill is marvellous. . . . The conceptions of the great West are surely far ahead of other doctrines. It is simply a shame that they speak of a Lord of Heaven, a crude and obnoxious conception that leads them into absurdities and which our literati have a great deal of difficulty accepting. If they could only put aside this conception, they would be very close to our Confucian tradition.[14]

Chinese intellectuals were troubled by the notion of an unseen 'creator' who remained outside the creation. Some scholars suspected that Christianity had stolen Confucian terms to name its god and had borrowed the language of the Buddhist transmigration of the soul. Furthermore, they found it hard to understand why an all-powerful deity should have created an evil spirit who made humans do evil things. To some scholars steeped in Neo-Confucian cosmology and the concept of the innate goodness of man's nature, Christian ideas such as the transcendent God, the need for individual prayer for God's forgiveness of sin and the hope for other-worldly salvation appeared egotistically motivated and 'perverse'. Such an un-Confucian 'profit-oriented mind' had much in common with indi-genous heterodox sects. Indeed, Christianity appeared to many to be an absurd and subversive philosophy that devalued the world, destroying the Three Relationships between ruler and subject, father and son, and husband and wife that constitute the core of the Confucian view of individual and society.

Fears of Christianity's subversiveness, real or imagined, virtually ended early hopes of success in the Confucian world of China. Matters were not helped by the decision of Pope Clement XI to bring the long Rites Controversy to a conclusion by ruling against the Jesuit compromise in the Constitution *Ex illa die* of 1715. The ruling was finalized in 1742 by Pope Benedict XIV in the bull *Ex quo singulari*. The refusal by Rome to allow Christians to take part in the Confucian and ancestral rites was to have grave consequences, for the Christians of China were, in effect, cut off from the Confucian cultural tradition, and thereby from society at large. Reflecting the state's hostility to anything perceived as a threat to the ideological orthodoxy and social unity of the empire, Christianity was now identified as a deviant ideology. From 1724, following the fateful edict of the Emperor Yongzheng, there was a significant intensification of persecution of converts. Christians were commanded to renounce their faith. Foreign missionaries, except those attached to the Bureau of Astronomy in Beijing, were expelled from China.[15] Church properties were confiscated and used for secular purposes. The papal abolition of the Jesuit order in 1773 and continuing quarrels amongst the China mission-aries (e.g. the Beijing Schism) merely aggravated the precarious position of the Church in the Middle Kingdom. For the next 120 years Christianity was officially proscribed as a heterodox cult. Catholicism retreated into the remoter parts of rural China, increasingly vulnerable to suppression. The few priests (Chinese and European) operating secretly in the country were able to provide rather inadequate pastoral supervision. An eighteenth-century Bishop of Nanjing, Gottfried Laimbeckhoven SJ, described the priests' problems thus:

> During the greater part of the year, we are confined to the prison of a narrow boat in which we wander here and there . . . During the deep silence of the night we slip into the houses of the Christians, quickly and in all haste we administer the Sacraments, baptize infants, and adults, if there are any. After saying Mass, we have to disappear at once in order not to be discovered by the infidels.[16]

In the absence of regular priestly care, congregations were left to their own devices for years if not decades.

Although not explicitly stated in missionary accounts, successful evangelization had from the beginning depended upon the generous assistance of Chinese Christians. The first three prominent Christian scholar-officials, Xu Guangqi (Paul Hsü), Li Zhizao (Leo Li) and Yang Tingyun (Michael Yang) not only supported and defended the Western priests, they also funded flourishing Churches in their native Jiangnan localities.[17] Thus Xujiahui (Zi-ka-wei), the estate of the Xu family outside the old city of Shanghai, became the major Jesuit mission station in China and still is the centre of Christian life in the Shanghai region. Later on other Chinese Christian literati collaborated in important translation projects, wrote on Christian theology as they understood it, and sought to mediate between the contending European parties in the Rites Controversy, correcting certain misconceptions concerning Chinese rites and advocating the coexistence of Confucianism and Christianity.[18]

At the same time, most Catholic missionaries came to recognize the importance of training a native clergy, given the size of the country and the many social and linguistic problems for foreign priests. Luo Wenzao [Gregorio Lopez] (1611–91) has the distinction of being the first Chinese priest. A native of Fujian province, he entered the Dominican order and was ordained in Manila in 1654. He was subsequently consecrated Bishop of Nanjing but, till the twentieth century, remained the only Chinese to hold an episcopal office. Bishop Luo in turn ordained the first Chinese priests on Chinese soil on 1 August 1688.[19] Other Chinese clerics were trained in Macao by the Jesuits, in Manila by the Dominicans and in the Seminary General in Siam by the Paris Missionaries.[20] The Propaganda missionary Matteo Ripa (1682–1746) founded the College of the Holy Family in Naples in 1732 for the purpose of training Chinese secular clergy.[21] In time more native clergy would receive training in China itself. All of these Chinese priests pursued their apostolic work during the periods of persecution in the eighteenth century. But their number remained rather small. Thus we find that the remarkable Li Ande [Andreas Ly] (1693–1774), who had been trained at the MEP Seminary General in Siam, was the only priest in the large province of Sichuan to minister to the many Christian communities in the late 1740s.

Given the nature of the evangelistic task and the paucity of clergy, the mission enterprise had to rely on various kinds of lay personnel to manage Church affairs, conduct religious services and evangelization, instruct the young and arrange the priests' all too infrequent clandestine visits to their communities: catechists, congregational leaders (*huizhang*) and women known as 'virgins'.[22] Since Chinese mores made it impossible for priests to establish direct contact with the often pivotal female elements in particular households, Christian women became a vital element in the apostolate from the beginning of the missionary enterprise in China. Certain single laywomen consecrated their lives to the service of God and the mission. These so-called Chinese virgins, while taking their vows, continued to live with their families, where they taught the women and children and during times of persecution became the true pillars of the faith within the community.[23]

While printed instructions were circulated in some parts of China to instruct local lay leaders of parishes deprived of their priests as to how to conduct Church affairs and propagate Catholicism, many Christian congregations relied on the accumulated body of religious knowledge, catechisms, songs, biblical stories or simply local Christian tradition to preserve the faith. Nevertheless, some congregations must have succumbed to the syncretistic pressures of local folk religion or indigenous sectarianism.[24] Yet, in spite of the many vexations and periodic persecutions, some 200,000 Christians are said to have existed nationwide in scattered communities at the beginning of the nineteenth century. These congregations of 'Old Christians' formed the vital base from which the next phase of Christian expansion in China would be launched.

The origins of the Church in Vietnam

Although there had been some earlier missionary contacts, a more fruitful Christianizing effort started in Vietnam in 1624 with the arrival at the Faifo mission of the French Jesuit Alexandre de Rhodes (1591–1660). He was a gifted linguist, producing the first catechism in the Vietnamese language. It was written in vernacular Vietnamese (*quōc-ngu*) in the Latin alphabet. Between 1627 and his expulsion in 1630, Rhodes was active in Tongking, the northern part of Vietnam, controlled by the Trinh. Here he made his greatest contribution to the Vietnamese Church by establishing the Domus Dei, an organization of seminary-trained catechists.[25] These celibate laymen also received elementary medical training and were encouraged to work in the villages. In fact, the organization was based on an existing Buddhist institution, evidence of Rhodes' willingness – following the examples set by Valignano and Ricci – to adapt to established indigenous religious customs and practices. In local communities there was already a high regard for celibacy and a common belief that illness was due to possession by evil spirits. Many traditional indigenous religious specialists who became catechists often brought their followers into the Church *en masse*. During a second sojourn in Vietnam from 1640, Alexandre de Rhodes applied the same methods in the Nguyen territories in the south, albeit with less success. In 1645 he was forced to abandon the work in Vietnam as both the Nguyen and Trinh factions had become apprehensive about Christianity. Still, parts of the country continued to witness remarkable Christian growth in spite of the very limited number of European clergy. In 1658 the whole of Vietnam was said to have some 300,000 Catholics, but only two priests. It was the lay leadership of the Domus Dei which was primarily responsible for this rapid growth and survival of the Vietnamese Church.

In consequence of this remarkable expansion, Father de Rhodes, upon his return to Europe from the East in 1649, sought to gain approval for the formation of a strong native clergy as necessary for the promotion of Catholicism. To this end, he played a significant role in the foundation of the Foreign Mission Society of Paris (Missions Étrangères de Paris) in 1659. In part intended to undermine the Portuguese and Spanish patronage monopolies,[26] this new society of secular priests enjoyed the support of the French Church, French mercantile interests and the court of Louis XIV. From the outset, the newly appointed French vicars apostolic, Pierre Lambert de la Motte MEP (1624–79) and François Pallu MEP (1626–84),[27] were interested in South-east Asia as a whole, in part because the Portuguese authorities prevented French priests from entering China through Macao. In 1666 the MEP opened a central seminary in Ayutthaya, the capital of Siam, to prepare Chinese, Vietnamese and other East Asians for the priesthood.

While the MEP priests continued to follow the Jesuit policy of promoting the formation of a native clergy, these bearers and representatives of Catholicism as well as French culture were less willing to practise accommodation in Vietnam. On the contrary, in 1672 the Synod of Tourane (Da Nang) forbade Catholics to participate in ceremonies revering Confucius, thus creating a major obstacle to the conversion of significant sections of Vietnam's Confucian elite. Moreover, this decision could not but increase the animosity toward Christianity of the Vietnamese authorities in both the Trinh and Nguyen areas, culminating in the expulsion of the missionaries in 1750. Although the mixture of French political, commercial and religious activities – promoted in South-east Asia since the 1660s – could not be sustained at this time, it laid the foundations for more aggressive French imperialist and missionary penetration of Vietnam in the nineteenth century. Indeed, at the end of the eighteenth century some French priests were able to enter the country once more by acting as intermediaries in military affairs. Thus Bishop Pierre Pigneau de Behaine MEP (died 1799)[28] assisted Nguyen Anh in his ultimately successful effort to reunite Vietnam. Nguyen Anh, who in 1802 proclaimed himself emperor under the reign title Gia Long, subsequently tolerated the presence of Christian communities as a debt of gratitude. In spite of periodic persecutions, the Catholic Church was more successful in Vietnam at this time than in any other part of Asia except the Philippines.

This is primarily due to the important contribution and perseverance of native Christians, led by indigenous clergy and a strong lay leadership.

1800–1945

In the course of the nineteenth century, the missionary enterprise – in which Catholics had now to compete with Protestants – became increasingly associated with expanding Western colonialism and imperialism. However, at the beginning of the nineteenth century much of East and South-east Asia was still beyond the reach of any European power. Only Penang, Melaka, Java, some of the Maluku and the northern part of the Philippines could really be said to be under direct foreign control. However, by the early twentieth century virtually all of South-east Asia had at least been nominally integrated into the colonial order, as the Dutch extended their control over the Indonesian islands, while the British absorbed Burma and Malaya in several stages, and the French took possession of Indo-China (Vietnam, Cambodia and Laos). Still, colonial domination remained rather uneven and never complete. For instance, a number of the outer regions under nominal Dutch sovereignty were in reality controlled by overseas Chinese economic interests. Although none of the East Asian states were formally integrated into Western colonial empires, in the middle of the nineteenth century China and Japan – and later Korea also – were forced to accept treaty settlements that entailed foreign penetration of hitherto relatively closed societies. Zealous missionaries, products of European and American revival movements, were quick to take advantage of the new opportunities created by Western imperialism.

The Church, colonialism and nationalism in South-east Asia

As we have seen, only the Philippines had largely been converted to Christianity by 1800. Elsewhere the foreign evangelists were struggling to overcome Muslim resistance in Malaya and parts of Indonesia, and Theravada Buddhist opposition in Burma and Thailand. But it was developments in Vietnam that demonstrated a new, more aggressive side of Christian expansion. Initially prospects looked rather better here, for the influence of Pigneau de Behaine and his French military associates in helping to establish the Nguyen dynasty of the Gia Long emperor in the 1790s carried over into the second decade of the 1800s. The emperor respected the Catholic faith espoused by his French friends and permitted the unimpeded functioning of the missionaries. These were mainly Spanish friars in the north (Tongking) and French priests in the south

(Annam and Cochin-China). There were an estimated 300,000 Christians in Tongking and some 60,000 in Cochin-China by 1820.

However, after Gia Long's death, the new ruler, dominated by conservative Confucianists and patriotic elements, inaugurated in 1825 a policy of harassment of missionaries and converts. The court at Hué was particularly alarmed by the arrival of new French missionaries in the 1820s, representatives of the vigorous revival which characterized the post-Napoleonic period in Europe and which found expression in the daring missionary penetration of various countries in Asia. The missionaries accepted personal risks and sacrifices, were contemptuous of any political barriers imposed, and were also oblivious to the feeling of local alarm which their aggressive actions might arouse.[29]

It is, therefore, not surprising that persecution of Christians became more violent in Vietnam after 1833, developing into a feud between King Minh Mang and French missionary leaders, who requested the aid of French naval vessels visiting Eastern Asia. In response, Minh Mang ordered all foreign priests to assemble at the capital, where they were held as virtual prisoners. Some escaped, but seven French and three Spanish missionaries were killed between 1833 and 1840. Nevertheless, these also were the years of the rapid expansion of French evangelistic activity in Vietnam. Catholic missionaries were able to enter Tongking secretly and quite easily from Macao. By encouraging greater French naval intervention, these priests argued that it would encourage disaffected partisans of the old Lê dynasty to challenge the established rulers. Once in power, the missionaries asserted, the new rulers would grant more missionary concessions, as well as the desired naval base for France. However, the French took little concrete action at this time and conditions deteriorated for foreign missionaries and indigenous Catholics. It was not until the reign of Napoleon III that the concerted clerical campaign succeeded in obtaining the armed intervention of France in Vietnam. The French emperor decided to take advantage of French participation in the Second Opium War in China (1856–60) to start the process of territorial acquisition in Vietnam, which was completed in 1885. Henceforth Vietnamese Catholicism came to be associated with French colonialism.

As Dutch control and influence expanded in what is now Indonesia in the seventeenth and eighteenth centuries, missionary activities as such were not encouraged. Indeed, such Christianizing efforts as had been undertaken were essentially confined to the conversion of indigenous Catholics to Protestantism, if need be by force. However, since Christians were favoured over non-Christians in Dutch East India Company service, some non-Muslims had found it useful to join the Protestant Church. After 1800, when evangelization was no longer discouraged by the Dutch authorities, active Protestant missionary work commenced amongst the non-Islamic peoples, and to a lesser extent amongst nominal Muslims. Thus more permanent work was initiated in eastern Java in 1814 by affiliates of the London Missionary Society. The Rhenish Missionary Society worked from 1836 in South Borneo and from 1862 among the Toba Bataks in northern Sumatra and on Nias, where in time the largest Indonesian Protestant Church, the Huria Kristen Batak Protestan, was to emerge. The Indische Kerk (the popular name of Protestantische Kerk in Nederlandsch-Indie), which originally had been the official Church of the Dutch East India Company, from around 1900 began substantial mission-ary activity in central Sulawesi, Maluku and the Timor archipelago. But it remained a kind of state Church, since its ministers and lay officials continued to be paid as government servants. In view of the strong link with the colonial system, this was to have disastrous consequences for them during the Japanese occupation 1942–45. Roman Catholic missions became possible again in the Dutch East Indies only after 1807, but at first remained limited to the pastoral care of European Catholics. However, in time a number of societies were able to resume mission work, especially amongst the surviving congregations in Maluku, northern Sulawesi, Solor, Flores and the Dutch part of Timor.

In the fiercely Islamic parts of the Indonesian archipelago, on the other hand, opposition to the Dutch rulers and their religion remained strong, as indicated by the fanatical resistance of Acheh in northern Sumatra in a war which started in 1873. The Muslim populations of the Malay peninsula proved equally unresponsive. Here the Christianizing effort remained largely confined to the British possessions of Melaka, Penang and Singapore, where evangelistic work among the Chinese migrant communities became an important part of the missionary enterprise.

In Siam and the Burmese kingdoms of Ava and Pegu relatively little progress was made. In particular, the Protestant version of Christianity proved too alien in the heartland of Theravada Buddhism and almost impossible to reconcile with traditional social and religious norms and practices. The only important Christian missionary impact was achieved among non-Buddhist minority groups such as the Karens and Kachins.

While traditional political and cultural opposition had accompanied the extension of European colonialism, in time an emerging national consciousness produced new forms of resistance. These forces developed quite early in the Philippines, the most Christianized colonial possession in Asia. After 1800 the Spanish began to experience increasing political and social unrest, especially in areas where the reactionary regular clergy had control over most of the land. Moreover, these friars (Augustinian Eremites, Franciscans and Dominicans) formed the most reliable pillar of Spanish rule in the Philippines. Indebted peasants came into conflict with the friars over access to undeveloped land. Although passivity more often than not was the norm, from time to time rustic reaction became violent. Such belligerent responses frequently developed strong millenarian dimensions in which magic played a powerful part, including the belief in charms, amulets and symbols of invulnerability deriving from pre-Spanish traditions, but modified by popular Catholicism.

While much of the rural unrest remained traditional in character, some of the millenarian anti-friar movements in central Luzon were coloured by patriotic sentiments. They were led by Filipino clergy who felt discriminated against in parish appointments which far too often went to regular clergy from Spain. Thus Apolinario de la Cruz, a frustrated Filipino layman who had been refused membership in a religious order in 1841, transformed what had originally been a Church-approved confraternity, the Cofradía de San José, into a separate organization. It became known as the Colorum movement, in which Spaniards and mestizos were explicitly denied membership. Although essentially a social movement, it did develop certain heterodox religious ideas. Consequently, when Apolinario was captured, he was horribly dismembered, presumably to disprove his supernatural pretensions. The survivors went into the mountains and there founded their 'New Jerusalem'. Christian names and terminology were used by the rebels, but the doctrines and rites were of pre-Spanish origin.[30]

The important contribution of native priests to the rise of Filipino nationalism became particularly evident in a schismatic religious movement led by Father Gregorio Aglipay who had been excommunicated in the 1890s because of his condemnation of foreign domination of the Philippine Church. Emilio Aguinaldo, leader of Katipunan (Sons of the People), made him vicar-general of the nationalist army, and after the break with Rome in 1902 he assumed the role of supreme bishop of the new Philippine Independent Church. This new religious organization enlisted only Filipinos as clergy, permitted them to marry, conducted services in the local dialects and itself participated actively in national political affairs.[31] It should be stated though that the great majority of Filipino Catholics remained loyal to the orthodox Catholic faith. Under American rule the dominant friar landholdings were dissolved and clerical influence in government was eliminated. At the same time, health and educational facilities were much improved. It should also be noted that American imperialist expansion was enthusiastically supported and taken advantage of by many American Protestant missionaries who finally saw a chance to commence evangelistic work in the Philippines after 1900.

Although conversion to Christianity often implied collaboration in colonial rule, the emerging indigenous Protestant Churches could also become a focus of resistance to foreign secular and religious domination. The movements by the Javanese mystics Paulus Tosari and Sadrach in central Java were the earliest and most remarkable examples of indigenous use of Christianity to resist Dutch dominance in the nineteenth century.[32] But it was not until the 1930s that a number of autonomous Churches emerged in various parts of Indonesia, such as the Batak Church in 1930, the Christian Church of East Java in 1931, the Pasundan Church in West Java, the Minahasa Church in 1934, the Moluccan Church in 1935. The Dutch missionary theologian Hendrik Kraemer deserves some of the credit, for he recognized the impact of the growing Indonesian nationalism on native Christians and was instrumental in effecting a change of attitude among missionaries. As he reminded the delegates to the 1938 Tambaran Conference of the International Missionary Council, the 'younger' Churches are the fruit of missionary labour, not the possession of mission societies.[33]

However, as the history of the Batak Church in northern Sumatra indicates, the organization of autonomous Churches had more to do with the indigenous Christians' desire to rid themselves of the tight grip of missionary control than with the early stirrings of a national consciousness. Since Christianity was the faith of the colonial rulers, it was in any case virtually impossible for native Christians to be actively involved in the early national independence struggles – except, of course, in the Philippines. It was the Japanese wartime occupation of South-east Asia which gave local Christians the opportunity to assume prominent leadership positions and manage Church affairs while the Europeans were interned or expelled.

From mission to Church in modern China

Following the Napoleonic Wars, renewed Catholic – as well as the emerging Protestant – interest in the West in missions brought about the gradual expansion of the missionary enterprise in the Middle Kingdom during the first four decades of the nineteenth century. Indeed, China would become the primary focus of the Western missionary movement in East Asia and a major object of the hopes of Christians around the world. However, the Chinese people remained suspicious of and hostile toward Christianity. Probably few missionaries in the nineteenth century realized the depth and strength of the Chinese state's historical obsession with preserving orthodoxy, and the resulting immense suspicion of Christianity as a heterodox doctrine that would undermine the traditional social order. Thus missionary activities in the interior of China continued to be illegal and precarious. Nevertheless, the clandestine operations saw the reassembly of scattered surviving Christian congregations and the reorganization of Catholic ecclesiastical territories, involving the final replacement of the *padroado* arrangement with vicariates apostolic controlled by the Congregation of Propaganda Fide in Rome.

The reintegration of Chinese Catholics into the expanding missionary enterprise was not achieved without resistance. There are some indications that local communities and their lay leaders were loath to give up the autonomy they had achieved as a result of infrequent or non-existent priestly supervision. Certainly in the Shanghai area (vicariate apostolic of Jiangnan) there was considerable resistance to the reassertion of foreign missionary power. In particular, the *huizhang*, having become accustomed to complete financial autonomy, clashed with the missionaries over the question of local financial control.

The newly arrived missionaries also objected to the ecclesiastical power of women, especially the virgins' liturgical and religious role in the local community. They appreciated their dedication, but also considered them a source of scandal. Thus Pierre Lavaissière CM wrote in 1840 that he was endeavouring to eliminate night visits by the virgins and to compel them to show less familiarity with their relatives and neighbours. In the prefectural city of Songjiang a confrontation between missionaries and Chinese arose over virgins' participation in the liturgy. The latter were accustomed to chanting prayers in Chinese during Mass. When Bishop Ludovico de Besi ordered the prayers to be recited by the entire congregation, men and women alternately, a storm of protest broke out, since such 'public conversation' between men and women offended Chinese moral sensibilities.

After the Jesuits had taken charge of the Jiangnan mission in the 1840s, they determined to solve these problems by 'regularizing' the virgins' life. Thus, in 1869 a group of French nuns founded a native Chinese congregation, the Association of the Presentation of the Blessed Virgin (Presentadines). The new congregation, as well as those subsequently established in other parts of the country, was intended to replace the virgins. They were placed under the authority of the mission superior, which contributed to greater foreign ecclesiastical control. However, it proved impossible to eliminate the ancient institution of virgins entirely and thus a degree of local autonomy was preserved.[34]

The privileged status Christians gained as a result of the so-called 'unequal treaties' probably more than made up for the loss of autonomy. Certainly proselytization in China was greatly facilitated. Under the treaty settlements of 1842–44, following the First Opium War (1839–42), the old 1724 prohibition against belief in Christianity was lifted. In addition, the French special envoy Théodose de Lagrené obtained an imperial edict in 1846 that provided for the return to the Christians of certain Church properties of the pre-1724 era. More important concessions were gained by the missionaries in the treaties of 1858–60. These permitted travel and the propagation of Christianity anywhere in the interior of China. Particularly noteworthy here is the French treaty (especially the notorious Article VI, containing surreptitiously inserted additional rights in the Chinese version, of the 1860 Beijing Convention), permitting the purchase of land and erection of buildings anywhere, not just in the designated treaty port cities, and associated agreements which exempted Christians from contributing to communal endeavours that were thought to have a 'superstitious' component. Most importantly, the French government assumed a religious protectorate over all Catholics in the Qing Empire, including foreign missionaries regardless of nationality as well as Chinese converts. Thus the physical expansion of the Christian presence was delimited by treaties, foreign diplomatic intervention and from time to time threatened or actual military action.

The emergence of muscular Christianity in China coincided with the Taiping Rebellion (1851–64) against the alien Manchu dynasty, one of the most devastating civil wars in human history. The Qing state considered the Taipings to be dangerous ideological heretics. Moreover, in the eyes of government officials and the gentry class, the Taipings were 'Christians'. Perhaps they are best understood as a Chinese heterodox millenarian sect with a syncretic Christian veneer derived from limited contact with Protestant missionaries (at best a premature and misguided example of indigenous Christianity).[35] What is important is that China's ruling class identified the Taipings with Christianity, thereby intensifying opposition to the foreign religion which certainly made it more difficult for Western missionaries to enter the country and the Chinese Church to flourish.

The presence of Protestant evangelists had in fact added a new dimension. Prior to the treaties, Robert Morrison of the London Missionary Society, who had arrived in 1807, and the handful or so subsequent early missionary arrivals were confined to a precarious existence in Macao and seasonal residence in Guangzhou (Canton). In both locations their religious activities were severely restricted. In the 1830s the Prussian Lutheran independent missionary Karl Friedrich August Gützlaff (1803–51) made several attempts to gain direct access to the Middle Kingdom. His reckless operations in foreign ships smuggling opium to points along the Chinese coast have been especially severely criticized. But essentially all missionaries, Protestant as well as Catholic, had to depend on the opium connection: many travelled out to China in ships carrying opium, their funds were remitted via opium traders and their charitable or educational work relied on donations from resident Western firms connected with the opium trade. Certainly in the minds of many Chinese, opium and Christianity were closely associated.

As a result of the first treaty settlements the Protestant missionaries, mostly of American and British nationality, had better opportunities to establish themselves in the five treaty ports and Hong Kong. After 1860 missions were established in all the new coastal and riverine treaty ports, and from there began to spread into the interior. The missionary presence grew rapidly in size and complexity. By 1900 there were over two thousand foreign Protestant missionaries in China. The main point here, too, is that all these developments, as well as the status and activities of the increasing numbers of Chinese who converted to Christianity, were ultimately dependent on the treaties imposed by the foreigners on the Qing state, and therefore had political implications.

Whereas Protestant missionaries, with the exception of Hudson Taylor's interdenominational and international China Inland Mission,[36] established themselves primarily in cities and from there itinerated in the surrounding villages, the returning Roman Catholic priests re-established control over the surviving rural congregations and worked and lived among the ordinary peasants. In time they, too, would reclaim former urban church premises and erect major residences and imposing structures in the cities of China, essentially for reasons of prestige and security. But a large number of European priests continued to reside at many of the growing number of rural stations. Indeed, in the nineteenth century 'conversion' to Christianity remained overwhelmingly a rural phenomenon. In the increasingly unstable social situation, especially after the devastating mid-century rebellions, some groups within rural communities became amenable to mass 'conversion'. It is difficult to know whether and to what extent spiritual motivations came into play. Certainly individual 'seekers after truth' entered the Church for religious reasons. There are also many documented cases of indigenous 'heterodox' sectarian groups who were attracted by the Christian message of salvation in an uncertain world. Nevertheless, perhaps in the majority of cases adherence to the Catholic Church provided a basis for social integration and self-protection in the competition for survival and resource control in rural China, where groups had to rely on their own cohesiveness and strength. Clearly, some of the individuals and families who became Christians in this chaotic social situation were able directly or indirectly to use the influence of foreign missionaries to increase their leverage in local society.

The competition for scarce resources naturally gave rise to violent conflict. There are hundreds of documented cases of disputes involving local Christians in the late nineteenth century: the refusal of Christians to pay taxes and contributions to 'heathen' temple upkeep and village theatricals; lawsuits between Christians and non-Christians; problems over property rights; intra-lineage or inter-lineage disputes. Since Catholic missionaries could rely on the often willing support of the French government, their effective intervention not only created powerful new solidarities or reinforced existing ones but made the Church attractive to other groups as well. The group identity of Christians helped them protect their interests at the expense of their adversaries.

Anti-Christian feeling derived from other sources as well. In spite of the continuous growth of rural Christianity, its adherents amounted to only a fraction of 1 per cent of the total population of China. Nevertheless, its increasingly powerful social and political role was seen as harmful by both rural elites and common people. It undermined long established traditions, thereby provoking the anger of non-Christians in the locality.

Conflict occurred also in urban settings. Here missionaries had an even greater political and cultural impact. It should be noted that missionaries saw themselves as engaged in a civilizing mission, as part of the general expansion of Western domination. The foreign missionaries were a profound threat to the local cultural and social hegemony and status monopoly of the gentry class. Indeed, much more, for with their status as literate teachers and having access to political authorities and thus the ability to protect their followers, missionaries encroached on the specifically political prerogatives of the gentry. Protestants especially set up schools for boys and girls, hospitals and printing presses, producing both secular and religious works. Chinese women found employment in schools and hospitals or worked as Bible women. Implacable gentry hostility to missionaries and Christianity, and the prominent gentry role in fomenting and leading anti-Christian violence, is therefore not difficult to understand. It was they who generated fear and suspicion, fed by rumours and inflammatory placards, that from time to time burst into anti-Christian violence. These increasingly endemic local tensions reached a climax in the intensely xenophobic Boxer Uprising of 1900 in which many missionaries and thousands of Christians were killed.

The disastrous 'summer madness' of 1900 brought about significant changes in China's relations with the West. Traditional anti-Christian sentiments subsided significantly, and missionaries and Christians were able to play a more constructive role in subsequent Chinese reform efforts. On the Protestant side, Christianity became much more diverse than it had been before 1900. A great variety of new Christian mission groups established themselves, some of them in theology or practice quite new, such as Pentecostals or Adventists. Many more independent or 'faith' missionaries came to China; these were not part of the traditional mission societies. Meanwhile those established mission societies, who had not only churches but other institutions such as schools or hospitals, also grew substantially. By 1925, there were over 8,000 foreign Protestant missionaries in China, nearly four times as many as in 1900.

A portion of the Protestant mission community attempted, with some success, to overcome their traditional denominational divisions and to promote a unified Protestant Church. But other missionaries refused to participate in this trend, and kept their activities and organizations separate. One reason for this was the theological split between evangelicals and social reformers. After the First World War this split became quite severe and bitter, and took on the terms 'conservative' and 'modernist' to designate its two theological poles. As a result of the influx of new mission groups and ideological differences, the Protestant mission bodies tended to be less united by the 1920s than they had been in the 1890s.

As another important development, the contours of an emerging Chinese Christianity began to take shape after 1900, as indicated by the growth of independent Chinese Protestant forces, both inside and outside the established mission Churches. Towards the end of the nineteenth century, some foreign missionaries as well as Chinese Christian leaders had already begun to promote the 'three-self' principle, that is to say, Chinese Christians would be responsible for 'self-management, self-support and self-propagation' in the Churches. From the early 1910s and the formation of the China Continuation Committee (of the Edinburgh Conference of 1910), this goal was pursued gradually, reaching its high point in the National Christian Conference of 1922. Out of this historic meeting came the interdenominational Church of Christ in China, a Sino–foreign body with a significant degree of Chinese leadership and responsibility. The National Christian Council, a Protestant co-ordinating and liaison body, was also a product of this period. However, these changes did not really constitute a great deal of movement towards an authentically independent or indigenous Chinese Church. Attitudes of paternalism remained strong among foreign missionaries, and the power of foreign financial subsidy remained a potent, if usually an implicit, factor in most Christian organizations.

A rather more independent sector of Chinese Protestantism also came into being in the period between 1900 and the 1920s. At best it had rather tenuous links with foreign missions, was autonomous in operations and truly indigenous in ideas and leadership. It is a diverse sector, made up of a combination of organized Church groups (some nationwide with hundreds of congregations) and of individual congregations or even individual Christian workers who made their mark in a more local setting. Some of these coexisted with and interacted with the mission Churches; others were quite separatist and had almost no contacts with other Christians, Chinese or foreign. Some of its major components were the following. (1) Church federations made up of self-supporting and self-governing congregations which had broken away or distanced themselves from foreign missionary bodies. One of these, the Chinese Christian Independent Church, had started as an independent, all-Chinese congregation, formed in Shanghai in 1906 by the Presbyterian pastor Yu

Guozhen and others. By the 1920s it had become a federation with over one hundred affiliated congregations. A smaller North Chinese movement emerged in 1912 in Shandong. The Tianjin congregation of this federation was led by Zhang Boliang (1876–1951), the founder of Nankai University. Cheng Jingyi (1881–1939), who subsequently held important offices in the mainstream Sino–foreign Protestant establishment, was the leader of the Beijing independent Church. (2) The True Jesus Church, a Pentecostal Church founded in 1917 that may have been the largest of the independent groups nationwide by the 1930s. (3) The Assembly Hall (or 'Local Church', or 'Little Flock') organized in the mid-1920s and led by Ni Tuosheng ('Watchman Nee', 1903–72). This was a strongly proselytizing Church and rather anti-foreign. (4) The Jesus Family, a unique Pentecostal communitarian Church started by Jing Dianying (1890–1953?) in rural Shandong province in the 1920s. (5) Several other independent but more loosely organized groups such as the Spiritual Gifts Church which emerged as a revival movement in Shandong in the 1930s, as well as individual evangelists and teachers such as Wang Mingdao (1900–91), famous for his conservative theological stance and outstanding moral rectitude, and the radical revivalist preacher Song Shangjie [John Sung] (1901–44).[37]

In spite of the growing number of Chinese priests in Catholic missions, the move towards a greater leadership role for them was rather slower than among the Protestant establishments. The Belgian Lazarist missionary Vincent Lebbe (1877–1940) noted in 1901, for instance, that the European clergy and Chinese priests ate at different tables in the Beijing Seminary. The course of study was far less advanced for Chinese seminarians than for European clerics. 'The missionaries were haunted by the fear that pride would drive the Chinese to revolt, and so the great thing was to keep them in a state of humility . . . And of course they were expected to fill only subordinate positions in any case.'[38] Later Lebbe pleaded passionately for greater involvement of indigenous clergy in the running of the Catholic enterprise. Towards the end of the First World War, he began to send alarming reports to Rome, criticizing Church policy in China and demanding the separation of missions from politics, the advancement of Chinese priests and the transfer of responsibility to them. The Vatican, having made several attempts since the 1880s to bypass French government control of Catholic missions and establish direct contacts with the Chinese government, sent Bishop Jean-Baptiste-Marie Budes de Guébriant MEP (1860–1935) on a fact-finding mission to China in 1918–19. As a result, Pope Benedict XV issued on 30 November 1919 his apostolic letter *Maximum illud*, 'the Magna Carta of the modern [Catholic] missions', which deplored, among other things, the effects of European nationalism on the Catholic Church in China and called for the elimination of the entrenched prejudices of the Western clergy, as well as the eventual transfer of ecclesiastical administration to the Chinese clergy. From 1922 this Vatican policy was vigorously promoted by the new apostolic delegate to China, Monsignor Celso Costantini (1876–1958). The lack of enthusiasm among the foreign missionary community notwithstanding, the process gained momentum with the consecration of six Chinese bishops, three of whom had been recommended by Lebbe, by the Pope in Rome on 28 October 1926. When Lebbe returned to China in 1927, he acquired Chinese citizenship and started his evangelistic work at Anguo, Hebei province, under a Chinese bishop. There he founded two Chinese religious societies, the Little Brothers of Saint John the Baptist in 1928 and the Little Sisters of Saint Theresa.

Although Chinese Catholicism continued to be dominated by foreign priests, Chinese believers were beginning to play a greater role in the running of the Church. Ma Xiangbo (1840–1939), probably the most influential modern Chinese Catholic thinker, made important contributions to religion, politics and education. He had entered the Society of Jesus in 1862 and was ordained a priest in 1869, but left the order in 1874, married and engaged in various forms of public service. Having been reconciled with the Church and the Jesuits in 1898, he established Aurora University (now Zhendan University) in Shanghai in 1903 as China's first Catholic establishment of higher learning. Furen University, which opened in Beijing in 1925, likewise owes its existence to Ma's initiatives. Another influential twentieth-century Catholic was Lu Bohong [Joseph Lo Pa Hong] (1874–1937), a wealthy Shanghai businessman. He established hospitals and schools and in 1928 founded and became president of Catholic Action in Shanghai. He was assassinated by Chinese nationalists.

René Lu Zhengxiang [after 1927 Dom Pierre-Celestin Lou] (1870–1949) was a Chinese diplomat during the late imperial and early republican years (and several times China's foreign minister). Born into a Protestant family in Shanghai, he converted to Catholicism in 1911. After his Belgian wife died, he entered a Belgian Benedictine abbey in 1927. As a result of both his diplomatic contacts and his extensive literary output, Lu was influential in promoting the cause of Christianity in China and acting as cultural intermediary between East and West.

The rise of an indigenous Christian identity, including the formation of independent Churches, was to a considerable extent part of the rise of a Chinese national consciousness after 1900, which found its most radical expression in the 1920s. As the tide of anti-imperialist and revolutionary sentiment increased after the May Fourth Movement of 1919, one of its most convenient targets was the thousands of foreign missionaries, and their property and institutions, still protected by extraterritoriality under the 'unequal' treaties. The most visible parts of the Chinese Church, closely allied with foreign mission operations, also came under attack by those who denounced imperialism and all its accomplices in China. Many Chinese Christians did not remain unaffected by the widespread and emotionally charged patriotic currents at this time. They demanded and indeed achieved a greater degree of participation and leadership in Church affairs.

It should be noted, however, that the great Anti-Christian Movement[39] was relatively short-lived and essentially confined to the major urban centres. Except for areas in the control of Communist revolutionaries, in many rural parts of China Christianity was able to adapt and even flourish during the chaotic 1920s. A mission station was now rarely a target, but often a safe haven for people suffering from famine or fleeing from warlord conflict and bandit depredations.

The prospects of Church planting improved further during the brief period of relative stability in many parts of China during the early 1930s, following the establishment of the Guomindang (Nationalist) government under Chiang Kai-shek. Not that the Nationalists were encouraging religious work. On the contrary, they passed laws intended severely to curtail such activities. However, preoccupation with the dual threat of Japanese aggression and Communist revolution, poor enforcement and appeals to fellow-Christians in the government ensured the continuation of Christian endeavours. It should be noted that Chiang Kai-shek, after his marriage to the American-educated Methodist Song Meiling, had himself become a nominal Christian. The various Christian organizations were thus able to expand their routine social service operations. At the same time, rural areas in particular became the scene of extensive revivalistic movements. Another important development occurred on 8 December 1939 when Pope Pius XII reversed the fateful ruling of 1715 and permitted Catholics to participate in ceremonies revering Confucius and observe ancestral rites. Thus the way was clear for the emergence of a Chinese Catholic Church.

In contrast to the countryside, Church life became rather more politicized in the cities in the 1930s. In the face of Japan's aggressive advances in China since 1931, YMCA student leaders like Zhao Zizhen [T. C. Chao], an advocate of Chinese Christian nationalism, not only lost confidence in the Guomindang government, but also became critical of the Christian community's ethical approach to China's national predicament. Another YMCA leader, Wu Yaozong [Y. T. Wu] (1893–1979), was even more critical of the Chinese Church and favoured social revolution and support for the Chinese Communists as the only means of national salvation.

During the War of Resistance against Japan (1937–45), the Christian

Churches were once again endeavouring to afford relief of suffering and distress. In the early years of the war, their foreign connections gave them access to relief funds and supplies that came from the British Commonwealth and the United States. Millions of refugees were fed and housed, and many more sick or injured treated. In the Japanese-occupied areas of the country, German and French missionaries provided relief and protection from Japanese oppression. The Japanese, for their part, sought to exert control over Chinese Christian establishments and remove all other foreign influences. As a result of these restrictions – as well as the internment or repatriation of many missionaries from enemy countries – Chinese Christians had to assume greater responsibility for maintaining Church life in occupied China during the Anti-Japanese War. In many ways, this proved another important step towards realization of the 'three-self' ideal.

Japan: the second encounter

During the last decades of the Tokugawa shogunate, the continuing policy of seclusion and prohibition kept Japan firmly closed to foreign missionary activities. When Western countries began to press for renewed contact with Japan in the early nineteenth century, the implicit danger of trade and Christianity was put forward as a powerful argument against such contacts. As one apprehensive writer pointed out in 1825:

> When those barbarians plan to subdue a country not their own, they start by opening commerce and watch for a sign of weakness. If an opportunity is presented, they will preach their alien religion to captivate the people's hearts. Once the people's allegiance has been shifted, they can be manipulated and nothing can be done to stop it. The people will be only too glad to die for the sake of the alien God ... The subversion of the people and overthrowing of the state are taught as being in accord with the God's will. So in the name of all-embracing love the subjugation of the land is accomplished.[40]

The long period of Japanese seclusion ended with the arrival of the American 'Black Ships' under Commodore Matthew C. Perry in 1853. Under the Treaty of Amity and Commerce of 1858 and similar agreements signed with other Western powers, Americans and Europeans were permitted freely to exercise their religion in Japan. In 1859 representatives of three Protestant missionary societies arrived, ostensibly to serve the foreign residents, but their true aim was to begin direct work among the Japanese. In 1859 the Catholic priest Prudence Girard MEP (1821–67) became attached as interpreter to the French consulate general in Edo (Tokyo), while another priest settled in Hakodate. But language difficulties and the anti-Christian regulations still in force prevented much progress during the first few years.

Yet it was during these difficult years that communities of 'hidden Christians' (*Kakure Kirishitan*) were discovered in the Nagasaki area in 1865. Living in remote areas where government surveillance was at its weakest and where the early Christian faith had had time to send down deep roots, these communities had preserved their religion in secret for more than two centuries. Not surprisingly, their understanding of Christian doctrine had become corrupted in the course of time. Their biblical account called *Tenchi hajimari no koto* is a remarkable document incorporating both Shintō and Buddhist elements, while retaining passages from the Bible with remarkable accuracy. Of the approximately 60,000 'hidden Christians' discovered at that time, about half chose to return to the newly introduced Catholic Church; the rest preferred to continue with their centuries-old underground tradition. Since the anti-Christian laws were still in effect, many of the newly discovered believers were imprisoned or deported to other parts of the country, and their leaders executed. Finally, following the Meiji Restoration in 1868, the government withdrew religious sanctions and allowed the uprooted peasants to return to their homes. The majority of the inhabitants of the small island of Ikitsuki, off western Kyūshū, are *Kakure Kirishitan* even today.[41]

During the last years of the Tokugawa shogunate, Western missionaries established themselves under the protection of the foreign powers, often resorting to diplomatic pressure and violating what the Japanese authorities regarded as an indisputable agreement about non-interference in religious matters. The aggressive spirit of the missionary enterprise naturally provoked fear and opposition among many sections of Japanese society. The missionaries' strict injunctions against idol worship brought them into conflict with traditional religious practices. The Buddhists, in particular, had long regarded Christianity as the fatal enemy, and did so with renewed vehemence right up to the end of the nineteenth century.[42]

After the Japanese government removed the notices proscribing Christianity in 1873, Christian missionary efforts – Catholic, Protestant and also Russian Orthodox – met with some successes. But in the longer run attempts to implant this foreign religion in Japan have not been particularly successful. The converts to Protestant Churches during the Meiji period were mostly individuals from the former samurai class, attracted by the non-theological, ethical and biblical approach in the missionary presentation of Christianity. Furthermore, the missionaries, especially some Protestants, attached particular importance to education, including in time higher education. At a time when leading Japanese were generally interested in things Western, missionary teachers were often regarded as the representatives of a new and superior civilization. Early Protestant

Christianity in Japan was, however, for the most part an intellectual religion for a small segment of elite that looked down on the masses (who remained attracted to Buddhism).

While the very 'Westernness' of Christianity appealed to some Japanese during the Meiji period, in time many converts felt that their new faith was unnecessarily bound to foreign organizational forms, denominational loyalties and dissensions. Consequently, a number of independent indigenous Christian sects came into being.[43] The first of these bodies outside Western missionary control, the Mukyōkai (Non-Church Movement), was founded in 1901 by Uchimura Kanzō (1861–1930) as a religious community of the intellectual elite. However, the majority of such new bodies did not emerge until after the Second World War. Some of the more popular sects combined strands of Japanese folk religion with Pentecostal elements in reaction to Uchimura's intellectual movement. While this development contributed to the process of indigenization of Christianity amongst the Japanese lower classes, it was a rather unstable process. Often these groups were held together by their charismatic founders and tended to decline and split after a leader's death.

Against the background of a rising nationalist spirit, aggravated by the Western reluctance to abrogate the 'unequal treaties', Christians made notable contributions to the modernization of the country. After 1900 the Churches sponsored a variety of social and medical projects, such as hospitals, sanatoria, leprosaria, orphanages, old people's homes, etc. Christians were also instrumental in the foundation and development of the socialist and trade union movements. Yet the steady increase of nationalism during the 1930s raised difficult problems of conscience for Christians. Their refusal to participate in certain official ceremonies was interpreted as a Christian lack of loyalty and patriotism. This became painfully apparent at the time of the 'Yasukuni Incident' in May 1932, when a few students refused on religious grounds to bow at the Yasukuni Shrine in Tokyo.

Although a compromise was reached to the effect that such ceremonies constituted 'a civil manifestation of loyalty' and 'reverence toward the imperial family', many Christians felt uneasy, especially during the Pacific War. With the approach of the war, the foreign Catholic bishops resigned their offices, and since that time members of the hierarchy have been Japanese. Foreign missionaries of all Churches were interned or repatriated during the war or at best allowed very limited freedom to continue their work. Government pressure led to the formation in 1941 of the United Church of Christ in Japan (*Nihon Kirisuto Kyōdan*), a union of some 30 Protestant Churches entirely administered by Japanese.

In spite of a remarkable post-war recovery, the Christian religion has not entered the mainstream of Japanese life. In the popular mind, it is still a 'foreign creed', preaching admirable ideals but not suitable for ordinary Japanese people. Christian teachings are too much at variance with the more traditional patterns of Japanese thought and outlook. The present situation of Christianity in Japan is characterized in general by unobtrusive activity, with emphasis still placed on education as a means of spreading the Gospel message.

Korea

Korea was the last East Asian country to be opened to direct Christian proselytization, yet ultimately it produced the most remarkable results. Being a vassal state of China, the 'Hermit Kingdom' remained closed to the outside world until the late nineteenth century. As a consequence, early missionary attempts from Japan, China and the Philippines ended in failure and direct missionary work did not begin until the very end of the eighteenth century. However, Christianity did have an indirect influence on some members of the scholar-elite as early as the seventeenth century, through Chinese-language works produced by the Jesuits in China and taken to Korea by the periodic Korean tribute embassies to Beijing.

The last quarter of the eighteenth century represents the actual formative period of Korean Catholicism. It is at this time that we first find definite evidence for the existence of a body of professing Christians and the beginnings of an organized Church. This period of Korean Catholicism was dominated by Confucian scholars following the line of the *Sirhak-p'a* (School of Practical Learning), perhaps not surprising, since the Jesuits' Chinese writings included many scientific works. Many of these men were in turn connected to the Southern or Nanmin political faction, which was out of power at the time. Consequently, the formative stage of the Church was dominated by the aristocracy and typified by intellectual and scholastic concerns. However, some young scholars began to take a *religious* interest in Catholicism. In 1777 one group gathered in the grounds of a Buddhist temple to study the religious tracts put out by the Jesuits in China. It is to this group that the Korean Church traces its origins. In 1784 one of the principal members of the group, Yi Pyŏk [Lee Pyok] (1754–86), convinced Yi Sŭnghun [Peter Lee Seung-hun] (1756–1801), who was accompanying his father on an official mission to the imperial court in Beijing, to make contact with the Catholic priests there. While in the Chinese capital, Yi Sŭnghun was baptized by the ex-Jesuit Jean-Joseph de Grammont (1736–1812), and upon his return to Korea he and Yi Pyŏk began to evangelize amongst their friends and neighbours. Thus it was Korean intellectuals who introduced Christianity to Korea, not Western missionaries. In other words, from the first the Korean Catholic Church has been a self-evangelized Church.

Government opposition to the spread of Christianity notwithstanding, the aristocratic members of the group began to create a Church based on what they knew of the Church in Beijing. A bishop and priests were elected, and these appointments remained in force for two years until 1789. In that year a letter from the Bishop of Beijing informed them that what they were doing was illegal according to canon law. Another letter in 1790 discouraged Christians from participating in the ancestral ceremonies, which caused many people to drift away from the Church. In 1791 two cousins, *yangban* converts (i.e., members of Korea's bureaucratic class), were arrested and executed for not performing the ancestral rites and for burning the ancestral tablets in their possession. These executions for belief in Catholicism set the pattern for the persecutions which were to typify the history of the Korean Catholic Church in the nineteenth century.

It was not until 1795 that a Chinese priest, James Zhou Wenmo (1752–1801), secretly entered the country and revived the fortunes of the new faith during a brief period of tacit tolerance. Whereas in 1795 there were some 4,000 adherents, the number had increased to 10,000 five years later. However, the very growth of the foreign sect caused grave concern in certain circles. In common with Confucian scholars in China and Japan, Koreans mostly judged Christianity to be an absurd and subversive philosophy. It was condemned as a 'barbarous', 'beastly' and 'heterodox' creed 'without king or parents', which destroys the state and the family. The involvement of prominent Catholic converts with the *Sip'a* (Party of Expediency) clique, which happened to lose power in the wake of King Chŏngjo's sudden death in 1800, also made the Church the scapegoat for factional politics. Attacks on Catholicism became more pronounced, culminating in the bloody Sinyu Persecution of 1801. Many prominent Korean Catholics were killed, as well as the Chinese priest Zhou Wenmo.

As James Huntley Grayson has argued, the Sinyu Persecution 'is a watershed in Korean Catholic history, marking the end of the scholarly Church of the aristocracy and the beginning of the persecuted underground Church of the people'.[44] The ferocity of this first persecution was in part due to the famous 'silk letter' sent by a young scholar, Hwang Sayŏng (1775–1801), to Bishop Alexandre de Gouvea (1751–1808) in Beijing, appealing for a Western navy and army to compel the Korean rulers to grant religious freedom. The interception of this letter convinced the Korean authorities that Catholicism was a dangerous heterodox creed which threatened Korea's political independence and traditional ties with China.

Fearing the threat Catholicism posed to the state as well as to traditional social and religious norms and practices, the authorities launched periodic anti-Christian campaigns, such as the Ŭrhae Persecution of 1815, the Chŏnghae Persecution of 1827 and the Kihae Persecution of 1839. The last was the result of the discovery of foreign missionaries on Korean soil, which once again raised the fear of subversion by foreign powers of the Korean state. The three foreign priests, members of the Missions Étrangères de Paris, had arrived in Korea – which had been established as a vicariate apostolic separate from Beijing in 1831 – to minister to the Christians who had been without priestly supervision for a generation. They were amongst the many Catholics who were executed in 1839. Disregarding the hostile atmosphere in the peninsula, twelve new French missionaries entered the country in the 1840s and 1850s. The Catholic community began to grow once more, now attracting an increasing number of people from the lower social classes. However, at this time the Western powers began to take a greater interest in the Hermit Kingdom as well, wishing to establish trade links. Being aware of the fate that had befallen China as a result of the opium wars, the Korean government rejected Western demands. Suspecting that the spread of Catholicism was part of a foreign plot to undermine the country's strict isolation policy, the Korean leaders launched another full-scale persecution early in 1866, in the course of which nine French missionaries and some 8,000 Korean converts were slain. In response, a French naval force launched a punitive attack but was forced to withdraw in the face of stubborn Korean resistance. However, the Catholic position improved considerably in the 1880s, following Korea's reluctant decision to establish links with the outside world.

The end of isolation also gave Protestant missions the opportunity to embark on direct proselytization. The first American Presbyterian and Methodist missionaries entered Korea in the mid-1880s. Much of the success of the Protestant Churches in the first 25 years after the arrival of the missionaries was due to the association of Christianity with the 'progressive' West, to the policy of social outreach – most notably in the area of education – and to the emphasis which the first generation of missionaries placed on the responsibility of local Christians for the growth and support of their Churches. In the Presbyterian case, this resulted in the formal organization of the Presbyterian Church in Korea into a self-governing independent national presbytery by the four Western missions operating in Korea at that time.

During the years of Japanese colonial rule in Korea between 1910 and 1945, Christianity became increasingly associated with Korean nationalism. Conflict arose from Japanese attempts to impose their own system of 'patriotic' schools, with Japanese the national language and religious instruction and worship banned. The Conspiracy Trial of 1912 and the March First Movement of 1919 both had strong Christian links. As a result, Christians were often singled out for harsh treatment by the Japanese. There are many examples of churches being burnt and Christians killed by Japanese troops. A major conflict flared up between the Protestant Churches and the Japanese colonial government over the question of compulsory attendance at services of worship at Shintō shrines to honour the Japanese emperor and his divine ancestors. The Catholic Church seems to have more readily acquiesced in the Japanese attempt to impose Shintō nationalism on the Korean nation, but many Protestant ministers and laymen were imprisoned and foreign missionaries deported for their refusal to support the shrine edict.

1945 onwards

The rise of nationalism since the late nineteenth century notwithstanding, the Christian enterprise in East and South-east Asia continued for long to be dominated by foreign missions. However, the Second World War initiated a process that brought about decolonization and the elimination of the more direct forms of imperialist domination throughout the region. Asian Christians now had the opportunity to free themselves from colonial and missionary domination and engage in independent Christianization. During the early post-war decades, Church growth was particularly encouraging in Korea, Taiwan and Hong Kong. More recently, other parts of East and South-east Asia experienced a growing interest in Christianity, mainland China being the most remarkable case.

The Chinese Church under Communism

When the Anti-Japanese War ended in August 1945, the resumption of vigorous Christian proselytization was anticipated. Chinese Christians were to assume greater responsibility in this work. To this end, the Catholic Church established an ecclesiastical hierarchy in China in 1946. Twenty ecclesiastical provinces were erected, the vicariates and prefectures were raised to dioceses, twenty of them to archdioceses, and the ordinaries, many of them Chinese, were made bishops or archbishops, respectively. Bishop Thomas Tien [Tian Gengxin] SVD (1890–1967) of Tsingtao became China's first cardinal and was soon afterwards appointed Archbishop of Beijing. However, implacable opposition to Communism and Rome's decision to back the Guomindang during and after the Civil War (1946–49) precluded any accommodation with the CCP. While the Communists had tolerated Christians and missionaries during the Anti-

Japanese War, their attitude changed dramatically after 1945. In the Communist-controlled so-called 'liberated zones', anti-missionary struggle meetings were organized, mission stations materially ruined and foreign missionaries routinely accused of certain crimes. Among other things, the old xenophobic tales of child murder and mutilation of children's bodies for evil purposes were revived and circulated in inflammatory placards and newspaper reports.[45] After the Communists had gained control of state power in 1949, these campaigns were extended to the entire country. With the governmental decree of 23 June 1950 on the suppression of 'counter-revolutionary activity' began the systematic struggle against the Church. By 1954 most foreign missionaries had been expelled from the country, often after ignominious show trials, mistreatment and imprisonment, and the confiscation of foreign-run establishments. Since missionary activity had become impossible on the Chinese mainland, a significant number of the foreign personnel were redeployed to work in Taiwan, Hong Kong and amongst the Chinese diaspora in South-east Asia.

However, ideologically and organizationally, the Catholic Church in particular continued to constitute an implicit challenge to the Chinese state even after the elimination of the foreign missionaries. Eric O. Hanson writes:

> The People's Republic considered the latent Catholic political opposition much more serious. Catholicism threatened to block effective government penetration, regulation, and control of its organization . . . The new government demanded not only the public obedience of key Church figures, but also their sincere total allegiance. This demand, of course, followed the Chinese political tradition, but the Communists had the will and the means to pursue this objective with greater force than Ming or Ch'ing dynasties.[46]

To this end the CCP's Central Committee, in January 1951, established the Religious Affairs Office (later, Bureau), staffed with specialists to oversee religious affairs, its function being to penetrate, regulate and control religious organizations. To this end the government sponsored the Catholic Three Self Movement of 1950–51 to establish a self-governing, self-supporting, self-propagating Church free of all foreign influence. The state obtained its objective with the establishment of the National Patriotic Catholic Association (now known as the Chinese Catholic Patriotic Association, CCPA) in 1957 and the consecration of government-sponsored bishops in 1958. Officially, the Chinese Catholic Church had severed all links with the Vatican.

In contrast to the belligerent anti-Communist stand of the Catholic hierarchy, many Chinese Protestants welcomed the Communist victory and were actively involved in setting up a national Church body in 1951, for which the name Three-Self Patriotic Movement (TSPM) was adopted in 1954. It is nominally an autonomous organization that is co-opted and utilized by the state to eliminate foreign influence, unite Protestants in one organization and promote CCP policies within the Church. Many of its leaders had been active in the YMCA and YWCA in the 1930s and 1940s, including the highly controversial Wu Yaozong. In spite of the willingness of many liberal Protestants to co-operate with the Communists, oppositionist sentiments prevailed amongst more conservative elements. Many of the indigenous Protestant sects and charismatic evangelical leaders, in consequence of the dissolution of denominational structures, resisted coerced unification or collaboration with the new state. In response, the TSPM organized a series of denunciation campaigns against unaffiliated groups and individuals in the 1950s. Zhao Zizhen, Jing Dianying, Wang Mingdao and Ni Tuosheng were some of the prominent victims.

Indeed, the period from the mid-1950s to the late 1960s was a time of great suffering for Christianity as a whole. The nationwide mobilization campaigns such as the Great Leap Forward (1958–60) and the calamitous Cultural Revolution (1966–69), in particular, adversely affected the Christian Churches. Bob Whyte has aptly described the impact of the Cultural Revolution on the faithful as follows:

> All religious personnel were forbidden to engage in religious activities and many were subjected to abuse and ill-treatment. Such abuse was conducted on an arbitrary basis, and it was much worse in some places than in others. In the early stages many clergy and also lay believers had their homes ransacked, their religious books taken and burnt, and their movements and activities watched. As social chaos mounted so the tides of the factional struggles could sweep up people on a random basis. Priests, pastors, Buddhist monks, imams, found themselves sharing in manual labour with intellectuals, democrats, and disgraced Communist officials, including the former cadres of the Religious Affairs Bureaus. This shared suffering was to influence the future attitudes of many in more tranquil times. There is no doubt of the suffering experienced by Christians during these long years, but Christians were by no means the prime targets of the persecutions.[47]

These terrible events led many outsiders to believe that Christian faith was doomed in China. Yet by the late 1970s it became clear that it had survived, essentially in the form of clandestine 'underground Churches' and family prayer meetings. Since then an explosive growth of Christianity has occurred in many parts of the country. This so-called 'Christianity fever' has been particularly prevalent in Chinese Protestantism. Exact figures are difficult to establish, since many Christians do not wish to register with the TSPM because of the latter's close collaboration with the government. Similar problems exist between the 'official' Catholic Church regulated by the CCPA and the 'pro-Rome' underground movement led by the so-called 'little black priests'. Yet in spite of these divisions, the tight control exercised by the Religious Affairs Bureaux and sporadic bouts of harassment, the Catholic and Protestant Churches continue to grow.

Post-colonial South-east Asia

In South-east Asia, Christians played at best a marginal role in the liberation struggles and nation-building processes after the Second World War. For one thing, Christianity was the religion of outsiders, that is to say, Europeans, Indians and Chinese. But as the Malaysian experience has shown, independence was seen as a Malay, and thus a Muslim rather than a Christian, issue. In areas where Islamization has intensified in recent decades, for example in Acheh, Muslims are demanding government intervention against Christianity. In such localities contextualization is in any case virtually impossible. Similar cases could be made with respect to Buddhist domination in the post-colonial nation-states of Burma and Thailand.

In other independent countries of South-east Asia, the greater centralizing efforts of post-colonial governments are threatening ethnic minority groups and the residual autonomy of tribal communities. It was among the ethnic minorities on the peripheries or margins of centralizing colonial states that modern forces were first introduced in significant ways as part of the missionizing effort. From the late nineteenth century Protestant missionaries brought communities like the Karen in Burma and the Batak in Sumatra into contact both with Christianity and, through mission schools, with the modern world. Yet in the newly independent states the existing Christian infrastructure amongst minority peoples, often with separatist tendencies, is perceived to undermine state control.

In spite of these many obstacles, Christianity has experienced further growth in South-east Asia. Concerns about the rise of Communism (the victory in China; the Emergency in Malaya; the conflict in Vietnam) induced many diaspora Chinese to join the Church. In this connection, following the government's attack on Communism in 1965, the growth of Protestantism has been quite remarkable in Indonesia. In Malaysia these developments have given some impetus to the formation of an ecumenical movement and regional Christian association, but cultural diversity and ethnic identity have also produced greater denominational fragmentation. In particular, Chinese-speaking congregations have preserved a strong sense of autonomy, as have the immigrants, including the

Mar Thoma and Syro-Malabarian Christians from India. At the same time, many local Chinese and Indians have joined groups associated with rapidly expanding charismatic Christianity.

For Vietnamese Catholics the post-war experience was rather tragic. In the past Catholics, a minority of 10 to 15 per cent of the population, had, with some exceptions, remained aloof from the nationalist and anti-foreign sentiments that had inspired the non-Catholic majority. Vietnam's declaration of independence following the Japanese surrender in August 1945 gave them the opportunity to prove their patriotism. Indeed, Catholics supported and served in the short-lived Communist-dominated Vietminh government. But in time the Communists initiated a pro-gramme designed to gain them undisputed domination of the country through the elimination of non-Communist resistance forces. Initially the strongly Christianized area around Phat Diem and Bui Chu in northern Vietnam retained their special administrative status under Bishop Le Huu Tu (1897–1967), who was also a member of Ho Chi Minh's government. However, anti-Catholic harassment increased, culminating in general anti-Christian persecution in North Vietnam following the division of the country in 1954. This caused between 600,000 and 800,000 Catholics to flee to the South.

This large influx of Catholics strengthened the newly formed southern government of Ngo Dinh Diem, a devout Catholic and ardent anti-Communist. These refugees became the most enthusiastic supporters of his increasingly ruthless dictatorship. While the official Church hierarchy was rather prudent in its relations with Diem, this cannot be said of Bishop Ngo Dinh Thuc, the brother of the president. At the same time, Vietnamese Catholics held a disproportionate number of official posts in the national and provincial governments, as well as in the army. The privileged position of Catholicism and its attendant triumphalism in turn alienated the majority Buddhists. Indeed, it was the Buddhist crisis of the summer of 1963 that contributed to Diem's fall in November of that year and the subsequent 'settling of accounts' with the Catholics. Although the South Vietnamese Church recovered from the crisis, Christians experi-enced a new setback following the Communist victory and reunification of the country in 1975.[48]

South Korea

During the immediate post-war years, local Korean Churches in the American-controlled south began to play a significant role in providing social services and rebuilding institutional facilities. This was necessitated by the influx of Christians from North Korea as a consequence of the severe suppression of Christianity by the Russians and the Korean

Communists. On the eve of the outbreak of the Korean War, a large number of Catholic priests and believers were arrested, imprisoned and executed in the North. The subsequent Korean War (1950–53) had, of course, an even more devastating impact. Nevertheless, Church membership continued to grow in the South, as many Koreans looked for new certainties during and following the terrible ordeal. It was, however, in the 1960s that spectacular Church growth commenced. This decade saw the expansion of social and evangelistic outreach, involving projects such as urban industrial mission, work with prostitutes, the development of Korean missions overseas,[49] and provision of relief supplies to foreign countries. Church membership has continued to grow and today nearly one-fifth of the South Korean population is Protestant.

The Catholic Church also experienced rapid growth after the end of the Korean War. By 1962 membership had increased to 575,000 from 166,000 in 1953. At the same time, it began to change from a rural ghetto Church to one part of the mainstream of Korean society, and Catholics have shown greater social concern than in the past, supporting students' protest movements and demanding social justice for Korean workers. Moreover, the Second Vatican Council created the conditions for co-operation with other Christian Churches in Korea. The new ecumenical spirit became particularly evident in the joint struggle of liberal Church leaders against the undemocratic, military authoritarianism of Presidents Pak Chŏnghŭi [Park Chung-hee] and Chŏn Tuhwan [Chun Doo-hwan].

The phenomenal growth of Christianity has in recent decades been accompanied by three tendencies: fragmentation, indigenization and the rise of syncretistic sects. The Presbyterian Church of Korea, for instance, split into four major groups between 1952 and 1959, and since then these four bodies have further fragmented into 87 different Presbyterian factions.[50] While little attempt was made until recently to adapt Christianity to Korean culture by removing, for instance, non-essential Western accessories, there are now indications that elements of Korean folk tradition are coming to the fore in Christian religious practices. One increasingly prominent characteristic of Church life are the faith healing services, often in connection with revival meetings, including features reminiscent of shamanistic practices. Moreover, charismatic preachers tend to emphasize the blessings of temporal prosperity in this life in their sermons. The related phenomenon of 'newly emerged religions', that is to say, syncretic religions, constitutes another noteworthy aspect of modern Korea. The two major examples of syncretic sects with a high Christian content are the Olive Tree Church, founded by Pak Taesŏn, and the Holy Spirit Association for the Unification of World Christianity (Unification Church or 'Moonies'), founded by Mun Sŏnmyŏng [Moon Sun-myung].

Concluding comments

It is remarkable indeed that Christianity, following severe persecution in the nineteenth century, has become the predominant religious movement in South Korea at the end of the twentieth. Christians have proved themselves adequate to the task of self-support, self-development and survival under harsh conditions of foreign colonial and indigenous military rule. In this respect, the Korean experience appears as a significant departure from the predominant pattern in East Asia. Christianity struggled for centuries to gain a foothold in the face of strong states everywhere attempting to penetrate, regulate and control institutional religion. Confucianism, primarily the Neo-Confucian Zhu Xi philosophy, with its static view of social life and its emphasis on loyalty and filial piety, provided the official philosophy and contributed to the stability of intellectual life in China, Korea, Japan and Vietnam. It dominated all levels of intellectual and social activity of the government and the ruling class and regulated the pattern for social relations and family life. Foreign religious influence was tolerated only during periods of social, economic and political crisis. The more the old legitimacy failed to provide security and sustenance, the more people were disposed to accept both universal religions and heterodox sects. But as soon as strong central power was re-established, the state set out once more to regulate and control the Churches, as occurred in modern times in Meiji Japan, in Taiwan after 1949, and even in South Korea, but most powerfully in the People's Republic of China. Hanson has argued that this was one of the most enduring aspects of the Chinese polity: 'The Chinese politico-religious culture discourages independent religious organizations. The difficulties of the Catholic Church in the People's Republic are not primarily due to Peking's Marxist ideology, but to the re-emergence of a strong Chinese state with a continental [as opposed to a more open maritime] political ideology.'[51]

Yet the iron hand of the Communist state notwithstanding, mainland China has experienced a remarkable revival of Christianity and phenomenal growth during the last twenty years, within both officially recognized Church organizations and unaffiliated autonomous communities. Estimates for 1996 put the number of baptized Protestants at 33 million (Chinese government estimate: 19 million) and of Roman Catholics at 18 million (government estimate: 6 million). Seen in the context of China's enormous population, even on the basis of the higher estimate, Christians (Catholics and Protestants) account for only 4.3 per cent of the total. However, this is a significant increase over the 1 per cent in 1949. Moreover, in the global context Chinese Christians represent a significant component of world Christianity, especially when fellow Chinese believers in Hong Kong, Taiwan and the South-east Asian diaspora are taken into account.

Similar revivals have also been noted in other parts of the region, including Indonesia, Malaysia and Singapore, where Pentecostal and charismatic currents have been particularly powerful. The vitality of Korean Christianity has already been noted. At the higher echelons, international ecumenical and interdenominational structures have been established (but with little progress at the grass roots) which are encouraging the emergence of an Asian form of Christianity, with an intra-Asian cross-cultural apostolate. A significant step towards an Asian theology was taken in the mid-1970s, when an indigenous Korean theology began to develop among Korean Protestants overseas and imprisoned theologians in Korea. This led to the emergence of the distinctive *minjŭng sinhak* (Theology of the People). Reflecting the experiences of urban workers, especially during the years of oppressive military rule, the focus of minjung theology is on the politically oppressed, the economically exploited and socially alienated. Thus it has much in common with Latin American Liberation Theology.

In spite of these many positive developments, Christianity faces a number of problems in East and South-east Asia. As far as China is concerned, the process of improving Sino–Vatican relations has been painfully slow. This in turn has prevented the coming together of the official and underground Churches. At the same time, the severe shortage of priests has placed great responsibility on the laity, not only in China, but also in the Philippines. Protestant Churches are facing similar problems. The re-emergence of denominationalism (in China this development explains in part the persistence of unregistered 'house Churches') and Church affiliation along ethnic lines (especially in South-east Asia) hamper moves towards greater unity and co-operation. Moreover, rapid Christianization has also encouraged certain sectarian tendencies, extreme doctrines and immoral practices. Nevertheless, if some of the internal and external problems can be overcome, Asian Christianity as a whole may well emerge as a major force in world Christianity in the twenty-first century.

Notes

1 Text in P. Y. Saeki, *The Nestorian Documents and Relics in China* (2nd rev. and enlarged edn; Tokyo, 1951), pp. 57–8.
2 Samuel Hugh Moffett, *A History of Christianity in Asia*, vol. I: *Beginnings to 1500* (New York, 1992), p. 313.

3 Charles F. Beckingham and Bernard Hamilton (eds), *Prester John, the Mongols and the Ten Lost Tribes* (Aldershot, 1996).

4 The travel narratives of Carpini, Rubruck and others are found in Christopher Dawson (ed.), *Missions to Asia: Narratives and Letters of the Franciscan Missionaries in Mongolia and China in the Thirteenth and Fourteenth Centuries* (New York, 1966; repr. from 1955 edn entitled *The Mongol Mission*). See also William of Rubruck, *The Mission of Friar William of Rubruck: His Journey to the Court of the Great Khan Möngke 1253–1255*, trans. Peter Jackson, ed. Peter Jackson with David O. Morgan (London, 1990).

5 Quoted in Rubruck, p. 213.

6 Indeed, Markos rather unexpectedly became the Catholicos Yaballāhā III, to preside over the whole Nestorian Church in Asia. The most recent study is Morris Rossabi, *Voyager from Xanadu: Rabban Sauma and the First Journey from China to the West* (Tokyo, New York and London, 1992). See also E. A. Wallis Budge (trans.), *The Monks of Kûblâi Khân, Emperor of China* (London, 1928).

7 Erica C. D. Hunter, 'The conversion of the Kerait to Christianity in A.D. 1007', *Zentralasiatische Studien*, 22 (1989/91), pp. 142–63.

8 Quoted in Dawson, *Missions to Asia*, p. 224.

9 See Franz Josef Schütte SJ, *Valignano's Mission Principles for Japan*, trans. John J. Coyne SJ (2 vols; St Louis, 1980).

10 Quoted in C. R. Boxer, *The Christian Century in Japan, 1549–1650* (2nd corrected printing; Berkeley and Los Angeles, 1967), p. 318.

11 See Johannes Laures SJ, *Takayama Ukon und die Anfänge der Kirche in Japan* (Münster, 1954).

12 See e.g. Bernward H. Willeke OFM, 'Did Catholicism in the Yuan Dynasty survive until the present?', *Tripod*, 47 (October 1988), pp. 64–9.

13 For biographies of the 'Three Pillars of the Early Christian Church', see Willard J. Peterson, 'Why did they become Christian? Yang Ting-yün, Li Chih-tsao and Hsü Kuang-ch'i' in Charles E. Ronan SJ and Bonnie B. C. Oh (eds), *East Meets West: The Jesuits in China, 1582–1773* (Chicago, 1988); Nicolas Standaert SJ, *Yang Tingyun, Confucian and Christian in Late Ming China* (Leiden, 1988).

14 Quoted in Jacques Gernet, 'Christian and Chinese visions of the world in the seventeenth century', *Chinese Science*, 4 (1980), p. 17.

15 For a detailed discussion of a major episode of persecution, see Bernward H. Willeke OFM, *Imperial Government and Catholic Missions in China During the Years 1784–1785* (St Bonaventure, NY, 1948).

16 Joseph Krahl SJ, *China Missions in Crisis: Bishop Laimbeckhoven and His Times, 1738–1787* (Rome, 1964), p. 139.

17 The origin of the church at Hangzhou, the capital of Zhejiang, is told in D. E. Mungello, *The Forgotten Christians of Hangzhou* (Honolulu, 1994).

18 Lin Jinshui, 'Chinese literati and the Rites Controversy' in D. E. Mungello (ed.), *The Chinese Rites Controversy: Its History and Meaning* (Nettetal, 1994), pp. 65–82.

19 H. Jedin and J. Dolan (eds), *History of the Church* (London, 1981), vol. VIII, pp. 314–15.

20 When the Burmese invaded Ayutthia, then the capital of Siam, in 1767, the seminary was moved, first to Hon-dat in Vietnam, then in 1770 to Virampatnam near Pondichéry in French India. It was closed in 1781 and not reopened until 1807, in Penang, Malaya. Robert E. Entenmann, 'Chinese Catholic clergy and catechists in eighteenth-century Szechwan', *Actes du VIᵉ Colloque International de Sinologie de Chantilly* (Paris, 1995), p. 396.

21 Until its closure by the Italian government in 1869, the college had graduated

106 Chinese priests. See *Elenchus Alumnorum, Decreta et Documenta quae spectant ad Collegium S. Familiae Napolis* (Shanghai, 1917), pp. 1–10.

22 For a discussion of the role of Catholic 'virgins' in Sichuan province, see Robert Entenmann, 'Christian virgins in eighteenth-century Sichuan' in Daniel H. Bays (ed.), *Christianity in China, the Eighteenth Century to the Present: Essays in Religious and Social Change* (Stanford, 1996), pp. 180–93.

23 B. Biermann OP, *Die Anfänge der neueren Dominikanermission in China* (Münster, 1927), pp. 163–5.

24 For an account of Chinese sectarian groups becoming adherents of the Catholic Church, see R. G. Tiedemann, 'Christianity and Chinese "heterodox sects": mass conversion and syncretism in Shandong Province in the early eighteenth century', *Monumenta Serica*, 44 (1996), pp. 339–82. See also Robert Entenmann, 'Clandestine Catholics and the state in eighteenth-century Szechwan', *Proceedings of the First International Symposium on Church and State in China: Past and Present* (Danshui, Taiwan, 1987), pp. 123–52. The low level of life among the Chinese Christians is a constant complaint in Andreas Ly's Latin diary. See Adrien Launay MEP, *Journal d'André Ly, prêtre chinois, missionnaire et notaire apostolique, 1746–1763* (2nd edn; Hong Kong, 1924).

25 Alexandre de Rhodes SJ, *Rhodes of Viet Nam: The Travels and Missions of Father Alexander de Rhodes in China and Other Kingdoms of the Orient*, trans. by Solange Hertz (Westminster, MD, 1966). On the Domus Dei, see Nikolaus Kowalsky OMI, 'Die Anfänge der "Domus Dei" in Tongking und Cochinchina' in Johann Specker SMB and Walbert Bühlmann OFMCap (eds), *Das Laienapostolat in den Missionen* (Schöneck-Beckenried, 1961), pp. 155–60.

26 Parallel to this development, Rhodes had obtained approval from Rome in 1653 for introduction of the vicariate system to the eastern missions which would permit direct papal action, bypassing Portuguese *padroado* claims. The first French vicars apostolic under the direct authority of the Pope were appointed in 1658.

27 De la Motte was appointed vicar apostolic for Cochin-China (i.e. the southern part of Vietnam) with the administration of several provinces of south-eastern China; Pallu had jurisdiction over Tongking and administration over central and south-western China.

28 For an account of Pigneau de Behaine's career, see Charles B. Maybon, *Histoire moderne du pays d'Annam, 1592–1820* (Paris, 1920), chs V–IX.

29 John F. Cady, *The Roots of French Imperialism in Eastern Asia* (Cornell, 1954), pp. 28–38.

30 The Cofradía de San José and other Christianized protest movements are discussed in Reynaldo Clemeña Ileto, *Pasyon and Revolution: Popular Movements in the Philippines, 1840–1910* (Quezon City, 1979); Setsuho Ikehata, 'Popular Catholicism in the nineteenth-century Philippines: the case of the Cofradía de San José' in Takahishi Shiraishi (ed.), *Reading Southeast Asia: Translation of Contemporary Japanese Scholarship on Southeast Asia* (Ithaca, NY, 1989), pp. 109–88; David Sweet, 'A proto-political peasant movement in the Spanish Philippines: the Cofradía de San José and the Tabayas Rebellion of 1841', *Asian Studies*, 8.1 (1970), pp. 94–119.

31 Pedro S. de Achútegui SJ and Miguel A. Bernad, *Religious Revolution in the Philippines: The Life and Church of Gregorio Aglipay 1860–1960* (3 vols; 2nd edn; Manila, 1961).

32 On the incorporation of Christianity into Javanese religion, see Ph. Quarles van Ufford, 'Why don't you sit down? Sadrach and the struggle for religious independence in the earliest phase of the Church of Central Java (1861–1899)' in

Reimar Schefold, J. W. Schoorl and J. Tennekes (eds), *Man, Meaning and History: Essays in Honour of H. G. Schulte Nordholt* (The Hague, 1980), pp. 204–29.

33 Hendrik Kraemer, *The Christian Message in a Non-Christian World* (London, 1947; first published 1938), p. 426.

34 Eric O. Hanson, 'Political aspects of Chinese Catholicism' in James D. Whitehead, Yu-ming Shaw and N. J. Girardot (eds), *China and Christianity: Historical and Future Encounters* (Notre Dame, IN, 1979), pp. 138–9.

35 The most recent account of the Taiping Rebellion and its religious dimension is Jonathan Spence, *God's Chinese Son: The Taiping Heavenly Kingdom of Hong Xiuquan* (New York and London, 1996). See also Rudolf G. Wagner, *Reenacting the Heavenly Vision: The Role of Religion in the Taiping Rebellion* (Berkeley, 1982).

36 The early history of the China Inland Mission, the first 'faith mission' and ultimately largest Protestant society in China, is outlined in A. J. Broomhall, *Hudson Taylor and China's Open Century* (7 vols; Sevenoaks, 1981–89).

37 For further details, see Daniel H. Bays, 'The growth of independent Christianity in China, 1900–1937' in Bays, *Christianity in China* (Stanford, 1996), pp. 307–16.

38 Jacques Leclerq, *Thunder in the Distance* (New York, 1958), pp. 55–6.

39 Ka-che Yip, *Religion, Nationalism and Chinese Students: The Anti-Christian Movement of 1922–1927* (Bellingham, WA, 1980); Jessie G. Lutz, *Chinese Politics and Christian Missions: The Anti-Christian Movement of 1920–28* (Notre Dame, IN, 1988).

40 Aizawa Seishisai (1782–1863) in *Shinron* (New proposals), quoted in Ryusaku Tsunoda, Wm. Theodore de Bary and Donald Keene (comps), *Sources of Japanese Tradition* (4th printing; New York, 1968), vol. II, pp. 95–6.

41 For a history of the 'hidden Christians' and an account of their beliefs and practices, see Ann M. Harrington BVM, *Japan's Hidden Christians* (Chicago, 1993); Stephen Turnbull, *The Kakure Kirishitan of Japan: A Study of Their Development, Beliefs and Rituals to the Present Day* (Richmond, Surrey, 1998). The *Tenchi hajimari no koto* has been translated and annotated by Christal Whelan as *The Beginning of Heaven and Earth: The Sacred Book of Japan's Hidden Christians* (Honolulu, 1996).

42 Notto R. Thelle, *Buddhism and Christianity in Japan: From Conflict to Dialogue, 1854–1899* (Honolulu, 1987).

43 Carlo Caldarola, *Christianity the Japanese Way* (Leiden, 1979).

44 James Huntley Grayson, *Korea: A Religious History* (Oxford, 1989), p. 181.

45 A selection of such illustrations is found in Johannes Schütte SVD, *Die katholische Chinamission im Spiegel der rotchinesischen Presse. Versuch einer missionarischen Deutung* (Münster, 1957).

46 Eric O. Hanson, *Catholic Politics in China and Korea* (Maryknoll, NY, 1980), pp. 32–9; quotation on pp. 36–7.

47 Bob Whyte, *Unfinished Encounter: China and Christianity* (London, 1988), p. 292.

48 On the development of Catholicism in modern Vietnam, see Piero Gheddo, *The Cross and the Bo-Tree: Catholics and Buddhists in Vietnam* (New York, 1970).

49 The first Korean Presbyterian cross-cultural mission was, in fact, established in Shandong, China, as early as 1912. Kim Hwal-young, *From Asia to Asia: A Study on Mission History of the Presbyterian Church in Korea (1876–1992)* (Manila, 1994), pp. 25–62.

50 Yim He-Mo, *Unity Lost – Unity to be Regained in Korean Presbyterianism* (New York and Frankfurt, 1996).

51 Hanson, *Catholic Politics*, pp. 85–6.

11

North America

Robert Bruce Mullin

The story of Christianity in North America is a story both like and unlike the story of Christianity elsewhere. Issues of Catholicism versus Protestantism, learning versus heartfelt religion and adaptation versus resistance to culture, pepper the narrative here as they do elsewhere. But Christians in North America, perhaps more than any other Christian community, have been forced to confront two overarching challenges. The first concerned the great task of Christianizing a vast continent. The second concerned the balancing of unity and diversity.

Both factors stem from the unique situation in which North American Christians found themselves. Christianity entered North America through the great folk migration of Europeans from the Old World to the New. On the new continent all of the carefully constructed supports of a Christian culture were eerily absent. The landscape bespoke the awesomeness of nature rather than the architectural presence of Christian civilization, and laws and customs, long considered foundational, were lacking. To Christianize the landscape and to transform the natural order formed a great concern. Nor was this simply the task of the first generations. As the frontier progressed the challenge of Christianization progressed along with it. Yet it was not one 'Christianity' but many 'Christianities' which were dutifully transported to the New World by the myriad of settlers. The particularities of these inherited faiths became a cherished sense of self-identification in the new environment. Writing in the early twentieth century, the British observer James Bryce noted 'each race has, as a rule, adhered to the form of religion it held in Europe'.[1] How to fashion a sense of religious unity in the face of such diversity would be a recurring theme in North American religious life. In both of these ways the pattern of Christianity in North America would differ from that of Europe.

Seventeenth-century beginnings

When the Genoese navigator Christopher Columbus landed on (what is now probably) San Salvador in the Caribbean Sea and claimed all he found for the King and Queen of Spain, he reflected that what had occurred was no mere discovery, but an inauguration of a new era in sacred history. 'Let Christ rejoice on earth, as he rejoices in heaven, in the prospect of the salvation of the souls of so many nations hitherto lost.'[2] Conquest and conversion were interlocking themes in the founding of the Americas, and they were themes about which Christianity would play a key role.

Spain, France, Britain, Sweden and the Netherlands all laid claims to parts of what is now North America, and planted their Church life there. Spain brought to the west, south-west and other parts of what is now the United States its vision of Roman Catholicism. France brought its own form of Catholicism to Canada and parts of the great American heartland. Sweden and the Netherlands for a time exercised control of what is now Delaware and New York, and there attempted to establish their own Reformation Churches. Finally Britain exported the confusions of its own Reformation settlement to different parts of what are now the United States and Canada.

Yet in all of these plantations, the Christian life that emerged was shaped by tensions between the vision of the founders and the distinctive nature of the environment. Let us take three examples: the English colony in Virginia, the settlements in the St Lawrence River valley in New France and the English Puritan settlements in New England. In each case, vision and environment shaped Christian development.

The Virginia colony attempted to reconstitute the English Protestant Church of the early Jacobean period. A theological loyalty to the Reformed faith was combined with a fealty to the practices and observances of the Prayer Book tradition. In instructions to an early governor it was stated: 'You shall take principal order and care for the true and reverent worship of God, that his word be duly preached and his holy sacraments administered according to the constitution of the Church of England in all fundamental points . . . and all atheism, prophaneness, popery or schism be exemplary punished to the honour of God and the peace and safety of his Church.'[3] Despite the lofty ideal, however, the early history of the colony was as troubled and halting as was its religious life. At times governors such as Thomas Dale attempted to use religion to enforce discipline on the colony. His 'Lawes Divine Morall and Martiall' made blasphemy a capital offence, while at other times the colony's General Assembly likewise attempted to enforce details of moral action. Yet

417

despite these attempts, colonial Virginia was never to be known as a particularly godly commonwealth.

The established Church served still another purpose. From early on (perhaps to overcome the vastness of the virgin continent and the distance from familiar institutions) the ceremonies and dignities of the old established religion were kept. As one contemporary account recalled, every Sunday, when the Lord Governor went to church, he was accompanied by his councillors, captains, 'and all the gentlemen, and with a guard of fifty Halberdiers in the Lordship's living, fair red cloaks, on each side and behind him'. There in worship, governors and councillors sat 'each in their place'. For the settlers of Virginia, to be connected to their homeland, symbols of sacred authority were necessary.[4]

Thus the Church in Virginia was established by law. At first the parent London Company, and later the General Assembly of the colony, set up parishes and set forth requirements for the support of a ministry. Yet the Anglican model in the South was shaped over the course of the colonial period by the absence of bishops in America. The lack of a resident bishop resulted in crucial authority devolving upon laypersons. This was the background for the famous 'vestry system', one of the distinctive features of the colonial Church in Virginia. Vestries were charged to elect ministers to parishes, levy tithes, care for indigents and orphans and perform other social functions. But quickly vestries took upon themselves the authority of hiring and firing of clergy. Still another peculiarity of the established Church in Virginia was its legal status: although religiously connected to the Church of England through the Bishop of London, it was legally subservient to the Virginia Assembly.

If the established Church of Virginia attempted to transplant the Reformed faith of sixteenth-century Anglicanism, the Church of New France strove to transplant the Catholic religion of the French homeland. But even here the simple picture unravels with close analysis. Despite the historic interconnection between French Canadian culture and the religion of Roman Catholicism, in its origins the story of Christianity in New France was never simply a story of French immigrants, but included missions to the native peoples. Far more so than almost any other colonizing nation, the French were concerned with the evangelization and conversion of the native populations. The names of the famous missionaries – such as Claude Allouz, Jacques Marquette and the North American Martyrs – have come down as a memorial to the sacrificial spirit of the early clerics. Furthermore, among the Huron of southern Ontario, French Jesuit missionaries responded far more positively to native religious sentiments than did either contemporary English or Spanish missionaries. Unlike the English and Spanish, who on the whole believed that Christianization and enculturation went together, the French showed a surprising cultural sensitivity towards native society.

Nor, at its beginning, were the settlements exclusively Catholic. At the onset of the Christianization of French Canada, a degree of toleration between Catholics and Huguenots was maintained. Henry IV of France was interested in transporting the tolerant spirit of the Edict of Nantes to the New World, and accordingly in both Acadia and Québec until the 1620s Catholics and Protestants lived in harmony. By the end of this decade, however, the policy had begun to change. Cardinal Richelieu reorganized the Company of Québec to ensure Catholic dominance and to remove official toleration of Protestantism. He also entrusted the missions of the colony to the Jesuits. These middle decades of the seventeenth century witnessed not only Protestant/Catholic tensions, but also intra-Catholic ones. The French Catholic world was divided between Gallicans who emphasized the subservience of the Church to the state, and an Ultramontane or Tridentine party which emphasized loyalty to Rome and a centralized Roman Catholicism. Which vision would triumph in the New World?

In this struggle François de Montmorency Laval (1623–1708) played a crucial role. Appointed vicar apostolic of New France, he arrived in Québec in 1659, and left an indelible mark on the Church in New France. Both as vicar apostolic and later (1674) as Bishop of the newly constituted diocese of Québec, he exercised discipline over clergy, maintained the independence of the Church over against the state, and extended the Church's role in education and reform. One of his tireless crusades was against the alcohol trade with the native peoples. Laval's endeavours, along with those of his successor Jean Baptiste de Saint Vallier, gave a rigour to the Church in New France, as well as a spiritual and intellectual conservatism that would continue well into the twentieth century. When fellow religionists in the old country became attracted to Enlightenment ideas, Catholicism in New France remained united and conservative. This factor would be of crucial importance when New France fell under the dominion of Protestant England in the next century.

Of all the religious traditions transplanted in seventeenth-century North America, the English Puritan experiment in New England was to have the most far-reaching effect. Both on the level of institution and symbol, the Puritan experience was to shape Christianity in North America profoundly. Puritans were British Protestants who saw their Church as incompletely reformed in a number of areas. First, they found the willingness of English prelates to continue old practices such as vestments and saints' days debilitating to true Christianity. The Church must be fully purified (hence their appellation 'Puritan'). More importantly, Puritans reflected a distinct view of the true Church. The Church for them was to be a disciplined community concerned with the building up of the faithful. Such a Church (and community) ought to be governed rigorously by the rules of Scripture. Finally, Puritans emphasized a new way of understanding the Christian life. The transformed heart, manifested in a conversion experience, came to be seen as the mark of a true believer or saint. Such an experience could help answer the question that plagued many within the Reformed or Calvinistic tradition – how could one be certain of one's own predestined status? By the seventeenth century, conversion, which provided personal assurance, also increasingly became the criterion for full Church membership.

As the dissatisfaction increased over the inadequacies of the Elizabethan settlement, and the religious policies of the Stuart monarchs offered little hope of change, the New World beckoned as a refuge. In 1620 a small group of radical Puritans, or Separatists, led by William Bradford, established an outpost in southern Massachusetts, which they named Plymouth in honour of the town they had left. These 'pilgrims', as they later came to be known, were never a significant factor in seventeenth-century religious life. But as a symbol they became a crucial part of the American national faith. Far more important was the large-scale migration of English Puritans to the New World beginning in 1630. Between 1630 and 1643 over 20,000 Puritans flocked to Massachusetts. These Puritans brought along with them a distinctive vision of their place in divine providence. In the famous words of John Winthrop (1588–1649), their first governor, 'We must consider that we shall be as a city upon a hill, the eyes of all people are upon us'.[5] The invocation of such biblical imagery was not accidental. Puritans saw themselves as the 'new Israel' and their experiment as 'God's new Israel'.

The Puritan holy commonwealth was a vision of the Christian society unlike that found earlier. Convinced that in the experience of the holy spirit upon the heart of the individual one could divine who were the true saints, Massachusetts Bay in the mid-1630s required a narration of the experience of regenerating grace as a prerequisite for Church membership, and hence indirectly for citizenship in the colony. All other persons would be merely 'attendees' of the Church and 'inhabitants' of the commonwealth. But if Puritans strove to establish 'holy commonwealths', they were 'holy' in ways unlike earlier Christian societies. Church and state were separated to a degree unheard of in English society, and institutions and practices such as Church courts and the public use of excommunication were excluded. The 'holiness' stemmed from the fact that magistrates as well as ministers saw themselves under a solemn covenant with God and saw their secular duties as part of their religious calling. Although, as its subsequent history was to demonstrate, New England Puritan society was as capable of serving the world and the flesh as any other society, its religious vision, and in particular its conception of itself as a 'city upon a hill', would be a recurring theme in American history.

The presence of such vastly different religious visions would result in conflict, and in particular the conflict between Catholicism and Protestantism would be an overriding theme in North American religious life well into the twentieth century. But these three great visions do not do justice to the complexity of the story of Christianity in North America. From early on, the New World was a place not only to attempt to re-establish the religious ideals of seventeenth-century Europe, but also to strike out on new paths. From New England itself, Roger Williams helped in the establishment of the colony of Rhode Island, a 'shelter for persons distressed for conscience'. For Williams, no society could ever be a 'new Israel' and hence none ought to enforce godliness. Likewise in the area between New England and the Anglican southern colonies – in the middle colonies of New York, New Jersey and Pennsylvania – a religious pluralism began to take root that would make them distinct. There, Dutch, Swedes, Germans and Scotch Irish coexisted along with English-speaking Puritans and Anglicans. It was furthermore in the colony of Pennsylvania, under the leadership of William Penn and Quakers, that this religious and cultural pluralism reached its most vivid expression. The dual Quaker emphasis upon non-violence and the recognition of the inner light in each human soul provided the justification for this policy of toleration.

New challenges

The North American colonies had been founded as part of that great outpouring of religious excitement associated with the Reformation era. As this fervour began to recede it inevitably affected colonial religious life, and hence by the early eighteenth century none of the distinctive visions were quite what they had been. Just as in the Old World the era of religious wars was succeeded by an age of reason, so too in the New World one found a growing interest in the natural world and the potency of human reason. Such trends, although never dominant, would play their role.

Much of colonial Anglicanism drank deeply of the new spirit. Eschewing its Reformation theology, colonial Anglicanism emphasized reason, balance, human freedom and morality. These emphases played an important role in the growth of Anglicanism in the northern colonies, where it was embraced as a religious alternative to Puritanism. The emphasis upon humanitarianism also bore practical fruit in a wide variety of actions. The Society for the Propagation of the Gospel in Foreign Parts, founded in

1701, emphasized the evangelization and catechesis of the slave community. The new humanitarian spirit of the eighteenth century perhaps culminated in the founding of the colony of Georgia (1733) by James Oglethorp. Established as a second chance for honest debtors, Georgia was conceived of as a model society. Slavery and spirituous beverages, for example, were both outlawed. The colony, however, did not prosper, and by mid-century had largely abandoned its higher moral vision, but it nonetheless stood as a symbol of the new spirit of natural philanthropy.

The new spirit of reason and morality would have an even greater effect upon the Puritan commonwealths. The failure of Puritanism in England with the Restoration, and a loss of a sense of eschatological expectation, led to soul-searching among New England Puritans. Preachers denounced the decline in vitality since the founding of the colony. These 'jeremiads', as the sermons were called, may have spoken more to perception than to reality, but by the early eighteenth century changes had taken place that modified the Puritan pristine vision of the true Church and true state. The notion of a Church of 'visible saints' was tempered in 1662 when Massachusetts clergy accepted a 'Half-Way Covenant' that allowed unconverted individuals (that is, the children of Church members) a half-way Church membership. Although unable to receive communion or vote in Church elections, they could have their children baptized. Similarly the Puritan vision of the godly commonwealth received a severe blow in the issuing of a new charter for the Massachusetts colony in 1691 that shifted the condition for voting privileges from Church membership to property. These tensions may have lain behind the infamous Salem Witch Trial (1692) at which nineteen people were hanged.

On still another front, the 'new learning' of post-1660 Europe was beginning to find favour at institutions such as Harvard and Yale College. All of these trends were vague, but the result was that from the heart of New England there began to be heard claims for 'Arminianism'. Arminianism in the New World, however, bore little parallel with the technical theological debates among seventeenth-century Dutch Calvinists. Rather it was a movement to elevate the role of reason, conscience and human freedom in the religious life.

Wars and the Great Awakening

Christianity in North America would be profoundly affected by religious and political changes in the middle of the eighteenth century. Wars and awakenings would leave their mark on both Canada and the United States, and largely transform the older colonial religious visions. Like their European compatriots, North American Protestants felt the effects of the movement known as Pietism, with its emphasis on vital piety and a zeal for missionary outreach. In the middle colonies of America the message of Continental Pietism found voice in ministers such as Theodore Freling-huysen (1691–1747). Other channels of transmission also operated, and the result was a resurgence of heartfelt religious revivals, known as either the Great Awakening or Great Awakenings. Whether this was a unified movement (as subsequent generations understood it to be) or rather a series of disconnected local events linked only by later memory (as some scholars now argue) is unclear, but the effect was truly 'great'. It reshaped the religious topography of Protestant North America as individuals from Nova Scotia to Georgia felt the impact of the new preaching and piety.[6]

One can see the Awakening reflected in a number of phases. The first is often referred to as the 'Frontier Revival' and was rooted in rural New England. There in the mid-1730s, as preachers railed against the new spirit of Arminianism, they began to experience large numbers of conversions and 'a great and earnest concern about the great things of religion . . . became universal . . . and among persons of all degrees and all ages'.[7] The revival was duly recorded by the pastor-theologian Jonathan Edwards (1703–58) in *A Faithful Narrative of the Surprising Work of God*. Although it was only a brief and relatively small affair, the revival generated great excitement. As the British hymn writer Isaac Watts noted, 'never did we hear or read, since the first ages of Christianity, any event of this kind so surprising as the present narrative has set before us'.[8]

The Frontier Revival was only a prelude, however, to the great stir caused by the preaching of George Whitefield. Whitefield, an Anglican priest and associate of John Wesley, made numerous visits to America, but his second visit of 1739–41 was perhaps his most celebrated. One of the great preachers of the century (of whom it was said that he could bring a crowd to tears by simply pronouncing the word 'Mesopotamia'), Whitefield created a stir wherever he went. His dramatic forceful preaching style and his emphasis upon the new birth drew crowds of tremendous size, culminating in his outdoor sermons on the Boston Common to as many as 30,000 people. Whitefield's preaching and fame spread the case for heartfelt religion throughout the colonies. But in Whitefield one sees another effect of the Great Awakening. In his journal, published after his return to England, he lamented the 'darkness' he had found at Harvard and Yale and the lack of vital piety among many of the colonial clergy.

Others took up Whitefield's practice of itinerancy as well as criticism of colonial clergy. The Presbyterian Gilbert Tennant preached on the dangers of an 'unconverted ministry' and urged believers to separate from such clergy. He argued 'if the Ministry of natural Men be as it has been represented; Then it is both lawful and expedient to go from them and hear Godly Persons.'[9] The challenge to the established ministry naturally increased the controversial nature of the Awakening. By the mid-1740s parties had developed within the northern colonies over the new message of the Awakening. Northern Anglicans and many Congregationalists cautioned against the unleashing of enthusiasm. But others saw in the Awakening a revitalization of religion.

If the message of the Awakening was controversial in the northern colonies, in the South it would prove to be revolutionary. There the message of heartfelt religion fell upon the colonists and created a crisis. The established Anglican Church (and its vision of society) was becoming more precarious, particularly among the small farmers of the piedmont or western areas. Various groups preached the new message: Presbyterians, and, by the 1770s, Methodists, but it was the Baptists who were to be the great apostles of the revivalist message in the colonial South. Missionaries from northern colonies, such as Shubal Stearns (1706–71), preached the new message with emotional warmth and fervour. Their message, however, was not merely one of evangelistic religion but also a democratic critique of the hierarchical social order reflected by colonial Anglicanism. This critique, when ultimately loosed by the American Revolution, would fundamentally transform southern culture and leave little remaining of the colonial Anglican vision.

A final phase of the Awakening can be called the Canadian phase, and would leave its mark upon maritime Canada. Through the preaching of Henry Alline (1748–84) the message of heartfelt religion would win over many Canadian Protestants, yet, as we will see, the social implications of the Canadian awakening would be far different from that of the lower colonies.

The Awakening was to have profound long-term effects. If on the one hand it was a divisive movement – spawning separatism, and critics – it was to have a unifying effect as well. The message of evangelical Protestantism increasingly became the religious cement binding together the different parts of the colonies. The diverse religious visions of the early colonial period were ultimately undermined by this new evangelical understanding. Likewise the new spirit of evangelical awakening quickened an interest in missions, and along with this a concern to spread the message to the outcasts of the colonial social order. David Brainerd (1718–47), son-in-law of Jonathan Edwards, began a mission to Native Americans, though with comparatively little success. Of greater importance, the message began to spread to the African slave community. The issue of the evangelization of the slave community had been a thorny one, and before the middle of the century the few efforts at Christianization had been under the auspices of colonial Anglicans. But the new message found favour among African-Americans, and increasingly the message of a heartfelt gospel became the common piety of both blacks and whites.

But perhaps the most far-reaching effect of the Great Awakening was on the understanding of history and destiny. The era of the Awakening also saw a rising popularity in the idea of 'post-millennialism', or the belief that the golden age of the kingdom of God would occur before the return of Jesus. This belief was taken up by the Awakening's proponents and engendered a degree of excitement and possibility in the view of the future. Furthermore, some writers such as Jonathan Edwards speculated concerning the possibility of this hoped-for golden age beginning in the New World. By the 1750s this expectation was given a political twist, and the millennial expectation began to affect the way in which particularly New England Protestants viewed the course of current events. Language of liberty and virtue became enmeshed with the prospect of the millennium, and the result was what has been called a 'civil millennialism' which saw the triumph of the divine kingdom not only in the success of true Protestant piety and religion but also in the advance of liberty and freedom.

This way of reading the signs of the times would be crucially important because there appeared to be many such 'signs'. The first six decades of the eighteenth century witnessed continual clashes between the empires of Catholic France and Protestant Britain, and this struggle had religious corollaries. As might be expected, the cross often followed the Crown, and British successes in wresting the maritime provinces away from France were quickly followed by plantings of Protestant Churches. With the British presence in Acadia (Nova Scotia), Protestantism took root in Canada. Although French Catholics were guaranteed free exercise of their religion by the treaty of Utrecht (1713), by mid-century a process of Protestantization was under way. In 1755 British administrators ordered the evacuation of the Acadians from Nova Scotia, and in 1758 the Church of England was made the established Church. These apparent triumphs of Protestantism over Rome excited many New England Protestants. When the fortress of Louisburg, on Cape Breton Island, fell in 1745 to a New England army, it was announced that God had 'triumphed gloriously over his and our anti-Christian enemies'.[10] The final triumph of Britain over the French Catholic empire was greeted with equal celebration.

Britain had the more difficult task, however, of incorporating Canada into its haphazardly gained empire. Part of this necessitated a religious policy. What should be done with the French Catholic community? During the first decade of British rule of Canada its policies were marked by ambivalence. The formal goal (as implied in the Royal Proclamation of 1763) was Anglicization, particularly since many feared the French Catholic clergy as agents of disloyalty. Yet the practical difficulties of forcing such a large alien population to abandon its historic ways were likewise recognized. A formal British policy was finally established in the

Québec Act (1774). In it Catholics were granted free exercise of religion; the Church's hierarchy was recognized, and the right to receive customary dues was affirmed; and the property rights of seminaries and religious orders (except for the Jesuits, who were suppressed and dissolved) acknowledged. The Act also implicitly allowed for French Catholic participation in the political life of the province. Thus it seemed as if the problem of French Canada had been solved.

These events, however, were viewed far differently by the lower colonies. The acceptance of the Catholic hierarchy by the Québec Act was viewed as scandalous, and the Act's extending of the province down to the Ohio River (lands on which the colonies also had claims) was seen as sinister. Furthermore, at the same time, colonial Anglicans renewed their campaign to establish a colonial episcopate. The campaign for an American bishop evoked in northern colonists memories of Charles I and William Laud, while in the South fears arose that resident bishops would threaten the vestry system. The struggle over bishops convinced many that tyranny and the destruction of liberty lay at the root of the imperial agenda, while the acceptance of Roman Catholic claims in the Québec Act raised the fear of Catholic influence.

These religious paranoias fed into the American Revolutionary War and left their mark upon the religious life of North America. In the thirteen colonies Christians found themselves divided. Some were Patriots, particularly among the Puritans of New England, the Presbyterians of the Middle Colonies, and to a lesser degree the Southern Anglicans. Others, particularly but not exclusively Northern Anglicans, were Loyalists. Many others remained neutral. The two regions most affected by the war would be the American South and Canada. In Virginia, for example, the privileged status of the Anglican Church was removed by degrees between 1776 and 1785. Furthermore, with the withdrawal of public support many clergy left the state. The result was the large-scale collapse of Southern Anglicanism. The once proud established Church of Virginia shrank from over 90 clergy to only thirteen. The vacuum created by the collapse of Anglicanism allowed for the rapid growth of evangelical denominations. Even more than Baptists, the Methodists grew in the South.

The war propelled Canadian Church life in a very different direction. The magnanimity of the Québec Act assured the loyalty of the French Catholic community to Britain during the war. The Bishop of Québec, Jean Olivier Briand, for example, instructed his clergy to refuse the sacraments to Canadians siding with the American Patriots. Likewise, the influx of over 35,000 Loyalists did much to bolster Canadian Protestantism. Convinced that the problems of the thirteen colonies had stemmed from an inadequate linking of Church and empire, the British Crown took steps to put the Church of England on a firm legal footing in English-speaking Canada. Charles Inglis was appointed Bishop of Nova Scotia in 1787, and in 1791 the British Parliament established the Church of England in British Canada and endowed it with resources.

Finally the American struggle forced Canadian Christians to begin to reflect upon their distinctiveness. One sees this in the career of Henry Alline. Alline was one of the many New Englanders who began settling in the Canadian maritime region at the end of the Seven Years War. Converted in 1775, he began a vigorous preaching ministry emphasizing the theme of the new birth, and became known as the leader of the Great Awakening in Nova Scotia. But part of Alline's message involved the exceptionalism and mission of the maritime community. They were a 'people highly favoured of God'[11] for whom loyalty to Christ necessitated abstention from the great conflict between Britain and her colonies to the south. The war, he argued, was a judgement on both Britain and the colonies. Thus if the influence of the Awakening was to light fires of revolution in the lower colonies, in Canada its influence was to dampen them.

Like most wars, the American Revolution disturbed much of the settled religious life of the areas affected. Populations were dispersed, property was destroyed and the long-established rhythms of piety were disturbed. At the end of the eighteenth century the different religious communities began the process of picking up the pieces. For some, such as the Congregationalists, who were the heirs of the New England Puritans, the transition was a relatively smooth one. With their 'Standing Order' or establishments still intact, they continued in their traditional role. Other communities were much more adversely affected. In particular, Anglicans and Quakers suffered as a result of the Revolution and did not fully rebound until the next century.

But if these early years of the republic were years of dislocation for some, for others they provided the opportunity for organization. The small American Catholic community, largely concentrated in Pennsylvania and Maryland, throughout the colonial period had been under various legal restraints. The new state constitutions springing up after the Revolution, however, included articles on religious freedom. Accordingly in 1783 clergy in Maryland began working on a plan for the organization of the Catholic community. The next year John Carroll (1735–1815) was appointed 'Superior of the Mission', and in 1790 was consecrated Bishop of Baltimore.

Still another group that began to organize during these years was the free African-American Community. Many African-Americans had been affected by the evangelistic message of Great Awakening preaching, and in the Chesapeake Bay area they enthusiastically supported the young

Methodist movement. Racial tensions, however, were never absent. After a particularly unpleasant incident in which African-American worshippers were pulled from their knees while in prayer because they were occupying the wrong part of St George's Methodist Episcopal Church (Philadelphia), African-Americans established independent worshipping communities. The story of the institutional development of these communities is somewhat convoluted, but by the early nineteenth century two independent African-American denominations had taken root: the African Methodist Episcopal Church, and the African Methodist Episcopal Church Zion. During these years independent African-American Baptist Churches also began to be established. These Churches quickly became the centres for the free African communities.

The Second Great Awakening

The early years of the republic confronted still one more question. What was to be the religious foundation of the new nation? As a result of the Revolution not only were kings set aside but so too was the traditional idea of the relationship of religion and society. The new national constitution rejected any idea of religious tests for public office, and the First Amendment to the new Constitution stated 'Congress shall make no laws respecting an establishment of religion, or prohibiting the free exercise thereof'. But what would take the place of established Churches in anchoring morality and providing ultimate meaning? The last years of the eighteenth century saw a flurry of interest, particularly among elites, in rational forms of belief such as Freemasonry and Deism. But the religious direction of the young republic would be finally shaped not so much by any of these forces as by a resurgence of evangelical Protestantism.

This resurgence is generally known as the Second Great Awakening, and if anything, it was more diverse than the revivals of the mid-eighteenth century. Indeed, the early nineteenth-century revival was fundamentally paradoxical, combining both conservative and radical elements. Similarly, it both placed evangelical Protestantism into the centre of early national culture while transforming it through the triumph of popular democratic impulses. This mixed heritage would leave an indelible mark on American religious life as well as American culture.

One way of understanding this paradox is to see the Second Great Awakening flowering in different locations. One place of origin was among the Congregationalist Churches of New England, particularly Connecticut. There a body of clergy by the end of the century was dedicating itself to preaching a message of 'New Divinity' and defending the Standing Order. Particularly with the commencement of Timothy Dwight's presidency, Yale College became the centre of this phase of the Awakening. Dwight (1752–1817) tirelessly worked to convert his students away from the sceptical attitudes associated with the French Enlightenment and towards a conversion-oriented piety. If Dwight was the intellectual captain of the eastern phase of the revival, his chief lieutenant, Lyman Beecher (1775–1863), was the active embodiment of it. This eastern awakening had two goals. It both attempted to salvage the traditional Reformed theology by allowing for a greater degree of human agency and a larger role for divine justice and also emphasized moral reform. Individuals such as Beecher became actively involved in campaigns against duelling and the use of alcoholic beverages. In all, the thrust of the eastern revival was fundamentally conservative, and it attempted to buttress both the established Congregationalist Churches and the traditional social order.

The Awakening took a completely different turn outside New England. In both the rapidly expanding trans-Appalachian West and the post-Anglican South, the Awakening served not to buttress an already existing order but to fill a cultural and psychological void. In this context the revivals were neither moderate nor contained. One sees this in the famous revival meeting at Cane Ridge. In August of 1801 up to 25,000 persons gathered for a season of preaching and sacrament. But the result was not what might have been expected, and the emotional excesses of the event have become legendary. Commentators both at the time and since have luxuriated on the running, jerking, singing and barking 'exercises' which were exhibited there. As a result of such revivals there occurred not only the large-scale evangelization of the trans-Appalachian population, but a significant transformation in American religious life, since the great beneficiaries of the revival were not the older colonial Churches but the new popular denominations.

No group benefited more from the new revivalism than did the Methodists. Having their roots in America in the 1760s, they underwent a period of phenomenal growth in the decades after their organization in 1784. In that year they numbered 14,000. Sixty years later their numbers had swollen to over one million, making them the largest Church in America and easily dwarfing the old colonial Churches. Indeed, it was not only other Churches which the Methodists dwarfed. By the 1840s there were more Methodist Churches in the United States than there were federal post offices!

If Methodists grew furiously during these years, so too did other groups such as the Baptists, who increased tenfold in the decades after the Revolution. By the early 1840s Methodists and Baptists constituted two-thirds of the Protestant ministers and Church members in the United States.

The Second Great Awakening in the west was both vitalizing and divisive. It emphasized themes of populism, volunteerism, competition and plain preaching that would reverberate through American religious life. But the divisiveness and competition were troubling to many. Some offered solutions to recover the lost unity. The Christian Association, spearheaded by Alexander Campbell (1788–1866), attempted to recapture the unity of the Christian community through a form of radical restorationism. Arguing that the New Testament was the only true guide for the Church, they offered as their maxim 'where the Scriptures speak, we speak; where the Scriptures are silent, we are silent'. Such movements, however, rather than overcoming the divisions, contributed to them.

The extreme divisiveness of American Protestantism as a result of the Second Great Awakening was mind-boggling to foreign visitors. But, as observers noted, these divisions, rather than weakening the power of religion, ironically strengthened it. As the historian Philip Schaff observed, 'In Berlin there are hardly forty Churches for a population of four hundred and fifty thousand, of whom, in spite of all the union of Church and state, only some thirty thousand attend public worship. In New York, to a population of six hundred thousand, there are over two hundred and fifty well-attended churches.'[12]

The divisiveness of the Second Great Awakening is only part of the story. Visitors also recognized that beneath these divisions lay a larger unity. Scripturalism, a conversion-oriented piety, moral urgency and a missionary spirit were shared presuppositions of this great evangelical Protestant community, and by the 1820s Protestants of different denominations found themselves slowly coming together for common purposes. Symbolically, the collapse of the Connecticut Standing Order in 1818 ended the colonial idea that religion and morality required an established Church. All religious communities were now denominations, free competitors in the market place. In this competition evangelical Churches, despite their differences, increasingly found common purpose. As the Presbyterian Robert Baird noted, 'I hesitate not to affirm that . . . the Evangelical Churches . . . manifest a remarkable degree of mutual respect and fraternal affection. While earnest in maintaining . . . their own views of Truth and Church order, there is rarely any thing like denunciation and unchurching other orthodox communions, but every readiness, on the contrary, to offer help when needed.'[13]

This spirit of co-operation allowed members of the evangelical Churches to come together in voluntary societies for the purposes of advancing education, mission and social reform. Particularly in the great campaigns for Bible distribution and the war against alcohol, a functional ecumenicity reigned among American evangelical Protestants. Indeed by the 1830s it came to be argued that this paradox of co-operation and competition was the precise meaning of the Constitution's language of separation of Church and state. The Constitution did not wish to define America as anything other than a Christian republic, but wished to forestall the establishment of any particular Church. 'The real object of the amendment', explained Supreme Court Justice Joseph Story, 'was not to countenance . . . Mahometanism, or Judaism, or infidelity, by prostrating Christianity, but to exclude all rivalry among Christian sects, and to prevent any national ecclesiastical establishment.'[14]

The Second Great Awakening refashioned an American Protestantism far more active, more revival oriented, more voluntaristic and more dedicated to moral reform than earlier. At least one scholar has referred to this period as the 'Methodist Age' in American Christianity, during which human freedom, warm-hearted emotion and romantic perfectionism carried the day.[15] No figure embodied these themes, nor reflected both the possibilities and limitations of nineteenth-century American Protestantism, more than did the revivalist Charles G. Finney. Finney (1792–1875) brought a lawyer's eloquence, an impatience with theological niceties and a vision of the possibility of moral transformation to his ministry. Converted in 1821, he soon entered the ministry. Although technically a Presbyterian (and accordingly a Calvinist), theology hung loosely upon him. He was far more concerned with the need for conversion, and the power of the converted individual to triumph over sin, than with any of the traditional Calvinist teachings. Indeed he exalted the idea of human freedom, and believed that by means of the right techniques free individuals could be persuaded to accept the evangelical message. These new techniques became known as the 'new measures' and involved the use of special prayers, and an 'anxious bench' for would-be converts. Finney's confidence in technique was reflected in his famous saying that revivals were not 'prayed down' but 'worked up'. Finney, however, did not merely exalt human freedom in conversion, but also in the ability to triumph over sin. Accordingly, by the 1830s Finney began linking his revivalist ministry with two of the great moral reform campaigns in ante-bellum America, the crusades against alcohol and slavery. The truly converted individual, Finney claimed, would forswear both. Finney epitomized much of the spirit of the new American Protestant evangelicalism: loyalty to biblicism and a conversion-oriented piety, with an increasing emphasis upon innovation, free will and moral reform.

To be sure, not all American Christians accepted the message of this evangelical united front. In New England, some of the heirs of the New England Puritans, chastened by the emotional excesses of the First Great Awakening, moved in a fundamentally opposite direction. Their message involved divine goodness, human rationality and the transforming power of culture. By the early nineteenth century these Churches had begun organizing into a separate Unitarian movement, largely located in eastern New England and spiritually centred at Harvard College. From a different perspective, many Episcopalians (the heirs of the colonial Anglicans) used distinctive liturgical practices and emphasis upon the historic succession of ministry to offer a refuge from democratic evangelicalism. Likewise non-English-speaking Protestant immigrants, such as German-speaking Lutherans and Reformed, were critical of the American Protestant evangelical world-view. Finally, outside the boundaries of traditional Christianity even more radical alternatives were offered by Shakers, Mormons and Transcendentalists. But the evangelical culture functioned as the hegemonic religious vision of the young republic.

Canadian developments

Religious developments in Canada during these years moved in subtly different directions. In key ways the religious development of the early nineteenth century grew out of two fundamental aspects of Canadian society. The first was that Canada possessed not one but two distinctive cultures – French and British – and religion played a crucial role in both. The second was that Canada, rather than seeing itself as a unique 'city upon a hill', attempted to emphasize the interconnections between the Old World and the New.

The dual nature of Canadian culture was reflected in the establishment in 1791 of Upper Canada (Ontario) and Lower Canada (Québec). The vision of incorporating Lower Canada more fully into the British Protestant empire was never completely abandoned. The Anglican bishopric of Québec, for example, was designed on the English model, and there was continuing talk of the Anglicization (both culturally and religiously) of Québec. But the necessities of maintaining the loyalty of the French-speaking community compelled the British to grant more and more authority to the Roman Catholic Church. Particularly after the American invasion of Canada during the War of 1812, in which the French-speaking community proved overwhelmingly loyal, the British government relaxed efforts to control the Catholic Church. The Catholic Bishop of Québec, Joseph-Octave Plessis (1763–1825), was made a member of the legislative council of the province. During these years French Canadian Catholicism continued to be marked by a conservative, Ultramontane spirit, only made more dominant by the influence of French émigré priests fleeing from their country's revolution.

In English-speaking Canada, imperial plans to shape the ecclesiastical life of Canada along English lines were ultimately no more successful. The Constitutional Act of 1791, while not establishing the Church of England, did endow it. Some individuals, like the Bishop of Nova Scotia, were paid directly by parliament. Additionally, 675,000 acres of property were set aside as a 'Clergy Reserve' to support 'Protestant' (i.e., Anglican) clergy. Anglicans such as John Strachan (1778–1867), Bishop of Toronto, argued that the special status of the Church of England, which the Clergy Reserve allowed, was essential for the well-being of British Canada. But increasingly the Clergy Reserve became a source of controversy, particularly as Anglicans became only a minority of the Canadian Protestant population. In the maritime provinces the spirit of Henry Alline continued to flourish and Baptists multiplied. Likewise, as in America, Methodists made great strides during the early decades of the century. Finally, large numbers of Presbyterians, many from Scotland, emigrated to Canada. These latter individuals argued in particular that, as representing one of the established Churches of the British Isles, they deserved part of the revenue of the Clergy Reserve. Strife over the reserves did not end until they were at last secularized in 1854.

But Canadian Protestant Church life would furthermore be marked by its interconnection with the Old World. During these years British Churches were active in sending missionaries, and Canadian Churches self-consciously chose to model themselves upon British, rather than American, patterns. The case of Canadian Methodists illustrates this. At first Canadian Methodism was an offshoot of the American movement, and emphasized the popular vernacular style of American Methodists. But as a result of the War of 1812 and British Methodist missions, Canadian Methodists began to draw closer to their British counterparts, and stress formality and a more decorous worship. Identification with Britain was a unifying force throughout large parts of English-speaking Canada. Protestantism functioned as a culturally centripetal force, in marked contrast to the American model.

Catholics and controversy

The stability of the American Protestant voluntary establishment was to be substantially challenged by the growing presence of the Roman Catholic community. Indeed by the 1850s Catholics constituted the largest single Church body in America. Along the way the American Catholic community grappled with the perennial question of adaptation, while Protestants wrestled with the presence of a large Catholic community in the land of the pilgrims' pride.

A small Catholic community had been present in the American colonies since the 1630s. Although English recusants were never the majority component, their ethos shaped the colonial Catholic community. But by the early nineteenth century the American Catholic community began to be transformed by the great flow of immigration, particularly from Germany and Ireland. The result was an increase in both size and strife, the latter often upon ethnic lines. French émigré clergy found themselves at loggerheads with their Irish congregations. But these clashes were more than ethnic; they can be seen as the Catholic phase of the great early nineteenth-century debate over the democratization of Christianity. For émigré priests, the spirit of republicanism was antithetical to true Catholicism. In contrast, Irish and German immigrants often responded more favourably to the republican egalitarianism of nineteenth-century culture. The point of clash often became the question of Trusteeism. From as early as the eighteenth century, American Catholics often organized their congregations in a manner similar to their Protestant neighbours. A committee of lay trustees were chosen who were responsible for Church property and other temporalities. Indeed some trustees also claimed the right to employ clergy. The use of trustees, it was argued, helped the Church adapt to the practices of the larger culture. Traditionalists, in turn, argued that Trusteeism was antithetical to true Catholicism, and was a surrender of the historic vision of the Church to the corrosive tendencies of popular democracy. The clash over Trusteeism was a dominant question in ante-bellum Catholicism and symbolized the question of the relationship of Catholicism to American culture. By mid-century the hierarchy had largely consolidated its position and had gained control over ecclesiastical properties. Thus Catholicism stood as something of an outsider to the broader religious culture.

But it was an attractive outsider, and during the early decades of the nineteenth century it attracted a bevy of converts drawn to it as an alternative to evangelical America. Elizabeth Seton, later the first American-born canonized saint, found in Catholicism a spiritual depth which she had not found in Protestantism. Orestes Brownson, the Transcendentalist, found in the Catholic view of society an alternative to the materialistic and atomistic tendencies in American culture. Levi Silliman Ives, an Episcopalian bishop, found in Rome's claims to religious truth a rock of certainty in the surfeit of competing claims found within democratic Protestantism. Such converts were a continuing presence in American Catholicism, and it has been estimated that up to 700,000 persons voluntarily entered the Catholic Church between 1813 and 1893.[16]

By the 1840s the steady stream of Catholic immigration had become a torrent. Propelled by the catastrophic failure of the potato crops in both Ireland and Germany, immigration reached unheard-of numbers. Between 1846 and 1851 one million people left Ireland for America, and even after the end of the famine the flow continued. Germans arrived in almost as massive numbers, though many of these were not Catholics. This massive migration of European Catholics would have a tremendous effect upon American Catholicism. Although many of these individuals (particularly among the Germans) settled in agricultural communities in the Midwest, most took up residence in urban areas, and found employment in menial labour. Thus the American Catholic community began to take on social characteristics that would define it for a century: urban and working-class. The expansion of the nation into the south-west as a result of a series of conflicts with Mexico further added to the American Catholic community. These numerical increases were both a boon and a challenge for the American hierarchy. They enhanced the visibility and importance of the Catholic Church, but the necessity of providing institutions for this burgeoning community was a constant drain upon Church resources. Some have referred to this as the 'brick and mortar' period of American Catholicism, when institution building demanded precedence over all other concerns.

But the rapid rise of the Catholic community created alarm among many Protestants. They saw a Protestant America as having a special place in the divine plan for the world and Rome as the very antithesis of republican principles and virtues. Furthermore, lurid 'accounts' of escaped nuns such as Rebecca Reed and Maria Monk convinced many a voyeuristic Protestant that life within the convent walls put far less emphasis upon chastity than it did on obedience. Indeed, some Protestants, such as the artist and inventor Samuel F. B. Morse, saw in the massive Catholic immigration evidences of a conspiracy for a papal takeover of the American republic. Throughout the 1830s nativist reaction to the growing Catholic presence increased, and occasionally loosed itself in acts of violence, such as the burning of an Ursuline convent near Boston in 1834.

Protestant–Catholic tensions entered a new phase during the 1840s with a protracted debate over education. Part of the 'establishment' of Protestant Christianity in ante-bellum society was in its shaping of public institutions, and nowhere was this more evident than in education. From the daily readings from the King James Bible to the schema of history taught – in which the Middle Ages were inevitably dark, and the Reformation a burst of light – Protestantism and progress were viewed as largely interchangeable concepts. Catholics objected to the religious bias of the public schools, and demanded public support for their own schools. This in turn provoked a tremendous nativist reaction which defended the propriety of the public schools against Catholic attacks. The conflict of words moved into actions in Philadelphia in 1844, where rioting occurred.

The nativist reaction to Catholic immigration peaked in the early 1850s with the rise of the Order of the Star Spangled Banner. Founded in

1849, and perhaps better known as the 'Know Nothing' party, the order was a secret society whose members dedicated themselves to opposing the election of Roman Catholics, and wherever possible their removal from public office. In the short run the movement was remarkably successful. By 1854 it had elected 75 representatives to the national Congress. Their success may have had more to do with political factors than religious, and their equally dramatic decline by the end of the decade may suggest that the movement benefited from a temporary vacuum in the political life of the republic. But the very fury of the movement is indicative of both how problematic the presence of a large Catholic community was to many Protestants, and how fragile the unofficial establishment of evangelical Protestantism was in ante-bellum America. A major Catholic presence in the American religious scene would be a *fait accompli* by the late 1850s. But perhaps as much by choice as by necessity, Catholics were outsiders to the larger religious life of the American republic.

The problem of slavery and division

Perhaps no question perplexed American Christians as much as the question of slavery. Slavery struck at the core confidence of America as a Christian society, and the great national debate it brought forth had major religious implications. Of course the debate over slavery took place in other realms, but because of the long and deep involvement of American Christians in the institution, the question in America was particularly wrenching.

One mark of Protestant evangelicalism was a spirit of moral reform. Reform was viewed as necessary both for the health of the republic and for the furtherance of the coming of the kingdom of God. One area that cried out for change was slavery. This had existed in English-speaking America since 1619, but already in the eighteenth century many were finding themselves uneasy with the institution. Quakers led the way in attacking it, and some theologians such as Samuel Hopkins (1721–1803) also criticized the practice. By the end of the eighteenth century there was an increasing consensus, in both the North and the South, that slavery was in some ways a blot upon the republic. But slavery in America was never merely a system of labour; it was also seen as a system of race control. Few if any white Americans (even among the opponents of the institution) were willing to admit the full equality of African-Americans. Slavery in addition played a crucial role in questions of social status. The presence of African chattel slavery not only increased the status of slave owners but ironically also allowed for a sense of republican egalitarianism among all white freemen.

Thus the American discussion of the question of slavery was always ambiguous and convoluted, and American Churches shared in this ambiguity. Methodists, for example, lived in a perpetual tension between their founder's adamant condemnation of slavery and the large-scale involvement in the institution on the part of laity. Thus at times they affirmed the abolitionism of their founder while at other times they provided solace to Methodist slave holders. Most other Churches were no more forthright in their positions. There were exceptions of course, and Quakers such as Sarah (1792–1873) and Angelina (1805–79) Grimké were adamant in their denunciation of the practice.

From such ambivalence sprang the evangelical enthusiasm for colonization. The American Colonization Society was founded in 1817 to raise money for the manumission of slaves and for the resettling of them in Africa. Such a scheme, it was argued, respected the property rights of slave holders, was least disruptive of the society and could aid in evangelizing the African continent. The plan, however, was doomed from the start. It succeeded in freeing and transporting less than 2,000 slaves, and was viewed by its critics as a means more of removing the freed African-American population than addressing the question of slavery itself.

By the 1830s the debate over slavery took on a new and more divisive character, which would have wide implications for the Churches. The slavery question had now become entangled in the growing antagonism between the northern and southern states of the union. Southerners saw the institution of slavery as their 'peculiar institution' and as a foundation for their distinctive way of life. Southern religious figures added to this defence, and claimed not only that was slavery a positive good, but that it was a Christian institution. The master/slave relationship, based on mutual trust and dependence, was morally superior to the northern exploitative employer/employee relationship. The South, they concluded, was a distinctively Christian society, and the attacks upon its way of life stemmed from the growing materialism and de-Christianization of the northern states.

In contrast, many northern Christians were growing impatient with the idea of gradual emancipation. Unlike the British Empire, which had successfully abolished slavery in 1833, the American anti-slavery campaign seemed bogged down. In the early 1830s anti-slavery advocates began to demand immediate, rather than gradual, emancipation. This campaign rested on a key religious principle. Slavery by its very nature was a sin, a *malum in se*, and not merely an occasion for sin. Accordingly, Christians ought to reject it fully and completely as they did all other sins. The idea of slavery as a *malum in se* was quickly taken up by the revivalist Charles G. Finney, who argued that an opposition to slavery was one of the fruits of a true conversion.

This argument largely transformed the American debate, giving it a specific religious dimension. But it thrust upon northern Protestants a difficult question – how was slavery a sin? Did the Bible ever condemn slavery as sinful in its very nature, and if not, were there actions which were in fact sinful which the Bible did not recognize as sin? A close reading of Scripture demonstrated that the biblical authors seemed to accept slavery as an institution and nowhere explicitly condemned it, and this theological question became a troubling aspect of the American crisis. Particularly when opponents of slavery sought to disfellowship slave holders, some Americans questioned the appropriateness of dividing Churches over issues concerning which the Bible had no clear teaching. As the Presbyterian theologian Charles Hodge (1797–1878) insisted, 'nothing is obligatory upon the conscience but what [the Bible] enjoins; nothing can be sin but what it condemns'.[17]

For one group, African-Americans, the debate over slavery served a unifying function. Before the Civil War, there existed two distinct types of African-American religious communities. In the South, slave holders fearing rebellion attempted to keep strict controls over the religious life of their slaves. In response, many slaves resorted to clandestine worship, which has been referred to as the 'invisible institution'. In the North, independent Baptist and Methodist Churches served the needs of the freed black community. Both in the North and in the South, African-Americans did what they could to resist slavery. Free black Churches in the North were often centres of abolitionist activity, while in the South the 'invisible institutions' provided solace and hope for the enslaved community.

The debates were particularly intense because they often involved interconnected questions of moral reform and Church order. Presbyterians, for example, were divided between traditionalist 'Old School' followers who thought modern reform endeavours like abolition were unscriptural and hence not concerns of the Church, and 'New School' members who defended the moral campaign against slavery. Such debates ultimately split the great evangelical Churches. Presbyterians divided in 1837. Among Methodists, the question of slavery became entangled with the question of the authority of bishops vis-à-vis General Conference, and in 1844 they divided along regional grounds. In the same year the Baptists split over slave-holding missionaries. These divisions continued among Methodists until 1939, among Presbyterians until 1983, and among Baptists probably until judgement day.

In all of the crisis over slavery, Christianity was intricately involved. Works like Harriet Beecher Stowe's *Uncle Tom's Cabin*, the most influential anti-slavery publication of its age, were filled with religious images and discussions, just as southern defences of slavery were peppered with biblical citations. What this generation might have lacked in self-reflection, they more than made up for in heartfelt devotion. As Abraham Lincoln observed, both North and South 'read the same Bible and pray to the same God, and each invokes His aid against the other'. This heightened religious perspective only increased with the outbreak of the American Civil War. Southerners saw their cause as that of God's. The constitution of their new confederacy was explicitly Christian (unlike the national constitution). As one southern writer said of it, 'When . . . I read in the first lines of our organic and fundamental law a clear, solemn, and official recognition of Almighty God, my heart swelled . . . [with] gratitude and joy'. In contrast, many northern clergy saw the war as the 'Armageddon of the Republic', or as part of a final epic struggle between gospel freedom and despotism before the ushering in of the millennium. In the famous words of Julia Ward Howe, the war was to be seen in apocalyptic terms:

Mine eyes have seen the glory of the coming of the Lord,
He is trampling out the vintage where the grapes of wrath are stored.
He has loosed the fateful lightning of His terrible swift sword,
His truth is marching on.

The war was in key ways the culmination of the millennial themes of ante-bellum evangelicalism. America, as God's new Israel, was at the banks of the Red Sea and was called to cross it in order to enter into the promised land. These heightened expectations helped catalyse northern religious opinions, and helped transform a war to save the union into a war to eradicate slavery.[18]

The Civil War left its mark on the various Christian communities in America. For Catholics, their participation in the struggle played an important part in their growing social acceptance. For African-Americans, the war allowed for the rapid organization of religious life in the South and a tremendous expansion of the black denominations. After the war the 'invisible' slave Churches quickly took on the bodies of independent Methodist and Baptist Churches. As patterns of racial segregation descended upon southern culture, these black Churches became the centres of their communities. Among white southerners, the defeat and despair led to an increased emphasis upon the distinctiveness of the southern way of life, including its emphasis upon religion. As southerners attempted to shore up a distinctive southern culture in the wake of the war, evangelical Protestantism played a crucial role in regional self-identity. Finally, for the victorious northern Protestants, success dealt an ironic blow. Rather than finding themselves in a promised land as they had hoped, these individuals found themselves in a culture and intellectual world different from ante-bellum society. The task of responding to this new culture thrust upon northern Protestants difficult and divisive decisions.

Crisis days/halcyon days

Late Victorian and early twentieth-century America was paradoxical. Like the world of Charles Dickens's *A Tale of Two Cities*, it was the best of times and the worst of times. The average Protestant denomination more than tripled in membership during the last four decades of the century. Indeed the lusty growth of the Churches is reflected by one Methodist's response to the sceptic Robert Ingersoll's claim that Christianity was dying. ' "All hail the power of Jesus' name." We are building more than one Methodist Church for every day of the year and propose to make it two a day.' Confident Christians could sing 'All hail the power of Jesus' name, we're building *two* a day'.[19]

Despite the statistics, all was not right with the faith itself and its relation to the society. Both intellectual issues of the meaning of the faith, and existential questions of its reality, loomed. Thus Americans in their own way participated in the Victorian crisis of faith. Like others, American Christians were forced to address the interlocking intellectual issues of Darwin and history. These two fundamental questions, concerning the relationship of God to the world and the role of God in history (and in particular in the record of Scripture), became acute concerns during these decades. At first, critics of Darwin could appeal to scientific authorities, but by the 1880s the scientific debate had largely ebbed. If Darwin had not triumphed completely, the notion of evolution and the transformation of species had. This new scientific position called into question the traditionally understood biblical view of creation. In response, a number of clerical popularizers such as Henry Ward Beecher (1813–87) and Lyman Abbott (1835–1922) set forth schemes of 'Christian evolution' reconciling biological evolution with divine plan and purpose. A similar endeavour was undertaken by the Catholic priest and scientist John A. Zahm (1851–1921). Although Christian evolution probably never took root among average churchgoers, late nineteenth-century American Protestants seemed to take the question of evolution remarkably in their stride.

The question of biblical history proved more troublesome. Many American Protestants had inherited the strict Reformed theological views of the Westminster Confession, which affirmed that the Bible was 'authentical' because it was 'immediately inspired by God', and was 'kept pure in all ages'. As a result, they held an extremely high view of biblical inspiration. A very different picture of the Scriptures emerged as students took up the new approach to biblical criticism known as higher criticism. Approaching the study of the Scriptures as one might approach the study of other ancient texts, higher critics argued that the Bible contained archaic world-views, human elements and evolving understandings of the nature of God and morality. Higher biblical criticism created a controversy when it surfaced in the 1880s. In response, scholars like Archibald A. Hodge (1823–86) and his Princeton colleague Benjamin Warfield (1851–1921) began formulating a formal theory and defence of biblical inerrancy. They argued that the Bible was fully and completely inspired by God down to its very words, and was accordingly free from error (at least in its original manuscripts). This Hodge/Warfield doctrine of inspiration would become a rallying position for conservative Protestants for over a century, and would be a key point of division between liberal-leaning and conservative-leaning Protestants.

Another vexing question concerned what anchored religious faith. Since the days of the Puritans, personal religious confidence was anchored in the transforming experience of the conversion. From the eighteenth-century Awakening, corporate religious life was further anchored in conversion writ large – or revivalism. Revivalism continued to play an important role in late nineteenth-century Protestantism. One of the best-known figures in America was Dwight L. Moody (1837–99), revivalist extraordinaire. Looking like a moderately successful businessman, Moody preached his revival message on both sides of the Atlantic. His message was summarized by the '"Three Rs" – Ruin by sin, Redemption by Christ, and Regeneration by the Holy Ghost'. Moody's preaching, albeit simple, was attractive, and his revivals were tremendously popular. Moody served as a unifying figure in American evangelical Protestantism, holding it together programatically and symbolically.

But for some – particularly urban, educated, middle-class individuals – the conversion-oriented anchor began to slip. In this context, the Congregationalist Horace Bushnell (1802–76) published *Christian Nurture* (1861), which set forth a new theory of how the Christian life was to be anchored. Bushnell's argument was simple yet revolutionary: a child was to be brought into the Christian community by nurture rather than conversion. 'The child is to grow up a Christian, and never know himself as being otherwise.'[20] Bushnell's ideas, although revolutionary, found favour among many, in part because he appealed to two of the most important elements of late-Victorian life. *Christian Nurture* took the idea of evolution and transferred it into the religious life. Evolution and not revolution was the model of the Christian life, and God was seen as acting through culture rather than intervening immediately. Likewise Bushnell harnessed Christian development to perhaps the most powerful institution in Victorian culture, the family. The family, and in particular the Christian mother, was the chief evangelizing agent.

Others found themselves moving in very different directions in anchoring Christian faith in the modern world, by emphasizing the continuing availability of direct supernatural intervention. Throughout the 1870s and 1880s some American Protestants began to emphasize the possibility of divine healing as promised in the Bible. By the late 1890s this interest in the supernatural embraced the gifts of the Holy Spirit described by St Paul in 1 Corinthians 12. This is the background for the emergence of modern Pentecostalism, traditionally seen as beginning on 1 January 1901, in the small Bethel Bible School (or College) in Topeka, Kansas. There Charles F. Parham (1873–1929) and his students prayed for a 'baptism of the Holy Ghost', and began to speak in strange tongues. Among the Pentecostalists, the baptism of the Holy Spirit became a central part of the Christian experience. It allowed for a 'Full Gospel', and endowed individuals and communities with the power of the apostolic generation. The movement quickly spread and was popularized through the famous 'Azusa Street revival' in Los Angeles (1906–09). The Pentecostal movement would flourish throughout the twentieth century, both within North America and outside it, and would become a major force in modern Christianity.

Roman Catholics during these years likewise struggled with the question of responding to the new challenges, and their debates broadly paralleled those of their Protestant contemporaries. By the end of the nineteenth century the Catholic clerical community divided over the question of how much their Church could adapt itself to the spirit of the age. Americanists, like John Ireland (1838–1918), Archbishop of St Paul (Minnesota), argued that America was a fruitful environment for the flowering of Catholicism. He advocated, accordingly, a policy of cautious adaptation on issues such as education and social reform. He experimented with ways of combining Catholic educational concerns and public education. Conservatives, such as Michael Corrigan (1839–1902), Archbishop of New York, saw the Catholic Church as an alternative to the larger cultural trends of the society. How far this division would have developed is open to debate, but the papal condemnation of 'Americanism' in the bull *Testem Benevolentiae* (1899) effectively ended the debate. The subsequent papal condemnation of 'modernism' in 1907 further assured that, until the 1960s, American Catholics and Protestants would inhabit quite different intellectual worlds.

The Social Gospel

The challenges of the end of the nineteenth century were not all on the individual or intellectual levels. By this period there was an increased awareness that urbanization and industrialization were changing the face of America in troubling ways. Religious leaders lamented the violent clashes which characterized labour disputes as well as a perceived loss of civic virtue. In the new social order, it came to be argued, Christianity must take the lead. This was the background to the Social Gospel movement.

On one level it was neither unique to the end of the nineteenth century, nor unique to America. Since the days of the apostles, Christians had recognized that there was a social dimension to their gospel. But the Social Gospel movement was dependent upon presuppositions drawn from both late nineteenth-century theological liberalism and a number of uniquely American emphases. From theological liberalism, proponents of the Social Gospel drew their confidence in the possibility of rational reform, their emphasis on the 'latent perfectibility' of human nature and their belief that the core of the gospel was the ethical message of Jesus. From the American Protestant tradition they drew upon the popular spirit of post-millennialism, and the belief that through human labour the kingdom of God might be achieved. Hence unlike many European Christian social critics who attacked modern industrial society from the perspective of an idealized Christian past, American proponents of the Social Gospel looked to the imminent coming of the kingdom.

The movement offered both practical criticism of American society and a vision of the true Christian life. Its proponents attacked the overly competitive nature of American economics, advocated co-operation between capital and labour and called for increased governmental involvement in maintaining a just and proper way of life. The theological elements of the movement can be seen in its most famous representative, Walter Rauschenbusch (1861–1918). Rauschenbusch was the premier theologian of the kingdom of God. The fruits of the kingdom would be a social redemption that would complement spiritual redemption. As he explained, the coming of the kingdom 'will be the regeneration of the super-personal life of the race, and will work out a social expression of what was contained in the personality of Christ'. Social redemption would be marked by the triumph of co-operation over competition, fraternity over coercion and public good over private gain.[21] The Social Gospel movement was controversial. Its challenge to the social and political order upset economic conservatives, just as its reconceptualization of the Gospel troubled religious conservatives. As much as the issue of the higher biblical criticism, it served to exacerbate liberal/conservative tensions.

If there were forces pulling American Protestants apart, there were other forces knitting them more closely together. The end of the nineteenth century witnessed a number of these pan-Protestant undertakings, perhaps none more important than the foreign missionary movement. North American enthusiasm for missions was so great that by the early twentieth century over a third of the Protestant missionaries, and over 40 per cent of the missions' financial support, came from there. The Student Volunteer Movement for Foreign Missions, founded in 1886, became a popular symbol of both missionary enthusiasm and pan-Protestant unity. Through groups such as this and the Foreign Missions Conference of North America. founded in 1893, and through the influence of individuals like John R. Mott (1865–1955), head of the Student Volunteer Movement, a vision of a unified and expanding Christianity was set forth. The concern for unity resulted in the founding of the Federal Council of Churches in 1908, which provided a unified Protestant voice on many of the social issues of the day.

Canada: organization and union

During these years Canada also underwent great changes. In 1867 the dominion of Canada was established and national life was formalized. These social changes shaped religious developments. Canadian Church leaders saw confederation as an opportunity for further Christianizing the nation, and spoke of the new state as 'His dominion'. At the same time Canadians also grappled with many of the same social and intellectual changes as their southern neighbours, though usually with more moderation and restraint.

By the time of confederation, the denominational pattern was firmly established among Canadian Churches. The selling of the Clergy Reserves in 1854 symbolized the end of the earlier attempt to maintain a special status for Canadian Anglicans. All Churches hereafter would be on a largely equal footing. This factor, coupled with a lessening of British support in the years after confederation, resulted in a large-scale concern for national organization. The major Protestant groups – the Methodists, Presbyterians, Anglicans and Baptists – all scurried to tie together their far-flung communities. Even Roman Catholics, though still centred in Québec, had large (and often English-speaking) communities elsewhere. By the century's end this endeavour at organization was largely accomplished.

Like Americans, Canadians confronted the issues of science, biblical criticism, and social Christianity. What is distinctive about the Canadian story, however, is that these debates did not provoke the discord that they did in America. Canadian Protestants on the whole were able to maintain a mediating evangelicalism that was respectful both of tradition and of the new concerns. One sees this in career of the Methodist Nathaniel Burwash (1839–1916), Professor of Natural Theology at the Methodist Victoria College. Burwash combined a traditional Methodist interest in the experience of regeneration and personal morality with a tentative openness to the new Darwinian science and higher criticism. Likewise, Canadians were greatly attracted to the growing concern for the social message of Christianity, and were particularly concerned with attempting to continue to make a Christian presence felt in the industrial cities. Protestants were particularly successful in maintaining the public reverencing of the first day of the week, and the 1906 Lord's Day Act was a fruit of this concern to combine both traditional ideas about Sabbath observance with the new concerns for the rights of workers.

In one area, Canadian Protestants were more successful than their American counterparts, and that was concerning Church union. The possibility of a united Protestant Church was frequently mooted in the late nineteenth-century Anglo-American world and these discussions bore fruit in Canada. Inspired by works such as *The Church Idea* by the American Episcopalian William R. Huntington, many Canadians broached the possibility of Church union. While Anglicans and Baptists ultimately demurred, the idea took root elsewhere. In 1902, William Patrick (1852–1911), a Presbyterian fraternal delegate to the Methodist General Conference, proposed union between their two denominations. Methodists responded, as later did the Congregationalists. During the early twentieth century representatives of these three denominations hammered out a basis for union. The eventual compromise attempted on the level of theology to balance a mild Presbyterian Calvinism with a mild Methodist Arminianism, and on the level of ecclesiology it attempted to balance the different traditions of ministry.

In 1910, the Congregationalists accepted the Basis of Union, and in the next year the Methodists did so as well. Presbyterians, however, had more difficulties, and a significant minority balked at the plan. Many of these were of Scottish origin, for whom Presbyterianism was not simply a set of religious beliefs, but also a crucial part of their ethnic self-identity. Presbyterians postponed their decision, and the outbreak of the First World War put the question of Church union off even more. The Presbyterian discussion was not renewed until 1920, with a final decision being made in 1925. Approximately two-thirds of Canadian Presbyterians decided to enter into the United Church of Canada, while a third refused.

Robert Bruce Mullin

Challenges for the soul of America

The era of the First World War was a watershed in North American culture. It was also a key turning point in the story of Christianity. America entered the war an inward-looking, idealistic nation, confident in its values which were rooted in Victorian culture and the inherited Protestant faith. Indeed, despite an increasing social pluralism, the pre-eminence of the Protestant heritage was still largely unchallenged. Politicians freely used biblical imagery in their speeches, and rallies often ended with the singing of 'Onward, Christian Soldiers'. America carried these confidences into the war. After years of indecision, when the nation finally entered the conflict it did so on quasi-religious terms. As President Woodrow Wilson (himself the child of a Presbyterian manse) explained, it would be the war to end all wars.

The aftermath of the war, with the victorious nations greedily dividing the spoils, proved disillusioning. Even more disheartening were two other factors. The war radically displayed the gap between the traditional American Protestant perception of their society, and the reality. The war years showed America to be far more pluralistic and secular than Protestants had heretofore imagined. Secondly, the war catalysed the existing divisions between conservative and liberal Protestants, and began a period of acrid controversy.

American Protestants had always recognized that there were others in 'their' country, but for many, particularly small-town, Americans there was a soothing solidarity everywhere the eye could see. One might recognize that there were large urban areas with mixed populations, but these did not seem like real America. However, the war experience showed an America far more complex. Indeed the census of 1920 for the first time recorded more persons living in urban areas than rural. Furthermore, the new modes of communication, such as radio and moving pictures, made rural America aware not only that urban America existed, but that its cultural and moral presuppositions, particularly concerning sexuality, were at odds with the countryside. Since the cities were seen as the locations of both immigrants and an emerging crisis of morality, they were often lumped together.

One reaction to this threat was the passage of Prohibition in 1919, abolishing the manufacture and sale of alcoholic beverages. As we have seen, the campaign against alcohol was a long-standing element of Protestant reform. By the late nineteenth century it was also taken up by many political reformers who saw in the institution of the saloon a source of political corruption. Alcohol poisoned both the body human and the body politic, and its eradication would allow the forces of morality to reassert themselves over the larger society. Canadian Protestants also helped pass prohibition laws in the various Canadian provinces during the war, but afterwards they were repealed. The prohibition campaigns often pitted native Protestants against the new immigrants.

Still another reaction to the crisis of the city was a turning off of the spigot of immigration. A series of immigration laws, culminating in the National Origins Act of 1924, set up annual quotas based upon the profile of the American population in 1890. These quotas not only insured a drastically reduced number of immigrants, but that the bulk would be from the more Protestant northern Europe, rather than from central or southern Europe. These formal actions were coupled with other, more nasty, turns of nativism, ranging from quotas at elite colleges and universities to keep out the new immigrants, to the emergence of the Ku Klux Klan designed to protect '100% Americanism'. All of these actions can be seen as attempts by English-speaking Protestants to maintain the traditional patterns of the society.

The issues of urbanization, immigration and alcohol came to a head in the presidential campaign of 1928. In that year the Democratic Party chose New York governor Al Smith for its nominee. Smith was an Irish Catholic from New York City and a notorious critic of Prohibition. He was in some sense the native Protestants' nightmare. Although he was defeated in the general election, his candidacy was a sign of how the nation was changing and how the days of the Protestant hegemony were numbered.

Meanwhile the post-war era saw an intensifying of the conservative/liberal divide within Protestantism. As we have seen, a long-standing question of American Christianity had been that of adaptation – or to what degree older understandings and practices could be modified to respond to new cultural settings. If during the first half of the nineteenth century the cultural setting facing Protestants had been democratic populism, by the end of the century it had become the new intellectual milieu characterized by the questions of science and history. Since the 1880s some American Protestants had been engaged in modifying aspects of the inherited faith, particularly in their views on divine intervention in the world. Yet these liberalizers were always a minority, and the further one moved from institutions of learning and power the more scarce they appeared. The perceived crisis of the post-war world – manifested in everything from radical politics to short skirts – convinced many conservatives that American was failing because it had jettisoned its traditional biblical heritage. It had done so because the leaders of the great Protestant Churches, stewards of this heritage, had let it slip away. This reaction became known as Fundamentalism, the belief that true Christianity was marked by a number of basic or fundamental beliefs. The inerrancy of

Scripture, the miraculous birth and resurrection of Jesus and his sacrificial death were all considered essential to true Christianity. Those who could not affirm them should be excluded from the Churches.

The Fundamentalist/Liberal debate involved two very different visions of the nature of the true Church. Fundamentalists offered a combative vision reflecting a strict doctrinal orthodoxy, while Liberals suggested an inclusivist vision. Fundamentalists such as the Presbyterian J. Gresham Machen (1881–1937) argued that no compromise could be made between biblical Christianity and Liberalism. In contrast, Liberals such as Harry Emerson Fosdick (1878–1979) called for toleration and discussion. The controversy affected large sections of American and Canadian Protestantism, but the two communities in which the battle raged most intensely were Northern Presbyterians and Baptists.

In the South, however, the Fundamentalist controversy took a different form. By the 1920s the American South was beginning to emerge from its largely self-imposed isolation stemming from its defeat in the Civil War. The era of the First World War had brought the South far more in touch with larger national concerns. Southern Fundamentalists shared with their northern co-religionists the sense of crisis, but for them the focus of the crisis was not Liberalism but the theory of evolution. Evolution was seen as undergirding a naturalistic world-view, and undermining the idea of a Christian democracy. If the book of Genesis offered the foundational principle of democracy, that all citizens were endowed with the image of God, evolution justified theories of elitism such as Friedrich Nietzsche's superman. Significantly, the great champion against the teaching of evolution was both a Presbyterian layman and a populist politician, the perennial presidential candidate, William Jennings Bryan.

Throughout the early 1920s a number of southern state legislatures began to pass legislation banning the teaching of evolution in public schools. It was the Tennessee law that was challenged in the infamous Scopes Trial of 1925. There in rural Tennessee, before the press in full force, the trial took place. It seemed to manifest the intellectual limitations of Fundamentalism, and associated the movement for many with rural and anti-intellectual themes. As a result, the Fundamentalist campaign collapsed. Rather than forcing out the Liberals, Fundamentalists themselves began abandoning the historic Protestant denominations. This denouement, however, was tinged with irony. Fundamentalism did not disappear but retreated to separatist communities. There it licked its wounds and prepared for its next clash with liberal Protestantism.

Let the Church be the Church

In 1929, with the great stock market crash, North America (like the rest of the world) entered into the Great Depression, which affected North American Christians both socially and psychologically. On the social level, the economic collapse threatened Church institutions from local to national. If the loss of revenues was a tangible blow, North American Protestants were perhaps even more profoundly affected by the psychological blow. Many Canadian and American Protestants had viewed their societies as distinctive contributions to the idea of Christian civilization. The cultural values of progress, uplift, co-operation and rationality were assumed to be part of a proper Christian world-view. The social and economic collapse caused many to re-examine these presuppositions. As one chastened cleric admitted, 'Our conception of God is that he is sort of a magnificent Rotarian. Sometimes, indeed, one wonders whether the social movement and the uplift in general have not become among Protestants a substitute for devotion; worse than that a substitute for real religion.'[22] The social and economic crisis made words like 'uplift' and 'progress' ring hollow.

The economic crisis provoked radical social nostrums from left and right. From the left, individuals such as the Methodist Harry F. Ward urged the Churches to reject capitalism outright, and to move in the direction of Communism. Others, such as the Fellowship of Socialist Christians, advocated a fundamental reformation of American society. From the right, figures like the Disciples of Christ minister Gerald L. K. Smith espoused nativism and vigorous anti-Communism. Still others, such as the Catholic priest and radio broadcaster Charles Coughlin, combined attacks upon bankers, politicians and international conspirators. In a class by himself was the Canadian William Aberhart (1878–1943), radio preacher and premier of Alberta, who combined fundamentalism and monetarist reform.

The decade of the 1930s saw increased visibility for American Catholics. The election of Franklin D. Roosevelt to the presidency in 1932 brought to national prominence not only Catholic politicians, but also Catholic ideas. Inspired by medieval ideas of the just wage, Catholics like John A. Ryan (1869–1945) had long advocated the idea of a 'living wage', or the setting of labour costs on the basis of justice rather than upon market conditions. This was institutionalized in minimum wage legislation. Other Catholics, emboldened by papal pronouncements like *Quadragesimo Anno*, advocated the rights of labour and the view of a corporate state that would transcend the alternatives of both capitalism and Communism. Still others, like Dorothy Day (1897–1980) and the Catholic

Worker movement, emphasized solidarity with the poor and a radical social vision. Yet the prestige of Catholicism during these years was not limited to its social teachings. The 1930s saw perhaps the fullest flowering of neo-Thomism, the revival of the philosophy of Thomas Aquinas, with its emphasis upon the integration of reason and revelation. The assertion that Catholicism offered an alternative to both American capitalism and culture-bound Protestantism attracted many to the Church of Rome.

Themes of social and intellectual crisis were likewise taken up by advocates of Protestant Neo-Orthodoxy. Having its roots in post-First World War Europe, particularly in the insights of the Swiss theologian Karl Barth, Neo-Orthodoxy strove to reclaim basic Christian themes, while addressing the modern human predicament. Neo-Orthodox writers such as Reinhold Niebuhr (1892–1971) and H. Richard Niebuhr (1894–1962) criticized American Protestantism for both its social thinking and its theology. Both reflected nineteenth-century cultural idealism more than the world of the Bible. American Protestants had all too often viewed the world through rose-coloured glasses, believing that co-operation, human effort and reform could bring about the kingdom of God. In contrast, Neo-Orthodox writers emphasized the hard reality of sin and selfishness that polluted human endeavours and kept justice at bay. Likewise in their view of the human predicament, they returned to the biblical categories of sin and grace which earlier liberals had seemed to de-emphasize in favour of ideas of uplift and nurture. Nineteenth-century American Protestantism had attempted to model itself after the patterns of the world, but now the world was bankrupt. One of the Neo-Orthodox watchwords became 'let the Church be the Church'. Although open to ideas of modern science and history, writers like Reinhold Niebuhr saw the modern world as tragically confirming the biblical view of human nature as marked by sin rather than giving any view of the latent perfectibility of humanity.

Neo-Orthodoxy might have been only an academic movement if it had not been for the impact of the Second World War. As the secret history of the First World War, the 'war to end all wars', came to be learned, it appeared that it had been fought more to make the world safe for those American banks that had lent huge sums to the Allies than for any lofty purpose. Disillusion convinced many leading American Protestants to renounce warfare all together. Even in the face of the rise of Adolf Hitler and Nazism, many (if not a majority) of leading Protestants supported a policy of pacifism. One who did not was Reinhold Niebuhr. A realistic view of the world, he argued, showed that injustice had to be met with force. While the peace which Christ promised could only be brought about by prayer, that did not imply pacifism, a refusal to resist evil and injustice.

Niebuhr's view of social responsibility took on great importance as America entered the Second World War. With it, the Neo-Orthodox view of the world and human nature as broken and sinful, and emphasis upon individuals as responsible moral agents, gained in attractiveness. The strains felt during the post-1945 Cold War added to the popularity of Neo-Orthodoxy, and for two decades it reigned as the pre-eminent theology and social philosophy of American Protestants. The Neo-Orthodox revitalization of intellectual Protestantism can further be seen in the heightened status of institutions such as Union Theological Seminary (New York) and Yale Divinity School. In the post-war decades they emerged as important centres of international Protestantism.

The Post-War Revival

America's entrance into the war also inaugurated a revival of interest in religion. This revival gained speed in the post-war decades, and the Post-War Revival represented a high-water mark of public religiosity in American history. By 1960, 69 per cent of Americans were associated with a religious community. Furthermore, in 1957, 96 per cent of Americans surveyed identified themselves as either Christian or Jewish.

The Post-War Revival, however, was unlike other revivals in American history. Even during its heyday commentators noted that it was inspired by a number of non-traditional factors, one being a surge in anti-Communism. The tensions of the Cold War, in which Americans saw themselves as pitted against a 'godless Communism', convinced many that patriotism and religion were intricately interconnected. Religion was a necessary bulwark against Communism both at home and abroad. A second factor in the growth of religious identification were demographic changes in American society. The post-war era was a time of burgeoning suburbanization, and in these new suburbs Churches were key institutions for socialization. Furthermore, as the sociologist Will Herberg, noted, suburban Church identification was one of the few socially acceptable ways for new suburbanites to maintain a degree of ethnic self-identity, that had been so important in the cities which they had left.[23] Finally, the Post-War Revival benefited from a strong social interest in peace of mind. A therapeutic rather than reformist element became a defining aspect of public religiosity, and works like Norman Vincent Peale's *The Power of Positive Thinking* (1952) which emphasized the practical value of religion for successful living proved enormously popular.

Still another factor behind the Post-War Revival was the resurgence of conservative evangelicalism. After a decade of retrenchment, conservative Protestants re-entered the public scene in the 1940s. The National

451

Association of Evangelicals was founded in 1942 as a voice for conservative evangelicalism. By the end of that decade, writers such as Carl F. H. Henry and Edward J. Carnell began articulating a self-conscious 'Neo-Evangelicalism' that attempted to separate from the central evangelical emphases of conversion-oriented piety and biblicism some of the cultural quirks of earlier Fundamentalism. The movement of Neo-Evangelicalism would be most popularized by its leading figure, the evangelist Billy Graham, through whom the revivalist message of conservative Protestantism again began to compete for the loyalty of the American religious public.

At first glance American Christianity seemed stronger than ever. On the international scene it was taking the lead in institutions like the World Council of Churches (which met in Evanston, Illinois, in 1954), and on the local scene it seemed to be growing everywhere. Critics, however, observed that the swelling churches were in a peculiar position. Sunday school and Sunday morning attendance were surging, while other services such as Wednesday evening prayer services were withering. Likewise, as a professed loyalty to the Bible was advancing, the actual knowledge of its content was embarrassingly slight. The religious revival rested upon the shallowest of foundations. It was often more a revival of 'faith in faith', than of the historic faith itself. The traditional cultural loyalties that had bound people to religion were being torn asunder by demographic changes, and the slightest tremor might upset the edifice of the religious revival.

The 1960s and the second disestablishment

The events of the turbulent decade of the 1960s proved more than a tremor. Rather they were a profound eruption that transformed the religious landscape. Even from a distance of 30 years it is hard to have a full picture of the effects of this decade upon the lives of American and Canadian Christians, but its impact was to be felt in at least four different areas.

First, the decade witnessed the final collapse of the Protestant hegemony in America. It began with the election of John F. Kennedy to the presidency of the United States, as the first Catholic president. Kennedy's election may also be seen as a symbol of the coming of age of the American Catholic community. Demographic changes, such as suburbanization and upward economic mobility, were largely removing many of the social barriers that had long divided Protestant and Catholic Americans, and given to the latter their sense of minority status.

Second, there occurred a radicalization of the concept of the separation of Church and state. For nineteenth-century figures such as Joseph Story, the First Amendment primarily served to prevent an established Church. Courts had not held that the government be disengaged from, or neutral regarding, religion. Many twentieth-century legal commentators argued that such a neutrality and even total separation was the true meaning of the Amendment. In the 1960s, in a series of Supreme Court decisions, both formal prayer and devotional Bible reading were banned from the public schools. Subsequent cases have treated the permissibility of prayer at other public gatherings and the permissibility of displaying religious symbols on public property.

Third, the idea that America had a special religious mission came increasingly under attack. As has been shown, from very early on religion and nationalism were interconnected in the American experience, and Americans often understood themselves as a 'city upon a hill'. Such religious imagery, always more ideal than real, fell especially short in race relations. During the 1960s a great campaign for the full civil rights of African-Americans arose to make good such ideals. At first the message of individuals like Martin Luther King, Jr (1929–68) combined biblical themes and appeals to American traditions of justice, and the campaign attracted the active support of many clergy. But by the late 1960s, social critics in the movement were both more critical and pessimistic of American society and questions of race. At the same time, opponents of the war in Vietnam faulted America for its imperialism and presumption. These criticisms badly damaged the heretofore accepted notion of America as a shining city on a hill. It was seen as more sickly than shining. Accordingly, prophetic denunciation rather than patriotic celebration seemed to be the proper religious response.

Finally, these years also saw many Americans begin to call into question a number of cultural and ethical assumptions. On questions of sex and gender, society was faulted for its traditional view that certain sexual orientations and certain models of gender relationship were 'natural'. Others issues concerned the lack of respect for the environment. In all of these areas major challenges were presented to the traditional Christian communities.

How to respond to these challenges became a pressing concern, and since the 1960s the North American Christian communities have been increasingly divided. On the whole, the older English-speaking Protestant communities, such as the Methodists, Presbyterians, Northern Baptists and Episcopalians, began haltingly to come to grips with the revolution. In liturgical revisions, in moral teachings and in social statements the influence of the revolution of the 1960s began to be felt. Perhaps most dramatically the impact was seen in questions of gender. The ordination of women to the varying levels of ministry was largely accepted by the late 1970s. Other questions, such as the use of inclusive language and the questioning of the metaphor of the fatherhood of God have been more controversial.

The cultural revolution furthermore transformed the attitudes of many Christians to the Native American community. From the seventeenth century, North American Christians had usually assumed that evangelization and Westernization went hand in hand. The new perspective of the 1960s not only led to a rejection of this presupposition, but also a new positive appreciation of the religious heritage of Native Americans themselves. Particularly on questions of spirituality and respect for nature, the European American community realized it had much to learn from its Native American neighbours.[24]

The questions of the 1960s left their mark on the older Protestant denominations in one other way. Since the early 1960s there has been a significant loss in membership here and in the three decades after 1965 they have all lost between one-sixth and one-third of their members.

No religious community, however, was more affected by the turmoil of the 1960s than was Roman Catholicism. Before the 1960s, Catholics in both America and Canada had the reputation for conservatism, docility and loyalty to Rome. Yet as has been suggested, during the post-war years the Catholic community underwent a profound demographic revolution. Upward social and economic mobility and suburbanization created a very different Catholic laity, one in which the traditional moorings of a tightly-knit Catholic culture were being eroded. In this context, the *aggiornamento* (an 'opening of windows') of the Second Vatican Council was followed with enthusiasm by North American Catholics. The teachings of Vatican II delighted, puzzled and frustrated these individuals. They applauded the Declaration on Religious Liberty which affirmed the American experience of freedom of conscience, and owed much to an American Jesuit, Courtney Murray. Likewise most American and Canadian Catholics responded favourably to the Decree on Ecumenism which allowed a freer interchange between Catholics and their non-Catholic neighbours. Other changes seemed more puzzling. Changes in liturgy, devotional practices and such long-standing marks of social identification as the Friday fast, seemed to upset traditional assumptions and practices. Finally, many Catholics were frustrated at the halting nature of the changes. Nowhere was this more expressed than in the reaction to the papal pronouncement affirming the traditional rejection of birth control, *Humanae Vitae* (1968). Despite the pronouncement, polls indicated that the papal view was rejected or ignored by large numbers of American Catholics. Perhaps the 'crisis' of North American Catholicism was as much an effect of time warp as anything else, as Catholics began wrestling with a whole variety of questions that other Christians had been confronting for a century, but the effect was great. One symbol was the decline in priestly vocations. In the two decades after Vatican II the number of seminarians in the United States dropped by 75 per cent, and 241 seminaries were forced to close.[25]

If the 1960s had a dramatic effect on American Catholics, they were to have an even greater effect on French-speaking Canadian Catholics. For nearly three hundred years, Québec had viewed itself as a society held together by its Catholicism. The role of the Catholic Church in shaping education and morals was legendary, as was the loyalty of Québecois to the Church. In the late 1950s 93 per cent of Québecois attended weekly Mass. But the patterns of urbanization and dislocation weakened the traditions of the society. In 1960 Québec labour unions broke their ties with the Catholic Church, and by 1964 the Catholic dominion over education was also challenged. All of this has been referred to as the 'Quiet Revolution', in which the place of the Catholic Church in French-speaking Canada was largely transformed. Increasingly Francophone culture and not Catholicism became the badge of identification. One result of this quiet revolution has been that weekly Mass attendance plummeted from 93 per cent to 30 per cent in 30 years.

The decades after the 1960s have finally witnessed a remarkable growth in the movements of conservative evangelicalism where themes of biblical inerrancy and conversion-oriented piety continue to find a hearing. Both in numbers and influence these Churches began to challenge the traditional status of the older Protestant denominations. Particularly fast-growing have been the Pentecostal Churches such as the Assemblies of God. By the end of the 1980s evangelical Protestant Churches equalled in size the older mainline Churches. These Churches on the whole have rejected the revolution of the 1960s on questions such as sexuality, gender roles and civil religion. The post-1960s revival of conservative Protestantism has also involved a political dimension, and many of these individuals, through movements like the Moral Majority or Christian Coalition, have attempted to shape public policy.

Christianity in North America at the end of the twentieth century

As the century comes to an end, the story of Christianity in North America shows signs of both continuity and discontinuity. In America, 43 per cent of Christians still attend church weekly. Although this is below the unusually high levels of the Post-War Revival, it is approximately the average of most decades in the twentieth century. The story in Canada is a bit different. In 1940 Canadians were more likely than Americans to attend church, while by 1980 this pattern had reversed. But whether this shift marks a fundamental change in religious life is difficult to determine. In both nations people baptize children, support churches and perform religious duties in large numbers.

But there are signs of discontinuity as well. The new challenges have in many ways polarized North American Christians into conservative and liberal camps. Indeed, the conservative/liberal split has become more profound than earlier. Because the issues have become largely cultural, the division has transcended the customary dividing lines of Protestantism and Catholicism, and the conservative/liberal split has largely replaced the earlier Catholic/Protestant divide that for so long characterized North American Christianity. By century's end, on issues of theology, morality and social policy, liberals and conservatives within both Protestantism and Catholicism often find more in common with their ideological soulmates than with their co-religionists. As these divisions have spilled forth into the political arena, and as issues of abortion, gender roles and homosexuality have become a regular part of American political debates, Christians both from the left and right have become more politically active.

Finally, the notion of an unofficial establishment of religion, that had played such an important role in the story of Christianity in North America, has been largely abandoned. As one Canadian historian has observed, by the 1960s Canadian Christians were forced to recognize 'a situation in which churches were no longer moral policemen, but pressure groups or even interest groups'.[26] This recognition of a new role for Christianity in society, no longer as official leaders, but as witnesses, has been perhaps the greatest transformation within North American Christianity in the last decades of the twentieth century.

Notes

1 James Bryce, *The American Commonwealth* (new edn; 2 vols; New York: Macmillan Co., 1911), vol. 2, p. 773.

2 Paul Leicester Ford (ed.), *Writings of Christopher Columbus* (New York: C. L. Webster and Co., 1892), p. 50.

3 'Instruccions Orders and Constitucions . . . to Sr Thomas Gates' in Samuel Bemiss (ed.), *The Three Charters of the Virginia Company of London* (Williamsburg: Virginia 350th Anniversary Celebration Corporation, 1957), p. 57.

4 William Strachey, quoted in George MacLaren Brydon, *Virginia's Mother Church: And the Political Conditions Under Which It Grew* (2 vols; Richmond: Virginia Historical Society, 1947), vol. 1, p. 16.

5 'A Modell of Christian Charity' in Perry Miller and Thomas H. Johnson (eds), *The Puritans* (2 vols; New York: Harper Torchbooks, 1963), vol. 1, p. 199.

6 On the question of Awakening versus Awakenings, see Jon Butler, 'Enthusiasm described and decried: the Great Awakening as interpretative fiction', *Journal of American History*, 69 (1982–83), pp. 305–25.

7 Jonathan Edwards, *A Faithful Narrative of the Surprising Work of God . . . in The Works of President Edwards* (4 vols; New York: Robert Carter and Brothers, 1879), vol. 3, p. 234.

8 Quoted in Clarence Goen (ed.), *The Works of Jonathan Edwards: The Great Awakening* (New Haven: Yale University Press, 1972), p. 130.

9 Gilbert Tennant, 'The dangers of an unconverted ministry' in H. Shelton Smith, Robert T. Handy and Leffert A. Loetscher (eds), *American Christianity: An Historical Interpretation with Representative Documents* (2 vols; New York: Charles Scribner's Sons, 1960), vol. 1, p. 328.

10 Quoted in Nathan O. Hatch, *The Sacred Cause of Liberty: Republican Thought and the Millennium in Revolutionary New England* (New Haven: Yale University Press, 1977), p. 36.

11 Gordon Stewart and George Rawlyk, *A People Highly Favoured of God: The Nova Scotia Yankees and the American Revolution* (Hamden, CT: Archon Books, 1972), pp. 154–78.

12 Philip Schaff, *America: A Sketch of its Political, Social and Religious Character*, ed. Perry Miller (Cambridge, MA: The Belknap Press of Harvard University Press, 1961), p. 78.

13 Robert Baird, *Religion in America*, a Critical Abridgment and Introduction by Henry Warner Bowden (New York: Harper Torchbook, 1970), p. 255.

14 John F. Wilson and Donald L. Drakeman (eds), *Church and State in American History* (2nd edn; Boston: Beacon Press, 1987), p. 93.

15 Winthrop Hudson, 'The Methodist Age in America', *Methodist History*, 12 (1974), pp. 3–15.

16 Sydney E. Ahlstrom, *A Religious History of the American People* (New Haven: Yale University Press, 1972), p. 548.

17 Charles Hodge, 'Retrospect of the history of the *Princeton Review*', *Biblical Repertory and Princeton Review: Index Volume* (Philadelphia, 1871), p. 15.

18 Benjamin M. Palmer, *National Responsibility Before God*, reprinted in David M. Chesebrough (ed.), *God Ordained This War* (Columbia, SC: University of South Carolina Press, 1991), p. 208. The Lincoln quotation is from his Second Inaugural Address; the Julia Ward Howe quotation is from 'The Battle Hymn of the Republic'.

19 Frank Milton Bristol, *The Life of Chaplain McCabe* (New York: Jennings and Graham, 1908), pp. 259–60.

20 Horace Bushnell, *Christian Nurture* (New Haven: Yale University Press, 1967), p. 4. Bushnell had published versions of this book in 1838 and 1847.

21 Walter Rauschenbusch, *A Theology for the Social Gospel* (Nashville: Abingdon, 1945), p. 226.

22 Charles Fiske, *Confessions of a Puzzled Parson* (New York: Charles Scribner's Sons, 1928), p. 14.

23 Will Herberg, *Protestant–Catholic–Jew: An Essay in American Religious Sociology* (New York: Doubleday and Co., 1955).

24 On these questions see James Treat (ed.), *Native and Christian: Indigenous Voices on Religious Identity in the United States and Canada* (New York and London: Routledge, 1996).

25 Jay P. Dolan, *The American Catholic Experience* (Notre Dame: University of Notre Dame Press, 1992), p. 437.

26 John Webster Grant, *The Church in the Canadian Era: The First Century of Confederation* (Toronto: McGraw-Hill Ryerson Limited, 1972), p. 202.

12

Christianity in Western Europe from the Enlightenment

Mary Heimann

Introduction[1]

At some point between the late seventeenth century and the present day there occurred an important shift in the way in which the Christian message was viewed by most Western Europeans. The most succinct way of expressing the contrast between the general attitude of mind of the 1690s and that of the 1990s would be to say that in the late seventeenth century Christianity was generally presumed to be true unless there seemed good reasons to doubt; whereas in the late twentieth century Christianity was usually presumed to be untrue unless good reasons could be given to believe. Exactly how and when the burden of proof shifted from the non-Christian to the Christian position is not the sort of question which can be answered precisely, let alone authoritatively, by any historian. But it is probably the question which is most central to understanding the post-Enlightenment period in the West.

Every historical period has its own prejudices and unverified assumptions, uncritically held beliefs which together make up what one historian has aptly termed the 'climate of opinion'.[2] Since our own period is no exception to this rule, any account which we offer of the past is bound to be partial, to betray modern concerns and beliefs at least as much as it reflects those of earlier times. To this fundamental problem, which is rooted in the nature of historical writing, there does not seem to be any satisfactory solution. The best that can be hoped is that the inevitable distortion will be minimized through a deliberate attempt to follow the lead of contemporary sources in order to recapture distinctive attitudes as they were expressed in the eighteenth, nineteenth and twentieth centuries. The intention is to discuss the issues in a way which focuses primarily on the intellectual, rather than the political, institutional or even sociological aspects of Christianity. The reader whose interests lie in the relationship between religion and social class, or in the political behaviour of the institutional Churches, will find many excellent surveys to complement or to replace the present study;[3] the aim here will be to place religious beliefs at the centre of discussion.

Enlightenment

At the end of the seventeenth and beginning of the eighteenth century, the religious map of Western Europe was more or less the same as it is today. France, Poland, Spain, Portugal and the territories which are now called Belgium, Italy, Austria and Hungary were Catholic by majority; Britain, the Scandinavian countries and much of Switzerland were Protestant. The German states were roughly divided between a Protestant north and a Catholic south; and the Dutch republic, although officially Protestant, was similarly split.

The post-Reformation division of what had once been Christendom into two mutually suspicious and antagonistic ideological blocks is so familiar that we may easily forget how unnatural religious disunity seemed to Europeans at the time. Neither the Protestant nor the Catholic side believed that truth was divisible, or that religious differences among Europeans were anything less than a scandal. For nearly two centuries after Martin Luther's new interpretation of Faith had caught the imagination of Christians throughout Europe, civil and international wars of religion, interspersed with periods of cold war and détente, had been the ordinary state of affairs in Europe as each side tried to impose religious hegemony throughout the Continent. It was only in 1648 that what might be seen as the last full-blown war of religion between European states, the Thirty Years War, was concluded by the Peace of Westphalia. Memories of the dream of a unified Christian West lingered on in official documents well beyond that date: the Treaty of Utrecht of 1713 still described the geographical area afterwards known only as Europe as 'Christendom'; the 'Holy Roman Empire' staggered on until its eventual abolition by Napoleon I in 1806. But from the late seventeenth century, and certainly by the opening years of the eighteenth, it seemed clear to most Europeans that a stalemate in the wars of religion had been reached: the notion that Protestantism might be obliterated no longer seemed tenable, and it did not appear plausible that Catholic countries would reform themselves in a Protestant direction.

The problem of whether religious integrity within national borders could be achieved remained a more open question. All Western European governments appeared to feel, at least at times, that this would be both a desirable and a possible end, and took measures designed to further it. In order to accord special status to a single denomination which was understood to represent the nation's religion, governments chose to approve and uphold a single established Church whose functions were mingled, to a greater or lesser degree, with those of the government. The timing and details of establishment, which depended partly on the historical background of Church–State relations, varied from country to country; so did the degree of toleration which it seemed right or expedient to accord to those who fell outside the umbrella of the established faith.

The division of Europe into states associated with a single Christian denomination made good political sense in the aftermath of the sixteenth- and seventeenth-century wars of religion. In the longer term, the policy created new problems, particularly those of how religious minorities ought to be accommodated and how far governments should intervene in matters of religion. The very fact that irreconcilable divisions of opinion existed in a realm of thought as fundamental as religious belief and practice posed difficulties for faith. A good deal of the history of Christianity in Europe from the Enlightenment onwards was taken up with these social, political and intellectual problems, whose tone and detail varied over time, but whose difficulties could all be traced back to the break-up of what had once been Christendom.

It is now a long-standing convention to use the expression 'the Enlightenment' to describe the climate of Western opinion – intellectual, political and religious – which dominated Europe from the end of the seventeenth century until the outbreak of the French Revolution in 1789. Like all such historical abstractions – the 'Renaissance', the 'Reformation' and others – the term encourages one particular perspective to be applied to what is seen as a discrete period of history. It seems entirely appropriate that it should have been Immanuel Kant who, in 1793, first coined the phrase *Aufklärung* (translated as Enlightenment in English and *Lumières* in French) to describe the European state of mind of the previous hundred years. The term carries with it a number of unspoken assumptions which one might expect a philosopher, who was also a Protestant, a Prussian and a member of an educated and cultured elite, to have taken as axiomatic.

Embedded in the term Enlightenment, as in its common alternative, the Age of Reason, lie a number of hidden assumptions both about how history ought to be approached and about the distinctive features of the eighteenth century in the history of Western Europe. Among these are the beliefs that developments in philosophy are of the utmost significance; that those whose frame of mind was affected by such developments, mainly the well-to-do and educated, are the people whose outlook ought to be taken to characterize a particular culture; and that the Western world was in the vanguard of human thought at this particular time.

Over the course of the twentieth century, each of these assumptions has been tacitly called into question. One of the legacies of Marxist approaches to history has been to challenge the notion that elites may be taken as typical of any given historical period. Were one to ignore the upper echelons of eighteenth-century society and focus instead on its peasants, artisans and labourers, one might indeed find that Enlightenment seems less appropriate an appellation than some other term which would imply continuity rather than a sudden break with the past.

An analogous problem is presented by the notion that the thought of whole peoples can be described in terms of intellectual progress, or indeed that there exists such a thing as intellectual 'progress' at all. The dangers of the so-called Whiggish approach to history, of the historian's tendency to select and interpret evidence in ways which 'emphasize certain principles of progress in the past' in order 'to produce a story which is the ratification if not the glorification of the present',[4] were first put forward by the historian Herbert Butterfield in 1931. More recently, they have found an emphatic endorsement in the arguments of postmodernist critics that no historical writing can really be disinterested, and that value judgements about the past reveal little more than present-day prejudices.

There are at least two compelling reasons why the familiar account of the eighteenth century as the 'Enlightenment' or the 'Age of Reason' should put us on our guard. The first is that we have a vested interest in believing in it. All that we consider most modern and progressive in Western society is generally agreed to owe its origins to the 'enlightened' thought of the eighteenth-century philosophers: political democracy and the possibility of advancement through merit; the achievements of science and technology; and the freedom of individual conscience from the tyrannies of any single religion or other state-imposed ideology.

There is a second reason why we should exercise caution in accepting the common view that the eighteenth century heralded the dawn of progress, humane values and intellectual enlightenment in the West. The idea has not come to us from impartial witnesses but rather from crusaders or propagandists of the time who called themselves philosophers, *Aufklärer, philosophes*, the enlightened ones. These self-appointed intellectual elites of the eighteenth century were self-publicists as well as critics of the *status quo*: denouncing religious intolerance, the implication seemed to be that they alone were tolerant; reiterating that experience and reason were their sole guides to thought, they vilified their opponents as prejudiced and irrational; presenting themselves as the intellectual equals of the Ancient Greeks, they proclaimed that they offered the sure and universal method for discovering certain truths.

Their method, induction, was not new. Its origins could be traced back to Aristotle. But developments in 'natural philosophy' (what would today be called 'science') which had occurred during the seventeenth century appeared to give the empirical method new validity. It would be misleading to regard the natural philosophers whose names are associated with the Scientific Revolution of the seventeenth century – Newton, Kepler, Halley, Harvey, Galileo, Robert Boyle and others – as 'scientists' in the modern sense, still less as technocrats. Nor would it be wise to separate their philosophies from their 'discoveries' or, more accurately, theories about aspects of the natural world. Yet it was the claims of these natural philosophers to be able to describe mechanisms believed to operate in the real world, and not only to make logical sense within the covers of philosophical treatises, which particularly excited their eighteenth-century descendants.

The self-consciously enlightened thinkers of the eighteenth century made heroes of the seventeenth-century natural philosophers. According to their accounts, methods of enquiry as propounded by Francis Bacon (in his *Proficience and Advancement of Learning* (1605), *Novum Organum* (1620), *De Augmentis Scientiarum* (1623), as well as in his better-known *Essays*) and developed in seventeenth-century works of physics, chemistry and astronomy, had led to the discovery of universally valid natural laws. Galileo's law of dynamics and new theory of the solar system; Kepler's laws of planetary motions; Boyle's laws about the properties of gases: all of these theories were regarded as the fruits of rational enquiry which added to the sum of objective human knowledge about the workings of nature. All seemed likely to lead both to further theoretical insights and, in that favourite eighteenth-century phrase, to the development and diffusion of 'useful knowledge'.

The supposed heroism of the great men of the seventeenth century did not, however, rest solely on the quality of their scientific contributions. Their credibility in eighteenth-century eyes stemmed just as much from their advocacy of particular kinds of theology which, being described as 'natural' or 'reasonable', could be contrasted with the supposed irrationality and arbitrariness of forms of religion associated with absolutist and 'backward' European states. Wishing to criticize what were seen as corruptions in the traditional pillars of society – monarchy, aristocracy and the Church – while at the same time upholding Christian ethics, most philosophers were far from socially radical. Only those seventeenth-century natural philosophers who had clearly and explicitly defended traditional morality were safe from public opprobrium for most of the eighteenth century. Among those who were omitted from the pantheon of the enlightened were Baruch Spinoza (whose denial of miracles and of the reality of evil had put him beyond the pale of respectable philosophy from the end of the seventeenth century), Thomas Hobbes and Nicolas Malebranche, who were considered to hold dangerously equivocal stances on morality as well as serious errors in theology.[5]

Natural philosophers who had steered away from controversial religious subjects were likely to fare much better. Boyle's law did indeed appear, from an eighteenth-century perspective, to represent an increase in knowledge which would no doubt lead to useful applications. But his insistence that scientific truth was in perfect harmony with a rational view of Christianity was every bit as important in raising him to the status of an enlightened predecessor. Galileo's merit as an astronomer was certainly an important factor in his rise to fame; but his heroism was chiefly seen in what was presented as his martyrdom to truth. It was because his investigations into the workings of the solar system were pursued even when he was accused of heresy by a 'bigoted' Catholic Church that the enlightened gave him their highest accolade of a true philosopher. In taking upon themselves the title of 'philosopher' while quietly dropping the qualifier of 'natural', the self-consciously enlightened of the eighteenth century did more than pay their respects to the likes of Boyle and Galileo: they also claimed to be their intellectual heirs, choosing to see themselves as martyrs to truth who fearlessly applied objective and rational methods of enquiry to the metaphysical realm as their heroes had to the physical world.

Of all the intellectual giants who found a place in the eighteenth-century pantheon of true philosophers, Isaac Newton was undoubtedly the most acclaimed. Only, perhaps, his fellow-countryman the philosopher John Locke came as close to universal esteem and admiration. The words composed by Alexander Pope in 1730 for Newton's epitaph in Westminster Abbey offered a simple tribute, as if further explanation could only detract from the greatness of the man: 'Nature, and Nature's Laws lay hid in Night / God said, *Let Newton be!* and All was *Light*.'[6] Among the international set of intellectuals who called themselves philosophers, Newton and Locke were as widely acclaimed abroad as they were at home: just as England's constitutional government was favourably contrasted with arbitrary rule elsewhere, so the new philosophy which coincided with England's 'Glorious Revolution' of 1688 was held up as an example, first in France, and then among self-consciously advanced thinkers throughout the Western world.

At first glance, Newton's overwhelming importance to the eighteenth-century critics, wits, writers and dabblers in science who adopted the name of 'philosopher' may seem puzzling. That a physicist should have become a household name even among cultured people is surprising, especially since the most celebrated of Newton's works, *Philosophiae Naturalis Principia Mathematica* or *Mathematical Principles of Natural Philosophy* (1687), was incomprehensible to those without mathematical training. Ironically enough, this fact probably helped rather than hindered his rise to fame: it meant that would-be philosophers had to rely on second-hand accounts of the *Principia Mathematica* such as that offered by

François-Marie Arouet (better known by his pseudonym Voltaire) in his far more accessible and engaging *Lettres Philosophiques* or *Lettres sur les Anglais* (*Philosophical Letters* or *Letters on the English*) of 1733, which were eagerly read in coffee houses, salons and drawing rooms throughout continental Europe and its colonies in the New World.

As explicated and popularized by Voltaire and other *philosophes*, Newton seemed to teach a number of valuable lessons, most of which were only tangentially concerned with physics. First of all, the *Principia* showed that logical sense could be made of a variety of apparently disconnected phenomena, and that the symbolic language of mathematics could account for aspects of reality as diverse as orbiting spheres and falling apples. To the philosophers, this seemed to prove that universal laws were not paper fictions, but the key to all knowledge, providing insights into humanity as well as understandings of the natural world. Newton's work was also seen to demonstrate that the new philosophy, which was grounded firmly in a rational belief in God, supported what tended to be called the 'essentials' of Christianity, although arguments were later to emerge over precisely which aspects of Christianity were central and which peripheral.

The methods which Newton was thought to have used in the realm of physics were endorsed by John Locke in the branch of philosophy known as epistemology or the theory of knowledge. In his *An Essay Concerning Human Understanding*, published in 1690 (just three years after Newton's *Principia Mathematica*), Locke argued that all human beings were born in a state of ignorance, their minds as empty of ideas as a clean slate or blank page. By living in the world they accumulated experiences – at first only simple sensory experiences such as feeling hot or cold or perceiving softness or hardness. Through their innate ability to reason, these merely animal sensations were abstracted into simple ideas such as 'solidity', 'cold' or 'whiteness'. From such simple ideas, more complex ideas were developed, including, according to Locke, the concept of number, the notion of the immaterial soul and the existence of God, all of which his *Essay* claimed to have proved.[7] All human knowledge, including knowledge of God and of the supernatural dimension of life, therefore, was argued to be demonstrable through experience of the world as filtered through mental reflection.

Locke's highly influential argument managed to accommodate the earlier philosopher Descartes's insistence upon the intellectual necessity of applying systematic doubt to common-sense truths while at the same time refuting the notion that innate ideas existed in the mind. It thus opened up the possibility of applying the empirical methods advocated by natural philosophers like Francis Bacon to the sphere of all philosophical speculation. To the enlightened, this seemed to show that inductive reasoning could conclusively establish the independent existence of the world and begin to unravel its mechanisms. It also seemed to prove the objective reality of both God and the soul while at the same time endorsing the methods and findings of modern philosophical or 'scientific' thought. Small wonder that Locke and Newton were accorded a special niche in the eighteenth-century temple of fame, or that the philosophers who saw themselves as their disciples felt confident that their new methods of reasoning would eventually lead to the establishment of a rationally ordered world, a Utopia in which ignorance would be banished, virtue flourish and enlightenment spread to all corners of the still darkened world.

Rational religion

The history of Christianity in Western Europe from the Enlightenment is often presented as a story of steady and inevitable decline. This view presupposes at least two highly dubious assumptions. Firstly, it takes for granted that the Middle Ages represented an Age of Faith in which everyone believed wholeheartedly in orthodox Christianity as preached by the Catholic Church. This assumption hardly seems to be borne out by the recurrence of doctrinal disputes and heretical movements throughout the Middle Ages and by the later emergence of Protestantism, a reformist movement important enough to tear European society apart for most of the sixteenth and seventeenth centuries.

The second assumption which underlies deterministic views of the decline of religion is that forces loosely described as 'progress', 'rationality' and 'the rise of science' ushered in a revolution in European thought which inevitably, if gradually, overwhelmed the heritage of Christian teaching and its expression in Christian society. At their crudest, such accounts imply that the Christian view of the world, being false, could not help but admit defeat in the face of the inexorable advance of scientific and secular truth. There are a number of problems with this view, not least that the long-predicted 'secularization' of Europe has yet to have occurred in any unambiguous way: the signs of advancing atheism, which seemed so clear to liberals of the 1960s and 1970s, seem far less certain in the 1990s. As for the notion that widespread loss of faith was caused by the 'rise' of science, it is just as easy to take the opposite view, arguing that the new 'scientific' thinking of the Enlightenment period rose to prominence precisely because it appeared to contemporaries to offer irrefutable proofs of what were held to be the central truths of Christianity.

In our own age, which tends to treat religion and science as belonging in separate compartments, it is perhaps difficult to imagine how they

465

could ever have been subsumed in the same branch of study. For most of the history of Western Europe, however, 'science' (which meant nothing more than what would now be called systematic 'knowledge'), comprised numerous branches: these included logic and mathematics, the study of the physical world, and intellectual speculations which would today be divided firmly into the 'philosophical' and the 'theological'. Since truth was the object of all knowledge, and truth was indivisible, all of these branches of knowledge were held to complement each other. Mathematical formulae presupposed a divine origin just as the existence of a rational creator presupposed the truth of mathematical logic. Natural philosophers looked for ordered patterns in the world; but the discovery of such patterns could only be understood as endorsements of the fact of creation and the rationality of the creator.

Evidences of God's existence and attributes were traditionally divided into the 'natural' and the 'supernatural'. The natural were those which were held to be open to rational enquiry, to the application of human reason to observed phenomena in the world. Supernatural evidences were those which came in the shape of revealed knowledge – principally through that revelation which was delivered in the Scriptures, but also through the continued operation of the Holy Spirit as safeguarded in Church doctrine and traditions. Protestants tended to emphasize the Bible as the prime source of spiritual knowledge and Catholics to give more stress to the tradition of the Church; but neither side, for all its posturings, could dispense altogether with either historical or scriptural evidence.

Rational proofs for the existence of God had, of course, been put forward by theologians and scholastics throughout the Middle Ages. There was nothing new in the simple fact of their existence in the seventeenth and eighteenth centuries. But in a Europe which had suffered over a century of religious warfare and was still torn by deep religious divisions, there were new reasons why intellectual proofs which claimed to argue from first principles and to rely on reason alone for their persuasiveness were much more likely to find a popular audience in the period which has come to be known as the Enlightenment. Although differences between Catholic and Protestant justifications for religious knowledge can be seen as differences of degree rather than of kind, arguments over the relative importance of the Bible and Christian tradition from the Reformation onwards had caused, and continued to cause, much bitterness and mutual misunderstanding.

Armed with the inductive methods of the natural sciences, the eighteenth-century philosophers declared themselves to have certain grounds for knowledge of the essentials of Christianity. A large part of their intellectual mission, as they saw it, was to purge the Christian faith of its irrational accretions, those stubbornly held beliefs and practices which had divided Catholics from Protestants and had led to what were disparaged as 'enthusiasm' (meaning fanaticism), bigotry and intolerance. Although this missionary zeal could, and often did, lead to anticlericalism, to hatred of the 'irrational' aspects of both Protestant and especially Catholic belief and to contempt for a good deal of the legacy of the Middle Ages, it was not intended to undermine belief in what were seen as the fundamentals of the Christian message. Far from hoping to debunk what they saw as true Faith, the philosophers set out to defend it with the most up-to-date intellectual materials. They did so in the sanguine belief that their interpretation, since it was held to be accessible to reasonable men and women of all backgrounds, Catholic or Protestant, was innately uncontroversial as well as demonstrably true.

When Locke wrote his *Essay Concerning Human Understanding* he did not feel it necessary to dwell too long on proofs for the existence of God, since God's existence seemed to him to be 'the most obvious truth that reason discovers'.[8] Newton's physics, too, was firmly predicated on the belief in a divine creator, one 'very well skilled in mechanics and geometry'.[9] To those whose view of the universe was an increasingly mechanical one, the evidence that an intelligent mind must have created it seemed almost too obvious to be worth stating: here, if anywhere, was a point upon which all rational people might agree. As even the notorious 'infidel' Voltaire marvelled, contemplating the starry night sky, 'One would have to be blind not to be dazzled by this sight; one would have to be stupid not to recognize its author; one would have to be mad not to worship him'.[10] The more certain and detailed knowledge of the world was thought to be, and the more rational in its workings, the less plausible it seemed to maintain that it could have come about by any means other than the deliberate creation of a supreme intelligence. Boyle summed up the general appeal to common sense by asking rhetorically how 'so curious an engine' as this world could possibly have been produced by a 'casual concurrence of the parts it consists of?'[11] The very intricacy of the workings of the universe seemed to reveal its creation by a deliberate divine act.

The beauty of enlightened or rational Christianity was that its tenets were thought to be as self-evidently true as geometrical proofs or the laws of physics: God's existence and his purposes for creation could, it claimed, be established beyond the shadow of a doubt or the possibility of dispute. But such proofs, however elegantly and persuasively stated, did not go beyond the first premises of traditional Christianity. They therefore offered an implicit, if unintended, invitation to reductionism, since it is only a small step from the belief that the existence of a divine creator can be proved to the position that only those tenets which can be logically proved are true.

Locke had insisted in his *Letters Concerning Toleration* of 1689, 1690 and 1692 that all religions, except those whose dogmatism made them intolerant of others, ought to be allowed to exist unmolested. Similarly, Jean-Jacques Rousseau (who had reason to mistrust religious dogmatism through his own experience of converting from Calvinism to Catholicism and back again) argued in his *Du Contrat Social* (*The Social Contract*) (1762) that a perfect state would uphold natural religion but forbid all creeds which refused to tolerate the others. Voltaire, fulminating against sectarianism in his *Philosophical Dictionary*, pointed out that 'there are no sects in geometry; we don't say, a Euclidian, an Archimedian. When the truth is evident, it is impossible for parties and factions to arise. People have never argued over whether it was daytime at noon.'[12] In seeking to find a version of Christianity as self-evident as its being daytime at noon, the enlightened philosophers were certainly optimistic. They were also liable to stir up precisely the sort of controversy which they sought to avoid, since their arguments could not conclusively prove the validity of the tenets either of traditional Catholicism or of orthodox Protestantism, but at best only a lowest common denominator ultimately unsatisfactory to both sides.

The most minimalist interpretations of Christianity which arose out of attempts to establish a rational basis for faith have traditionally been classified under the umbrella term 'deism'. In his *A Discourse concerning the Being and Attributes of God, the Obligations of Natural Religion, and the Truth and Certainty of the Christian Revelation* of 1713, the Anglican clergyman Samuel Clarke identified four strands of contemporary 'deist' thought which he felt needed urgently to be refuted. At its starkest, deism suggested that all that could be known of the divine was that a creator must have existed, since the evidence of his creation was plain for all to see. Other deists were not quite so reductionist, arguing with Newton that this creator must continue to interfere occasionally in the universe, if only to keep the stars in their places, since not all aspects of the physical universe were capable of self-regulation. Still others argued that an all-powerful creator, with no obvious motive to create a world, could be deduced to be good, just and merciful as well as all-powerful, through his bountiful act of creation. The deists who came closest to a fully Christian position were those who believed that rationally defensible or 'natural' religion could confirm the reality of good and evil, the existence of the soul and the certainty of an afterlife.[13] But even these writers, who were prepared to accept all that could be reasonably deduced of God, morality and the supernatural through the natural channels of the intellect, fell well short of orthodox Christian belief by explicitly rejecting the evidence of revelation.

It is all too easy to exaggerate the importance of the deists and to imagine that their extreme positions were characteristic of enlightened thought of the day; even that they anticipated the beliefs of a secular modern world. It would probably be closer to the truth to see most thinking people of the time as having felt intuitively that reason and revelation must be compatible, but as believing that stronger intellectual justifications were needed to prove Christianity – or its essentials – to be true beyond the possibility of doubt.

It was not only extreme deists who struggled to reconcile inherited ideas about the Christian message with the self-imposed rigours of newly fashionable philosophical systems. The Anglican John Locke, for example, tried in *The Reasonableness of Christianity as Delivered in the Scriptures* (1695) to show how much of Christianity could be ascertained by the use of natural reason. Locke stopped just short of deism by insisting that biblical miracles offered proof of the divine origin of the Scriptures, thus protecting the notion of supernatural evidence or revelation. John Toland's more radical *Christianity Not Mysterious* (1696) agreed that God's existence and even the validity of his revelation could be rationally deduced, but argued that the traditional mysteries associated with Christianity had been introduced through pagan superstitions and priestly corruptions. Both works, which were seen by many orthodox Christians as invitations to infidelity, were received with widespread horror when they were first published. But Locke's *The Reasonableness of Christianity* meant only to establish a basis for agreement among a majority of Christians; and even Toland's work, though certainly deist, seems, with hindsight, to have been closer in spirit to a piece of seventeenth-century Protestant polemic than to a nineteenth-century anti-religious tract. The supposed secularism of many eighteenth-century thinkers seems to have been far more superficial than is often supposed: beneath the gloss of rational objectivity usually lay continued sectarian hostility or else the dream of re-establishing unity of faith within the old borders of Christendom. Both seem more aptly described as legacies of the Reformation than as anticipations of modern forms of secularism.

The unintended effect of a proliferation of rational defences of theism and the first principles of Christianity was to present many thinking people with the uneasy sense that their intuitive belief in the truth of the Christian message and their habits of Christian worship needed somehow to be squared with recent currents in philosophical thinking. As one humorist put it, 'no one had doubted the existence of God until the Boyle lecturers undertook to prove it'.[14] Increasingly, aspects of traditional Christianity which could not be grasped immediately, or which did not seem to accord with common sense, began to seem dubious. Monks and nuns in Catholic countries began to be judged by human rather than by other-worldly standards: their care of the sick and the poor, which clearly served a useful social purpose, seemed perfectly commendable; but the contemplative life, the notion of doing good both in this world and the next through prayer, began to seem like a self-indulgent delusion. Tales of corruption among the religious, of cruelty on the part of Catholic schoolteachers, of self-interest on the part of clergymen and particularly bishops, were no longer restricted to Protestant critiques of Catholicism, but became the standard fare of satires and exposés penned by philosophers, often themselves at least nominally Catholic and even, like Voltaire and Diderot, Jesuit-educated. Diderot and d'Alembert's *Encyclopédie* (1751–65), the foremost piece of Enlightenment polemic undertaken by the *philosophes*, was riddled with anticlerical sentiment: even the definition of a term as apparently neutral as 'cowl', for example, offered an excuse for exposing absurdities within the Catholic Church, this item of religious clothing being dismissed as 'once the cause of a major war among the Franciscans'.[15] In a Protestant country like England, too, Edward Gibbon's authoritative *The History of the Decline and Fall of the Roman Empire* (1776–88) portrayed early Christianity as an intolerant, superstitious and barbarous fanaticism which was largely to blame for the loss of the genuinely civilizing effects of the classical world so admired by both Protestant and Catholic philosophers.[16]

The more earnestly would-be defenders of rational religion and natural theology sought to prove their case, the more scandalously they viewed the actual practice of Christianity, whether in the absolutist regimes of their own day, or in the remote Christian past. Mischievous contrasts were drawn with other cultures, the Tahitians, Persians or Chinese being presented as morally superior to the Europeans, Islam being held up as a better civic religion than Christianity or Confucianism as a more rational creed than Catholicism. In Germany, Gotthold Lessing's *Nathan der Weise* (1779) presented a Jew as the archetypically tolerant, rational and benevolent enlightened man. Freemasonry, whose Lodges offered 'reasonable' forms of Christianity in England and Germany, or more frankly anticlerical deism in France and Italy, began to rise in membership. Everywhere, the philosophers' idealized notion of what rational people should believe and how they ought to behave came increasingly into tension with how Christianity was actually lived. In their high ideals, coupled with increasing intolerance of what they saw as the corruptions, superstitions and idiocies of the unenlightened, the rhetoric of the philosophers took on many of the characteristics of those Christians whose reforming zeal had ushered in the Reformation of the sixteenth century. The Enlightenment of the eighteenth century was ultimately to prove as damaging to the restoration of Christian consensus as the Reformation had been instrumental in breaking it.

The unenlightened

As long ago as 1939 an historian of the Enlightenment observed that virtually no scholarly attention had been paid to conservative and reactionary thinkers of the eighteenth century, those people who disagreed with the positions so emphatically put forward by the *philosophes* on questions of religion. 'In the picture we usually receive [of the Enlightenment]', he mused, 'certain bold and progressive men, who are outlined with great distinctiveness, do battle with vague but powerful adversaries who are rarely described but are indicated as extremely unenlightened.'[17] The criticism still seems every bit as valid today.

Although their views are seldom given an airing, a large number of eighteenth-century Christians disagreed absolutely with the point of view of the philosophers. Among these dissenters from prevailing opinion were traditionalists, whose understanding of the Faith remained more or less unchanged in the new climate but who were willing to enter into debate with the philosophers; and newer groups, whose refusal to engage with Enlightened thought drove them to what might today be described as 'fundamentalist' positions. Of the first group, perhaps the most vocal were conservative Catholic thinkers in France, who argued that the *philosophes* were fundamentally misguided, and even dishonest, in their arguments. Accepting that faith could in principle be reconciled with reason, they argued that anticlericals who claimed reason and empirical knowledge as their guides were in practice relying upon common-sense prejudice rather than advancing philosophically valid positions. Central to the arguments of these apologists for orthodoxy was one irreducible piece of evidence to which there seemed ample testimony in Scripture: the fact of the Incarnation. Eschewing natural religion, with its tendency towards deist reductionism, conservatives like A. de Malvin de Montazet, Archbishop of Lyons, were quick to admit that 'revelation is the sole foundation of our faith', but defended revealed truth as 'based on facts which we consider to be as indubitable as any that history reports'.[18] The supposedly enlightened, he argued, far from being impartial, were clouded by prejudices of the very kind they deplored in others. Rather than examining the historical evidence for miracles with genuine objectivity, they simply asserted that miracles were impossible on the grounds that they had not witnessed any, taking it as an article of faith that the laws of nature could never be suspended. Were the philosophers really interested in establishing the truth, rather than simply finding a stick with which to beat the

Catholic Church, they would not presume to know more than their evidence could support, nor would they 'resort to anecdote, burlesque, and vulgarity to amuse the fops of Paris'.[19]

Defenders of Catholic orthodoxy who entered into debate with the philosophers characteristically stressed that it was the testimony of history, not the natural sciences, which offered the surest guide to truth. History, rather than natural philosophy, appeared to support the notion that it was the Catholic Church which preserved 'the faith once delivered to the saints' through its conservatism of doctrine. Over the particularly contentious issue of miracles, for example, orthodox Catholics argued that there existed no positive scientific evidence to discount reports of miracles in the past, whereas there was a great body of historical writing to attest to their reality; the onus therefore seemed to be on those who wished to disprove rather than to prove the supernatural. When the philosophers retaliated by pointing to similar claims of the miraculous which were made by non-Catholic heretics and infidels, apologists for Catholicism like Nicolas-Sylvestre Bergier (1718–90), priest of Besançon, were led into the position of stoutly maintaining that genuine miracles could only be performed by the orthodox and that all other historical or contemporary claims were the result of deliberate frauds. As Robert Palmer has pointed out, such a defensive position could lead to absurdly anachronistic portrayals of the apostles and saints of Scripture as cool and impartial observers who, like their idealized eighteenth-century counterparts, accepted reports of the supernatural only after the most searching and exhaustive of empirical tests.[20] This was a position which it was not difficult for anticlerical philosophers to ridicule.

Not all apologists for Christian orthodoxy tried to shift the terms of the debate from one which stressed the uniformity of natural laws to one which focused on the problems of historical evidence. An increasingly common response among 'reasonable Christians' was to accept the philosophers' premises, but to increase the sphere of natural religion to include more of traditional Christianity than was usually allowed by the enlightened. This most popular of approaches, which seemed to accommodate the latest philosophical trends while at the same time maintaining faith, characteristically drew analogies from nature to validate the reality and benign purpose of God's plan for mankind. Seizing on the exciting new theories of microscopists that all matter had existed from the beginning of the world in germ form, intellectually progressive Christians argued that the universal pattern of growth from simple to complex organisms revealed that there was a premeditated purpose in design. Innumerable religio-scientific treatises which appeared throughout the eighteenth century took this line of argument, works like the best-selling eight-volume *Spectacle de la Nature* (*The Spectacle of Nature*), first published by Abbé

Pluche in 1732, Lesser's *La lithothéologie, ou La théologie des pierres* (1735) and *La théologie des insectes* (1738) (*The Theology of Stones* and *The Theology of Insects*), to name but a few.

It is all too easy for the modern reader to be tempted to take sides in the eighteenth-century debate over topics like the possibility of miracles, the grounds for religious knowledge or the substance and scope of the Christian message, eagerly following, as if at a tennis match, the critiques and rejoinders, points and counterpoints, which were made by anticlerical philosophers on the one hand and defenders of orthodoxy on the other. In our desire to applaud what may seem like clinching arguments on one side or the other, the amount of common ground between them may easily be overlooked. For although frequently, and sometimes bitterly, opposed in their conclusions, clerics and anticlerics came to substantial agreement in their premisses and adopted a remarkably similar tone to defend their positions, whether of belief or unbelief in traditional Christianity. Both sides invited reasonable people, possessed only of the capacity to reflect on their experience, to follow the logic of what were presented as unassailable arguments. Both sides claimed to be scrupulous to avoid dogmatic statements or arguments from the authority of tradition alone, and appealed instead to abstractions like 'reason' and 'nature' to convince the ordinary educated reader. It was not only the celebrated *philosophes* or radical deists whose utterances created the distinctive intellectual atmosphere of the Age of Reason or Enlightenment; most upholders of Christian orthodoxy who lived and preached in eighteenth-century Europe deserve an equal share of the blame or praise for its pervasive influence.

Not everyone shared in this most characteristic and distinctive outlook of the age, however. Even at the high point of the Enlightenment there were some who went to the heart of the matter by rejecting the authority of reason itself. Groups like the Methodists in Britain, the Jansenists in France and the Pietists in Germany are often treated as if their dissent from rational religion was simply the exception which proves the rule, as if the philosophers were correct to brand them as out of step with the times, the unfortunate relics of a superstitious past. A more helpful way of understanding these groups would be to see them as genuine dissidents from elite intellectual opinion whose radicalism was increased, even in part created, by the intolerance implicit in a rationalist monopoly of learned discussion.

Jansenism, a spiritual movement within the Catholic Church which had its origins in the writings of Cornelius Jansen (1585–1638) and owed its organization first to Jean Duvergier de Hauranne, the Abbé de Saint-Cyran (1581–1643), and then to Antoine Arnauld (1612–94), was as dangerous to the position of the philosophers as it was to that of orthodox Christians. From the point of view of traditional Catholics, and particularly the increasingly morally 'lax' Jesuits, Jansenism, which took an almost Calvinistic approach to predestination, seemed at once too rigorous and pessimistic an outlook to be appropriate to a Church whose aim was to save everyone, not only the elect. It was accordingly treated as a heresy and, partly due to Jesuit pressure, formally condemned by the papal bull *Unigenitus* of 1713. The unpopularity of this measure was later to rebound in the expulsion of the Society of Jesus from Portugal (1759), France (1764) and Spain (1767), and ultimately in the formal dissolution of the Jesuit order in 1773.

At the core of Jansenist theology lay a serious criticism which was applicable not only to Catholics but to all those who believed in the compatibility of Christianity with Enlightened philosophy. This criticism was that natural religion and natural morality, far from being identical with Christian faith and morals, offered rival, 'pagan' systems of belief and ethics. Such a view could hardly have been calculated to be more offensive to the enlightened, whether Christian or deist. It is therefore understandable that when the French government began to persecute Jansenists in earnest from the 1730s, no voice was raised in their defence, even by the supposed champions of religious toleration. As if in illustration of their contempt for the prevailing doctrine of reason, thousands of Jansenists gathered at the Saint-Médard cemetery in Paris between 1730 and 1732, writhing convulsively, prophesying doom, claiming miracles and generally disturbing the peace until the cemetery was forcibly closed by the first minister of France, André-Hercule de Fleury (1654–1743), who was also a cardinal of the Catholic Church. It is surely revealing of the eighteenth-century climate of opinion that the orthodox clergy, whose business it was to defend the Faith, could be joined by philosophical advocates of religious toleration in ridiculing and condemning the Jansenists. The very existence of these theological and intellectual rebels was an affront to those who felt in their bones that faith should be expounded by means of rational argument and expressed through decorous forms of piety.

In England the comparable thorn in the side of both the established Church and enlightened forms of Christianity developed somewhat later in the brand of religion first put forward by the Anglican clergyman John Wesley (1703–91) in the 1730s and soon derided as 'Methodism', an insulting term which meant to suggest that the emotionally charged outpourings of its members were merely formulaic. Methodists returned the insult by arguing that Anglicanism was dry, unfeeling, overly intellectual, an unreal creed which had everything to do with social convention and almost nothing to do with the realization of personal salvation offered by Christ through his death on the cross.

Wesley's condemnations of the reliance upon natural religion, rationalism and conventional piety to save souls had been largely inspired by the writings of German Pietists and Moravian Brethren of the late seventeenth century whose arguments, like his own, attempted to renew religious fervour within an established Church rather than to overturn it. But whereas Pietism gradually took hold in Lutheran Churches throughout the German states and spread, via German immigrants, to America, Methodism in England, like Jansenism in France, was generally derided as 'enthusiastic' and its adherents presented in polite society as sinister devils or raving lunatics. It was a presage of things to come that, even in England and France, where Enlightened views had their origins and ran deepest, neither Methodism nor Jansenism could be entirely ignored or was successfully extinguished over the course of the eighteenth century.

The importance of what one might think of as 'fundamentalist' groups like the Methodists and Jansenists lay in their tacit but powerful critique of the underlying assumptions of the *philosophes*. Anti-rationalists were potentially far more dangerous enemies than defenders of orthodoxy, who could at least be counted upon to engage in gentlemanly debates which agreed most terms of reference and kept to the subject under discussion. Methodists, who harangued from the pulpit or met in open fields to proclaim the Gospel, like Jansenists who writhed convulsively at the Saint-Médard cemetery, seemed to be wild, unpredictable folk, rabble-rousers and hysterics who, as often as not, were drawn from the most dangerous ranks of society – those who had least to lose by its overthrow. It is therefore not altogether surprising that the 'religion of the mob' which they seemed to represent was generally attacked with satire rather than with reasoned debate and treated to loathing rather than to measured criticisms, even by those who prided themselves on their universality, toleration and advocacy of open debate.

Another tacit criticism of rational religion came through a current of taste, later dubbed 'Romanticism', which began to make itself felt in the second half of the eighteenth century. Although notoriously difficult to define precisely, this primarily artistic and literary movement found something approaching unity in its instinctive rejection of the regular and predictable, the harmonious and the overly cerebral aspects of neoclassicism, prizing irregularity in beauty and quirkiness in architecture as it emphasized the importance of feeling over the intellect in poetry, painting and music. Whereas the *philosophes*, who drew inspiration from Ancient Greece and Rome, believed in the universality of good taste, delighting to demonstrate the mathematical logic of the rules of proportion or to find satisfaction in the symmetrical, Romantics found Enlightenment rationalism, like neoclassical aesthetics, shallow and inadequate. Increasingly, they turned to the 'barbarous' Middle Ages to recover the importance of awe, mystery and the sublime. Edmund Burke's *Philosoph-*

ical Enquiry into the Origin of Our Ideas of the Sublime and Beautiful (1756) made the case for the power of awe in aesthetic appreciation, while Horace Walpole's estate of Strawberry Hill in Twickenham, a medievalist folly (complete with a resident hermit to surprise guests on tours of its deliberately wild landscape), offered an early experiment in its fulfilment. The high point of Romanticism was to coincide with the early years and immediate aftermath of the French Revolution, but the beginnings of the dissatisfaction with the dominance of Reason which it represented began to be expressed in a number of disciplines from about the middle of the eighteenth century.

In the last quarter of the century, even some philosophers began to expose what they saw as the fallacies of Enlightened thinking. The Scottish thinker David Hume's posthumously published *Dialogues Concerning Natural Religion* (1779) followed the deists' empirical methods with a remorseless logic which exposed the limitations of reason, effectively undermining the intellectual foundations of natural religion. The inadequacies of rational religion could also be grasped from Immanuel Kant's *Kritik der reinen Vernunft* (*Critique of Pure Reason*) (1789) which stressed the inadequacies of reason alone to establish the central tenets of Christianity. As natural religion was increasingly felt to offer only one part of religious truth and to ignore too many aspects of human sentiment and imagination, a new stress began to be placed on religious feeling as a proper concern of the faithful.

Criticisms of rational religion which were presented over the course of the eighteenth century – first by orthodox defenders of tradition, then by sects claiming the authority of private religious experience and finally by the most thoroughgoing of the philosophical sceptics – all combined to cast doubt on the complacent arguments for the inherent reasonableness and universality of Enlightened Christianity which had set the tone of polite religion for about a hundred years. Methodists, Jansenists, Pietists, Romantics and even some philosophers suggested that reason could not account for all aspects of human motivation, establish all forms of knowledge or offer unassailable safeguards of religious truth. The final hammer-blow which was to discredit the Enlightenment approach to Christianity, however, did not appear in the form of a religious pamphlet, a philosophical treatise or even an open-air sermon, but rather through the shocking events of the French Revolution.

Revolution and reaction

Nothing was ever to be quite the same after the French Revolution. Although it had begun, rather in the spirit of a seventeenth-century civil war, as a protest against 'tyrannical' excesses of the government of the day, it soon emerged as a movement whose avowed aim was to revolutionize European society. In the development from constitutional monarchy to republic, from civil war to Terror, and from the dictatorship of the Directorate to the empire of Napoleon I, virtually no aspect of the *ancien régime* was left untouched. Aspects of traditional society as fundamental as political organization, social place and attitudes towards the Church, each representing a pillar of the established order, had all been challenged or actually overturned. Even the familiar way of ordering time was suspended for several years when the Gregorian calendar (which marked time from Christ's birth) was replaced with a new revolutionary calendar which dated the years from 22 September 1792, the day of the Proclamation of the first French Republic. Not content with overthrowing the social and political order at home, the French Jacobins also exported their ideology abroad, giving confidence to would-be revolutionaries throughout the Continent and spreading Enlightenment propaganda with their armies.

The French Revolution brought to pass every possible nightmare which might have been dreamed up by even the most alarmist eighteenth-century conservative. Monasteries and convents had been forcibly suppressed and mock religious processions, complete with Republicans dressed up as monks or priests and leading mitred donkeys, had paraded through the streets.[21] Priests had been forced to swear oaths of loyalty to a puppet Church; those who refused had been imprisoned, exiled or executed. Hundreds of faithful lay Catholics had been drowned, stabbed, lynched or guillotined. A spurious Religion of Humanity, complete with blasphemous temples to Reason and Liberty, or to an abstracted Supreme Being, had, for a time, been put in the place of traditional Catholic worship. The revolutionary government had even gone so far as to substitute its own 'martyrs of liberty' for canonized saints, to replace the Christian Sabbath with the tenth day or *décadi*, and to set up 'rational' civil ceremonies of marriage and divorce which undermined the sacrament of holy matrimony. Even after the worst of the Terror and de-Christianization campaigns had subsided, and Napoleon I had made his formal reconciliation with the Catholic Church in the Concordat of 1801, the possibility of calm discussion between defenders of the Church and enlightened sceptics had been irrevocably damaged.[22]

The immediate reaction of governments throughout Europe after Napoleon's defeat by the allied British, Prussian and Belgian/Dutch forces at

Waterloo was to seek to reverse the spirit as well as many of the practical results of the Revolution. This policy, exemplified by the peace settlement drawn up at the Congress of Vienna in 1815, remained the favoured political solution until repeated revolutions, first in France in 1830 and then in the Kingdom of the Two Sicilies, France, Poland and most parts of the Habsburg Empire in 1848, gradually drove home the point that conservative reaction was not necessarily the best safeguard of stability. But in the decades immediately following the French defeat, when even moderate reform appeared inherently dangerous to many, ultra-conservatives seemed to be trying to return the whole of the Continent to some idealized point in time before the storming of the Bastille, while governments attempted to maintain the new *status quo* as established by the Vienna settlement.

It was to maintain a balance between what were seen as the twin extremes of ultra-reaction and revolutionary sentiment that monarchies explicitly linked to Churches were restored in 1815, the Catholic and Bourbon King Louis XVIII returning to the French throne and Pope Pius VII being restored as ruler of the Papal States. Both Pius VII and his Secretary of State, Ercole Consalvi, while anxious to undo the worst excesses of the French Revolution, were determined not to give in to the most reactionary elements in the papal court, the *zelanti*. Many monasteries and convents were restored and the particularly contentious Jesuit order was formally reconstituted. The notion that a firmer alliance between throne and altar would prevent the recurrence of revolution became a platitude among those who upheld the Vienna settlement, but seemed to would-be progressives to represent a regression from Enlightenment ideals of religious toleration and internationalism. In Prussia, the Reformed and Lutheran Churches were brought together to form a single Evangelical Church supported by the state in 1817; in Britain, which had escaped revolution though not war, pressure for reform, whether in Church or state, was delayed for years; when the first, politically unavoidable, concession came in the shape of the Catholic Emancipation Bill of 1829, it was taken as a reluctant ministerial decision to avert civil war in Ireland.

European clergymen and aristocrats who had fancied themselves advanced thinkers or had dabbled in Enlightenment philosophy until the shocks of the French regicide, the expulsion of the clergy or the reign of Terror, had grown disillusioned with progressivism. They now gave their wholehearted support to established Churches and royalist regimes as the bedrock of their security and the protectors of their deepest social, political and religious values. In this new climate, atheism and anticlericalism could no longer be seen as legitimate topics for learned debate or light-hearted repartee; they had become politically subversive as well as heretical. The revolutionary slogan of 'liberty, equality, fraternity', along with the related ideas that human beings are innately reasonable and entitled to natural rights, could hardly continue to resonate among the privileged as they had in the years of pre-revolutionary innocence. A safer course for the preservation of society now seemed to many to lie in the legal protection of a single state Church, in the curbing of the press, in the exclusion of social inferiors from the franchise and in the barring of religious dissenters from holding political office. Salutary doses of dogmatic theology (with the emphasis firmly placed on the unregenerate nature of fallen man and the Christian duty of civil obedience) seemed more appropriate lessons for society at large than the Utopian pipe dreams of the *philosophes*.

A comparable reaction to that which took place in the political sphere could be detected in the religious message which began to be preached in most European Churches and insisted upon by many ordinary Christians. In Northern Germany, the Protestant revivalist movement known as the Awakening rejected both the Enlightenment and the French Revolution as works of the devil; the message was equally well preached by Joseph de Maistre, whose *Considérations sur la France* (1796) made the same point on behalf of Catholic priests who had suffered exile, assault or imprisonment during the revolutionary years. Natural religion, dismissed by many as little more than an intellectual assent to an abstraction, hardly seemed an appropriate response to the realization of the depth of human sin and the miracle of Christ's redeeming sacrifice on the cross.

Among Protestants, early calls to the devout life included those of the German Evangelical Friedrich Schleiermacher, whose *Reden über die Religion (On Religion: Speeches to its Cultured Despisers)* (1799) called the genteel sophisticates of European society to 'turn back from those enlightened religions to the despised positive religions where everything real, powerful, and determinate appears'.[23] Rigorous Protestant groups like the Methodists in Britain, who had seemed beyond the pale of polite Georgian society, became more socially acceptable in the general climate of evangelical revival: indeed, some members of the new denomination thought too much social and theological radicalism was being compromised in the process of integration and left to form new Methodist communions – the Independents broke away in 1805, the Primitives in 1810 and the Bible Christians in 1815, partly because they wished to preserve such unconventional features of the early movement as an itinerant ministry, preaching by women and 'love-feasts' or open-air revivalist meetings.

The view that rational theology was inadequate to express the felt truths of revelation was equally widely popularized in Catholic circles. An early work by François René, Vicomte de Chateaubriand, entitled *Génie du Christianisme, ou beautés de la religion chrétienne (The Genius of Christianity or the Beauties of the Christian Religion)* (1802) presented the Catholic

Church as both the repository of Christian truth and the safeguard of European civilization. Félicité Robert de Lamennais's *Réflexions sur l'état de L'Église* (*Reflections on the State of the Church*) of 1808 warned that solitary contemplation could only lead to atheism. As he elaborated in his best-selling *Essai sur l'indifférence* (1817), the state could not be indifferent to religion, since it was only through obedience to the teaching of the Catholic Church that the individual could be saved from error, a lesson reiterated in de Maistre's pro-papal tract *Du Pape* (*On the Pope*) of 1819. In France, Italy, Southern Germany, Prussia and elsewhere, thousands of ordinary Catholics chose to pursue the religious life in one of many reopened or newly established religious houses: the number of nuns involved in teaching and charitable activities in France alone doubled during the period between the Restoration and the Revolution of 1830, rising from about 12,500 sisters in 1814 to 25,000 in 1830.

A new kind of Christian apologetic, born out of reaction to the Revolution, set the tone of conservative orthodoxy for most of the nineteenth century. This tone was at once more dogmatic and emotive than the 'rational religion' which had dominated the established Churches in the eighteenth century. It not only followed the Romantics in placing feeling above what was now discredited as cold logic, but also focused attention on the personal relationship believed to exist between God and the believer as an antidote to what was seen as the religious indifference of the previous age. Formerly unfashionable eighteenth-century works which stressed the importance of religious feelings, like the non-juror William Law's *Serious Call to a Devout and Holy Life* (1728), or which pointed to the futility of attempting to deduce revelation directly from nature, like Joseph Butler's *The Analogy of Religion, Natural and Revealed, to the Constitution and Course of Nature* (1736), were now revived by Protestants. The Anglican clergyman Charles Simeon's (1759–1836) emotive sermons on themes drawn from religious experience made a lasting impression on generations of ordinands at the University of Cambridge and helped to spread the new religious tone throughout the Church of England. In Germany, Schleiermacher and others advocated a return to the native Pietist tradition to renew faith since the 'proud islanders' of Britain, whose 'zeal for the sciences, for the wisdom of life and for holy freedom, is merely an empty sham battle', seemed nearly as morally bankrupt as the French, 'whose sight the lover of religion can hardly bear, for in every act, in every word, they all but trample on its most holy laws'.[24]

Protestant groups which proclaimed an evangelical message and acknowledged the validity of dramatic conversion experiences, sometimes accompanied by extraordinary manifestations of the Holy Spirit such as speaking in tongues or being miraculously healed, swelled in membership. Evangelically minded laymen within national Churches – like those in

Prussia and Germany who had absorbed Schleiermacher's message or the religiously earnest group who formed London's influential 'Clapham Sect' or 'Hackney Phalanx' — began to move from the periphery to the centre of respectable religion, influencing the characteristic expression of religiosity even in high society. As one English lady noted in 1828, 'the doctrines called Evangelical make all the noise now', or as Lord Melbourne complained to Queen Victoria in 1837, 'Nobody is gay now; they are so religious'.[25]

As enthusiastic reappropriations of religion became more socially acceptable in polite circles, pressures for reform came to be instinctively resisted by most established churchmen. It was a year after the passage of the Great Reform Bill of 1832 in England, for example, that a group of Anglican clergymen at the University of Oxford, alarmed by the prospect of governmental interference in Church affairs, began to launch a series of pamphlets on religious subjects known as 'Tracts for the Times'. The intention of these 'Tractarians', in what came to be known as the Oxford Movement, was to protect the Church of England from reform by affirming its claims to authority as given in the Thirty-Nine Articles, a series of doctrinal statements which constituted the post-Reformation theology of the Anglican Church. They soon discovered that the Thirty-Nine Articles were neither clearly Protestant nor formally Catholic, but offered what was in effect a compromise position between the twin extremes of sixteenth-century Calvinism and Catholicism. In seeking to make the articles appear internally consistent, the Tractarians increasingly stressed their Catholic rather than their Protestant legacy, thus reopening old theological controversies and alienating both evangelical and liberal groups within the established Church. The growing suspicion that the Tractarians were crypto-Catholics appeared to be borne out when one of the leaders of the Movement, John Henry Newman, published his celebrated *Tract 90* (1841), which argued that the Thirty-Nine Articles were 'patient of a Catholic interpretation'.[26] Newman's conversion to Catholicism in 1845, along with a number of other prominent Tractarians, shattered the confidence of the Oxford Movement and left the Church of England factionalized into mutually mistrustful Evangelical, Anglo-Catholic and liberal or Broad Church groupings whose public disputes helped to undermine the Church's credibility.

The validity of direct religious experience tempered by doctrinal authority was emphasized with as much fervour in Catholic as in Protestant circles. Claims of miracles, which in the pre-revolutionary period had been liable to be loudly ridiculed as relics of a superstitious past, were afterwards seen in a very different light. When a nun called Catherine Labouré had a vision of the Virgin Mary at her home in the rue du Bac in Paris, the very city which had launched the Revolution, she was neither pilloried in the press nor despised as the deluded tool of priests. Rather, the vision which she saw, of the Virgin shedding light on a penitent world above a caption reading 'O Mary, conceived without sin, pray for us who have recourse to thee', seemed an uncannily apposite call to repentance and prayer. The vision was engraved on a medal which was first struck in France in 1832 and widely distributed from 1834; many claimed mysterious healings, especially of cholera, from this 'miraculous medal'.

A second apparition of the Virgin Mary, to two young cowherds near the French Alpine village of La Salette in 1846, although afterwards discredited, helped to prepare popular opinion to accept a number of further nineteenth-century apparitions. The most enduring and renowned of these visions were those which took place at Lourdes in 1858; but over the course of the century Marian apparitions were claimed in virtually every country which boasted a Catholic population. Among the more celebrated were those which were said to have taken place at Pontmain (France) in 1870, Marpingen (Germany) and Pompeii (Italy) in 1876, Mettenbuch (Germany) in 1877, Knock (Ireland) in 1879 and Tilly-sur-Seulles (France) from 1896 to 1899. The pattern was to continue throughout the twentieth century, some of the more famous apparitions taking place at Fatima in Portugal in 1917, at Ezquioga in the Spanish Pyrenees in 1931, at Beauraing (1932) and Banneux (1933) in Belgium, at Pfaffenhofen in Germany in 1945–46 and at Medjugorje in Yugoslavia (Bosnia) in 1981.

In a climate in which direct religious experiences and even revelations were more readily accepted by the Church, there was at the same time an increasing stress on doctrine and authority. The need to place uncompromising doctrine at the centre of the Catholic faith seemed especially urgent, not only because of the traumatic experience of the French Revolution but also because of the more recent threats to faith of creeds like liberalism, socialism and nationalism as well as resurgent Protestantism. Catholics who were worried by liberal tendencies within the Church, or by the division of the Faith into national variants which could seem like so many potential heresies, urged Catholics throughout the world to seek direct guidance from the Vatican and to support the authority of the Pope against that of individual national bishops. This tendency to look to Rome for increased authority, known as 'Ultramontanism', gradually won over many Catholic adherents and became the dominant Catholic outlook of the age, although it also had influential critics within the Catholic world, particularly in the Liberal Catholic movements of the Netherlands, Austria, Germany and, to a lesser extent, Switzerland and England.

When the Vatican declared that an ecumenical or general council of all Catholic bishops would be held in Rome in 1869 and the issue was raised as to whether the doctrine of papal infallibility should be defined,

Ultramontanes, led by the French Catholic Louis Veuillot in his newspaper *L'Univers*, and Liberal Catholics, who found spokesmen in the German historian Ignaz von Döllinger and the English historian Lord Acton, became increasingly divided from one another. A propaganda war, which was of as much interest to liberal Protestants as to Catholics, raised the temperature of the debate over papal authority and ensured that reactions to the outcome of the council would be heated.

In the end, the First Vatican Council of 1869–70 decided, against the wishes of the liberal minority, to declare papal infallibility to be a tenet of the Catholic faith. Although the definition of papal infallibility which was eventually agreed circumscribed the Pope's powers, sharply distinguishing infallibility from inerrancy, and limiting *ex cathedra* statements to those concerned with faith and morals, it was nevertheless felt as a blow by Liberal Catholics, who wished for all authority to be retained by the council of bishops, or who believed any definition of papal infallibility to be 'inopportune' since it would play into the hands of anti-Catholic polemicists. Especially in non-Catholic circles, where papal infallibility in faith and morals was popularly understood to mean papal inerrancy in everything, the decrees of the First Vatican Council were seen to represent an aggressive aggrandizement of papal power. They therefore helped to galvanize support for Bismarck's *Kulturkampf*, a repressive campaign against indigenous Catholics in Germany, and to revive anti-Catholic feeling within the British Isles. A small number of Swiss, Dutch and German Catholics felt strongly enough about the outcome of the council to break away from the Catholic Church and join together in a body known as the 'Old Catholics'. Most Catholics, however, either approved of the definition (which won further sympathy after the loss of the Pope's temporal power in 1870 and particularly because of the anticlericalism of the recently unified Italian nation), or else resigned themselves to acceptance. Yet the presentation of the First Vatican Council as the symbolic triumph of a reactionary party over liberal opinion within the Catholic Church, which prompted outraged pamphlets by many non-Catholics (including the British Prime Minister William Gladstone, who published his *The Vatican Decrees in their Bearing on Civil Allegiance: A Political Expostulation* in 1874), was to affect perceptions of Catholicism by outsiders for at least the next hundred years.

It was the urgent desire to establish what were thought to be fundamental aspects of Catholicism in correct theological form which led the Catholic Church to pronounce on the question of the Immaculate Conception of the Virgin Mary in 1854 and to define the doctrine of papal infallibility in 1870. For the same reasons, it attempted to steer the spontaneous piety surrounding Marian apparitions into orthodox channels, eventually approving some pilgrimage sites, like Lourdes, while rejecting others, such as Marpingen. In what was seen by many to be a revival of Counter-Reformation intolerance, the Church, fuelled by the energetic proselytizing of the Ultramontanes, sought both to stimulate greater religious commitment and to stamp out practices which it believed to be unorthodox or 'pagan' superstitions.

Through the increased zeal of priests, missionaries and lay societies, and through the insistence of both popes and bishops that Catholics be educated in religious schools, married within the denomination and discouraged from mixing with those outside the community, the experience of being a Catholic in the nineteenth century became increasingly distinct from that of being another sort of Christian. In addition to the formal requirements of Catholics to hear weekly Mass and to take the sacrament at least once a year, new or newly revived lay societies called 'confraternities' or 'sodalities' urged their members to aspire to sanctity, imitating the holy poverty of St Francis of Assisi or preparing themselves for a 'Happy Death'. Revivalist missions held by Jesuits, Redemptorists, Passionists and others encouraged more frequent confessions and communions than had been standard in the eighteenth century, and recommended lay people to take part in exclusively Catholic devotions like the public recitation of the rosary, meditations on the Sacred Heart of Jesus or the thrice-daily recitation of the Marian prayer, the *Angelus*. Although missionary Catholicism resembled contemporary Evangelical Protestantism in its intensity and emotionalism, it also became more distinctively Catholic through its increased insistence upon doctrinal rigour and denominationally-specific devotional practices.

As Christians throughout Europe returned to what they believed to be the fundamentals of Christianity as transmitted by their own distinctive denominational traditions, they inevitably became less tolerant of the equally exclusive claims of others. Increasingly, religious identity came to be mingled not only with political affiliation but also with idealized forms of ethnic and national self-definitions. In Britain, periodic no-popery riots, particularly acute after the alarms caused by the Oxford Movement of the 1830s and formal re-establishment of the English Catholic ecclesiastical hierarchy (the so-called Papal Aggression) in 1850, expressed the popular sense that Protestantism was an integral part of national identity, a notion which continued to complicate the problems of the predominantly Catholic island of Ireland. In the kingdom of the Netherlands, the overwhelmingly Catholic territory of the south broke away in 1830 to form the independent nation of Belgium, which was to feel the stresses of political and ethnic divisions once religious solidarity began to fade in the twentieth century. In Germany, Bismarck's aim to unite the new nation under the banner of Protestantism in the *Kulturkampf* made as strong an initial appeal to agnostic liberals as it did to zealous Protestants, but was abandoned when Catholic support was needed to combat what was coming to be seen as a greater threat, that of socialism.

Over the course of the nineteenth century, Schleiermacher's contempt for what he had scorned as early as 1799 as the 'poorly stitched together fragments of metaphysics and morals that are called rational Christianity'[27] came to be shared by Protestants and Catholics of all nationalities. Emotive, Romanticized apprehensions of religious identity which replaced 'enlightened' Christianity tended of their nature to be more distinctive and exclusive. The eighteenth-century ideal of mutual tolerance, along with the willingness of many Christians to join across denominational and national boundaries in order to seek a universal 'natural' and 'rational' religion, appeared to be disintegrating politically and socially as well as theologically and devotionally.

Liberalism

However much some devout Christians, conservatives and political reactionaries may have wished to return to a golden pre-revolutionary age, it is never really possible to turn the clock back. One way of viewing the progress of institutional Churches and theological developments over the course of the nineteenth century would be to say that the immediate reaction to the French Revolution went too far, thus provoking a recurrence of the very dangers it sought to avoid. Attempts to protect the Church with the arm of the state may have been successful in reversing the effects of revolution in the short term, but inevitably led to the alienation of substantial numbers of ordinary people from both pillars of the old order. Among those most likely to nurture political grievances were religious minorities or dissenters from the Establishment (who resented having to support a Church to which they did not belong) and remaining sympathizers with the radical aims of the Revolution, who were unlikely to be impressed by a Church dominated by what they saw as unfair privilege. Those who disapproved of the governments who ruled them were equally likely to resent national Churches as symbols of the hated state. As conservative politics began to be associated with the faith of those who worshipped in state-protected Churches, and liberalism or radicalism with those who were excluded, or chose to exclude themselves, from establishment, religion as a whole became more politicized.

Much of what happened to the Christian Churches over the course of the nineteenth century was akin to what happened to the conservative or ultra-conservative governments with which they had come to be so closely associated. Just as the spectre of revolution haunted monarchical governments throughout the period, leading them to alternate between reaction and pragmatic concessions to liberal – but not republican or socialist – demands, so the national Churches feared widespread atheism and the wholesale rejection of Christian morality and practice as the religious counterpart to revolution and the natural accompaniment of political radicalism. When liberal or radical theological opinions were expressed by clergymen or laymen within established Churches, the choice presented to Church authorities seemed equally stark: to reject unorthodox opinion altogether, thus preserving ecclesiastical authority at the expense of Church membership, or else to concede the necessary minimum to conserve as much doctrine as could be reconciled with current intellectual fashion. The gradual polarization of opinion between the twin extremes of radicalism on the one hand and ultra-conservatism on the other, particularly after the European revolutions of 1848–51, was to make liberalism a pragmatic compromise for increasing numbers of ordinary Christians. It was to influence their understanding of the Faith as well as of contemporary politics.

Loosely known as 'liberals' because of their insistence on freedom from governmental constraints, self-conscious 'progressives' demanded religious toleration, constitutional government, elective assemblies, trial by jury, laissez-faire economic policies and the abolition of press censorship. Their unofficial manifesto was John Stuart Mill's *On Liberty* of 1859, which declared that 'the sole end where mankind is warranted . . . in interfering with the liberty of action of any of their number is self-protection'.[28] Apart from being recognizable through their opinions on a cluster of political and social issues, and by appearing to place their faith in an indefinable good called 'progress', liberals are not easily defined as a group. At times represented by political parties calling themselves Liberal and at others simply existing as a voice of protest in journals, newspapers and books, they continued to present intellectual and sometimes overtly political challenges to those whose dream was to maintain the post-revolutionary *status quo*.

Although political liberalism was associated in Catholic countries with anticlerical opinion, the philosophy of liberalism was, in theory at least, neither religious nor anti-religious, since it claimed only the right to freedom of expression for all – or most – shades of opinion, without seeking to define which opinions were best. In countries like England or the Netherlands, where there existed a wide variety of Christian denominations to choose from, many religious minorities, although instinctively conservative theologically, pressed for religious toleration as government policy in order to advance their own interests. In Britain, for example, it was pressure from religious dissenters, anxious to transmit what they saw as correct theological beliefs to future generations, which eventually forced the government to recognize nonconformist forms of marriage, to introduce civil registration of births and deaths, and to permit only non-sectarian religious teaching in state schools.

The liberal slogan of 'a free Church in a free state', which advocated a separation of powers on the American constitutional model, became a rallying cry not only for religious but also for irreligious thinkers, being championed by men as different in their aims and beliefs as Cavour and Montalembert. Particularly in countries where Church and state were so closely tied that the national Church appeared to represent little more than privilege, anti-state sentiment could easily turn to anti-Christian polemic, and political frustration go hand in hand with atheism. Radical opinion seemed most likely to flourish where there was least denominational choice, as in France, Prussia, Italy, Spain and Portugal, where those who became alienated from established Churches could find alternative ethical codes and teleologies in socialism, communism or scientific materialism, creeds which were to gain substantial numbers of converts over the course of the nineteenth and twentieth centuries.

Intended primarily as a safeguard of religious liberty and as a protection from the interference of state-supported Churches, liberal religious policies nevertheless had the effect of leaving room for the freedom to be irreligious as well as merely nonconformist. As Owen Chadwick has put it, 'from the moment that European opinion decided for toleration, it decided for an eventual free market in opinion'.[29] The very doctrine of pluralism held dangers for the unity of Christian faith, since the existence of alternative systems of thought tacitly challenged the notion that the truth was the same for all people and helped to erode both legal and social pressures to conform to any single variety of Christian practice. To conservative thinkers, liberalism could therefore appear as a sort of cancer within the Christian body politic which might, without warning, spread, undoing all the good work of the post-revolutionary settlement and ending in widespread atheism, social levelling and the collapse of the established order. It was to this perspective that Pope Pius IX appealed when, in 1864, his *Syllabus Errorum* (*Syllabus of Errors*) condemned as a false proposition the notion that the supreme pontiff ought to reconcile or adjust himself to 'progress, liberalism and modern civilization' and declared the teachings of socialism and communism to be injurious to Faith. It is a measure of the change which occurred in the dominant European climate of opinion between about 1830 and 1860, however, that Pope Pius IX's pronouncement, which would have seemed nothing more than a commonplace conservative response in the immediate aftermath of the French Revolution, made him a laughing-stock in the liberal heyday of the 1860s. A cartoon which appeared in the English magazine *Punch* in 1864, depicting the 'papal bull' as a deranged steer charging headlong into a brick wall, seemed to many to sum up the future of ultra-conservative opinion, whether in politics or in religion.

The central tenet of liberalism, that all opinions should be allowed to be freely voiced, had theological as well as political and economic implications. Liberals characteristically claimed for themselves the fearless and impartial examination of received wisdoms as part of a broadly progressive movement which held it as an axiom that open debate was the most effective means of arriving at the truth. Enlightenment debates over aspects of the Christian tradition which had seemed embarrassingly irrational to the eighteenth-century philosophers – especially scriptural and contemporary miracles – were soon reopened under the confident banner of nineteenth-century liberalism. Theologians at the University of Tübingen, led by F. C. Baur and deeply influenced by the historical philosophy of G. W. F. Hegel, began, as early as the 1830s and 1840s, to argue that several of the books of the New Testament were written too long after the events which they described to be of any historical value. According to this new school of biblical criticism, which came to be known as 'neology', the significance of the Christian story was increasingly seen as one of poetic myth or moral excellence rather than of literal truth.

Like so many other 'progressive' intellectual movements which shocked orthodox sensibilities, the primary aim of the Tübingen school was to establish Christianity on a more secure footing. The movement meant rather to prove the existence of the historical person of Jesus than to undermine the credibility of the Christian faith. But when David Friedrich Strauss, one of a number of Hegelians to emerge from the Tübingen school, published his *Leben Jesu* (*The Life of Jesus Critically Examined*) in 1835–36, the work appeared deeply damaging to Christianity. By attempting to detach the stories of miracles which had grown up around the historical person of Jesus, Strauss intended to prove beyond the shadow of a doubt that the carpenter's son had really lived and preached, and that he had been a moral and rational person, so that his Gospel might be approached with confidence. But by discrediting the supernatural and miraculous element in Scripture, Strauss's Jesus was presented as merely a man, not the son of God or 'Christ'. Such a fundamental critique of the central message of Christianity was hardly likely to be received with acclaim, and Strauss was immediately dismissed from his academic post as Professor of Theology at Tübingen. Although he never taught again, Strauss's work brought to the surface what was to become an intellectual problem for many in the second half of the nineteenth century, namely the apparent difficulties in reconciling scriptural revelation with what were coming to be thought of as the scientifically impeccable methods of historical investigation and textual criticism.

A more immediate difficulty for many believers from about the middle of the nineteenth century came in the form of moral revulsion from aspects of Christian teaching – like the small number of the elect and the existence of a material hell – which seemed to many to be unworthy of a compassionate God. Such criticisms voiced what was perhaps an inevitable reaction to the severity of much preaching during the evangelical and missionary revivals which followed the French Revolution, through sermons which could be terrifying in their evocations of hellfire and threats of eternal damnation. Children who had suffered acute terror of the Day of Judgement or who, like John Addington Symonds, were convinced that 'the devil lived near the doormat, in a dark corner by the passage of my father's bedroom',[30] were perhaps among the most vulnerable to losing their faith altogether when they outgrew their childish fears, although others adapted their understanding of Christianity as they grew up.

Christians who were prey to intellectual or moral doubts about Christianity were not likely to be reassured by the widespread publication, in the 1860s, of the notion that the New Testament might not offer a dependable account of the Incarnation. In England, long sheltered from Continental neology, a sensation was caused by the publication by a group of university dons and Anglican clergymen of a series of short articles known collectively as *Essays and Reviews* (1860), which presented French and German criticisms of sacred texts to a largely devout public. One of the most disturbing chapters was written by Benjamin Jowett, a celebrated figure in English society and Regius Professor of Greek at the University of Oxford (at that time primarily an institution for the training of Anglican clergymen), whose 'On the Interpretation of Scripture' suggested that the textual methods which were routinely applied to classical texts should also be used in interpreting the Bible. The imperative which Jowett delivered to theology students and laymen alike, and which he italicized for the greatest possible emphasis, was: '*Interpret the Scripture like any other book.*'[31] The publication by established churchmen and theologians of a work which appeared to discredit the literal truth of much of the New Testament launched decades of controversy over how the Bible ought to be approached and what the essence of its message was. The Church of England, which had already lost many of its more dogmatically-minded churchmen in the Oxford Movement and had alienated a good deal of Evangelical opinion through its increased Catholicity, gradually absorbed the central message of biblical criticism over the course of the nineteenth and twentieth centuries, though not without difficulty or heated controversy.[32]

It was in France that the most devastatingly reductionist of all approaches to Scripture was penned, by a respected theologian. Joseph Ernest Renan's *Vie de Jésus (The Life of Jesus)* (1863) attacked each of the New Testament miracles in turn, ignored the ethical content of the

Gospel message and left a portrait of Jesus as an amiable but otherwise undistinguished preacher from Galilee who was presented as entirely and exclusively human. Biblical criticism, combined with widespread unease about the validity of a good deal of traditional Christian preaching, confronted believers who wished to reconcile their faith with the new learning with two unpalatable choices: to cling to their creeds and doctrines despite liberal claims that these were unreliable, or else to accept the new 'scientific' theories and adjust the nature of their faith accordingly. The problem, which provoked crises of faith among many educated Christians, was to continue to disturb Christians of varying degrees of religious commitment throughout the twentieth century.

Science and religion

When people in the first half of the nineteenth century spoke of a conflict between 'science' and 'religion' the sciences which they had in mind were primarily the historical sciences. Attacks on the authority of Scripture which had been launched by Continental textual critics and Hegelian philosophers of the Tübingen school appeared at first to be easily rebutted by evidence drawn from the natural sciences. Liberal theologians who returned to the most sceptical eighteenth-century critiques of revealed religion to restate the terms of their faith were opposed by equally confident defenders of orthodoxy who revived Enlightenment arguments for God's reality from the evidence of the natural world. Neither side simply reproduced the old arguments verbatim, however, but reappropriated them, subtly altering their tone and emphasis.

In England, which had escaped revolution, and where enlightened defences of Christianity were therefore least disturbed, one of the most popular works of religious orthodoxy throughout the nineteenth century was William Paley's *Natural Theology; or Evidences of the Existence and Attributes of the Deity, collected from the Appearances of Nature*, which was first published in 1802. Paley's thesis, essentially nothing more than a restatement of the old argument from design, was that the intricate wonder of creation demonstrated the existence of a creator who was both intelligent and benign. 'Were there no example in the world, of contrivance, except that of the eye', he wrote, 'it would be alone sufficient to support the conclusion which we draw from it, as to the necessity of an intelligent Creator.'[33] Paley's argument, although presented in the language of scientific observation and structured by an overwhelming number of detailed examples of the marvels to be found in nature, did not offer a formal philosophical proof of God's existence, but rather a hymn of praise to the creator. That the eyes of mammals were formed in the darkness of the womb; that milk was produced by mothers at exactly the time that it was required; that the number of lactating teats in different animals corresponded to the number of offspring they would produce: all seemed to offer overwhelming evidence that every aspect of creation was perfectly attuned to needs which only an all-powerful creator could have anticipated. It was because Paley's statement of the case was redolent of piety, as well as appearing to be systematic, that it exercised such a spell over the English-speaking world: at one English university, *Natural Theology* remained required reading for all undergraduates well into the nineteenth century, and at another until the First World War.

Natural theology was influential not only in the biological sciences, but also among geologists, who argued that the study of the earth could support the factual accuracy of the Pentateuch (the first five books of the Old Testament whose authorship was traditionally ascribed to Moses). Such arguments were particularly influential in England, where the Evangelical revival had heightened the importance of Bible-reading for all sections of society, and the need to establish the objective truth of the Scriptures seemed correspondingly acute.

A bequest left to the Royal Society of London by the Earl of Bridgewater for £8,000 to be spent on the publication of a work which would demonstrate the 'power, wisdom and goodness of God, as manifested in the Creation'[34] led to a series of lectures by Anglican natural scientists, afterwards published as the Bridgewater treatises. Influential lectures by the geologist William Buckland argued that natural evidence supported Old Testament accounts of the creation and of Noah's flood. Some sleight of hand was needed to prove the consistency of Scripture with the evidence of fossil remains and the relics of dinosaurs: a number of scholars posited an enormous gap between the initial act of creation and the first day as given in Genesis, while others suggested that each 'day' referred to a geological age, rather than to a mere twenty-four hours. Yet Buckland felt able to conclude cautiously in his inaugural lecture as Reader in Geology at the University of Oxford, published a year later as *Vindiciae Geologicae; or the Connexion of Geology with Religion Explained* (1820), that 'it may be safely affirmed, that no Geological theory has yet been proposed, which is not less reconcilable to ascertained facts and conflicting phenomena, than to the Mosaic history'.[35]

With hindsight, what seems most important about the Bridgewater treatises is not so much the detail of their theses, but rather that they unwittingly helped to shift the grounds for faith from the evidence of revelation to that of scientific theory. For all their pious intent, attempts to support Christianity by means of the natural sciences set the stage for religion to be put on the defensive, since the corollary of allowing theology to be based on up-to-date theory was to make rational arguments for faith vulnerable to changing scientific fashions.

The celebrated confrontation between Science and Religion of the middle and late nineteenth century has long been associated with the publication of Charles Darwin's *On the Origin of Species by Means of Natural Selection* in 1859, which effectively demolished the common-sense appeal of natural theology by offering a rival, religiously agnostic, model to account for the variety of species to be found in nature. Darwin's arguments, which were deeply damaging to the beliefs of biblical literalists as well as natural theologians, created serious intellectual difficulties for a number of Protestant groups, particularly those in the English-speaking world who relied on Paley's works or who stressed biblical inerrancy. Darwinian notions of evolutionary development were much more easily reconciled with Faith, both in 1859 and afterwards, in a number of other Christian traditions. The notion, particularly well developed in the Catholic Church, that Christian doctrine had not been delivered all at once, but gradually became manifest over time (a view which Newman had found so compelling that writing his *Essay on the Development of Christian Doctrine* in 1845 helped to convince him to become a Catholic) allowed Darwin's ideas to be accommodated much more easily by some scientists, like the Catholic St George Mivart or the Unitarian William Carpenter, who, although they found fault with Darwin's precise mechanisms for natural selection, did not see any difficulty to Faith in accepting the notion of the evolution of species. Liberal Protestants, increasingly inclined to defend the spirit rather than the letter of biblical texts, were similarly cushioned from the blow.

It was Darwin's *The Descent of Man* (1871), which explicitly included mankind in the evolutionary scheme and could be seen as raising doubts about the reality of the soul and the origins of human conscience, which troubled most Christians and took longest to be absorbed. It was partly because doubts about traditional Christian faith and ethics had been raised by *The Descent of Man* that spiritualism (and, later, its more academically respectable cousin psychical research), both of which aimed to prove the existence of the soul empirically, became so widespread throughout Europe in the 1860s and 1870s, being treated as a serious object of intellectual enquiry by, among others, Arthur Conan Doyle (the creator of Sherlock Holmes) and Alfred Russel Wallace, the co-discoverer of Darwin's evolutionary theories.

In retrospect, Darwin's most famous work seems less significant for its thesis than for the symbolic importance which was attributed to it in what gradually came to be seen as an antithesis between something loosely called 'religion' and something equally loosely termed 'science'. Despite the continued popularity of Whiggish accounts of the history of science, which see modern developments as a series of inspired discoveries by intellectual heroes like Galileo, Giordano Bruno, Isaac Newton, Charles Darwin, Albert Einstein and others, a number of recent historians have pointed to the absurdity of maintaining that 'revolutions' in scientific thinking could ever emerge out of an intellectual vacuum or come to be widely accepted in an intractably hostile environment. The criticism certainly appears to be borne out in the case of Darwin, whose theories, although they effectively undermined one particularly fashionable reconciliation of natural with revealed evidences for God, did not come out of nowhere, nor was their supposed incompatibility with Faith broadcast without ulterior motives.

The components which made up Darwin's argument for the evolution of species were not, as he admitted with characteristic candour, original: theories of evolution of different kinds had been put forward by, among others, his own grandfather (Erasmus Darwin), Jean-Baptiste Lamarck and Robert Chambers; even natural theologians like William Buckland, Adam Sedgwick and William Whewell had advanced the notion of 'progressive creation' to account for the apparent extinction and renewal of some species. The work of Charles Lyell, a personal friend as well as a scientific colleague, had established the scale of geological time required for Darwin's modification of species, and a theoretical economist, Thomas Malthus, supplied the mechanism by which favourable variations might be preserved and unfavourable ones lost.[36] But although Darwin admitted his intellectual debts and acknowledged frankly that 'many and grave objections' could be advanced against his 'theory of descent with modification through natural selection',[37] his recombination of familiar elements led to a theory which was at once as evocative as Paley's while at the same time being more economical, since it could account for apparently useless variations and solve the moral problem of suffering in the world without having recourse to divine agency.

Darwin, who had once intended to become a clergyman and was an admirer of Paley's rhetorical methods as well as his meticulous observational powers, used both to good effect in the *Origin of Species*, which offered a literary, as well as a scientific, *tour de force*. Although he sometimes liked to think that he worked on 'true Baconian principles', following the evidence wherever it might lead, he readily acknowledged that the moment of theoretical inspiration came from reading Thomas Malthus's *An Essay on the Principle of Population as it Affects the Future Improvement of Society* (1798) some twenty years before the publication of his thesis. It was while reading Malthus, which was also the trigger for Alfred Russel Wallace, that the thought struck him that the extraordinary variety in nature need not have come about through the ingenuity of an infinitely imaginative God. Rather, the same phenomena could be explained in purely natural terms by positing the idea that the world was characterized by a Malthusian struggle for existence in which only those specimens which were best adapted to changing environments would live to replicate themselves and so, by gradual modifications, evolve into separate species.

For all its intrinsic merits, it seems unlikely that Darwin's *Origin of Species*, which was, after all, a hypothesis about the past rather than a law which could ever be demonstrated experimentally, would have created the sensation which it eventually did had it not been seized upon by anticlerical polemicists and presented to an audience already made uneasy by the results of biblical criticism. When Darwin's theory was first presented to scientists at London's Linnean Society in a joint paper with Alfred Russel Wallace (who, although ready to publish first, was generous enough to share the credit with Darwin), it seemed of so little consequence that the Society concluded its annual report with the sad reflection that 1858 had not been a year 'marked by any of those striking discoveries which at once revolutionize, so to speak, the department of science on which they bear'.[38] It was not until the same theories were presented in the *Origin of Species*, which was published in book form in 1859, that Darwin's rhetorically powerful argument was made easily accessible to non-scientists. More important for its sales was the furore surrounding the publication of *Essays and Reviews* a few months later, which brought out the implications of Darwin's work for natural theologians, whose arguments for purposeful design appeared to be undermined by its central thesis, and for biblical literalists, whose acceptance that all species had been created in the first week described in Genesis was flatly contradicted. Had Darwin's work not become embroiled in disputes between those who wished to promote or to denounce theological liberalism it might never have come to be known outside of a narrow circle of natural scientists.

History textbooks throughout the twentieth century have perpetuated the idea that Darwin's arguments, usually presented as the 'discovery' of an objective truth rather than the presentation of a scientific hypothesis, dealt an immediate blow to the credibility of the Christian Churches. The symbolic moment of the supposed triumph of progressive science over backward religion is invariably cited as having taken place at a meeting of the British Association for the Advancement of Science which was held in Oxford in 1860. This famous meeting, at which papers by the natural scientist Charles Daubeny 'On the Final Causes of the Sexuality of Plants, with Particular Reference to Mr. Darwin's work on the *Origin of Species*' and by the chemist John William Draper on the 'Intellectual Development of Europe considered with Reference to the Views of Mr. Darwin' were read, was important because it allowed Darwin's theories to be presented to a mixed audience of theologians and scientists. Since Darwin was too ill to attend, an aspiring scientist called Thomas Huxley defended his views, while attacks upon them were led by a more established figure, the natural scientist Samuel Wilberforce. Because T. H. Huxley (who in 1869 coined the term 'agnostic' to describe his intellectual position) was already an avowed religious sceptic and Samuel Wilberforce was an Anglican bishop, it was easy for the discussion to be presented afterwards as a symbolic battle between obscurantist religion and objective science.[39] The clinching moment of the debate was supposed to have come when Wilberforce asked Huxley whether he would claim an ape for his ancestor, at which Huxley was reported to have whispered 'the Lord hath delivered him into my hands!' before retorting, to tumultuous applause, that he would prefer to be descended from an ape than from a bishop who used his talents and influence to obscure the truth.[40]

Although something approximating to the notorious exchange between Wilberforce and Huxley undoubtedly occurred, neither its symbolic importance nor the outcome of the debate seemed so clear-cut at the time. Eyewitnesses, none of whom could recall the precise wording of the exchange, evidently understood the subject under discussion to be the scientific validity of Darwin's theories, not their theological implications. Furthermore, if anyone emerged as the clear 'winner' of the debate, it was Wilberforce rather than Huxley: the earliest known report of the meeting concluded that 'the most eminent naturalists assembled at Oxford' supported Wilberforce, while most members of the audience bestowed 'bitter looks of hatred' on Huxley who, they felt, had treated the bishop 'abominably'.[41] Even Darwin admitted that the review of the *Origin of Species* which Wilberforce afterwards published 'pick[ed] out with skill all the most conjectural parts, and br[ought] forward well all the difficulties' of his argument.[42] Nor did the pro-Darwinian minority have better scientific credentials than the anti-Darwinians: perhaps the most prominent member to be convinced by Huxley was the liberal theologian and contributor to *Essays and Reviews*, Frederick Temple.

Although there seems little historical evidence to support the claim of T. H. Huxley's son Leonard (in 1903) that the Oxford debate represented 'not merely the contradiction of one anatomist by another, but the open clash between Science and the Church',[43] this is the version of the debate which has passed into modern folklore. Reasons for later interpretations of the significance of the Oxford debate seem to have had less to do with Darwin's science and the Churches' immediate reactions to it than with the anticlerical position of some who found his theories potentially congenial to their cause. The paper which Draper presented to the same meeting of the Association, for example, argued that 'science' was the progressive force which had guided Western civilization forward, despite the repeated opposition of reactionary Churches. The moral was one which advocates of liberalism were quick to seize. Subsequent works like Draper's highly influential *History of the Intellectual Development of Europe* (1862) and *History of the Conflict between Religion and Science* (1875) further expanded on what was to become a familiar model of the supposed 'warfare' between science and religion, one in which Darwin began to be presented as a martyr to scientific truth.

The notion that the natural sciences – now significantly called Science – held the key to certain knowledge and human progress was to be aggressively publicized in the latter years of the nineteenth century and broadly accepted by most Europeans over the course of the twentieth. As anticlericals increasingly appealed not only to the familiar Enlightenment rallying cries of 'rationality' and 'progress' to defend their positions, but to something like scientific determinism as the final arbiter of intellectual and spiritual disagreements, Science began to be described in a semi-mystical light and to be championed by anticlerical liberals with all the fervour of a new religion. John Tyndall, who declared prophetically at a meeting of the British Association held at Belfast in 1874 that Science had 'already to some extent leavened the world', and would continue to 'leaven it more and more',[44] was matched in his confidence by T. H. Huxley, whose aptly named *Lay Sermons* preached liberalism, Darwinism and scientific progressivism to packed halls throughout the British Isles. In Germany, racist interpretations of Darwinism (like those which were propounded in the English-speaking world by Herbert Spencer) were preached with particular fervour by Ernst Haeckel; in France, where the *Origin of Species* had been translated into French by Clemence Royer in 1862, Darwinism was taken up by the Third Republic to justify the purging of 'clerical' opinion from universities and to establish the importance of 'modern' and 'scientific' education for the nation.

The Enlightenment, which had been disparaged for nearly a century as the quintessential age of shallow thinking and superficial understandings of religious truth, now began to be reclaimed by historians, scientists and politicians alike as an important chapter in the steady march of progress from the superstitions of a so-called 'primitive' age towards the bright future of scientific knowledge and technological advancement. This new scientist creed, which drew upon the positivist arguments of Auguste Comte that all knowledge passed though primitive stages of theological and metaphysical understandings before finally arriving at scientific or 'positive' knowledge, was deeply flattering to those who believed that nineteenth-century knowledge surpassed that of all other historical periods. It also offered a convenient anticlerical weapon with which to justify the increasing dominance of a liberal intellectual elite. That Darwin's theories were valued more for what they seemed to claim for modern Western civilization than for their contribution to biology seems evident from the bewildering array of arguments which they were afterwards claimed to support. Marxism, laissez-faire capitalism, racist theories or 'social Darwinism' and nationalism, among many other (often mutually exclusive) philosophies, all came to be justified through their supposed promotion of the 'survival of the fittest'. As well as appearing to lend support to a wide variety of nineteenth- and twentieth-century ideologies, the popular notion that Darwin had 'disproved the Bible' was to convince many that the authority of something called 'Science' was weightier than the authority of something called 'Religion'.

Pluralism and diffusion

Widespread doubts as to the possibility of a secure future for Christian society began to be expressed, from about the 1880s, in ways which were to become all too familiar in the twentieth century. Clergymen and other committed Christians complained that fewer people, especially middle-class men and working people of both sexes, were turning up for weekly Sunday services. The poor were said to be shockingly ignorant of Christian doctrine and often no better than pagans in their attachment to super-stitious beliefs and practices. The fear that they might be seduced away from the Faith by the secular creeds of socialism, materialism and communism seemed increasingly acute. The preaching of the main Churches was thought by some to be doctrinally suspect, and the atmosphere of a Sunday less reverent. Established Churches, faced with intense interdenominational competition as well as rival forms of belief, appeared to be struggling harder to retain the loyalty of their nominal members, many of whom had lost the habit of regular Church attendance and seemed to prefer to spend their leisure hours in cafés, music halls and theatres, or else taking part in newly popular sports like football, cricket or bicycling. Agnostic, materialist and positivist opinions, which circu-lated freely in newspapers, learned journals, novels and political pam-phlets, seemed to be espoused by people in all walks of life, from the proletarian to the bourgeois, and were said to be rife in many European universities.

In addition to what seemed to many to be the secularizing effects of modern, and particularly urban, life, the institutional Churches appeared to be becoming politically marginal. In Italy, Catholic welfare organiza-tions had been secularized; in France, Republicans had restored divorce to the civil code, allowed work on Sundays, removed prayers from the opening of national assemblies and insisted that priests be considered eligible for military service. The Anglican Church, although still estab-lished in England, had lost its status in Ireland and its practical monopoly in Wales and, despite valiant attempts to reach the slums of the great industrial cities, appeared to leave most working people cold. In Germany, the intransigence of a majority of firmly established evangelical *Landeskirchen* towards adapting to theological liberalism and even to moderate forms of socialism left them open to the charge of representing little more than an ideology for conservatives.

The sense that society was becoming more secular was not restricted to social and political developments. The work of scholars in a number of academic disciplines appeared to cast doubt on the exclusivity and objectivity of the Christian message by suggesting that religions were merely social and cultural artefacts and therefore legitimate subjects for scrutiny by 'social scientists'. Almost no one went as far as Friedrich Nietzsche, retired as professor in philology at Basel, who argued in *On the Genealogy of Morals* (1887) that the so-called Christian virtues were not only historically conditioned but motivated by the resentment of the weak for the strong. But arguments which stressed the contingency of religious beliefs were being voiced in a number of newly confident disciplines from about the turn of the century.

The conclusions of early anthropologists like E. B. Tylor and James Frazer, who attempted to account for the existence of common features in all religions, could be taken to imply that the Christian faith was nothing more than an evolved form of superstitious magic. Frazer's immensely influential *The Golden Bough: A Study in Magic and Religion* (1890), like Emile Durkheim's sociological study of Aboriginal totemism in *Les formes élémentaires de la vie religieuse* (*Elementary Forms of the Religious Life*) (1912), treated the sacred beliefs of 'primitive' people with an apparent reductionism which was soon to be applied to the origins of Christian beliefs as well. The works of the linguist Max Müller, who did more than anyone to present the sacred texts of Buddhism and Hinduism to the educated European public, claimed that religion and morality, which were universal in all cultures, represented only a stage in societal development. The ultimate end of advanced civilizations, he argued, lay beyond religion in the realm of 'philosophy, or a critique of the powers of reason in their legitimate working on the data of experience'.[45]

Works which seemed to imply that religious faith represented little more than an evolutionary stage, and which invited unflattering parallels to be drawn between the supernatural beliefs of 'savages' and those of European Christians, were joined by works which stressed the subjectivity of religious experience. In a series of lectures delivered at the University of Edinburgh and afterwards published as *The Varieties of Religious Experience* (1902), the American psychologist William James stressed the value of 'healthy-minded' religious approaches in promoting individual fulfilment, but explicitly excluded the question of whether such beliefs were true as unverifiable and, by implication, irrelevant. The theories of the Viennese physician Sigmund Freud, whose investigations into hysteria led him to conclude that psychological disturbances or 'neuroses' were the result of the repression of the libido by the ego, had serious implications for the Christian notion of sin as well as for traditional conceptions of the will. Freud's *Totem and Taboo* of 1912–13, which sought to account for the development of primitive religious beliefs in psychoanalytic terms, seemed to many to hold equally reductionist implications for more 'developed' faiths. While relatively few works of the late nineteenth and early twentieth centuries directly challenged the truth of Christianity or spoke of its doctrines with anything less than respect, readers might have been forgiven for imagining that, once methodologically rigorous disciplines had accounted for the development of world religions and established the unconscious motivations of believers, there might be nothing left of Faith to be explained.

As public opinion appeared to be growing more secular, many Churches tried hard to adapt to new social and intellectual trends, while others continued in the old ways, gradually reconciling themselves to the fact of smaller, although not necessarily less fervent, congregations. Since denominations could no longer rely on the pressure of social convention to fill their Churches, or on the state wholeheartedly to support their activities, many began to sponsor more leisure outings, social clubs and sporting events to compete with secular alternatives. They also began to advertise their services more aggressively, and to target groups whose members seemed most alienated from the institutional Churches: the young, men of all social classes and working people. This was the quintessential age of boys' clubs, swimming baths, walking holidays, 'socials' and youth movements, not only in the secular but also in the Christian world.

To reach the apparently indifferent, and sometimes hostile, working classes, many Churches also made a concerted effort to accommodate criticisms offered by socialism into their presentations of the Gospel message. A number of priests and religious went to live with the poor in industrial slums, sharing their hardships as they tried to follow the example of Christ; a group in the Church of England became convinced that the only solution to the social injustices of modern society lay in the creed of 'Christian Socialism'; some Catholics, encouraged by papal social teaching in Leo XIII's encyclical *Rerum Novarum* (1891), helped to set up Catholic trade unions among French, Dutch and Belgian factory workers, or saw a future in the spread of 'Christian Democracy'. A number of attempts to find Christian alternatives to secular forms of socialism, most of which were revived in the period between the Bolshevik revolution and the Second World War, laid the foundations for the rise of the Labour party in Britain and the growth of Christian Democratic parties throughout the continent of Europe. But although Christian answers to the social questions of the day were to have a deep influence on post-war movements towards European unity, and despite the fact that a substantial proportion of middle-class Protestants and Catholics continued to practise their faith, social groups and geographical areas which had become most 'de-Christianized' over the course of the nineteenth century remained on the whole unresponsive to calls to return to the fold.

Those who tried to make Christianity more obviously relevant to the 'modern' world by reconciling traditional Christian teaching with fashionable intellectual currents of the day appear to have run into similar difficulties. Although Liberals and Socialists tended to think of the Churches as obscurantist, many Christian theologians felt perfectly able to integrate the results of historical and biblical criticism, scientific and social evolutionary theories, and even socialist and ethical critiques, into their understanding of the Faith. The Protestant patristic scholar Adolf Harnack, for example, argued in his *Lehrbuch der Dogmengeschichte* (*History of Dogma*) (1886–89) that the Gospels offered, not metaphysics, but a system of ethics which clearly endorsed the notion of universal human brotherhood. The French Catholic Alfred Loisy agreed in his *L'Évangile et l'Église* (*The Gospel and the Church*) (1902), that Christ had neither founded the Christian Church nor instituted its sacraments, but suggested that this posed no obstacle to faith in the Catholic Church, whose doctrines and sacraments had evolved over time under the protective influence of the Holy Spirit. Encouraged by Pope Leo XIII's encyclical *Providentissimus Deus* (1893), which stressed the importance of biblical study for Catholics, Alfred Loisy, Maurice Blondel, Friedrich von Hügel, George Tyrrell and other prominent priests and laymen undertook to bring Catholic understandings up to date by incorporating some of the most radical conclusions of biblical criticism. Since their work ended by calling into question almost every aspect of traditional Catholic teaching, from the inspiration of the Bible to Church doctrine and authority, it is not altogether surprising that the movement, which was officially described as 'the synthesis of all the heresies', was eventually condemned as 'Modernism' by Pius X in the decree *Lamentabili* (3 July 1907) and the encyclical *Pascendi* (8 September 1907). The Anglican authors of a collection of essays entitled *Lux Mundi* (1889), while less radical than the Modernists in their claims, caused similar controversy within the Church of England when they applied 'higher criticism' to biblical texts and adopted popular theories of evolution and 'social Christian' ethics, even though they maintained a firm insistence on the literalness of the Incarnation and in the reality of the supernatural.

Although a number of believing Christians felt able to incorporate late nineteenth- and early twentieth-century criticisms of Christianity into their understandings of it, others felt that the essence of the Faith was being undermined in the process. As increasing numbers of Christians attempted to reconcile traditional theology with liberalism, biblical authority with scientism, natural ethics with Christian morality, sin with Freudian psychology and the exclusivity of Christianity with the relativism of the new social sciences, they were apt to become idiosyncratic in the blend of beliefs which constituted their understanding of the Faith. The philosopher Bertrand Russell, when sent to gaol for promoting conscientious objection to the First World War, remembered how the prison warder 'asked my religion, and I replied "agnostic". He asked how to spell it, and remarked with a sigh: "Well, there are many religions, but I suppose they all worship the same God." '[46] Even anticlericals could not agree as to what Christianity, as opposed to the teaching of the Churches, meant, some seeing it as an endorsement and others as an obstacle to their policies. When Eleanor Marx, the daughter of Karl Marx, explained to Beatrice Potter (later Beatrice Webb) that the working classes must rid themselves of religion since it was 'an immoral illusion', the prominent English Fabian could only reflect that it seemed pointless 'to argue with one who had no idea of the beauty of the Christian religion and read the gospels as the gospel of damnation'.[47]

The sense that pluralism was leading modern society into a Babel of conflicting opinions in which no moral truth was safe and the very fabric of society might come apart, was an acute worry for many Christians and non-Christians alike. It was this widespread mood of alienation and alarm which helped to win sympathy for the great collectivist movements of the 1930s which sought to build a better world, among them Fascism and Communism. The Vatican's willingness to negotiate with Mussolini in the 1920s and even, albeit more reluctantly, in the 1930s, like the initial welcome given to the National Socialists by most German clergy (including Pastor Martin Niemöller, who was later sent to a concentration camp for his outspoken opposition to Nazism), reflected the feeling among many Christians that Communism was the greatest contemporary danger both to faith and to the security of the Christian Churches. The course of the Spanish Civil War (1936–39), whose widely publicized clerical and anticlerical atrocities helped to further polarize political opinion throughout Europe, was particularly important in allying virtually all Christian Churches, and many, perhaps even most, individual Christians, with the political Right in the years leading up to the Second World War.

When Hitler came to power in 1933, over half the German Protestant *Landeskirchen* chose to adopt the theological synthesis of Nazism and Christianity put forward by the so-called *Deutsche Christen* (German Christians). This government-supported faction within the Protestant

Churches, whose stated aim was to 'complete' the Lutheran Reformation, was from the beginning accompanied by suggestions for radical reforms, including the elimination of the Old Testament, the teaching of St Paul and the doctrines of St Augustine as despised 'Jewish' elements within Christianity. Although a few German clergymen, like the Catholic Cardinal Faulhaber and the Protestant theologian Karl Barth (1886–1968), preached against the Nazis from the first, the overwhelming majority at the very least tolerated a party implacably opposed to Communism and dedicated to restoring the economy and standing of the German nation, while many others gave the Third Reich their enthusiastic support. When, in 1933, the German Christians attempted to introduce the 'Aryan paragraph' to exclude pastors of Jewish descent from the Prussian Church, Niemöller, sensing danger, called together a Pastors' Emergency League of the 'Confessional' or 'Confessing' Church (*Bekenntnis-Kirche* or *Bekennende Kirche*), a body consisting of German Protestants who were worried by the interference of the government in Church affairs. The neo-pagan and Erastian elements of German Christian theology became more obvious when the Evangelical Youth was incorporated into the *Hitler Jugend* (Hitler Youth) in 1934, and Niemöller's 'Confessional Christians' met for their first synod at Barmen in 1934, where they issued a theological declaration, largely inspired by the work of Karl Barth, which stressed the importance of the freedom of the Gospel and of the grace of God. After war broke out, and the Confessing Church was forced underground, a few notable Christian leaders in Germany, in particular Dietrich Bonhoeffer (1906–45), made clear their absolute opposition to the Nazi regime. Bonhoeffer's attempts to mediate between anti-Nazi Germans and the British government through his friend George Bell, the Anglican Bishop of Chichester, were as unsuccessful as Bell's own attempts to persuade the British government to stop bombing German civilians. After being imprisoned in Buchenwald in 1943, Bonhoeffer was eventually hanged by the Gestapo at Flossenbürg in 1945.

The full horror of Nazi brutality made itself plain over the course of the war, not only to the Allied forces, but also to many German citizens – not least those who were the targets of its campaigns for systematic extermination, most notably Jews and people of partly Jewish descent, but also gypsies, the handicapped, homosexuals, Communists, anarchists and other groups deemed 'undesirable'. After the Holocaust, programmes of enforced euthanasia and the imprisonment of hundreds of thousands of Christians in German-occupied territories, it was less easy to defend the notion that Christian values could ever be safe in the hands of autocratic governments, however much they claimed to uphold established Churches. The lesson was one which was also drawn from the widespread publicity given to the Stalinist purges of the 1930s and the annexation of virtually all of the countries of Eastern Europe at the end of the Second World War by the 'godless' Soviet Union.

After Fascism was widely discredited by the experience of German Nazism, and Communism called into question for many by the example of Marxism-Leninism as practised in the Soviet Union and its satellites, secular socialism and Christian democracy were left as the dominant political ideologies of Western Europe. The belief that only political democracies could safeguard liberty and that pluralism was the mark of any civilized society, an opinion which had come to be shared by believers as well as unbelievers, was enshrined in declarations of human rights, in charters which endorsed the ideal of 'united nations' and in treaties which sought the integration of Europe. But because liberal democracies held it as an axiom that all forms of belief must be treated in law as if they were equally valid, Christian faith was increasingly left to fend for itself as one intellectual option among many alternatives.

Partly because committed Christians appeared to be in a shrinking minority, and partly because divisions among Christians had always been felt as a scandal, ecumenical movements, whose origins lay in the late nineteenth and early twentieth centuries, began to gather momentum throughout the inter-war period. Protestant groups, which were particularly fragmented, had already begun to form coalitions in the nineteenth century through joint missionary endeavours overseas such as those sponsored by numerous interdenominational Bible societies and which developed into organizations like the International Missionary Council (1910). The first Universal Christian Conference on 'Life and Work' (1925), which aimed to promote Christian values in political, economic and social life, was soon matched by a World Conference on 'Faith and Order' (1927), which aimed to pursue the goal of Christian unity through theological rapprochements. At conferences held in Edinburgh and Oxford in 1937, the 'Faith and Order' and 'Life and Work' movements agreed to join together in a single World Council of Churches, whose constitution was drafted in 1938, but only put into practice in 1948, as part of a popular movement of the revival of Christian values which followed the Second World War.

That all Christian Churches would immediately unite after four centuries of mutual hostility was never very likely. Increased tolerance and greater sympathy among Protestants and Catholics as they emerged from their respective denominational 'ghettos' was nevertheless a marked development of the second half of the twentieth century. The Catholic Church, which had seemed most alien to the other Christian denominations through its claims to special authority and its separate liturgical language, took steps to modernize its teaching, liturgy and organization at the Second Vatican Council (1962–65). It also began its cautious approach to the World Council of Churches, first through a Joint Working Group, established in 1965 and then, in 1968, by accepting full membership in the Faith and Order Commission. The increasing sense that traditionalist Christians had much in common with each other was made particularly acute by the social and sexual revolutions of the 1960s and 1970s, which tended to divide Christians from non-Christians over especially contentious ethical issues like divorce, homosexuality and abortion, although the equally explosive moral and theological questions surrounding birth control and the role of women in both Church and society tended to arouse as much controversy within Christian denominations.

Despite the confident predictions of many liberals of the 1960s and 1970s that Christianity, evidently in serious decline, would soon be as defunct as the religion of the Ancient Greeks, Western Europe not only continued to contain many believing Christians but also remained at least latently Christian in many other respects. Not only did most people continue to believe in God (however vaguely and sometimes heretically defined), but many non-believers or semi-believers continued to wish to marry in church, to have their children baptized and to feel that a church burial was somehow more reverent than a secular cremation. Even pervasive unofficial non-Christian creeds, like socialism, popular psychology and scientism, bore a distinct family resemblance to traditional Christianity in their moral earnestness, their claims to universality and their hopes for human redemption. As the familiar joke had it, even atheists could be clearly divided into Protestant atheists and Catholic atheists.

From about the 1980s, as socialist movements appeared to be losing their self-confidence, and the progressivist optimism associated with technological, medical and material advances of the long post-war economic boom – and particularly the 1960s – seemed to be running out of steam, there were also distinct signs of Christian revival. These could be sensed in a number of ways: in the spread of charismatic movements among the young, both Protestant and Catholic; in the sales of popular theological works like those of best-selling authors C. S. Lewis and Pierre Teilhard de Chardin; in at least occasionally less hostile appraisals of the Churches in the media; and in widespread admiration for at least a few contemporary religious figures, among them Mother Teresa of Calcutta and Archbishop Desmond Tutu of South Africa. At the same time, publicity given in the West to Liberation Theology helped to remove the stigma of right-wing politics with which the Christian Churches had come to be associated by the political Left.

For Christians who remained fully committed to their faith at the end of the twentieth century, the sea change which had taken place throughout Western Europe in the role of the institutional Churches, in theological developments and above all in the formation of an instinctively sceptical and relativist outlook, had a number of important effects. Thoughtful

Christians, like thoughtful agnostics, could no longer unquestioningly accept the faith, or anti-faith, of their parents. As C. S. Lewis mused in the 1940s, 'The ancient man approached God (or even the gods) as the accused person approaches his judge'. In modern times, however, 'the roles are reversed. He is the judge: God is in the dock. He is quite a kindly judge: if God should have a reasonable defence for being the god who permits war, poverty and disease, he is ready to listen to it. The trial may even end in God's acquittal. But the important thing is that man is on the bench and God is in the dock.'[48]

By the end of the twentieth century, the primacy of individual conscience had been raised to a point where it appeared to overshadow the older virtue of obedience to Church teaching. The onus of proof which had once rested on the religious sceptic now seemed to lie with the conservative believer. But although this change of emphasis made Christians far more vulnerable to shifts in prevailing secular opinion, it also meant that Faith, once accepted or painfully reappropriated, was arguably more likely to last. It seems absurd to presume that there could ever have been a time when the entire population of Europe would spontaneously and wholeheartedly have chosen to commit itself to Christianity had it been presented with a series of distinct and mutually contradictory ethical and philosophical systems and been free of any legal pressure or social incentive to choose only one. Despite the prevalence of romantic fictions about the European past, there never was an age of perfect Christian faith. To those who, noting an overall decline in church attendance from the 1880s to the present day, feel certain that the territory which was once called Christendom will one day be fully atheist, Christians might well reply that faith, never universal, has been known to survive in even less promising conditions than those of the present.

Notes

1 For comments and helpful criticisms, I am deeply grateful to John Bossy, David Goodall, Hugh McLeod, Sheridan Gilley, Dinos Aristidou, Peter Biller and Jim McMillan. My thanks also to Donald Olsen, who taught me ten years ago, and to the students at the University of York who took part in the 'Climates of Opinion 1750–1870' and 'Religion and Science in Victorian England' seminars in 1995–96.

2 C. L. Becker, *The Heavenly City of the Eighteenth-Century Philosophers* (New Haven and London: Yale University Press, 1932; 1960), pp. 1–28.

3 See the bibliography for details. For the student unfamiliar with the outlines of modern European history, helpful introductory surveys include William Doyle, *The Old European Order 1660–1800* (Oxford: Oxford University Press 1978; 1990), Robert Gildea, *Barricades and Borders: Europe 1800–1914* (Oxford, 1987) and Norman Davies, *Europe: A History* (Oxford, 1996). For those with little back-

ground in the history of Christian thought, Alister McGrath, *Christian Theology: An Introduction* (2nd edn; Cambridge, MA, 1997), Jaroslav Pelikan, *Jesus Through the Centuries: His Place in the History of Culture* (New Haven, 1985) and Owen Chadwick, *The Secularization of the European Mind in the Nineteenth Century* (Cambridge, 1975) offer useful introductions.

4 H. Butterfield, *The Whig Interpretation of History* (1931; Harmondsworth: Penguin Books Ltd, 1973), p. 9.

5 For a brief summary of their views, see Doyle, *The Old European Order*, pp. 175–6.

6 A. Pope, 'Epitaph. Intended for Sir Isaac Newton in Westminster-Abbey' (1730) in J. Butt (ed.), *The Poems of Alexander Pope* (London: Methuen & Co. Ltd, 1963; 1965), p. 808.

7 J. Locke, *An Essay Concerning Human Understanding* (1690), ed. A. D. Woozley (London and Glasgow: The Fontana Library, Fontana/Collins, 1976), Book II, ch. xv, pp. 153–6; Book II, ch. xxiii, pp. 187–97; Book IV, ch. x, pp. 379–87.

8 Locke, *Essay*, Book IV, ch. x, p. 379.

9 J. H. Brooke, *Science and Religion: Some Historical Perspectives* (Cambridge: Cambridge University Press, 1991; 1993), p. 146.

10 Lively, 'Voltaire's deism' in *The Enlightenment*, pp. 43–5, as cited in Davies, *Europe: A History*, p. 601.

11 As cited in Brooke, *Science and Religion*, p. 134.

12 'Secte, Sect' in Voltaire, *Dictionnaire Philosophique* (1734), trans. P. Gay, *Philosophical Dictionary* (New York: Basic Books, 1962), pp. 463–4.

13 D. A. Pailin, 'Rational religion in England from Herbert of Cherbury to William Paley' in S. Gilley and W. J. Sheils, *A History of Religion in Britain* (Oxford: Basil Blackwell Ltd, 1994), p. 221.

14 Cited in Brooke, *Science and Religion*, p. 194.

15 'Cowl' in D. Diderot, J. Le Rond d'Alembert, *et al.*, *Encyclopédie ou Dictionnaire raisonné des Sciences, des Arts et des Métiers* (1751–65), trans. N. S. Hoyt and T. Cassiver, *Encyclopedia: Selections; Diderot, d'Alembert and the Society of Men of Letters* (Indianapolis, IN: Bobbs-Merrill, 1965), p. 84.

16 See especially the famous sections on early Christianity in chapters 15 and 16 of E. Gibbon, *The History of the Decline and Fall of the Roman Empire* (1776) (London: Penguin Books Ltd, 1995), vol. 1, pp. 446–580.

17 R. R. Palmer, *Catholics and Unbelievers in Eighteenth Century France* (Princeton: Princeton University Press, 1939), p. 4.

18 A. de Malvin de Montazet, *Instruction pastorale sur les sources de l'incrédulité* (Paris, 1776), pp. 58–9, as cited in Palmer, *Catholics and Unbelievers*, p. 84.

19 Palmer, *Catholics and Unbelievers*, p. 84.

20 See descriptions of N.-S. Bergier, *Le déisme réfuté par lui-même* (1771) and *Certitude des preuves du Christianisme* (1767) and also J. F. de La Baume-Desdossat, *La Christiade, ou le Paradis reconquis, pour servir de suite au Paradis Perdu de Milton* (1753), as summarized in Palmer, *Catholics and Unbelievers*, pp. 96–102, 105.

21 H. McLeod, *Religion and the People of Western Europe 1789–1970* (Oxford: Oxford University Press, 1981), p. 3.

22 For an excellent summary of the effects of the French Revolution on the Church, see J. McManners, *The French Revolution and the Church* (London: SPCK, 1969).

23 F. Schleiermacher, *On Religion: Speeches to its Cultured Despisers* (1799), trans. R. Crouter (Cambridge: Cambridge University Press, 1988; 1994), p. 207.

24 Schleiermacher, *On Religion*, pp. 85–6.

25 As cited in I. Bradley, *The Call to Seriousness* (London: Cape, 1976), p. 108.

26 See Newman's defence of the Tract in J. H. Newman, *Apologia Pro Vita Sua*, (1864; 5th edn, London: J. M. Dent & Sons, Ltd, 1912), p. 123.

27 Schleiermacher, *On Religion*, p. 89.

28 As cited in Davies, *Europe: A History*, p. 803. See also J. S. Mill, *On Liberty* (1859; Harmondsworth: Penguin Books Ltd, 1974).

29 O. Chadwick, *The Secularization of the European Mind in the Nineteenth Century* (Cambridge: Cambridge University Press, 1975), p. 21.

30 As cited in W. Houghton, *The Victorian Frame of Mind* (New Haven and London: Yale University Press, 1957; 1985), p. 63.

31 B. Jowett, 'On the interpretation of Scripture' in *Essays and Reviews* (1860; 5th edn, London: Longman, Green, Longman and Roberts, 1861), p. 377.

32 O. Chadwick, *The Victorian Church*, vol. 2 (London: SCM Press Ltd, 1972), pp. 75–111.

33 W. Paley, *Natural Theology; or Evidences of the Existence and Attributes of the Deity, collected from the Appearances of Nature* (1802; 19th edn, London, 1819), p. 69.

34 As cited in D. C. Goodman, *Science and Religious Belief 1600–1900* (Dorchester, Dorset: The Open University, 1973), p. 401.

35 W. Buckland, *Vindiciae Geologicae; or the Connexion of Geology with Religion Explained* (Oxford: Oxford University Press, 1820), p. 26.

36 C. Darwin, *The Autobiography of Charles Darwin 1809–1882* (1876), ed. N. Barlow (London: Collins, 1958), pp. 116–45.

37 C. Darwin, *The Origin of Species by Means of Natural Selection, or the Preservation of Favoured Races in the Struggle for Life* (1859), ed. J. W. Burrow (London: Penguin Books, 1985), p. 435.

38 From T. Bell, Presidential Address to the Linnean Society on the anniversary of Linnaeus's birth, 24 May 1859, *Proceedings of the Linnean Society of London*, vol. 4 (1858–59), p. viii, as cited in D. R. Oldroyd, *Darwinian Impacts: An Introduction to the Darwinian Revolution* (Milton Keynes: Open University Press, 1980; 1983), p. 84.

39 For a painstaking reconstruction of the debate and a fascinating discussion of its significance, see T. Cosslett (ed.), *Science and Religion in the Nineteenth Century* (Cambridge: Cambridge University Press, 1984), pp. 145–55.

40 For one of a number of recent reiterations of this familiar account, see V. Green, *A New History of Christianity* (Stroud: Sutton Publishing Ltd, 1996), p. 231.

41 From the *Athenaeum* (1860), as cited in A. Ellegård, *Darwin and the General Reader: The Reception of Darwin's Theory of Evolution in the British Periodical Press, 1859–1872* (Göteborg, 1958; Chicago and London: University of Chicago Press, 1990), pp. 68–9.

42 As cited in Brooke, *Science and Religion*, p. 42.

43 L. Huxley, *Life and Letters of Thomas Henry Huxley* (1903), as cited in Cosslett, *Science and Religion*, p. 149.

44 J. Tyndall, 'The Belfast Address', *Nature* (20 August 1874), as reproduced in Cosslett, *Science and Religion*, p. 186.

45 F. Max Müller, *Contributions to the Science of Mythology* (1897), vol. I, p. v, as cited in N. Smart, *Nineteenth Century Religious Thought in the West* (Cambridge: Cambridge University Press, 1985), vol. III, p. 184.

46 B. Russell, 'Experiences of a pacifist in the First World War' in *Portraits from Memory and Other Essays* (Nottingham: Spokesman, 1956; 1995), p. 34.

47 As cited in O. Chadwick, *The Victorian Church*, vol. 2, p. 263.

48 C. S. Lewis, 'God in the dock' (1948) in *God in the Dock: Essays on Theology*, ed. W. Hooper (London: HarperCollins Publishers, 1971; 1979), p. 100.

13

Australasia and the Pacific

David Hilliard[1]

Christianity entered the Pacific Ocean in two different forms. The first was the Catholicism of imperial Spain, brought by the first European explorers in the sixteenth and early seventeenth centuries. The second was English and Protestant. The Church of England from 1788 provided a chaplaincy to the British colony of New South Wales on the east coast of Australia, and the English Dissenting tradition was planted by the London Missionary Society in eastern Polynesia in 1797. This chapter explores some themes in the expansion of Christianity from these beginnings in three distinct geographical regions: the Pacific Islands, the continent of Australia, and the islands of New Zealand. Australia and New Zealand (sometimes collectively called Australasia) form a natural unit for this study. As British settler colonies, their religious histories share many common features. In the island Pacific, Christianity has been shaped by a very different environment and has developed according to its own rhythms.

The Spanish navigators Mendaña and Quiros, accompanied by Franciscan friars, voyaged in the South Pacific in a search for lands to conquer for Spain and peoples to convert to Catholic Christianity. They conferred on islands and geographical features the names of popular saints, symbols and Christian feasts. In their encounters with the islanders they exchanged words from each other's languages, which they hoped would lead to the teaching of 'our holy Catholic Faith'.[2] They also showed them how to make the sign of the cross and took away a small number of young people for baptism. The first Catholic missionaries in the Pacific Islands were Spanish Jesuits from the Philippines, who went to the Mariana Islands in Micronesia, north of the equator, in 1668. In the South Pacific, however, the Spanish initiated no permanent missionary work. In Vanuatu (formerly known as the New Hebrides) Quiros believed he had discovered the edge of a southern continent which he called Austrialia del Espiritu Santo, and from this the name Australia was later derived.

Christian beginnings in Australia

At the end of the eighteenth century the largest number of baptized Christians in the region between South America and the Philippines lived on the east coast of Australia, in the British territory of New South Wales. This colony had been founded at Sydney in 1788 as a penal settlement for convicts brought from British gaols and as a strategic base in a remote part of the world where Britain could keep a protective eye on the lucrative trade route to China. The original convict settlement spread to Norfolk Island in 1789 and Van Diemen's Land (later named Tasmania) in 1803. In Western Australia, on the opposite side of the continent, the Swan River colony began in 1829 and the province of South Australia was founded in 1836. The Port Phillip district was separated from New South Wales to become the colony of Victoria in 1851 and in the north the colony of Queensland was proclaimed in 1859. Aboriginal people, who had first arrived in Australia more than 50,000 years earlier, were pushed aside.

In the convict colonies of eastern Australia for the first 30 years the only officially sanctioned religion was that of the Church of England (the Anglican Church). Its clergy, paid by the government as chaplains, were expected to provide a ministry to the whole population and until the 1820s they were the only legally authorized marriage celebrants. The early clergy were evangelicals who preached a message of salvation from sin through personal conversion and faith in Christ as saviour. However, there was no religious idealism in the decision to found New South Wales, and it was hard to recruit chaplains for a penal colony. The military and civil officers who held power there mostly saw Christianity as the means to create a disciplined and moral social order. They were slow to allocate money and labour for the building of churches. Nor were many convicts moved by evangelical exhortations to repent and amend their lives. The majority of them came from those sections of English working-class society that conformed to the established Church without being regular churchgoers. They professed Christianity and had their children baptized, but when compelled by government orders to attend Sunday worship they endured the Prayer Book service and the long sermon as part of their punishment. They resented the Anglican clergy for their formality, their strict moral teachings, and their alliance with the government and the property-owning gentry. Samuel Marsden, the most prominent of these early chaplains, was also a magistrate and successful pastoralist; he became a symbolic and controversial figure.[3]

About one-third of the convicts transported to Australia came from Ireland. Nine in every ten of these were Catholics who regarded the

Church of England as alien, oppressive and heretical. The government did not trust them. Because of the fear that Catholic priests might encourage sedition and rebellion among their Irish flock, it was not until after the Napoleonic Wars that the British government allowed priests into the convict colonies as official chaplains. During the 1820s the Roman Catholic Church began adjusting to its new status of a legally free – though socially inferior – religious minority in a predominantly Protestant society.

Organized Christianity had a presence in the convict colonies, but its influence was limited. In New South Wales in 1836 there were 35 clergymen, of all denominations, in a population of 77,000.[4] The level of church attendance was lower than in England, and clergy frequently lamented the 'godless' and 'immoral' society in which they lived. However, during the 1830s, and especially after the cessation of transportation to New South Wales in 1840 and Van Diemen's Land in 1853, the Australian colonies became more attractive to free and government-assisted immigrants. These were much more likely than the convicts and ex-convicts (emancipists) to be churchgoers. With financial aid from the government, the number of church buildings and clergy multiplied. The proportion of the population which habitually attended church rose to about one in five in Sydney in the late 1840s. As European settlement expanded along the coastal belt and into the interior, new congregations were formed in almost every locality. The presence of a church was seen as a sure indication of a community's piety, prosperity and moral tone. Church buildings ranged from handsome stone structures with towers and spires, modelled on the medieval parish churches of England, to temporary chapels of timber slabs in newly settled districts. The building of a permanent church, like the introduction of a regular postal service, the opening of a bank and the arrival of a railway, was seen as a sign that civilization had arrived.

Sydney became a base for Christian missionary activity. Until the 1830s, when wool became the main export, much of the wealth of the New South Wales colony was derived from the whaling and sealing industries, and Sydney was a centre for trade with the islands of the South Pacific. In 1814 Samuel Marsden sailed across the Tasman Sea to New Zealand with the first group of missionaries of the Church Missionary Society (CMS), an evangelical society in the Church of England. They founded a mission among the Maori at the Bay of Islands, in the far north of the North Island. This venture was followed in 1822 by a Wesleyan Methodist mission, led by Samuel Leigh, who had been the first Methodist missionary in New South Wales.

Evangelical missionaries were optimistic about the potential of the Maori to understand and receive Christianity. On the other hand, they had a very low view of the status and capacity of the Aborigines, who were being dispossessed from their tribal lands and food supplies by British settlers and devastated by introduced European diseases. In 1814 Governor Macquarie of New South Wales founded a Native Institution near Sydney where Aboriginal children, under the guidance of a missionary clergyman and his wife, could be integrated into civilized society. When this assimilationist approach seemed to fail, the government moved towards a policy of protection and segregation. From the 1820s Christian missions were granted land on the frontiers of the colony, with the object of persuading semi-nomadic Aborigines to detach themselves from traditional tribal society and settle in stable agricultural communities. For the next hundred years almost all Aboriginal missions were organized on similar lines. They depended on governments for land and finance and, through the separation of children from their parents, sought to create closed institutions based on Christianity, the English language and farming. Most of these missions in south-eastern Australia failed. Aborigines remained on the periphery of the white Australian missionary vision, and an Aboriginal Church with its own leadership and style of worship did not begin to emerge until the mid-twentieth century.

Christianity in the Pacific Islands

Four thousand miles away from New South Wales, in the eastern Pacific, a contingent of missionaries sent by the London Missionary Society (LMS) was attempting to preach Christianity to the people of Tahiti. The largest of the Society Islands, Tahiti had been 'discovered' by British and French explorers in the late 1760s. Literary people were fascinated by what they read of this exotic 'island of love', but evangelicals were moved to prayer by the plight of the 'perishing heathen'. The LMS, founded in 1795 by Calvinistic Methodists and evangelical Dissenters, therefore decided to send its first mission to the islands of the 'South Seas'.[5] The founding party of missionaries – young 'godly artisans' who were to teach civilization as well as Christianity – was delivered by the ship *Duff* to Tahiti in 1797, during the first phase of European contact by naval and trading vessels. The missions begun by the LMS on Tonga and the Marquesas Islands were abandoned and the Tahitian mission came close to collapse. However, its success was assured in 1815 when the principal chief Pomare II, having changed his allegiance from the god Oro to Jehovah, gained paramountcy over the islands of Tahiti and Moorea. This was followed by a general movement in favour of Christianity in which hundreds of Tahitians were enrolled as candidates for baptism, observed the Christian Sabbath as a holy day and formed village congregations led by pastors and deacons. The missionaries put the Tahitian language into written form, taught their converts to read, write and tell the time, and translated the Bible, catechisms, hymns and other religious works. This pattern of a popular movement, eventually embraced and supported by the chiefs, within the traditional social structure, was to be repeated throughout the island Pacific. It produced a communal Church in which the Christian religion was fused with chiefly authority and island custom. The Church community reflected the village, so that pastors generally had high social standing and men of rank were given a prominent position in the local congregation.

The spread of the Christian Church in the Pacific Islands in the nineteenth century was shaped by geography. The overall movement was towards the north and west. In a vast region flecked with hundreds of small islands, missionary journeys had to be made by ship: each mission body required a vessel for the placing and provisioning of its agents. The different Protestant missions did not usually compete against each other but, by mutual agreement, worked in separate island groups. This meant that when the community eventually turned to Christianity the mission which introduced Christianity became the religion of the great majority of the population. The LMS had an early monopoly in eastern Polynesia, from where it expanded westwards to the Cook Islands and Samoa. The CMS introduced Christianity into New Zealand in 1814. The Wesleyan Methodists were the first to undertake continuing work in Tonga and Fiji. The American Board of Commissioners for Foreign Missions, supported mainly by New England Congregationalists, founded a mission in Hawaii in 1820 and later extended its work to the Gilbert Islands (now Kiribati) and other islands in Micronesia. In Polynesian societies, in the eastern and central Pacific, the movement of conversion was often very rapid. In Samoa, for example, seven years after the introduction of Christianity in 1830 there was a LMS or Wesleyan chapel in almost every village and more than 20,000 people – half the population – were under instruction. By contrast, in the Melanesian islands of the south-west Pacific, where people lived in small and mutually suspicious communities, fragmented by geography and language, Christianity spread very slowly. From 1848 Presbyterians from Nova Scotia and Scotland sent missionaries to the New Hebrides (Vanuatu), and in 1849 Bishop G. A. Selwyn of New Zealand began the Melanesian Mission, in a grandiose but unworkable plan to claim for the Church of England the remainder of the south-west Pacific. These missions gained small footholds, but they had less influence in the region than sandalwood traders and recruiters of island labour for the sugar plantations of Queensland and Fiji. In the twentieth century, after the establishment of colonial rule and the arrival of other missionary bodies, the process of Christianization speeded up. The Presbyterians became pre-eminent in the southern New Hebrides, while the largest body of Anglicans in the South Pacific was in the Solomon Islands.

The Protestant missions did not have the Pacific Islands to themselves. After the Napoleonic Wars Spain was supplanted by France as the centre of Catholic missionary activity and many new religious congregations were founded. Two of these undertook work in the Pacific: the congregation of the Sacred Hearts of Jesus and Mary (Picpus Fathers) and the Society of Mary (Marists), which was to become the most widespread religious order in the South Pacific and New Zealand. The Marists, imbued with the lush piety of post-revolutionary France and even relishing the prospect of martyrdom – between 1841 and 1855 six of them met violent deaths in the South Pacific – established their first bases in 1837 on the remote islands of Wallis and Futuna, west of Samoa. From there they extended their activities to places where the Protestant 'heresy' had already been planted, starting with New Zealand in 1838. In 1843 they began a mission on the large island of New Caledonia, which was later annexed by France and became a settlement colony. Competition between British Protestants and French Catholics – as followers of the Pope, they were called *popis* – was often intense. The French missionaries did not succeed in dislodging the Protestants from their Polynesian strongholds, but they endured and gained a minority following. Priests and nuns, living in great poverty, often stayed in one island group for life and gained a profound knowledge of the local language and customs. The liturgical worship, feast days and devotional practices of nineteenth-century French Catholicism coalesced easily with many aspects of traditional religion. As an alternative version of Christianity, it also provided a way for the islanders to express long-standing rivalries and feuds between neighbouring chiefs and villages.

There is no single or simple explanation for the conversion of the Pacific Islanders to Christianity. Reasons that were decisive in some areas did not apply in others. Almost everywhere, however, acceptance of the Christian God occurred in the context of changes in island societies and cultures that followed the arrival of the Europeans: new epidemic diseases; the disruption of economic life caused by the production of food and other items for sale rather than local consumption; the impact of new ideas and values. Many islanders were impressed by the personal possessions, trade goods and technology of the Europeans. A Samoan chief was recorded as saying:

> Only look at the English people. They have noble ships while we have only canoes. They have strong, beautiful clothes of various colours while we have only *ti* leaves; they have iron axes while we use stones; they have scissors, while we use the shark's teeth; what beautiful beads

they have, looking glasses, and all that is valuable. I therefore think
that the god who gave them all things must be good, and that his
religion must be superior to ours. If we receive this god and worship
him, he will in time give us these things as well as them.[6]

The expectation that the new religion would bring material blessings to
its followers was a common theme. So was the association of Christianity
with books and the arts of reading and writing.

Christianity had political implications. Although the English evangelical missionaries had been instructed to avoid 'politics', they believed that
civil society should be regulated in accordance with the laws of God. This
coincided with the political needs of Christian chiefs who, after their
rejection of the old gods, saw the need of a new form of divine justification
for their authority. With missionary advice, therefore, Christian chiefs
promulgated written codes of law which in the name of 'the true God'
forbade behaviour which the missionaries regarded as immoral and
'heathen' and laid down new punishments for old offences. The fullest
expression of missionary intervention in matters of government was in
Tonga where in 1875 the chief Taufa'ahau (King George Tupou I)
introduced a constitution, drawn up by the Methodist missionary Shirley
Baker, which made Tonga a constitutional monarchy. Its declaration of
rights included equality under the law, freedom of worship and the strict
observance of Sunday: 'The Sabbath Day shall be sacred in Tonga for ever
and it shall not be lawful to work, or artifice, or play games, or trade on
the Sabbath.'[7]

The English Protestant missionaries respected the authority of these
indigenous governments and supported their independence. They were
reluctant imperialists. It was only after French intervention in Tahiti in
the 1840s and the visible support given by French warships to Catholic
missionaries that they began to turn to Britain for protection and aid.
Until the end of the century they were usually on friendly terms with
visiting British warships, providing advice and local information, and
they welcomed British rule when it came. By the end of the nineteenth
century most of the Pacific Islands had been absorbed into the colonial
empires of Britain, France and Germany, and of the former missionary
kingdoms only Methodist Tonga maintained its political independence.

The missionaries did not question the right of the imperial powers to
rule in the Pacific. In island Melanesia and New Guinea, British and
Australian colonial administrators encouraged the extension of Christianity because it brought an end to warfare and spread a little knowledge of
law and 'civilization', thus making their own task so much easier. In
almost every Pacific Island colony the missions provided whatever there
was of schooling in the villages. At the local level the relationship

between missions and the government was typically one of collaboration, but at a distance. Government officials, always outnumbered by missionaries, were inclined to resent the rival influence, while the missions usually preferred to see their role as defenders of indigenous rights and mediators between governments and the local people.

Almost everywhere the introduction of Christianity into Pacific Island villages was undertaken by 'native teachers' who were the ground-breakers and founders of the local church. Beginning in the 1820s hundreds of Pacific Island Christians, with their wives, volunteered to be missionaries themselves in distant places. Tahitians went to the Cook Islands, Hawaii, Fiji and Samoa; Cook Islanders and Samoans worked in New Caledonia and the New Hebrides; Tongans largely evangelized Fiji. Living in island cultures that had many similarities with their own, they taught through daily conversation in the food gardens and around the cooking fire and gave explanations of the new religion in a familiar idiom. Ta'unga from Rarotonga in the Cook Islands, one of the few teachers whose own writings have survived, recalled that in New Caledonia:

> I preached about what God was like and His creation of the first man in this world. I spoke about Jehovah, who created that first man; the sinning of that man and the death of mankind because of that sin; also about God's great love in giving His Son to absolve that sin so that all men should live.[8]

At a later stage European missionaries would arrive to set up a mission station, school and training institution where the process would be continued with local converts being prepared to become teachers themselves. These mission seminaries, such as Malua in Samoa, founded in 1844, were the first institutions to provide islanders with a Western-style education, though at an elementary level.

In the Pacific Islands a distinctive style of Christianity emerged. The evangelical religion of the early Protestant missionaries led to an emphasis on the experience of conversion, as liberation from the power of Satan, and 'happiness in Jesus'. At the village level, everywhere in the South Pacific the style of Church life was remarkably similar. In every settlement the church was led by a pastor–teacher or catechist, who was appointed by the supervising missionaries. He led daily worship, taught school and conducted Sunday services. Symbolizing its place in the life of the village, the church was usually the largest building and located in a central position. In most places it was built in the style of a village dwelling, with a roof of thatched palm leaf. From the late nineteenth century, on islands where Christianity was well established, villages demonstrated generosity and sought prestige by building new churches in Western style, in wood or whitewashed coral-cement with galvanized iron roofs.

The large and mountainous island of New Guinea, with its adjacent islands, north of Australia, contains half the population of the island Pacific, but its history of Christianity has been very different. The Christianization of New Guinea has extended over a century from 1872, when the first continuing mission was commenced in Papua by the LMS, to the present day. After the Second World War there was a 'mission rush'. Missionary organizations proliferated in a scramble to enter the newly contacted and populous New Guinea highlands, so that by the early 1970s, a scholar of Melanesian Christianity observed, the eastern highlands 'had all the appearances of being the most missionized province on earth'.[9] The missionary force in New Guinea was more diverse than elsewhere in the Pacific. The LMS initially drew its recruits from England and Scotland; the Methodist, Anglican and Seventh-day Adventist missions were mostly from Australia; the Catholic missionaries came almost entirely from France, Holland and Germany; the Lutherans of the Neuendetteslau and Rhenish missions were Germans, with a few Australians. About one-third of these early missionaries were women. In the LMS and Methodist missions, from the 1870s to the 1930s, the pioneering work was largely undertaken by Pacific Island teachers. The majority of them came from the Cook Islands, Samoa, Fiji and Tonga. They introduced foods, methods of cooking and weaving, church customs, dances and songs from their home societies, as well as the Polynesian word *lotu* for Gospel or worship.

The expansion of Christianity in the Pacific produced a roll of heroes and martyrs. The great majority were Pacific Islanders who are known only by name and are remembered locally by the island churches. The British missionary martyrs, on the other hand, became the subject of an immense literature. The most famous of these were John Williams of the LMS, killed in the southern New Hebrides in 1839, Bishop J. C. Patteson of the Melanesian Mission in 1871 and James Chalmers of the LMS in Papua (south-eastern New Guinea) in 1901. Missionary biographies did much to foster a romantic image of Pacific missions – idyllic 'coral islands' of reefs and palm trees, faithful island Christians, the 'darkness' of paganism, heroic missionaries opposed by wicked traders.[10]

Christianity in New Zealand

Christianity in New Zealand had a dual origin. The first strand was brought by evangelical Anglican and Methodist missionaries to the Maori. Since the 1830s the Maori had accepted Christianity in large numbers and with enthusiasm. This process of 'going *mihinare*' began with coastal tribes in the north of the North Island then spread southwards, sometimes in advance of direct missionary contact. Within twenty years about three-quarters of the Maori population were attending Christian worship and had access to the Bible in their own language. In the villages an indigenous Christian leadership of catechists and teachers was emerging. Meanwhile, through the Treaty of Waitangi of 1840 the Maori chiefs had ceded a protective sovereignty to Queen Victoria. In return, the Crown guaranteed to the Maori people the ownership of their lands and granted them the 'rights and privileges' of British subjects. The English missionaries, led by Henry Williams of the CMS, played a crucial role in the Treaty. Convinced that the Maori needed protection from an unrestrained influx of land-hungry settlers, they acted as interpreters and negotiators, advising the tribal chiefs to sign and emphasizing the benefits they would receive from British rule. Through the explanations given by the missionaries, the Treaty of Waitangi came to be understood by the tribes as a covenant between the Maori people and the Queen of England.[11]

The second wave of Christianity came to New Zealand with European ('Pakeha') settlers. They emigrated from the British Isles and the Australian colonies to trade and farm in the various settlements that were founded by private colonization groups in the years after 1840. The colony's first capital was the northern port town of Auckland. Clergymen sent to New Zealand from England and Scotland encouraged lay people to form congregations. French missionary priests, mostly of the Marist order, ministered to Catholics. Churches were built in local timber with shingled roofs in adaptations of the English gothic style. Two Church-based colonies were founded in the South Island. In 1848 a lay association of the newly-formed Free Church of Scotland planted the Otago colony at Dunedin. Two years later the Canterbury colony was set up at Christchurch by a group of conservative Anglicans, influenced by the Oxford Movement, who hoped that a purified Church of England would emerge there, far away from social and political crisis at home. Although neither colony was able to remain religiously exclusive, Otago retained a predominantly Scottish and Presbyterian character, while Canterbury was deeply influenced by its English and Anglican origins.

The Maori national movement that emerged among the tribes of the central North Island in the 1850s was led by Christian converts, and the idea of having a Maori king to unite the different tribes was inspired by the Old Testament stories of the kings of Israel. An influential group of Anglican clergy and lay people supported Maori tribal rights to land and protested against the government's 'native policy': the CMS missionary Octavius Hadfield had three pamphlets published in London, appealing for justice for the Maori. For this, the 'philo-Maori' party was attacked by colonists as traitors who encouraged rebellion against British authority. In the early 1860s, however, alignments changed. Almost all Church leaders and missionaries supported the government's use of British troops against the Maori 'rebels' as necessary for the advance of Christianity and British civilization. The New Zealand Wars, and the resulting confiscation of large areas of Maori land for Pakeha settlement, were disastrous for the mission Churches. Disillusioned with the missionaries, whom they saw as treacherous allies of the government, many Maori Christians were attracted to new faiths led by Maori prophets and visionaries who claimed to have special revelations from Jehovah. In 1867 Te Kooti, the founder of Ringatu, recorded a vision from the 'Spirit of God':

> I again became unconscious when the voice again appeared to me and raised me up and spoke to me as before. I then called out saying, Speak Lord, and He said to me, Fear not because thy cry hath reached unto God, and God hath heard thy crying, hearken, I will strengthen thee . . . thou must tell my words and make them known to my people, it is only my words that thou must speak.[12]

Indigenous religious movements such as Pai Marire, Ringatu and, in the 1920s, Ratana synthesized Christian ideas and practices with elements of traditional Maori religion. They showed the extent to which biblical stories and concepts, transmitted orally, had been absorbed into the mental world of the Maori people. It was part of the appeal of the Latter-day Saints (Mormons), who began missionary work among the Maori in the 1880s, that they stressed the similarities between their own faith and Maori mythology, prophecy and religion. They taught that the Maori, and all Polynesians, were descendants of the 'Lamanites' of North America whose history was recounted in the Book of Mormon.

Adaptation and innovation

Christianity in the Australian and New Zealand colonies in the nineteenth century was derived almost entirely from Great Britain and Ireland. It was an offshoot of the metropolitan religious culture into a new environment where it was modified and subtly transformed. In every religious body there were tensions between traditionalists who sought to perpetuate the forms of worship and devotion, theological emphases and Church life they had known at 'home' and those who welcomed the opportunity to adapt them, to meet the needs of a new land. The former outlook was reinforced by the constant recruitment of clergy from England and Wales, Scotland and Ireland to minister to immigrants and their children. Locally born clergy were a minority until the early decades of the twentieth century. Almost every Catholic diocese was led by an Irish bishop, appointed by Rome, while the Anglicans preferred to import Englishmen as bishops. Despite the distance, the links did not diminish. With faster shipping from the 1850s it took only a few months for letters, newspapers, new books and new ideas from Britain and Europe to reach the opposite side of the world; from 1872 Australia was linked to Europe by telegraph. The result was that colonial clergy were usually well informed on theological controversies, liturgical developments and ecclesiastical gossip in their parent Churches. Visitors to Australia and New Zealand, who were looking for something obviously new and innovative, often remarked on the unoriginal character of colonial religion. When an English Congregationalist leader addressed meetings of ministers in Adelaide and Melbourne in 1887 he found that the questions he was asked 'would probably have been proposed at a similar meeting in Nottingham or Leeds . . . It was all too much like home.'[13] New religious organizations and institutions, such as the Young Men's Christian Association, the Salvation Army, the Mothers' Union, the Keswick 'holiness' conventions and the Student Christian Movement, were transplanted from Britain to Australia and New Zealand and did well.

Another strand of religious influence came from North America, after the opening of regular shipping services across the Pacific to California in the late 1840s. American Mormon missionaries began work in New South Wales and New Zealand in the early 1850s. However, they encouraged the first generation of converts to 'gather to Zion' by emigrating to Utah, so that there were no permanent Mormon congregations in the colonies until later in the century. The Churches of Christ, which sought to recover the Church's lost unity through the restoration of authentic 'primitive Christianity', looked to the Restoration movement in the United States for inspiration and, from the 1860s, were deeply influenced by American evangelists. Links developed, too, between Australian Lutherans, whose first group had emigrated from Germany to South Australia in 1838, and several Lutheran synods in the United States. During the latter decades of the nineteenth century the first Seventh-day Adventist missionaries came to Australia and New Zealand, and during the 1890s the 'prophetess' of the movement, Mrs Ellen G. White, lived near Sydney. The Women's Christian Temperance Union (whose members were soon active in the colonial campaigns for women's suffrage) and the Christian Endeavour movement were introduced from the United States. From the end of the century, with the advent of faster steam ships, all the colonies were visited by a succession of American revivalists – R. A. Torrey, Charles Alexander and J. Wilbur Chapman were the most famous – who popularized a new style of evangelistic campaign, marked by advertising, large-scale organization and cheerful gospel songs. In religion, as in popular culture, during the twentieth century the United States has overshadowed Britain as a primary source of religious innovation.

At the same time, everyone recognized that Christianity in the colonies was slowly developing its own shape and style. Both Australia and New Zealand were quite unlike any particular part of the British Isles, for in almost every region the population embraced significant proportions of Anglicans, Roman Catholics, Presbyterians and Methodists. Until the 1960s some 80 per cent of the population of each country identified themselves with one or other of these four religious bodies. The denominational pattern was remarkably stable: the relative size changed little over time. In both Australia and New Zealand the Church of England had a strong public presence and the largest number of self-described adherents, but their level of regular church attendance was much lower than other denominations. In New Zealand Presbyterians formed a greater proportion of the population than in Australia and made up the largest body of regular churchgoers, while the Irish Catholic community was relatively smaller. The Baptists and Congregationalists had expected to flourish in new societies where there was no established Church and no social disadvantage in belonging to a minority religious group, but as unions of autonomous congregations they found it difficult to sustain church extension outside the towns and their numbers remained quite small. Methodism, by contrast, with its centralized organization, circuit system and use of lay preachers, was well adapted to an expanding society, and it had an informal style of worship which many ordinary people found attractive. The percentage of Methodists in the population, and the number of attenders at Methodist churches, rose steadily during the second half of the century. In eastern Australia, during the nineteenth century Catholics grew in numbers and confidence. The appointment in New South Wales in 1836 of a Catholic Attorney-General illustrates that it was easier for a Catholic in the Australian colonies to achieve prominence in public life than it was in England at the time. A sense of hope was encouraged by promoters of Irish colonization when they reminded intending emigrants that 'Our people are to be the founders of a great nation'.[14] The increased Irish presence aroused Protestant fears of a 'popish plot' to undermine the British and Protestant character of the colonies. The bellicose Presbyterian minister and politician John Dunmore Lang called for limits to the number of Irish Catholic immigrants and wrote pamphlets such as *The Question of Questions! or, Is this Colony to be transformed into a Province of the Popedom?*

There was a new relationship between Church and state. Initially it was taken for granted that when the Church of England was transplanted to the colonies it was the state Church there too. By the 1830s, however, when adherents of the Church of England comprised less than half the population of New South Wales, the government was compelled to recognize religious pluralism. In 1836 Governor Bourke's Church Act (as it was generally known) authorized grants from public funds to the Church of England, the Church of Scotland and the Roman Catholic Church to assist the building of churches and the payment of clergy, and to any other Christian body that wished to receive it, in proportion to the funds raised locally by their adherents. This was followed by similar legislation in the other colonies. The formal alliance between Church and state lasted until the abolition of state aid in each of the Australian colonies between 1851 and 1895. Thereafter each religious body had to rely entirely on the voluntary support of its own lay members and from whatever funds it could obtain from missionary societies in its parent Church. In New Zealand the trend was the same. Non-Anglicans demanded religious equality; the Church of England relinquished its privileges; state aid for religion was phased out. In 1854 the newly established colonial parliament, on its first sitting day, asserted 'the privilege of a perfect political equality in all religious denominations'.[15]

The prevailing temper of the Australian and New Zealand colonies was democratic. During the 1850s the British government gave the older colonies self-government through bicameral parliaments. In the area of Church government each religious body found that its inherited structures required adjustment to new conditions. As a voluntary religious society, how was the Church to be organized? To what extent should lay people participate with clergy in the processes of government? The Anglican and Roman Catholic Churches established dioceses which were subdivided as European settlement spread. In 1835 J. B. Polding, an English Benedictine monk, was appointed by Rome as the first Catholic bishop in Australia. In the following year the British government created for the Church of England a diocese of Australia. This was headed by W. G. Broughton, who was the first Anglican bishop in the southern hemisphere. A diocese of New Zealand was formed in 1841, with G. A. Selwyn – an influential figure in the history of Anglicanism in the nineteenth century – as its first bishop. For the Church of England, no longer the official Church, the problem of organization was very pressing. As in the United States and Canada, the answer was found in elected assemblies or synods. From the 1850s each colonial Anglican diocese formed a synod, comprising bishop, clergy and (male) lay representatives, which met annually to discuss Church affairs and pass resolutions on matters of importance. A provincial (national) general synod was formed in New Zealand in 1857 and in Australia in 1872. The Catholic bishops, likewise, had to deal with newly vocal laity who had absorbed the ideas of colonial democracy and wanted more of a say in Church affairs. Yet the bishops gave nothing away: the structures of the Roman Catholic Church in Australia remained hierarchical, and the style of its clerical leaders was authoritarian.

The Methodists were the first major denomination to achieve autonomy.

David Hilliard

In 1854 the British Wesleyan Methodist Conference formed an Australasian Conference, controlling the five Australian colonies, New Zealand
and the Pacific missions. In 1902 the three branches of Australian
Methodism – Wesleyans, Primitive Methodists and Bible Christians –
came together to form one Church; this was 30 years before Methodist
union was achieved in Britain. A united Methodist Church of New
Zealand was formed in 1913. Presbyterians, despite their Scottish and
Ulster origins, found it harder to work together. The majority of Scots
who came to Australia were members of the established Church of
Scotland. However, the ideal of one Church was soon fractured by the
formation of new congregations committed to the position of the Scottish
free Churches, and there were further splits. The differences between them
were not doctrinal; the forces working for unification were strong. Within
a generation the main Presbyterian groups within each Australian colony
had joined together, and in 1901 national Churches were created in both
Australia and New Zealand.

The six colonies of Australia and the ten provinces of New Zealand
were competitors, often jealous of their neighbours and proud of their
material achievements. As a result of different patterns of immigration
and settlement, each colony and province acquired, and long retained, a
subtly distinctive denominational mixture and religious ethos. In
addition, there were many regions and localities where one particular
religious denomination had a dominating public presence. Presbyterians,
for example, were numerous and influential in the pastoral districts of
western Victoria and in the southern region of New Zealand. There was a
high proportion of Methodists in mining towns where Cornish miners
had settled and in the agricultural districts of South Australia, the
'paradise of dissent'. South Australia also contained some rural communities where Lutherans predominated and the majority of church services
until the First World War were conducted in the German language.
Evangelicalism was strong in Sydney, but with something of a siege
mentality, inherited from the convict era, resisting the influence of both
Roman Catholicism and the secular liberalism of many colonial intellectuals. The religious climate was different in Melbourne, which during the
1870s and 1880s, as a result of the Victorian gold rushes, became the
largest and richest English-speaking city in the southern hemisphere. The
level of churchgoing was higher there than in Sydney, its metropolitan
churches were the most imposing in the colonies and its leaders of
religious opinion were more willing to accommodate the new ideas
flowing in from overseas on science and the Bible. The study of theology
did not flourish in Australia or New Zealand, and it was excluded from
the colonial universities, but Melbourne provided a more hospitable
environment than anywhere else.

At the end of the nineteenth century half the population of Australia and two-thirds of the population of New Zealand lived outside the capital cities and provincial towns, in small townships and scattered communities or on isolated farms. In Australia this was the 'bush', in New Zealand the 'backblocks'. The description by an Australian journalist of a Sunday service at a rural church in New South Wales in the 1880s could have been written in either country at any time over a hundred years:

> The church stands a little apart from the few houses that form the infant township. It is generally built of wood, and surrounded by tall gum-trees, which, however, afford a very scanty shade from the burning heat. Here is gathered on the Sunday morning a collection of buggies and horses, for the people come long distances, and it is necessary in Australia to drive or ride. The congregation stand in groups before the door, chatting over the week's news, and waiting for the clergyman to arrive. The Day of Rest is the only day in the week in which they have an opportunity of meeting, and many come early and loiter with their neighbours till the service begins. They are all browned and tanned by scorching suns, but they speak with the self-same accent that they learnt at home.[16]

It was always hard to provide an effective pastoral ministry in country areas where the population was too sparse to build a church or maintain a resident clergyman in the traditional style. The rough-living and single men who worked there – drovers, shepherds, shearers, stockmen and timber cutters – had a reputation for being cynical and scornful about organized religion. Their folk songs contained scarcely any religious imagery; bush ballads steered clear of God or the supernatural. 'There is no Sunday in the bush' was a common Australian saying, but this was not quite true. Even without religious observances, Sunday was almost invariably a day without regular work, when itinerant rural workers washed their clothes, had a shave and wrote letters. Rural women taught religion to their children within the household.

Many different models of ministry emerged to meet the needs of outback Australia. Several Churches set up bush missions. In the north-east of South Australia, for example, in the 1890s the Bible Christians had three young lay missioners who were paid a few pounds a year and travelled hundreds of miles along sandy tracks on bicycles that were called the 'Way', the 'Truth' and the 'Life'.[17] High Church Anglicans founded 'bush brotherhoods' of unmarried clergymen who itinerated on horseback or by battered motor car from a central community house.[18] They left a strongly Anglo-Catholic imprint on the rural dioceses where they worked. Another approach was pioneered by the Australian Inland Mission. This was founded in 1912 by the Presbyterian Church on the initiative of John

Flynn ('Flynn of the Inland') to minister to settlers, though not to Aborigines, on the cattle stations and mining townships of the vast interior. The Flying Doctor medical service, which it introduced in the 1920s as a service to the community (later a separate organization), caught the national imagination and became a symbol of outback Australia.

Everywhere in the Australasian colonies the mobility of the population, and the mixing together within the same community of people of different religious allegiances, encouraged a lowering of inherited barriers. Marriage between members of different religious groups was more common than in Britain. Children of non-churchgoing families were often sent to the nearest Sunday school, regardless of denomination. In country towns, Protestants who privately regarded Romanism as a distortion of biblical Christianity and a threat to British liberties quite often subscribed to the building funds of Catholic churches or allowed their daughters to be taught music by a nun at the local convent. Catholics who lived in places where priests visited only at rare intervals sometimes attended a Protestant church rather than none at all. In some rural areas the settlers built a 'union church' where Sunday services were conducted by any available Protestant clergyman for the whole community. An Anglican clergymen who went to the town of Gilgandra in the wheat-growing central-west of New South Wales in 1902 recalled:

> At that time Gilgandra had five services a month. The Roman Catholics and Presbyterians visited it, and held service on the first Sunday in the month; the Anglican priest had evensong on the second Sunday; the Presbyterians came again on the third, and the Wesleyans on the fourth. The Roman Catholics had a church of their own; the others shared the Union Church, hence the name. The people attended indiscriminately any, all, or none of the services, according to their tastes.[19]

Although the gulf between Protestants and Roman Catholics was deep, and the history of each of the Australasian colonies was punctuated by noisy sectarian clashes, lay people were often sympathetic to the idea that the religious divisions and hostilities of the Old World ought not to be transferred to new societies. All denominations, it was often said, were part of one family, united by a 'common Christianity' and divided only by secondary matters of doctrine and worship: 'We are all going to the same home though by different roads.'[20] By the late nineteenth century the frequency with which High Church Anglican clergy warned against 'undenominationalism' and Catholic priests condemned 'indifferentism' indicates that the attitudes described by such terms had become well entrenched. Co-operative action by people of different denominations was already an important part of colonial religious life.

The tension between undenominational and denominational Christianity came to a head over education. In the middle decades of the nineteenth century, in each colony, the state began a system of 'national' or public schools, open to all children. These schools included a component of 'non-sectarian' Christian instruction, usually in the form of Bible readings. They were opposed by those bishops and clergy who held that true education could not be separated from doctrinal teaching. This dual system – public and denominational schools – lasted until the 1870s when one by one each colonial government introduced a system of free, compulsory and 'secular' (meaning non-sectarian) education and withdrew state aid from denominational schools.

In both Australia and New Zealand, unlike Britain, state secular education was widely accepted as the only workable solution in a growing and religiously mixed community. To give religious instruction to the young, the Protestant Churches built up their own Sunday schools, which at their peak enrolled the majority of eligible children of school age. Anglicans, Presbyterians and (in Australia) Methodists also founded a number of fee-paying secondary schools for boys and girls. Modelled on the English public schools, these were intended to educate the children of the upper middle classes for leadership in the community. They played an important role in the creation and reinforcement of ruling elites.

The Roman Catholic Church took a different course. The bishops – one much-quoted pastoral letter in 1879 denounced secular public schools as 'seedplots of future immorality, infidelity, and lawlessness'[21] – set to work to create a complete system of schooling for Catholic children under the sole control of the Church. These Catholic schools were to be staffed by religious sisters and teaching brothers, recruited initially from Ireland and France, and funded by the Catholic laity. Teaching orders multiplied. Of the indigenous congregations, the most widespread was the Sisters of St Joseph of the Sacred Heart. This order was founded in South Australia in 1866 by Mary MacKillop and Father Julian Tenison Woods specifically to teach the children of the Catholic poor.[22] By the end of the century, in the towns and closely settled areas, almost every Catholic parish had at least a primary school, with a convent next door for the teaching nuns. By the 1950s only one in every five Catholic children attended state schools. The maintenance of separate schools reinforced the bonds of the Catholic community: fund-raising and raffles for the school were a central part of parish life. Because of the failure of successive campaigns to obtain state aid, it also created a sense of grievance that was not removed until the 1960s when Australian and New Zealand governments conceded the aid principle and introduced state funding for private schools.

The leadership of the colonial Churches was in the hands of men, and their activities dominate the written records, but women were the majority of regular churchgoers.[23] In connection with their local churches, women did charitable work and district visitation, taught religion to the young in Sunday schools, decorated church interiors, provided suppers and cups of tea. Through fêtes and trading tables, they raised much of the money that kept churches afloat. In the latter decades of the nineteenth century some women found freedom to enlarge their sphere of activity in the Church. In country districts, where there were few resident priests, teaching nuns often exercised an informal pastoral role in the local Catholic community. In New Zealand Suzanne (Mary) Aubert, born in France, undertook missionary work among the Maori and then social work among the urban poor, for which she founded in 1892 an indigenous religious order, the Daughters of Our Lady of Compassion. In some small religious bodies such as the Bible Christians, the Salvation Army and the Unitarians women were able to take their place alongside men as preachers. The larger Protestant Churches introduced the order of deaconesses, and in the 1890s women were first admitted to the annual assemblies of colonial Congregational Unions. About the same time, the Australian and New Zealand Churches were expanding their support of overseas missions. The majority of those who volunteered to become full-time missionaries were single women. In the Pacific Islands, China, India and East Africa they filled positions of religious leadership that at home were held only by men. In 1886 Florence Young, from an intensely evangelical background, founded the Queensland Kanaka Mission which twenty years later extended its work to the Solomon Islands as the South Sea Evangelical Mission. The first woman minister in either country was Winifred Kiek, who was ordained in the Congregational Church in South Australia in 1927, but the number of women in the ordained ministry remained very small until the 1970s.

Church and society

'It is the counsel and pleasure of God . . . to raise up here a Christian nation', declared Archdeacon Broughton in his first sermon after his arrival in New South Wales in 1829.[24] Many Church leaders shared his vision. A central theme in Protestant activity in both Australia and New Zealand until the mid-twentieth century was the hope of creating 'a Christian country'.[25] The first and essential step, it was said, was the conversion and moral reform of individuals, but it was also the duty of the secular state to pass laws that would strengthen the moral environment, making it easier for citizens to obey the laws of God and harder to do wrong. In the latter half of the nineteenth century the issues that received the most attention were the regulation of the liquor trade, gambling, the sanctity of Sunday, prostitution, the raising of the age of consent and indecent publications. As the result of successful lobbying, in every colony the number of legal prohibitions multiplied: most of them remained on the statute books until the 1960s. In popular speech the Protestant moral reformers attracted the abusive epithet 'wowser', meaning censorious and prudish. In Australia during the 1890s, largely in response to the results of economic depression, drought and a series of strikes among maritime workers and miners, there was a shift in thinking within the Churches towards 'social Christianity'. A few progressive clergymen – lone voices – advocated radical reform of the economic and social system. The Methodist Church, following a British model, founded its first Central Missions for evangelism and relief work among the unchurched of the inner cities. These developed into large, and sometimes innovative, social welfare organizations.

In the Australasian colonies the emergence of organized labour as a political force in the 1890s polarized religious opinion. Methodists and other evangelicals had been prominent in the early leadership of the trade and mining unions, but from the 1900s the Protestant presence in the labour movement declined. The prevailing temper of the Protestant Churches was respectful of the existing social order and the majority of their churchgoers – small business owners, skilled workers and professional people – voted for conservative parties. Meanwhile, despite the warnings of bishops who feared that organized labour was tainted with the 'deadly heresy' of irreligious socialism, an unofficial Catholic alliance with the Labor Party (spelled Labour in New Zealand) grew stronger. Catholics, who were strongly represented in working-class communities, readily identified with a party that grew out of the trade union movement, and in any case the non-Labor parties were dominated by Anglicans and Presbyterians. So during the first decades of the twentieth century, in both Australia and New Zealand, Catholics came to play an important role in the Labor Party, especially at the local level, and a Labor politician who was a Catholic (or a lapsed Catholic) was a familiar figure.

During the 1890s the six Australian colonies agreed to federate. In 1901, on the first day of the new century, the Commonwealth of Australia was inaugurated, with a population of almost four million. New Zealand, whose population was only a quarter of Australia's and conscious that its outlook and interests were different, stayed apart. Although the federal movement in Australia was not inspired by religious motives, the mood of the Churches was favourable to the idea of a nation for a continent. Church leaders expounded their ideas on Australia's religious destiny and pressed successfully to have the words 'Humbly relying on the Blessing of Almighty God' inserted into the preamble of the federal constitution.[26] But that was as far as the constitution went in recognizing Australia as a

Christian nation: the Commonwealth was explicitly prohibited from favouring or hindering the practice of any religion. Meanwhile, in New Zealand a sense of national identity was emerging without reference to religion, apart from a conceited conviction that it was indeed 'God's own country' and a celebratory hymn 'God defend New Zealand' which became popular around the turn of the century and was later adopted as the national song.

The First World War illustrated the complex relationship between religion and national identity. In both countries, Church leaders and representative assemblies of all denominations urged support for the British Empire's cause as a religious duty. Christian pacifists, few in number, were badly treated. In 1915 troops of the Australian and New Zealand Army Corps (ANZAC) landed in the Dardanelles, in Turkey; the plan was to open the way to Constantinople. The campaign became a military disaster, but the event immediately became a legendary story of heroism and endurance. After the war the date of the dawn landings at Gallipoli, 25 April, was set apart as a sacred day for commemorating the war dead. The public ceremonies for Anzac Day – the form of service was devised by a Queensland Anglican clergyman – and the memorials of the war blended a subdued Christian imagery with classical ideas of war as a heroic and ennobling ordeal.[27] At the same time, the tensions of a society at war led to an upsurge of sectarian strife between Protestants and Catholics ('the Roman menace') that reverberated even 40 years later. This was triggered by the 1916 Easter Rising in Dublin and the resulting Anglo-Irish war, and by debates over conscription. In Australia the symbolic figure was the Irish nationalist, Daniel Mannix, who was Catholic Archbishop of Melbourne from 1917 until his death in 1963. In New Zealand, where feelings had been inflamed by the Protestant Political Association, in 1922 Bishop Liston in Auckland was prosecuted for sedition after a speech at a St Patrick's Day concert supporting the cause of Irish nationhood.[28]

Between the 1920s and the mid-1960s the religious landscape changed only slightly. About three in every ten Australians and one in four New Zealanders were weekly churchgoers. The majority of children were baptized and more than 90 per cent of all marriages were conducted by clergymen.[29] The Anglican, Presbyterian and Methodist Churches enjoyed close connections with a large section of the political, business and community leadership. Religious institutions were expected to offer moral guidance. During the inter-war years the active membership of the Protestant Churches and their influence in society gradually declined, but during the 1950s there was a series of evangelistic crusades and missions to regain lost ground, a wave of church building and a modest upturn in regular attendance, comparable to the post-war religious boom in North

America. From the mid-1960s the pace slowed. The international theological debates of the period produced a noisy eruption in New Zealand, where Lloyd Geering, a professor at the Presbyterian theological hall, was attacked for doctrinal error and became the best-known minister in the country. Meanwhile, at the national level there were moves towards interdenominational co-operation and Church union. The cause of institutional ecumenism gained wide support among Protestant leaders. Negotiations for structural union in New Zealand were unsuccessful, but in Australia they led in 1977 to the formation of the Uniting Church in Australia from a merger of Methodists, Congregationalists and the majority of Presbyterians.

The relationship of Catholics to the wider society was less clearly defined. Increasingly they formed a separate community, with their own network of schools, charitable institutions, devotional associations and social clubs. At the same time, they wanted to harmonize and conform with the general community, to become insiders. The tension could be both negative and creative. It has found literary expression in a remarkable cluster of semi-autobiographical novels and plays on the theme of a Catholic upbringing in the 1940s and 1950s, acutely observed, sometimes hilarious and sometimes painfully remembered.[30] In Australia a certain distance from the centres of political power gave the Catholic bishops an opportunity to be social critics. From 1940 to 1966 they issued an annual social justice statement, which applied to Australia the principles of the papal social encyclicals and called upon Catholics to mobilize against the threat of Communism.[31] The Catholic campaign against Communism in the trade unions was implemented through 'the Movement', a militant and secretive organization led by B. A. Santamaria in Melbourne and supported by the Australian bishops. Eventually its activities produced a harsh reaction from the (mainly secular) left and in 1955 a split in the Australian Labor Party. This resulted in the formation of the vigorously anti-Communist Democratic Labor Party, which in some states received wide support from Catholics and for fifteen years weakened Labor at the elections.

The Pacific Churches since the Second World War

The Second World War was a traumatic dividing line in the history of the Pacific Islands in the twentieth century. The Japanese invasion of New Guinea and the Solomon Islands early in 1942 was followed by American and Australian counter-attacks, with huge loss of life on land and sea. In the south-west Pacific, in what before the war had been sleepy corners of empire, the island Churches were in the front line. Christians who had been taught by missionaries about the God of peace found themselves in battlefields. Mission stations, schools and coconut plantations were bombed. In New Guinea some 330 Church workers – both foreign missionaries and indigenous people – were war victims.[32] When the war ended in 1945 the colonial powers resumed control, but their policies were set in a new direction. They wanted the post-war world to be different. More money was spent on health and education, air travel reduced the isolation of island communities and the British, Australian and New Zealand governments took the first steps towards the eventual goals of self-government or independence. In 1962 Western Samoa was the first former colony in the Pacific to become an independent state, choosing as the motto on its national insignia 'Samoa is founded on God'. Within twenty years there were eleven independent or self-governing Pacific Island states. Only France and the United States (and Chile, with Easter Island) retained control over their island territories.

The achievement of self-government in the Pacific Island Churches preceded national independence. The process began in the central Pacific – in Samoa, Tonga and Fiji – where Christianity had been planted in the early nineteenth century. Much of the initiative came from overseas mission boards, influenced by international thinking on indigenization, whereas some local missionaries had misgivings and dragged their feet. After the Second World War the atmosphere changed and the pace speeded up. In 1948 the Presbyterian Church of the New Hebrides was inaugurated. During the next 30 years the LMS, Methodist, Anglican, Lutheran, South Sea Evangelical and French Reformed missions became autonomous national Churches. In the Roman Catholic Church the transfer of leadership was slower, for until the 1980s the number of Pacific Island priests was very small. Although indigenous sisterhoods have flourished, in the majority of island dioceses the locally born clergy are still outnumbered by expatriate missionary priests.

At the end of the twentieth century Christianity remains a dominant force in Pacific Island cultures. Since the 1960s, however, there have been four new developments. In the first place, the sharpness of the denominational divisions brought by Western missionaries has largely dissolved. The historic Protestant Churches, having achieved autonomy and cut links with their parent bodies, found they shared aspirations and problems with other denominations in their region. New organizations and institutions have been founded, with overseas financial support, for cooperative action and advanced theological education. The most comprehensive of these regional associations is the Pacific Conference of Churches, founded in 1966. Secondly, there has been the search for 'the Pacific way' in Christianity. Both Protestants and Catholics have begun working towards expressions of worship, theology and art rooted in the traditions and belief-patterns of the Pacific Islanders.[33] Thirdly, the membership of the historic Churches, formerly based on unified village communities, has been eroded by migration to towns, the expansion of tourism, the alternative influence of radio and television and the arrival of new religious movements, mostly from the United States. Pacific Christianity is more diverse, with more options available, than ever before. In Fiji, for example, where Christianity among the indigenous Fijians was once dominated by Methodism, there are in the 1990s some 30 different religious denominations and evangelical–fundamentalist organizations.[34] Fourthly, the Pacific Churches, because of their close ties with indigenous peoples and particular regions, have played an important role in nationalist causes. The involvement of Protestants in independence movements in French Polynesia, New Caledonia and the New Hebrides (the first prime minister of independent Vanuatu was an Anglican priest, Walter Lini), the support given by the majority of Fijian Methodists to the military coup in Fiji in 1987 and the role of the Catholic bishop and his clergy in the Bougainville independence movement in the nation of Papua New Guinea, illustrate the problems inherent in any alliance of Churches with secular political movements.

Recent trends in Australia and New Zealand

In Australia and New Zealand the shape of Christianity is changing. In the 1990s, as a result of large-scale immigration in the post-war years from southern and eastern Europe and since the 1970s from Asia, the Roman Catholic Church is the largest religious denomination in Australia, while the Orthodox Church, in its various national communities, has a strong presence in some inner urban areas. In New Zealand, where the Pakeha population is more homogeneous, a new stream in the country's religious life has derived from the immigration of Pacific Islanders, mainly from Samoa, Tonga and the Cook Islands, who brought the style of worship, choral music, annual festivals and Church organization of their homes. Immigration from Asia has led to the formation in the cities of both countries of Chinese, Korean and Vietnamese congregations.

Other religious trends since the 1960s reflect broader shifts in Western Christianity. The historic Protestant Churches have declined in active membership and as a proportion of the total population, and they comprise a less significant component of organized Christianity than previously. Catholic life, worship and relationships with other Christians have been transformed by the reforms of the Second Vatican Council and Catholic cohesion has loosened. Denominational boundaries are less important than before; new movements and special-purpose organizations of all kinds cut across traditional borders. Evangelical, Pentecostal and fundamentalist Christian groups have grown in size. To a much greater extent, so has the proportion of the population that has no Church affiliation and claims to have no religion.[35] Women participate more fully in Church government and in the study of theology. In New Zealand women were ordained to the ministry of the Methodist (1959), Presbyterian (1965) and Anglican (1977) Churches before this occurred in the Australian or British Churches. In 1990 the Anglican diocese of Dunedin elected as its bishop Penny Jamieson, the first woman diocesan bishop in the world. Among Australian Anglicans, by contrast, the debate over the ordination of women was bitter and divisive; the first women priests were ordained in 1992.[36] In both countries there has been a secularization of public life, in which the Churches have a more marginal role and less influence with politicians and in the mass media than ever before.

Among historians and sociologists who have studied the cultural role of religion in the experience of Australia and New Zealand there are two main interpretations of the evidence.[37] One view emphasizes the failure of organized Christianity to put down roots and its irrelevance to the mainstream of national life; indeed, one influential historian wondered if modern Australia could be understood best as 'the first genuinely post-Christian society'.[38] But there is an alternative and more optimistic interpretation: that the religious history of European Australia is 'by and large – a success story'.[39] Transplanted Christianity, it is argued, has had a profound influence on the social environment and in the creation of moral order, and the majority of Australians and New Zealanders continue to hold significant religious beliefs and, at the census, describe themselves as belonging to a Christian denomination.

At the end of the twentieth century, reflecting a renewed sense of nationalism, Christianity in Australia and New Zealand has a stronger sense of identity than ever before. The process of engagement with the local society and culture has gone furthest in New Zealand (now often called Aotearoa New Zealand), where the Treaty of Waitangi of 1840 is now widely regarded as the foundation document of bicultural partnership. Liturgical worship regularly incorporates Maori language and imagery, and in each major denomination the Maori Church has its own structures of government.[40] In the 1989 prayer book of the Anglican Church an adaptation of an ancient hymn of praise calls upon local trees, animals, fish and birds:

> Rabbits and cattle, moths and dogs,
> kiwi and sparrow and tui and hawk:
> give to our God your thanks and praise.[41]

In Australia the voices of indigenous forms of Christianity are more muted, but they can be found in art, music, literature and theological reflection.[42] Many of those who are exploring the Australian experience of God and the relationship of Christianity to Australian culture point towards a rediscovery of the religious significance of place and land – the beach, the desert and the bush – and show a new appreciation of the traditional religion of Aboriginal Australians. This process is only beginning.

Notes

1 For assistance in the preparation of this chapter, I am grateful to the Revd Professor Ian Breward, the Revd Dr Allan Davidson, Associate Professor Brian Dickey, Dr Julie-Ann Ellis, the Revd Dr John Garrett, Dr Katharine Massam and Dr Walter Phillips.

2 *The Discovery of the Solomon Islands by Alvaro de Mendaña in 1568*, ed. Lord Amherst of Hackney and Basil Thomson (Hakluyt Society, series II, vols 7–8; London, 1901; reprint edn, 1967), pp. 113, 146.

3 Alan Atkinson, *The Europeans in Australia: A History*, vol. 1: *The Beginning* (Melbourne, 1997), ch. 9, on 'God and humanity'; A. T. Yarwood, *Samuel Marsden: The Great Survivor* (2nd edn; Melbourne, 1996).

4 John Barrett, *That Better Country: The Religious Aspect of Life in Eastern Australia, 1835–1850* (Melbourne, 1966), pp. 14–15.

5 Niel Gunson, *Messengers of Grace: Evangelical Missionaries in the South Seas, 1797–1860* (Melbourne, 1978), includes a list of all missionaries sent to the Pacific Islands by the evangelical missionary societies before 1860.

6 Recorded by John Williams in 1832, in R. P. Gilson, *Samoa, 1830 to 1900: The Politics of a Multi-Cultural Community* (Melbourne, 1970), pp. 72–3.

7 Sione Latukefu, *Church and State in Tonga: The Wesleyan Methodist Missionaries and Political Development, 1822–1875* (Canberra, 1974), p. 253.

8 'Establishing the Tuauru Mission' (1842) in *The Works of Ta'unga: Records of a Polynesian Traveller in the South Seas, 1833–1896*, ed. R. G. and Marjorie Crocombe (Canberra, 1968), p. 42.

9 G. W. Trompf, *Melanesian Religion* (Cambridge, 1991), p. 157.

10 For example, David Hilliard, 'The making of an Anglican martyr: Bishop John Coleridge Patteson of Melanesia' in Diana Wood (ed.), *Martyrs and Martyrologies* (*Studies in Church History*, vol. 30; Oxford, 1993), pp. 333–45.

11 Claudia Orange, *The Treaty of Waitangi* (Wellington, 1987), pp. 60–91.

12 'Te Kooti's prophetic call' in Allan K. Davidson and Peter J. Lineham (eds), *Transplanted Christianity: Documents Illustrating Aspects of New Zealand Church History* (3rd edn; Palmerston North, 1995), p. 157.

13 R. W. Dale, *Impressions of Australia* (London, 1889), p. 219.

14 Patrick O'Farrell, *The Irish in Australia* (Sydney, 1986), p. 135.

15 G. A. Wood, 'Church and state in New Zealand in the 1850s', *Journal of Religious History*, 8, no. 3 (1975), pp. 255–70, at p. 255.

16 Howard Willoughby, *Australian Pictures: Drawn with Pen and Pencil* (London, 1886), p. 32.

David Hilliard

17 Arnold D. Hunt, *This Side of Heaven: A History of Methodism in South Australia* (Adelaide, 1985), p. 114.

18 R. M. Frappell, 'The Australian bush brotherhoods and their English origins', *Journal of Ecclesiastical History*, 47, no. 1 (1996), pp. 82–97.

19 C. H. S. Matthews, *A Parson in the Australian Bush* (London, 1908; reprint edn, Adelaide, 1973), p. 52.

20 Patrick Dowling, 'Some dangers and difficulties of Australian Catholics', *Proceedings of the Third Australasian Catholic Congress ... 1909* (Sydney, 1910), pp. 112–14, at p. 112.

21 Joint pastoral letter of the Catholic bishops in New South Wales (July 1879), quoted in Ronald Fogarty, *Catholic Education in Australia, 1806–1950* (Melbourne, 1959), vol. 1, p. 250.

22 Marie Therese Foale, *The Josephite Story: The Sisters of St Joseph: Their Foundation and Early History, 1866–1893* (Sydney, 1989). In 1995 Mary MacKillop became the first Australian to be beatified by the Roman Catholic Church, as a step towards her canonization.

23 Janet West, *Daughters of Freedom: A History of Women in the Australian Church* (Sydney, 1997); Mark Hutchinson and Edmund Campion (eds), *Long Patient Struggle: Studies in the Role of Women in Australian Christianity* (Sydney, 1994), includes a substantial bibliography; Jane Simpson, 'Women, religion and society in New Zealand: a literature review', *Journal of Religious History*, 18, no. 2 (1994), pp. 198–218.

24 Quoted in G. P. Shaw, *Patriarch and Patriot: William Grant Broughton, 1788–1853: Colonial Statesman and Ecclesiastic* (Melbourne, 1978), p. 21.

25 Walter Phillips, *Defending 'A Christian Country': Churchmen and Society in New South Wales in the 1880s and After* (Brisbane, 1981).

26 Richard Ely, *Unto God and Caesar: Religious Issues in the Emerging Commonwealth, 1891–1906* (Melbourne, 1976), p. 74.

27 K. S. Inglis, 'The Anzac tradition', *Meanjin Quarterly*, 24, no. 1 (1965), pp. 25–44; Maureen Sharpe, 'Anzac Day in New Zealand, 1916–1939', *New Zealand Journal of History*, 15, no. 2 (1981), pp. 97–114.

28 Rory Sweetman, *Bishop in the Dock: The Sedition Trial of James Liston* (Auckland, 1997).

29 For an evocative account of Australian religion in the 1930s, F. B. Smith, 'Sunday matters' in Bill Gammage and Peter Spearritt (eds), *Australians: 1938* (Sydney, 1987), pp. 391–405. On the post-war years, David Hilliard, 'God in the suburbs: the religious culture of Australian cities in the 1950s', *Australian Historical Studies*, 24, no. 97 (1991), pp. 399–419.

30 For example, Ron Blair, Jennifer Dabbs, Nick Enright, Thomas Keneally, Peter Kenna, Gerald Murnane, Barry Oakley, Penelope Rowe, Gerard Windsor. For collections of autobiographical essays on this theme, Kate Nelson and Dominica Nelson (eds), *Sweet Mothers, Sweet Maids: Journeys from Catholic Childhoods* (Melbourne, 1986); Jane Tolerton, *Convent Girls* (Auckland, 1994); Jim Sullivan, *Catholic Boys* (Auckland, 1996).

31 Michael Hogan (ed.), *Justice Now! Social Justice Statements of the Australian Catholic Bishops: First Series, 1940–1966* (Sydney, 1990).

32 Theo Aerts (ed.), *The Martyrs of Papua New Guinea: 333 Missionary Lives Lost During World War II* (Port Moresby, 1994).

33 Horst Rzepkowski, 'Stepping stones to a Pacific theology', *Mission Studies*, 9, no. 17 (1992), pp. 40–61. For a pioneering collection of essays from Melanesia and

Aboriginal Australia, G. W. Trompf (ed.), *The Gospel Is Not Western: Black Theologies from the Southwest Pacific* (Maryknoll, NY, 1987).

34 Manfred Ernst, *Winds of Change: Rapidly Growing Religious Groups in the Pacific Islands* (Suva, 1994), pp. 197–223.

35 Michael Hogan, 'Australian secularists: the disavowal of denominational allegiance', *Journal for the Scientific Study of Religion*, 18, no. 4 (1979), pp. 390–404.

36 Muriel Porter, *Women in the Church: The Great Ordination Debate in Australia* (Melbourne, 1989); Mavis Rose, *Freedom from Sanctified Sexism: Women Transforming the Church* (Brisbane, 1996).

37 The pioneeering work is Hans Mol, *Religion in Australia: A Sociological Investigation* (Melbourne, 1971).

38 Patrick O'Farrell, 'Writing the general history of Australian religion', *Journal of Religious History*, 9, no. 1 (1976), pp. 65–73, at p. 70.

39 Bruce Mansfield, 'Thinking about Australian religious history', *Journal of Religious History*, 15, no. 3 (1989), pp. 330–44, at p. 331; also Ian Breward, *A History of the Australian Churches* (Sydney, 1993), ch. 15.

40 For an archbishop's account of changes since the 1960s in the Anglican Church in New Zealand, Brian Davis, *The Way Ahead: Anglican Change & Prospect in New Zealand* (Christchurch, 1995).

41 *A New Zealand Prayer Book: He Karakia Mihinare o Aotearoa* (Auckland, 1989), p. 64.

42 For example, Rosemary Crumlin, *Images of Religion in Australian Art* (Sydney, 1988); Tony Kelly, *A New Imagining: Towards an Australian Spirituality* (Melbourne, 1990).

Bibliography

General

There have been various multi-volumed histories of the Church in English during the last 40 years. The ten-volume *History of the Church*, ed. H. Jedin and J. Dolan (London, 1965–81), first appeared in German and represents a scholarly but somewhat old-fashioned approach to the subject from a Roman Catholic viewpoint. The *Pelican History of the Church* in six volumes began to be published in the early 1960s under the general editorship of Owen Chadwick. More ecumenical and also more readable, some of its volumes too are now somewhat dated, but volume 1 by Henry Chadwick on *The Early Church* and volume 2 by R. W. Southern on *Western Society and the Church in the Middle Ages* remain very usable. Another series begun at much the same time, *The Christian Centuries*, edited by David Knowles and others, was intended to include five volumes but only three actually appeared. The most useful now is probably the fifth in the plan, Roger Aubert's *The Church in a Secularised Society* (London, 1978). The latest and by far the largest and most authoritative series is *The Oxford History of the Christian Church* (general editors, Henry and Owen Chadwick). Planned to include about 25 large volumes, some ten have so far appeared, beginning with Robert Handy, *A History of the Churches in the United States and Canada* (1976).

The most indispensable reference work is F. L. Cross and E. A. Livingstone, *The Oxford Dictionary of the Christian Church* (3rd edn, 1997). Other valuable tools covering the whole or a large part of our history are Henry Bettenson and Christopher Maunder (eds.), *Documents of the Christian Church* (3rd edn; Oxford, 1999); N. P. Tanner (ed.), *Decrees of the Ecumenical Councils* (2 vols; London, 1990); J. N. D. Kelly, *The Oxford Dictionary of Popes* (1986); H. Chadwick and G. Evans, *Atlas of the Christian Church* (London, 1988); D. H. Farmer, *The Oxford History of Saints* (1978); and Edward Carpenter and Adrian Hastings, *Cantuar: The Archbishops in Their Office* (3rd edn; London, 1997). The one-volume *Oxford Illustrated History of Christianity*, ed. John McManners (1992), is wonderful for its pictures.

Chapter 1: The emergence of Christianity

For good general accounts of the early period see H. Chadwick, *The Early Church* (2nd edn; London, 1993), C. Rowland, *Christian Origins: From Messianic Movement to Christian Religion* (London, 1985), and N. Hyldahl, *The History of Early Christianity* (Frankfurt, 1997). The more detailed account in W. H. C. Frend, *The Rise of Christianity* (London, 1984), deals mostly with institutional and theological issues. The standard reference work for Jewish history in this period is E. Schürer, rev. G. Vermes, F. G. B. Millar, M. Black and M. Goodman, *The History of the Jewish People in the Age of Jesus Christ (175 BC–AD 135)* (3 vols; Edinburgh, 1977–87); a useful summary of the current state of scholarship on most issues can be found in L. L. Grabbe, *Judaism from Cyrus to Hadrian* (2 vols; London, 1992). On the Roman background, see M. Goodman, *The Roman World 44 BC–AD 180* (London, 1997). The political relations between Jews and Romans are surveyed in E. M. Smallwood, *The Jews Under Roman Rule* (Leiden, 1976). Roman views on Jews and Judaism are discussed in the magisterial collection of texts by M. Stern, *Greek and Latin Authors on Jews and Judaism* (3 vols; Jerusalem, 1974–84); a selection of these texts may also be found in M. Whittaker, *Jews and Christians: Graeco-Roman Views* (Cambridge, 1984). On paganism in the Roman Empire, R. Lane Fox, *Pagans and Christians* (Harmondsworth, 1986), may be singled out as a rare attempt to empathize with ancient polytheistic beliefs and practices. Many other studies reduce the study of ancient paganism to a set of puzzles about the popularity of particular cults. R. MacMullen, *Paganism in the Roman Empire* (New Haven and London, 1981), tries to bring home to readers the complexities of paganism.

Research into the historical Jesus, which was dormant for much of the twentieth century because of radical doubts about the historicity of the Gospels, is now rampant. Among more successful recent efforts are E. P. Sanders, *Jesus and Judaism* (2nd edn; London, 1987), and J. D. Crossan, *The Historical Jesus: The Life of a Mediterranean Jewish Peasant* (Edinburgh, 1993). On the social and economic problems of Judaea in the first century CE, see M. Goodman, *The Ruling Class of Judaea* (Cambridge, 1987). On the history of Galilee, S. Freyne, *Galilee from Alexander the Great to Hadrian, 323 BCE to 135 CE* (Notre Dame, 1980), continues to be useful although intensive excavation in the region over recent years has much increased the evidence for contacts with surrounding areas. On the Jewish diaspora see now most conveniently J. M. G. Barclay, *Jews in the Mediterranean Diaspora* (Edinburgh, 1997). By far the best study of common Judaism in Judaea is by E. P. Sanders, *Judaism: Practice and Belief, 63 BCE–66 CE* (London and Philadelphia, 1992). Varieties within Judaism are surveyed in a clear and balanced account by S. J. D. Cohen, *From the Maccabees to the Mishnah* (Philadelphia, 1987); L. H. Schiffman, *From Text to Tradition: A History of Second Temple and Rabbinic Judaism* (Hoboken, NJ, 1991), starts from the assumption that the rabbinic tradition was normative except where there is evidence to the contrary. For a translation of the Dead Sea Scrolls see G. Vermes, *The Complete Dead Sea Scrolls in English* (Harmondsworth, 1997). The best introduction to the philosophy of Philo is by S. Sandmel, *Philo of Alexandria: An Introduction* (New York and Oxford, 1979). Study of Jewish messianism is divided between those who minimize its importance in first-century Judaea and those who emphasize it: the chapters in J. Neusner, W. S. Green and E. S. Frerichs (eds), *Judaisms and Their Messiahs at the Turn of the Christian Era* (Cambridge, 1987), belong to the former tendency, the monograph by J. J. Collins, *The Scepter and the Star* (New York and London, 1996) to the latter. There is a clear discussion of the relation between Jesus and contemporary Jewish law in E. P. Sanders, *Jewish Law from Jesus to the Mishnah* (London and Philadelphia, 1990), chapter 1. On the trial of Jesus the standard work is still P. Winter, *On the Trial of Jesus*, rev. T. A. Burkhill and G. Vermes (Berlin, 1974); see also D. R. Catchpole, *The Trial of Jesus* (Leiden, 1971).

The bibliography about St Paul is vast and many of the basic issues about his career and theology are disputed, but for introductions to the subject see F. Watson, *Paul, Judaism and the Gentiles* (Cambridge, 1986), and E. P. Sanders, *Paul* (Oxford, 1991). On Jewish Christians in the Holy Land see the sceptical comments by J. E. Taylor, *Christians and the Holy Places: The Myth of Jewish-Christian Origins* (Oxford, 1993). Reconstruction of the history of the Jerusalem Church depends entirely on the view taken of the historicity of Acts, on which see the differing views of J. Knox, *Chapters in a Life of Paul* (Nashville, 1950), E. P. Sanders, *Paul and Palestinian Judaism* (London and Philadelphia, 1977), and M. Hengel, *Acts and the History of Earliest Christianity* (London, 1979). On the reasons for Christian missionary enthusiasm, J. Gager, *Kingdom and Community: The Social World of Early Christianity* (Englewood Cliffs, NJ, 1975), provides a sociological explanation; see also M. Goodman, *Mission and Conversion* (Oxford, 1994). The social origins of early Christians are examined in W. A. Meeks, *The First Urban Christians: The Social World of the Apostle Paul* (New Haven and London, 1983), and R. Stark, *The Rise of Christianity: A Sociologist Reconsiders History* (Princeton, 1996). On the development of Christian views on martyrdom and on its role in the history of Christianity in this period, W. H. C. Frend, *Martyrdom and Persecution in the Early Church* (Oxford, 1965), remains fundamental. There have been many studies on the relations between Jews and Christians in this period. Among important works are D. R. A. Hare, *The Theme of Jewish Persecution of Christians in Matthew* (Cambridge, 1967), some useful contributions in J. D. G. Dunn (ed.), *Jews and Christians: The Parting of the Ways, AD 70 to 135* (Tübingen, 1992), and J. T. Sanders, *Schismatics, Sectarians, Dissidents, Deviants: The First One Hundred Years of Jewish–Christian Relations* (London, 1993).

On persecution by the Roman state the fundamental discussion remains the exchange between G. E. M. de Ste Croix and A. N. Sherwin-White first published in the journal *Past and Present* in 1963 and 1964 and reprinted in M. I. Finley (ed.), *Studies in Ancient Society* (London, 1974). The outstanding reference work on the geographical spread of Christianity is still the remarkable A. von Harnack, *The Mission and Expansion of Christianity in the First Three Centuries* (2 vols; 2nd edn, Edinburgh, 1908). On the influence and extent of heresy the view of W. Bauer, *Orthodoxy and Heresy in Earliest Christianity* (Philadelphia, 1971), that there was almost unrestricted variety in the first century of Christianity, is now unfashionable, but the book remains well worth reading; for a more recent account, see H. Chadwick, *Heresy and Orthodoxy in the Early Church* (Aldershot, 1991). On the gradual emergence of hierarchies within the Church, see H. von Campenhausen, *Ecclesiastical Authority and Spiritual Power in the Church of the First Three Centuries* (London, 1969). On the state of Christianity by the end of the New Testament period, see the useful summary by R. Lane Fox in *Pagans and Christians*. The creation of a distinctively Christian ethical system in the first generation is discussed by W. A. Meeks, *The Origins of Christian Morality* (New Haven and London, 1993). On the early history of Christian liturgy, see E. Schwelzer, *Church Order in the New Testament* (London, 1961), and P. Bradshaw, *The Search for the Origins of Christian Worship* (London, 1992). On Christology in this early period, see C. F. D. Moule, *The Origin of Christology* (Cambridge, 1977); P. Fredriksen, *From Jesus to Christ* (New Haven, 1988).

Chapter 2: 150–550

W. H. C. Frend, *The Rise of Christianity* (London, 1984), is the best one-volume introduction to the first six centuries. It can be supplemented by Jean Daniélou and Henri Marrou, *The First Six Hundred Years* (London, 1964), and the shorter, but extremely reliable, study by the greatest modern scholar of this period, Henry Chadwick, *The Early Church* (Harmondsworth, 1967). *Christian Spirituality: Origins to the Twelfth Century*, ed. Bernard McGinn and John Meyendorff (New York, 1985), is a wonderful guide to its side of things. J. Stevenson, *A New Eusebius: Documents Illustrating the History of the Church to AD 337* (2nd edn; London, 1987), and J. Stevenson, *Creeds, Councils and Controversies, AD 337–461* (London, 1966), remain incomparable as well-selected source books for the period, but E. Giles, *Documents Illustrating Papal Authority AD 96–454* (London, 1952), is also useful. F. Van Der Meer and Christine Mohrmann, *Atlas of the Early Christian World* (London, 1958), goes as far as the end of the sixth century and is splendidly illustrated.

Robin Lane Fox, *Pagans and Christians* (Harmondsworth, 1986), discusses the interaction within the Roman Empire of the two religions up to the mid-fourth century; Derwas Chitty, *The Desert a City* (London, 1966), provides a magisterial account of early Egyptian and Palestinian monasticism. Two other recent scholars whose work is both wide-ranging and highly authoritative are W. H. C. Frend and Peter Brown. Besides *The Rise of Christianity*, Frend is the author of *The Donatist Church* (3rd edn; London, 1985), *Martyrdom and Persecution in the Early Church* (London, 1965) and *The Rise of the Monophysite Movement* (Cambridge, 1972). Peter Brown is the author of a classical biography, *Augustine of Hippo* (London, 1967), *Religion and Society in the Age of Saint Augustine* (London, 1972), *The Cult of the Saints* (Chicago, 1981), *The Body and Society: Men, Women and Sexual Renunciation in Early Christianity* (New York, 1988) and *The Rise of Western Christendom* (Cambridge, MA, 1996).

For Constantine, N. H. Baynes, *Constantine the Great and the Christian Church* (Oxford, 1929; 2nd edn, 1972), has never been surpassed, but is supplemented by T. D. Barnes, *Constantine and Eusebius* (Cambridge, MA, 1981). The *Ecclesiastical History* of Eusebius, the supreme text of the time, appeared in a two-volume English edition, ed. H. J. Lawlor and J. E. Oulton (London, 1928), and in a Penguin edition, ed. G. A. Williamson (Harmondsworth, 1965). For the great doctrinal controversies of the Eastern Church in the fourth and fifth centuries, see Frances Young, *From Nicaea to Chalcedon* (London, 1983), an excellent introduction to the literature; Henry Chadwick, *Early Christian Thought and the Classical Tradition* (Oxford, 1966); R. A. Norris, *God and World in Early Christian Theology* (London, 1966); R. Williams, *Arius: Heresy and Tradition* (London, 1987); T. D. Barnes, *Athanasius and Constantius* (Cambridge, MA, 1993); P. Rousseau, *Basil of Caesarea* (Berkeley, 1994); John McGuckin, *St Cyril of Alexandria and the Christological Controversy* (Leiden, 1994); and R. V. Sellers, *The Council of Chalcedon* (London, 1953).

Augustine's *Confessions* have been translated many times, most accessibly by Henry Chadwick (Oxford, 1991), who has also written a brief life, *Augustine* (Oxford, 1986). For longer lives, see Peter Brown (above) and John Rist, *Augustine* (Cambridge, 1994); and for his thought, E. Gilson, *The Philosophy of St Augustine* (London, 1960); J. J. O'Meara, *The Young Augustine* (London, 1954); and R. A. Markus, *Saeculum: History and Society in the Theology of St Augustine* (Cambridge, 1970). For Jerome there is J. N. D. Kelly, *Jerome: His Life, Writings and Controversies* (New York, 1976), and for

Boethius there is Henry Chadwick, *Boethius: The Consolations of Music, Logic, Theology, and Philosophy* (Oxford, 1981).

J. M. Wallace-Hadrill, *The Barbarian West, 400–1000* (London, 1967), the same author's *The Frankish Church* (Oxford, 1983), Judith Herrin, *The Formation of Christendom* (Oxford, 1987), and Douglas Dales, *Light to the Isles: Missionary Theology in Celtic and Anglo-Saxon Britain* (Cambridge, 1997), all in their different ways can introduce one to the way things were in the Western Church at the start of the sixth century.

Chapter 3: The Orthodox Church in Byzantium

General introductions to the subject include J. M. Hussey, *The Orthodox Church in the Byzantine Empire* (Oxford, 1986), and, from an Orthodox perspective, John Meyendorff, *Byzantine Theology: Historical Trends and Doctrinal Themes* (New York, 1974; repr. 1987), and Alexander Schmemann, *The Historical Road of Eastern Orthodoxy* (Crestwood, NY, 1963). The Orthodox Church from the late Roman period to the modern day, with valuable discussions of all the Chalcedonian Churches in Eastern Europe and Russia, is covered in Timothy Ware, *The Orthodox Church* (2nd edn; Middlesex, 1993). For a good introduction to the organization of the Byzantine Church and its relationship with the secular government see J. M. Hussey (ed.), *The Cambridge Medieval History*, vol. IV, part II, pp. 1–18; 105–118 (Cambridge, 1967). On Byzantine political philosophy and the organization of the Church, see N. Baynes, 'Eusebius and the Christian Empire' in his *Byzantine Studies and Other Essays* (London, 1955), pp. 168–172 and F. Dvornik, *Early Christian and Byzantine Political Philosophy*, vols I–II (Washington, DC, 1966). Byzantine philanthropy is treated in D. Constantelos, *Byzantine Philanthropy and Social Welfare* (New Brunswick, NJ, 1968).

For the reign of Justinian and the sixth century, see Pauline Allen and Elizabeth Jeffreys (eds), *The Sixth Century: End or Beginning?* (Brisbane, 1996); J. W. Barker, *Justinian and the Later Roman Empire* (Madison, 1966); John Meyendorff, *Imperial Unity and Christian Divisions: The Church 450–680 AD* (Crestwood, NY, 1989); and P. N. Ure, *Justinian and His Age* (Harmondsworth, 1951). The history of the Byzantine liturgy is well covered in Robert F. Taft, *The Byzantine Rite: A Short History* (Collegeville, MN, 1992). The background and development of the Oriental Orthodox Churches may be found in Aziz S. Atiya, *A History of Eastern Christianity* (2nd edn; Millwood, 1980); while the following books deal with the Syriac tradition and Monophysite movement: Sebastian Brock, 'Syriac spirituality' in E. J. Yarnold *et al.* (eds), *The Study of Spirituality* (London, 1986), pp. 199–215; W. H. C. Frend, *The Rise of the Monophysite Movement* (Cambridge, 1972); R. Murray, *Symbols of Church and Kingdom: A Study in Early Syriac Tradition* (Cambridge, 1975). The sixth-century contribution to Orthodox Christology has been treated extensively in the recent English translation of A. Grillmeier, *Christ in Christian Tradition*, vol. 2, part 2: *The Church of Constantinople in the Sixth Century*, trans. Pauline Allen and John Cawte (London, 1995). See also P. Charanis, *Church and State in the Later Roman Empire: The Religious Policy of Anastasius the First, 491–518* (Madison, 1939); J. Meyendorff, *Christ in Eastern Christian Thought* (Crestwood, 1975) and *Imperial Unity and Christian Divisions: The Church 450–680 AD* (Crestwood, 1989). On the rise of the cult of icons and the Virgin Mary, see A. Cameron, 'The Theotokos in sixth-century Constantinople', *Journal of Theological Studies*, n.s. 29, part 1 (1978), pp. 79–108; A. Cameron, 'Images of authority: elites and icons in late sixth-century Byzantium', *Past and Present*, 84 (1979), pp. 3–35; Hilda Graef, *Mary: A History of Doctrine and Devotion* (London, 1965; repr. 1987). The seventh century has received a recent re-evaluation in John Haldon, *Byzantium in the Seventh Century: The Transformation of a Culture* (Cambridge, 1990). On Maximos the Confessor and Monothelitism, see Andrew Louth, *Maximus the Confessor* (London and New York, 1996).

Iconoclasm has received extensive treatment and provoked much controversy. The most interesting works on the causes of Iconoclasm are Leslie W. Barnard, 'The Emperor cult and the origins of the Iconoclastic controversy', *Byzantion*, 43 (1973), pp. 7–13; P. Brown, 'A Dark-Age crisis: aspects of the Iconoclastic controversy', *English Historical Review*, 88 (1973), pp. 1–34; J. F. Haldon, 'Some remarks on the background to the Iconoclastic controversy', *Byzantinoslavica*, 38 (1977), pp. 161–84. For general background, see also P. J. Alexander, 'Religious persecution and resistance in the eighth and ninth centuries', *Speculum*, 52 (1977), pp. 238–64; A. A. M. Bryer and J. Herrin (eds), *Iconoclasm* (Birmingham, 1977); R. Cormack, *Writing in Gold: Byzantine Society and Its Icons* (London, 1985), pp. 95–140; S. Gero, 'Notes on Byzantine Iconoclasm in the eighth century', *Byzantion*, 44 (1974), pp. 23–42. On women and icons, see Judith Herrin, 'Women and the faith in icons in early Christianity' in R. Samuel and F. Stedman Jones (eds), *Culture, Ideology and Politics: Essays for Eric Hobsbawm* (London, 1982), pp. 56–83. The rise of the cult of icons and the theological arguments for and against are well treated in E. Kitzinger, 'The cult of images in the age before Iconoclasm', *Dumbarton Oaks Papers*, 8 (1954), pp. 85–150; Kenneth Parry, *Depicting the Word: Byzantine Iconophile Thought of the Eighth and Ninth Centuries* (Leiden, 1996); J. Pelikan, *The Christian Tradition: A History of the Development of Doctrine*, vol. II: *The Spirit of Eastern Christendom (600–1700)* (Chicago and London, 1974) and *Imago Dei: The Byzantine Apologia for Icons* (New Haven and London, 1990).

On Byzantine relations with the papacy and the issue of the *filioque*, see F. Dvornik, *The Photian Schism* (Cambridge, 1948) and *Byzantium and the Roman Primacy*, trans. E. A. Quain (New York, 1966); Judith Herrin, *The Formation of Christendom* (Oxford, 1987); A. Papadakis with J. Meyendorff, *The Christian East and the Rise of the Papacy* (Crestwood, 1994); and S. Runciman, *The Eastern Schism* (Oxford, 1955).

Middle Byzantine monasticism has recently been the subject of an excellent new study by Rosemary Morris, *Monks and Laymen in Byzantium, 843–1118* (Cambridge, 1985). See also J. P. Thomas, *Private Religious Foundations in the Byzantine Empire* (Washington, DC, 1987). On the background of asceticism and holiness in late Roman and Byzantine society see P. Brown, 'The rise and function of the holy man in late antiquity', *Journal of Roman Studies*, 61 (1971), pp. 80–101, and S. Hackel, *The Byzantine Saint* (London, 1981).

Ninth-century missions to the Slavs are discussed in F. Dvornik, *Byzantine Missions Among the Slavs: Sts Constantine-Cyril and Methodius* (New Brunswick, 1970); and Dimitri Obolensky, *Byzantium and the Slavs* (Crestwood, 1994) and *The Byzantine Commonwealth: Eastern Europe, 500–1453* (London, 1971). The Kievan period of the Russian Church has recently received a new study in Nicholas Fennell, *A History of the Russian Church to 1448* (London and New York, 1995). On Armenia, see Sirapie Der Nersessian, *Armenia and the Byzantine Empire* (Cambridge, MA, 1945).

Eleventh- and twelfth-century Byzantine Church history is introduced in Michael Angold, *Church and Society in Byzantium Under the Comneni, 1081–1261* (Cambridge, 1995), and Paul Magdalino, *The Empire of Manuel I Komnenos, 1143–1180* (Cambridge, 1993), pp. 367–72. On the heresies and trials in this period see L. Clucas, *The Trial of John Italos and the Crisis of Intellectual Values in the Eleventh Century* (Munich, 1981); N. Garsoïan, *The Paulician Heresy* (The Hague, 1967) and 'Byzantine heresy: a reinterpretation', *Dumbarton Oaks Papers*, 25 (1971), pp. 85–113; Dimitri Obolensky, *The Bogomils* (Cambridge, 1948).

Basic bibliography on the Crusades includes K. M. Setton (ed.), *A History of the Crusades*, vols I–VI (Madison, 1969–89), and S. Runciman, *A History of the Crusades*, vols I–III (Cambridge, 1951–54). On the period of Latin occupation between 1204 and 1261, see D. M. Nicol, *The Despotate of Epiros, 1267–1479: A Contribution to the History of Greece* (Cambridge, 1984), and A. D. Karpozilos, *The Ecclesiastical Controversy Between the Kingdom of Nicaea and the Principality of Epiros (1217–33)* (Thessalonica, 1973).

The later (Palaeologan) period of Byzantine history is covered in S. Ćurčić and D. Mouriki, *The Twilight of Byzantium: Aspects of Cultural and Religious History in the Late Byzantine Empire* (Princeton University Press, 1991), pp. 15–26; D. M. Nicol, *Church and Society in the Last Centuries of Byzantium* (Cambridge, 1979); and K. M. Setton, *The Papacy and the Levant (1204–1571)*, vols I–II (Philadelphia, 1976–78).

The Byzantine Orthodox (and Western) mystical tradition is introduced in Andrew Louth, *The Origins of the Christian Mystical Tradition from Plato to Denys* (Oxford, 1981). See also V. Lossky, *The Mystical Theology of the Eastern Church* (London, 1957); John Meyendorff, *St Gregory Palamas and Orthodox Spirituality* (New York, 1974) and *Byzantine Hesychasm: Historical, Theological and Social Problems* (London, 1974); G. E. H. Palmer, P. Sherrard and K. Ware (trans.), *The Philokalia*, vols I–IV (London, 1979–95).

Chapter 4: The medieval West

Background and general works

R. W. Southern, the supreme master of medieval Christian studies, has written two surveys, *Western Society and the Church in the Middle Ages* (Harmondsworth, 1970) and *The Making of the Middle Ages* (London, 1953), an early but classic work. See also D. Knowles and D. Obolensky, *The Middle Ages* (London, 1969); Judith Herrin, *The Formation of Christendom* (Oxford, 1987); and Peter Brown, *The Rise of Western Christendom* (Cambridge, MA, 1996). M. F. Hedlund and H. H. Rowley, *Atlas of the Early Christian World* (London, 1980), has text, maps and illustrations which apply beyond the first six centuries; Colin McEvedy, *Penguin Atlas of Medieval History* (Harmondsworth, 1961), often reprinted, has simplified maps from the fourth century to the fifteenth and useful explanations.

The Church and mission in Europe

Bede, *Ecclesiastical History of the English People*, ed. B. Colgrave and R. A. B. Mynors (Oxford, 1969): this edition of the primary source for the conversion of the Anglo-Saxons has both Latin and English text; for an English translation only, with excellent notes, J. McClure and R. Collins, *Ecclesiastical History of the English People* (Oxford, 1994). J. Campbell, P. Wormald and E. John, *The Anglo-Saxons* (Harmondsworth, 1991), has excellent text with good illustrations. F. Stenton, *Anglo-Saxon England* (Oxford, 1943), remains the fundamental study for this period. Henry Mayr-Harting, *The Coming of Christianity to Anglo Saxon England* (3rd edn; London, 1991), provides an extended study of the mission to England, while R. A. Markus, *Gregory the Great and His World* (Cambridge, 1997), is a vivid portrayal of the man who sent it. See also B. Ward, *The Venerable Bede* (2nd edn; London, 1998); G. Evans, *The Thought of Gregory the Great* (Cambridge, 1986); Gregory of Tours, *History of the Franks*, trans. L. Thorpe (Harmondsworth, 1974); M. Wallace-Hadrill, *The Frankish Church* (Oxford, 1983); and C. H. Talbot, *The Anglo-Saxon Mission to Germany* (London, 1954).

The Church and the Bible

Introductions in English to the medieval use of the Bible are not numerous but useful volumes are: G. W. H. Lampe (ed.), *The Cambridge History of the Bible: The West from the Fathers to the Reformation*, vol. 2 (2nd edn; Cambridge, 1976); B. Smalley, *The Study of the Bible in the Middle Ages* (Oxford, 1952); G. Evans, *The Language and Logic of the Bible* (2 vols; Cambridge, 1984–85); M. T. Gibson, *The Bible in the Latin West* (Notre Dame, 1993).

Authority in Church and state

The *Cambridge History of Medieval Political Thought, c. 350–1450* (Cambridge, 1988), is indispensable. C. Morris, *The Papal Monarchy: The Western Church from 1050 to 1250* (Oxford, 1989), is a magisterial study with admirable bibliography on the whole period; W. Ullmann, *A Short History of the Papacy in the Middle Ages* (London, 1972), a pungent approach; G. Barraclough, *The Medieval Papacy* (London, 1968), a sound text with illustrations. See also J. E. Sayers, *Innocent III, Leader of Europe 1198–1216* (London, 1987); E. H. Kantorowicz, *The King's Two Bodies* (Princeton, 1951); G. Constable, *The Reformation of the Twelfth Century* (Cambridge, 1996); and B. Hamilton, *Religion in the Medieval West* (London, 1986).

The Church and the individual

C. Morris, *The Discovery of the Individual, 1050–1200* (London, 1972); R. Brooke and C. Brooke, *Popular Religion in the Middle Ages: Western Europe 1000–1300* (London, 1984); T. Head, *Hagiography and the Cult of the Saints* (Cambridge, 1990); C. Brooke, *The Medieval Idea of Marriage* (Oxford, 1989); E. Duffy, *The Stripping of the Altars: Traditional Religion in England 1400–1580* (New Haven, 1992); B. Ward, *Miracles and the Medieval Mind* (2nd edn; London, 1987); *Prayers and Meditations of St Anselm with the Proslogion*, trans. B. Ward (Harmondsworth, 1973); J. Le Goff, *The Birth of Purgatory* (London, 1984); R. C. Finucane, *Miracles and Pilgrims* (London, 1977); J Sumption, *Pilgrimage: An Image of Medieval Religion* (London, 1975); E. W. Kempe, *Canonisation and Authority in the Western Church* (Oxford, 1948).

Religious life in the Church

Rule of St Benedict: there are many translations of this basic text. A recent version is *RB 1980: The Rule of St Benedict in Latin and English* with notes, ed. T. Fry OSB (Collegeville, MN, 1981). C. N. L. Brooke and W. Swaan, *The Monastic World 1000–1300* (London, 1974), is an excellent book for both text and photographs. Jean Leclercq, *The Love of Learning and the Desire for God: A Study of Monastic Culture* (New York, 1961), is still the best account of medieval monastic spirituality. D. Knowles, *The Monastic Order in England* (Cambridge, 1940) and *The Religious Orders in England*

(3 vols; Cambridge, 1948, 1957, 1959), together contain the insight of a master into monastic life as a whole, with England as the basis. A brief outline is contained in the same author's *Christian Monasticism* (London, 1977). *The Cistercian World: Monastic Writings of the Twelfth Century*, trans. P. Materasso (Harmondsworth, 1993), is an excellent selection from Cistercian sources. C. Lawrence, *Medieval Monasticism: Forms of Monastic Life in Western Europe in the Middle Ages* (2nd edn; London, 1989), is a recent outline of religious orders, complemented by the same author's outline account of the orders of friars, *The Friars* (London, 1989). Michael Robson, *St Francis of Assisi: The Legend and the Life* (London, 1997), is a fine introduction to the most perennially evocative religious figure of this period. J. R. H. Moorman, *A History of the Franciscan Order* (Oxford, 1968), is the classic study of that order. See also S. Tugwell (ed.), *Early Dominicans: Selected Writings* (London, 1982); H. Leyser, *Hermits and the New Monasticism, 1000–1150* (London, 1984); R. B. Brooke, *The Coming of the Friars* (London, 1975); G. Constable (ed.), *Medieval Monasticism: A Select Bibliography* (Toronto, 1976).

The Church and war

S. Runciman, *History of the Crusades* (3 vols; Cambridge, 1951–54), is a standard work, with very full bibliography. J. Riley-Smith, *The Crusades* (London, 1987) and *The First Crusade and the Idea of Crusading* (London, 1986), provide the most authoritative accounts of the subject, for which see also E. Christiansen, *The Northern Crusades* (London, 1980).

Education and theology

Etienne Gilson, *History of Christian Philosophy in the Middle Ages* (London, 1955); Hastings Rashdall, *The Universities of Europe in the Middle Ages*, ed. F. M. Powicke and A. B. Emden (2 vols; Oxford, 1936); J. Catto (ed.), *History of the University of Oxford*, vol. 1: *The Early Oxford Schools* (Oxford, 1984); J. Marenbon, *Early Medieval Philosophy, 480–1150* (London, 1983). The best life of Thomas Aquinas is James Weisheipl, *Friar Thomas d'Aquino* (2nd edn; Oxford, 1983), while Brian Davies, *The Thought of Thomas Aquinas* (London, 1992), introduces his philosophy. A. Murray, *Reason and Society in the Middle Ages* (2nd edn; Oxford, 1986). R. W. Southern has vastly assisted understanding of the medieval mind with a number of remarkable studies: *Medieval Humanism and Other Studies* (New York, 1970), *Scholastic Humanism and the Unification of Europe*, vol. 1: *Foundations* (Oxford, 1995) and *Western Views of Islam in the Middle Ages* (Cambridge, MA, 1962), together with two superb biographies, *Robert Grosseteste* (Oxford, 1986) and *Anselm: A Portrait in a Landscape* (Cambridge, 1990). See also G. R. Evans, *Old Arts and New Theology* (Oxford, 1980) and *Anselm and a New Generation* (Oxford, 1980).

Reform and revolution

M. Reeves, *The Influence of Prophecy in the Later Middle Ages* (Oxford, 1969), is a good place to start looking at the impact of Joachim of Fiore, and R. Moore's two books, *The Origins of European Dissent* (Harmondsworth, 1977) and *The Birth of Popular Heresy* (London, 1975), provide another. See also W. L. Wakefield and A. P. Evans, *Heresies of the High Middle Ages* (New York, 1969); J. Sumption, *The Albigensian Crusade*

(London, 1978); B. Hamilton, *The Medieval Inquisition* (London, 1981); and B. Tierney, *The Crisis of Church and State, 1050–1300* (with selected documents) (New Jersey, 1964). Anthony Kenny has written two books on Wyclif, a short *Wyclif* (Oxford, 1985) and a longer *Wyclif in His Times* (Oxford, 1986). See also M. Lambert, *Medieval Heresy: Popular Movements from Bogomils to Huss* (2nd edn; London, 1992).

Chapter 5: India

General

No satisfactory general history of Christianity in India has yet been produced. Volumes of the *History of Christianity in India*, being produced under the auspices of the Church History Association of India and published in Bangalore, where already in print, are located within appropriate periods (see Mundadan *et al.*). Some *Indian Church History Review* articles are useful. James Hough, *History of Christianity in India* (5 vols; London, 1839–60), is a useful but dated source. John W. Kaye, *Christianity in India* (London, 1855), was (with Hough) another early and useful attempt to comprehend how Christians came to India. Samuel Hugh Moffat, *A History of Christianity in Asia*, volume I (San Francisco, 1992), covers the whole of the East up to 1500. Stephen Neill, in old age, began a three-volume work: *A History of Christianity in India: The Beginnings to AD 1707* (Cambridge, 1984); *A History of Christianity in India: 1707–1858* (Cambridge, 1985); the third volume, never completed, was intended to cover the rest. See also Julius Richter, *A History of Missions in India* (Edinburgh and London, 1908) (translated from the German *Indische Missionsgeschichte* (1906) by Sydney H. Moore); Leslie W. Brown, *The Indian Christians of St Thomas: An Account of the Ancient Syrian Church of Malabar* (Cambridge, 1956); P. J. Podipara, *The Thomas Christians* (Madras, 1970); and Robin E. Waterfield, *Christians in Persia: Assyrians, Armenians, Roman Catholics and Protestants* (London, 1973).

Pre-1500

For the earliest documentation including the 'Acts of Thomas', see the following: [Abgar Legend], *Something concerning Abgarus, Prince of the Edesseans with his epistle to Christ, and Christ's epistle in answer thereto: also Paul's epistle to the Laodiceans, with the manner of his death and his exhortation to his persecutors: a catalogue of those Scriptures mentioned but not inserted in the Bible: as also how several Scriptures are corrupted by the translators, with the difference betwixt the old and new translations* ([London, 1675?]); William Cureton, *Ancient Syriac documents relative to the earliest establishment of Christianity in Edessa and the neighbouring countries, from the year after Our Lord's ascension to the beginning of the fourth century* (Amsterdam, 1867), discovered, edited, translated and annotated; A. F. J. Klijn, *The Acts of Thomas: Introduction, Text and Commentary* (Leiden, 1962), translated from a surviving Syriac text, derived from earlier originals; E. Hennecke, *New Testament Apocrypha* (London, 1963–5), vols 1 and 2, edited by W. Schneemelcher and translated by R. M. Wilson; J. K. Elliott (ed.), 'The Acts of Thomas', *The Apocryphal New Testament: A Collection of Apocryphal Christian Literature in an English Translation* (Oxford/New York, 1993 [1924]), with revised bibliographical references and indexes.

The origins and early history of the Thomas Christians and their Syriac connections are discussed in G. E. Medlycott, *India and the Apostle Thomas: An Inquiry* (London,

1905); Henry Hosten, *Antiquities from San Thome and Mylapore* (Madras, 1936). On the traditional site of martyrdom and tomb of the Apostle Thomas also see Hosten's *The Song of Thomas Rabban* (Madras, 1931); B. A. Figredo, *Bones of St Thomas and the Antique Casket at Mylapore* (Madras, 1972); H. J. W. Drijvers, *East of Antioch: Studies in Early Syriac Christianity* (London, 1984); Jacob Kollaparambil, *The Babylonian Origin of the Southists Among the St Thomas Christians* (Rome, 1992); George Mark Moraes, *A History of Christianity in India, from Early Times to St Francis Xavier: AD 52–1542* (Bombay, [1964]); A. Mathias Mundadan, *History of Christianity in India*, vol. I: *From the Beginning up to the Middle of the Sixteenth Century* (Bangalore, 1982) and *Sixteenth Century Traditions of St Thomas Christians* (Bangalore, 1970); S. G. Pothan, *The Syrian Christians of Kerala* (New York, [1963]); J. P. M. van der Ploeg, *The Christians of St Thomas in South India and Their Syriac Manuscripts* (Bangalore, 1983). See also Avadh Kishore Narain, *The Indo-Greeks* (Oxford, 1957), Bibliography, and J. B. Segal, *A History of the Jews of Cochin* (London and Portland, 1993).

1500–1800

Joseph Thekkedath, *History of Christianity in India*, vol. II: *From the Middle of the Sixteenth Century to the End of the Seventeenth Century* (Bangalore, 1982), provides a general history for the first part of this period. The Jesuit mission is covered by Georg Schurhammer, *Francis Xavier: His Life, His Times* (*Franz Xavier, sein Leben und seine Zeit*), translated into English by M. Joseph Costelloe (Rome, 1973–82), in four volumes; E. Maclagan, *The Jesuits and the Great Mogul* (London, 1932); also see the popular work by Vincent Cronin, *A Pearl to India: The Life of Roberto de Nobili* (London, 1959), and Sundararaj Manickam, *The First Oriental Scholar* (Tirunelveli, 1972).

For the Tranquebar Mission and other early Protestant work, see Bartholomaeus Ziegenbalg, *The Propagation of the Gospel in the East* (London, 1709; 1710; 1718), ed. and introductory notes by A. H. Bohme, 'Preliminary discourses concerning the character of Missions . . .'; Erich Beyreuther, *Bartholomaeus Ziegenbalg: A Biography of the First Protestant Missionary in India, 1682–1719* (Madras, 1956), translated by S. G. Lang and H. W. Gensichen; John Foster, 'The significance of A. H. Boehme's [Böhme's] "The Propagation of the Gospel in the East"', *Oecumenia* (1968). Robert Caldwell, *Records of the Early History of the Tinnevelly Mission* (Madras, 1881). Johannes Ferdinand Fenger, *History of the Tranquebar Mission, Worked out from the Original Papers* (Tranquebar, 1863), from the German by Emil Francke, with biographies of 98 Evangelical Lutheran missionaries in India. Wilhelm Germann, *Missionar Christian Schwartz – Sein Leben und Wirken aus Briefen des Halleschen Missionsarchiv* (Erlangen, 1870). Dennis Hudson, *The Kingdom of God Is Not Food and Drink: The Beginnings of Evangelical Christianity Among the Tamils, 1706–1830* (London/Grand Rapids, in press). Daniel Jeyaraj, *Inkulturation in Tranquebar: Der Bertrag der frühen dänisch-halleschen Mission zum Werden einer indisch-einheimischen Kirche (1706–1730)* (Erlangen, 1996). E. Arno Lehmann, *Es begann in Tranquebar* (Berlin, 1955); and abridged English translation, *It Began in Tranquebar* (Madras, 1956). Hugh Nicholas Pearson [Dean of Salisbury], *Memoir of the Life and Correspondence of the Reverend Christian Frederick Swartz, to which is prefixed, a sketch of the History of Christianity in India* (2 vols; London, 1834, 1835, 1839), the standard work, consists mainly of letters. Indira Viswanathan Peterson, 'European science and German missionary education in the lives of two Indian intellectuals of the eighteenth century: the Cabinet of Curiosities (Kunstkammer) in Halle and Tanjavur', unpublished Conference paper (Copenhagen,

21 August 1996). Julius Richter, *Die deutsche Mission in Südindien* (Gütersloh, 1902). SPCK, *An Abstract of the Annual Reports and Correspondence of the SPCK* (London, 1814); *Notices of Madras {and the Coast of Coromandel} and Cuddalore in the last Century, from the Letters and Journals of Earlier Missionaries of the Society for Promoting Christian Knowledge* (London, 1858), beginning with Benjamin Schultze in 1726 and ending with John Sartorius in 1738.

Post-1800

C. M. Agur, *History of the Protestant Church in Travancore* (Madras, 1903). Thomas Anchukandam, *Catholic Revival in India in the 19th Century: Role of Mgr. Clement Bonnard (1796–1861)*, vol. one (Bangalore, 1996). Frederick S. Downs, *History of Christianity in India*, vol. V, part 5: *North East India in the Nineteenth and Twentieth Centuries* (Bangalore, 1992). Timothy George, *Faithful Witness: The Life and Mission of William Carey* (Birmingham, AL, 1991). Hugald Grafe, *History of Christianity in India*, vol. IV, part 2: *Tamilnadu in the Nineteenth and Twentieth Centuries* (Bangalore, 1990). E. Daniel Potts, *British Baptist Missionaries in India, 1793–1837: The History of Serampore and Its Missions* (Cambridge, 1967). Brian Stanley, *The History of the Baptist Missionary Society, 1792–1992* (Edinburgh, 1992). Alvin Texas Fishman, *Culture Change and the Underprivileged: A Study of Madigas in South India Under Christian Guidance* (Madras, 1941), an anthropological study. Dennis Hudson, 'The life and times of H. A. Krishna Pillai (1827–1900): a study of the encounter of Tamil Sri Vaishanava Hinduism and Evangelical Protestant Christianity in nineteenth-century Tirunelveli District' (Claremont Graduate School PhD dissertation, 1979), a study of perhaps India's greatest nineteenth-century writer. Sundararaj Manickam, *The Social Setting of Christian Conversion in South India* (Wiesbaden, 1971), a study of the impact of the Wesleyan Methodist missionaries on the Trichy-Tanjore Diocese with special reference to the Harijan communities of the Mass Movement Area, 1820–1947. James Stuart, *Swami Abhishiktananda: His Life Told Through His Letters* (Delhi, 1995). Bror Tiliander, *Christian and Hindu Terminology: A Study of Their Mutual Relations with Special Reference to the Tamil Area* (Uppsala, 1974). Susan Visvanathan, *The Christians of Kerala: History, Belief and Ritual Among the Yakoba* (Madras, 1993). John C. B. Webster, *A History of Dalit Christians in India* (San Francisco, 1992). Richard Fox Young, *Resistant Hinduism: Sanskrit Sources on Anti-Christian Apologetics in Early Nineteenth-Century India* (Vienna and Delhi, 1981); *The Bible Trembled: The Hindu–Christian Controversies of Nineteenth-Century Ceylon* (1995); and *Vain Debates* (1996).

On Bishop Azariah and the Church of South India see Susan Billington Harper, *In the Shadow of the Mahatma: Bishop V. S. Azariah and the Travails of Christianity in British India* (London/Grand Rapids, 1998); Bengt Sundkler, *Church of South India: The Movement Towards Union, 1900–1947* (London, 1954); Constance Millington, *An Ecumenical Venture: The History of the Nandyal Diocese in Andhra Pradesh (1947–1990)* (Bangalore, 1993) and *Led by the Spirit: A Biography of Arthur Michael Hollis* (Bangalore, 1996). Benny M. Aguiar, 'India and Sri Lanka' in *Modern Catholicism*, ed. Adrian Hastings (London, 1991), pp. 377–86, provides an introduction to the Catholic Church's history since the Second Vatican Council.

Chapter 6: Africa

The most wide-ranging and magisterial work is Adrian Hastings, *The Church in Africa 1450–1950* (Oxford, 1994). This is the basic resource for all students of the history of African Christianity, with extensive bibliographies. Elizabeth Isichei, *A History of Christianity in Africa* (London, 1995), is a very useful introductory account. A general history widely available in Africa is John Baur, *2000 Years of Christianity in Africa* (Nairobi, 1994), written with seminarians particularly in mind. The *Journal of Religion in Africa* (edited at Leeds and published by Brill of Leiden) is of great importance as a forum for contemporary scholarship in the field.

Two books which help to locate Christianity within the larger context of religion in Africa are: Thomas Blakely, W. van Beek and D. L. Thompson (eds), *Religion in Africa* (London, 1994), and Benjamin Ray, *African Religions* (New Jersey, 1976). John Iliffe, *Africans: The History of a Continent* (Cambridge, 1975), provides a masterly summation of African history, always sensitive to the significance of religion. John Middleton (Editor in Chief), *Encyclopedia of Africa South of the Sahara* (4 vols; New York, 1997), contains much material of interest to the student of Christianity in Africa. For a theological assessment of Africa's Christian history, see Kwame Bediako, *Christianity in Africa: The Renewal of a Non-Western Religion* (Edinburgh, 1995).

Three wide-ranging collections of essays on the development of Christianity since the 1960s are C. G. Baeta (ed.), *Christianity in Tropical Africa* (London, 1968); T. O. Ranger and J. Weller (eds), *Themes in the Christian History of Central Africa* (London, 1975); and E. Fasholé-Luke *et al.* (eds), *Christianity in Independent Africa* (London, 1978). Adrian Hastings, *A History of African Christianity 1950–1975* (Cambridge, 1979), provides a fascinating historical account of this period. P. Gifford (ed.), *The Christian Churches and the Democratization of Africa* (Leiden, 1995), is a useful series of essays on even more recent events. Fiona Bowie, Deborah Kirkwood and Shirley Ardener (eds), *Women and Missions: Past and Present: Anthropological and Historical Perceptions* (Oxford, 1993), has a number of interesting contributions both on missionaries and on African women. Nathaniel Ndiokwere, *Prophesy and Revolution: The Role of Prophets in the Independent African Churches and in Biblical Tradition* (London, 1981), provides a convenient Africa-wide survey of founders and movements of African independent churches.

A. S. Atiya, *A History of Eastern Christianity* (London, 1967), provides a good general survey of the Church in Egypt. For Ethiopia, see Taddesse Tamrat, *Church and State in Ethiopia 1270–1527* (Oxford, 1972); Edward Ullendorff, *Ethiopia and the Bible* (London, 1968); Steven Kaplan, *The Monastic Holy Man and the Christianization of Early Solomonic Ethiopia* (Wiesbaden, 1984); and Donald Crummey, *Priests and Politicians: Protestant and Catholic Missions in Orthodox Ethiopia 1830–1868* (Oxford, 1972). For Nubia, see Giovanni Vantini, *Christianity in the Sudan* (Bologna, 1981). For Christianity in Kongo, see two works of general history: Anne Hilton, *The Kingdom of Kongo* (London, 1985), and John Thornton, *The Kingdom of Kongo, Civil War and Transition* (Madison, 1983). There is also a chapter on Kongo in Richard Gray, *Black Christians and White Missionaries* (Yale, 1990), a work which has general importance for understanding the dynamics of African Christianity.

For a general account of West African Christianity, see Lamin Sanneh, *West African Christianity: The Religious Impact* (New York, 1983). Sanneh is a prolific writer on a variety of religious themes relating to Africa: *Translating the Message: The Missionary Impact on Culture* (New York, 1989); *Encountering the West: Christianity and the Global*

Cultural Process: The African Dimension (London, 1993); *Piety and Power: Muslims and Christians in West Africa* (NY, 1996). W. L. Williams examines the the role of African American missionaries in West Africa in *Black Americans and the Evangelisation of Africa 1877–1900* (Madison, 1982). For Nigeria see Elizabeth Isichei, *Varieties of Christian Experience in Nigeria* (London, 1982), and the pioneering works of modern Nigerian historiography: J. F. A. Ajayi, *Christian Missions in Nigeria 1841–1891* (London, 1966), and E. A. Ayandele, *The Missionary Impact on Modern Nigeria, 1842–1914* (London, 1966). J. B. Webster, *The African Churches Among the Yoruba* (Oxford, 1964), Harold Turner, *History of an African Independent Church: The Church of the Lord (Aladura)* (Oxford, 1967), and John Peel, *Aladura: A Religious Movement Among the Yoruba* (London, 1968), are important for the study of independent churches in Nigeria.

For an autobiographical account of the anti-slavery era by an African – an Igbo – read Paul Edwards (ed.), *The Interesting Narrative of the Life of Olaudah Equiano* (London, 1969). E. Isichei, *Entirely for God* (London, 1980), is a fine biography of another Igbo Christian, Michael Tansi, a Catholic priest of this century, who became a contemplative monk. The impact of Prophet Harris can be gauged in the two accounts by G. M. Halliburton, *The Prophet Harris* (London, 1971), and David Shank, *Prophet Harris: The Black Elijah of West Africa* (Leiden, 1994). For Ghana see F. L. Bartels, *The Roots of Ghana Methodism* (Cambridge, 1965), and N. Smith, *The Presbyterian Church of Ghana* (Accra, 1966). For an account of Liberia in the late twentieth century, see P. Gifford, *Christianity and Politics in Doe's Liberia* (Cambridge, 1993).

Two books on Congo in the colonial period can be recommended: Ruth Slade, *English-Speaking Missions in the Congo Independent State* (Brussels, 1959), and S. Axelson, *Cultural Confrontation in the Lower Congo* (Uppsala, 1970). W. de Craemer, *Jamaa and the Church: A Bantu Catholic Movement in Zaire* (Oxford, 1977), describes this Catholic renewal movement both in colonial times and since independence. For the life of Simon Kimbangu and the Kimbanguist Church, see M. L. Martin, *Kimbangu* (Oxford, 1975).

There is a wealth of material on Southern African history. Richard Elphick and Rodney Davenport, *Christianity in South Africa: A Political, Social and Cultural History* (Cape Town and London, 1997), provides an excellent synthesis of recent research, giving a general overview of important developments, and full of fascinating detail, for which see also H. Bredekamp and R. Ross, *Missions and Christianity in South African History* (Johannesburg, 1995). Two works by J. B. Peires are important for an understanding of Xhosa Christian history: *The House of Phalo* (Johannesburg, 1981) and *The Dead Shall Arise: Nongqawuse and the Great Cattle-Killing of 1856–7* (Johannesburg, 1989). N. Etherington, *Preachers, Peasants and Politics in Southeast Africa* (London, 1978), focuses on the social and economic impact of Christianity in Kwazulu-Natal; J. and J. Comaroff, *Of Revelation and Revolution*, vol. 1: *Christianity, Colonialism and Consciousness* (Chicago, 1991) and vol. 2: *The Dialectics of Modernity on a South African Frontier* (Chicago, 1997), is seminal, dealing with the interaction between missionary ideology and the African appropriation of Christianity from anthropological perspectives. See also Paul Landau, *The Realm of the Word: Language, Gender and Christianity in a Southern African Kingdom* (London, 1995).

Brian Willan's biography, *Sol Plaatje: South African Nationalist, 1876–1932* (Berkeley, 1984), gives a good account of this writer, political activist and Christian. Bengt Sundkler's two works on 'Zionism' in South Africa, *Bantu Prophets in South Africa* (London, 1948) and *Zulu Zion and Some Swazi Zionists* (London, 1976), have been widely influential. Mia Brandel-Syrier, *Black Woman in Search of God* (London, 1962), was a pioneering work in highlighting the role of women in South African Christianity. There is a large literature on apartheid and the theological issues it raises: for example, J. de Gruchy, *The Church Struggle in South Africa* (London, 1986) and (edited with others) *Apartheid Is a Heresy* (Grand Rapids, 1983).

Terence Ranger, *Are We Not Also Men? The Samkange Family and African Politics in Zimbabwe 1920–64* (London, 1995), is a delightful account of a prominent Christian family. M. Daneel has written extensively and with great insight on independency in Zimbabwe in the three volumes of *Old and New in Southern Shona Independent Churches* (The Hague, 1971, 1974, 1988). For Malawi, see G. Shepperson and T. Price, *Independent African: John Chilembwe and the Origins, Setting and Significance of the Nyasaland Native Rising of 1915* (Edinburgh, 1958); J. McCracken, *Politics and Christianity in Malawi, 1875–1940: The Impact of the Livingstonia Mission in the Northern Province* (London, 1977); T. J. Thompson, *Christianity in Northern Malawi: Donald Fraser's Missionary Methods and Ngoni Culture* (Leiden, 1995); and Kenneth Ross (ed.), *Christianity in Malawi: A Source Book* (Gweru, 1996). For Zambia, see B. Garvey, *Bembaland Church* (Leiden, 1993), and R. Henkel, *Christian Missions in Africa: A Social Geographical Study of the Impact of Their Activities in Zambia* (Berlin, 1989).

For Eastern Africa, see Z. Nthamburi, *From Mission to Church: A Handbook of Christianity in East Africa* (Nairobi, 1991), and for Kenya see: A. Temu, *Protestant Missions* (London, 1972); R. Strayer, *The Making of Mission Communities in East Africa* (London, 1978); D. Sandgren, *Christianity and the Kikuyu* (New York, 1989); and John Baur, *The Catholic Church in Kenya: A Centenary History* (Nairobi, 1990). Aylward Shorter and Edwin Onyancha, *Secularism in Africa* (Nairobi, 1997), explores religion in the 'secular city' of Nairobi. Sandra Wallman, *Kampala Women Getting By: Wellbeing in the Time of AIDS* (London, 1996), has useful material on women and religion in another African capital. Uganda, and particularly Buganda, has a rich historiography, including J. V. Taylor, *The Growth of the Church in Buganda* (London, 1958); H. P. Gale, *Uganda and the Mill Hill Fathers* (London, 1959); L. Pirouet, *Black Evangelists: The Spread of Christianity in Uganda 1879–1914* (London, 1978); H. Hansen, *Mission, Church and State in a Colonial Setting* (London, 1984); and J. Waliggo, *A History of African Priests* (Masaka, 1988).

For Tanzania, see C. H. Hellberg, *Missions on a Colonial Frontier* (Lund, 1963); B. Sundkler, *Bara Bukoba: Church and Community in Tanzania* (London, 1980); and T. O. Beidelman, *Colonial Evangelism: A Socio-Historical Study of an East African Mission at the Grassroots* (Bloomington, 1982). Carl-Erik Sahlberg, *From Krapf to Rugambwa – A Church History of Tanzania* (Nairobi, 1986), provides a convenient summary. F. Welbourn, *East African Rebels* (London, 1961), and F. Welbourn and B. Ogot, *A Place to Feel at Home* (London, 1966), are important accounts of independency in East Africa. Ian Linden, *Church and Revolution in Rwanda* (London, 1977), provides insights into the background of conflict in this area, discussed also in Gerard Prunier, *The Rwanda Crisis: History of a Genocide* (London, 1995). Andrew Wheeler (ed.), *Land of Promise: Church Growth in a Sudan at War* (Nairobi, 1997), contains a number of stimulating essays on the recent history of Christianity in the Sudan.

Novels are often a good way into religious themes in Africa, e.g. Chinua Achebe, *Things Fall Apart;* Ngugi wa Thiongo, *The River Between;* Stanlake Samkange, *The Mourned One;* Mongo Beti, *The Poor Christ of Bomba* (all published in the Heinemann Africa Writers Series); and Alan Paton, *Cry the Beloved Country* (Penguin).

Chapter 7: Reformation and Counter-Reformation

Recent general treatments of the subject include Euan Cameron, *The European Reformation* (Oxford, 1991), and Carter Lindberg, *The European Reformations* (Oxford, 1996). On the Pre-Reformation Church, Steven Ozment, *The Age of Reform, 1250–1550* (New Haven, 1980), is the best introduction. Johann Huizinga's classic *Waning of the Middle Ages* is now reissued in a new translation as *The Autumn of the Middle Ages* (London, 1996). On England, see Eamon Duffy, *The Stripping of the Altars* (New Haven, 1992). For the ideas of the Reformation era, Heiko Oberman, *Masters of the Reformation* (Cambridge, 1981), and Alister McGrath, *Reformation Thought: An Introduction* (Oxford, 1988). For collections of original documents in translation, Hans J. Hillerbrand, *The Protestant Reformation* (New York, 1968), William Naphy, *The Continental Reformation* (Basingstoke, 1996), and Alastair Duke, Gillian Lewis and Andrew Pettegree, *Calvinism in Europe, 1540–1610* (Manchester, 1992).

On Luther and Germany, the classic A. G. Dickens, *The German Nation and Martin Luther* (London, 1974), is stimulating and readable; Heiko Oberman, *Luther, Man Between God and the Devil* (New Haven, 1989), is the best Luther biography. On the Reformation controversies, Mark Edwards, *Luther and the False Brethren* (Stanford, 1975), and on Luther's public appeal, Steven Ozment, *The Reformation in the Cities* (New Haven, 1975), and Robert Scribner, *For the Sake of Simple Folk* (Cambridge, 1981). R. Po-Chia Hsia, *The German People and the Reformation* (Ithaca, 1988), is an outstandingly useful collection. For the conservative response to Luther, David Bagchi, *Luther's Earliest Opponents: Catholic Controversialists, 1518–1525* (Minneapolis, 1991). Peter Blickle, *The Communal Reformation* (New Jersey, 1992), provides an alternative explanatory framework; see also his *The Revolution of 1525* (Baltimore, 1981), on the German Peasants' War. On the radicals, Hans Jürgen Goertz, *The Anabaptists* (London, 1996), and for the Protestant Reformation's radical reorganization of the visual arts, Carl Christiansen, *Art and the Reformation in Germany* (Athens, OH, 1979) and his *Princes and Propaganda: Electoral Saxon Art of the Reformation* (Kirksville, 1992).

On the Reformation outside Germany, the essays collected in Andrew Pettegree, *The Early Reformation in Europe* (Cambridge, 1992), provide an introduction. See also Mark Greengrass, *The French Reformation* (Oxford, 1987), Francis Higman, *Censorship and the Sorbonne* (Geneva, 1979), and Alastair Duke, *Reformation and Revolt in the Low Countries* (London, 1990). Pending an up-to-date study of the Swiss Reformation, G. R. Potter, *Zwingli* (Cambridge, 1976), is a fine study of the Zurich reformer. On Scandinavia, Ole Grell, *The Scandinavian Reformation* (Cambridge, 1995); on Eastern Europe, Karin Maag (ed.), *The Reformation in Central and Eastern Europe* (Aldershot, 1997). Jean-François Gilmont, *La Réforme et le Livre* (Paris, 1990), provides an invaluable series of surveys; a translation of this work is to be published in 1998.

The best work on England is contained in specialist works and monographs. Susan Brigden, *London and the Reformation* (Oxford, 1989), is the definitive account of events in England's capital. Diarmaid MacCulloch, *Thomas Cranmer* (New Haven, 1996), offers a fine account of the period of early success for English Protestantism; Andrew Pettegree, *Marian Protestantism: Six Studies* (Aldershot, 1996), charts survival under persecution. It is now generally accepted that English Protestantism only finally became a majority faith during the reign of Elizabeth. On this period, see Patrick Collinson, *The Birthpangs of Protestant England* (Basingstoke, 1988); Tessa Watt, *Cheap Print and Popular Piety, 1550–1640* (Cambridge, 1991); David Cressy, *Bonfires and Bells* (London, 1989); and Martin Ingram, *Church Courts, Sex and Marriage in England,*

1570–1640 (Cambridge, 1987). The full history of the Scottish Reformation is still to be written. See, meanwhile, Michael Lynch, *Scotland: A New History* (London, 1991), and Michael Graham, *The Uses of Reform: 'Godly Discipline' and Popular Behaviour in Scotland and Beyond, 1560–1610* (Leiden, 1996).

On Calvinism, William G. Naphy, *Calvin and the Consolidation of the Reformation in Geneva* (Manchester, 1994), is a bold revisionist portrait. Andrew Pettegree, Alastair Duke and Gillian Lewis, *Calvinism in Europe, 1540–1620* (Cambridge, 1994), offers an introduction to Calvinism as an international movement. On France, see Mack Holt, *The French Wars of Religion* (Cambridge, 1995), Philip Benedict, *Rouen During the French Wars of Religion* (Cambridge, 1981), and Nicola Sutherland, *The Huguenot Struggle for Recognition* (New Haven, 1980). On French Catholicism and the massacre of St Bartholomew's Day, Barbara Diefendorf, *Beneath the Cross: Catholics and Huguenots in Sixteenth-Century Paris* (New York, 1991), and on the end of the wars, Michael Wolfe, *The Conversion of Henri IV* (Cambridge, MA, 1993). For the Netherlands, Jonathan Israel, *The Dutch Republic, Its Rise, Greatness and Fall, 1477–1806* (Oxford, 1995), provides an introduction; see also Andrew Pettegree, *Emden and the Dutch Revolt* (Oxford, 1992), and Guido Marnef, *Antwerp in the Age of Reformation: Underground Protestantism in a Commercial Metropolis, 1550–1577* (Baltimore, 1996). Raymond Mentzer, *Sin and the Calvinists* (Kirksville, 1994), is the best introduction to Calvinist social discipline.

Later Lutheranism is not well served in the English-speaking literature. The two collections by Heinz Schilling, *Civic Calvinism* (Kirksville, 1991) and *Religion, Political Culture and the Emergence of Early Modern Society* (Leiden, 1992), contain important work and a useful introduction to the issue of confessionalization. See also R. Po-Chia Hsia, *Social Discipline in the Reformation: Central Europe, 1550–1750* (London, 1989). Gerald Strauss, *Luther's House of Learning* (Baltimore, 1978), initiated one of the most important debates of recent times; the issue is more starkly put in his 'Success and failure in the German Reformation', *Past and Present*, 67 (1975). On the rural Reformation, Scott Dixon, *The Reformation and Rural Society: The Parishes of Brandenburg-Ansbach-Kulmbach* (Cambridge, 1996). On German Calvinism, Bodo Nischan, *Prince, People and Confession: The Second Reformation in Brandenburg* (Philadelphia, 1994). See also Bob Scribner and Trevor Johnson, *Popular Religion in Germany and Central Europe, 1400–1800* (Basingstoke, 1996).

The Catholic Reformation still requires a definitive study. N. S. Davidson, *The Catholic Reformation* (Oxford, 1987), and R. Po-Chia Hsia, *The World of Catholic Renewal, 1540–1770* (Cambridge, 1997), are useful as introduction. There is no modern study of the Council of Trent but see *The Canons and Decrees of the Council of Trent*, ed. H. J. Schroeder (Rockford, IL, 1978), for a good edition of the text. Against this a host of important local studies now chart the progress of Catholic Reform at a local level. See especially Marc Forster, *The Counter-Reformation in the Villages: Religion and Reform in the Bishopric of Speyer* (Ithaca, 1992); David Gentilcore, *From Bishop to Witch: The System of the Sacred in Early Modern Terra d'Otranto* (Manchester, 1992); William A. Christian, *Local Religion in Sixteenth-Century Spain* (Princeton, 1981); and Henry Kamen, *The Phoenix and the Flame: Catalonia and the Counter-Reformation* (New Haven, 1993). Recent research has also permitted a more realistic evaluation of the work and impact of the Inquisition. See particularly Stephen Haliczer, *Inquisition and Society in the Kingdom of Valencia, 1478–1834* (Berkeley, 1990), and William Monter, *Frontiers of Heresy: The Spanish Inquisition from the Basque Lands to Sicily* (Cambridge, 1990). On the new religious orders and missions, see A. D. Wright, *The Counter-Reformation: Catholic Europe and the Non-Christian World* (London, 1982), and John W. O'Malley, *The First Jesuits* (Cambridge, MA, 1993).

On the revitalized Catholicism of the seventeenth century, Jean Delumeau, *Catholicism Between Luther and Voltaire* (London, 1977), and Louis Châtellier, *The Europe of the Devout: The Catholic Reformation and the Formation of a New Society* (Cambridge, 1989). For France, Roland Mousnier, *The Assassination of Henry IV* (London, 1973), and Joseph Bergin, *The Making of the French Episcopate* (New Haven, 1996). The intellectual background to the Revocation of the Edict of Nantes is the subject of E. I. Perry, *From Theology to History: French Religious Controversy and the Revocation of the Edict of Nantes* (The Hague, 1973). Its effects are painstakingly chronicled in Samuel Mours, *Les Églises réformées en France* (Paris, 1968).

For England, the best introduction to the religious politics of the pre-Civil War period is now Derek Hirst, *Authority and Conflict: England 1603–1658* (London, 1986). The essays in Kenneth Fincham (ed.), *The Early Stuart Church* (Basingstoke, 1993), review admirably the current state of a complicated historical debate. Christopher Hill's *Oliver Cromwell* (London, 1958), is rightly admired as a classic.

For the Habsburg diplomacy of the Thirty Years War, see Robert Bireley, *Religion and Politics in the Age of the Counter-Reformation: Emperor Ferdinand II, William Lamormaini, SJ, and the Formation of Imperial Policy* (Chapel Hill, 1981). The best general study of the conflict is Geoffrey Parker, *The Thirty Years' War* (London, 1984). On Eastern Europe, see R. J. W. Evans, *The Making of the Habsburg Monarchy, 1550–1700* (Oxford, 1977). For the creation of the Polish Catholic identity, Norman Davies, *God's Playground: A History of Poland* (2 vols; Oxford, 1982).

Chapter 8: Eastern Europe since the fifteenth century

A useful handbook enabling the reader to gain an overall view, through maps, of the complex history of the region, with due attention to the religious aspect, is Paul Robert Magocsi, *Historical Atlas of East Central Europe* (Seattle and London, 1993). For background to divided Christendom the reader should consult Steven Runciman, *The Eastern Schism* (Oxford, 1955), and, for more recent reflections, Aidan Nichols OP, *Rome and the Eastern Churches: A Study in Schism* (Collegeville, MN, 1992). Good introductions to the teachings, spirituality and worship of the Orthodox Church are: Vladimir Lossky, *The Mystical Theology of the Eastern Church* (London, 1955); Nicholas Arseniev, *Mysticism and the Eastern Church* (Crestwood, 1979); John Meyendorff, *The Orthodox Church* (London, 1962); and Timothy Ware, *The Orthodox Church* (London, new edn, 1993). A readable introduction to the history of the Eastern Churches is Nicolas Zernov, *Eastern Christendom* (London, 1961); it provides orientation and pointers to further reading, but is in itself not free from tendentiousness and inaccuracy. More comprehensive coverage is to be found in Donald Attwater, *The Christian Churches of the East* (London, 1961), in two volumes, the first dealing with those Churches in communion with Rome and the second with the rest; older sources are the three volumes by A. Fortescue, *The Orthodox Eastern Church* (London, 1907), *The Lesser Eastern Churches* (London, 1913) and *The Uniate Eastern Churches* (London, 1923); and from the mid-nineteenth century John Mason Neale, *A History of the Holy Eastern Church* (5 vols; London, 1847–73). Steven Runciman, *The Orthodox Churches and the Secular State* (New Zealand, 1971), is an accessible short history of Orthodoxy in relation to secular power. J. Meyendorff, *The Byzantine Legacy in the Orthodox Church* (Crestwood, 1982), contains discussion of positive and negative features of autocephaly and of the future of the Ecumenical Patriarchate. F. Dvornik, *National Churches and the Church Universal* (Westminster, 1994), is a short introduction to the theme of its title in relation to the whole of Christendom. Histories of particular areas are Boris Gasparov and Olga Raevsky-Hughes (eds), *Christianity and the Eastern Slavs* (3 vols; Berkeley, Los Angeles and Oxford, 1993–95), and Robert Brenton Betts, *Christians in the Arab East* (rev. edn, Atlanta, 1978). O. Halecki, *From Florence to Brest* (Fordham, 1958), covers the historical background to the Union of Brest in 1596.

For the political and social history of the Ottoman period see L. S. Stavrianos, *The Balkans Since 1453* (New York, 1961), and Peter F. Sugar, *Southeastern Europe Under Ottoman Rule, 1354–1804* (Seattle and London, 1977). A basic work on religion in the Ottoman Empire is Frederick W. Hasluck, *Christianity and Islam Under the Sultans* (2 vols; Oxford, 1929), and more recent studies are Benjamin Brande and Bernard Lewis, *Christians and Jews in the Ottoman Empire: The Functioning of a Plural Society* (New York and London, 1982), and Charles A. Frazee, *Catholics and Sultans: The Church and the Ottoman Empire, 1453–1923* (Cambridge, 1983).

The history of the Greek Orthodox Church throughout the Ottoman period to the early nineteenth century is covered in Steven Runciman, *The Great Church in Captivity: A Study of the Patriarchate of Constantinople from the Eve of the Turkish Conquest to the Greek War of Independence* (Cambridge, 1968), and the story is continued by Charles A. Frazee, *The Orthodox Church and Independent Greece 1821–1852* (Cambridge, 1969). An illuminating approach is Timothy Ware, *Eustratios Argenti: A Study of the Greek Church Under Turkish Rule* (Oxford, 1964). Two substantial works covering the period to the end of the nineteenth century are A. H. Hore, *Eighteen Centuries of the Orthodox Greek Church* (London, 1899), and A. H. Hore, *Student's History of the Greek Church* (London, 1902). Euphrosyne Kephala, *The Church of the Greek People: Past and Present* (London, 1930), brings coverage into the twentieth century. P. Hammond, *The Waters of Marah* (London, 1955), presents a somewhat idealized picture of the Greek Church in the late 1940s. The implications of modern secularization for the Greek Church are explored in Mario Rinvolucri, *Anatomy of a Church: Greek Orthodoxy Today* (London, 1966); and the story is brought almost up to date by chapters in Richard Clogg (ed.), *Greece in the 1980s* (London 1983), and in Pedro Ramet (ed.), *Eastern Christianity and Politics in the Twentieth Century* (Durham and London, 1988).

In the absence of solid English-language studies of the Churches of the other Balkan peoples in the Ottoman Empire and afterwards, the best means of access is through general histories of the particular countries, some useful recent examples of which are: Richard Clogg, *A Short History of Modern Greece* (2nd edn; Cambridge, 1986); C. M. Woodhouse, *Modern Greece: A Short History* (5th edn; London, 1991); R. J. Crampton, *A Short History of Modern Bulgaria* (Cambridge, 1987); Anton Logoreci, *The Albanians: Europe's Forgotten Survivors* (London, 1977); Noel Malcolm, *Bosnia: A Short History* (London, 1994); and Fred Singleton, *A Short History of the Yugoslav Peoples* (Cambridge, 1985). Older, but still useful, is R. W. Seton-Watson, *A History of the Roumanians: From Roman Times to the Completion of Unity* (Cambridge, 1934). For the political history of the Balkan states in the context of the decline of the Ottoman Empire in Europe see Charles and Barbara Jelavich, *The Establishment of the Balkan National States, 1804–1920* (Seattle and London, 1977). For the history of the Caucasus see W. E. D. Allen, *A History of the Georgian People* (London, 1932); Ronald Grigor Suny, *The Making of the Georgian Nation* (London, 1989); and Christopher Walker, *Armenia: the Survival of a Nation* (London, 1980). Adrian Hastings, *The Construction of Nationhood: Ethnicity, Religion and Nationalism* (Cambridge, 1997), while treating principally of Western Europe, has much of relevance to Eastern, particularly the South Slavs.

Some books specifically on the religious history of these regions are: Keith Hitchens, *Orthodoxy and Nationality: Andreiu Saguna and the Romanians of Transylvania*

(Cambridge and London, 1977); Dennis P. Hupchick, *The Bulgarians in the Seventeenth Century: Slavic Orthodox Society and Culture Under Ottoman Rule* (Jefferson, NC, and London, 1993); Leon Arpee, *A History of Armenian Christianity from the Beginning to Our Own Time* (New York, 1946); Bishop Karekin Sarkissian, *The Armenian Church in Contemporary Times* (New York, 1970).

The history of Russian Orthodox theology and spirituality is addressed in Georges Florovsky, *Ways of Russian Theology* (in *The Collected Works of Georges Florovsky*, (Belmont, MA. and Vaduz, Liechtenstein, 1979)); in G. P. Fedotov, *The Russian Religious Mind* (2 vols; Belmont, MA, 1975), which takes the story up to the fifteenth century; and in Nicholas Arseniev, *Russian Piety* (London, 1964). See also Nadejda Gorodetsky, *The Humiliated Christ in Modern Russian Thought* (London, 1938). The most comprehensive and authoritative account of the Slavophiles and their heritage is Andrzej Walicki, *The Slavophile Controversy: History of a Conservative Utopia in Nineteenth-Century Russian Thought* (Oxford, 1975). See also Peter K. Christoff, *An Introduction to Nineteenth-Century Russian Slavophilism* (2 vols; The Hague, 1961 and 1972). On the subject of cross-fertilization between monks and intellectuals in nineteenth-century Russia see Nadejda Gorodetsky, *Saint Tikhon Zadonsky: Inspirer of Dostoevsky* (London, 1951); John B. Dunlop, *Staretz Amvrosy: Model for Dostoevsky's Staretz Zossima* (Belmont, MA, 1972); and Donald Nicholl, *Triumphs of the Spirit in Russia* (London, 1997).

On the seventeenth-century disputes in Russia involving Patriarch Nikon, see Paul Meyendorff, *Russia, Ritual and Reform* (New York, 1991). For the Petrine period see James Cracraft, *The Church Reform of Peter the Great* (Stanford, 1971). Gregory L. Freeze, in *The Russian Levites: Parish Clergy in the Eighteenth Century* (Cambridge, MA, 1977) and *The Parish Clergy in Nineteenth-Century Russia: Crisis, Reform, Counter-Reform* (Princeton, 1983), covers the imperial period, as do Robert L. Nichols and Theofanis G. Stavrou (eds), *Russian Orthodoxy Under the Old Regime* (Minneapolis, 1978). For a general overview of Orthodox mission, including that of the Greeks, see James J. Stamoolis, *Eastern Orthodox Mission Theology Today* (Maryknoll, 1986). John Shelton Curtiss, *Church and State in Russia: The Last Years of Empire 1900–1917* (New York, 1940), covers the immediate pre-revolutionary period but includes a 30-page introduction outlining the history of the Church to 1900. Histories covering other denominations are Rolf R. Robson, *Old Believers in Modern Russia* (Illinois, 1995), and Sophia Senyk, *A History of the Church in Ukraine* (Rome, a continuing series from 1993).

The period of religious ferment in Russia at the turn of the century and the leading personalities, many of whom he knew, are introduced by Nicolas Zernov, *The Russian Religious Renaissance of the Twentieth Century* (London, 1963); a deeper analysis of the main issues is George F. Putnam, *Russian Alternatives to Marxism: Christian Socialism and Idealistic Liberalism in Twentieth-Century Russia* (Knoxville, 1977). There is a good selection of material relating to this period in Alexander Schmemann (ed.), *Ultimate Questions: An Anthology of Modern Russian Religious Thought* (New York, 1965). Christopher Read, *Religion, Revolution, and the Russian Intelligentsia, 1900–1912: The 'Vekhi' Debate and its Intellectual Background* (London, 1979), looks at the political and social contribution of those involved, while James W. Cunningham, *A Vanquished Hope: The Movement for Church Renewal in Russia 1905–1906* (New York, 1981), examines the consequences for the Church.

On the tribulations for religious denominations in the Soviet Union see: Walter Kolarz, *Religion in the Soviet Union* (London, 1961); William C. Fletcher, *A Study in Survival: The Church in Russia, 1927–1943* (London, 1965); Nikita Struve, *Christians in Contemporary Russia* (London, 1967); Gerhard Simon, *Church, State and Opposition in the USSR* (London, 1974); and Sabrina Petra Ramet (ed.), *Religious Policy in the Soviet*

Union (Cambridge, 1993). Specifically on the Russian Orthodox Church, see Michael Bourdeaux, *Patriarch and Prophets: Persecution of the Russian Orthodox Church Today* (London, 1969); Dimitry Pospielovsky, *The Russian Church Under the Soviet Regime 1917–1982* (2 vols; Crestwood, 1984); and Jane Ellis, *The Russian Orthodox Church: A Contemporary History* (London, 1986). On the Ukrainian Catholics in the Soviet period, see Serge Keleher, *Passion and Resurrection: The Greek-Catholic Church in Soviet Ukraine* (Lviv, 1993).

A valuable introduction to the Churches of Eastern and Central Europe under Communism is Trevor Beeson, *Discretion and Valour: Religious Conditions in Russia and Eastern Europe* (rev. edn; London, 1982). Their situation on the eve of the changes of 1989 is described in Philip Walters (ed.), *World Christianity: Eastern Europe* (Eastbourne, 1988). Three magisterial volumes offer detailed analyses of Church–state relations in twentieth-century Eastern Europe across the denominational spectrum: Pedro Ramet (ed.), *Eastern Christianity and Politics in the Twentieth Century* (Durham and London, 1988); see also Pedro Ramet (ed.), *Catholicism and Politics in Communist Societies* (Durham and London, 1990), and Sabrina Petra Ramet (ed.) [same person], *Protestantism and Politics in Eastern Europe and Russia: The Communist and Post-Communist Eras* (Durham and London, 1992). An important single-country study is Stella Alexander, *Church and State in Yugoslavia Since 1945* (Cambridge, 1979).

Books dealing with the period since the onset of *glasnost'* in the Soviet Union are Nathaniel Davis, *A Long Walk to Church: A Contemporary History of Russian Orthodoxy* (Boulder, CO, 1995), and Jane Ellis, *The Russian Orthodox Church: Triumphalism and Defensiveness* (Basingstoke, 1996). The collapse of former Yugoslavia has produced many attempts to analyse the role of religion in the conflict, including Paul Mojzes, *Yugoslavian Inferno: Ethnoreligious Warfare in the Balkans* (New York, 1995), and several chapters in Sabrina Petra Ramet, *Balkan Babel: The Disintegration of Yugoslavia from the Death of Tito to Ethnic War* (Boulder, CO, 1996). An understanding of the complex religious situation in Bosnia-Hercegovina is facilitated by John Fine, *The Bosnian Church: A New Interpretation. A Study of the Bosnian Church and Its Place in State and Society from the 13th to the 15th Centuries* (Boulder and New York, 1975); Robert J. Donia, *Islam Under the Double Eagle: The Muslims of Bosnia and Hercegovina, 1878–1914* (Boulder and New York, 1981); and Mark Pinson, *The Muslims of Bosnia-Herzegovina: Their Historic Development from the Middle Ages to the Dissolution of Yugoslavia* (Cambridge, MA, 1994).

Coverage of all aspects of religious life in the Communist and post-Communist world is to be found in the journal published by Keston College, now Keston Institute (Oxford), under the titles *Religion in Communist Lands* (1973–91) and *Religion, State and Society: The Keston Journal* (1992–).

Chapter 9: Latin America

General works

The most wide-ranging and authoritative work of recent scholarship is the *Cambridge History of Latin America*, ed. Leslie Bethell (11 vols; Cambridge, 1984–95). It has, however, devoted rather limited space specifically to the Church. There are essays in volume I on the colonial period by Josep Barnadas and Eduardo Hoornaert, a note in volume III by L. Bethell on the Church and Independence and longer articles in volume IV by John Lynch on the Catholic Church 1830–1930, and in VI, 2 by Enrique Dussel on Catholicism and José Miguez Bonino on Protestantism since 1930.

Robert A. McNeil has edited *Latin American Studies: A Basic Guide to Sources* (2nd edn; London, 1990), while the University of Texas Press produces an invaluable annual *Handbook of Latin American Studies*, ed. Dolores Moyano Martin, with sections on religion and the Church.

E. Dussel (ed.), *The Church in Latin America: 1492–1992* (Maryknoll, 1992), provides an up-to-date review of the whole subject, while Hans Jürgen Prien, *Die Geschichte der Christentums in Latinamerika* (Göttingen, 1978), is the most comprehensive single volume to date. The standard general history in English remains Lloyd Mecham, *Church and State in Latin America* (Chapel Hill, 1966). The 11-volume *Historia General de la Iglesia en América Latina*, edited by Enrique Dussel, is in course of publication (Mexico).

For the Spanish background see J. N. Hillgarth, *The Spanish Kingdoms 1250–1516* (Oxford, 1978), and John Lynch, *Spain 1516–1598* (Oxford, 1991). An outstanding guide to much of the period is David Brading, *The First America: The Spanish Monarchy, Creole Patriotism and the Liberal State* (Cambridge, 1991). Among other general books on the colonial period are Jacques Lafaye, *Quetzalcóatl and Guadalupe: The Formation of Mexican National Consciousness 1531–1813* (Chicago, 1976), W. E. Shiels, *King and Church: The Rise and Fall of the Patronato Real* (Chicago, 1961), and C. R. Boxer, *The Church Militant and Iberian Expansion, 1440–1770* (Baltimore, 1978). Edward Norman's *The House of God* (London, 1990) splendidly illustrates the development of architecture.

For the first hundred years, the following is a selection of work available in English: J. L. Phelan, *The Millennial Kingdom of the Franciscans in the New World* (Berkeley, 1970), and N. Wachtel, *The Vision of the Vanquished* (Sussex, 1977). For Las Casas and the debates to which he was central, see Juan Friede and Benjamin Keen, *Bartolomé de Las Casas in History* (De Kalb, IL, 1971), Henry Raup Wagner and Helen Rand Parish, *The Life and Writings of Bartolomé de Las Casas* (Albuquerque, 1967), and B. de Las Casas, *In Defence of the Indians*, ed. Stafford Poole (Illinois, 1974; 2nd edn, 1992), as well as Lewis Hanke, *The Spanish Struggle for Justice in the Conquest of America* (Philadelphia, 1949) and *Aristotle and the American Indians* (London, 1959). Other aspects of sixteenth-century religious life are discussed in Richard E. Greenleaf, *Zumárraga and the Mexican Inquisition 1536–1543* (Washington, 1961); Robert Ricard, *The Spiritual Conquest of Mexico: An Essay on the Apostolate and Evangelizing Methods of the Mendicant Orders in New Spain* (Berkeley, 1966); Munro S. Edmonson (ed.), *Sixteenth-Century Mexico: The Work of Sahagún* (Albuquerque, 1974); Victoria Bricker, *The Indian Christ, the Indian King: The Historical Substrate of Maya Myth and Ritual* (University of Texas, 1981). Guaman Poma de Ayala's *El primer nueva corónica y buen gobierno* has been edited by John V. Murra, Rolena Adorno and Jorge L. Uriosto (Mexico, 1980) but not, as yet, translated into English. For Peru at this time, see Steve Stern, *Peru's Indian Peoples and the Challenge of Spanish Conquest: Huamanaga to 1640* (Madison, WI, 1982).

The seventeenth and eighteenth centuries

Stafford Poole, *Our Lady of Guadalupe: The Origins and Source of a Mexican National Symbol 1531–1797* (Tuscon, 1995), argues that the apparition story, though not the devotion to Mary at Tepeyac, is all a mid-seventeenth-century invention. David Brading, *Church and State in Bourbon Mexico: The Diocese of Michoacán 1749–1810* (Cambridge, 1994), and William B. Taylor, *Magistrates of the Sacred: Priests and Parishioners in Eighteenth-Century Mexico* (Stanford, 1996), provide two remarkable studies of the late colonial Mexican Church, for which see also Nancy M. Farris, *Crown and Clergy in Colonial Mexico 1759–1821: The Crisis of Ecclesiastical Privilege* (London, 1968), and Michael Costeloe, *Church Wealth in Mexico* (Cambridge, 1967), though the last in particular is a study of early nineteenth-century evidence. For Brazil in this period see John Hemming, *Red Gold: The Conquest of the Brazilian Indians* (London, 1978), A. J. R. Russell-Wood, *Fidalgos and Philanthropists* (London, 1968), and R. Cantel, *Prophétisme et messianisme dans l'oeuvre d'António Vieira* (Paris, 1960). Vieira was the most outstanding Portuguese Jesuit of the period. For the Jesuits more widely see Magnus Mörner, *The Political and Economic Activities of the Jesuits in the La Plata Region: The Hapsburg Era* (Stockholm, 1953); Philip Caraman, *The Lost Paradise: An Account of the Jesuits in Paraguay* (London, 1975); Herman W. Konrad, *A Jesuit Hacienda in Colonial Mexico: Santa Lucia 1576–1767* (Stanford, 1980); and David Block, *Mission Culture on the Upper Amazon: Native Tradition, Jesuit Enterprise and Secular Policy in Moxos, 1660–1880* (London, 1994).

Nineteenth and twentieth centuries

The first half of Edward Norman, *Christianity in the Southern Hemisphere: The Churches in Latin America and South Africa* (Oxford, 1981), provides a coherent introduction to this period. William Coleman, *The First Apostolic Delegation in Rio de Janeiro and Its Influence in Spanish America: A Study in Papal Policy 1830–1840* (Washington, 1950), is a close account of a fundamental moment of ecclesiastical change. For a number of country studies see J. L. Klaiber, *Religion and Revolution in Peru, 1824–1976* (Notre Dame, 1977); J. L. Kennedy, *Catholicism, Nationalism and Democracy in Argentina* (Notre Dame, 1958); Austen Ivereigh, *Catholicism and Politics in Argentina 1810–1960* (London, 1995); Michael Costeloe, *Church and State in Independent Mexico: A Study of the Patronage Debate 1821–1857* (London, 1978); R. E. Quirk, *The Mexican Revolution and the Catholic Church, 1910–1929* (Bloomington, 1973); S. Mainwaring, *The Catholic Church and Politics in Brazil, 1916–1985* (Stanford, 1986); D. H. Levine, *Religion and Politics in Latin America: The Catholic Church in Venezuela and Colombia* (Princeton, 1981); K. M. Schmitt (ed.), *The Roman Catholic Church in Modern Latin America* (New York 1972). Jean Meyer, 'The *Cristiada*: peasant war and religious war in revolutionary Mexico, 1926–9' in *Religion and Rural Revolt*, ed. Janos M. Bak and Gerhard Benecke (Manchester, 1984), pp. 441–52, is based on the same author's major three-volume study in Spanish, *La Cristiada* (Mexico, 1980). Alceu Amoroso Lima, 'Brazil' in Adrian Hastings (ed.), *The Church and the Nations* (London, 1959), pp. 193–206, offers an interesting account by a distinguished lay intellectual of how Brazilian Catholicism looked in the later 1950s; see also William J. Coleman, *Latin American Catholicism: A Self-Evaluation* (Maryknoll, 1958).

   For the 30 years following the Second Vatican Council there is a vast literature, much of it inevitably a little partisan. See in particular Edward L. Cleary and Hannah Stewart-Gambino (eds), *Conflict and Competition: The Latin American Church in a Changing Environment* (Boulder, Colorado, 1992); Edward Cleary (ed.), *Born of the Poor: The Latin American Church Since Medellín* (Notre Dame, 1990); Enrique Dussel, *A History of the Theology of Liberation* (New York, 1976); Paul Sigmund, *Liberation Theology at the Crossroads: Democracy or Revolution?* (New York, 1990); Thomas C. Bruneau, *The Political Transformation of the Brazilian Church* (Cambridge, 1974) and *The Church in Brazil: The Politics of Religion* (Austin, Texas, 1982); Brian Smith, *The Church and Politics in Chile* (Princeton, 1982); Emilio Mignone, *Witness to the Church: The Complicity of the Church and Dictatorship in Argentina* (Maryknoll, 1988); Margaret

Crahan, *The Church and Revolution in Cuba and Nicaragua* (Bandoora, Australia, 1988); W. E. Hewitt, *Base Christian Communities and Social Change in Brazil* (Lincoln, NE, 1991); and Teresa Whitfield, *Paying the Price: Ignacio Ellacuría and the Murdered Jesuits of El Salvador* (Philadelphia, 1994).

For the two CELAM meetings and official documents see CELAM, *The Church in the Present Day Transformation of Latin America in the Light of the Council* (2 vols; Bogota, 1970), and Edward Cleary (ed.), *Path from Puebla: Significant Documents of the Latin American Bishops Since 1979* (Washington, 1988).

Protestantism

John Sinclair (ed.), *Protestantism in Latin America: A Bibliographical Guide* (South Pasadena, 1976); E. Willems, *Followers of the New Faith: Cultural Change and the Rise of Protestantism in Brazil and Chile* (Nashville, 1967); Deborah Baldwin, *Protestants and the Mexican Revolution: Missionaries, Thinkers and Social Change* (Urbana, 1990); Rubem Alves, *Protestantism and Repression: A Brazilian Case Study* (New York, 1979); David Stoll, *Is Latin America Turning Protestant? The Politics of Evangelical Growth* (Berkeley, 1990); David Martin, *Tongues of Fire: The Explosion of Protestantism in Latin America* (Oxford, 1990); and David Lehmann, *Struggle for the Spirit: Religious Transformation and Popular Culture in Brazil and Latin America* (Oxford, 1996).

Chapter 10: China and its neighbours

There is as yet no general English-language history of Christianity covering East and South-east Asia. The following selected readings are for specific countries or regions.

China

Although published nearly 70 years ago, the following work is still the best general outline history of Christianity in China: Kenneth Scott Latourette, *A History of Christian Missions in China* (New York, 1929). A recent account, with an emphasis on more recent decades, is Bob Whyte, *Unfinished Encounter: China and Christianity* (London, 1988). Columba Cary-Elwes OSB, *China and the Cross: Studies in Missionary History* (London, 1957), provides a popular account of Catholicism in China.

The history of the Nestorian Church in China is traced in the following, mostly older, studies: P. Y. Saeki, *The Nestorian Monument in China* (London, 1916); P. Y. Saeki, *The Nestorian Documents and Relics in China* (2nd edn; rev. and enlarged; Tokyo, 1951); Samuel Hugh Moffett, *A History of Christianity in Asia*, vol. I: *Beginnings to 1500* (New York, 1992), chapter 15: 'The first Christian mission to China'; John Foster, *The Church of the T'ang Dynasty* (London, 1939); James Legge, *The Nestorian Monument of Hsi-An Fu* (London, 1968); Charlotte Eliza Couling, *The Luminous Religion: A Study of Nestorian Christianity in China* (London, 1925); Arthur Christopher Moule, *Nestorians in China: Some Corrections and Additions* (London, 1940).

The following texts provide information on the rise and fall of Christianity in Mongol China: Christopher Dawson (ed.), *Missions to Asia: Narratives and Letters of the Franciscan Missionaries in Mongolia and China in the Thirteenth and Fourteenth Centuries* (New York, 1966, reprinted from the 1955 edition entitled *The Mongol Mission*);

William W. Rockhill, *The Journey of William of Rubruck to the Eastern Parts, 1253–55, with Two Accounts of the Earlier Journey of John of Pian de Carpine* (London, 1900); Arthur Christopher Moule, *Christians in China Before the Year 1550* (London, 1930).

Many studies exist for the early modern period. The following selection affords a comprehensive introduction: Jacques Gernet, *China and the Christian Impact: A Conflict of Cultures* (2nd edn; Cambridge, 1987); D. E. Mungello (ed.), *The Rites Controversy: Its History and Meaning* (Nettetal, 1994); David E. Mungello, *Curious Land: Jesuit Accommodation and the Origins of Sinology* (Stuttgart, 1985); Charles E. Ronan and Bonnie B. C. Oh (eds), *East Meets West: The Jesuits in China, 1582–1773* (Chicago, 1988); Wang Xiaochao, *Christianity and Imperial Culture: Chinese Christian Apologetics in the Seventeenth Century and Their Latin Patristic Equivalent* (Leiden, 1998); Jonathan D. Spence, *The Memory Palace of Matteo Ricci* (New York, 1984); D. E. Mungello, *The Forgotten Christians of Hangzhou* (Honolulu, 1994).

Early Protestant work in China is discussed in the following studies: Ralph R. Covell, *Confucius, the Buddha, and Christ: A History of the Gospel in China* (Maryknoll, 1986); Suzanne Wilson Barnett and John King Fairbank (eds), *Christianity in China: Early Protestant Missionary Writings* (Cambridge, MA, 1985); Daniel H. Bays (ed.), *Christianity and China, The Eighteenth Century to the Present: Essays in Religious and Social Change* (Stanford, 1996).

Paul A. Cohen, *China and Christianity: The Missionary Movement and the Growth of Chinese Antiforeignism, 1860–1870* (Cambridge, MA, 1963), is the first major academic study of nineteenth-century Chinese Catholic Church history in the English language. The same author's influential article, 'Christian missions and their impact to 1900' in John K. Fairbank (ed.), *The Cambridge History of China*, vol. 10: *Late Imperial Ch'ing 1800–1911*, part 1 (Cambridge, 1978), pp. 543–90, provides an excellent framework for the study of anti-Christian conflict. Eric O. Hanson, *Catholic Politics in China and Korea* (Maryknoll, 1980); Jessie G. Lutz, *Christian Missions in China: Evangelists of What?* (Boston, 1965) and *China and the Christian Colleges, 1850–1950* (Ithaca, 1971); Jane Hunter, *The Gospel of Gentility: American Women Missionaries in Turn-of-the-Century China* (New Haven, 1984); Kwok Pui-lan, *Chinese Women and Christianity, 1860–1927* (Atlanta, 1992); John K. Fairbank (ed.), *The Missionary Enterprise in China and America* (Cambridge, MA, 1974). A historical survey of evangelistic work among China's national minorities is Ralph R. Covell, *The Liberating Gospel in China: The Christian Faith Among China's Minority Peoples* (Grand Rapids, 1995).

Scholarly surveys of Christianity in contemporary China include Alan Hunter and Chan Kim-Kwong, *Protestantism in Contemporary China* (Cambridge, 1993); Alan Hunter and Don Rimmington (eds), *All Under Heaven: Chinese Tradition and Christian Life in the People's Republic of China* (Kampen, 1992); Tony Lambert, *The Resurrection of the Chinese Church* (London, 1991); Raymond Fung, *Households of God on China's Soil* (Geneva, 1982). For a rather more positive assessment of the CCP and its religious policy, see Philip L. Wickeri, *Seeking the Common Ground: Protestant Christianity, the Three-Self Movement, and China's United Front* (Maryknoll, 1990). The recent history of the Chinese Catholic Church is treated in James T. Myers, *Enemies Without Guns: The Catholic Church in the People's Republic of China* (New York, 1991); Edmond Tang and Jean-Paul Wiest (eds), *The Catholic Church in Modern China: Perspectives* (Maryknoll, 1993); Beatrice Leung, *Sino-Vatican Relations: Problems in Conflicting Authority, 1976–1986* (Cambridge, 1992); Chan Kim-Kwong, *Struggling for Survival: The Catholic Church in China from 1949–1970* (Hong Kong, 1992). The growth of Protestantism in Taiwan is discussed in Murray A. Rubinstein, *The Protestant Community in Modern Taiwan: Mission, Seminary, and Church* (Armonk, NY, 1991).

South-east Asia

The following works deal with the early history of the Catholic Church in South-east Asia: Manuel Teixeira SJ, *The Portuguese Missions in Malacca and Singapore (1511–1958)* (3 vols; Lisbon, 1961–63); Georg Schurhammer SJ, *Francis Xavier: His Life, His Times*, vol. 3: *Indonesia and India 1545–1549*, trans. M. Joseph Costelloe (Rome, 1980); Achilles Meersman, *The Franciscans in the Indonesian Archipelago* (Louvain, 1967). The history of Philippine Christianity is outlined in Peter G. Gowing, *Islands Under the Cross: The Story of the Church in the Philippines* (Manila, 1967); Miguel A. Bernad, *The Christianization of the Philippines: Problems and Perspectives* (Manila, 1972); Horacio de la Costa SJ, *Church and State: The Philippine Experience* (Manila, 1972); Pablo Fernandez OP, *History of the Church in the Philippines (1521–1898)* (Manila, 1979); Gerald Anderson (ed.), *Studies on Philippine Church History* (Ithaca and London, 1968).

The following outline the history of Catholic and Protestant Christianity in South-east Asia after 1800: Winburn T. Thomas and Rajah B. Manikam, *The Church in Southeast Asia* (New York, 1956); Gerald H. Anderson (ed.), *Christ and Crisis in Southeast Asia* (New York, 1968); Brian Harrison, *Waiting for China: The Anglo-Chinese College at Malacca, 1818–1843, and Early Nineteenth-Century Missions* (Hong Kong, 1979); Herman G. Tegenfeldt, *A Century of Growth: The Kachin Baptist Church of Burma* (South Pasadena, CA, 1974); Alexander Garnett Smith, *Siamese Gold: A History of Church Growth in Thailand: An Interpretive Analysis 1816–1982* (Bangkok, 1982); Kenneth E. Wells, *History of Protestant Work in Thailand, 1828–1958* (Bangkok, 1958); Samuel I. Kim, *The Unfinished Mission in Thailand: The Uncertain Christian Impact on the Buddhist Heartland* (Seoul, 1980); P. J. N. Tuck, *French Catholic Missionaries and the Politics of Imperialism in Vietnam, 1857–1914* (Liverpool, 1987); W. J. Roxborough, *A Short Introduction to Malaysian Church History* (Kuala Lumpur, 1986); Robert Hunt, Lee Kam Hing and John Roxborough (eds), *Christianity in Malaysia: A Denominational History* (Petaling Jaya, 1992); M. Northcott, 'A survey of the rise of charismatic Christianity in Malaysia', *Asia Journal of Theology*, 4, no. 1 (April 1990), pp. 266–78; Bobby Sng, *In His Good Time: The Story of the Church in Singapore, 1819–1978* (Singapore, 1980).

The beginnings of Protestant work in the Philippines are considered by Kenton J. Clymer, *Protestant Missionaries in the Philippines 1898–1916* (Urbana, 1986). On the rise of indigenous Christianity in the Philippines, see John N. Schumacher SJ, *Revolutionary Clergy: The Filipino Clergy and the Nationalist Movement, 1850–1903* (Quezon City, 1981); Horacio de la Costa SJ and John N. Schumacher SJ, *The Filipino Clergy: Historical Studies and Future Perspectives* (Quezon City, 1979); John N. Schumacher SJ, *Readings in Philippine Church History* (2nd edn; Quezon City, 1987) and 'Syncretism in Philippine Catholicism: its historical causes', *Philippine Studies*, 32 (1984), pp. 261–9; Lewis Bliss Whittemore, *Struggle for Freedom: History of the Philippine Independent Church* (London and Greenwich, CT, 1961); Arthur Leonard Tuggy, *The Philippine Church: Growth in a Changing Society* (Grand Rapids, 1971) and *Iglesia ni Cristo: A Study in Independent Church Dynamics* (Quezon City, 1976).

The history of indigenous Christianity and particular churches in Indonesia is traced in the following works: Philip van Akkeren, *Sri and Christ: A Study of the Indigenous Church in East Java* (London, 1970); Th. Sumartana, *Mission at the Crossroads: Indigenous Churches, European Missionaries, Islamic Association and Socio-Religious Change in Java 1812–1936* (Jakarta, 1994); Hendrik Kraemer, *From Mission Field to Independent Church: Report on a Decisive Decade in the Growth of Indigenous Churches in Indonesia*

(London, 1958); R. A. F. Paul Webb, *Palms and the Cross: Socio-Economic Development in Nusatenggara, Indonesia 1930–1975* (Townsville, 1986); D. G. McKenzie, *The Mango Tree Church: The Story of the Protestant Christian Church in Bali* (Brisbane and Melbourne, 1988); James Haire, *The Character and Theological Struggle of the Church in Halmahera, Indonesia, 1941–1979* (Frankfurt am Main, 1981); Avery T. Willis, *Indonesian Revival: Why Two Million Came to Christ* (Pasadena, 1977); Frank L. Cooley, *Indonesia: Church and Society* (New York, 1968).

Japan

An older but still useful history of Christianity in Japan is Otis Cary, *A History of Christianity in Japan: Roman Catholic, Greek Orthodox, and Protestant Missions* (new edn; Rutland, VT, and Tokyo, 1976; first published in 1909). For a useful collection of articles covering various aspects of Christianity in Japan, see John Breen and Mark Williams (eds), *Japan and Christianity: Impacts and Responses* (Basingstoke and New York, 1996). The following titles provide comprehensive information on the early history of the Catholic Church in Japan: Charles Ralph Boxer, *The Christian Century in Japan: 1549–1650* (Berkeley, 1951; rev. edn, Manchester, 1993); George Elison, *Deus Destroyed: The Image of Christianity in Early Modern Japan* (Cambridge, MA, 1973; 1988); Georg Schurhammer SJ, *Francis Xavier: His Life, His Times*, vol. 4: *Japan and China 1549–1552* (Rome, 1982); J. F. Moran, *The Japanese and the Jesuits: Alessandro Valignano in Sixteenth Century Japan* (London, 1992); Franz Josef Schütte SJ, *Valignano's Mission Principles for Japan*, trans. John J. Coyne SJ (2 vols; St Louis, 1980); Michael Cooper (ed.), *The Southern Barbarians: The First Europeans in Japan* (Tokyo, 1971); Michael Cooper, *Rodriguez the Interpreter: An Early Jesuit in Japan and China* (New York and Tokyo, 1974, 1994); Joseph Jennes CICM, *A History of the Catholic Church in Japan: From Its Beginnings to the Early Meiji Era (1549–1873)* (rev. edn; Tokyo, 1973); Joseph J. Spae CICM, *Catholicism in Japan* (Tokyo, 1964); Stephen Turnbull, *The Kakure Kirishitan of Japan: A Study of Their Development, Beliefs and Rituals to the Present Day* (Richmond, Surrey, 1998).

The following works deal with Protestant Christianity: Charles W. Iglehart, *A Century of Protestant Christianity in Japan* (Rutland, VT, 1959); Carl Michalson, *Japanese Contributions to Christian Theology* (Philadelphia, 1960); J. M. Phillips, *From the Rising of the Sun: Christians and Society in Contemporary Japan* (New York, 1981); Irwin Scheiner, *Christian Converts and Social Protest in Meiji Japan* (Berkeley and Los Angeles, 1970); Yamamori Tetsunao, *Church Growth in Japan: A Study in the Development of Eight Denominations, 1859–1939* (South Pasadena, 1974); Carlo Caldarola, *Christianity the Japanese Way* (Leiden, 1979); David Reid, *New Wine: The Cultural Shaping of Japanese Christianity* (Berkeley, CA, 1991).

Korea

Wi Jo Kang, *Christ and Caesar in Modern Korea: A History of Christianity and Politics* (Albany, NY, 1997); Joseph Chang-mun Kim and John Jae-sun Chung, *Catholic Korea: Yesterday and Today* (Seoul, 1964); Allen D. Clark, *A History of the Church in Korea* (1961; rev. edn, Seoul, 1971); Donald N. Clark, *Christianity in Modern Korea* (Lanham, MD, 1986); Samuel H. Moffett, *The Christians of Korea* (New York, 1962); Kenneth M. Wells, *New God, New Nation: Protestants and Self-Reconstruction Nationalism in Korea, 1896–1937* (Honolulu, 1991); Ro Bong-rin and Marlin Nelson (eds), *Korean*

Church Growth Explosion: Centennial of the Protestant Church (1884–1984) (Taichung, Taiwan, 1983); Everett Nichols Hunt, *Protestant Pioneers in Korea* (New York, 1980); Lee Kun-sam, *The Christian Confrontation with Shinto Nationalism 1868–1945* (Philadelphia, 1966); Martha Huntley, *Caring, Growing, Changing: A History of the Protestant Mission in Korea* (New York, 1984).

Chapter 11: North America

The literature on the story of Christianity in North America is enormous and growing annually. A few studies, such as Robert T. Handy, *A History of the Churches in the United States and Canada* (New York, 1976), and Mark A. Noll, *A History of Christianity in the United States and Canada* (Grand Rapids, 1992), integrate American and Canadian developments. Most studies treat the religious histories of the two nations separately. Sydney E. Ahlstrom, *A Religious History of the American People* (New Haven, 1972), and Martin E. Marty, *Pilgrims in Their Own Land: 500 Years of Religion in America* (Boston, 1984), explore long-term themes in the story of religion in America. Roger Finke and Rodney Stark, *The Churching of America: Winners and Losers in Our Religious Economy* (New Brunswick, 1992), offers a provocative (and controversial) reinterpretation of the same terrain. Jay P. Dolan, *The American Catholic Experience: A History from Colonial Times to the Present* (Garden City, NY, 1985), is the standard historical survey of American Catholicism, while Philip Gleason's collection of essays, *Keeping the Faith: American Catholicism Past and Present* (Notre Dame, 1987), offers many provocative insights on selected issues in the history of American Catholicism. Rosemary R. Ruether and Rosemary S. Keller (eds) strive to reintroduce the role of women into the narrative of American religious history in *Women and Religion in America: A Documentary History* (3 vols; New York, 1981–86). C. Eric Lincoln and Lawrence H. Mamiya do the same for African-Americans in *The Black Church in the African-American Experience* (Durham, NC, 1990).

Scholarship on Canadian religious life is not as advanced. The standard history of Christianity in Canada is John W. Grant *et al.*, *A History of the Christian Church in Canada* (3 vols; Toronto, 1966–72). A re-evaluation of the history of Protestantism is found in George A. Rawlyk (ed.), *The Canadian Protestant Experience: 1760–1900* (Burlington, Ontario, 1990).

Some of the best scholarly work has focused on the early period of colonization. On the general question of Christianization see: Jon Butler, *Awash in a Sea of Faith: Christianizing the American People* (Cambridge, MA, 1990); E. Brooks Holifield, *Era of Persuasion: American Thought and Culture, 1521–1680* (Boston, 1989); and Henry Warner Bowden, *American Indians and Christian Missions: Studies in Cultural Conflict* (Chicago, 1981). No aspect of North American religion has been as carefully studied as has Puritanism. In addition to the classic works of Samuel Eliot Morison and Perry Miller see (among many): Stephen Foster, *The Long Argument: English Puritans and the Shaping of New England Culture, 1570–1700* (Chapel Hill, 1990); Edmund S. Morgan, *Visible Saints: The History of a Puritan Idea* (New York, 1963); and Harry S. Stout, *The New England Soul: Preaching and Religious Culture in Colonial New England* (New York, 1986).

Henry F. May, *The Enlightenment in America* (New York, 1976), is a masterly account of eighteenth-century American intellectual life. Edwin S. Gaustad, *The Great Awakening in New England* (New York, 1957); Rhys Isaac, *The Transformation of Virginia, 1740–1790* (Chapel Hill, 1982); and George A. Rawlyk and Gordon T.

Stewart, *A People Highly Favoured of God: The Nova Scotia Yankees and the American Revolution* (Hamden, CT, 1972), interpret the Great Awakening(s) from the perspectives of New England, Virginia, and Canada. Norman Fiering, *Jonathan Edwards' Moral Thought and Its British Context* (Chapel Hill, 1981), is perhaps the best account of the thought of America's greatest theologian. On religious issues and the revolution see (in addition to Rhys Isaac), Nathan O. Hatch, *The Sacred Cause of Liberty: Republican Thought and the Millennium in Revolutionary New England* (New Haven, 1977); Patricia U. Bonomi, *Under the Cope of Heaven: Religion, Society and Politics in Colonial America* (New York, 1986); and Peter Doll, 'Imperial Anglicanism in North America' (DPhil dissertation, University of Oxford, 1989).

The question of the Second Great Awakening and the ante-bellum religious world has also generated much scholarship. Nathan O. Hatch in *The Democratization of American Christianity* (New Haven, 1989) sees the democratic impulse as profoundly transforming American Protestantism. Donald G. Mathews in *Religion and the Old South* (Chicago, 1977) sees this period to be similarly crucial for southern religion. Both Conrad Cherry's *Nature and the Religious Imagination: From Edwards to Bushnell* (Philadelphia, 1980) and Paul K. Conkin, *The Uneasy Center: Reformed Christianity in Antebellum America* (Chapel Hill, 1995), explore intellectual questions during this era. Our understanding of the religious life of this period has been aided by an upswing of scholarship on both evangelicalism and the African-American experience. On the former see Leonard I. Sweet (ed.), *The Evangelical Tradition in America* (Macon, 1984); on the latter, Albert J. Raboteau, *Slave Religion: The 'Invisible Institution' in the Antebellum South* (New York, 1978).

On the question of slavery and the Civil War, Bertram Wyatt Brown, *Lewis Tappan and the Evangelical War Against Slavery* (Cleveland, 1969), explores the Northern evangelical world, while James O. Farmer, *The Metaphysical Confederacy: James Henley Thornwell and the Synthesis of Southern Values* (Macon, 1986), sketches the southern outlook. African-American responses can be found in Raboteau and Lincoln/ Mamiya. James H. Moorhead, *American Apocalypse: Yankee Protestants and the Civil War* (New Haven, 1976), discusses the transformation of northern clerical attitudes as a result of the war, and William J. Wolf, *The Almost Chosen People: A Study of the Religion of Abraham Lincoln* (Garden City, NY, 1959), sheds light upon the religious reflections of Lincoln.

William R. Hutchison, *The Modernist Impulse in American Protestantism* (Cambridge, MA, 1976), and George M. Marsden, *Fundamentalism and American Culture: The Shaping of Twentieth Century Evangelicalism, 1875–1925* (New York, 1980), both treat key aspects of the intellectual and cultural world of late nineteenth-century religion. Jon H. Roberts, *Darwinism and the Divine in America: Protestant Intellectuals and Organic Evolution, 1859–1900* (Madison, 1988), is the most complete account of the debate over Darwin. On the rise of the Social Gospel Movement, see Ronald C. White, Jr, and C. Howard Hopkins, *The Social Gospel: Religion and Reform in Changing America* (Philadelphia, 1976). On the missionary impulse see William R. Hutchison, *Errand to the World: American Protestant Thought and Foreign Missions* (Chicago, 1987). Canadian developments are traced in Phyllis D. Airhart, *Serving the Present Age: Revivalism, Progressivism, and the Methodist Tradition in Canada* (Montreal, 1992). On the rise of the Holiness-Pentecostal Tradition, see Vinson Synan, *The Holiness-Pentecostal Movement in the United States* (Grand Rapids, 1971).

For twentieth-century issues, in addition to Marsden and Hutchison, see Martin E. Marty, *Modern American Religion: The Noise of Conflict, 1919–1941* (Chicago, 1991). The cultural world of 'mainline' Protestantism is intriguingly explored in William R. Hutchison (ed.), *Between the Times: The Travail of the Protestant Establishment in America,*

1900–1960 (Cambridge, 1989). The Catholic response to the cultural crisis of the early twentieth century is examined in William M. Halsey, *The Survival of American Innocence: Catholicism in an Era of Disillusionment, 1920–1940* (Notre Dame, 1980), while Donald B. Meyer's *The Protestant Search for Political Realism, 1919–1941* (Berkeley, 1960) focuses upon the rise of neo-Orthodoxy. Gerald P. Fogarty SJ, 'North America' in *Modern Catholicism*, ed. Adrian Hastings (London, 1991), pp. 326–33, discusses the state of American Catholicism since the Second Vatican Council. Will Herberg's *Protestant, Catholic, Jew: An Essay in American Religious Sociology* (Garden City, NY, 1955) is both an analysis and a product of the post-Second World War religious revival. Finally, Pamela W. Darling, *New Wine: The Story of Women Transforming Leadership and Power in the Episcopal Church* (Cambridge, MA, 1994), recounts how one religious community responded to the changing understandings of gender.

Chapter 12: Christianity in Western Europe from the Enlightenment

General accounts of the Western European Churches in the modern period include Gerald Cragg, *The Church and the Age of Reason* (Harmondsworth, 1960), and Alec R. Vidler, *The Church in an Age of Revolution* (Harmondsworth, 1961); Owen Chadwick, *The Popes and European Revolution* (Oxford, 1981), is admirably clear on politics, and Hugh McLeod, *Religion and the People of Western Europe 1789–1970* (Oxford, 1981), offers an excellent social survey. A number of stimulating essays on modern religious themes may be found in Jim Obelkevich, Lyndal Roper and Raphael Samuel, *Disciplines of Faith: Studies in Religion, Politics and Patriarchy* (London, 1987).

The most engaging history of philosophical ideas in the West is probably still Bertrand Russell, *History of Western Philosophy* (London, 1946; many modern editions). The classic study of the Enlightenment is Peter Gay, *The Enlightenment: An Interpretation* (2 vols; New York, 1971); other introductory surveys include Norman Hampson, *The Enlightenment* (Harmondsworth, 1968), and Roy Porter, *The Enlightenment* (Basingstoke, 1990). Carl Becker, *The Heavenly City of the Eighteenth-Century Philosophers* (New Haven, 1932), offers a valuable corrective to the anticlerical slant of many accounts of the Enlightenment, while Joseph Chinnici's *The English Catholic Enlightenment: John Lingard and the Cisalpine Movement 1780–1859* (Shepherdstown, WV, 1980) is a particularly interesting case study.

Collections of essays which stress the importance of national politics include H. M. Scott (ed.), *Enlightened Absolutism: Reform and Reformers in Later Eighteenth-Century Europe* (London, 1990), Roy Porter and Mikulas Teich (eds), *The Enlightenment in National Context* (Cambridge, 1981), and Stuart Mews (ed.), *Religion and National Identity* (Oxford, 1982). On mesmerism and freemasonry, see Robert Darnton, *Mesmerism and the End of the Enlightenment in France* (Cambridge, MA, 1968), Margaret Jacob, *The Radical Enlightenment: Pantheists, Freemasons and Republicans* (London, 1981), and J. M. Roberts, *The Mythology of the Secret Societies* (London, 1972). On Jansenism see especially Robert Palmer, *Catholics and Unbelievers in Eighteenth Century France* (Princeton, 1939), and D. Van Kley, *The Jansenists and the Expulsion of Jesuits from France 1757–1765* (New Haven, CT, 1975); on French attitudes towards Jesuits, see Geoff Cubitt, *The Jesuit Myth: Conspiracy Theory and Politics in Nineteenth-Century France* (Oxford, 1993).

For differing interpretations of Methodism, see David Hempton, *The Religion of the*

People: Methodism and Popular Religion c. 1750–1900 (London, 1996); Deborah Valenze, *Prophetic Sons and Daughters: Female Preaching and Popular Religion in Industrial England* (Princeton, 1985); and Alan Gilbert, *Religion and Society in Industrial England: Church, Chapel and Social Change 1740–1914* (London, 1976). On Romanticism, see especially Bernard Reardon, *Religion in the Age of Romanticism* (Cambridge, 1985).

The clearest introduction to the Catholic Church and the French Revolution is probably still John McManners' excellent *The French Revolution and the Church* (London, 1969); on the Huguenots, see B. C. Poland, *French Protestantism and the French Revolution* (Princeton, 1957).

An outstanding collection of essays on post-revolutionary religious thinkers is Ninian Smart, John Clayton, Patrick Sherry and Steven Katz (eds), *Nineteenth Century Religious Thought in the West* (3 vols; Cambridge, 1985). On religious revivalism in the English-speaking world, see Ian Bradley, *The Call to Seriousness* (London, 1976); David Bebbington, *Evangelicalism in Modern Britain: A History from the 1730s to the 1980s* (London, 1989); Richard Carwardine, *Trans-Atlantic Revivalism: Popular Evangelicalism in Britain and America, 1790–1865* (Westport, 1978); and John Kent, *Holding the Fort: Studies in Victorian Revivalism* (London, 1978). The literature on the Oxford Movement is enormous; a concise account may be found in Owen Chadwick, *The Victorian Church* (2 vols; London, 1970; 1972), and a good bibliography in Laurence Crumb, *The Oxford Movement and Its Leaders: A Bibliography of Secondary and Lesser Primary Sources* (Metuchen, NJ, 1988; supplement 1993). The first chapter of David Blackbourn's *Marpingen: Apparitions of the Virgin Mary in Bismarckian Germany* (Oxford, 1993) gives an excellent survey of the existing literature on Marian apparitions while Sandra Zimdars-Swartz, *Encountering Mary from La Salette to Medjugorje* (Princeton, 1991), discusses the most famous cases.

The most balanced account of the First Vatican Council is still Cuthbert Butler, *The Vatican Council* (2 vols; London, 1930), and J. T. Ford, 'Infallibility: a review of recent studies', *Theological Studies*, 40 (1979), pp. 273–305, gives a survey of works on the subject of papal infallibility. On changes in Catholic practice in the nineteenth century, see Ralph Gibson, *A Social History of French Catholicism, 1789–1914* (London, 1989); Jonathan Sperber, *Popular Catholicism in Nineteenth-Century Germany* (Princeton, 1984); Mary Heimann, *Catholic Devotion in Victorian England* (Oxford, 1995); and P. J. Corish, *The Irish Catholic Experience: A Historical Survey* (Wilmington, DE, 1985).

On Liberalism, Bernard Reardon's *Liberal Protestantism* (Stanford, 1968) and *Liberalism and Tradition: Aspects of Catholic Thought in Nineteenth-Century France* (Cambridge, 1975) are stimulating and informative, while Alister McGrath, *Christian Theology: An Introduction* (London, 1994), offers a clear introduction. On politics and Protestant Nonconformity in England, see especially David Bebbington, *The Non-conformist Conscience: Chapel and Politics, 1870–1914* (London, 1982). For debates surrounding biblical criticism and nineteenth-century lives of Jesus, see Albert Schweitzer's classic, *The Quest of the Historical Jesus* (London, 1954); Jaroslav Pelikan, *Jesus Through the Centuries: His Place in the History of Culture* (New Haven, 1985); James Robinson, *A New Quest of the Historical Jesus and Other Essays* (Philadelphia, 1983); and Alister McGrath, *The Making of Modern German Christology* (2nd edn; Grand Rapids, 1993). On changing attitudes to hell and the afterlife, see Geoffrey Rowell, *Hell and the Victorians* (Oxford, 1974), Ralph Gibson, 'Hellfire and damnation in nineteenth-century France', *Catholic Historical Review* (1988), and Thomas Kselman, *Death and the Afterlife in Nineteenth-Century France* (Princeton, 1993). For a detailed discussion of *Essays and Reviews*, see Ieuan Ellis, *Seven Against Christ: A Study of Essays and Reviews* (Leiden, 1980).

An excellent and highly accessible survey of the relations between science and religion is John Brooke, *Science and Religion: Some Historical Perspectives* (Cambridge, 1991); collections of relevant source material for the eighteenth and nineteenth centuries may be found in D. C. Goodman (ed.), *Science and Religious Belief 1600–1900* (Dorchester, 1973), and Tess Cosslett (ed.), *Science and Religion in the Nineteenth Century* (Cambridge, 1984), which also gives succinct introductions to each source. On natural theology, see especially John Brooke, 'Natural theology in Britain from Boyle to Paley' in John Brooke and R. Hooykaas (eds), *New Interactions Between Theology and Natural Science* (Milton Keynes, 1974), and Dan LeMahieu, *The Mind of William Paley: A Philosopher and His Age* (Lincoln, NE, 1976). On geology, Charles Coulton Gillispie, *Genesis and Geology: The Impact of Scientific Discoveries upon Religious Beliefs in the Decades Before Darwin* (Cambridge, 1959), is clear and helpful. Useful introductions to Darwin and Darwinism, too numerous to cite, include David Oldroyd, *Darwinian Impacts: An Introduction to the Darwinian Revolution* (Milton Keynes, 1980), and James Moore, *The Post-Darwinian Controversies: A Study of the Protestant Struggle to Come to Terms with Darwin in Great Britain and America, 1870–1900* (Cambridge, 1979). On the theme of evolutionary religion and the cultural dimension of scientific thought, see especially Susan Cannon, *Science and Culture: The Early Victorian Period* (Folkestone, 1978); Frank Turner, *Between Science and Religion: The Reaction to Scientific Naturalism in Late Victorian England* (New Haven, 1974); and Gillian Beer, *Darwin's Plots: Evolutionary Narrative in Darwin, George Eliot and Nineteenth Century Fiction* (London, 1983). On positivism, see Charles Cashdollar, *The Transformation of Theology, 1830–1890: Positivism and Protestant Thought in Britain and America* (Princeton, 1989), and L. Kolakowski, *Positivist Philosophy from Hume to the Vienna Circle* (Harmondsworth, 1972). On the 'warfare' between science and religion, see Colin Russell, 'The conflict metaphor and its social origins', *Science and Christian Belief*, 1 (1989), pp. 59–80, and David Lindberg and Ronald L. Numbers, 'Beyond War and Peace: a reappraisal of the encounter between Christianity and science', *Church History*, 55 (1986), pp. 338–54.

Lively studies of nineteenth-century superstition include Judith Devlin, *The Superstitious Mind: French Peasants and the Supernatural in the Nineteenth Century* (London and New Haven, 1987), and Thomas Kselman, *Miracles and Prophecies in Nineteenth-Century France* (New Brunswick, NJ, 1983). Differing interpretations of spiritualism may be found in Janet Oppenheim, *The Other World: Spiritualism and Psychical Research in England, 1850–1914* (Cambridge, 1985), Logie Barrow, *Independent Spirits: Spiritualism and English Plebians, 1850–1920* (London, 1986), and Alex Owen, *The Darkened Room: Women, Power and Spiritualism in Late Victorian England* (London, 1989).

On the predominantly middle-class 'crisis' of faith, see especially Owen Chadwick, *The Secularization of the European Mind in the Nineteenth Century* (Cambridge, 1975), and Susan Budd, *Varieties of Unbelief: Atheists and Agnostics in English Society* (London, 1977); for working-class attitudes, Hugh McLeod, *Piety and Poverty: Working-Class Religion in Berlin, London and New York 1870–1914* (New York, 1996), is engaging and helpful. An interesting study of the British case is Alan Gilbert, *The Making of Post-Christian Britain: A History of the Secularization of Modern Society* (London, 1980), and particularly stimulating local studies include Jeffrey Cox, *The English Churches in a Secular Society: Lambeth, 1870–1930* (Oxford, 1982), and James Obelkevich, *Religion and Rural Society: South Lindsey, 1825–75* (Oxford, 1976).

An excellent survey of religious thought in the twentieth century is David Ford (ed.), *The Modern Theologians* (2 vols; Oxford and Cambridge, 1990). On specific theological developments, see Alec Vidler, *A Variety of Catholic Modernists* (Cambridge, 1970); Peter Hebblethwaite, *The Christian–Marxist Dialogue* (London, 1977); C. K. Murphy, *The Spirit of Catholic Action* (London, 1943); Oscar Arnal, *Priests in Working Class Blue: The History of the Worker-Priests 1943–1954* (New York, 1986); and M. P.

Fogarty, *Christian Democracy in Western Europe 1820–1953* (London, 1957). On the Churches and Fascism, see John Pollard, *The Vatican and Italian Fascism, 1929–32: A Study in Conflict* (Cambridge, 1985); F. H. Littell and H. G. Locke (eds), *The German Church Struggle and the Holocaust* (Detroit, 1974); James Bentley, *Martin Niemöller* (Oxford, 1984); and Eberhard Busch, *Karl Barth* (London, 1976). On Catholic politics see Martin Conway, *Catholic Politics in Europe, 1918–1945* (London, 1997), and on the Cold War, see especially Owen Chadwick, *The Christian Church in the Cold War* (London, 1992).

On ecumenicalism and moves towards European unity, David Armstrong, *The Rise of International Organisation: A Short History* (London, 1982), is helpful for background; H. E. Fey, *The Ecumenical Advance 1848–1968* (London, 1969); A. Perchenet, *The Revival of the Religious Life and Christian Unity* (English trans., London, 1969); and John McDonnell, *The World Council of Churches and the Catholic Church* (New York, 1985), offer more specific studies.

Additional works on religion in specific countries include: Norman Ravitch, *The Catholic Church and the French Nation 1589–1989* (London, 1990); D. G. Charlton, *Secular Religions in France 1815–70* (Oxford, 1963); Frank Tallett and Nicholas Atkin (eds), *Catholicism in Britain and France Since 1789* (London, 1996); John Groh, *Nineteenth-Century German Protestantism: The Church as a Social Model* (Washington, DC, 1982); William Callahan, *Church, Society and Politics in Spain, 1750–1874* (Cambridge, MA, 1984); Frances Lannon, *Privilege, Persecution and Prophecy: The Catholic Church in Spain, 1875–1975* (Oxford, 1987); and A. C. Jemolo, *Church and State in Italy, 1850–1950* (Oxford, 1960). For the Scandinavian countries, L. S. Hunter (ed.), *Scandinavian Churches: A Picture of the Development of the Life of the Churches of Denmark, Finland, Iceland, Norway and Sweden* (London, 1965), offers an introduction, and a list of more specialist works may be found in Stewart Oakley (ed.), *Scandinavian History: 1520–1970: A List of Books and Articles in English* (London, 1984). The Benelux countries are treated in K. S. Latourette, *Christianity in a Revolutionary Age* (London, 1963); for more recent works, see Carl Strickwerda, *A House Divided* (1997), and Michael Wintle, *Pillars of Piety: Religion in the Netherlands in the Nineteenth Century 1813–1901* (Hull, 1987). On the British Isles, see especially Sheridan Gilley and W. J. Sheils (eds), *A History of Religion in Britain* (Oxford, 1994); Gordon Rupp, *Religion in England 1688–1791* (Oxford, 1986); Gerald Parsons (ed.), *Religion in Victorian Britain* (4 vols; Manchester, 1988); Adrian Hastings, *A History of English Christianity 1920–1990* (London, 1991); and Terence Thomas (ed.), *The British: Their Religious Beliefs and Practices 1800–1986* (London, 1988). On Ireland, see Sean Connolly, *Religion and Society in Nineteenth Century Ireland* (Dundalk, 1985), and Desmond Keenan, *The Catholic Church in Ireland* (Dublin, 1983). Steve Bruce, *God Save Ulster! The Religion and Politics of Paisleyism* (Oxford, 1989), gives a highly readable introduction to modern religion and politics in Northern Ireland, and a helpful volume on Scotland is Callum Brown, *Religion and Society in Scotland Since 1707* (Edinburgh, 1997).

Chapter 13: Australasia and the Pacific

Recent general histories of Christianity in Australia and New Zealand are Ian Breward, *A History of the Australian Churches* (Sydney, 1993), and Allan K. Davidson, *Christianity in Aotearoa: A History of Church and Society in New Zealand* (2nd edn; Wellington, 1997). Roger C. Thompson, *Religion in Australia: A History* (Melbourne, 1994), provides a short and stimulating survey. For a study of Australian Christianity from an evangelical perspective, see Stuart Piggin, *Evangelical Christianity in Australia: Spirit, Word and World* (Melbourne, 1996). Michael Hogan, *The Sectarian Strand: Religion in Australian History* (Melbourne, 1987), explores the effects of religious division and rivalry on Australian society. Hilary M. Carey, *Believing in Australia: A Cultural History of Religions* (Sydney, 1996), covers Aboriginal religion and new religious movements, as well as Christianity. Religious practice and belief in the Protestant and Catholic churches are examined in H. R. Jackson, *Churches and People in Australia and New Zealand, 1860–1930* (Wellington and Sydney, 1987). Peter Donovan (ed.), *Religions of New Zealanders* (2nd edn; Palmerston North, 1996), comprises essays on many different faiths and religious groups.

A wide-ranging collection of primary sources with introductory essays is Allan K. Davidson and Peter J. Lineham (eds), *Transplanted Christianity: Documents Illustrating Aspects of New Zealand Church History* (Auckland, 1987; 3rd edn, Palmerston North, 1995). The nearest Australian equivalent is Patrick and Deirdre O'Farrell (eds), *Documents in Australian Catholic History* (2 vols; London, 1969). For bibliographies, Lawrence D. McIntosh, 'Religion' in D. H. Borchardt (ed.), *Australians: A Guide to Sources* (Sydney, 1987), and Peter J. Lineham, *Religious History of New Zealand: A Bibliography* (4th edn; Palmerston North, 1993).

For denominational histories, see Patrick O'Farrell's influential work, *The Catholic Church and Community: An Australian History* (Sydney, 1985). At a more popular level, Edmund Campion, *Australian Catholics* (Melbourne, 1987) and *Rockchoppers: Growing Up Catholic in Australia* (Melbourne, 1982). For a history of lay Catholics, see Naomi Turner, *Catholics in Australia: A Social History* (2 vols; Melbourne, 1992). Katharine Massam, *Sacred Threads: Catholic Spirituality in Australia, 1922–1962* (Sydney, 1996), is a pioneering study of lay Catholic piety. On the Lutherans, Everard Leske, *For Faith and Freedom: The Story of Lutherans and Lutheranism in Australia, 1838–1996* (Adelaide, 1996). At the time of writing, the other major denominations in Australia lack substantial national histories, but there are many studies at the state or regional level. Among these, see David Hilliard, *Godliness and Good Order: A History of the Anglican Church in South Australia* (Adelaide, 1986); Arnold D. Hunt, *This Side of Heaven: A History of Methodism in South Australia* (Adelaide, 1985); Stephen Judd and Kenneth Cable, *Sydney Anglicans: A History of the Diocese* (Sydney, 1987); Brian Moore (ed.), *Baptists of Western Australia: The First Ninety Years, 1895–1985* (Perth, 1991); Brian Porter (ed.), *Melbourne Anglicans: The Diocese of Melbourne, 1847–1997* (Melbourne, 1997); Don Wright and Eric G. Clancy, *The Methodists: A History of Methodism in New South Wales* (Sydney, 1993). On Christianity and the Australian Aborigines, see John Harris, *One Blood: 200 Years of Aboriginal Encounter with Christianity: A Story of Hope* (Sydney, 1990) and Tony Swain and Deborah Bird Rose (eds), *Aboriginal Australians and Christian Missions: Ethnographic and Historical Studies* (Adelaide, 1988). New Zealand denominational histories include Michael King, *God's Farthest Outpost: A History of Catholics in New Zealand* (Auckland, 1997); Dennis McEldowney (ed.), *Presbyterians in Aotearoa, 1840–1990* (Wellington, 1990), W. P. Morrell, *The Anglican Church in New Zealand: A History* (Dunedin, 1973); and [various authors], *A Handful of Grain: The Centenary History of the Baptist Union of New Zealand* (4 vols; Wellington, 1982–84).

The sociological literature on Christianity in Australia and New Zealand is extensive and includes Hans Mol's authoritative survey, *The Faith of Australians* (Sydney, 1985). Alan W. Black and Peter E. Glasner (eds), *Practice and Belief: Studies in the Sociology of Australian Religion* (Sydney, 1983), and Alan W. Black (ed.), *Religion in Australia: Sociological Perspectives* (Sydney, 1991), are useful collections of essays.

Bibliography

On Christianity in the Pacific Islands, an outstanding general history in three parts by John Garrett, *To Live Among the Stars: Christian Origins in Oceania*; *Footsteps in the Sea: Christianity in Oceania to World War II*; *Where Nets Were Cast: Christianity in Oceania Since World War II* (Suva and Geneva, 1982, 1992, 1997). For the establishment of independent national churches, see Charles W. Forman, *The Island Churches of the South Pacific: Emergence in the Twentieth Century* (Maryknoll, 1982). For analyses of religious and cultural changes resulting from Christian missionary activity, James A. Boutilier, Daniel T. Hughes and Sharon W. Tiffany (eds), *Mission, Church, and Sect in Oceania* (Ann Arbor, 1978); Darrell L. Whiteman, *Melanesians and Missionaries: An Ethnohistorical Study of Social and Religious Change in the Southwest Pacific* (Pasadena, 1983). A collection of essays on Pacific Islanders as missionaries is Doug Munro and Andrew Thornley (eds), *The Covenant Makers: Islander Missionaries in the Pacific* (Suva, 1997). Studies of individual missions include David Hilliard, *God's Gentlemen: A History of the Melanesian Mission, 1849–1942* (Brisbane, 1978); David Wetherell, *Reluctant Mission: The Anglican Church in Papua New Guinea, 1891–1942* (Brisbane, 1977); Hugh Laracy, *Marists and Melanesians: A History of Catholic Missions in the Solomon Islands* (Canberra, 1976); J. Graham Miller, *Live* (a history of the Presbyterian Church in Vanuatu; 7 vols; vols 1–2, Sydney, 1978–81; vols 3–7, Port Vila, Vanuatu, 1985–90); Herwig Wagner and Hermann Reiner (eds), *The Lutheran Church in Papua New Guinea: The First Hundred Years, 1886–1986* (Adelaide, 1986); A. Harold Wood, *Overseas Missions of the Australian Methodist Church* (5 vols; vols 1–4, Melbourne, 1975–80; vol. 5, Sydney, 1987).

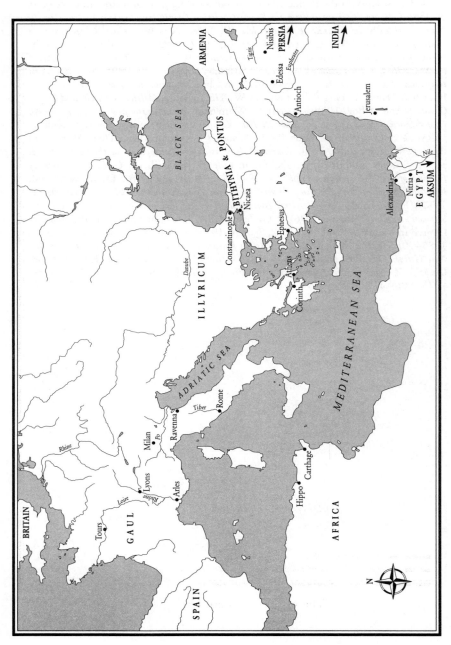

The central Christian world in the fourth century

The world of Eastern Orthodoxy

Western Christianity in the early Middle Ages: monasticism and conversion

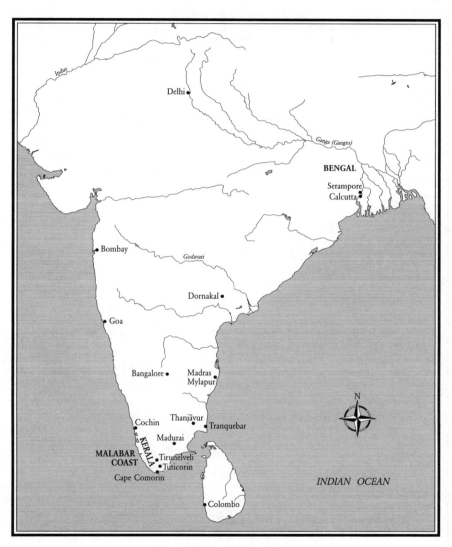

Christianity in India

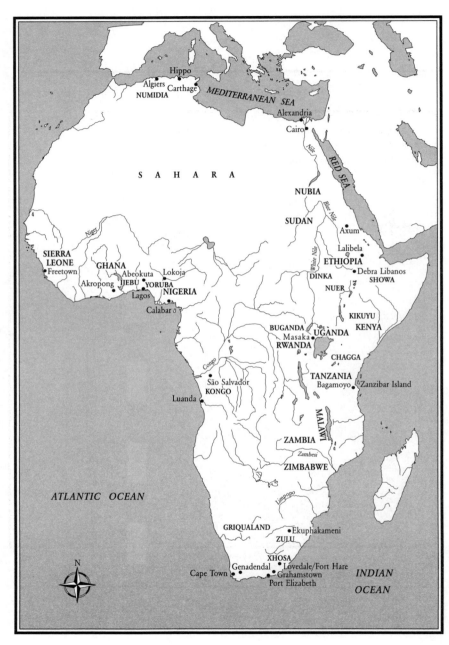

Africa

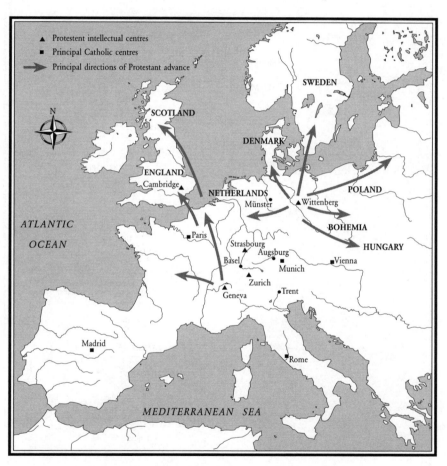

Sixteenth-century Europe

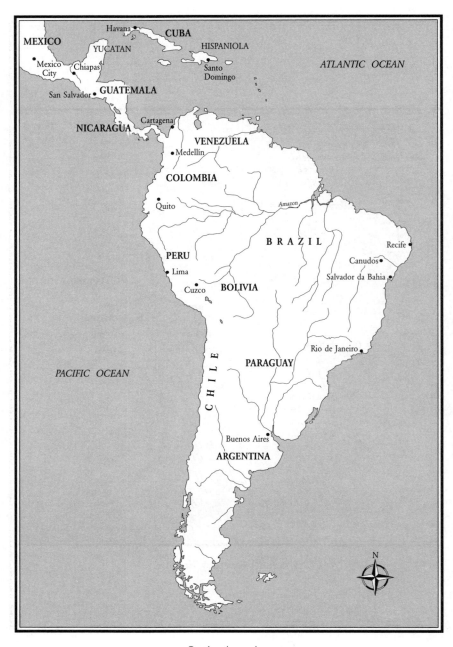

Latin America

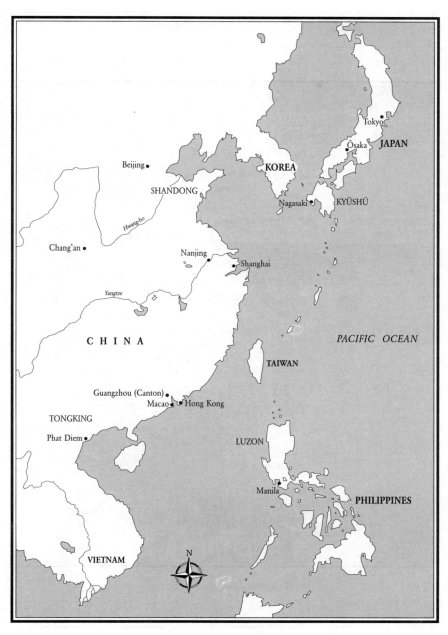

China and its neighbours

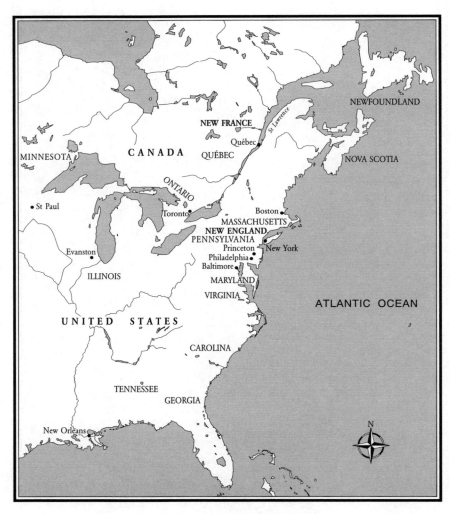

Eastern North America

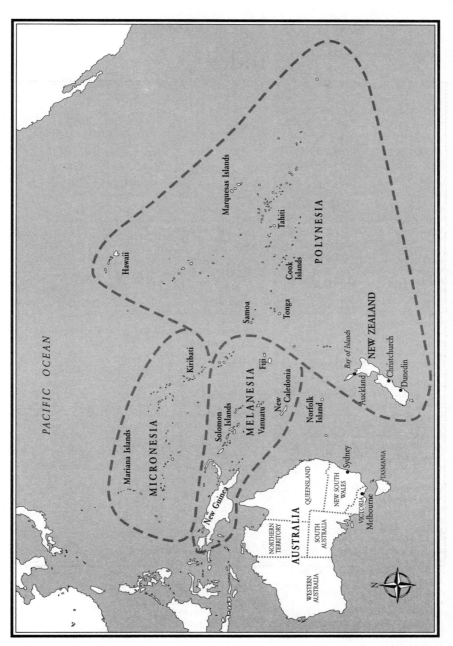

Australasia and the Pacific

Index

Index

Index

Index

Index

Index

Index